GW00746078

**HARDPRESS**.NET
HOME OF HARD-TO-FIND BOOKS

# Lives of the British Admirals
by John Campbell

Copyright © 2019 by HardPress

Address:
HardPress
8345 NW 66TH ST #2561
MIAMI FL 33166-2626
USA
Email: info@hardpress.net

BE JUST AND FEAR NOT

Aaron Arnold

NYPL RESEARCH LIBRARIES

3 3433 00848811 0

BE JUST AND FEAR NOT

Aaron Arnold

THE NEW YORK
PUBLIC LIBRARY

ASTOR, LENOX AND
TILDEN FOUNDATIONS.

Hamilton Delin!                                                    Page Sc

**NEPTUNE** refigning the **REINS** of his **CHARIOT** to **BRITANNI**

Lond.ⁿ Jan.ʸ 1ˢᵗ 1779. Publish'd as the Act directs. by A.Donaldson St Pauls Churchyard.

# LIVES

OF THE

# BRITISH ADMIRALS:

CONTAINING A NEW AND ACCURATE

# NAVAL HISTORY,

FROM THE EARLIEST PERIODS.

By Dr. J. CAMPBELL.

WITH A CONTINUATION DOWN TO THE YEAR 1779,

INCLUDING THE

NAVAL TRANSACTIONS OF THE LATE AND PRESENT WAR, AND AN ACCOUNT OF THE RECENT DISCOVERIES IN THE SOUTHERN HEMISPHERE.

WRITTEN UNDER THE INSPECTION OF

# DOCTOR BERKENHOUT.

THE WHOLE ILLUSTRATED WITH CORRECT MAPS, AND FRONTISPIECES ENGRAVED FROM ORIGINAL DESIGNS.

IN FOUR VOLUMES.

A NEW EDITION.

VOL. IV.

LONDON:

PRINTED FOR ALEXANDER DONALDSON, No. 48, ST. PAUL's CHURCH-YARD.
M. DCC. LXXII.

THE NEW YORK
PUBLIC LIBRARY

ASTOR, LENOX AND
TILDEN FOUNDATIONS.

# CONTENTS

## OF

## VOLUME FOURTH.

### CHAP. XXIII.

THE *Naval History of Great Britain, from the accession of King George II. to the end of the war in 1763.*

# CONTENTS.

## C H A P.   XXIV.

The Naval History of Great Britain, from the end of the war in 1763 to the year 1779.

# CONTENTS.

## APPENDIX.

# CONTENTS.

LIVES

THE NEW YORK
PUBLIC LIBRARY

ASTOR, LENOX AND
TILDEN FOUNDATIONS

4 5

THE NEW YORK
PUBLIC LIBRARY

ASTOR, LENOX AND
TILDEN FOUNDATIONS

# L I V E S

## OF THE

# A D M I R A L S:

### INCLUDING A NEW AND ACCURATE

# N A V A L   H I S T O R Y.

## C H A P.   XXIII.

The Naval Hiftory of GREAT-BRITAIN, from the
acceffion of King George II. to the end of the war
in the year 1763.

K ING GEORGE II. afcended the throne of Great-
Britain in the year 1727, and in the forty-fourth year
of his age. All the European powers were now at
peace; neverthelefs, fome of them were fo little fatisfied with
the terms to which neceffity had compelled them to accede, that
a future war was eafily forefeen. The late king had engaged
in an unnatural alliance with France, and, under a pretence of
adjufting the balance of power, had burdened the nation with
fubfidies to Sweden and the landgrave of Heffe-Caffel. The
Emperor Charles VI. for whom we had fo lately wrefted Sicily
from the Spaniards, was now leagued with the court of Madrid, and the political fcheme of our miniftry, fome time before
the death of George I. was to humble this very emperor, in

VOL. IV.                    A                         whofe

A. D. whofe caufe we had fo lately expended fuch fums of Britifh
1727. treafure.

Before I proceed to the occurrences which are the immediate
objects of a naval hiftory, it feems neceffary to bring the reader
acquainted with the men in power at the beginning of this
reign. Lord Townfend and the duke of Newcaftle were generally fuppofed to conduct the important concern of foreign negotiations. The firft of thefe is allowed to have poffeffed knowledge and talents equal to the tafk. As to the latter, he was
certainly not a man of great abilities; but he had diftinguifhed
himfelf as a fteady and indefatigable friend to the houfe of Hanover, and his parliamentary intereft was very confiderable.
Lord Carteret, though not oftenfibly in the adminiftration,
was frequently confulted, and his advice generally followed.
He was a man of fome genius and learning, and, having been
much abroad, was fuppofed to be well acquainted with the general fyftem of Europe. The interior government of the kingdom was principally conducted by Sir Robert Walpole, who
was at the head of the treafury, and leader of the Whigs in the
houfe of commons. He was well verfed in the myftery of finan-
cing, funding, and in the effectual application of money, as a
powerful engine of government. He fpoke in parliament,
though not elegantly, yet with eafe, fluency, and perfuafion.
He knew mankind, and on that knowledge he is faid to have
laid the foundation of that uniform plan of influence, fo very
agreeable to fubfequent parliaments, and fo indifpenfibly ufeful
to future minifters. The principal fpeakers in the oppofition
were Sir William Wyndham, Mr. Shippen, Mr. Hungerford,
and Mr. Pulteney.

The reader has feen, in the laft page of the preceding volume,
that the navy of England was, at this period, exceedingly formidable. Our chief naval commanders, who were at this time
employed, were Sir Charles Wager, Sir John Norris, and Admiral Hofier: the firft commanded a fleet in the Mediterranean,
the fecond in the Baltic, and the third in the Weft-Indies,
where he died about two months after the king's acceffion.
Sir Charles Wager had been fent to fecure Gibraltar, then befieged by the Spaniards. He afterwards continued upon the coaft
of Spain, in order to perfuade that nation, by the *ultima ratio
regum*,

*regum*, if neceffary, to acquiefce in the general plan of peace A. D
to which the other confiderable powers had already acceded. 1727
Sir John Norris had been fent with a fleet into the Baltic, with
a defign to protect Sweden from the Czarina, who threatened
that country with an invafion. And Admiral Hofier had failed,
in April 1726, to the Weft-Indies, in order to block up the
Spanifh galleons, and thereby prevent that treafure from being
brought to Europe, without which, it was imagined, the courts
of Vienna and Madrid could not profecute the war.

Such was the fituation of the Britifh navy at the acceffion of
George II. who, as I have before obferved, found his kingdom at peace with all the world. No immediate change was
made, either of minifters or meafures; but, before the expiration of the year, Lord Torrington was placed at the head of
the admiralty, and the earl of Weftmoreland made firft lord of
trade [a].

A new parliament was called. The two houfes met on the 1728
twenty-third day of January. The commons unanimoufly
chofe for their fpeaker Arthur Onflow, Efq; member for the
county of Surrey; a man whofe abilities and integrity rendered
him fingularly qualified for that important office. The king,
in his fpeech from the throne, informed his parliament, that the
difficulties, which had hitherto prevented the execution of the
preliminaries to the eftablifhment of a general peace, were now
removed, and that a congrefs would foon be opened for that
purpofe, in which he hoped the peace of Europe would be effectually fecured; but that neverthelefs, in order to prevent the
poffibility of an open rupture, it was neceffary to continue the
preparations for war. He wifhed that fome fcheme might be
formed for the increafe and fecurity of feamen, that they might
rather be invited than compelled into the fervice. He promifed
economy as foon as the public fafety would permit, and concluded his fpeech, as ufual, with recommending unanimity and defpatch. The two houfes prefented moft dutiful addrefles on the
occafion. They voted 22,955 men for guards and garrifons,
and 15,000 feamen for the fervice of the year. They granted
231,000 l. for the maintenance of 12,000 Heffians; a fubfidy

[a] Smollet's hiftory, 3d edition. vol. vii. p. 172.

of

A. D.  of 50,000 l. to the king of Sweden, and 25,000 l. to the duke
1728.  of Brunſwick [b].

The congreſs, which met at Soiſſons to eſtabliſh peace, having
yet determined nothing, the fate of Europe remained ſuſpend-
ed.   Spain had ſecretly ſhook hands with France, and was
now allied to Portugal by means of a double marriage; ſhe
therefore grew indifferent as to peace with England. She continued her depredations on our commerce in the Weſt-Indies,
where our fleet remained inaſtive and rotting, and our ſailors
periſhed miſerably, inſulted and unrevenged.

The parliament of England met, according to their proroga-
1729. tion, on the 21ſt of January.   They voted 15,000 ſeamen for
the ſervice of the year : the number of land-forces was alſo
continued, as likewiſe the ſubſidies to foreign princes.
The merchants of London, Briſtol, and Liverpool preſented
petitions to the houſe of commons, complaining of the repeated injuries they had ſuſtained by the depredations of the Spaniards in the Weſt-Indies ; upon which the houſe ordered the
lords of the admiralty to produce every ſimilar memorial which
they had received ; and they addreſſed the king, praying, that
the inſtruſtions and letters ſent to Admiral Hoſier and his ſuc-
ceſſors in command, might be laid before them.  A committee
of the whole houſe took this important affair into conſideration,
and after examining evidence, and amply debating the matter,
reſolved, that the Spaniards had violated the treaties ſubſiſting
between the two crowns ; that they had treated the crews of
ſeveral Engliſh ſhips with inhumanity ; and that the inſtruſtions
given to Admiral Hoſier, to ſeize and detain the Spaniſh galleons, were juſt and neceſſary.   The houſe of commons then
addreſſed the king, requeſting his majeſty to demand ſatisfaſtion
from Spain ; and he anſwered them by a promiſe to comply
with their requeſt [c].

Meanwhile the houſe of lords deliberated on the poſitive demand made by the Catholic king, of the reſtitution of Gibraltar,
founded on the contents of a letter written by King George I.
to the king of Spain. From an authentic copy of this letter, it
appeared, that his late majeſty had aſtually conſented to this re-

b Smollet, vol. vii. p. 173.
c Ibid. p. 180.

ſtitution.

ftitution. Their lordships then refolved, that the houfe did A. D firmly rely, that his majefty would, in fupport of the honour 1729 and trade of this kingdom, take effectual care to preferve his undoubted right to Gibraltar and Minorca.

The year 1730 produced nothing worthy the attention of a 1730 naval hiftorian. The king, in his fpeech to parliament, which met on the 13th of January, informed them, that the peace of Europe was now eftablifhed by a treaty concluded at Seville; that the uninterrupted commerce of Great Britain was reftored; and that the nation was to be amply indemnified for the Spanifh depredations in the Weft-Indies. Neverthelefs I find, that on the 2d of March 1731[d], feveral mafters and failors of mer- chant-fhips, who had been taken by the Spanifh guarda-coftas, came to London to give an account to parliament of the cruel treatment they had received from the Spaniards. In 1733 the houfe of commons addreffed the king, to know what fa- tisfaction had been made by Spain for the depredations above- mentioned[e]; and by his majefty's anfwer it appeared, that the commiffioners had not yet made their report. In the fpeech from the throne, which put an end to the preceding feffion of parlia- ment, the nation was told, that all difputes with foreign powers were fettled, and the public tranquillity eftablifhed. However, twelve fhips of the line were put into commiffion, and prefs- warrants were iffued for manning the fleet. Meanwhile Rear- admiral Stewart demanded of the governors of Campeachy and the Havanna, reftitution for three fhips plundered by Spanifh guarda coftas. In confequence of this peremptory demand, one of the guarda coftas was fold at St. Jago de Cuba, and the money paid to the South-fea factors: one of the Spanifh governors was fent home, and another confined in the caftle of Cuba.

That we may in fome degree preferve the chain of fuch pub- 1733 lic events as are connected, though indirectly, with our naval hiftory, it is neceffary to inform the reader, that, in the year 1733, the king of France concluded a treaty with Spain and Sardinia, by which they mutually agreed to declare war againft

d Gentleman's Magazine, March, 1731.
e Smollet's hiftory, vol. vii. p. 207.

the

A. D. the emperor.    Accordingly a war in Germany and in Italy im-
1734. mediately commenced.

In 1734 the navy of England confifted of ninety-two men of
1735. war, fixty of which were of the line.    In the following year
a mifunderftanding, on a frivolous occafion, happening between
the courts of Spain and Portugal, the latter applied to Great-
Britain for protection; in confequence of which, Sir John Norris failed with a powerful fleet, and arrived at Lifbon on the
ninth of June, where he was joyfully received as their deliverer.

Regardlefs of the frequent complaints and remonftrances delivered to the court of Spain by the Britifh ambaffador at Madrid, the Spaniards in America continued audacioufly to infult
and moleft our commerce.  They pretended that we had no right
either to cut logwood in the bay of Campeachy, or to gather
falt on the ifland of Tortugas.   Their guarda coftas boarded
and plundered every Englifh fhip they met, under a pretence of
fearching for contraband goods.  They even feized feveral Englifh veffels, confifcated their cargoes, and threw the failors into
prifon.    Fired by fuch reiterated provocation, the people of
England began now to lofe all patience.    Petitions to the houfe
of commons were tranfmitted from various parts of the kingdom.   The houfe again addreffed the king, and the king again
returned a promiffory anfwer.    It is difficult, even at this diftance of time, to reflect with patience on the pufillanimity of
the Britifh miniftry at this period; nor is it poffible to imagine
the Spaniards would have carried their infolence fo far, if they
had not depended on the pacific difpofition of Sir Robert Walpole [f].    That able minifter dreaded the confequences of a war
to himfelf and friends.    He had other ufes for the treafure
which fleets and armies would confume; and therefore he left
nothing unattempted to avert, or, at leaft, to procraftinate the

[f] One of the moft fhocking inftances of Spanifh infolent barbarity appeared in
the cafe of one Jenkins, mafter of a Scotch merchant fhip, who at the bar of the
houfe of commons held his ear in his hand, which had been torn from his head
by the crew of a guarda cofta, who declared they would do the fame by his mafter.  They tortured him with the moft wanton inhumanity, and threatened him
with inftant death. Being afked by a member, what were his thoughts when he was
in the hands of thefe barbarians? he anfwered, " I recommended my foul to God,
" and my caufe to my country."  This evidence made a ftrong impreffion on the
houfe.

ftorm.

form. For this purpose, he patched up a convention with the A. D court of Spain, importing, that the difputes between the two 1739 crowns fhould be fettled by two plenipotentiaries  This convention was feverely cenfured by the oppofition in both houfes of parliament.  The city of London, the Weft-India merchants, and the merchants of Briftol, prefented petitions, juftly complaining, that their indifputable right to pafs unmolefted to and from the Britifh colonies, was, in this convention, left, as a dubitable privilege, to be determined by plenipotentiaries.

The convention above mentioned ftipulated, that 95,000l. being a balance due from Spain to the crown and fubjects of Great-Britain, fhould be paid in London before the expiration of four months after the ratification. The time was now expired, and the money not yet paid.  The houfe of lords appointed a day for taking the ftate of the nation into confideration, and when the day arrived, Lord Carteret moved for a refolution, that this failure of payment was a high indignity to the king, and an injuftice to the nation [g]. The previous queftion was put, and the motion loft.  But though the minifter yet retained a fufficient majority in both houfes, the nation in general was too much exafperated to afford any hopes of preventing a war with Spain [h]. Letters of marque and reprifal were granted ; the army was augmented ; an embargo was laid on all outward-bound veffels ; a fleet was affembled at Spithead, and a reinforcement was fent to Admiral Haddock, who at this time commanded a fleet in the Mediterranean.  Our whole fleet in commiffion confifted of eighty-four men of war, befides thirty-two ready to be put into commiffion [i]. The entire navy of Spain amounted to thirty-three fhips of war, thofe of the flota, which are properly merchant-fhips, included.

[g] Smollet, vol. vii. p. 268.

[i] The fhips in commiffion were,

|  | of | 90 guns, |
|---|---|---|
| 1 | of | 90 guns, |
| 5 | —— | 80 |
| 12 | —— | 70 |
| 20 | —— | 60 |
| 19 | —— | 50 |
| 9 | —— | 44 |
| 18 | —— | 20 |

[h] Gent. Mag June, 1739.

Ships ready for commiffion.

| 2 | of | 100 guns, |
|---|---|---|
| 2 | —— | 90 |
| 6 | —— | 80 |
| 4 | —— | 70 |
| 10 | —— | 50 and 60 |
| 3 | —— | 44 |
| 5 | —— | 20 and 22 |

Both

Both nations began to make vigorous preparations for war. The court of Spain at this juncture revived its alliance by a marriage between the Infant Don Philip and Madam de France; and the French ministry did not scruple to declare, that if Spain were oppressed by any power whatsoever, they should not remain idle spectators. The States-General, on the other hand, did not scruple to signify by their ministers at the courts of France and Spain, that they were under certain mutual engagements to England, which, if required, they thought themselves in honour obliged to fulfil.

Vice-admiral Vernon sailed on the 20th of July for the West-Indies with nine men of war. This gentleman had rendered himself conspicuous in the house of commons by his blunt opposition to the ministry. In the debate concerning the Spanish depredations in the West-Indies, he had affirmed, that he could take Porto-Bello with six men of war. He had formerly commanded a fleet on the Jamaica station, and was therefore supposed to be well acquainted with those seas. His offer was echoed by the members in the opposition, and the whole nation resounded his praise. The minister embraced this opportunity of acquiring some popularity, and, at the same time, of removing a troublesome opponent in the house of commons. Besides, it was generally imagined that he was not without hopes that the admiral might disgrace himself and his party by not succeeding in the adventure. Vernon sailed for the West-Indies.

The English fleet cruising on the coast of Spain was particularly intended to intercept the Assogues ships from Vera Cruz [k]. These ships, however, arrived safe at St. Andero. Having received information of the situation of affairs in Europe, instead of coming by the Madeiras for Calais, as usual, they sailed by the Bahamas, and went north about; then steering westward, and doubling the Lizard, they made Ushant, and thence creeping along shore, crossed the bay of Biscay, and so to St. Andero.

On the 23d day of October, Great Britain declared war against Spain, and in the same month intelligence was received that Admiral Haddock had taken two rich ships from the Cara-

[k] Gent. Mag. vol. ix. p. 443.

caos,

caos, having on board 2,000,000 pieces of eight. He was foon A. D after joined by Admiral Balchin with fix fhips of the line. 1739

Vice-admiral Vernon arrived at Jamaica the 23d of October, the day on which war was proclaimed in England. On his arrival off Port-Royal in that ifland he had the fatisfaction to fee the Diamond man of war ftanding into the harbour with two Spanifh veffels in tow, one of which was a regifter fhip with 120,000 pieces of eight, and clothing for 6000 men, on board. The admiral failed from Jamaica on the 5th of November with fix fhips of war[m]. Having met with contrary winds, he did not come in fight of Porto-Bello till the 20th in the evening. He was apprehenfive of driving to the eaftward during the night; he therefore anchored about fix leagues from fhore. Porto-Bello is a town in the Spanifh Weft-Indies, fo called from the beauty of its harbour. It is fituated on the north coaft of the ifthmus of Darien, which divides the kingdom of Mexico from Terra Firma. The town ftands at the bottom of a fmall bay, defended by a caftle and two forts, one of which, called the Iron Fort, is fituated on the north fide of the mouth of the harbour; and the other, St. Jeronimo, near the town, with a battery facing the entrance into the bay. The caftle, called Gloria, ftands on the weft fide of the town.

On the 21ft, in the morning, the admiral weighed and plied to windward in line of battle[n]. The fhips entered the bay in the following order, viz. the Hampton-Court, Norwich, Worcefter, Burford, Strafford, Louifa. Orders had been given for a general attack; but, the wind coming to the eaftward, the admiral was obliged to confine his attack to the Iron Fort, clofe to which the fquadron was piloted by Captain Rentone. When the Hampton-Court came within about a cable's length of the fort, fhe was fuddenly becalmed by the high land to windward, and, before fhe could bring her guns to bear, was

[m] Viz.

| | | | |
|---|---|---|---|
| Burford | of | 70 guns and 500 men. | |
| Hampton-Court, | 70 | 495 | Capt. Watfon. |
| Worcefter, | 60 | 400 | Main. |
| Louifa, | 60 | 400 | Waterhoufe. |
| Strafford, | 60 | 400 | Trevor. |
| Norwich, | 50 | 300 | Herbert. |

[n] London Gazette, March 15, 1740.

A. D.
1739.

exposed to a smart fire from the enemy. But as soon as she was in a situation to return the salute, after having dropped her anchor, she seemed, in a moment, a cloud of perpetual thunder. She appeared to the rest of the fleet to be all on fire. In the space of twenty-five minutes she is said to have fired 400 balls. The Norwich and the Worcester were not long before they came up, and fired upon the fort with vast alacrity. These were followed by the Burford, on board of which was the admiral, who, perceiving that the Spaniards began to fly from several parts of the fort, made a signal for landing. Meanwhile he luffed up as near the fort as possible, and, by means of his small arms, drove the garrison from the lower battery. As the boats full of sailors and marines passed the admiral, he called to them to land immediately under the walls of the fort, though there was no breach made. The sailors were no sooner on shore than they scaled the wall, and, pulling up the soldiers after them, struck the Spanish colours in the lower battery, and hoisted an English ensign. This was no sooner perceived by the garrison in the upper part of the fort, than they hoisted a white flag, a signal for capitulation, and surrendered at discretion. The garrison of this fort consisted of 300 men, out of which, at the time of surrender, there remained only thirty-five privates and five officers.

The ships which sailed in before the admiral were now fallen to leeward; but the Burford being exposed to the Gloria-Castle, it continued firing at her till night, without, however, doing her any other damage than wounding her fore-top-mast a little above the rigging. The admiral then pointed some of his lower-deck guns at this castle, and sent several shot over it into the town, one of which went through the governor's house.

On the morning of the 22d the admiral called a council of war, and, it being thought not adviseable to attack the Gloria-Castle by day, orders were issued for warping the ships up the following night. This circumspection proved unnecessary. The Spaniards hoisted a white flag, and immediately sent a boat with a flag of truce, with terms on which they wished to capitulate: in answer to these the admiral returned other articles, and allowed them a few hours for deliberation. They accepted
                                                                    his

his terms*, and the British troops took immediate possession of A. D. the Gloria and St. Jeronimo forts.

There were in the harbour of Porto-Bello two Spanish guarda-costas of twenty guns each, and an armed snow. The crews of these vessels, chusing to anticipate the British sailors, plundered the town in the night, and committed great outrages on the inhabitants. The English seamen and soldiers, on the contrary, behaved with great decency and humanity, after they

---

* *Articles of capitulation granted by Edward Vernon, Esq; vice-admiral of the blue, and commander in chief of his majesty's ships and vessels in the West-Indies, and Commodore Brown, to Don Francisco Martinez de Retez, governor of Porto-Bello, and Don Francisco de Abared, commandant of the guarda-costas at the same place, the 22d of November, 1739, O. S.*

I. That the garrison be allowed to march out, as desired, upon condition the king of Great Britain's troops be put into possession of the Gloria-Castle before four o'clock this evening, and the garrison to march out by ten o'clock to-morrow morning. That the inhabitants may either remove or remain, under a promise of security for themselves and their effects.

II. That the Spanish soldiers may have a guard, if they think it necessary.

III. That they may carry off two cannons mounted with ten charges of powder each, and their match lighted.

IV. The gates of the Gloria-Castle must absolutely be in possession of the king our master's troops by four o'clock, and the Spanish garrison shall remain in all safety, for their persons and effects, till the appointed time for their marching out, and to carry with them the provisions and ammunition necessary for their safety.

V. That the ships, with their apparel and arms, be absolutely delivered up to the use of his Britannic majesty; but that all the officers, soldiers, and crews, shall have three days allowed them to retire with all their personal effects, only one officer being admitted on board each ship and vessel, to take possession for the king our master, and to see this article strictly complied with.

VI. That provided the articles above mentioned are strictly complied with, and that possession is given of Castle St. Jeronimo, in the same manner as is stipulated for the Castle Gloria, then the clergy, the churches, and town, shall be protected and preserved in all their immunities and properties; and that all persons already taken shall be set at liberty before our leaving the port.

Given under our hands on board his majesty's ship Burford, in Porto-Bello harbour, this 23d of November, 1739, O. S.

E. VERNON,
CHA. BROWN.

I presume it will not be thought inconsistent with the dignity of history to record a piece of genuine wit in a common sailor, who, when the officer who commanded at the scaling of the Iron-Castle, ordered the troops to *halt,* cried, " Damn " my eyes, captain, don't let's *halt* till we are *crippled.*"

became

A. D. became poffeffed of the town; and, as a reward for their mo-
1739. deration and gallantry, the admiral diftributed among them
10,000 dollars, which were juft arrived in order to pay the Spanifh troops. The admiral, having taken on board his fleet all
the brafs cannon and ammunition found in the feveral forts, he
proceeded to demolifh the fortifications; which was completely
effected in three weeks, at the expence of 122 barrels of Spanifh gun-powder [p]. On the 27th of November the Diamond,
Captain Knowles, and on the 29th the Windfor, Captain Berkley, and the Anglefea, Captain Reddifh, arrived at Porto-Bello,
in confequence of orders, left by the admiral at the Leeward
iflands, for thefe fhips to follow him. On the 13th of December the admiral, with his fquadron, failed for Jamaica, and on
the 28th, being then off Carthagena, he defpatched Captain
Rentone, in the Spanifh fnow, with the news to England.

Admiral Vernon, and the fleet under his command, certainly
deferved the honour they acquired by the fuccefs of this expedition; neverthelefs, it muft be confeffed, that their eafy conqueft muft be in part attributed to the cowardice of the Spaniards in furrendering the firft fort before a breach was made,
and the other two before they were attacked. The Gloria-Ca-
ftle was garrifoned by 400 men, and was fo regularly fortified,
that it might have fuftained a long fiege. Its lower battery had
two baftions, and a curtain which mounted 22 guns, befides a
line of eight guns facing the mouth of the harbour. There
were alfo feveral other batteries both in the Gloria and St. Jeronimo, in the fame direction, which, if properly ferved, would
have rendered the entrance into the harbour exceedingly dangerous, if not impracticable.

The taking of Porto-Bello, whilft it did honour to the Britifh
navy, reflected at the fame time no inconfiderable degree of praife
on the Englifh miniftry. There was an evident propriety in punifhing the infolence of the Spaniards in the offending part.
Porto-Bello was an afylum for the guarda-coftas, two of which
were found in the harbour, and carried off by the admiral. But
this was not the only fervice he rendered to his country in the

---

[p] The admiral took on board, from the feveral batteries, 40 pieces of brafs
cannon, 10 brafs field-pieces, four brafs mortars, 18 brafs pattereroes, and fpiked
80 pieces of iron ordnance.

deftruction

destruction of Porto-Bello. His success enabled him to extend his influence to Panama, where some of the factors and servants of the South-sea company were confined. He wrote to the president of that place in the language of a conqueror, and the factors and servants were immediately sent to Porto-Bello.

Captain Rentone, in the Triumph sloop, arrived in England on the 12th of March, 1740, with the news of this expedition [q]. The whole nation became frantic with joy. Congratulatory addresses were presented by parliament, by the cities of London, Bristol, &c. The commons granted every demand of the crown. They voted 28,000 land-forces, besides 6000 marines; they provided for a powerful navy, and several men of war were added to those already in commission [r].

There were at this time two considerable squadrons of English men of war in the Mediterranean; one at Gibraltar, commanded by Sir Chaloner Ogle, consisting of twelve sail, and the other on the Minorca station, commanded by Rear-admiral Haddock. But these fleets were only employed in cruising on the coast of Spain and Italy, without any attempt to attack or annoy the enemy, except by now and then seizing a poor defenceless fly that happened unfortunately to fall into their web. The reader needs not be informed, that I allude to the capture of unarmed trading vessels by ships of war. A contemplative mind, reflecting on these maritime depredations, is naturally led to inquire, by what law of nature, or of nations, or on what principle of justice, princes at war thus seize the private property of each others subjects, in ships trading to other king-

---

[q] The news was known in England before his arrival. On the 11th Mr. Baker, master of Lloyd's coffeehouse, waited on Sir R. Walpole with a letter, containing an account of Vernon's success. It was brought from Jamaica by a ship which sailed from thence, in company with Captain Rentone; and arrived at Dover a day before him.

[r] Viz. Colchester, of 80 guns, and 600 men, Captain Garlington.

| | | | | |
|---|---|---|---|---|
| Torbay, | — 80 | —— | 600 —— | Parker. |
| Cambridge, | — 80 | —— | 600 —— | Whorwood. |
| Pr. Frederic, | — 70 | —— | 480 —— | Clinton. |
| Oxford, | — 70 | —— | 480 —— | Ld. Aug. Fitzroy. |
| Seven fire-ships. | | | | |

doms?

doms? This procedure feems more extraordinary when we confider, that their land-forces generally obferve a different conduct. A general, in marching through an enemy's country, fo far from robbing and imprifoning every peafant he meets, gives pofitive orders, that the perfon and property of individuals, not in arms, fhall not be molefted. He makes war againft the prince, and not againft the people individually. An admiral, on the contrary, takes every trading veffel he meets, robs the owners of their property, and fends the crew home to be confined as prifoners of war. Here then is a heavy punifhment inflicted on perfons who had neither intention nor power to commit any offence, or in any wife to injure thofe by whom the punifhment is inflicted. I do not obtrude thefe reflections with any hope of influencing the conduct of the rulers of the earth: reafon, juftice, and humanity are not the privy-counfellors of kings. But perhaps the reader may not totally difregard thefe counfellors, and will therefore pardon this fhort interruption of the thread of our hiftory.

1740. We now return to Admiral Vernon, the hero of this period. I have related above, that in the laft month of the year 1739, he failed with his fquadron from Porto-Bello to Jamaica. He continued at Port-Royal, in that ifland, till the 25th of February (1740) following, on which day he failed for Carthagena, which he bombarded at intervals during three days, with no other effect than that of terrifying the inhabitants, and injuring fome of their churches and convents[a]. What was intended by this bombardment is not very evident. On the 10th of March the fquadron weighed anchor, and failed in line of battle weftward along the coaft. In paffing by Boca Chica, they were faluted with a few fhot from three fmall forts near the mouth of the harbour; but they fell fhort of the fhips. The admiral, having ordered the Windfor and the Greenwich to cruize off Carthagena, proceeded with the reft of his fleet to Porto-Bello, in order to repair the damages fuftained by the fmall craft in the late bombardment. This bufinefs being compleated, and the fleet watered in about eight days, he failed on the 22d, and fteering fouth-weft along fhore, entered the river

[a] London Gazette, June 19.

Chegre,

Chegre, which is but a few leagues diftant from Porto-Bello. A. D. At the mouth of this river there was a caftle, or fort, called 1746 St. Lorenzo, under whofe protection the guarda-coftas ufed to ride fecure. The only two of thefe Spanifh pirates (for they were little better) which now remained on this coaft, were at this time in the river. The admiral, in going in, had the mif-fortune to be retarded by an accident which happened to his fore-top-fail-yard. He was on board the Strafford. This ac-cident obliged him to make a fignal for the Norwich to fail in before him, with the bomb-ketches, fire-fhips, and tenders. The Norwich was then commanded by Captain Herbert, and the bomb-ketches, &c. were conducted by Captain Knowles, who came to an anchor at three in the afternoon, and began to bombard the fort that evening. The admiral's fhip did not come to an anchor till ten o'clock at night. Far be it from me to infinuate that there was any want of perfonal courage in Ad-miral Vernon; but I beg leave to advife all future admirals, to whom fuch an accident in the fore-top-fail-yard may happen, immediately to hoift their flag on board the leading fhip. This, however, does not appear to have been a fervice of much danger. The caftle mounted only eleven brafs cannon, and as many pattereroes. Neverthelefs it fuftained a furious bombard-ment, and a continued cannonade from three of the largeft fhips in the fleet, till the morning of the 24th, when the gar-rifon furrendered, and the fort was immediately poffeffed by the Britifh troops [t].

---

[t] *Articles of capitulation between Edward Vernon, Efq; vice-admiral, &c. and Don Juan Carlos Zavellos, captain of foot, &c.*

I. That, upon his Britannic majefty's troops being put in poffeffion of the fort St. Lorenzo, at the mouth of the river Chegre, the faid captain, and all his gar-rifon, be at free liberty to march out without any moleftation, and may retire into the village of Chegre, or where elfe they pleafe.

II. That the inhabitants of Chegre may remain in all fafety in their own houfes, under a promife of fecurity to their perfons and houfes.

III. That the guarda-cofta floops be delivered up in the condition they are, and the cuftom-houfe.

IV. That the clergy and churches in Chegre fhall be protected and preferved in all their immunities.

E. VERNON.

There

There were found in the cuftom-houfe, on the oppofite fide of the river, 4,300 bags of Peruvian bark, and other merchandize, which were fhipped on board the fleet, together with the brafs ordnance above-mentioned. The cuftom-houfe was then fet on fire, the two guarda-coftas deftroyed, and the fort entirely demolifhed; after which the admiral returned to Porto-Bello, where he arrived on the firft of April.

Whilft Vernon was thus employed in the Weft-Indies, our fleets in Europe were unemployed. I mean to fay, that they atchieved nothing againft the enemy; for as to employment, they had enough of failing and counter-failing, and of fighting too, with adverfe winds. On the 23d of July a fleet of twenty-one fhips of the line, commanded by Sir John Norris, with two other admirals, viz. Sir Chaloner Ogle, and Philip Cavendifh, failed from St. Helen's with a fair wind, the duke of Cumberland ferving on board as a volunteer. But the wind fhifting, they were obliged, after being three days at fea, to put back into Torbay. On the 4th of Auguft they failed again, with the wind at north-eaft, and on the following day were within a few leagues of the Lizard; but on the 6th it blew fo violently from the weft, that they were obliged once more to return to Torbay. On the 22d they made a third attempt, and after five days obftinate contention with tempeftuous contrary winds, were a third time obliged to return to the fame place. What was the deftination of this fleet remains a matter of doubt. Probably the Spanifh fquadron, at that time at Ferrol, was the object. But, be the defign whatfoever it might, it was now relinquifhed, and the admiral, with the duke of Cumberland, returned to London. Thus began, and thus ended the naval hiftory of his Royal Highnefs, who probably concluded, from this inaufpicious effay, that he had miftaken his element.

In this year the celebrated Commodore Anfon began his voyage to the South-feas. He failed from St. Helen's with five men of war on the 18th of September. About two months after, Sir Chaloner Ogle failed for the Weft-Indies with twenty-one fhips of the line, and a confiderable body of land-forces, commanded by Lord Cathcart. This formidable fleet, which confifted of a hundred and feventy fail [u], had fcarce taken its

[u] Smollet's hiftory, vol. viii. p. 287.

departure

departure from the Land's-end, before it was fcattered and difperfed by a violent tempeft. The admiral neverthelefs purfued
his voyage, and came to an anchor in the neutral ifland of Dominica, in order to take in wood and water. In this ifland the
expedition fuftained an irreparable lofs in the death of Lord
Cathcart, a brave and experienced officer, who died of a dyfen-
tery. The command of the land forces now devolved upon
General Wentworth, an officer of no experience, and of very
moderate abilities. The admiral, in his voyage from Dominica
to Jamaica, failing near the ifland of Hifpaniola, difcovered four
large fhips of war. He made fignal for an equal number of
his fquadron to give them chace. The chace refufed to bring
to, and Lord Auguftus Fitzroy, who commanded the Englifh
detachment, gave one of them a broad-fide, and an engagement enfued, which continued during part of the night. In the
morning they boifted French colours, and confequently the firing ceafed, there being at this time no declaration of war between the two nations. The commanders appologized to each
other for the miftake, and parted, but with lofs of men on both
fides.

Sir Chaloner Ogle arrived off Jamaica on the 9th of January
1741, where he joined Admiral Vernon, who now commanded
a fleet of thirty fhips of the line, with a confiderable number
of frigates, bomb-ketches, firefhips, &c[a]. The number of
feamen was about 15,000, and that of the land-forces at leaft
12,000, including four battalions raifed in America, and 500
negroes from Jamaica. This very formidable armament, doubtlefs the moft tremendous that ever appeared in thofe feas, was
certainly equal to any attempt againft the Spanifh fettlements.
Their treafure might have been intercepted, and their colonies
eafily reduced. But this complete humiliation of Spain was prevented by the concurrence of a variety of circumftances. The
Britifh miniftry, for reafons beft known to themfelves, detained
the fleet at Spithead much too long. For the credit of human nature, I am willing to believe, that the prime minifter
was not fo exceedingly wicked as to endeavour, by retarding
the fleet, to fruftrate the expedition: and yet, to the difgrace

[a] Vide appendix, No. I.

A. 1
174
1741

A. D. of human nature, I fear there have been inftances of minifters 1741· fo diabolical as to be influenced by very ignoble paffions, in oppofition to the intereft and dignity of the nation, with whofe weal they were intrufted. It feems however a fafe maxim in politics, not to commit the management of a war to a minifter who fhall have repeatedly declared his difapprobation of the meafure. But be the defigns of the minifter what they might, it is fcarce poffible to fuppofe that the admiral was not hearty in the caufe; and yet it was near the end of January before he failed from Jamaica, though he certainly was not ignorant that the feafon was already two far advanced, in a climate where the rains, which begin about the end of April, render it impoffible for troops to keep the field.

I muft here take occafion to obferve, that the admiral's orders were difcretionary: he might therefore have made his attack on any of the Spanifh fettlements. The Havanna, which was certainly an objeét of the greateft importance, lay to leeward, and might eafily have been reached in lefs than three days. Neverthelefs, Mr. Vernon thought fit to beat againft the wind to Hifpaniola, with an intention, as it was faid, to obferve the French fleet. On the 15th of February he learnt, that this fleet had failed for Europe, having previoufly fent an advice-boat to Carthagena, to inform the Spaniards of Vernon's being in thofe feas. The admiral called a council of war, and it was determined to land on the continent of New Spain. Accordingly, after fpending fome days in taking in wood and water at Hifpaniola, the fleet failed, and, on the 4th of March, came to an anchor in a bay called Playa Granda, to windward of Carthagena. This fleet confifted of one hundred and twenty-four fail, the fight of which muft have ftruck fuch terror into the Spaniards, that nothing but want of refolution and defpatch could have prevented its fuccefs. There cannot be a truer maxim in the art of war, than, That hefitation in the affailant infpires the defendant with courage, which augments progreffively in proportion to the delay. But the commanders of this fleet and army, as if determined to give the enemy time to recover from their furprize, remained inaétive in the bay till the 9th. On that day the firft divifion of the fleet, commanded by Sir Chaloner Ogle, followed by Admiral Vernon with all the tranfports, moved forward

towards.

towards the entrance of the harbour called Boca Chica, which A. D was defended by several formidable batteries. The third divi- 1741 fion, commanded by Mr. Leftock, remained at anchor. The Norfolk, the Ruffel, and the Shrewfbury anchored very near two forts called St. Jago and St. Philip, which being filenced in lefs than an hour, were immediately poffeffed by a detachment of Britifh grenadiers.

On the 10th, the two regiments of Harrifon and Wentworth, with fix regiments of marines, landed on the ifland of Tierra Bomba, where, having pitched their tents, they began to erect a battery againft the caftle of Boca Chica. Five days more were employed in landing the artillery and neceffary ftores. But General Wentworth's want of knowledge in the art of war, foon difcovered itfelf in the choice of his ground: for the tents were no fooner pitched than the foldiers found themfelves expofed to the fire of a fafcine battery from the oppofite fide of the harbour, on the ifland of Varu. To remedy this evil, the admiral immediately detached a confiderable number of failors under the command of Captain Bofcawen, who landed about a mile to leeward of the battery, which mounted fifteen twenty-four pounders, under a raifed battery of five guns. Thefe intrepid fons of Neptune foon gained poffeffion of both batteries, and, having fpiked the cannon, returned to their fhips.

On the 22d, General Wentworth opened a battery of twenty twenty-four pounders againft the caftle of Boca Chica, and the next day Commodore Leftock with five fhips was ordered to attack it by fea. He renewed his attack on the 24th, and on that day fell Lord Aubrey Beauclerc, captain of the Prince Frederic, a very brave and experienced officer. Meanwhile the Spaniards had remounted their fafcine battery, which was a fecond time deftroyed by a detachment of failors. A fmall breach being now made on the land-fide of Boca-Chica caftle, the general acquainted the admiral with his refolution to ftorm it, who, in order to divert the attention of the enemy, manned his boats under the command of Captain Knowles. The failors landed near the caftle, and there waited for the general affault: The grenadiers, on the other fide, marched up in good order; but they no fooner began to mount the breach, than the garrifon fled without firing a fingle mufket. The garrifon of another

C 2                                    fort

fort, called St. Joseph, followed their example, and our sailors took immediate poffeffion of it. Emboldened by this fuccefs, and perceiving the enemy preparing to fink their fhips, they boarded the Spanifh admiral's fhip, the Galicia, on board of which they found the captain and fixty men. There were in the harbour, when the attack of Boca Chica began, fix Spanifh men of war, two of which were now funk, and one burnt by the Spaniards themfelves. The failors then proceeded to cut the boom, and thus opened a free paffage for our fhips into the lake. Next morning the fleet entered without moleftation, but the wind blowing frefh and contrary, it was feveral days before they reached the narrow entrance into the harbour near the town. This entrance was defended by a confiderable fortrefs, called Caftillo Grande, mounting fifty-nine guns, which the enemy abandoned as foon as the fhips approached.

Thus far all went well. The caftles, forts, and batteries, which commanded the lake, were now in poffeffion of the Englifh. The entrance into this lake, was doubtlefs an enterprize of no fmall danger and difficulty, the channel being commanded by two hundred cannon, thofe from the enemy's fhips included. So far the admiral feems to have done every thing neceffary on his part, by removing all obftacles in the way to conqueft; and he was fo confident of fucceeding, that, on the firft of April, he fent an exprefs to the duke of Newcaftle, with an account of his progrefs; on the receipt of which his grace, with the reft of the people of England, became frantic with joy and exultation. But with pain I proceed to record, that here our fuccefs ended. The next exprefs brought a tale as humble as the former was triumphant. On this lucklefs *firft of April*[c], the failors having opened a channel through the funken wrecks of the enemy, the bomb-ketches covered by two frigates, entered the harbour, and were, on the fucceeding day, followed by three fire-fhips, which were fo pofted as to cover the intended landing of the troops. The Weymouth, Captain Knowles, got into the harbour on the third, and on the fifth, early in the morning, the troops began to land at a place called la Quinta, from whence General Wentworth, at the head of 1500 men, pufhed forward,

[c] London Gazette, June 20.

through

through a narrow defile, to an open ground about a mile from A. I fort St. Lazar, which fort entirely commanded the town of 174: Carthagena. He met with some interruption on his march from a body of six or seven hundred Spaniards, and lost a few of his men; but the enemy soon retired, and, in the evening of the sixth, the remainder of the English army were disembarked, and, having joined their general, the whole encamped on the plain above mentioned.

Fort St. Lazar, the only remaining fortress, was well forti-fied, and defended by a numerous garrison. The general was of opinion, that any attempt to take it without regular ap-proaches would be attended with much danger and difficulty. The admiral, on the contrary, was positive that it was practi-cable by escalade. From this time the demon of discord pre-sided in their councils, and they began to entertain a sovereign contempt for each other's opinions. The general upbraided the admiral for not cannonading the town, and the latter reproach-ed the former for not storming the fort. It was at length re-solved in a council of war to attack St. Lazar by storm, the season being now too far advanced to allow time for erecting a battery of cannon in order to open a breach. In consequence of this resolution, on the ninth, before break of day, Brigadier-General Guise, with 1200 men, marched to the attack. Un-fortunately his guides were slain before he reached the walls. His scaling-ladders, being applied at random, proved too short. The officers were disconcerted for want of orders. A general confusion ensued, and the troops were obliged to retire with the loss of 600 men killed or wounded. By this time the rains began to fall very heavily, and disease became so universal in the camp, that it was determined in a general council of war to re-linquish every idea of a farther attempt. The remnant of the army retired to their ships, and were re-embarked on the 16th. The admiral, in order to clear himself from any imputation of neglect, and to demonstrate the impracticability of taking the place with ships after the unsuccessful attack on St. Lazar, having previously converted the Spanish admiral's ship, Galicia, into a floating battery, warped her into the harbour as near to the town as possible. In this station she fired upon the town for some hours; but it appearing that she was at too great a distance to injure the

walls,

A. D. walls, she was suffered to drive, and soon struck upon the san:
1741. This experiment, how plausible soever it might seem, was by n :
means allowed to be satisfactory.   An historian [d], who was pre-.
sent, affirms, that in another part of the harbour there was
space and water sufficient for four or five men of war to lie within pistol-shot of the walls of Carthagena.   If this be true, the
admiral was certainly inexcusable for not bringing his ships to
bear upon the town during the attack upon St. Lazar.

The shattered remnant of this ill-fated army having returned
to their ships, diseases, peculiar to the climate, raged with inconceivable malignity, and many brave men who had escaped
the enemy died in their hammocks.   The jarring chieftains were
unanimous as to the expediency of retiring from this scene of
destruction and disgrace.   A few days were spent in destroying
the forts already taken, and then the fleet sailed for Jamaica.

As the rational design of historical writings is not merely to
gratify the reader's curiosity, but rather to exhibit examples of
vice and folly, virtue and sagacity, for his occasional abhorrence
or imitation, I shall endeavour to point out the causes of the
miscarriage of this important expedition.   Some future commander of an attack upon Carthagena may possibly deem this
investigation worthy of his attention.

The old adage, That a bad beginning commonly produces a
bad ending, is more frequently verified in the catastrophe of
naval expeditions, than in any other species of human transactions.   It is always in the power of a malignant prime minister
to frustrate the best-concerted attempt, if he be influenced by passions or policy to wish that it may not succeed : and I fear there
have been very few prime ministers so uninterestedly dispassion-
ate, as sincerely to wish the success of measures adopted in opposition to their advice.   Sir Robert Walpole's consent to a war
with Spain, was evidently an involuntary compliance with the
clamour of opposition, and of the nation in general.   The fleet
was not only unnecessarily retarded at Spithead, but the troops,
which were put on board, were raw and undisciplined.   The
fleet ought certainly to have sailed at least a month earlier ; for
though there might be barely time to execute the plan proposed,

d Smollet's hist. vol, vii, p. 187.

naval

th val expeditions are, in their nature, liable to fo many caufes A. D.
fc f delay, that they wi.l not admit of nice calculation in point 1741.
c f time. But, if this minifterial delay was inexcufable, what
fhall we fay of the dilatory proceedings of the admiral, who was
certainly better acquainted with the climate?

From the above account of this unfuccefsful expedition we
learn, that our fleet and army were no fooner in poffeffion of
all the forts, which defended the lake, than the admiral and
general began to quarrel: their animofity daily increafed, and
their mutual contempt became at laft fo exceffive, that the glorious caufe in which they were engaged feemed lefs the object
of their attention, than the means of effecting each other's difgrace. But the mifchief did not end with the commanders;
each had his feparate cabal, and the fpirit of difcord was diffufed through the whole fleet and army. This fatal, childifh
mifunderftanding is an evident proof, that both the admiral and
general, to fay no worfe of them, were weak men. If either
of them had poffeffed the foul of a great commander, he would
not have fuffered the folly of the other to ruin an enterprize of
fuch importance. Fools, it is true, are fometimes obftinate;
but it is feldom difficult for difpaffionate wifdom to flatter them
into compliance; and certainly, on fuch an occafion, fomewhat
of punctilio fhould have been facrificed to patriotifm.

The attack upon St. Lazar was certainly abfurd, and the hope
of fucceeding was doubtlefs founded folely on the facility with
which the other forts had been poffeffed. This was a falfe conclufion; for that facility had rendered this fortrefs more formidable by an accumulation of troops. But, in order to give the
leaft degree of probability to the fuccefs of this attack, the admiral ought at the fame time to have cannonaded and bombarded the town with all the power of his fleet. He might certainly have brought more fhips into the harbour, and they might
with fafety have brought up much nearer to the walls. When
the French took Carthagena in 1697, the firing from the fhips
contributed effentially to their fuccefs; but they landed a confiderable train of artillery, with which they made a breach in the
walls of the town, and then bravely fought their way into it.
I alfo beg leave to remind the reader, that, in the year 1740,
Admiral Vernon bombarded the town of Carthagena from the
fea.

fea. As therefore he had now fo many fhips more than he wanted, why did he not leave fome of them on the coaft, with orders to co-operate with the fleet in the harbour and the army, in the moment of a general attack? Upon the whole, Wentworth appears to have done all in his power, and his troops do not feem in any ways to have difgraced their country; but, alas! the refolutions by which they had the misfortune to be directed, were the refult of jarring deliberations among the incongruous inhabitants of different elements. The general might be culpable in not treating the admiral with that degree of refpect which his late victory gave him fome reafon to expect; but the latter was certainly inexcufable in not affifting the former in the reduction of the town. This conduct in the admiral will appear exceedingly reprehenfible, if, upon a careful furvey of the forts and harbour, it fhould appear, that, after the reduction of the feveral fortreffes commanding the lake, the town might be reduced by a fleet without the affiftance of a land army: and the truth of this fuppofition feems fo extremely probable, that I verily believe Vernon would have taken it, if the troops had never been landed, or if he had had no troops to affift him in the attempt. It is very evident that the town of Carthagena may be eafily bombarded both from the fea and from the harbour; and it is equally certain that no town, in which there are any number of opulent inhabitants, will fuftain that fpecies of deftructive infult for any length of time; they will rife upon the garrifon, and oblige them to capitulate.

Be this as it may, though the Englifh failors and foldiers were difappointed of their expected fpoils of the enemy, they retired with the fatisfaction of having done the Spaniards great injury in the deftruction of many confiderable fortifications, in fpiking a number of cannon, and in annihilating fix men of war and fix galleons, befides many other veffels.

Let us now follow the Englifh fleet to Jamaica, where it arrived on the 19th of May. The climate of this ifland did not contribute much towards the recovery of the fick, many of whom died after their arrival; among the reft Lord Auguftus Fitzroy, captain of the Orford. Vernon, on his arrival at Jamaica [c], having received orders from England to retain in the

[c] London Gazette, July 25, 1741.

Weft-

West-Indies no more ships than were necessary, sent home seve- A. D
ral men of war under the command of Commodore Lestock f. 1741
The remainder of his fleet were deemed quite sufficient, there
being at this time but one Spanish squadron at the Havanna,
and a small French fleet at Hispaniola. It is very certain that
the admiral was so exceedingly dissatisfied with his colleague
Wentworth, that he ardently wished to return to England; but
the king had conceived so high an opinion of his abilities, and
the letters which the admiral received from the duke of Newcastle were so extremely flattering, that he determined to continue in his station. On the 26th of May he called a general
council of war, the members of which were himself, Sir Chaloner Ogle, General Wentworth, General Guise, and Governor
Trelawny. The four first of these gentlemen were unanimous
in opinion, that St. Jago on the island of Cuba was the proper
object of attack. Governor Trelawny, on the contrary, thought
Cuba of little importance, and strenuously advised an expedition
against Panama on the isthmus of Darien. The governor, however, acquiesced, and raised a corps of a thousand negroes, which
were put on board the fleet with all possible expedition.

This armament, which sailed from Jamaica on the first of
July s, consisted of eight ships of the line, one of 50 guns,
twelve frigates, &c. h and about 40 transports, on board of

---

f These were the Carolina, Russel, Norfolk, Shrewsbury, Amelia, Torbay,
Chichester, Hampton-Court, Burford, Windsor, and Falmouth, besides five frigates.

g London Gazette, Oct. 27.

h Viz.

VICE-ADMIRAL VERNON.

*Frigates.*

| | | | |
|---|---|---|---|
| Shoreham, | Chester, | Captain Long, | 50 guns. |
| Alderney, | Grafton, | Rycaut, | 70 |
| Strombolo, | Boyne, | (Admiral) Watson, | 80 |
| Phaeton, | Worcester, | Cleland, | 60 |
| Bonetta, | Tilbury, | Dent, | 60 |
| Princess Royal, | | | |
| Pompey, | | | |
| Triton. | | | |

REAR-ADMIRAL SIR CHALONER OGLE.

| | | | |
|---|---|---|---|
| Experiment, | Kent, | Mitchel, | 70 |
| Sheerness, | Cumberland, (Adm.) | Norris, | 80 |
| Vesuvius, | Tyger, | Herbert, | 60 |
| Scarborough, | Montague, | Chambers, | 60 |

A. D. which, including blacks, were 3400 land forces. The fleet came
1741. to an anchor on the 18th in Walthenham harbour on the south
side of the isle of Cuba. The admiral, fully determining to
annex for ever this fine island to the dominions of his Britannic
majesty, began by changing the name of *Walthenham* into that
of *Cumberland* harbour, in compliment to his Royal Highness
the duke. With submission to commanders of fleets, invading
an enemy's country, I should think it most advisable to avoid
this parade of giving names to places which were named before,
unless they are perfectly certain of being able to maintain their
conquest, because the spurious appellation, after their departure, will be recollected only as a memorandum of their disgrace. This harbour, howsoever called, was a very capacious
and secure asylum against the hurricanes so frequent in the
West-Indies at this season of the year: it was therefore a de-
sirable possession, particularly as it was acquired without molestation. The island of Cuba is not only the largest of the An-
tilles, but it is also said to be the most fruitful and healthy of
any in the West-Indies.

There were, at this time, twelve Spanish ships of the line
at the Havanna, a populous city on the west side of the island,
where the governor resides, and where there were strong forti-
cations and a numerous garrison. For these reasons, though
the conquest of the whole island was ultimately intended, it was
thought advisable to begin with St. Jago, a less considerable
city on the eastern coast. Walthenham harbour lies about eleven
leagues south-west from St. Jago, and distant by land about sixty
miles, on which side the city is almost entirely defenceless. Its
fortifications to the sea were not formidable, but the entrance
into the harbour is so extremely narrow, and the navigation so
dangerous, that nature has sufficiently secured it from a naval
attack. On these considerations it was resolved, in a general
council of war, held on board the admiral, on the 20th of July,
to land the troops immediately, and take the city of St. Jago
by surprise.

The troops were accordingly disembarked, and, meeting with
no opposition, marched some miles up the country, and encamped on the banks of a navigable river. From this encampment
General Wentworth detached several reconnoitring parties,
which

which falling in with fmall bodies of the enemy, repulfed them A. D with very little lofs on either fide. One of thefe reconnoitring 174 parties, confifting of 150 Americans and negroes, commanded by Major Dunfter, penetrated as far as the village of Elleguava, where he continued fome time; but not being fupported by the main army, he returned to the camp. Meanwhile Admiral Vernon defpatched part of his fleet to block up the port of St. Jago, and to watch the motions of the Spanifh admiral at the Havanna, expecting with the utmoft impatience the progrefs of the army. But, on the 5th of October, he had the mortification to receive a letter from General Wentworth, expreffing his doubts of being able either to advance farther, or even to fub- fift his army much longer in the part which they then poffeffed. On the 9th the general called a council of war, the members of which were unanimoufly of opinion, that it was impoffible to march farther into the country, without expofing the troops to certain ruin. The army neverthelefs continued in its encamp- ment till the 7th of November, when another council of war, confifting of the land-officers only, refolved, that the troops ought to be re-embarked with all poffible expedition; and they were accordingly put on board their tranfports on the 20th, without the leaft moleftation from the enemy.

Thus ended the *conqueft* of the ifle of Cuba, the inhabitants of which were, from the incomprehenfible conduct of the Bri- tifh troops, at laft perfuaded that they landed without any ho- ftile intentions. The good people of England grew extremely diffatisfied, impatient of news, and as much aftonifhed at the cautious inactivity of General Wentworth, as they are at this moment (October the 5th, 1777 *) at the manœuvres of their general who is to conquer America. But the people of Eng- land, who reafon only from appearance, and are guided folely by common fenfe, are very incompetent judges of the actions of great generals and great minifters. A general, though abfolute at the head of his army, is a mere inftrument in the hands of the prime minifter, and muft fight or not fight according to his private inftructions. Some of the politicians, of the period of which I am now writing, were of opinion, that our making

---

* General Howe failed from New-York on a fecret expedition in Auguft, and no accounts of him had arrived in England at this period.

conquefts

A. D. conquests in the West-Indies was disagreeable to France, and
1741. that a French war was to be avoided at all events : others did
not scruple to infinuate, that the minister did all in his power to
fruftrate every attempt in the profecution of a war into which
he had been forced by the oppofition ; and a third clafs of people attributed this mifcarriage entirely to the general's want of
fkill and refolution.    Whatever might be the real caufe of this
very extraordinary fupinenefs in the Britifh troops, there are
very few incidents in hiftory which afford more apparent foundation for cenfure.    St. Jago, which was not above four days
march, for light troops, from Cumberland harbour, was in a
great meafure defencelefs on the land fide, and therefore might
have been eafily furprifed.    There was no army in the country
to oppofe an enemy, therefore why it was not immediately attempted is very difficult to conceive ; unlefs we fuppofe that the
officers had no inclination to make conquefts in fo fatal a climate, where, if they had fucceeded, they would have been left
in garrifon.    As to their refolution of returning to their fhips,
after remaining four months on the ifland, it was certainly proper ; for by this time their number was fo exceedingly decreafed,
by the difeafes of the climate, that probably, in another month,
there would fcarce have been a man left to bring home the tale
of their difafters.

When we confider the number of men facrificed to the climate in this, and in the preceding attempt againft Carthagena,
one cannon help wifhing, if humanity be admiffible in politics,
that future minifters would not wantonly tranfport fo many
thoufands of Europeans to a climate where it is almoft impoffible for them to exift.    Poffibly the political fyftem of Great
Britain may fometimes require fuch facrifices ; but one would
hope, that nothing but the moft inevitable neceffity would au-
thorife fuch deftruction of the human fpecies.

Before we quit this expedition, we cannot avoid inquiring into
the defign of it.  That General Wentworth did not act his part
in the reduction of St. Jago is pretty evident.  But fuppofe that
town had been taken, what then?  Would the ifland have fallen
in confequence?  By no means.  The Havanna was ftrongly fortified, well garrifoned, and defended by twelve fhips of the line :
fo that any idea of reducing the whole ifland feems to be entire-

ly

ly out of the queftion. What poffible advantage could therefore refult from taking St. Jago? It may be anfwered, That a rein-forcement of 2000 marines was expected from England. This fupply, however, was a precarious expectation. They did not arrive at Jamaica till the 15th of January: and had they even arrived two months fooner, the army would ftill have been inadequate to the reduction of the Havanna, and confequently infufficient to conquer the ifland, or even to maintain their ground for any length of time; and yet the heroes of this expedition were fo confident of fuccefs, that they not only entered upon it, by giving Englifh names to the enemy's harbours and rivers, but they actually invited new fettlers from North America, and promifed them grants of land [l].

From thefe confiderations it follows, that, though General Wentworth may be juftly cenfured for performing nothing, yet all he could poffibly have done would have anfwered no rational purpofe; and the expedition was no lefs injudicioufly planned than pufillanimoufly executed.

The troops were re-embarked on the 20th of November, and on the 25th it was refolved in a general council of war, that the general, with the troops under his command, fhould return to Jamaica, and that the fleet fhould continue to cruize off Hifpaniola in fearch of the expected reinforcement from England. The tranfports failed on the 28th, and the admiral on the 6th of December, with the remaining fquadron, confifting of eight fhips of the line, a fire-fhip, an hofpital-fhip, and two tenders. But before we take an entire leave of Cuba, it is neceffary, in juftice to the navy, to inform the reader, that, whilft the troops were on fhore, the fleet was not quite inactive. The Worcefter took a Spanifh man of war of 24 guns, the Defiance took a regifter fhip laden with provifions for Carthagena, and the Shoreham took another veffel with 70,000 pieces of eight on board.

Having clofed the naval tranfactions of the year 1741, in the Weft-Indies, I muft recal the reader's attention to the progrefs of Mr. Anfon, who, I before mentioned, had failed from St. Helen's on the 18th of September, 1740 [k], with a fquadron of

[l] See Governor Shirley's fpeech to the council at Bofton, September 23, 1741.
[k] Anfon's voyage by Walter, chap. 1.

A. D. five men of war, a fmall floop, and two victuallers[1]. This ex-
1740. pedition was originally planned prior to the declaration of war
with Spain, and was rationally founded on a defign of feizing
the wealth of that kingdom at its fource, and thereby depriving
the enemy of the means of executing their hoftile intentions.
There were indeed at firft two feparate fleets deftined for this
fervice ; one of which was to have been commanded by Mr.
Cornwall, and the other by Mr. Anfon. The firft was to have
failed round Cape Horn into the South-feas, and the other directly to the Eaft-Indies. Thefe two fquadrons were to have
met at Manilla, where they were to expect farther orders. This
project feemed well calculated to humble the pride and infolence
of Spain ; becaufe their remote fettlements were, at this time,
almoft entirely defencelefs, and feveral of the moft important
of them might probably have been furprifed before they had
intelligence of a war between the two nations. The original
fcheme, however, was laid afide, and it was determined that
one fquadron only fhould be fent to the South-feas, of which
Mr. Anfon fhould have the command.

This deviation from the original plan was no lefs difpleafing
to Mr. Anfon than to Sir Charles Wager, by whom it was firft
propofed, and who was equally ignorant of the reafons which
induced the miniftry to lay it afide. However, on the 10th of
January Mr. Anfon received his commiffion as commodore of
the fquadron above mentioned. The king's inftructions were
dated the 31ft of the fame month, which, neverthelefs, Mr.
Anfon did not receive before the 28th of June following. He
then went down to Portfmouth, where his fquadron lay, in full
expectation of failing with the firft fair wind ; for though he
knew that he was at leaft 300 men fhort of his compliment,
he had been affured that the deficiency would be fupplied
from Sir John Norris's fleet then at Spithead. But Sir John
did not chufe to part with any of his failors. This difappoint-

| [1] *Viz.* The Centurion, | 60 guns, | 400 men, | George Anfon commander. |
|---|---|---|---|
| Gloucefter, | 50 | 300 | Richard Norris. |
| Severn, | 50 | 300 | Edward Legge. |
| Pearl, | 40 | 250 | Matthew Mitchell. |
| Wager, | 28 | 160 | Danby Kidd. |
| Tyrell, | 8 | 100 | Hon. George Murray. |

ment

ment was another cause of delay, and all that Mr. Anson could A. D at last obtain, was 170 men, ninety-eight of which were ma- 1740 rines, and thirty-two from the hospitals.

According to the first plan, Bland's entire regiment of foot and three independent companies were to have embarked on board this fleet. But it was afterwards resolved, that the land forces should consist of 500 out-pensioners of Chelsea hospital, of which only 259 of the most feeble were embarked, all those who were able to walk having deserted. On such occasions it is not easy to determine which most to execrate, the heads or hearts of those who are entrusted with the management of public affairs. It surely requires a very moderate degree of understanding to know that such troops, so far from being serviceable, must necessarily prove a burdensome obstruction to the success of an expedition, which, from its nature, required health, strength, and vigour, in their utmost degree of perfection. As to heart, can any thing be imagined more inhuman, than treacherously to drag from their peaceful habitations, and from the enjoyment of the scanty reward of past services, a number of decrepid old men, conscious of their inability to render further service to their country, and certain of an inglorious catastrophe? To supply the place of the 240 invalids who had deserted, 210 marines, new raised and totally undisciplined, were ordered on board, the last detachment of which embarked on the 8th of August, and on the 10th the squadron sailed from Spithead to St. Helen's, there to wait for a fair wind.

If Mr. Anson's squadron had now been suffered to proceed, he might have tided it down the channel without waiting for a fair wind; but the Lords Justices (the king being then at Hanover) ordered him to sail from St. Helen's in conjunction with the two fleets commanded by Admiral Balchen and Sir Chaloner Ogle, amounting, in all, to 145 sail. Now it being impossible for so numerous a fleet to proceed, with safety, without an easterly wind, forty days more were spent in hourly expectation of a favourable breeze. At last, on the 9th of September, Mr. Anson received orders to proceed with his own squadron, independent of the rest. He sailed on the 18th, and in four days got clear of the channel.

I have

A. D.
1740.

I have dwelt a little upon this very extraordinary delay, and its several causes, because to this very unaccountable conduct of administration may rationally be ascribed the many hardships, dangers, and disappointments experienced in the progress of this expedition. It seems indeed exceedingly inconceivable, that an expedition appointed early in the month of January, should not have proceeded till late in September. But so it was, and the consequences were such as might easily have been foreseen. The squadron was not only, by this delay, obliged to double Cape Horn in the most tempestuous season of the year, but the Spaniards, in every part of the globe, were informed of its destination.

Having cleared the channel, Mr. Anson steered for the island of Madeira; but, as if all nature as well as art had conspired to retard his progress, he was forty days on a passage which is frequently made in ten. However, at last, after this tedious contention with adverse winds, he arrived at Madeira on the 25th of October. He immediately visited the governor, who informed him, that several days past there had appeared to the westward of the island seven or eight men of war, which he supposed to be Spanish. Mr. Anson despatched a sloop to reconnoitre this squadron, and the sloop returned without any intelligence. This was in truth a Spanish squadron of seven ships of the line and a Patache, which were sent for the sole purpose of counteracting Mr. Anson's operations in the South-seas. They had on board a regiment of foot, intended to strengthen some of their garrisons, and two of the ships were destined for the West-Indies. Their commodore was Don Joseph Pizarro. Of the five ships that sailed for the South-seas, but one returned to Europe, the rest having either foundered at sea, or were wrecked or broken up in the course of the voyage.

On the 3d of November Mr. Anson left Madeira, and crossed the line on the 28th. He arrived at the island of St. Catherine, on the coast of Brazil, on the 21st of December, where he repaired such of his ships as had suffered in the voyage, took in wood and water, and regaled his people with fresh provisions, and recovered some of his sick. But he neither found the climate so healthy, nor the Portugueze so hospitable,

as reprefented by former voyagers. The governor of the ifland A. D
perfidioufly defpatched a veffel to the Spanifh admiral, then at 1741
Buenos-Ayres, with an account of Mr. Anfon's ftrength and
condition, during his continuance in this neutral port.

The fquadron failed from St. Catherine's on the 18th of January, fteering fouthward along the coaft of America, towards
Cape Horn. In fo hazardous a voyage, at this feafon of the
year, it was more than probable that the fleet would be feparated, the commodore therefore appointed three feveral places of
rendezvous: the firft at St. Julian on the coaft of Patagonia,
the fecond at the ifland of Socoro in the South-feas, and the
third at Juan Fernandez. Soon after their departure from St.
Catherine's, the Pearl was feparated, and did not rejoin the
fquadron till near a month after. On her return, Lieutenant
Salt informed Mr. Anfon, that Captain Kidd died on the 31ft of
January; that he had fallen in with the Spanifh fleet above
mentioned, and that, miftaking one of their fhips for the Centurion, he very narrowly efcaped being taken. The Englifh fquadron anchored in the harbour of St. Julian on the 18th of February, principally with a defign to repair the Tryal floop, which
had loft her main-maft in a fquall. This bufinefs being finifhed, they failed again on the 27th, and paffed the Streights Le
Maire on the 7th of March.

At this time their fhips were in good condition, and their
crews in tolerable health and fpirits. They flattered themfelves
that, as they were now entering into the Pacific Ocean, their dangers and difficulties would gradually vanifh, and that Spanifh
treafures would foon reward their labour. But delufive were
thefe expectations. They did not even clear the Streights without great danger, and they no fooner quitted the land than they
found themfelves expofed to all the horrors of impetuous winds,
and waves turbulent and mountainous beyond all conception.
They now began emphatically to execrate the caufes of their late
departure from Europe. This formidable fquadron foon feparated never more to unite! After ftruggling with infinite variety
of diftrefs during two long months, the Centurion, Mr. Anfon's
fhip on the laft day of April, found herfelf to the northward
of the Streights of Magellan, and therefore concluded that fhe
had fecured her paffage round Cape Horn. On the 8th of

A. D. May she arrived off Socoro, the first rendezvous in the Pacific
1741. Ocean. She cruized there, in extreme bad weather, above a
fortnight, in hopes of rejoining some of the squadron ; but being difappointed in this expectation, stood for the island of Juan
Fernandez, where she arrived on the 9th of June ; but in so
feeble a condition, that at this time not above twenty hands,
officers included, were left capable of assisting in working the
ship. The scurvy had made such terrible havock among the
crew, that out of 450, their complement when they passed
Streight Le Maire, scarce half that number were now living,
and most of these were sick in their hammocks. The Tryal
sloop reached the island about the same time, in the same di-
stressful situation, and they were joined by the Gloucester on
the 23d of July, which ship had lost three fourths of her crew,
and would certainly never have been able to reach the island,
but for the assistance sent her by the commodore after she was
in sight. The Anna Pink, their victualler, came in about the
middle of August, and this was the last ship of the squadron
they ever saw.

The missing ships were the Severn, the Pearl, and the Wager
store-ship. The two first parted company off Cape Noir, and
put back to the Brazils. The latter pursued her voyage towards
the island of Socoro, the first rendezvous in the Pacific Ocean.
She made the land on the western coast of South America, on the
14th of May, in latitude 47, and the next morning struck upon
a sunken rock, and soon after bulged. Most of the crew were
landed on this desolate island, where they remained five months,
and then about eighty of the sailors, in a schooner built by
lengthening the long-boat, sailed back for the Brazils, leaving
Captain Cheap and nineteen other persons on shore. These were
by various accidents at last reduced to four, who were landed
by an Indian on the coast of Chiloe, thence conveyed to St.
Jago, where they continued a year, and three of them were
finally sent to Europe on board a French ship, viz. Captain
Cheap, Mr. Byron *, and Mr. Hamilton.

We now return to Mr. Anfon's squadron at Juan Fernandez,
consisting of the Centurion, the Gloucester, the Tryal sloop,
and the Anna Pink. The last of these being found totally unfit
for service, was broken up. By the beginning of September

* Now Admiral Byron.

the

the crews were pretty well recovered, though the whole num- A. D
ber was, by this time, reduced to 335, boys included. 1741

On the 19th of September, Mr. Anson with his small squadron sailed from the island of Juan Fernandez, with a design to
cruize near the continent of Spanish America. On this cruize
he took three trading vessels of no great value; but from the
passengers on board he received such intelligence as determined
him to surprise the town of Paita, in latitude 50° 12' south.
It consisted of about 200 houses, and was defended by a small
fort mounting eight guns. Fearful of alarming the inhabitants
by the approach of his ships, he resolved to make the attempt
by means of his boats only. Whilst the squadron was yet at
too great a distance to be perceived by the enemy, about ten at
night he detached fifty-eight men, commanded by Lieutenant
Brett, and conducted by two Spanish pilots. They landed without opposition, and soon took entire possession of the place.
The governor, with most of the inhabitants, having had some
previous notice from the ships in the harbour, fled into the
country at their approach, and continued parading the hills.
The English remained three days on shore; during which time
they sent all the treasure they could find on board their ships.
They then set fire to the town and re-embarked, having lost
only two men in the enterprise. The booty they carried off
amounted to about 30,000 l. The loss sustained by the Spaniards was estimated at a million and a half of dollars.

Whilst Mr. Anson was thus engaged, the Gloucester, which
had been sent on a cruize, took two Spanish prizes with specie
on board amounting to 19,000 l. sterling. She joined the squadron two days after their departure from Paita, and they stood
to the northward with a design to water at the island of Quibo,
near the bay of Panama. At this island they arrived on the
4th of December. The commodore had indeed entertained
some hopes of being reinforced from Admiral Vernon's squadron across the isthmus of Darien; but he learnt, from the papers found on board one of his prizes, that the attack upon
Carthagena had failed. These hopes therefore immediately va-
nished, and he now determined to steer for the coast of Mexico,
in expectation of falling in with the galleon which he supposed
to be on her passage from Manilla to Acapulco. The squa-

E 2                           dron

dron failed from Quibo on the 12th of December, and did not make the coast of Mexico till the 29th of January. But, as this brings us to the transactions of the year 1742, we must now return to Europe, in order to take a view of the British navy nearer home to the end of the year 1741.

Whilst Vernon and Anson were thus employed in America, the admirals Sir John Norris and Haddock commanded two formidable fleets in Europe. The first of these commanders failed from Spithead on the 27th of July with sixteen ships of the line, and, steering for the bay of Biscay, began to cruize upon the coast of Spain. With this formidable fleet he might with the utmost facility have injured the enemy most essentially, by ravaging their coast and destroying their maritime towns, which were almost totally defenceless. Not only the British nation in general, but the Spaniards themselves, and every person on board, except the admiral, were confident that so powerful a fleet had some capital object in view. But, to the astonishment of all the world, except those who were admitted behind the curtain, in less than a month, Sir John Norris returned to Spithead with half his fleet, without having executed, or even attempted, any thing worth relating. Part of the squadron continued cruizing on the Spanish coast, and the Nassau and Lenox were sent to join Admiral Haddock, who, with thirteen men of war, spent the whole summer cruizing in the Mediterranean, without atchieving any thing sufficient to furnish a tolerable Gazette. The causes assigned for his being stationed in that sea were, to prevent the junction of the Spanish fleet at Cadiz with that of France at Toulon, and to intercept the troops which were intended to be transported from Barcelona to Italy, in order to act against the queen of Hungary. But unfortunately neither of these purposes were answered.

What were the private instructions given to Norris and Haddock will probably always remain a secret. Their respective characters, as men of abilities and resolution stand unimpeached; but abilities and resolution are not sufficient to complete the character of a naval commander. Probity is an indispensible ingredient. The man who is mean enough to accept of a command with ignominious restrictions, merits the obloquy which posterity will never fail to bestow.

On

On the 12th of October Sir John Norris sailed again for the coast of Spain with a fleet of ten men of war. The inhabitants of the towns along the shore were at first a little alarmed at his re-appearance; but, finding him now no less harmless than before, they beheld the English fleet as an agreeable spectacle, and were at length fully persuaded that he was sent to parade along their coast merely for their amusement.

Notwithstanding the formidable state of our navy at this period, our trade was so ill protected, that, since the commencement of the war, the Spaniards had taken no less than 372 of our trading vessels. The merchants of London and other ports were convinced that their losses were chiefly owing to neglect, and they remembered the declaration of the minister, That as the war was their own, they must take the consequences. I have before animadverted on the imprudence of entrusting the conduct of a war to a minister who is forced into it by opposition. Sir Robert Walpole did every thing in his power to avoid a war with Spain, which, with a little of that spirit which Cromwell on a like occasion would have exerted, he might have avoided. The Spaniards presumed on a knowledge of Sir Robert's pacific disposition. That nation had indeed great reason to be dissatisfied with the illicit trade carried on by English vessels in the West-Indies. If, instead of guarding their coasts by armed ships, they had complained to the British ministry, and if the British ministry had taken effectual methods to prohibit this illicit trade, in consequence of such complaint, peace between the two nations might have been preserved, and Sir Robert Walpole would have remained prime minister. He was averse to the war, because he foresaw that it would destroy his influence, and I am afraid he wanted magnanimity to exert a degree of patriotic zeal sufficient to render successful a war which he did not approve [m].

Sir Robert Walpole, though extremely unpopular, had hi- therto stood secure under the shelter of the throne. But the people of England were now so dissatisfied with this unsuccessful war with Spain, and particularly with his total neglect of the queen of Hungary in her distress, that, at the general election of a new parliament, a considerable majority of the inde-

[m] For the state of the navy in the year 1741, see the Appendix, N° 2.

pendent

A. D. pendent voters, throughout the kingdom, opposed the court; 1742. many of Sir Robert's members were thrown out, and when the parliament met, the complexion of the house of commons was such, that a change of ministry became unavoidable. Sir Robert Walpole was created earl of Orford; he resigned all his employments, and found an asylum in the house of lords. The leading patriots in both houses were either taken into the new administration, or silenced by titles, so that all inquiry into the conduct of the late minister fell to the ground. Mr. Sandys was appointed chancellor of the exchequer, the duke of Newcastle and Lord Carteret secretaries of state, and Mr. Pulteney was created earl of Bath.

These incidental matters being premised, we now return to the proper object of our history. Forty thousand seamen were voted for the service of the current year. The fleet in the Mediterranean, under Admiral Haddock, consisted of twenty-nine men of war. He resigned to Lestock on account of his declining health; but the new ministry gave the command to Admiral Mathews, who sailed from Spithead on the 16th of April, with the Namur, Caroline, Ruffel, and Norfolk. This admiral was also invested with the character of minister-plenipotentiary to the king of Sardinia and the states of Italy. As soon as he had assumed the command, being informed that five Spanish gallies lay at anchor in the bay of St. Tropez, he ordered Captain Norris to attack and destroy them[n]; which service was immediately and effectually performed. The united fleet of France and Spain was at this time in the harbour of Toulon: it consisted of thirty-six ships of the line. The British fleet, being joined by Rear-admiral Rowley, was somewhat superior in number of ships. Mr. Mathews's instructions were to block up the Toulon fleet, and by cruizing on the coast to prevent any supplies being sent to the army in Provence. For this purpose, on the 2d of June, he stationed his two rear-admirals, Lestock and Rowley, with twenty-four ships, off the islands of Hieres, with orders to cruize for six weeks. Whilst Mathews continued at Villa Franca, a French man of war, passing by that port, in sight of the fleet, neglected to pay a proper compliment to the British flag. The admiral fired a gun as a

_____
[n] Smollet's history of England, vol. vii. p. 314.

signal

fignal for her to bring to. The Frenchman continued obftinate. A. D. Upon which Mr. Mathews ordered one of his fhips to purfue 1742. and fink him; which was immediately executed by the firft broad-fide. Meanwhile a part of the Britifh fleet[*], cruizing on the coaft of Catalonia, bombarded the towns of Mataro and Palamos, in both which they deftroyed many houfes and many of their inhabitants. What had thefe wretched inhabitants done to offend the king of England? But fuch are the laws of war! If Chriftian princes believed in the religion they profefs, furely they would not wantonly involve their innocent fubjects in fuch calamities. But, if they muft needs quarrel and fight, it were devoutly to be wifhed, that, by fome general law of nations, the inoffenfive part of their fubjects might be fecured from infult and devaftation.

In the beginning of Auguft, Admiral Mathews detached Commodore Martin with a fquadron to the bay of Naples, with orders to compel his Sicilian majefty to recal his troops from the Spanifh army in Italy. The Neapolitans were thrown into the utmoft confternation at the appearance of an Englifh fleet; expecting every moment a more dreadful thunder than, that of Vefuvius. The king, however, to fave his capital, figned a paper delivered to him by Mr. Martin, by which he engaged immediately to recal his troops, and to obferve a ftrict neutrality during the war. Having performed this fervice, the commodore rejoined the admiral in the road of Hieres, which was now the general rendezvous of the Britifh fleet. Towards the end of Auguft Mr. Mathews, being informed that the Spaniards had collected a confiderable magazine at St. Remo, in the Genoefe territories, caufed a party of failors to be landed near that town in order to deftroy it; and they executed their commiffion without any danger or difficulty. He likewife fent two fhips with orders to take or deftroy a Spanifh man of war of the line, which lay at anchor at Ajaccio in the ifland of Corfica; but the Spaniard faved them the trouble, by firft fetting his men on fhore and then blowing up the fhip.

Let us now take a temporary leave of Europe, in order to review the Britifh fleet and army in the Weft-Indies. We are to recollect, that, after the retreat from Carthagena, the troops

[*] Rolt, vol. ii. p. 115.

under

A. D. under General Wentworth returned to Jamaica, and Admiral
1742. Vernon with his squadron continued cruizing off Hispaniola in expectation of a reinforcement from England. But not meeting with the convoy, he returned to Jamaica on the 5th of January, where, on the 15th, arrived also the Greenwich, St. Alban's, and the Fox, with the expected reinforcement from England of 2000 marines. The principal officers, both of the army and navy, ruminating, with regret, on their two last unsuccessful expeditions, were unanimously of opinion, that they could not, with any degree of credit, return to England without some farther attempt against the enemy. General councils of war were frequently held, and it was at last determined to land at Porto-Bello, march across the isthmus of Darien, and taken the rich town of Panama. But, though this resolution was taken early in January, it was upwards of two months before the troops and transports were ready for embarkation. However, they embarked at last, and the whole fleet came to an anchor in the harbour of Porto-Bello in the evening of the 28th of March. This fleet consisted of eight sail of the line, three fire-ships, and two hospital ships, with forty transports, on board of which were 3000 land-forces, and 500 negroes raised by Governor Trelawney, who himself attended the expedition. As soon as the fleet came to an anchor, the governor of Porto-Bello marched directly to Panama with three companies of Spaniards and two companies of Mulattoes. There being nothing to oppose the landing of the troops, the admiral imagined that they would proceed without delay; but, to his great surprise, a council of the land-officers [p] resolved that the scheme was impracticable, and that it was therefore necessary to return to Jamaica. The reasons assigned for this resolution were, the season being too far advanced, their numbers being diminished by sickness and the separation of some of the transports, and their having received intelligence that the garrison of Panama had been lately reinforced. These reasons did not appear quite satisfactory to Mr. Vernon; nevertheless, as, in their general councils of war, there was a majority of land-officers, his opi-

[q] The officers present at this council of war were, General Wentworth, Colonel Frazer, Governor Trelawney, Colonel Leighton, Colonel Cope, Colonel Duroure, and Colonel Martin.

I nion

hion of no importance. That their number was somewhat A. D.
reduced is moft certain; but there remained yet 2000 effective 1742
men; an army more than fufficient, under a general of fpirit
and abilities, to have fecured the treafure of Panama. Nothing
can be more contemptible than this prudent timidity, when we
confider that the attempt might have been made without the
leaft rifk, as there was no army in the whole country capable
of meeting them in the field, and confequently, in cafe of a
repulfe, they might have returned without the leaft danger of
being har.fed in their retreat. Poffibly thefe land-officers would
have had more refolution in a colder climate. The animal mercury in the human barometer feems to fall in proportion to its
approximation to the fun. Be this as it may, the whole fleet
failed from Porto-Bello in the beginning of April, and arrived
at Jamaica on the 15th of May. On the 23d of September
the Gibraltar man of war arrived at Port-Royal in that ifland,
with a letter from the duke of Newcaftle, ordering Vice-admiral
Vernon and General Wentworth to return immediately to England, and they returned accordingly.

Thus ended this vaft enterprife againft the Spanifh fettlements
in America! in which enormous fums were expended, and ten
thoufand lives facrificed, without the leaft benefit to the nation,
or glory to the commanders. To inquire into the caufe, or
caufes, of fuch a feries of difappointments cannot, at this diftance of time, be attributed to partiality or malevolence; and
to neglect fuch inquiry were to fruftrate the only rational defign of hiftory. The death of Lord Cathcart was the firft
misfortune, and probably the foundation of all that followed.
Though this could neither be forefeen nor prevented, yet it may
teach future minifters of ftate, that it is not fufficient to attend
folely to the abilities of the commander in chief; the fecond,
and even the third in command, fhould alfo be men equal to
the command of an army. That General Wentworth wanted
that determined intrepid alacrity fo neceffary in the execution
of fuch enterprizes is felf-evident. As to Vernon, he certainly
did not want refolution, but it is pretty certain that his contempt
for Wentworth prevented him from acting fo cordially and vi-
goroufly as he ought to have done. He wifhed to have had the
fole direction of every operation, and I muft do him the juftice

A. D. to believe, that, if that had been the cafe, he would generally
1743. have fucceeded.

I muſt now recal the reader's attention to Mr. Anſon, whom
we left in the Pacific Ocean, cruizing on the coaſt of Mexico[q],
in hourly expectation of falling in with the annual Spaniſh galleon in her paſſage from Manilla to Acapulco. In theſe hopes
he was diſappointed; for he was informed by three negroes,
whom he ſurpriſed in a canoe off the harbour of Acapulco,
that the galleon arrived on the 9th of January, about twenty
days before the ſquadron fell in with the coaſt. But he had
the ſatisfaction to learn alſo, that her return was fixed for the
3d of March. This information was joyfully received, as the
ſpecie for which ſhe had ſold her cargo would render her a
much more valuable prize than ſhe would have been before her
arrival at Acapulco.

All hands were now employed in preparing for the reception
of the galleon, not doubting but this immenſe reward of their
former ſufferings would foon be in their poſſeſſion; for though
the crews of the five ſhips amounted in all to no more than
330, boys included, and the hands on board the galleon were
generally almoſt double that number; yet there was not a perſon on board the ſquadron, who had any other doubt, or fear,
than that of her not ſailing at the time appointed. Mr. Anſon's fleet conſiſted of the Centurion, the Gloucefter, the Carmelo, the Carmin, the Tryal's prize, and two cutters. With
theſe five ſhips he formed a chain, commanding an extent of
about twenty leagues, at ſuch a diſtance from the harbour of
Acapulco as not to be ſeen from the ſhore, and ſent the two
cutters every night nearer the ſhore, with orders to ſtand off
again at the approach of day. In this diſpoſition they expected
the appointed day with the utmoſt impatience. The important
day dawned at laſt, and every eye in the fleet gazed perpetually
towards the land. The ſun ſunk beneath the horizon, and no
ſhip appeared. Another day paſſed, and then a third, in fruit-
leſs expectation. In ſhort, after waiting to no purpoſe till the
23d, the commodore rationally concluded, that the galleon was
detained till the year following; and this was really the caſe, in

[q] Anſon's voyage, p. 331.

consequence of his barge having been seen by the enemy when
she was sent to discover the harbour of Acapulco.

Having now remained on this station as long as his stores of wood and water would allow, Mr. Anson thought it expedient to prepare for his voyage to China, and it being determined to recruit his stores at Chequetan, about thirty leagues west of Acapulco, he steered directly for that harbour, where he arrived on the 7th of April. The first business here, after a vain attempt to open an intercourse with the natives, was to unload and destroy the Carmelo, the Carmin, and the Tryal's prize, in order to strengthen the crews of the men of war, so as to enable them to undertake, with any degree of safety, the voyage across the Pacific Ocean. The business of watering, &c. being now finished, the Centurion and the Gloucester weighed anchor on the 28th of April, and proceeded on their voyage to China. They lost sight of the American mountains on the 8th of May. After contending with repeated gales of contrary winds, the Gloucester, having lost most of her masts, became so leaky that, on the 15th of August, it was found impossible to keep her any longer above water. The crew was therefore removed to the Centurion, and the Gloucester was set on fire. On the 28th the Centurion arrived at Tinian, one of the Ladrone islands, in latitude 15° north, and 115° west of Acapulco. At this time, so many of their people had perished, or were sick of the scurvy, that not quite a hundred men remained fit for duty. The number of the sick amounted to 128, most of which recovered soon after landing on this fertile, healthy, and beautiful island. Here they remained till the 21st of October, on which day, the crew being now in good health, the Centurion stood out to sea, steering directly for the island of Macoa, a Portuguese settlement near the mouth of the river Canton in China. She made the land on the 5th of November, and came to an anchor on the 12th, in the road near the city of Macoa.

After many provoking delays and difficulties, Mr. Anson at last obtained permission from the Chinese government to repair his ship, and replenish his store of provisions. This business being at length effected to his satisfaction, he put to sea on the 19th of April 1743; and, though he had given out that he was

bound

A. D. bound for Batavia, he had refolved once more to try to inter-
1743. cept the Acapulco fhip in her paffage to Manilla. With this intention he returned to the Phillippine Iflands, and cruized off
Cape Efpiritu Santo on the ifland of Samuel, that being the firft
land generally made by the galleons. He continued cruizing
on this ftation till the 20th of June, when, early in the morning, to the inexpreffible joy of the whole crew, they difcovered
the long-expected galleon. The engagement foon began, and
continued about two hours; after which the Spaniard ftruck,
having fixty-feven men killed and eighty-four wounded. The
Centurion had only two killed and feventeen wounded, who all
recovered except one man. The treafure on board this galleon
confifted of 1,313,843 pieces of eight, and 35,682 ounces of
virgin filver, befides fome cochineal and other merchandife,
amounting in the whole to 313,000 l. fterling.

The commodore being now in poffeffion of the reward of his
toil, dangers, perfeverance and refolution, with a crew on board
whofe felicity cannot be eafily imagined, returned to the river
of Canton, where he came to an anchor on the 14th of July.
His fole intention being to lay in the ftores neceffary for his
voyage to England, he applied immediately to the Chinefe government for leave to victual his fhip; but fuch is the fufpicious
folly and abfurd policy of that people, that after five months
delay he was at laft obliged to infift on an audience of the viceroy of Canton, before he could be fupplied. Immediately after
this audience his ftores were fent on board, and on the 7th of
December the Centurion and her prize unmoored and fell down
the river. On the 12th they anchored before the town of
Macoa, where Mr. Anfon fold the Spanifh galleon for 6000
dollars, and on the 15th proceeded on his voyage. He arrived
at the Cape of Good Hope on the 11th of March, and failing
from thence on the 3d of April, came to an anchor at Spithead
on the 15th of June 1744.

Having thus brought the fortunate Centurion fafe to England,
let us inquire into the exploits of our fleet in the Weft Indies.
When Admiral Vernon returned home, the command of the
fleet devolved on Sir Chaloner Ogle, who in the month of February detached Captain Knowles with eight men of war, having 400 land forces on board, with orders to make an attack
                                                                on

on the town of La Guira on the coast of Caraccas. Mr. A. D
Knowles accordingly proceeded [r]; he began his attack on the 1743
18th about noon, and continued firing upon the town till night,
without any other effect than that of destroying some houses
and churches. His ships were so shattered that he was obliged
to desist, and to sail for Curacoa in order to refit. It was said
that the Spaniards lost 700 men on this occasion; it is however
certain that the English squadron had near a hundred men killed, and three times that number wounded.

Mr. Knowles having miscarried in this attack, was unwilling
to return without a farther attempt to revive the faded laurels of
his country. His ships being repaired [s], he resolved to make
an attack upon Porto Cavallo. The Spaniards were apprized
of his design, and had taken effectual measures for their defence. The garrison, consisting of sailors, Indians, Mulattoes
and Blacks, amounted to about 2000 men; and the entrance
into the harbour was secured by sunken vessels, and commanded by several fascine batteries. The squadron sailed from Curacoa on the 20th of March, but did not arrive off Porto Cavallo
before the 15th of April. It was resolved to send in two men
of war to cannonade the batteries, and the Lively and Eltham
being immediately ordered upon this service, silenced the guns
of the enemy before night. As soon as it was dark, the firing
on both sides having ceased, Major Lucas with 1200 men, sailors and soldiers, landed on the beach, and, marching along
shore, took possession of one of the fascine batteries. The Spaniards being now alarmed, two guns were fired from another
battery upon the assailants, which throwing them into confusion, they began to fire upon each other, and with great precipitation retired to their ships. The British spirit being not yet
quite subdued by this miscarriage, it was resolved in a council
of war to make a general attack upon the castle and batteries
at the same time: accordingly, on the 24th this general attack
was begun by seven men of war; the Assistance, Burford, Suffolk and Norwich battered the castle; and the Scarborough,
Lively and Eltham fired upon the fascine batteries. The cannonading continued with great fury till nine at night, at which time

---

[r] London Gazette, June 7.          [s] Ibid, June 14.

A. D.
1743.
the commodore made a signal to cut. It was indeed high time, for he had now lost 200 men, and most of his ships had sustained considerable damage. His disgrace being now complete, Commodore Knowles made the best of his way to Jamaica, where he remained inactive during the remainder of the year.

Such were the atchievements of the British navy in the West-Indies during the year 1743. We were indeed peculiarly unsuccessful in that part of the world, every attempt against the enemy, since the taking of Porto-Bello, having miscarried. Our commanders probably were not deficient in point of personal courage; but personal courage without abilities is frequently productive of disappointment and disgrace. In the Mediterranean the fleet under the command of Admiral Mathews continued still on its station at Hieres, without performing any signal service, except preventing the French and Spanish fleets from sailing out of the harbour of Toulon.

The Spaniards in the course of this year took 262 British prizes, valued at 567,000 l. sterling; and we took from them 146 ships, worth about 754,000 l. including the Acapulco ship taken by Mr. Anson.

The naval promotions in this year were these: Sir John Norris made admiral of the red; John Balchen, Esq; admiral of the white; Thomas Mathews, Esq; vice-admiral of the red; Nicholas Haddock, Esq; vice-admiral of the white; Sir Chaloner Ogle, vice-admiral of the blue; James Steuart, Esq; rear-admiral of the red; Richard Lestock, Esq; rear-admiral of the white; Sir Charles Hardy, rear-admiral of the blue.

744.    Though, in the preceding year, the French army was defeated by the king of Great-Britain in person; though the French and Spanish fleets were united in the Mediterranean, yet between England and France there was no war[c]. However, in the beginning of the year 1744, both nations threw off the mask. The dissentions in the British parliament at this time ran high, and the people in general were discontented. The Popish emissaries and Jacobites, in different parts of the kingdom, persuaded the French ministry, that a revolution in favour of the Pretender might easily be effected, and Cardinal Tencin gave

[c] Smollet's history, vol. vii. p. 333.

ear to their project, fully perfuaded that the attempt would, at A. I leaft, caufe a confiderable diverfion from the continent. Charles, 1744 the fecond fon of the Chevalier de St. George, was accordingly invited to Paris, where he arrived fome time in the month of January.   In the fame month a fleet of twenty French men of war failed up the Englifh channel, and 7000 men were actually embarked at Dunkirk with a defign to invade England. Thefe proceedings being immediately known in this kingdom, Sir John Norris was ordered to take the command of the fleet at Spithead, which being joined by feveral fhips from Chatham, became fuperior to that of France.   At the fame time proper meafures were taken for defending the coaft in cafe of an invafion.   The fleets of the two nations came within fight of each other; but the French admiral, confcious of his inferiority, thought fit to decline an engagement, and taking the advantage of a hard gale of wind, returned to the port from whence he failed.   Thus ended this famous invafion, which was intended to reftore the unfortunate family of Steuart to the throne of their anceftors, and the young adventurer was obliged to poftpone the affertion of his pretenfions to a more favourable opportunity.

I muft now conduct the reader to the grandeft fcene exhibited during the whole war : a fcene which for magnificence and importance hath rarely been equalled in any age, on any fea. Seventy-four men of war in the Mediterranean, all in view, at the fame time preparing to pour out their thunder, deftructive of the human fpecies, and decifive of the fate of nations !   The great, the anxious expectation raifed by fuch a profpect may be eafily imagined ; but the vaft machinery was too ftupendous for human management, and the heroic virtue of former ages was wanting to produce a glorious cataftrophe.

The French and Spanifh fleets, in the harbour of Toulon, confifted of twenty-eight fail of the line, and fix frigates ; that of England of twenty-eight fhips of the line, ten frigates and two fire-fhips, all moored in the bay of Hieres.   The number of guns in the conjunct fleet was 1820, and of men 16,500; the guns on board the Britifh fleet were 2490, and the number of men 15,000.   But the number of fhips of the line was equal, and thefe were equally manned.   However, on a comparative

view

A. D.
744.
view of the whole force of each squadron, there was an evident superiority in favour of the English, in justice to whom we must nevertheless remember, that, having been long at sea, their ships were foul, whilst those of the enemy were clean, and in fine sailing condition.

The courts of France and Spain, no longer able to support the disgrace of having their fleets blocked up in the harbour of Toulon, sent positive orders for them to proceed to sea at all events. On the 8th of February they were perceived to be under sail, the French admiral, De Court, having hoisted his flag on board the Terrible. Admiral Mathews immediately made a signal for unmooring, and the British fleet got under way on the 9th, with all possible expedition [u]. During this and the following day, these two tremendous fleets continued manœuvring in fight of each other, apparently endeavouring, like two land armies, to gain the advantage of situation. It was very evident that the French admiral had no great inclination to fight, and his ships failed so well that he might easily have escaped; but the Spaniards, either from want of skill or want of hands, proceeded so tardily, that it was impossible to bring them off.

On the 11th, at break of day, the two fleets were at a greater distance than on the preceding day, and Admiral Mathews had the mortification to find Mr. Lestock's division considerably astern. He now imagined that De Court's intention was to draw him towards the Streights, in expectation of a reinforcement from Brest; he therefore determined to engage the enemy as soon as possible, notwithstanding the irregularity of his line, his van and rear being at too great a distance from the centre. Accordingly, at half past eleven, Admiral Mathews made the signal to engage; which signal Lestock did not think proper to repeat. Indeed he was, at this time, so far astern, that he had no enemy to engage. Admiral Mathews, with the centre of the English, was opposite to the enemy's rear, consisting of the Spanish squadron; and Rear-admiral Rowley, who commanded the van, was abreast of the enemy's centre. Thus were the two fleets situated when Admiral Mathews hoisted the signal for engaging. Himself in the Namur, and Captain Cornwall in the Marlborough, bore down upon the Spanish admiral and the

[u] See the Appendix, No 3.

Isabella,

Isabella, and began the attack about ha'f paft one o'clock. At A. D
the fame time Captain Forbes in the Norfolk engaged the Con- 1744
ftant, and the Princeffa, Somerfet, Bedford, Dragon and King-
fton fired at the Poder. About two o'clock, Rear-admiral
Rowley in the Barfleur, and Captain Ofborne in the Caroline,
came up with the French admiral and the Ferme, and engaged
them fome time. The brave Captain Cornwall loft both his legs
by one fhot, and was afterwards killed by the fall of a maft
which was fhot by the board. The Norfolk obliged the Conftant to quit the line. Meanwhile the Princeffa and Somerfet
were difabled by the Poder; but fhe being afterwards engaged
by Captain Hawke, in the Berwick, was difmafted and obliged
to ftrike.

This irregular and partial conflict continued till night, when
the French admiral, having collected his fcattered fleet, bore
away. The Britifh fleet purfued them all the next day; but on
the 13th, though they were yet in fight, Admiral Mathews, being apprehenfive that they intended to decoy him from the coaft
of Italy, made a fignal to difcontinue the chace. The French
fquadron put into Alicant on the 16th, and the Spaniards into
Carthagena on the day following. The Britifh fleet, having
fpent fome days, to no purpofe, in looking out for the enemy,
and afterwards in vainly attempting to regain their former ftation off Toulon, were at length obliged, by contrary winds, to
bear away for the ifland of Minorca.

Thus ended, chiefly in fmoke, this memorable battle, which
feemed to threaten a moft tremendous conflict, and which, from
the fuperiority of the Britifh fleet, ought to have annihilated
the naval power of France and Spain. How it happened that
fo many of our captains were on that day *fafcinated*, I know
not; it is however very certain, that few of them were fairly
engaged. Admiral Mathews was fo diffatisfied with Leftock's
conduct, that he fufpended him from his command and fent him
to England. That Leftock did not fight is moft certain. He
faid in his defence, that he could not have engaged without
breaking the line, which he was not authorifed to do, becaufe,
though the fignal for engaging was made, yet that for the line
of battle was ftill abroad. That Mathews might be guilty of
inattention in this particular without any impeachment of his

A. D. abilities as a naval commander, may surely be admitted, when we
744. confider him bearing down upon the enemy and preparing to
engage; but it was an excufe for declining an attack which an
honeft and brave man would never have pleaded. The misfortune originated in a continued mifunderftanding, between Mathews and Leftock; the latter of whom facrificed his own reputation to the hope of ruining the former. In that hope he was
but too fuccefsful; for, by the fentence of a court-martial in
England, Admiral Mathews was difmiffed, and rendered incapable of ferving the king; Leftock was honourably acquitted.
The people of England were however of a very different opinion from the court, and pofterity will do juftice to both commanders. Mathews was doubtlefs a brave and an honeft man;
Leftock was an artful, vindictive difciplinarian. Whether he was
really a coward, cannot be pofitively determined; but if he was
not deficient in courage, he apparently wanted both honour and
honefty. As fecond in command, he had no bufinefs with the
propriety or impropriety of orders. The laft order, or fignal,
like a laft will and teftament, fuperfedes all the preceding fignals, and ought to be immediately obeyed, regardlefs of any
apparent impropriety or abfurdity. Every individual in a fleet
or army, except the commander in chief, is a mere machine;
whofe bufinefs it is to execute, not to reafon. The fignal for the
line of battle being abroad, when that for engaging was hoifted, was a pitiful excufe for not fighting. Leftock evidently
faw, that the enemy was in our power, and though the admiral's fignals might feem fomewhat inconfiftent, his intentions
were not equivocal. Mathews might want head: Leftock certainly wanted heart. The one might deferve cenfure; the other
ought to have been fhot. By what extraordinary evidence, or
other inftigation, the members of the courts-martial who determined the fate of thefe admirals, were influenced, I know not;
but their fentence muft for ever remain a blot in the annals of
this country.

The few naval commanders who diftinguifhed themfelves in
this fkirmifh (for it hardly deferves the name of a battle) were,
the Admirals Mathews and Rowley, the Captains Cornwall,
Forbes, Ofborne and Hawke. Few of the reft were much engaged. The Spaniards loft but one fhip, the Poder, and about
a thou-

a thoufand men killed and wounded. The Britifh fleet loft a
fire-fhip, and in killed and wounded about four hundred.

Notwithftanding this naval engagement in the Mediterranean
with the combined fleets of France and Spain, there was yet no
declaration of war between Great Britain and France. This
ceremony, however, was at laft performed. On the 20th of
March, war was declared at Paris, and on the 31ft of the fame
month, at London. The navy of France confifted, at this time,
of forty-five fhips of the line, fixty-feven frigates and fifty-five
gallies: that of England of ninety fhips of the line, eighty-four
frigates and fifty other veffels; in all two hundred and twenty-
four fhips of war. On the 23d of June the following promotions were made in the navy: Nicholas Haddock, Efq; and Sir
Chaloner Ogle, appointed admirals of the blue; James Stuart,
Efq; and Sir Charles Hardy, vice-admirals of the red; Thomas
Davers, Efq; and the honourable George Clinton, vice-admirals
of the white; William Rowley and William Martin, Efqrs.
vice-admirals of the blue; Ifaac Townfend, Efq; rear-admiral
of the red; Henry Medley, Efq; rear-admiral of the white;
George Anfon, Efq; rear-admiral of the blue.

The firft fleet which failed from England after the declaration of war with France, was commanded by Sir Charles Hardy; it confifted of eleven fhips of the line. He failed from
St. Helen's on the 18th of April, with a number of ftore-fhips
under his convoy for the relief of the Mediterranean fleet,
which was in great want of ftores and provifions. Having put
into the port of Lifbon, and being there detained by contrary
winds, the French miniftry, acquainted with his deftination,
fent immediate orders for the Breft fquadron, of fourteen fail
of the line, to block him up. This fervice was effectually performed, and Sir Charles remained in the Tagus.

On the 6th of July the Britifh navy was reinforced by the arrival of twenty Dutch men of war at Portfmouth, under the
command of Admiral Bacbereft. On the 15th they were joined by Admiral Balchen with fourteen fail of the line[x]. This
united

* BRITISH DIVISION.——Sir JOHN BALCHEN admiral.

| | | | |
|---|---|---|---|
| Hampton-Court, | 70 guns, | Victory, | 110 guns, |
| Augufta, | 60 | Princefs Amelia, | 80, |
| Captain, | 70 | | |

G 2                                                                 Vice-

A. D. united fleet failed from Spithead on the 7th of Auguft, to the
1744. relief of Sir Charles Hardy, and on the 9th of September came
to an anchor off the rock of Lifbon. The French admiral,
having had previous intelligence of Balchen's approach, quitted
his ftation. Sir Charles Hardy, with his convoy, joined the
fleet, which immediately proceeded to Gibraltar, and, having
reinforced the garrifon, returned in fearch of the Breft fquadron. But Mr. Rochambault, the French admiral, was, by this
time, fafe in the harbour of Cadiz. Sir John Balchen entered
the bay of Bifcay, in his return to England, on the 30th of
September, and, on the 3d of October, his whole fleet was
difperfed by a violent ftorm. Several of the fhips fuffered confiderably, particularly the Exeter and the Duke, the firft of
which loft her main and mizen mafts, and was under the neceffity of throwing twelve of her guns overboard; and the latter
had all her fails torn to pieces, and ten feet water in her hold.
The whole fleet, however, except the admiral, arrived at St.
Helen's on the 10th of October. The Victory was feparated
from the reft of the fleet on the 4th, after which fhe was never
feen or heard of more. It is generally fuppofed that fhe ftruck
upon a ridge of rocks, called the Cafkets, near Alderney, as
repeated fignals of diftrefs were heard by the inhabitants of that
ifland; but it blew fo violently that it was impoffible to give
her any affiftance. Thus perifhed the fineft firft-rate man of
war in the world, one of the beft admirals in the Britifh fervice, 1100 failors, and a confiderable number of volunteers,
many of whom were of families of diftinction.

Having now concluded the naval tranfactions in Europe during the year 1744, we direct our inquiries towards America,

| Vice-admiral MARTIN. | | Vice-admiral STEUART. | |
|---|---|---|---|
| Falkland, | 50 guns, | Sunderland, | 60 guns, |
| Suffolk, | 70 | Monmouth, | 70 |
| St George, | 90 | Duke, | 90 |
| Exeter, | 60 | Prince Frederick, | 60 |
| | | Princefs Mary, | 60 |
| DUTCH DIVISION. | | | |
| Haerlem, | 70 | Edam, | 54 |
| Dordrecht, | 54 | Affendelft, | 54 |
| Damiata, | 64 | Delfi, | 54 |
| Leeuwenhorft, | 54 | Two frigates. | |

where

where we left Sir Chaloner Ogle with the Britifh fleet in the A. D harbour of Port-Royal in Jamaica, and Admiral de Torres, 1744 with that of Spain, at the Havanna. In thefe refpective fitua-tions they both remained, not otherwife employed than in fend-ing out cruizers to interrupt the trade of each nation; till, on the 4th of November, de Torres, with five men of war and as many galleons, richly laden, failed for Europe, and arrived fafe at Corunna on the 29th of December. Thefe galleons brought a treafure of fifteen millions of piaftres.

During this year the navy of England fuftained fome confi-derable loffes. I have before mentioned the fate of the unfor-tunate Victory. On the 4th of June the Northumberland, a new fhip of 70 guns and 480 men, commanded by Captain Watfon, cruizing in the channel, fell in with three French men of war, viz. the Mars of 68 guns and 580 men, commanded by Monf. de Perrier; the Conftant of 60 guns and 480 men, commanded by Monf. Conflans; and the Venus of 26 guns and 250 men, commanded by Monf. de Dacher. The North-umberland fuftained this very unequal conflict for three hours, with amazing activity and refolution; till, unfortunately, Captain Watfon was mortally wounded: fhe then ftruck her colours by order of the mafter, who was therefore afterwards fentenced by a court-martial, to fpend the remainder of his life in the Mar-fhalfea prifon. The French fhips loft 130 men in the engage-ment, and their rigging was fo fhattered, that they intended to fheer off as foon as it was dark. They carried the Northum-berland in great triumph into Breft, where Captain Watfon died. The Seaford, Captain Pie, the Solebay, Captain Bury, both of 20 guns, and the Grampus floop, were likewife taken by part of the Breft fquadron in the courfe of this year.

Before I conclude the naval hiftory of the year 1744, it is neceffary to turn our eyes, for a moment, towards the Eaft-Indies. In confequence of an application to the lords of the ad-miralty, from the Eaft-India company, Commodore Barnet, with four men of war [r], failed from Portfmouth on the 5th of May,

| [r] Viz. Deptford, | Commodore Barnet, | 60 guns, |
|---|---|---|
| Medway, | Captain Peyton, | 60 |
| Prefton, | Lord Northefk, | 50 |
| Diamond, | Captain Moor, | 20 |

and,

A. D. and, after his arrival in the East-Indies, took a French fifty-
1744. gun ship, and three rich prizes.

At the close of this year it appeared [s], that, since the commencement of the war, the Spaniards had taken 786 British
vessels, which were valued at 2,751,000 l.; and the British
effects, seized in Spain on the declaration of war, were estimated at 50,000 l. On the other hand, the number of Spanish
ships taken by our men of war and privateers amounted to 850,
supposed to be worth 2,550,000 l. To this if we add 2,181,000 l.
the supposed amount of the prizes taken, fortifications destroyed, &c. by Admiral Vernon and Mr. Anson, the loss sustained
by Spain will exceed that of Great Britain 1,930,000 l. By a
similar estimate of the account with France, there appeared
above half a million sterling in our favour.

1745.     Notwithstanding this balance, the reader has doubtless
been disappointed to find our naval history of 1744 so unimportant, and, in the only engagement of consequence, so disgraceful. The fatal disagreement between Mathews and Lestock cannot be remembered without indignation; but the ministry, who knew their enmity, must have foreseen, and were
therefore answerable for the consequence. That ministry was
now changed. Lord Carteret resigned his place of secretary of
state to the earl of Harrington, and the duke of Bedford was
appointed first lord of the admiralty. Orders were immediately issued for every man of war in the several ports to be fitted
for service. Admiral Davers was sent to protect Jamaica, the
Mediterranean fleet was reinforced by Admiral Medley, and the
coast of Great Britain was secured by cruizers properly stationed.

Meanwhile a project was formed, in the general assembly of
Massachuset in New-England, to surprise the city of Louisbourg,
the capital of Cape Breton, and to drive the French entirely
from that island. The ministry, being made sensible of the importance of the enterprize, ordered Commodore Warren to quit
his station at the Leeward islands, and join the American expedition. This armament was raised with so much secrecy and
despatch, that an army of 3850 volunteers, under the command

---

[s] Rolt's history, vol. iii. p. 460.

of William Pepperel, Efq; was ready to embark at Bofton, be- A. E
fore the French government were apprized of their intention. 1745
They arrived at Canfo in Nova Scotia, under the convoy of ten
American privateers, on the 2d of April, and on the 25th were
joined by Commodore Warren in the Superbe of 60 guns, attended by the Lancefton, the Eltham, and the Mermaid, of
40 guns each. Canfo is within fight of Cape Breton, and yet
the inhabitants of that ifland were hitherto totally ignorant of
their danger, till, on the 30th of April, they beheld this hoftile
fleet come to an anchor in Gabarus bay, about a league from
Louifburg. The governor immediately fent a detachment of a
hundred men to oppofe the landing of the American troops;
but the French were foon obliged to retire in confufion, and
the invaders difembarked without the lofs of a fingle man.
General Pepperel immediately invefted Louifbourg, whilft Mr.
Warren blocked up the harbour, convoyed feveral veffels with
ftores and provifions from Bofton, and intercepted a French
man of war of 44 guns, and other fhips intended to relieve the
city. Meanwhile he was joined by the Canterbury, the Sunderland, and the Chefter; the two firft of fixty guns, and the
laft a fifty-gun fhip, and on the 11th of June the Princefs Mary,
the Hector, and the Lark, were alfo added to his fleet. On
the 15th of June Monf. Chambon, the governor of Louifbourg,
fent a flag of truce to the Britifh camp, and the ifland of Cape
Breton was furrendered to his Britannic majefty.

It is impoffible to confider, without aftonifhment, the rapid
fuccefs of this handful of undifciplined Northern Americans,
againft a city regularly fortified, with feveral very formidable
batteries, and defended by twelve hundred regular troops, and
fkilful engineers. But the activity and refolution of the befiegers was fuch, that fkill and difcipline fled before them like chaff
before the wind. Can thefe Americans be a race of cowards?
Are thefe a people to be bullied into obedience? Will the feeble attempts of a General Wentworth in the Weft-Indies bear
any comparifon with the conqueft of Louifbourg? It was indeed
a very important conqueft, as it difpoffeffed the French of the
fifhery on the banks of Newfoundland, and deprived them of
their only feaport in North-America.

After

After the departure of Commodore Warren for North-America, the Weft-India iflands were left in a great meafure defencelefs, Sir Chaloner Ogle having returned to England with fix men of war. For this reafon Vice-admiral Townfend was ordered from the Mediterranean to the Weft-Indies, with a fquadron of eight fhips[a]. He failed from Gibraltar on the 2d of Auguft, and arrived off Martinico on the 3d of October, when he was joined by the Pembroke of 60 guns, and the Woolwich of 50. Admiral Townfend having had information that the inhabitants of Martinico were in great diftrefs for provifions, determined to remain upon this ftation in order to prevent their receiving any fupplies from France: for though it be a maxim of honourable war, among Chriftian princes, not to murder fuch of each other's fubjects as do not bear arms, it is neverthelefs univerfally allowable to deftroy by hunger as many peaceable men, women and children as they can. Gofpel and political Chriftianity are very different religions.

On the 31ft of October Admiral Townfend difcovered a fleet of forty fail of French fhips turning the fouthern extremity of Martinico. It proved to be a fleet of merchantmen and ftorefhips fent to the relief of the French Weft-India iflands, under convoy of four men of war, commanded by Commodore M'Namarra; who, perceiving the fuperiority of his enemy, faved himfelf by running under the guns of Fort-Royal. The other three men of war alfo efcaped; but near thirty of the other veffels were either taken, burnt, funk, or drove on fhore. The admiral likewife took a large privateer and three Dutch veffels bound from St. Euftatia to Martinico with provifions, by which he had the *happinefs* of completing the famine on that ifland fo entirely, that many thoufand negroes and other inhabitants perifhed of hunger. Exploits of this nature muft afford infinite *satisfaction* on reflection; efpecially when they contribute nothing either to the glory or emolument of the ftate!

---

[a] *Viz.* Lenox,   70 guns,     Hampfhire,  50 guns;
     Dreadnought, 60         Argyle,   50
     Worcefter,  60          Severn,   50
     Kingftou,  60          Gibraltar,  20
                         Comet bomb.

Such

Such were our naval exploits in the West-Indies in the year A. D
1745, exclusive of some valuable prizes taken by our men of 1745
war and privateers; the most considerable of which were, the
Marquis d'Antin and the Lewis Erasmus, worth 70,000 l. taken by the Prince Frederic and the Duke privateers. In the
course of this year the British navy suffered the loss of one
sloop only, which was taken and carried into Martinico; whilst
the British cruizers, in that part of the world, made captures
of five French and two Spanish men of war.

In Europe nothing material happened to grace our annals.
Admiral Martin commanded a squadron in the Channel, attending the motions of the Brest fleet. Rear-admiral Medley sailed
from Spithead, with seven men of war, in order to reinforce
Admiral Rowley, who now commanded in the Mediterranean,
and arrived at Minorca on the 10th of April. Thus strengthened, the vice-admiral proceeded, with twenty-four ships of the
line, to block up the Spanish fleet at Carthagena, which he
thereby prevented either from transporting troops to Italy or
from joining the French squadron at Brest. The republic of
Genoa having declared against the queen of Hungary, Admiral
Rowley detached a part of his fleet, under the command of
Commodore Cooper, to bombard the towns upon their coast;
several of these towns suffered considerably, particularly St.
Remo, which he reduced almost to ashes.

The year 1746 affords not a single example of the naval su- 1746
periority of Great Britain. It is nevertheless necessary, in order to preserve the thread of our history, to inform the reader
where and how our several fleets were employed. Commodore
Barnet, who died in the East-Indies, was succeeded in the command of the squadron by Captain Peyton. This squadron consisted of six men of war [b], which were now stationed at Fort
St. David. At Pondicherry the French had eight ships of

---

[b] Viz. Medway,     Commodore Peyton, of   60 guns,
    Preston,        Lord Northesk,         50
    Harwich,        Captain Carteret,      50
    Winchester,     Lord Thomas Bertie,    50
    Medway's Prize, Captain Griffith,      40
    Lively,         Captain Stevens,       20

A. D. force, under the command of Monf. Bourdannais [c]. Commo-
1746. dore Peyton, cruizing between the coaft of Coromandel and
the ifland of Ceylon, on the 25th of June, fell in with Bourdonnais, whofe fquadron was fomewhat reduced by the lofs of
the Infulaire. Both fquadrons prepared to engage, and about
four in the afternoon they began to fire upon each other. The
battle lafted till feven, it being then almoft dark. The Englifh
had 14 men killed, and 46 wounded; the French 27 killed,
and 53 wounded. Next morning the two fleets appeared at no
great diftance from each other; but neither of the commanders
chofe to renew the engagement. At four in the evening Mr.
Peyton called a council of war, which determined, as councils
of war generally do, not to fight. When a commander in
chief, invefted with full power to act by his fole authority, calls
a council of war, it creates a ftrong fufpicion, that he wants to
divide the blame of an unjuftifiable action. The hiftory of
mankind affords innumerable examples of cowardice in collec-
tive bodies, of which every individual would have been horridly
afhamed. The Englifh fquadron proceeded to the ifland of
Ceylon, and the French to Pondicherry.

Our principal hiftorian of thefe times [d] afferts, that the Britifh
fquadron was fuperior to that of the enemy. This, however,
was evidently not the cafe: therefore the imputation of cowardice feems to fall more particularly on the French commodore.
But Monf. Bourdonnais had a greater object in view. The
reduction of Madrafs promifed a better harveft than difabling
a few men of war. He appeared before that fettlement on the
18th of Auguft, and fired upon one of the fhips belonging to
the Englifh Eaft-India company, chiefly with a defign to try
whether Mr. Peyton meant to defend the place. Our *brave*
commodore, for reafons beft known to himfelf, as foon as he
was informed of this infult, and confequently of the danger of
Madrafs, immediately difappeared, and failed the Lord knows
whither. Monf. Bourdonnais, with his whole fquadron, re-

---

c *Viz.* The Achilles, of 74 guns,    Phœnix,     of 44 guns,
         Duc d'Orleans,  56            St. Louis,      44
         Bourbon,        56            Infulaire,      20
         Neptune,        44            Lis,            40
d Dr. Smollet's hiftory, vol. vii. p. 387.

turned

turned to Madrafs on the 3d of September, and in a fhort time A. D made himfelf mafter of that important place. He would pro- 1746 bably have fucceeded in the reduction of every other Britifh fettlement on that coaft, if he had not been prevented by a violent ftorm, which difabled a confiderable part of his fleet.

In Europe, great defigns were formed in the refpective cabinets of England and France againft each other's fettlements in North America. The French determined to retake Louifbourg, and alfo to furprize Annapolis-Royal in Nova Scotia. The Englifh, on the other hand, planned the reduction of Quebec. Both kingdoms were difappointed in their expectations. The French fleet, confifting of eleven fhips of the line, three frigates, three fire-fhips, and two bombs, came out of Breft on the 7th of May, but was prevented, by contrary winds, from proceeding on the voyage till the 22d of June. This fleet, which, with privateers and tranfports, made in all ninety-feven fail, was commanded by the Duke d'Anville. He had on board 3500 land forces, under the command of brigadier-general Jonquiere. They did not make the coaft of Acadia till the 10th of September, and on the 13th a ftorm arofe, which, continuing fome days, difperfed the fleet, and deftroyed feveral of the tranfports; fo that, on the 27th, they muftered at Chiboctou, their place of rendezvous, no more than feven fhips of the line, two frigates, one fire-fhip, one bomb-veffel, twelve privateers and eighteen tranfports, in all fifty-fix fail. Whilft they lay in the harbour of Chiboctou, the mortality was fo great, that, in a fhort fpace of time, they buried their commander in chief, their fecond in command, 1500 of the land forces and 800 failors. The number of their fhips and of their men being thus reduced, they gave up every idea of conqueft, and failed for Europe on the 12th of October, where they arrived without farther accident.

Meanwhile the Britifh miniftry, as I have faid above, had planned an expedition for the reduction of Quebec. For this purpofe a confiderable fleet was affembled at Portfmouth, in the month of April, and feveral regiments were actually embarked under the command of General Sinclair. The duke of Newcaftle having previoufly communicated his intention of invading Canada to the northern provinces of America, requiring

H 2 their

A. D. their affiſtance, ten thouſand men were immediately raiſed, and
1746. waited impatiently for the arrival of the Britiſh fleet.   But ſuch
was the irreſolution of the miniſtry at this period of our hiſtory,
that the French were not only informed of their deſign, but
had time to equip a ſquadron ſufficient to counteract the entire
project.   This ſquadron, as we have ſeen above, ſailed from
France on the 22d of June.   It was indeed ready to ſail ſix
weeks ſooner, but was detained by contrary winds.

The Britiſh miniſtry, having now relinquiſhed their deſign
againſt Canada, reſolved to make a deſcent on the coaſt of Britany, in France, and particularly to deſtroy *Port l'Orient*, in
order to ruin the French Eaſt-India Company.   Lieutenant-
general Sinclair commanded the land forces, and the command
of the fleet was given to Admiral Leſtock, that very Leſtock
with whoſe conduct in the Mediterranean the reader is ſufficiently acquainted.   This armament conſiſted of ſixteen ſhips
of the line, eight frigates, and two bomb-veſſels, beſides ſtore-
ſhips and tranſports, on board of which were 5800 regular
troops, including matroſſes and bombardiers.   After various
unaccountable delays, during which the French were perfectly
acquainted with their deſtination, they ſailed at laſt from Plymouth on the 14th of September, and, ſteering directly for the
coaſt of Britany, came to an anchor in Quimperlay-bay on the
18th.   General Sinclair, with the troops under his command,
landed on the 20th in the evening, without the leaſt moleſtation,
and the next morning took poſſeſſion of a ſmall town called
Plemure, about a league from l'Orient, and there fixed his
head-quarters.   On the 22d, the Britiſh army having advanced
to a riſing ground about half a league from the city, General
Sinclair ſummoned it to ſurrender; but the governor, not liking
the conditions, determined to defend it.   On the 25th the beſiegers opened a battery of twelve cannon and a mortar, and
the next day began to throw red-hot balls into the town, which
took fire in ſeveral parts.   During this time the beſieged continued to fire from the ramparts with great alacrity: neverthelefs,
their fortifications were in ſuch bad condition, that on the 27th
they had reſolved to beat a parley; when, to their infinite ſurpriſe and joy, the firing of the beſiegers ceaſed.   General Sinclair and his army retreated to their camp, leaving behind them
four pieces of cannon, the mortar, and a conſiderable quantity
of

of ammunition, and on the 28th reimbarked without molesta- A. D. tion. Their lofs during the fiege amounted, in killed and 1746. wounded, to eighty men. Why the Britifh general fled, with fo much precipitation, from the arms of victory, is difficult to imagine, unlefs he was difcouraged on finding the enterprize not feconded by the admiral, who, according to the original plan, was to have brought his fhips to bear upon the town. Mr. Leftock faid, in his defence, that the enemy had rendered his entrance into the harbour of Port l'Orient impracticable. Probably the fignals for advancing, as with Mathews in the Mediterranean, were not made in due form. But the caufe of their mifcarriage feems to have originated in not landing the troops immediately, and ftorming the town without the lofs of a moment. When the Britifh fleet came to an anchor, the gar- rifon of Port l'Orient was very weak, and few of their guns were mounted on the ramparts. Some of our fubfequent at- tempts on the coaft of France have been fruftrated by the fame caufe. The principal damage done to the enemy in this expe- dition was the deftruction of the Ardent, a fixty-four gun fhip, by the Exeter, who, after an obftinate engagement, ran her on fhore, and afterwards fet her on fire. Admiral Leftock, with his entire fquadron, left the coaft of France on the 8th of Oc- tober, and returned to England, without having in any degree fulfilled the intentions of the miniftry, which were, to ruin the French Eaft-India company by deftroying l'Orient, and, by di- viding of the French troops, to facilitate the invafion of Pro- vence by the Auftrian army[e].

In the Weft-Indies[f] nothing of importance was attempted by any of the belligerent powers. We find, however, upon record one naval tranfaction, which, though it will not add much to our national renown, ought neverthelefs to be remembered *in terrorem*. Vice-admiral Davers, who commanded on the Ja- maica ftation, having received intelligence that Monf. Conflans, with four men of war[g] and ninety merchantmen, from France,

[e] The celebrated David Hume attended General Sinclair, as his fecretary, on this expedition.

[f] Ralt, vol. iv. p. 360.

[g] *Viz.* The Terrible of 74 guns,
———————— 64
———————— 54
———————— 44

A. D. was hourly expected at Martinico, detached Commodore Mit-
1746. chel with five men of war and a sloop[h] to intercept him. He
fell in with the French fleet on the 3d of August, and at seven
in the evening was about a league to windward of them, when,
instead of engaging the enemy, he made a signal to speak with
the captains of his squadron, a majority of whom were of opinion, that it were best to defer the battle till next morning.
These councils of war, as I have before observed, seldom forebode much heroism. When a man calls his friends about him,
to ask them whether he shall fight to-day or to-morrow, there
is great reason to believe that he had rather not fight at all.
However, general orders were given to keep the enemy in sight,
and to engage as soon as day-light should appear. But the
French merchant vessels, being so unpolite as not to wait to be
taken by the English, all escaped; and Monf. Conflans, after
exchanging a few shot with the British squadron, followed his
convoy. Mr. Mitchel's caution was so great, that when night
came on he ordered his ships to carry no lights, lest the French
should be so rude as to give him chase. Monf. Conflans, in his
return to Europe, fell in with an English fleet from the Leeward
islands, under the convoy of the Woolwich and Severn, of 50
guns each, the latter of which, after two hours engagement,
he took and carried into Brest. Mitchel, being afterwards tried
by a court-martial, was fined five years pay, and rendered incapable of future service.

The British fleet in the Mediterranean was this year commanded by Vice-admiral Medley, whose principal transaction
was the assistance which he gave to the Austrian general at the
siege of Antibes. Admiral Martin, who commanded in the
channel, was in the month of July succeeded by Admiral Anfon,
who was appointed vice-admiral of the blue.

The French, in the course of this year, took from the English one man of war of 60 guns, two sloops, nine privateers,
one East-Indiaman, and 466 merchant-vessels. The Spaniards
took 183 British ships. The British men of war and privateers

| | | | |
|---|---|---|---|
| [h] Viz. Stafford of | 60 guns, | Plymouth of 60 guns, | |
| Lenox | 64 | Worcester 60 | |
| Milford | 44 | Drake sloop. | |

**took**

took from the Spaniards twenty-two privateers, ten regifter- A. I
fhips, and eighty-eight merchantmen. From the French we 174(
took feven men of war, ninety-one-privateers, and 312 merchant-veffels.

The French miniftry, notwithftanding their late difappoint- 174'
ment in North America, were determined to increafe their
force in Canada, and, with the affiftance of Canadians and Indians, to extend their territories by incroachments on the
neighbouring provinces belonging to Great Britain. At the
fame time they formed a defign againft fome of our fettlements
in the Eaft-Indies. For thefe purpofes, in the beginning of the
year 1747, a confiderable armament was prepared at Breft;
the fquadron deftined for America, under the command of
Monf. Jonquiere, and that for the Eaft-Indies commanded by
Monf. de St. George. For greater fecurity, thefe two fleets
were to fail at the fame time.

The Britifh miniftry, being informed of the ftrength and deftination of this fquadron, fent a fuperior fleet to the coaft of
France, commanded by Vice-admiral Anfon. He failed from
Plymouth on the 9th of April, and, cruizing off Cape Finifterre,
on the 3d of May fell in with the French fleet, confifting of
thirty-eight fail, nine of which fhortened fail and prepared to
engage, whilft the reft bore away with all the fail they could
make. Admiral Anfon firft formed his fquadron in line of battle; but, perceiving the enemy begin to fheer off, he made a
fignal for his whole fleet to give chace, and engage promifcu-
oufly. The Centurion came up with the fternmoft fhip of the
enemy about four in the afternoon. She was followed by the
Namur, Defiance, and Windfor, who were foon warmly engaged with five of the French fquadron[1]. The Centurion had
her main-top-maft fhot away early in the action, which obliged
her to drop aftern; but fhe was foon repaired. The battle now
became general, and the French maintained this very unequal
conflict with great fpirit and gallantry, till about feven in the
evening, when the whole fleet ftruck their colours. The *Dia-
mant* was the laft French fhip that fubmitted, after fighting the
Briftol near three hours. In juftice to our enemy it is neceffary

[1] London Gazette, May 16.

A. D. to remember, that the fquadron commanded by Admiral Anfon
747. confifted of fourteen fhips of the line, a frigate, a floop, and
a fire-fhip, with 922 guns, and 6260 men on board; and that
Monf. de la Jonquiere had no more than five line of battle
fhips, and as many frigates, 442 guns, and 3171 men[k]. Admiral Anfon in the mean time detached the Monmouth, the
Yarmouth, and the Nottingham in purfuit of the convoy, and
they returned with the Vigilant and Modefte both of twenty-
two guns, the reft having made their efcape. But though we
acknowledge the great fuperiority of the Britifh fquadron, it is
neceffary to inform the reader, that no more than eight Englifh
fhips were engaged. Captain Grenville of the Defiance, a very
gallant officer, loft his life in this engagement. Our number of
killed and wounded amounted to 520; that of the enemy to

[k] Lond. Gaz. May 16.　　　E N G L I S H.

| Prince George, | Admiral Anfon, | Captain Bentley, | 90 guns, |
| Devonfhire, | R. Adm. Warren, | —— Weft, | 66 |
| Namur, | — | —— Bofcawen, | 74 |
| Monmouth, | — | —— Harrifon, | 64 |
| Prince Frederic, | — | —— Norris, | 64 |
| Yarmouth, | — | —— Bret, | 64 |
| Princefs Louifa, | — | —— Watfon, | 60 |
| Defiance, | — | —— Grenville, | 60 |
| Nottingham, | — | —— Saumarez, | 60 |
| Pembroke, | — | —— Fincher, | 60 |
| Windfor, | — | —— Hanway, | 60 |
| Centurion, | — | —— Denis, | 50 |
| Falkland, | — | —— Barradel, | 50 |
| Briftol, | — | Hon. Wm. Montague, | 50 |
| Ambufcade, | — | —— Jn. Montague, | 40 |
| Falcon Sloop, | — | —— Guynn, | 10 |
| Vulcan Firefhip, | — | —— Pattigrew. | |

I　F R E N C H.

| Le Serieux, | — | Monf. de Jonquiere, | 66 |
| L'Invincible, | — | de St. George, | 74 |
| Le Diamant, | — | Hoquhart, | 56 |
| Le Jafon, | — | Beccard, | 52 |
| Le Rubis, | — | M'Carty, | 52 |
| Le Gloire, | — | Saleffe, | 44 |
| L'Aollon | — | de Santons, | 30 |
| Le Philipert, | — | Cellie, | 30 |
| Le Thetis, | — | Maçon, | 20 |
| Le Dartmouth, | — | Penoche, | 18 |

I

700. Captain Boscawen was wounded in the shoulder by a A. I
musket-ball. Monf. de la Jonquiere was also wounded in the 1747
same part; one French captain was killed, and another lost a
leg.

Admiral Anson returned to England, and brought the cap-
tive squadron safe to an anchor at Spithead. He set out immediately for London, where he was graciously received by the
king, and afterwards created a peer. Rear-admiral Warren
was made knight of the Bath. The money taken on board of
the French fleet was brought through the city of London in
twenty waggons, and lodged in the bank.

About the middle of April, Captain Fox in the Kent, with
the Hampton-Court, the Eagle, the Lion, the Chester and the
Hector, with two fire-ships, sailed on a cruize, designing to
intercept a fleet of St. Domingo-men under the convoy of four
French men of war. After cruizing a month between Ushant
and Cape Finisterre, Captain Fox fell in with this French fleet
of 170 sail. They were immediately deserted by their men of
war, and forty-six of them were taken.

The British ministry having received intelligence, that nine
French men of war of the line [l] had sailed from Brest, in order
to convoy a large fleet of merchant-men to the West-Indies,
ordered Rear-admiral Hawke, with fourteen men of war [m], to

sail

[l] Viz. Le Tonant,        M. de Letenduer,        80 guns,
     L'Intrepide,          Conte de Vaudreuil,     74
     Le Terrible,          Conte Dague,            74
     Le Monarque,          M. de Bedoyerre,        74
     Le Neptune,           M. de Fromenticre,      70
     Le Trident,           M. Demblimont,          64
     Le Fougeux,           M. Davigneau,           64
     Le Severn,            M. Dur-urel,            56
     Le Content, belonging to the East-India Company, 60
     Besides several trigates.
     London Gazette, extraordinary, October 26.

[m] Viz. Devonshire, (Admiral) Captain Moore,     66 guns,
     Kent,            ———— Fox              64
     Edinburgh,       ———— Cotes,           70
     Yarmouth,        ———— Saunders,        64
     Princess Louisa, ———— Watson,          60
     Windsor,         ———— Hanway,          60
     Lion,            ———— Scot,            60

A. D. fail immediately in queft of them. The admiral, with the fleet
1747. under his command, left Plymouth on the 9th of Auguft. The
French fleet, confifting of the above-mentioned men of war
and 252 merchant veffels, failed from the ifle of Aix on the
6th of October, and on the 14th they had the misfortune to
fall in with the Britifh fquadron. As foon as the French admiral became fenfible of his fituation, he made a fignal for the
trade to make the beft of their way, with the Content and frigates, and for the reft of his fquadron to prepare for battle. Admiral Hawke firft made a fignal to form the line; but finding
the French begin to fheer off, he ordered his whole fleet to give
chafe, and engage as they came up with the enemy. The Lion
and the Louifa began the conflict about noon, and were foon
followed, by the Tilbury, the Eagle, the Yarmouth, the Windfor, and the Devonfhire, which fhips particularly fhared the
danger and confequently the glory of the day.

About four o'clock four of the French fquadron ftruck, viz.
le Neptune, le Monarque, le Fougeux, and the Severn; at five
le Trident followed their example, and le Terrible furrendered
about feven. Be it however remembered, to the credit of their
feveral commanders, that they maintained this unequal conflict
with great fpirit and refolution, and that they did not fubmit
until they were entirely difabled. Their number of killed and
wounded was about 800, and of prifoners 3300 men. M. Fro-
mentierre, who commanded le Neptune, was among the flain,
and their commander in chief was wounded in the leg and in
the fhoulder. The Englifh had 154 killed, and 558 wounded.
Captain Saumarez, of the Nottingham, was among the former.
We loft no other officer of diftinction. On the laft day of
October Admiral Hawke brought thefe fix French men of war
to Portfmouth in triumph, and, in reward for his fervices, was
foon after honoured with the order of the Bath. He was diffatisfied with the behaviour of Captain Fox in the engagment,

| Tilbury, | Captain Harland, | 60 guns, |
|---|---|---|
| Nottingham, | ———— Saumarez, | 60 |
| Defiance, | ———— Bentley, | 60 |
| Eagle, | ———— Rodney, | 60 |
| Gloucefter, | ———— Durel, | 50 |
| Portland, | ———— Stevens, | 50 |

London Gazette extraordinary, October 26.

who

who was tried by a court-martial, and deprived of his command;
but he was reftored about two years after.

Vice-admiral Medley, who commanded a fleet of fifteen fhips
of the line in the Mediterranean, died there on the 5th of Auguft, and was fucceeded by Rear-admiral Byng, who continued
to block up the Spanifh fquadron in Carthagena, and to act in
concert with the Auftrian general on the coaft of Italy. Rear-
admiral Chambers commanded nine men of war in the channel,
and on the 1ft of November Rear-admiral Bofcawen failed for
the Eaft-Indies with fix fhips of the line.

During this year the Englifh took from the French and Spaniards 644 prizes, among which were feventeen French and one
Spanifh men of war. The Englifh veffels, including one man
of war and a fire-fhip, taken by the French and Spaniards,
amounted to 551. The royal navy of Spain was now reduced
to twenty-two fhips of the line, and that of France to thirty-
one; whilft the navy of Britain amounted to 126 fail of the
line, befides feventy-five frigates.

Being arrived at the laft year of this general war, I fhall be- 1748
gin with the hiftory of our naval tranfactions in the Weft-
Indies, where the Britifh fleet was now commanded by Rear-
admiral Knowles. He failed from Jamaica, on the 13th of
February, with eight fhips of the line [a], on an expedition againft
St. Jago de Cuba; but being prevented by contrary winds from
approaching that ifland, Port Louis, in Hifpaniola, became the
object of his hoftile intentions, before which place he arrived
on the 8th of March. Port Louis was defended by a ftrong
fort, mounting feventy-eight guns, with a garrifon of 600 men,
commanded by M. de Chateaunoye. The admiral began his
attack immediately on his arrival, and after three hours violent
cannonading filenced the fort, which furrendered on the follow-

[a] Viz. Cornwall, (Admiral) Captain Chadwick,    80 guns,
    Plymouth,    ——— Dent,    60
    Elizabeth,    ——— Taylor,    64
    Canterbury,    ——— Brodie,    60
    Stafford,    ——— Rentone,    60
    Warwick,    ——— Innes,    60
    Worcefter,    ——— Andrews,    60
    Oxford,    ——— Toll,    50
    Weafel and Merlin floops.

I 2    ing

ing terms, *viz.* The garrifon not to ferve againft the king of Great-Britain or his allies during a year; that they fhould march out with their arms, but without cannon, mortars, or ammunition; that the officers fhould retain their private baggage and fervants; that the town fhould be fpared on certain conditions to be fettled next morning. The garrifon loft 160 men killed and wounded, and the fleet feventy. Among the flain were the Captains Rentone, and Cuft, the laft of whom was a volunteer in the expedition.

Admiral Knowles having entirely deftroyed the fort, refumed his former defign againft St. Jago de Cuba, where he arrived on the 5th of April. The Plymouth and the Cornwall were ordered to enter the harbour; but finding a boom acrofs, and four veffels filled with combuftibles, after firing a few broadfides at the caftle, they judged it prudent to defift, and the fquadron returned to Jamaica. Captain Dent of the Plymouth was afterwards, at the requeft of the admiral, tried by a court-martial for not forcing the boom, and was honourably acquitted.

From this time the Britifh and Spanifh fleets were folely employed in cruizing in detachments againft the trade of each nation. Towards the latter end of Auguft Admiral Knowles, having received intelligence that the annual fleet from Vera Cruz was daily expected at the Havanna, began to cruize off the banks of Tortuga. The Spanifh Admiral Reggio, being informed of the vicinity of the Englifh fquadron, and of the confequent danger of the expected fleet, failed from the Havanna, determined to give Admiral Knowles battle °. On the 29th of September,

° BRITISH SQUADRON.

| | | |
|---|---|---|
| Cornwall, (Adm. Knowles,) | Captain Taylor, | 80 guns, |
| Lenox, | —— Holmes, | 56 |
| Tilbury, | —— Pawlett, | 60 |
| Stafford, | —— Brodie, | 60 |
| Warwick, | —— Innes, | 60 |
| Canterbury, | —— Clarke, | 60 |
| Oxford, | —— Toll, | 50 |

426 ——Men 2,900

SPANISH

tember, Admiral Reggio saw, at a distance, fourteen sail of A. D English merchantmen, under convoy of two men of war; he 1748 gave them chase, but they had the good fortune to escape, and the Lenox, having made a signal for his convoy to save themselves by flight, joined Admiral Knowles, who, on the first of October, fell in with the Spanish squadron near the Havanna.

By a comparison of the two squadrons, it appears that in number of ships they were equal; that in number of guns the Spaniards were somewhat superior, and that in number of men they exceeded us by 1250 [P]. The English admiral, though he had the advantage of the wind, did not at first seem over anxious to engage. About two o'clock the Spaniards began to fire at a distance. Admiral Knowles then made a signal for his squadron to bear down upon the enemy, and in less than half an hour most of the ships were engaged. The two admirals fought each other about half an hour, when Admiral Knowles, having received some damage, fell astern and quitted the line. The Conqueftadore, being likewise injured in her rigging, was also obliged to quit the line of battle, and, before she had time to repair the damage she had sustained, she had the misfortune to be attacked by the British admiral, who had now replaced the yard and main-top-mast which he had lost in his engagement with the Africa. They fought for some time with great obstinacy. The Spanish captain was killed, and the Conqueftadore finally struck to the Cornwall. The general action continued till eight in the evening, when the Spaniards began to edge away towards the Havanna, and got safe into port, except the Conqueftadore and the Africa, which last, being entirely dismasted, was run on shore and blown up by the Spanish admi-

### SPANISH SQUADRON.

| Africa, | Admiral Reggio, | 74 guns, |
|---|---|---|
| Invincible, | Rear-admiral Spinola, | 74 |
| Conqueftadore, | Don de St. Justo, | 64 |
| Dragon, | de la Pas, | 64 |
| New Spain, | Birella, | 64 |
| Royal Family, | Terreftal, | 64 |
| Galga, | Garrecocha, | 36 |
| | | 440 ——Men, 4,150. |

[P] Rolt, vol. iv. p. 567.

ral.

A. D. ral. The Spaniards had in this action three captains and eighty-
1748. six men killed, and 197 wounded; among the latter were Admiral Reggio and fourteen other officers. The Englifh, though
they had fifty-nine killed and 120 wounded, were fo fortunate
as not to lofe a fingle officer.

After this action the Englifh captains were by no means fatif-
fied with each other's conduct. The admiral himfelf was accufed by fome of them, and he was afterwards tried by a court-
martial, and reprimanded for not hoifting his flag on board another fhip after his own was difabled. It feems indeed very
probable, notwithftanding the fuperiority of the enemy, that, if
the Englifh fleet had been commanded by a Hawke, not a fingle
Spaniard would have efcaped.

This was the laft naval action of importance previous to the
general peace, which was finally concluded in the month of
October, 1748. The Englifh, during this year, took three
French and one Spanifh men of war. The whole number of
veffels taken from the Spaniards fince the commencement of
the war amounted to 1249; from the French to 2185: in all
3434. The entire lofs of the Englifh amounted to 3238 fhips.

When we confider the immenfe value of thefe captures;
when we reflect that moft of this wealth was private property;
when we count the number of lives that have been facrificed
during the war, and recollect that all the people facrificed were
neither confulted nor concerned in the conteft; when we farther reflect, that all the princes who caufed this horrible deftruction of life and property, profeffed the religion of peace, cha-
rity, philanthropy, and concord, we are difgufted with human
nature, and laugh at the pretenfion of kings to Chriftianity.
But what will the reader think of thefe mighty potentates, when
he is told, that, after all this wafte of blood and treafure, the
war ended juft where it began. None of the contending powers
retained any part of their acquifitions, the fifth article of the
treaty of peace having ftipulated, that all conquefts whatfoever
fhould be reftored: confequently Cape Breton was reftored to
the French, and Madrafs to the Englifh. Great Britain had
now increafed her national debt to eighty millions, and her fole
confolation was her having reduced the navy of France to a
ftate of contemptible infignificance. As to that nation, the
                                                        terms

terms of peace were easily settled, because we fought with her A. D without any previous cause of quarrel or dispute; she began the 1748 war merely in consequence of her alliance with Spain: but against that nation we commenced hostilities, solely with a design to secure an uninterrupted navigation to our own settlements; nevertheless, strange as it may seem, this important article was entirely neglected, or forgotten, by our plenipotentiaries at Aix-la-Chapelle. Our right to cut logwood in Campeachy and Honduras, an article of equal consequence to this nation, was also left undetermined. But these were not the only examples of inattention (I cannot suppose it ignorance) in the British ministry at this very important period. The French, in consequence of possessing Canada, had, for many years past, been gradually extending the limits of that province, and, in open violation of the treaty of Utrecht, their incroachments were now flagrant and oppressive to our North-American colonies: yet the peace of Aix-la-Chapelle was concluded without this notorious cause of complaint being mentioned by the British plenipotentiaries. The limits of Nova Scotia, another doubtful point, were also left undetermined.

From this precarious state of affairs it was easy to foresee, that the peace of Aix-la-Chapelle would be of no long duration; and, from the conduct of the French immediately after, their latent intentions were obvious. But, before we proceed to develope the *principia* of the succeeding war, it is necessary to record certain transactions in the British parliament, which are immediately connected with our naval history.

The ministry[q], for very wise reasons no doubt, brought a bill into parliament, under the title of, " A bill for reducing into " one act the laws relating to the navy;" by which the half-pay officers were to be rendered subject to martial law. The sea-officers took the alarm: they assembled, and presented a petition to the house requesting to be heard by their counsel, and though the minister mustered sufficient strength to reject the petition, he thought proper to relinquish his unconstitutional attempt. Another plan[r], relative to the navy, was also offered

[q] Smollet's continuation of the history of England, vol. i. p. 19.

[r] Ibid. p. 32.

to the confideration of parliament, *viz.* to regifter a certain number of feamen, who, for an annual ftipend, fhould be liable to ferve when called upon. This project, being calculated to fuperfede the illegal neceffity of preffing, appeared rational; neverthelefs Mr. Pelham found it to be an unpopular meafure, and therefore gave it up.

In the courfe of this year, 1748, the earl of Halifax, who prefided at the board of trade, formed a defign of eftablifhing a colony in Nova Scotia. His project was approved, and four thoufand adventurers, under the protection of Colonel Cornwallis, failed from England, and landed in the harbour of Chebucton, in the neighbourhood of which they built a town and called it Halifax. The French were difpleafed with this exertion of our right, and, by way of counterbalance, attempted to make a fettlement on the ifland of Tobago in the Weft-Indies; but, in confequence of a fpirited remonftrance to the court of Verfailles, they thought proper to defift. They continued neverthelefs to affert their title to St. Lucia, Tobago, and other neutral iflands; and in North America their daily encroachments were fo daring, that the fubjects of Great Britain bordering on the French fettlements, became very loud in their complaints to our miniftry. The French miniftry, according to cuftom, endeavoured to exculpate themfelves by throwing the blame on the governor of Canada. After feveral ineffectual memorials and remonftrances delivered by our ambaffador at Paris, commiffaries, of each nation, were appointed, in the

year 1750, to fettle the limits of Acadia or Nova Scotia. Thefe commiffaries met at Paris, and proceeded with all that deliberate circumfpection which is generally obferved by fervants of the public whofe ftipends muft end with their commiffion. The French commiffaries, in order to gain time by evading the main queftion, drew their antagonifts into a difcuffion concerning the ifland of St. Lucia. Meanwhile the Indians bordering on the Britifh dominions in North America, were infligated by the French to commence their barbarous hoftilities againft the defencelefs inhabitants of our back-fettlements. The Spaniards,

in 1752, began again their former practice, of infolently interrupting our navigation in the Weft-Indies by their guarda-coftas, and in Europe the navy both of France and Spain were

           daily

daily augmenting. In 1753 the conference at Paris, concern- A. 1 ing the limits of Nova Scotia, ended without effect; and the 175 French continued to extend their dominions in North America, by erecting a chain of forts along the lakes of Erie and Ontario, so as to connect their settlements on the Mississippi with Canada. At length, presuming on the amazing supineness of the British ministry, they crossed Lake Champlain, and built a fort at Crown-Point, in the province of New-York. A reader of English history, who reflects as he reads, when he meets with such examples of inactivity, such want of vigilance, such impolitic procrastination, is necessarily led to inquire into the cause. Is this incelerity (if I may be allowed the word) to be attributed to our natural or political constitution? Be this as it may, what we lose in time, as in mechanics, we sometimes gain in power.

The French ministry, notwithstanding such flagrant acts of hostility in America, continued to amuse the court of London with repeated assurances of friendship. But early in the year 1755, certain intelligence was received, that a considerable fleet 175 of men of war was preparing to sail from different ports in France, to America, with a formidable number of land-forces on board. The British ministry, rouzed at this intelligence, gave immediate orders to equip a squadron of men of war, and, towards the latter end of April, Admiral Boscawen, with eleven ships of the line, sailed for America. He was soon after followed by Admiral Holbourne with fix line of battle ships and one frigate, the ministry having received subsequent intelligence that the French fleet, intended for America, consisted of twenty-five ships of the line, &c. This fleet sailed from Brest in the beginning of May; but, after sailing a few leagues beyond the mouth of the English channel, Monf. Macnamara, the commander in chief, returned to Brest, with nine of the capital ships, and the rest proceeded to North America under the command of Monf. Bois de la Mothe. Admiral Boscawen's orders were, to attack the French fleet wheresoever he should meet with it. Being joined by Admiral Holbourne, he continued cruizing off the banks of Newfoundland, in hopes of intercepting the French squadron in their attempt to enter the gulf of St. Lawrence. But the thick fog, so frequent on that coast,

A. D. favoured their enterprize, and Monf. de la Mothe arrived fafe
1755. at Quebec with his whole fquadron, except the Alcide and the
Lys, the firft of fixty-four guns and 480 men; the fecond of
twenty-two, though pierced for fixty-four, with eight companies of land-forces on board. Thefe two unfortunate fhips fell
in with the Dunkirk, Captain Howe, and the Defiance, Captain
Andrews, both fixty-gun fhips. After a refolute engagement of
five hours, the French fhips ftruck. On board the Lys were
feveral officers of diftinction, and about 80,000 l. fterling.

From the capture of thefe two fhips the commencement of
the war may properly be dated. As foon as it was known in
Europe, the French ambaffador left London, and the Britifh
miniftry iffued general orders for making reprifals in every part
of the globe. In confequence of this refolution, three hundred
French merchantmen were taken and brought into England, before the expiration of this year. On the 21ft of July, Sir Edward Hawke failed on a cruize to the weftward, with eighteen
fhips of the line, and, on the 14th of October, Admiral Byng
proceeded to fea with twenty-two fhips. Both thefe fleets returned without meeting with any thing worth their attention.
The French neverthelefs bore thefe infults with a degree of
patience which aftonifhed all Europe. But they were not yet
prepared for war : their alliances were yet unformed, and their
fleet was much inferior to that of Great Britain, which, at this
time, confifted of 213 men of war *; that of France, including
fhips upon the ftocks, amounted to no more than 113 ᵗ.

| * Viz. ENGLISH. | | | * FRENCH. | |
|---|---|---|---|---|
| 1 fhip of 110 guns and 1100 men. | | | 6 fhips of 80 guns each. | |
| 5 | 100 | 1000——each. | 21 | 74 |
| 13 | 90 | 700 | 1 | 72 |
| 8 | 80 | 600 | 4 | 70 |
| 5 | 74 | 500 | 31 | 64 |
| 19 | 70 | 480 | 2 | 60 |
| 39 | 60 | 400 | 6 | 50 |
| 3 | 54 | 350 | 31 frigates. | |
| 18 | 50 | 300 | —— | |
| 4 | 44 | 250 | 113 | |
| 35 | 40 | 250 | | |
| 42 | 20 | 140 | | |
| 31 from 18 to 10 | | 100 | | |

213, befides bomb-ketches, fire-fhips and tenders.

L3

In the beginning of this year Major-general Braddock failed A. D from Corke, with two regiments of foot, for Virginia, with 1755 orders to difpoffefs the French of the lands they had unjuftly ufurped. That general was totally defeated, and flain, by an ambufcade of Indians. I have before obferved, that three hundred French merchantmen were brought into the ports of England; and all this without a declaration of war. The Britifh miniftry intended, by this extraordinary conduct, to validate their defenfive alliances, and that the private property of the fubjects of France might not fuffer, the feveral cargoes of the fhips taken were ordered not to be touched. But this appearance of ftrict juftice was a mere chimera, becaufe many of thefe cargoes confifted of perifhable commodities, and confequently proved a lofs to the owners, without producing any profit to thofe by whom they were taken. The French had evidently, and flagrantly, broken the bonds of peace by their audacious encroachments in America, fo palpably contradictory to the tenour of treaties between the two nations. For the credit of England, I wifh that a formal declaration of war had preceded the firft act of hoftility on our part. Previous to fuch declaration, every act of hoftility is a piracy againft the fubjects of either nation. It is furely a fufficient hardfhip for fubjects to be ruinoufly involved in the quarrels of their fuperiors after fuch quarrels are notorious; but to feel the horrible effects of fuch quarrels, whilft thefe fuperiors wear the mafk of mutual friendfhip, requires a greater degree of patience than any fubjects can be fuppofed to poffefs. We now proceed to the naval hiftory of the year 1756.

About the clofe of the preceding year [u], overtures of accom- 1756 modation were made on the part of France by Monf. Rouille, fecretary of ftate, in a private letter to Mr. Fox, fecretary of ftate to his Britannic majefty. But as this application was calculated only to amufe the Englifh miniftry, in order to gain time, it produced no other effect. The French, having now augmented their navy very confiderably, ordered all the Britifh fubjects in France to depart the kingdom, publifhed an edict for the encouragement of privateers, feized every Englifh veffel in

[u] Smollet's hiftory, p. 315.

K 2

their

their ports, and fent their crews to prifon. They then began to threaten us with an invafion, and, in order to give this project an air of probability, were extremely bufy in their military preparations on the coaft of the Britifh channel. But the defign of thefe preparations was merely to divert our attention from their armaments in the Mediterranean, where the blow was really intended. The king, the miniftry, and their adherents in parliament, were, however, fo completely duped by this French manœuvre, that Heffian and Hanoverian troops were fent for to protect us, and the repeated authentic information concerning the equipment and deftination of the Toulon fleet totally difregarded. There never was a more flagrant example of obftinate infatuation.

At length the deftination of the armament at Toulon was fo certainly and univerfally known, that the Britifh miniftry ftarted fuddenly from their apathy, and, like men juft awoke from a found flumber, began to act before they had recovered their fenfes. It was known to all Europe, that the French fquadron at Toulon confifted of thirteen fhips of the line, and that 15,000 land-forces were there ready for embarkation : neverthelefs, only ten Britifh fhips were ordered for the Mediterranean, and the command was given to Admiral Byng, a man whofe courage and abilities were yet untried. With this fquadron, not completely manned, without either hofpital or firefhip, he failed from Spithead on the 7th of April. He had on board Major-general Stuart, Lord Effingham, Colonel Cornwallis, and about forty inferior officers, whofe regiments were in garrifon at Minorca ; alfo a regiment of foldiers to be landed at Gibraltar, and about a hundred recruits.

Admiral Byng arrived at Gibraltar on the 2d of May, where he found the Louifa, Captain Edgecombe, who informed him, that he had been driven from Minorca by a French fquadron of thirteen fhips of the line, commanded by Monf. Galiffoniere, who had landed 15,000 men on that ifland. Admiral Byng gave immediate orders for the fhips to complete their provifions and water with all poffible expedition. On the third day after his arrival he went on fhore to confer with General Fowke, the governor of Gibraltar, concerning a battalion to be tranfported

to

to Minorca When the admiral demanded this battalion, the governor produced three several letters of instruction from the war-office, which he could neither reconcile with each other, nor with the order given by the admiralty to Admiral Byng. These several orders, which were then compared and considered by a council of war at Gibraltar, being matter of importance to every future commander, whether at land or sea, I must entreat the reader, before he proceeds, to consider attentively Admiral Byng's instructions, which he will find in the Appendix, N° 4. and then to read carefully the orders sent from the war-office to General Fowke, which he will find at the bottom of this page [x].

The council of war, after mature deliberation, determined not to part with the battalion required; first, because it appeared by Lord Barrington's first letter, that the Fuzileers were to remain at Gibraltar; and, secondly, because it was the opinion of the engineers who were well acquainted with Minorca, that to throw succours into St. Philips would be extremely difficult, if not impossible. But this resolution of the council of war was certainly wrong: for though it appeared by Lord Barrington's first letter, that the Fuzileers were to remain at Gibraltar, that order was evidently contradicted by Admiral Byng's instructions of a later date, and the order for sending a battalion to Minorca was repeated and confirmed. However, the council of war consented that one captain, six subalterns, five drums, and 235 privates, should be embarked, to supply the deficiency of those left at Minorca by Captain Edgecombe, and without which his ships would have been of little service in case of an engagement. With regard to Admiral Byng's orders, though they were in many respects conditional, his orders to save Minorca, at all events, were positive and explicit, and that he ought to have

---

[x] Lord Barrington's letter to General Fowke, dated the 21st of March, says, " The king has ordered the royal regiment of Fuzileers to embark immediately " for Gibraltar, and that upon their arrival you are to make a detachment equal " to a battalion, from the four regiments in garrison, to Minorca." The second letter, without any reference to the first, repeats the order for embarking a battalion on board the fleet for the relief of Minorca, in case there was any probability of its being attacked; and the third letter, dated April 1st, orders the governor to receive such women and children, belonging to the Fuzileers, as Admiral Byng should think fit to land.

effected,

A. D. effected, even at the risk of sacrificing his whole fleet. Be this
1756. as it may, he sailed from Gibraltar on the 8th of May, and on
the 16th arrived at Majorca, where he was joined by the Phœnix, Captain Hervey, who confirmed the intelligence relative to
the French fleet and the siege of St. Philips. He then steered
for Minorca, but having contrary winds, did not make that
island until the morning of the 19th, when he saw the English
flag still flying on the castle of St. Philips, and several bomb-
batteries playing upon it from the enemy's works. There have
been British admirals who, at such a prospect, would have
sworn to relieve the garrison, or perish in the attempt! Early
in the morning the admiral despatched Captain Hervey, in the
Phœnix, with the Chesterfield and Dolphin, with orders to reconnoitre the entrance into the harbour, and, if possible, to convey a letter to General Blakeney ʸ. Captain Hervey got round

---

ʸ Though this letter from the admiral was not delivered, it is necessary that
the reader should know its contents; because no circumstance ought to be concealed which may, in any degree, tend to elucidate a transaction attended by such
serious consequences.

" To General BLAKENEY.

" Sir, I send you this by Captain Hervey, of his majesty's ship Phœnix, who
" has my orders to convey it to you, if possible, together with the inclosed packet,
" which he received at Leghorn. I am extremely concerned to find, that Captain
" Edgecombe was obliged to retire to Gibraltar with the ships under his com-
" mand, and that the French are landed, and St. Philips castle is invested; as I
" flatter myself, had I fortunately been more timely in the Mediterranean, that
" I should have been able to have prevented the enemy's getting a footing in the
" island of Minorca. I am to acquaint you that General Stuart, Lord Effingham,
" and Colonel Cornwallis, with about thirty officers, and some recruits belonging
" to the different regiments now in garrison with you, are on board the ships of
" the squadron, and shall be glad to know by the return of the officer, what
" place you will think proper to have them landed at. The royal regiment of
" English Fuzileers, commanded by Lord Robert Bertie, is likewise on board
" the squadron, destined, agreeable to my orders, to serve on board the fleet in
" the Mediterranean, unless it should be thought necessary, upon consultation
" with you, to land the regiment for the defence of Minorca : but I must also
" inform you, should the Fuzileers be landed, as they are part of the ships com-
" plements, the marines having been ordered by the lords commissioners of the
" admiralty on board of other ships at Portsmouth, to make room for them,
" that it will disable the squadron from acting against that of the enemy, which
" I am informed is cruizing off the island : however, I shall gladly embrace
" every opportunity of promoting his majesty's service in the most effectual man-
" ner, and shall assist you to distress the enemy and defeat their designs to the
" utmost of my power."

the

the Laire before nine o'clock in the morning: he made fignals A. D
to the garrifon for a boat to come off; but without effect, and 1756
the admiral, about this time, difcovering the French fleet, ordered him to return.

Admiral Byng now ftood towards the enemy, and about two
in the afternoon made a fignal for the line of battle a-head.
He then diftributed as many feamen as could be fpared from
the frigates, on board fuch fhips as were moft in want of hands,
and converted the Phœnix into a fire-fhip. At feven in the
evening the French fquadron, being then about two leagues diftant, tacked, in order to gain the weather-gage; and the Englifh admiral, not chufing to relinquifh that advantage, alfo put
his fhips about.

On the 20th, in the morning, the weather being hazy, the
French fleet could not be difcovered; but it became vifible
before noon, and at two o'clock Admiral Byng made a fignal
to bear away two points from the wind and engage. Rear-
admiral Weft was then at too great a diftance to comply with
both thefe orders; he therefore bore away feven points from
the wind, and with his whole divifion attacked the enemy with
fuch impetuofity, that feveral of their fhips were foon obliged to quit the line. Had Admiral Byng been equally alert
and eager to engage, it is moft probable that the French fleet
would have been defeated and Minorca faved; but the enemy's
centre keeping their ftation, and Byng's divifion not advancing,
Admiral Weft was prevented from purfuing his advantage, by
the apprehenfion of being feparated from the reft of the
fleet.

After engaging about a quarter of an hour, the Intrepid, the
fternmoft fhip of the van, loft her fore-top-maft, which, according to Byng's account of the action [z], obliged his whole
divifion to back their fails, to prevent their falling foul of each
other. But when this matter came to be examined by the
court-martial, it appeared, that immediately after the fignal for
engaging, whilft the van were bearing down upon the enemy,
Admiral Byng, in the Ramillies, edged away fome points, by
which means the Trident and Louifa got to windward of him,

---

[z] Byng's letter to the admiralty.

A. D. and that, in order to bring them again into their ſtations, he
1756. backed his mizen-topſail, and endeavoured to back his main-
topſail. This manœuvre neceſſarily retarded all the ſhips in his
diviſion, and gave the enemy time to eſcape. M. Galiſſoniere
ſeized the opportunity, and, his ſhips being clean, was ſoon out
of danger. But Admiral Byng, before the engagement, ordered the Deptford to quit the line, in order to reduce his line of
battle to the ſame number of ſhips as that of the enemy. For
this apparent generoſity he was cenſured by the court-martial:
nevertheleſs, there does not appear to be any great impropriety in reſerving one or more ſupernumerary ſhips in readineſs
to ſupply the place of thoſe which may happen to be diſabled.

From this relation of facts, the reader will eaſily perceive
that Admiral Byng's conduct was by no means juſtifiable. The
naval reader ſees very clearly, from the ſituation of the two
fleets, relative to the wind, that he might have fought if he
would ; and, from a compariſon of the two fleets [a], it will ſeem
more than probable, to thoſe who are acquainted with the ſuperior activity and ſkill of our ſailors in time of action, that a
deciſive victory might have been expected. Whether Admiral

| [a] ENGLISH. | | | FRENCH. | | |
|---|---|---|---|---|---|
| Ramillies, | 90 guns, | 730 men, | Foudroyant, | 84 guns, | 950 men, |
| Culloden, | 74 | 600 | La Couronne, | 74 | 800 |
| Buckingham, | 68 | 535 | Le Guerrier, | 74 | 800. |
| Lancaſter, | 66 | 520 | Le Temeraire, | 74 | 800 |
| Trident, | 64 | 500 | Le Redoubtable | 74 | 800 |
| Intrepid, | 64 | 480 | L'Hipopotham | 64 | 600 |
| Captain, | 64 | 480 | Le Fier, | 64 | 600 |
| Revenge, | 64 | 480 | Le Triton, | 64 | 600 |
| Kingſton, | 60 | 400 | Le Lion, | 64 | 600 |
| Defiance, | 60 | 400 | Le Content, | 64 | 600 |
| Louiſa, | 56 | 400 | Le Sage, | 64 | 600 |
| Portland, | 48 | 300 | L'Orphèe, | 64 | 600 |
| | 778 | 5875 | | 828 | 8350 |
| Frigates. | | | Frigates. | | |
| Deptford, | 48 | 280 | La Juno, | 46 | 300 |
| Cheſterfield, | 40 | 250 | La Roſe, | 30 | 250 |
| Phœnix, | 22 | 160 | Gracieuſe, | 30 | 250 |
| Dolphin, | 22 | 160 | La Topez, | 24 | 250 |
| Experiment, | 22 | 160 | La Nymph, | 24 | 200 |
| | 932 | 6885 | | 982 | 9600 |

Byng's

Byng's conduct is juftly to be afcribed to his exceffive prudence, A. I his want of fkill, or want of courage, is difficult to determine. 175⁶ Probably thefe three caufes operated in conjunction to produce the fatal effect. The only plaufible argument that can be urged in extenuation of this admiral's conduct is, that he might be too ftrongly impreft by the recollection of Mathews and Le-ftock; the firft of whom was punifhed for fighting, not accord-ing to rule, and the latter not punifhed, though he did not fight at all.

The Englifh had in this engagement 42 men killed, and 168 wounded; the French, 145 wounded, and 26 killed. Captain Andrews, of the Defiance was the only officer of diftinction, on board the Englifh fleet, who loft his life on this occafion. The French fleet foon difappeared, and at eight in the evening Admiral Byng made a fignal for his fquadron to bring to, at which time the Intrepid and the Chefterfield were miffing; the former, being difabled, had been left to the care of the latter. They joined the fleet next morning, and the admiral then find-ing that three of his fquadron were damaged in their mafts, called a council of war, at which General Stuart, Lord Effing-ham, Lord Robert Bertie, and Colonel Cornwallis were re-quefted to affift.

The council of war being affembled on board of the Ramil-lies, the following queftions were propofed by Admiral Byng:

1. Whether an attack upon the French fleet gives any pro-fpect of relieving Minorca? *Anfwer*. It would not.

2. If there was no French fleet cruizing off Minorca, whe-ther the Englifh fleet could raife the fiege? *Anf*. It could not.

3. Whether Gibraltar would not be in danger by any acci-dent that may befal this fleet? *Anf*. It would be in danger.

4. Whether an attack with our fleet, in the prefent ftate of it, upon that of the French, will not endanger the fafety of Gibraltar, and expofe the trade of the Mediterranean to great hazard? *Anf*. It would.

5. Whether it is not for his Majefty's fervice that the fleet fhould immediately proceed for Gibraltar? *Anf*. It fhould pro-ceed for Gibraltar.

Here I muft beg leave to retard the progrefs of our hiftory a few moments, for the fake of the naval reader, to whom the

A. D.
1756.
consideration of these five resolutions may prove of infinite importance; these volumes being written with an intention, not only to record the heroic virtues of our naval commanders in times past; not only to amuse the gentlemen who in the present age have the honour to serve on board the British fleet; but to animate, to inform, to warn them, by example. I have more than once observed, and the truth of my observation hath been frequently confirmed, that councils of war seldom forebode much heroism. When a commander in chief, whose power is absolute, condescends to ask advice of his inferiors, it is a tacit acknowledgment, that his abilities are inadequate to his power; or, that he is inclined to do that for which he dares not be responsible. I do not believe there was one member of this council of war, who, if the five resolutions had depended upon his single voice, would not have answered them all in the negative. I am also of opinion, that if Admiral Byng had been positively ordered to call no councils of war, but to relieve Minorca at all events, he would have destroyed the French fleet, saved the island, and would have returned triumphant to Britain; unless we are to suppose him constitutionally a coward; for, on such beings, the *present*, though *least*, danger always acts most powerfully.

How this council of war could determine, that it was impossible to relieve Minorca, without ever making the least attempt for that purpose, is incredibly astonishing! and indeed it afterwards appeared, that the troops on board might have been landed at the sally-port with little danger; for Mr. Boyd, commissary of the stores, actually went out to sea in a small boat in search of the English fleet, and returned safe to the garrison. As to their concern for the safety of Gibraltar, their apprehensions were in the highest degree ridiculous. According, however, to the fifth resolution of the council, Admiral Byng returned with his fleet to Gibraltar, and Galissoniere to his former station off Cape Mola. How the garrison of St. Philip's must have been affected, when they beheld the French squadron return triumphant, and afterwards heard a *feu de joye* in the enemy's camp, may be easily conceived. The besiegers had doubtless cause to rejoice at the safe return of their fleet, though not on account of any victory obtained by their admiral; for the

**two**

two admirals evidently ran from each other. But, though the A. D garrison were not a little difappointed at Byng's difappearance, 175( they neverthelefs defended the caftle till the 28th of June, when defpairing of relief from England, and rationally fuppofing that, in the great fyftem of politics, they were intended to be facrificed, after a gallant defence of ten weeks, the venerable Blakeney, on very honourable terms, furrendered Minorca to the *Duc de Richlieu.*

Admiral Byng arrived at Gibraltar on the 19th of June, where Commodore Broderick had come to an anchor four days before, with a reinforcement of five fhips of the line, which were fent from England in confequence of certain intelligence that the French were fitting out more fhips at Toulon. Thus reinforced, Admiral Byng determined to return to Minorca, in hopes of being yet in time to relieve the garrifon; but, whilft he was with great activity preparing for this fecond enterprize, the Antelope of 50 guns arrived at Gibraltar. On board of this fhip were Admiral Hawke, Admiral Saunders, and Lord Tyrawley, who were commiffioned to fuperfede and arreft Admiral Byng, Admiral Weft, and Governor Fowke. The three delinquents were accordingly fent on board the Antelope, and returned prifoners to England. Sir Edward Hawke, with the fleet under his command, failed immediately up the Mediterranean; but, upon his arrival off Minorca, he had the mortification to fee the French flag flying on St. Philip's caftle. As foon as the garrifon furrendered, Galiffoniere prudently retired to Toulon, where he remained in fecurity, whilft Sir Edward Hawke afferted the naval empire of Great Britain, in fight of an enemy elated with the conqueft of a fmall ifland, which they were afterwards obliged to relinquifh. This conqueft, though really infignificant, caufed fuch extravagant exultation in France, fuch an univerfal *Te Deum laudamus*, that one might rationally have fuppofed the Britifh empire totally annihilated.

The people of England, on the contrary, received the intelligence of Byng's retreat with general diffatisfaction, and, without the leaft inquiry into the conduct of the miniftry, pointed all their refentment againft that unfortunate admiral. The miniftry joined in the cry, doing every thing in their power to divert the refentment of the people from themfelves. That

Mr. Byng's conduct was, in many respects, extremely reprehen-
sible, is most certain; but it is not less certain, that the ministry were equally inexcusable, for not sending troops to Minorca much sooner, and for not giving Byng a superior fleet. If
the five ships, which afterwards sailed to his assistance, had
made part of his squadron, Galissoniere must have fled at his
approach, and Minorca would infallibly have been saved. But
these reflections, whilst they fix eternal obloquy on the administration, do not exculpate the admiral. The exigency and
importance of the service on which he was sent, required a sacrifice of prudence to necessity. Our history affords many examples of English fleets obtaining a complete victory over an
enemy far superior in number of guns and men; but these vic-
tories were gained by admirals who disdained to calculate the
exact weight of metal in each squadron.

Admiral Byng, Admiral West, and General Fowke, arrived
at Portsmouth on the 3d of July. The two latter were ordered
to London, where Admiral West was graciously received by
the king. The general was tried for disobedience of orders in
not sending a battalion to the relief of Minorca, and sentenced
to be suspended for a year. The king confirmed the sentence,
and afterwards dismissed him the service. Admiral Byng, after
continuing some time in arrest at Portsmouth, was escorted to
Greenwich-hospital, where he remained close prisoner till December, the time appointed for his trial, which began on the
28th of that month, on board the St. George in Portsmouth-
harbour. The court-martial consisted of four admirals, and
nine captains of the navy[b]. They sat a month, daily examining evidence for and against the prisoner. Admiral West deposed, that he saw no reason why the rear-division might not
have engaged the enemy as close as did the van, and that there
was no signal made for giving chace when the French sheered
off. General Blakeney deposed, that, on the 20th of May,
boats might have passed between the fleet and the garrison with
great security, and that, if the troops ordered for his relief had
been landed, he could have held out till the arrival of Sir Ed-

---

[b] *Admirals.* Smith, president; Holbourne, Norris, Broderick.
*Captains.* Holmes, Boys, Simcoe, Bentley, Dennis, Geary, Moore, Douglas,
Keppel.

ward

ward Hawke. Captain Young, of the Intrepid, declared, that
the loſs of his fore-topmaſt did not appear to prevent the rear-
diviſion from bearing down upon the enemy. Captain Gardiner depoſed, that he adviſed the admiral to bear down, but
without effect, and that, on the day of the action, the admiral
took the command of the Ramillies entirely upon himſelf.—
Theſe cogent depoſitions were corroborated by other witneſſes,
and not in the leaſt degree invalidated by any counter-evidence
in favour of the delinquent. But ſome of the officers who
were on board his ſhip, and near him during the engagement,
depoſed, that he diſcovered no ſigns of confuſion, or want of
perſonal courage, but that he gave his orders diſtinctly and with
apparent coolneſs. The admiral's ſpeech, in his defence, was
inadequate to the great purpoſe of effacing the impreſſion which
the powerful evidence againſt him had made upon the court;
they therefore found him guilty of a breach of that part of the
twelfth article of war, which ſays, —" or ſhall not do his ut-
" moſt to take or deſtroy every ſhip which it ſhall be his duty
" to engage; and to aſſiſt and relieve all and every of his Ma-
" jeſty's ſhips which it ſhall be his duty to aſſiſt and relieve."
He was therefore ſentenced to be ſhot, that being the puniſh-
ment poſitively ordained for a breach of this article. The court,
however, being of opinion, that Admiral Byng's miſconduct did
not proceed from want of courage or diſaffection, added, to
their report of their proceedings to the lords of the admiralty,
a petition, requeſting their lordſhips moſt earneſtly to recommend him to his majeſty's clemency.

The lords of the admiralty, having compared the ſentence of
the court-martial with the words of the twelfth article of war,
which are, " Every perſon in the fleet, who through *cowardice,*
" *negligence,* or *diſaffection,* ſhall," &c. and not finding the
crime of *negligence* (he being acquitted of the other two) imputed by the court, were in doubt concerning the legality of the
ſentence: they therefore preſented a memorial to the king, requeſting, that the opinion of the twelve judges might be taken.
This was accordingly done, and the judges pronounced it a legal ſentence. After the lords of the admiralty had ſigned a
warrant for Admiral Byng's execution, ſome of the members of
the court-martial expreſſed a wiſh to be releaſed, by act of parliament,

A. D.
1756.
liament, from their oath of fecrecy.   A bill for this purpofe
accordingly paffed the houfe of commons;  but, when it came
to a fecond reading in the houfe of lords, each member of the
court-martial was feparately afked, whether he had any thing
to reveal which might incline the king to pardon the delinquent.   Strange as it may feem, they all anfwered in the negative!  and, on the 14th of March, Admiral John Byng was fhot
on board the Monarque, in the harbour of Portfmouth.

This exemplary punifhment of a Britifh admiral was an event
fo fingular, and fo interefting to every gentleman of the navy,
that it feems to require a few reflections before we difmifs the
fubject.   That the admiral did not exert his utmoft power
againft the enemy, is very evident;  and it is equally apparent,
his fleet having the advantage of the wind, that his fighting or
not fighting was matter of choice.   Hence it neceffarily follows,
(allowing that he ought to have fought), that he either wanted
judgment or refolution.   As to judgment, it certainly required
very little, to comprehend the importance of the fervice on
which he was fent, and ftill lefs knowledge of the hiftory of
human events, not to know, that, when great atchievements are
required, fomething muft be left to fortune, regardlefs of the
calculation of chances.   In all battles, whether at fea or in the
field, fortuitous events have vaft influence;  but in naval com-
bats moft frequently, where a fingle accidental fhot from a frigate may difable a firft-rate man of war.   This confideration is
alone fufficient to determine any commander of a king's fhip
never to ftrike fo long as he can fwim, be the force of his antagonift ever fo fuperior.   Upon the whole, I believe we may
equitably conclude, that Admiral Byng was conftitutionally deficient in that degree of perfonal intrepidity, by no means effential to the character of a private gentleman, but which is the
*fine qua non* of a Britifh admiral.   The juftice of punifhing a
man for a conftitutional defect, refts folely on his accepting his
commiffion with the articles of war in his hand.   But admitting
we are fatisfied in regard to the juftice of his execution, in confequence of the fentence of the court-martial, we are not at all
fatisfied with the conduct of that, or thofe members of that
court, who were fo anxious to be releafed from their oath of
fecrecy as to pufh an act for that purpofe through the houfe of
                                                    commons,

commons, and who afterwards fpoke another language at the
bar of the houfe of lords.   Truth or calumny, I know not
which, have whifpered, that Lord Anfon's private remonftrances
deprived Byng of that laft ray of hope which fome fcruples of
confcience gave him reafon to expect, and the public of that
fatisfaction which they have ftill a right to demand.  I fay this,
on a prefumption that the perfon alluded to is now living.

The purfuit of this tragedy to its cataftrophe having carried
us fomewhat beyond the limits of the year 1756, it is neceffary
that we fhould now refume the thread of our relation of fuch
public tranfactions as were connected with the naval hiftory of
this kingdom.  Hitherto we have feen Great Britain and France
actually at war, without the ceremony of an open declaration.
Why this formality was fo long deferred, muft be afcribed to
political confiderations, by which the minifters of both countries
were influenced; but, how cogent foever thefe confiderations
might feem to a cabinet-council, a piratical war between two
polifhed nations is unjuft to the fubjects of both : the reafon is
obvious.   However, in the beginning of May, the Britifh miniftry, being no longer in doubt concerning the invafion of Minorca by the French, determined to throw off the mafk; accordingly a declaration of war with that nation was publifhed
in London on the 18th, and on the 9th of June war with
England was proclaimed at Paris.   The ftate of the navy of
Britain and of France, at this period, the reader will find in
the Appendix, N° V. and VI.

One principal defign of this hiftory being to perpetuate the
names of fuch naval commanders, as, by their gallant actions,
deferve to be recorded in the annals of Britain, I cannot omit
an engagement which happened on the 17th of May off Rochfort, between the Colchefter of 50 guns, commanded by Captain Obrian, and the Lime of 20 guns, with the Aquilon of
48 guns, M. de Maurville, and the Fidelle of 36 guns, M. de
Litardais. They were within gun-fhot about fix in the evening,
and foon came to fo clofe an engagement, that the forefail of
the Lime was fet on fire by the wads of the Fidelle, againft
whom, notwithftanding the great inequality of ftrength, fhe
maintained a glorious conteft upwards of five hours; when the
Fidelle retreated firing fignals of diftrefs, and the Lime was fo

fhattered

A. D.
1756.
fhattered as to be totally incapable of making any fail a-head; The Colchefter and the Aquilon fought with equal intrepidity till paft midnight, and then parted with mutual honour and fatisfaction. Previous to this action, the Warwick of 60 guns, Captain Shuldham, off Martinico, falling in with three French men of war, was taken after an obftinate running fight, in which fhe loft her captain and a confiderable number of men.

Our fleet in North America was, during this year, not totally inactive. A French man of war of 50 guns, called L'Arc-en-ciel, with troops and military ftores for Louifbourg, was taken off that port by the Norwich and Litchfield, both 50 gun fhips, belonging to Admiral Spry's fquadron. On the 26th of July, off the harbour of Louifbourg, Commodore Holmes on board the Grafton, with the Nottingham, and the Hornet and Jamaica floops, fell in with two French men of war, Le Hero, L'Illuftre, and two frigates, which were returning from Canada. The enemy being to windward, Commodore Holmes ftood towards them, as near the wind as he could ly. The French fquadron bore down upon him till within about two leagues diftance, when the Englifh tacked with a defign to cut the enemy off from the port of Louifbourg; but they hauled in for it, and came to an anchor about noon. Commodore Holmes purfued them to within a league of the harbour, where he laid to till four in the afternoon, and then made fail to the eaftward. As foon as it was dark, he defpatched the Hornet floop to Halifax, to requeft a reinforcement, being much inferior to the enemy. At eight next morning, the four French fhips above mentioned weighed anchor, failed out of the harbour, and gave him chafe. The Englifh fhips ftood from the enemy at firft, and fought them for fome time with their ftern chafe only; but the Grafton at length hauled up her courfers, bunted her main-fail, and bore down upon the French commodore, who was alfo attacked by the Nottingham. L'Illuftre was prevented from affifting his partner, by a fudden calm; but, a breeze fpringing up foon after, the French were again united about feven in the evening. At dufk the battle ended, and the two fquadrons feparated. According to the French account of this engagement, the two Englifh fhips fheered off when they faw the Illuftre coming up; and next morning Monf. Beaufier, the commodore,

2

commodore, finding the English at too great a distance, return- A. 1
ed to Louisbourg, with the loss of eighteen men killed, and 175
forty-eight wounded. The English account, on the contrary,
assures us, that, before it grew dark, the French sheered off,
and next morning prevented a renewal of the action, by bearing away right before the wind for Louisbourg. The Hero was
considerably injured. The Grafton had six men killed and
twenty-one wounded.

Spain, at this time, affected to entertain sentiments of sincere
friendship towards England, and declared herself determined to
maintain the strictest neutrality: nevertheless, she had so continued to augment her navy, that she had now forty-six ships
of the line and twenty-two frigates almost fit for service. Notwithstanding the pacific declarations of the Spanish ministry,
they were certainly determined, as soon as they were ready, if
not to break with England, at least to try her patience to the
utmost. Their guarda-costas began again to insult our trade in
the West-Indies, and private orders were sent to prevent our
cutting logwood in the bay of Honduras. But these insults
being insufficient to provoke the British ministry, the haughty
Spaniard resolved to seize the first opportunity of insulting us
nearer home. A French privateer, having taken an English
vessel on the coast of France, brought her to an anchor under
the guns of Algezire, a Spanish fort in the bay of Gibraltar.
Sir Edward Hawke, whose squadron was at this time riding in
the bay, and Lord Tyrawley governor of Gibraltar, immediately
sent to demand the restitution of the prize, which the governor of Algezire positively refused. The English officer who
carried this demand, being attended with a number of armed
boats, with orders to cut the ship out and to bring her off at all
events, proceeded to execute his orders, and carried his point;
but the castle gave him so warm a reception, that above a hundred of his men were either killed or wounded. The court of
Spain approved of the governor's conduct, and pretended to be
violently offended with that of Sir Edward Hawke. England
bore this outrage with Christian patience; and the impression
it made was soon obliterated by a greater.

Human nature, collected into states and kingdoms, is influenced by the follies, passions, and vices, by which individuals

are generally governed. The man who wants fpirit to refent the firft affront, muft foon expect a fecond: fo it is with nations. The Antigallican, an Englifh private fhip of war, of thirty carriage and fixteen fwivel guns, commanded by Captain William Fofter, cruizing in the bay of Bifcay, fell in with Le Duc de Penthievre, a French Eaft-Indiaman, on the 26th of December, about feven leagues from Ferrol. The Indiaman, mounting fifty guns, being to windward, bore down upon the Antigallican, and fired a gun to bring her to. She then hoifted her colours. The Frenchman fired a broadfide, and half another, with confiderable effect, before the Antigallican returned the compliment. A clofe engagement enfued, and continued three hours, when the Indiaman ftruck, her captain and twelve men being killed, and her fecond captain and twenty-feven men wounded. They were, at this time, five leagues and a half diftant from the light-houfe at Corunna. Captain Fofter attempted to carry his prize into Lifbon; but, finding it impoffible to make that port, he bore away for Cadiz, where, as foon as he came to an anchor, the officers of the Indiaman depofed upon oath, that their fhip was in all refpects a legal prize. Neverthelefs, incredible as it may feem, it was not long before orders were fent from Madrid, to the governor of Cadiz, to detain both the fhips, under pretence that the Indiaman was taken fo near a Spanifh fort, as to be within the diftance prefcribed by the law of nations: a palpable falfhood! The Spaniards pretended to inftitute a legal inquiry; but their proceedings were a difgrace to all law and equity. Sir Benjamin Keene at Madrid, and Mr. Goldfworth, the Englifh conful at Cadiz, in vain remonftrated. The court of Spain fent a pofitive order for the prize to be delivered to the French conful, and the governor of Cadiz, on Captain Fofter's refufing to ftrike the Englifh colours, fent a fixty-gun fhip and a thirty-gun frigate to reduce the Penthievre to obedience by force. They continued firing upon her near two hours without a fingle fhot being returned. They fhot away his enfign, killed the failor who was fent to ftrike his pendent, and wounded feven of his men. When the Spanifh commodore had thus amufed himfelf as long as he thought fit, Captain Fofter was told that he was not a prifoner, and fuffered to go on fhore, and was afterwards told

by

by the governor, that he had no farther commands for him : A. D
nevertheless, he was next morning dragged to prison, and his 1756
crew, after being robbed and abused by the Spanish soldiers,
were thrown into a loathsome dungeon, where they must inevitably have perished of hunger, but for the humanity of the
British consul. These unhappy men were not released till the
5th of March.

It is as painful to the British historian as to the British reader
to contemplate the infolent cruelty and injustice of Spain, in this
and the preceding example. In some periods of our history,
not a nation under heaven would have dared thus to provoke
the growling lion. If this had happened in the reign of Elisa-
beth, or during Cromwell's usurpation, Cadiz would have been
laid in ashes in less than a month. But the political fystem of
the British ministry prompted them rather to submit to any infult, than risk a Spanish war. The people of England grew
diffatisfied. Braddock's defeat, the reduction of Ofwego and
other forts in America; the loss of Minorca, and the absurd
disposition and employment of the navy, convinced them, that
the ministry were unequal to the importance of their several
offices. The nation became clamorous, and the king at last
confented to a partial change in the administration. Mr. Pitt
was appointed secretary of state for the southern department,
and Mr. Legge nominated chancellor of the exchequer.

The people in general were extremely delighted with this 1757
change of men, in full confidence that a change of measures
would follow ; but too much of the old leaven still remained,
to fuffer the full exertion of heroic patriotism. These new ministers began to act upon principles so diametrically opposite to
those of their colleagues in administration, that they were hardly feated in their places before it was determined to remove
them. They were represented to the king as two obstinate,
wayward servants of the people, rather than of the crown, and
totally ignorant of that political fystem by which Hanover could
possibly be preserved. This artful appeal to his majesty's natural affections produced the desired effect. On the 5th of April
Mr. Pitt [c], by the king's command, was difmissed the office of

[c] London Gazette.

secretary

A. D.
1757.

fecretary of ftate, and Mr. Legge, having alfo refigned, **was** fucceeded by Lord Mansfield in the office of chancellor of the exchequer. This fudden difmiffion of the two popular minifters furprized and alarmed the nation, and, inftead of difgracing them with the people, added infinitely to their popularity. Many of the principal cities in England complimented them with their freedom in gold boxes, and the whole nation became at laft fo clamorous, that it was foon thought advifable to folicit their re-acceptance of the places from which they had been fo lately difmiffed. Mr. Pitt refumed his office of fecretary of ftate for the fouthern department on the 29th of June, and Mr. Legge that of chancellor of the exchequer a few days after. From this time Mr. Pitt became prime minifter, though the principal perfons who compofed the late adminiftration remained in office. The duke of Newcaftle was appointed firft lord of the treafury, Mr. Fox paymafter-general of the army, and Lord Anfon firft lord of the admiralty.

The firft expedition in which the navy bore a part, after Mr. Pitt's reftoration, was that againft Rochfort on the coaft of France. This minifter conceived, that the moft effectual means of ftopping the progrefs of the French armies in Germany, was, by ravaging their coaft, to call their attention to the fecurity of their own dominions. Rochfort became the firft object of his attention in confequence of certain intelligence which he had received from a Captain Clerk, who informed him, that, returning from Gibraltar in the year 1744, he vifited Rochfort with a defign to make himfelf acquainted with its ftrength, in cafe of a war with France, and that he found its fortifications in fo ruinous a ftate, that the town might be eafily taken by a *coup de main*; prefuming that it remained in the fame fituation, becaufe the fortifications had not been repaired during the two laft wars with England. Captain Clerk's information was afterwards laid before the cabinet, and Tierry, a French pilot, was clofely examined, concerning the practicability of landing and protecting the troops.

The miniftry being now perfectly fatisfied, as to the feafibility and importance of the enterprize, a formidable fleet was immediately ordered to Spithead, and ten regiments of foot encamped on the Ifle of Wight. Sir John Mordaunt, knight of the

the Bath, commanded the troops, and Sir Edward Hawke the A. D
fleet of men of war ordered for this service. The destination 1757
of this formidable armament remained a profound secret for
some time; it was, however, at last, generally understood to
be intended against some part of the coast of France. Mr. Pitt,
perfectly sensible of the necessity of proceeding with all possible
expedition, repeatedly urged the departure of the fleet; but,
either by some unaccountable fatality, or by the malignant influence of men who would damn their country to thwart the
measures of an envied minister, the transports did not arrive at
St. Helen's till the 4th of September. The troops were embarked with all possible expedition, and the fleet got under sail
on the 8th. This entire armament consisted of sixteen ships of
the line, seven frigates, two bomb-ketches, two fire-ships, two
busses, one horse-ship [d], and fifty-five transports, besides the

|  | Viz. | Captain |  |
|---|---|---|---|
|  | Royal George, | Buckle, | 100 guns, |
|  | Ramillies, (Adm. Hawke), | Hobbs, | 90 |
|  | Neptune, | Galbraith, | 90 |
|  | Namur, | Dennis, | 90 |
|  | Royal William, | Taylor, | 84 |
|  | Barfleur, | Graves, | 80 |
|  | Princess Amelia, | Colby, | 80 |
|  | Magnanime, | Howe, | 74 |
|  | Torbay, | Keppel, | 74 |
|  | Dublin, | Rodney, | 74 |
|  | Burford, | Young, | 70 |
|  | Alcide, | Douglas, | 64 |
|  | America, | Byron, | 60 |
|  | Achilles, | Barrington, | 60 |
|  | Medway, | Proby, | 60 |
|  | Dunkirk, | Digby, | 60 |
| Frigate | Southampton, | Gilchrist, | 32 |
|  | Coventry, | Scrope, | 28 |
|  | Cormorant, | Clive, | 18 |
|  | Postillion, | Cooper, | 18 |
|  | Beaver, | Gascoigne, | 18 |
|  | Pelican, | O'Hara, | 16 |
|  | Escort, | Inglis, | 14 |
| Bomb | Firedrake, | Edwards, | 8 |
|  | Infernal, | Kenzie, | 8 |
| Fireship | Pluto, | Lindsey, | 8 |
|  | Proserpine, | Banks, | 8 |
| Buss | Canterbury, | Lampriere, | 6 |

Jason,

A. D. Jafon, a forty-gun fhip, in the capacity of a tranfport, and the
1757. Chefterfield man of war for the purpofe of repeating fignals. On
board of this fleet were ten regiments of foot, two regiments of
marines, fixty light-horfe, and a formidable train of artillery.
The admirals under Sir Edward Hawke were Knowles and
Broderick, and under Sir John Mordaunt were the Generals
Conway and Cornwallis.

This fleet failed from St. Helen's with a fair wind, and bore
away to the weftward.    The troops on board were totally ignorant of their deftination till the 15th, when the orders iffued
by Sir John Mordaunt relative to the nature of the fervice on
which they were fent, put the matter out of doubt. They flood
into the bay of Bifcay, and on the 20th made the ifle of Oleron,
Sir Edward Hawke fent immediate orders for Admiral Knowles
to proceed with his divifion to Bafque road, and to attack the
fort on the ifle of Aix ; but the execution of this order, though
pofitive, was fufpended by a very extraordinary accident. Admiral Knowles, as foon as he received thefe orders, made fail
with his divifion, and prepared his fhips for action ; but he had
fcarce taken leave of Sir Edward Hawke, before a French man
of war was obferved ftanding in towards the centre of the Englifh fleet. When this fingular phenomenon appeared[c], Admiral
Knowles was fo deeply engaged in the important occupation of
exhibiting the entertaining fpectacle of a clear fhip between
decks to General Conway, that he could not poffibly attend to
the firft information brought by his lieutenant. However, in
confequence of a fecond meffage, the admiral came upon deck,
and, with his fpy-glafs, difcovered this ftrange fail to be a two-
decked fhip.    Admiral Knowles recollecting that he was fent
on a different fervice, but not recollecting the comparative importance of that fervice, was in doubt whether he fhould make
a fignal for any of his divifion to chace. During this hefitation
the French fhip difcovered her miftake, tacked and bore away
with all the fail fhe could crowd.   The admiral continued ftill
to doubt, and doubted fo long, that all poffibility of coming up
with her before night vanifhed.   At laft, however, Admiral
Knowles ordered the Magnanime and the Torbay to give chace.

[c] Knowles's anfwer on Sir John Mordaunt's trial.

They

They chafed as long as they could fee their object, and next A. D.
morning rejoined the fleet. 1757.

On the 21ft Admiral Knowles, with the divifion under his
command, made fail towards the land; but the weather proving
hazy, the pilots refufed to carry the fleet in. This evening the
troops were in full expectation of landing; but about feven
o'clock the fhips tacked, and came to an anchor near the Ifle
of Rheè. On the 22d the fleet entered the bay called the Road
of Bafque, between the iflands of Rheè and Oleron, and there
remained at anchor during the night. About eight next morning, Admiral Knowles in the Neptune, with the Magnanime,
the Barfleur, America, Alcide, Burford, and Royal William,
made fail towards Aix, a fmall ifland in the mouth of the river
leading up to Rochfort. Captain Howe in the Magnanime led
the van. At half paft twelve, the fort upon the ifland began
to fire upon him, and his people foon grew impatient to return
the compliment. But he continued to advance with the utmoft
compofure, without firing a fingle fhot, continually urging his
pilot to lay the fhip as clofe to the fort as poffible. The moment he came abreaft of the battery, he let go his anchors, and
fired a broadfide, which drove moft of the Frenchmen from
their guns. From this time the fire from the battery gradually
ceafed. It was, however, near an hour before fhe ftruck her
colours. That this ifland fhould prove fo eafy a conqueft will
not appear furprifing, when the reader is informed, that the
battery fo furioufly attacked by the Magnanime confifted of no
more than fix iron cannons, mounted *en barbet:* fo that the
gunners were fo entirely expofed, that captain (now Lord) Howe
might have taken the fort in his long-boat. There were indeed near thirty pieces of cannon upon the ifland; but the fix
above-mentioned were all that were brought to bear upon the
fhips. The fortifications of Aix were planned by the great
Vauban; but the execution of that plan had been fo totally
neglected, that the ifland was, at this time, entirely defencelefs.

As foon as the French colours were ftruck, an Englifh regiment landed and took poffeffion of the *important* conqueft.
Aix is an ifland about five or fix miles in circumference, entirely covered with vines, which yield a meagre wine, the common
beverage

A. D.   beverage of the country.   The garrifon confifted of about five
1757.  hundred men, part foldiers and part failors, moft of which had
been landed from the continent on the day preceding the attack,
and were now made prifoners of war.   As to the behaviour
of the Englifh regiment which took poffeffion of the fort, I will
tell it in the language of a writer who ferved as a volunteer on
this expedition [f].—" I wifh," fays the author,  " I could with
" truth report, that our people behaved with the moderation
" they ought to have done: and I am forry, for the credit
" of our difcipline, that the fevere orders iffued by the gene-
" ral were not as feverely executed.   Both our foldiers and
" failors were fuffered to get abominably drunk, and, in con-
" fequence of that, cruelly to infult the poor fufferers.   This
" little ifland became, in a very few hours, a moft fhocking
" fcene of devaftation; even the church was fuffered to be pil-
" laged, the poor prieft robbed of his little library, and his
" robes became a mafquerading habit to the drunken tars."
Such behaviour is not furprifing in a clafs of men who act without reflection, and in whom reflection would be a misfortune
to themfelves and to their country; but that fuch conduct
fhould have been fuffered by their fuperiors, is wonderful indeed!   That men flufhed with wine and victory are with difficulty reftrained, I readily acknowledge; but the difficulty of
preventing a crime, which admits of no paliation, is a very
feeble apology.

The conqueft of the ifle of Aix [g], though of little importance,
confidered as an omen of fuccefs, gave vaft fpirits to the whole
fleet, and infpired the troops with fuch ardour, that, if they
had been immediately landed on the continent, they would probably have fucceeded in any poffible attempt.   Five days from
this period were fpent in founding the depth of water, in pru-
dential deliberations and fage councils of war; fo that eight
days were now elapfed fince the firft appearance of the fleet on
the coaft of France, during which time, we may rationally fuppofe, that the enemy had made no inconfiderable progrefs in
preparing for a vigorous defence.   But before we proceed to
the conclufion of this grand expedition, it is neceffary to relate,

[f] Genuine account of the late expedition, p. 44.          [g] Ibid.

more

more particularly, the transactions of the five days from the ta-  A. D
king of the isle of Aix.  1757

On the 23d, in the afternoon, immediately after the *glorious*
conquest of that *important* fortress, Sir Edward Hawke sent
Admiral Broderick, with Captains Dennis, Douglas, and Buckle,
to reconnoitre and sound the coast, in order to find a proper
place for landing the troops which were intended to destroy the
shipping, docks, and naval stores at Rochfort. These gentlemen, having spent the remainder of that day, and the following night, in the laborious execution of their commission, returned to the fleet about four in the evening of the 24th, and
reported, that from Angolin to Chataillon there was a hard
sandy beech; also a small bay farther to the eastward, at either
of which places troops might be conveniently landed, and that
there was sufficient depth of water and clear ground for the
transports to anchor at the distance of a mile and a half from the
shore. They also reported, that on the south side of the bay
there was a square fort, on the north-west side of which were
nine embrazures, and two on the north-east. This fort had
been previously reconnoitred by Colonel Wolfe, who was of
opinion, that it might easily be silenced by a single ship, or, at
least, so engaged, that the troops might land on each side of it
with very little interruption. The pilot of the Magnanime made
no doubt of carrying his ship near enough to batter the fort.
From these several reports Sir Edward Hawke and Sir John
Mordaunt seemed determined to proceed to the execution of
Colonel Wolfe's plan. But this resolution was afterwards stag-
gered by General Conway, who, after a tedious examination of
several prisoners from the isle of Aix, reported that, according
to the information of these prisoners, the attempt against Rochfort would be attended with danger and difficulty [h]. This suspicious information determined the two commanders to have
recourse to that bane of our national glory, a council of war.
If Wolfe had commanded these brave troops, would he, on
this occasion, have called a council of war? The report of
prisoners ought not to be entirely disregarded; but a wise general, or admiral, will listen to their information with the utmost

[b] Entick, vol. ii. p. 321.

A. D. fufpicion.    Be this as it may, if thefe prifoners produced the
1757. council of war, they ought to have been amply rewarded by
the king of France as the faviours of Rochfort.

The members of this memorable council were, Sir Edward
Hawke, Sir John Mordaunt, Admiral Knqwles, General Conway, Admiral Broderick, General Cornwallis, Captain Rodney,
Colonel Howard. They met on the 25th, on board the Neptune,
and, after mature deliberation, determined unanimoufly, that
an attempt upon Rochfort was neither *advifable* nor *practicable.*
That it was unadvifable, if impracticable, no body will prefume
to doubt. Neverthelefs, Admiral Knowles was fent next morning with two bomb-ketches and other fmall veffels to bombard
the fort, and to found the entrance into the river Charante;
who on his return reported, that one of the bombs ran a-
ground, and that the Coventry touched five times in attempting to protect her from two French row-gallies. This report
by Admiral Knowles can no otherwife be reconciled with that
of the officers firft employed in founding, and with the evidence
of the pilot of the Magnanime, than by fuppofing that the
French pilots, now employed, chofe to facrifice their reputation
as pilots to the fafety of their country. But, notwithftanding
this report, orders were iffued that night for the troops to hold
themfelves in readinefs to land next morning; yet that day paffed in perfect inactivity. However, another council of war,
confifting of the fame members, being called, it was now unanimoufly refolved, that it *was* advifable to land the troops.

In confequence of this refolution, on the 28th in the afternoon, the Ramillies hoifted a fignal for the commanders of regiments to come on board, and at eight the fame evening orders
were iffued [1] for the troops to prepare for landing in the night.

                                                          Twelve

---

1 I7z.                              " Ramillies, Sept. 28.
    " The troops are to be ready to go from the tranfports into the boats at twelve
" o'clock at night; a number of men of war's boats will be appointed to every
" regiment, under the command of a lieutenant; thefe, with the tranfport boats,
" (who are to be under the direction of a lieutenant of foot), are to receive the
" grenadiers, the piquet companies, one, two, or more, as the boats can contain
" them; the commander of every regiment lands with the firft detachment, if it
" amounts to three companies.
    " Particular care to be taken that the foldiers be not too much crowded in the
" boats.
                                                       " The

Twelve hundred men were accordingly crowded into boats, in A. I full expectation of a signal at midnight to put off. Indeed such 1751 was the alacrity of the troops on this occasion, and such their eagerness to land, that the boats were filled an hour before the time. In this situation they remained, the boats beating against each other, for it blew rather fresh, till about three in the morning; when, instead of a signal to put off, a laconic order came for the troops to return to their respective transports.

" The crews of the boats that row the transports long-boats, are to be chiefly
" composed of soldiers, who are to return to the corps after the first landing,
" and row backwards and forwards till the whole disembarkation is completed,
" and till the provisions, tents, baggage, &c. are landed, according to the orders
" of the 15th.

" When the first part of every regiment is embarked, it is to proceed silently
" and quietly to the place of rendezvous appointed for the division, and there
" the whole division receive their orders from a captain of a ship of war, which
" orders they are in every particular strictly to obey.

" The troops have had a great example before their eyes, and the general is
" confident that they will endeavour to imitate the coolness and determined va-
" lour that appeared in the attack of the isle of Aix.

" No soldier is to fire from the boats on any account, but to wait for the mo-
" ment to join the enemy with their bayonets.

" Eight mantlets per regiment will be distributed, and the commanding officers
" will dispose of them, so as to cover the landing boats and rowers from the
" musquetry, in case it be necessary.

" The troops are to land silently, and in the best order the nature of the thing
" allows of.

" The companies to form, and be ready to attack whoever appears before
" them.

" The chief engineer, the quartermaster-general, and his deputies, are to go
" on shore with the first body that lands.

" All the intrenching tools are to be landed immediately after the second em-
" barkation.

" Mr. Boyd, the comptroller of the artillery, is appointed to carry orders to
" the chief engineer, captain of the artillery, and to every branch of the ord-
" nance, and is to be obeyed.

" Each regiment to send a return immediately of the number of tents they
" have remaining after the calculating a tent for eight men, as ordered on the
" 15th.

" Colonel Kingsly to be ready to march with the grenadiers upon their landing,
" with two field-officers, Major Farquhar, and Lieutenant-Colonel Sir William
" Boothby.

" The regiments are each of them to receive from the store-keeper of the ord-
" nance, ten chevaux-de-frize, and to send for them forthwith."

N 2                              This

A. D. This order was obeyed, but not without a general murmur of
1757. diſſatisfaction.

If the reader be unacquainted with the real hiſtory of this
expedition, he will doubtleſs be at a loſs on what martial principle to account for all theſe apparent dilatory, irreſolute, incongruous, and even contradictory proceedings: in juſtice, therefore,
to the commanders on each element, I will endeavour to develope the motives by which they were influenced in their various
reſolutions, and, if poſſible, to point out the ſeveral cauſes to
which the miſcarriage of this enterprize is to be attributed.

Thoſe who are acquainted with the hiſtory of Great Britain,
muſt recollect many inſtances of our naval expeditions having
failed for want of alacrity in the preparation. It requires very
little nautical knowledge or experience to conceive, that the ſucceſs of naval enterprizes depends almoſt entirely upon the proper ſeaſon of the year. This diverſion on the coaſt of France
ſeems to have been firſt ſuggeſted by the king of Pruſſia and the
duke of Cumberland, who were at this time overpowered by
numerous French armies in Germany. Mr. Pitt adopted their
idea, becauſe he thought it rational; but he was principally influenced by the proſpect of giving a mortal ſtab to the naval
power of France, in the deſtruction of Rochfort. When he
firſt determined to carry this project into execution, there appeared to be time ſufficient. The troops, and the fleet of men
of war, were aſſembled early in the month of Auguſt, and their
not ſailing till the 8th of September was entirely owing to the
miſconduct of the contractors for the tranſports: ſo much is it
in the power of little beings to fruſtrate the deſigns of the wifeſt
of the human ſpecies!

That the fleet did not make the iſle of Oleron till the 20th,
was chiefly owing to contrary winds; but, from the above narrative, it is evident that they might, with great eaſe, have anchored in Baſque road next morning; that the remainder of that day
would have been ſufficient for reconnoitring the coaſt, and that
the troops might have been in poſſeſſion of Rochfort on the
evening of the 22d. The attack upon the iſle of Aix was a
mere waſte of time, nor would the taking of Fort Fouras have
anſwered any better purpoſe; becauſe neither of theſe forts were
ſo ſituated as to prevent the landing of the troops, or impede
their

their march to Rochfort, or render their retreat lefs fecure. A. D
By the king's private inftructions to Sir John Mordaunt [k], it ap- 1757.
pears, that the firft and principal object of the expedition was
to deftroy the docks, magazines, arfenals and fhipping at Rochfort. This was to be effected by furprife, or *coup de main ;*
therefore every hour of unneceffary delay was a fault, as it not
only gave the enemy time to recover from the confternation into
which the appearance of fuch an armament muft have thrown
them, but alfo gave them time to collect their troops, and add
ftrength to their fortifications.

We have feen above, from the report of Admiral Broderick,
that the tranfports might fafely ride at anchor within a mile and a
half of a firm beach, where the troops might have landed without the leaft moleftation from any fort or battery. Why were
not the tranfports, immediately upon this report, ordered to
that ftation, and the army landed upon the beach? If the tranfports had been thus fituated, the entire difembarkation would
have been effected in the fpace of a few hours, and the firft
divifion landed would have been fupported by the fecond in lefs
than an hour. This feems to have been an obvious, eafy, and
rational method of proceeding, and probably would have been
purfued, but for General Conway's interrogation of the French
prifoners which were taken on the ifle of Aix. The report of
thefe prifoners produced a council of war, and that council, on
the information of thefe and other Frenchmen, were perfuaded,
that, if the troops fhould land on the continent, they would
certainly all be drowned, for that, by opening certain fluices,
the whole country might be laid under water. With thefe terrible apprehenfions, the council unanimoufly determined, that
any attempt upon Rochfort was neither *advifable* nor *practicable.*
For this determination fome reafons were affigned; but it may
be fomewhat difficult to find any reafon for an apparent contrary determination at their next meeting, efpecially when we confider, that the report of Admiral Knowles, fubfequent to the
firft council, tended rather to increafe than diminifh the horrible
chimeras which guarded the coaft of France. But it is neceffary to obferve, that this fecond refolution meant nothing more

[k] Vide Appendix, Nº VII.

than

than an attack upon Fort Fouras, if it had any precife object
farther than that of mere bravado ; for, at this time, every idea
of attempting Rochfort was entirely relinquifhed.

We have feen above, that, in confequence of the refolution
of the council of war of the 28th, the troops were ordered to
land the fame night, and that, after remaining four hours in the
boats, they were ordered to return to their fhips. The only
reafon that can be affigned for this counter-order is, that, after
the firft order had been iffued, and in part executed, the commanders difcovered the abfurdity of attempting to land a numerous army from fhips which were at the diftance of two leagues
from the fhore. It is alfo probable that they now recollected, that, at this time, they had no motive, no object, which
could either diftrefs the enemy or ferve their country in the
fmalleft degree. We find, in the fourth article of the king's
private inftructions to Sir John Mordaunt [1], that Mr. Pitt's plan
extended to other towns on the coaft of France, particularly
L'Orient and Bourdeaux ; but we fee in the following article of
thefe inftructions, that the end of September was fixed for the
return of the fleet. Neverthelefs, left a fcrupulous obedience
to thefe orders might fruftrate the intent of the expedition, Mr.
Pitt, on the 15th of September, wrote to Sir Edward Hawke
and to Sir John Mordaunt, informing them, that his majefty's
commands were to continue upon the coaft of France as many
more days as might be neceffary to the completion of any
operation in which they were engaged.

Having thus endeavoured to give the reader a clue which may
enable him to pafs through this labyrinth of delays and councils,
to the feveral apparent caufes of our difappointment, I will now
prefume to affign the real caufe. The very able and patriotic
minifter who planned this admirable enterprize, notwithftanding
his fuperior fagacity, was miftaken in the character of Sir John
Mordaunt, of General Conway, and of General Cornwallis.
In military knowledge and perfonal courage they were by no
means deficient ; but there was in them all a want of that conftitutional fpirit of enterprize, that impetuofity of refolution,
bordering upon imprudence, without which an expedition of this

[1] Appendix, No VII.

nature

nature will never fucceed. If the minifter himfelf, or any ge- A. I
neral of equal conftitutional heroifm, had commanded this ar- 175
my, Rochfort would have been deftroyed in twenty-four hours
after the fleet came to an anchor on the coaft of France.

We now refume the thread of our narrative. Sir Edward
Hawke, at length difgufted with the irrefolute proceedings of
the army, on the 29th of September, informed Sir John Mordaunt, by letter, that if he had nothing farther to propofe, he
intended to proceed with the fleet to England. The land officers approved his refolution, and, on the firft of October, the
fleet failed with a fair wind for England, and came to an anchor
at Spithead on the fixth of the fame month.

The people of England were exceedingly difappointed and
diffatisfied at this inglorious return of fuch a fleet and fuch an
army. But no man in the kingdom had fo much reafon to be
difpleafed as the minifter himfelf. He now plainly perceived
that he had miftaken his generals, and, to fatisfy the people,
confented to an inquiry into their conduct. Accordingly, a
board of inquiry was appointed, confifting of the duke of
Marlborough, Lord George Sackville, and General Waldegrave.
Thefe gentlemen, after much examination, deliberation, and reflection, prefented to the king fo vague, fo unfatisfactory, fo
filly a report, that it was afterwards thought neceffary to bring
Sir John Mordaunt to a formal trial by a court-martial. But
before we proceed to fpeak of that court-martial, it is impoffible to avoid taking fome farther notice of this court of inquiry,
the firft article of whofe report to the king was, that—" The
" not attacking Fort Fouras by fea, at the fame time that it
" would have been attacked by land, was one caufe why the
" expedition failed."—That is, the expedition failed, becaufe
fomething was not done in conjunction with fomething which
was never attempted. The fecond article of their report was—
" That the council of war of the 28th was not juftifiable in the
" refolution not to make an attack upon Rochfort, becaufe they
" afterwards refolved to attack Fort Fouras." Their third article
of report was, " That the expedition failed, becaufe the fleet re-
" turned to England without any previous regular meeting of
" the council of war." If the three members of this board of
inquiry had been well informed as to the fituation of Rochfort,

Aix,

A. D. Aix, and Fouras, they would have difcovered that the firft
1757. ought to have been attacked without any attention to either of
the latter. Sir John Mordaunt was afterwards tried by a court-
martial, and honourably acquitted. The minifter and the admiral were alfo acquitted by the general voice of the people; fo
that this grand expedition mifcarried without a caufe.

Having, I hope, fatisfied the reader concerning the employment of the Britifh navy in Europe, let us now follow our fleets
and armies to other parts of the world. In the Eaft-Indies we
behold a fcene extremely different from that which we have juft
quitted; unanimity, refolution, and the genuine fpirit of enterprize in our commanders; intuitive military genius, and victory
its natural attendant. Admiral Watfon failed from Bombay on
the 30th of April, 1756. He arrived at St. David's on the
29th of May; failed from thence on the 20th of June, and
anchored in Madrafs road the day following [m]. Here he firft
learnt the dreadful fate of Calcutta. Having taken Colonel
Clive and his fmall army on board his fquadron, he failed on
the 6th of October, determined to revenge the horrid murder
of his countrymen. They anchored in Balafore road on the
5th of December, reached Fulta on the 15th, and on the 28th
proceeded to Calcutta, with the Kent, Tyger, Salifbury, Bridgewater, and King-fifher floop. Next day Colonel Clive, with a
fmall body of men, landed, in order to attack a fort called
Bufbudgia, which, being at the fame time cannonaded by the
fhips, was foon abandoned by the garrifon. Other forts and
batteries were likewife deferted as the fhips proceeded up the
river, and, on the 2d of January 1757, after a fmart cannonade
from the Kent and Tyger, the enemy were driven from their
guns, and the town of Calcutta reftored to the Eaft-India Company. No more than nine feamen and three foldiers were killed, and about thirty men wounded. Ninety-one pieces of cannon were found in the place, with a confiderable quantity of
ammunition and military ftores.

This important conqueft being finifhed, the Britifh commanders refolved to attempt Hughly, a city of great trade, higher up
the Ganges. The Bridgewater of twenty guns, and a floop,

---

[m] Smollet's continuation, vol. ii. p. 46.

with a detachment of troops under the command of Captain A. L Kirkpatrick, were deftined for this fervice. This armament 1757 proceeded up the river on the 5th of January, and reduced the place without much difficulty. Twenty pieces of cannon were found on the ramparts, befides a confiderable quantity of falt-petre and magazines of grain, which were immediately deftroyed by the conquerors. The nabob of Bengal, enraged at being thus rapidly driven from his moft important poffeffions, affembled an army of ten thoufand horfe and fifteen thoufand foot, and, on the 2d of February, encamped about a mile from Calcutta. Colonel Clive, though very inferior in number, refolved to attack the nabob in his camp, and requefted the admiral to affift him with all the failors he could fpare. Six hundred feamen were landed, under the command of Captain Warwick, on the 5th, at one in the morning; at three Colonel Clive marched his little army, and about five the attack began. The nabob, after a feeble refiftance, retreated, with the lofs of a thoufand men killed, wounded and taken. This action, though not decifive, obliged the nabob to fign articles of capitulation, very advantageous to the Eaft-India Company.

Having thus humbled this infolent nabob, the conquerors turned their attention towards Chandenagore, a capital French fettlement above Calcutta, on the fame river. Colonel Clive with feven hundred Europeans, and about fixteen hundred Indians, marched towards the place, and, after gaining poffeffion of the principal outpofts, waited for the arrival of the fleet. On the 18th of March, the Admirals Watfon and Pocock, with the Kent, Tiger, and Salifbury men of war, came to an anchor two miles below Chandenagore. They found their paffage obftructed by booms and chains acrofs the river. Thefe obftacles being removed, on the 24th in the morning they began to batter the fort, whilft Colonel Clive continued his approaches by land, and after three hours cannonading the enemy hoifted a flag of truce, and furrendered by capitulation. The garrifon confifted of five hundred Europeans and twelve hundred Indians, well provided with ammunition and fubfiftence, and a hundred and twenty-three pieces of cannon mounted on the ramparts. This important conqueft coft the victors no more than forty men. Colonel Clive's fubfequent atchievements are foreign to

VOL. IV.                    O                              the

A. D. the purpose of this history. It is sufficient to say, that he totally
1757. defeated the nabob Sulajud Dowla at the head of 20,000 men,
caused him to be solemnly deposed, and his prime minister Ali
Khan to be proclaimed viceroy in his stead.

We now take our leave of the East in order to inquire how
our fleets in the West-Indies and in North America were employed. We are to remember that Mr. Pitt's first administration, which commenced with the year 1757, was of short duration. It continued, however, long enough to convince the nation
of his spirit and political sagacity. Astonished at the negligence
of his predecessors in administration, he immediately conceived,
and in part executed, a plan of operation wisely calculated to
revive the faded laurels of Britain. He sent a squadron of men
of war under the command of Commodore Stevens to the East
Indies, another to Jamaica under Admiral Cotes, and a third
was ordered to be equipped for North America, the command
of which was to be given to Sir Edward Hawke. This third
squadron was destined, with a body of troops under Lord Loudoun then in America, for the reduction of Louisbourg; but
the design was scarce revealed to the privy-council, before it
was known in the French cabinet, and the preparations at
Portsmouth so flagrantly retarded, that the enemy had sufficient time to render the expedition abortive. One French fleet
of nine ships sailed from Brest in January, a second, of five
men of war, sailed from Toulon in April, and a third, of fourteen sail, left France on the third of May. The last of these
squadrons arrived at Louisbourg in June. The English fleet,
intended for Sir Edward Hawke, was given to Admiral Holbourne, who sailed from Corke a week after the departure of
the last French squadron from Brest, and arrived at Halifax in
North America on the 9th of July. Admiral Holbourne being
joined by Lord Loudoun with the troops from New York,
councils of war were frequently held; and, according to the
general issue of such councils, it was resolved to postpone the
attack upon Louisbourg to a more favourable opportunity.
Thus ended the naval expedition of Admiral Holbourne. The
troops under the command of Lord Loudoun were 12,000 effective men, and the fleet consisted of fifteen ships of the line,
and eighteen frigates, &c.

We

We have seen above, that early in this year a squadron sailed A. D to the West Indies, under the command of Admiral Cotes. 1757 Soon after his arrival on the Jamaica station, he detached Captain Foreft with three frigates to cruize off Cape François, in order to intercept the trade from the French iflands. Captain Foreft had fcarce made his appearance on that coaft before he fell in with four French men of war commanded by Monf. Kerfaint. An engagement immediately enfued, which was fuftained with mutual courage and obftinate refolution for two hours and a half; after which the enemy retreated to Cape François, and the Englifh frigates to Jamaica. Thus ends our naval hiftory of the year 1757: a hiftory equally unfatisfactory to the writer and to the reader; a year diftinguifhed folely by our conquefts in the Eaft-Indies, which are to be attributed entirely to the genius and intrepidity of one man. Our fleets and armies in Europe and in America were either totally inactive or failed in their attempts. Notwithftanding the fuperiority of our fleet, the number of prizes taken by the French exceeded the Englifh lift of captures by more than 200. Let us now haften to the year 1758, where we may expect to find the patriotic 1758 zeal, political abilities, and heroic fpirit of enterprize, fo confpicuous in the character of the new minifter, in full exertion of their influence. This intrepid minifter was fo extremely difgufted at the behaviour of fome of our commanders, that, in one of his fpeeches in the houfe of commons, he did not fcruple to declare, that, though the king would readily embrace any rational meafure for the honour of his crown, he doubted whether a man could be found, who might fafely be trufted with the execution of any enterprize of danger or difficulty.

The parliament voted, for the fervice of the year 1758, fixty thoufand feamen, fifteen thoufand marines included; and, for the land-fervice, near fifty-four thoufand men. Our fleet, at this period, confifted of three hundred and twenty fhips of war, one hundred and fifty-fix of which were of the line. Befides thefe, there were on the ftocks, four fhips of 74, two of 70, four of 64, fix of 36, and ten of 28 guns. The fupplies were raifed with the utmoft facility, and at a moderate intereft. The languid, latent fpirit of the nation, inflamed by that of the new minifter, was fuddenly roufed from the difgraceful apathy which,

except

A. D. except in the East-Indies, characterized the operations of the
1758. preceding year. The navy of France, at this time, consisted of
seventy-seven ships of the line and thirty-nine frigates; that of
Spain of fifty-two line of battle ships, twenty-six frigates from
30 to 16 guns, thirteen xebeques of 24, and four packet-boats
of 16 guns.

The reduction of Louisbourg being a principal object in Mr.
Pitt's plan of military operations, a naval armament, adequate
to the purpose, was prepared with all possible expedition, and
the command given to Admiral Boscawen, an officer of approved
abilities. The formidable French fleet, which had protected
Louisbourg the preceding year, had returned to France in a
shattered condition. These ships, being repaired, were intended
to return to their former station in North America; but their
intentions were effectually anticipated and prevented by the vigilant alacrity of the British minister. Admiral Boscawen sailed
from St. Helen's on the 19th February, with forty-one men of
war [a]. Meanwhile, a fleet under the command of Sir Edward

[a] Viz. Namur, (Admiral Boscawen), Captain Buckle, 90 guns.

| Ship | Commander-in-chief | Captain | Guns |
|---|---|---|---|
| Namur, | (Admiral Boscawen), | Captain Buckle, | 90 guns. |
| Royal William, | (Sir Charles Hardy), | Evans, | 80 |
| Princess Amelia, | (Philip Durell), | Bray, | 80 |
| Dublin, | — | Rodney, | 74 |
| Terrible, | — | Collins, | 74 |
| Northumberland, | — | Lord Colvil, | 70 |
| Vanguard, | — | Swanton, | 70 |
| Oxford, | — | Spry, | 70 |
| Burford, | — | Gambier, | 70 |
| Somerset, | — | Hughes, | 70 |
| Lancaster, | — | Edgecombe, | 70 |
| Devonshire, | — | Gordon, | 66 |
| Bedford, | — | Fowke, | 64 |
| Captain, | — | Amherst, | 64 |
| Prince Frederick, | — | Man, | 64 |
| Pembroke, | — | Simcoe, | 60 |
| Kingston, | — | Parry, | 60 |
| York, | — | Pigot, | 60 |
| Prince of Orange, | — | Ferguson, | 60 |
| Defiance, | — | Baird, | 60 |
| Nottingham, | — | Marshal, | 60 |
| Centurion, | — | Mantel, | 54 |
| Sutherland, | — | Ross, | 50 |

Besides eighteen frigates.

Hawke,

Hawke, blocked up the French ports in the bay of Biscay, and A. D
another squadron, commanded by Admiral Osborne, was sent 1758
to cruize between Cape de Gatte and Carthagena on the coast
of Spain. There were, at this time, three small squadrons of
French ships of war in the different ports of Toulon, Carthagena, and Brest; which squadrons, under the command of Monf.
du Quesne and Monf. de la Clue, had orders to steal away for
Louisbourg, jointly or separately. The former of these commanders, in order to join the latter at Carthagena, sailed from
Toulon on the 25th of April, on board the Foudroyant of 80
guns, attended by the Orphèe of 64, the Oriflamme of 50,
and Pleiade of 24 guns. Admiral Osborne, expecting the departure of this squadron from Toulon, had stationed the Gibraltar frigate in the offing of that harbour to watch their motions. As soon as du Quesne's squadron appeared, the Gibraltar sheered off, and gradually decoyed the enemy so effectually,
that on the 27th, about two in the morning, du Quesne found
himself in the midst of Osborne's fleet. In this critical situation, the French admiral made a signal for his squadron to dif-
perse: each ship immediately steered a different course, and
were as immediately pursued by detachments from Osborne's
fleet, who, with the remainder of his fleet, continued to block
up the harbour of Carthagena. The Pleiade, being a prime
sailer, escaped. The Oriflamme was chased by the Monarque
and Montague, and escaped destruction by running under the
guns of a small Spanish fort. The Orphèe was pursued by the
Revenge and Berwick, and was taken, by the first of these ships,
in fight of Carthagena. The Foudroyant was chased by the
Monmouth, Swiftsure, and Hampton-Court. About seven in
the morning the Monmouth and Foudroyant began to fire at
each other, the rest of the fleet being then totally out of fight.
The disproportion between the two ships was very great. The
Foudroyant had a thousand men on board, and mounted eighty
guns, 42 and 22 pounders; the Monmouth mounted only sixty-
four 12 and 24 pounders, and her complement of men was no
more than four hundred and seventy. This remarkable disparity notwithstanding, Captain Gardiner, who commanded the
Monmouth, resolved, at all events, to vanquish his enemy.
Thus determined, he brought his ship within pistol-shot of his
antagonist,

A. D. antagonift, and now the battle raged with infernal fury. About
1758. nine o'clock Captain Gardiner was fhot through the head by a
mufket-ball°. He lingered till the day following, and then
died univerfally regretted and lamented, particularly by the
officers and crew of his own fhip. The death of fuch a man
was a very great lofs to his country. Soon after the captain fell,
the Monmouth's mizen-maft came by the board; on which the
enemy gave three cheers. The crew of the Monmouth returned
the compliment a few minutes after, on the mizen-maft of the
Foudroyant being alfo fhot away. This difafter was foon followed by the fall of her main-maft, which giving frefh fpirits
to the Englifh, their fire became fo inceffant and intolerable,
that the French failors could no longer be kept to their guns,
and the mighty Foudroyant ftruck a little after one o'clock.
This action, which is one of the moft glorious in the naval hiftory of Britain, and which muft ever remain an inconteftable
proof of our naval fuperiority, I beg leave to recommend to the
conftant recollection of fuch of our fea-officers as may be inclined to calculate their comparative weight of metal before they
venture to engage

The Orphèe and Foudroyant being taken, and the commander in chief being a prifoner, Monf. de la Clue gave up all
thoughts of paffing the Streights of Gibraltar, and returned
from Carthagena to Toulon, where his fquadron was laid up.
But the French miniftry, not depending entirely on their Mediterranean fleet for the protection of Louifbourg and the reinforcement of their army in North America, had prepared a
confiderable fleet of tranfports and ftore-fhips at Rochfort,
Bourdeaux, and other ports in that neighbourhood. Thefe
tranfports, with three thoufand troops on board, were ordered
to rendezvous in April, and to fail under convoy of fix fhips of
the line and feveral frigates. Such, however, was the intelligence and alacrity of the Englifh minifter, that effectual meafures were taken to fruftrate the defign. Sir Edward Hawke,

---

° It is faid that Captain Gardiner, before he expired, fent for his firft lieutenant, and made it his laft requeft, that he would not give up the fhip. The
lieutenant affured him he never would, and inftantly went and nailed the flag to
the ftaff. He then took a piftol in each hand, and fwore, if any man in the fhip
fhould attempt to ftrike the colours, he would put him to death.

with

with feven fhips of the line and three frigates, failed down the
bay of Bifcay, and on the 3d of April brought up in Bafque
road, where he difcovered five French fhips of the line and
feven frigates at anchor near the ifle of Aix. They no fooner
faw the Englifh fleet than they began with the utmoft precipitation to flip their cables, and fly in great confufion. Some of
them efcaped to fea; but far the greater number threw their
guns and ftores overboard, and, running into fhoal water, ftuck
in the mud. Next morning feveral of their men of war and
tranfports were feen lying on their broad fides; but, being out
of the reach of his guns, Sir Edward Hawke left them to their
fate, perfectly fatisfied with having fruftrated their intention of
failing to America.

I have before obferved, that fome of the ftore-fhips and tranfports deftined for North America were to fail from Bourdeaux.
Thefe tranfports were twelve in number. They failed under
convoy of the Galathèe, a frigate of twenty-two guns; and a
letter of marque of twenty guns. In the bay of Bifcay they
had the misfortune to fall in with the Effex of fixty-four guns,
and the Pluto and Proferpine fire-fhips, which were on their
paffage to join Sir Edward Hawke. After a fhort but fmart
conflict, the French frigate, the letter of marque, and one of
the tranfports, were taken. But this advantage was dearly purchafed with the death of Captain James Hume, who commanded the Pluto. Two more of thefe tranfports were afterwards
taken by the Antelope and Speedwell floops.

Having feen every attempt of France for the protection of
Louifbourg entirely fruftrated, we now proceed to projects more
directly offenfive, planned and executed by Mr. Pitt. But a
melancholy event intervenes. On the 13th of April the Prince
George of eighty guns, commanded by Rear-admiral Broderick,
in his paffage to the Mediterranean, took fire between one and
two in the afternoon, and, notwithftanding the utmoft exertion of human fkill and labour, aided by defpair, burnt with
fuch rapidity, that in the fpace of a few hours fhe burnt down
to the water-edge. A little before fix in the evening fhe funk
entirely, and more than two thirds of her crew perifhed in the
ocean. The admiral, after buffeting the waves near an hour [P],

[P] Annual regifter, p. 306.

A. D.
1758. was at length taken up by a boat belonging to one of the merchantmen under his convoy. Captain Payton and the chaplain
were also among the few that were saved.

We now proceed to the circumstantial relation of an expedition to the coast of Africa; an expedition which, extraordinary
as it may seem, was planned and executed by a Quaker. Thomas Cuming, the projector of this enterprize, having made a
voyage, as a merchant-adventurer, to Portenderick, on the
coast of Africa, became personally acquainted with Amir the
Moorish king of Legibelli. This prince, being prejudiced in
favour of the English nation, and extremely dissatisfied with
the French, wished eagerly for an opportunity to drive them
from their settlements on the river Senegal, and promised all
the assistance in his power to the arms of Britain. Mr. Cuming,
during his residence on the Gum-coast, became perfectly acquainted with the nature, extent, and importance of the trade,
and was very assiduous in his inquiry concerning the situation
and strength of the French forts. On his return to England
he communicated his observations and ideas to the board of
trade, by whom his project was approved, and finally adopted
by the ministry. This was in the year 1757. A force which
was deemed adequate to the expedition, was ordered to be prepared; but before the ships were ready to sail, the season was
so far advanced that it was thought advisable to postpone the
design. In the beginning of the following year, Mr. Cuming
revived his application; the minister approved his plan, and a
small squadron was equipped with all possible expedition. The
ships ordered for this service were the Nassau of sixty-four, the
Harwich of fifty, and the Rye of twenty guns, attended by the
Swan sloop and two busses. They had on board two hundred
marines, commanded by Major Mason, and a detachment of
matrosses, under Captain Walker; ten pieces of cannon and
eight mortars.

This small squadron [q], commanded by Captain Marsh, and
conducted by friend Cuming, sailed from Plymouth on the
9th of March, and on the 24th of April came to an anchor in
the mouth of the river Senegal, and in sight of Fort Louis,

[q] Smollet's continuation of the history of England, vol. ii. p. 172.

I

which

which is situated on the island of Senegal, about four leagues A. D within the bar. The French governor of this fort, as soon as 1758 he discovered the English squadron, sent down an armed brig and six sloops to dispute the passage of the bar. A brisk but ineffectual cannonading ensued. Meanwhile the channel being discovered, and the wind blowing up the river, Captain Millar of the London buss passed the bar and came to an anchor, where he remained all night exposed to the fire of the enemy. He was followed next morning by the other small vessels, some of which ran a-ground and bulged. The troops on board these vessels immediately took to their boats, and landed on the east shore of the river. Apprehensive of being attacked by the natives, they threw up an intrenchment and disembarked their stores. Next morning they were reinforced by a detachment of 350 seamen, and now began to meditate an attack upon Fort Louis. But the governor, not chusing to wait the event, sent two deputies with offers of surrender. His proposals, after a little deliberation, were accepted by Captain Marsh and Major Mason. By the articles of capitulation, the natives of France were to be sent home with all their private effects. On the first of May the English took possession of Fort Louis, and all the settlements belonging to France on the river Senegal were at the same time ceded to the king of Great Britain. Thus this important conquest, which was planned and conducted by a Quaker, was achieved in a manner perfectly consonant with the principles of his religion, namely, without spilling a single drop of human blood. It is also worthy of remark, that it was our first successful expedition since the commencement of the war. There were found in the fort ninety-two pieces of cannon, some treasure, and a considerable quantity of goods. This business being accomplished, and Fort Louis garrisoned by English troops, the men of war proceeded to attack the island of Goree, about thirty leagues distant from Senegal; but their force being insufficient, the attempt miscarried.

On the 29th day of May, the Dorsetshire, Captain Dennis, of 70 guns, cruising in the bay of Biscay, fell in with the Raisonable, a French man of war of 64 guns and 630 men, commanded by le Prince de Mombazon, who defended his ship with great resolution till one hundred and sixty of his men were

A. D. killed or wounded, and his hull and rigging confiderably da-
1758. maged.

Mr. Pitt's comprehenfive plan of operation was too rational
to be difconcerted by fuch mifcarriages as were juftly to be attributed to a want of fpirit in the execution. The expedition
to the coaft of France, of the preceding year, having failed,
made no alteration in the minifter's opinion, that a diverfion of
the like nature was a proper meafure. For this purpofe, in the
month of May, near fourteen thoufand men were encamped on
the ifle of Wight. This army, commanded by the duke of
Marlborough, confifted of fixteen battalions of infantry, four
hundred artillery men, and five hundred and forty light horfe.
One of the regiments of infantry, being deftined for another
fervice, did not embark; fo that the number employed in this
expedition, amounted to about thirteen thoufand. The fubordinate general officers were Lord George Sackville, the earl of
Ancram, Major-generals Waldegrave, Moftyn, Drury, Bofcawen and Elliot. Two diftinct fleets were affembled at Spithead;
the firft commanded by Lord Anfon, of twenty-two fail of the
line; the fecond under Commodore Howe, confifting of feveral
frigates, floops, fire-fhips, bomb-veffels, tenders, cutters, and
tranfports.

This tremendous fleet failed from St. Helen's on the firft of
June [r]. Lord Anfon with the line-of-battle fhips ftood away
to the weft, and proceeded to block up the French fleet at Breft;
whilft Commodore Howe fteered athwart the channel with the
wind at fouth-eaft. The night proved fo tempeftuous, notwithftanding the feafon of the year, that one of the ftore-fhips rolled away her mafts. About eight next morning they made
Cape la Hogue, and that night anchored in the race of Alderney. On the third, about noon, one of the tranfports ftruck
upon a rock, near the ifland of Sark, and was loft, but the
troops on board were faved. On the fourth, Mr. Howe came
to an anchor within three leagues of St. Malo. Next morning he weighed before break of day, and ftood into the bay of
Cancalle, fo called from a village of that name, where the
troops were intended to land. At four in the evening the

[r] Account of the enterprife by an officer.

whole

whole fleet brought up, and in a fhort time after ten companies **A. D** of grenadiers landed near the village above-mentioned. The **1758** only oppofition was from a battery of two guns fired by a brave old Frenchman and his fon, who maintained their poft till the poor old man was wounded by a fhot from one of our frigates. If others of his countrymen had behaved with equal refolution, the difembarkation would have been more difficult; for there were at this time feven companies of foot and three troops of dragoons at Cancalle : but thefe troops retired to St. Malo. The Britifh granadiers landed a little before funfet, attended by five volunteers of diftinction, whofe names fhould be recorded and remembered with gratitude. Such fpirit in young men of rank and fortune raifes the military character of a nation more effectually than a victory over the enemy. Lord Down, Sir John Armitage, Sir James Lowther, Mr. Francis Blake Delaval, and Mr. Berkley, were the men. The entire difembarkation was completed on the fixth, and the whole army encamped near Cancalle ; the grenadiers and the light horfe being advanced about a mile in the front of the line.

The duke of Marlborough, fenfible of the ravages which are generally committed by the common foldiers on their landing in an enemy's country, iffued ftrict orders to prevent marauding. Neverthelefs, fome irregularities were committed. The offenders were brought to immediate trial, and two or three of them executed. This rigorous exertion of military law faved the inoffenfive peafantry from many acts of brutal licentioufnefs which they would otherwife have experienced.

On the 7th, at break of day, the army marched towards St. Malo in two columns. The left column, commanded by Lord George Sackville, fell into the great road ; but the lanes through which Lord Ancram's column marched were fo narrow, and the country fo inclofed and woody, that notwithftanding the previous labour of two hundred pioneers, the men were frequently obliged to pafs in fingle files ; fo that a fmall number of the enemy might eafily have deftroyed this column, or at leaft have made it impoffible for them to advance. But, fo far from meeting with any oppofition, they found the villages and hamlets through which they paffed entirely deferted. The army proceeded in good order without beat of drum, and, after a

march

A. D. march of fix miles, encamped at the diftance of little more than
1758. a mile from the town of St. Malo. Whilft they were employed in pitching their tents, the light horfe, with the piquets of
the whole army, marched towards the town, and were faluted
by a few fhot from the cannon on the ramparts. As foon as it
was dark, the piquets marched down to the harbour, where
they found a confiderable number of privateers and other fmall
veffels, moft of which, it being low water, were laid dry. Having fet fire to all the fhipping, they proceeded to communicate
the flames to the magazines of pitch, tar, ropes, &c. all which
were entirely deftroyed, except one fmall ftore-houfe, which, if
it had been fet on fire, muft from its fituation have deftroyed
moft of the houfes in the fuburbs. This building was fpared
from a noble principle of humanity, worthy the imitation of
all future invaders. The number of fhips deftroyed was about
one hundred and twenty. The piquets now rejoined the army,
which continued unmolefted in its encampment till the 10th,
when the tents were ftruck, and the army in one column marched back to Cancalle. Whilft the main body of the troops were
employed as I have related, a battalion of the guards, under the
command of Colonel Cefar, marched twelve miles up the country, to a town called Dolle, where they were politely entertained by the magiftrates. As their defign was merely to reconnoitre, they continued one night in the town without committing the leaft act of hoftility, and then returned. A party of
the Englifh light-horfe penetrating a few miles farther, fell in
with the videts of a French camp, two of which they took,
and brought prifoners to Cancalle.

The purpofe of this invafion being fully accomplifhed, the
troops were re-embarked, and the fleet failed on the 16th early
in the morning, and, after beating againft the wind during that
whole day, came to an anchor off the harbour of St. Malo.
The night proved fo tempeftuous, that many of the fhips drove,
and fome parted their cables. Next morning, the wind continuing contrary, the fleet returned to Cancalle bay, and there remained till the 22d, when they failed again, and next day paffed
the iflands Jerfey and Guernfey. On the 25th they made
the ifle of Wight, and on the 26th, the wind veering to the
northward, they fteered again for the coaft of France, and ran
in

In with the land near Havre; but towards evening it blew so
fresh, that, to avoid the danger of a lee-shore, they stood out
to sea. On the 27th, the weather becoming more moderate,
they ran in with the land a second time, and the duke of Marlborough and Mr. Howe went out in a cutter to reconnoitre the
coast. At their return, orders were given for the troops to
prepare for immediate disembarkation: nevertheless, the 28th
passed without any attempt to land, and on the 29th the fleet
bore away before the wind, and anchored within a league of
Cherbourg. Some of the transports which brought up nearer
in shore, were fired at from several batteries, but received no
damage. A few troops were seen parading on the strand, most
of which appeared to be militia.

Soon after the fleet came to an anchor, the duke of Marlborough signified his intention of making an attack upon the town
that night, and ordered the first battalion of guards to be in
their boats at eleven o'clock. The rest of the troops received
orders in what manner, and at what time they were to proceed,
and every necessary preparation was made for immediate disembarkation. But as night approached, the wind off shore gradually increased, and, before the appointed hour, became so
violent as to render the attempt impracticable. Next morning
the duke of Marlborough, upon inquiry into the stock of provisions, hay, and water, found these several articles so nearly
exhausted, that it would be dangerous, in so variable a climate,
to remain any longer on an hostile coast. He therefore resolved
to return to England. The fleet accordingly weighed anchor at
ten o'clock, and arrived at St. Helen's the next day in the evening. The troops were encamped on the isle of Wight, that
they might recover the effects of so long a confinement, on
board of transports by no means sufficient for the accommodation of so numerous an army. These troops were destined for
more expeditions of the like nature, the success of which will
be seen in due time; but a regular attention to a chronological
series of naval events now calls us to North America.

I am to remind the reader, that Admiral Boscawen sailed from
England, with a considerable fleet, on the 19th of April[*]. He

---

* Smollet's continuation, vol. ii. p. 179.

arrived

A. D. arrived at Halifax in Nova Scotia on the 9th of May ; from
1758. whence he failed on the 28th, with an army of fourteen thousand men, under the command of Major-general Amherst [t].
This fleet, confisting of a hundred and fifty-seven fail, anchored, on the fecond of June, in the bay of Gabarus, about two
leagues weftward of Louifbourg. The French governor, le
Chevalier Drucour, had taken every poffible precaution to prevent a furprife. He had thrown up feveral intrenchments,
erected batteries, and formed a chain of redoubts for two leagues
and a half along the coaft. There were in the harbour fix
fhips of the line and five frigates, three of which were, during
the fiege, funk at the entrance. The fortifications of the town
were not in good repair ; the garrifon confifted of two thoufand
five hundred regular troops, befides fix hundred burghers and
Canadians. When the fleet firft came to an anchor, and during
feveral fucceeding days, the furf ran fo high, that it was impoffible for the boats to come near the fhore. Thefe feveral obftacles appeared fo tremendous to many of the officers, that
they advifed the admiral to call a general council of war. Fortunately for the fervice, and for his own reputation, he difregarded fuch advice, and determined to land the troops at all
events.

On the 8th of June, the weather being more moderate, the
grenadiers and light-infantry were in the boats before break of
day. The frigates and armed floops began to fcour the coaft,
by an inceffant fire upon the enemy; and now the boats rowed
brifkly towards the fhore in three divifions, commanded by the
Generals Wolfe, Whitmore, and Laurence. When they approached the land they met with a warm reception from the
enemy, and the furf ran fo high that many of the boats were
ftaved, and fome of the foldiers drowned. General Wolfe leapt
into the fea, and, being followed by his whole divifion, formed
his people on the beach, and marched intrepidly to the neareft
battery. The other two divifions followed his example, and
the enemy foon fled in confufion. The remainder of the army,
cannon, and ftores were landed with all poffible fpeed, and the
town was regularly invefted. General Amherft having fecured

***

[t] Annual regifter, p. 70.

his

his camp by proper redoubts and epaulments, now began his A. D. approaches in form. In landing the troops, three officers, four 1758. ferjeants, one corporal, and thirty-eight private men, were killed or drowned; five lieutenants, two ferjeants, one corporal, fifty-one men wounded; and about feventy boats loft. The enemy, when they fled from their entrenchments, left behind them feventeen pieces of cannon, fourteen large fwivels, two mortars, a furnace for red-hot balls, fmall arms, ammunition, ftores, tools and provifions in confiderable quantity.

The Chevalier Drucour, having received his detachments into the town, deftroyed his out-pofts, and all buildings within two miles of the ramparts, prepared for a vigorous defence. The approaches of the Britifh general were at firft flow, owing to the difficulty of landing his ftores, the labour of dragging his cannon through a marfhy country, and the neceffity of fortifying his camp. Meanwhile General Amherft, being not a little incommoded by the fire from the enemy's fhips in the harbour, and alfo from the ifland battery, detached General Wolfe, with a confiderable body of troops, with orders to march round the north-eaft harbour and take poffeffion of the light-houfe point. This order was executed with great alacrity and defpatch, and a powerful battery erected, which on the 25th filenced that of the enemy on the ifland. On the 29th the befieged funk four fhips at the entrance of the harbour. They made feveral fallies from the town, and were repulfed with lofs. The Britifh army continued to approach the town in a regular and fcientific manner, and the enemy difplayed no lefs refolution and fkill in the fcience of defence. On the 13th of July the befiegers were about fix hundred yards from the covert way.

On the 21ft, a fhell from our battery on the light-houfe point fet fire to one of the enemy's fhips in the harbour. She immediately blew up, and two other men of war having caught the flames were alfo deftroyed. Thefe were the Entreprenant, the Capricieux, and the Celebre: fo that the Prudent and the Bienfaifant were the only fhips of force remaining. In the night of the 25th the firft of thefe two were fet on fire, and the other towed triumphantly out, by a detachment of feamen under the command of Captains Laforey and Balfour. This gallant exploit merits a circumftantial relation. The naval reader will
peruse.

A. D.
1758.

peruse it with pleasure; probably with advantage—By the admiral's orders, a barge and pinnace from every ship in the fleet assembled, about noon, under the stern of the Namur. These boats were manned only by their proper crews, armed chiefly with pistols and cutlasses, and each boat commanded by a lieutenant and midshipman. From thence they proceeded, by two or three at a time, to join Sir Charles Hardy's squadron near the mouth of the harbour. Being there reassembled in two divisions, under the two captains above mentioned, about midnight they paddled into the harbour of Louisbourg unperceived. The night was extremely dark, and the seamen were profoundly silent. They passed very near the island battery undiscovered, the darkness of the night, and a thick fog, prevented their being seen, whilst the perpetual din of bombs, cannon, and musquetry, both of the besieged and besiegers, effectually drowned the noise of their oars. As soon as each division came near enough to perceive the devoted object, the two men of war were immediately surrounded by the boats, and were first alarmed by the firing of their own centinels. All the boats fell a-board at the same instant, and the several crews, following the example of their officers, scrambled up every part of the ships, and, in a few minutes, took possession of their respective prizes. The resistance was very feeble, and consequently the loss of men on either side inconsiderable.

Day-light and the shouts of our sailors, having at length discovered to the enemy on shore, that their ships were in possession of the English, they immediately pointed every gun that could be brought to bear upon the boats and prizes, and a furious discharge of cannon ensued. Those who were in possession of the Prudent, finding her a-ground, set her on fire, and then joined the boats which were now employed in towing off the Bienfaisant, which, with the assistance of a favourable breeze, was triumphantly carried away and secured.

On the 26th, whilst Admiral Boscawen was preparing to send six ships into the harbour, he received a letter from the chevalier Drucour, offering to capitulate on the same terms that were granted to the English at Minorca. The admiral insisted on the garrison remaining prisoners of war, and with these terms the governor finally complied. He could not do otherwise. He

2            yielded

yielded to irrefiftible neceffity. His fhips were all deftroyed or
taken; his cannon were difmounted; his garrifon diminifhed,
and the remainder haraffed and difpirited; all his hopes of relief from Europe or from Canada were vanifhed, and his ramparts in many places battered to pieces. The capitulation being
figned, the Britifh troops took poffeffion of Louifbourg on the
27th, and the two iflands of Cape Breton and St. John were
ceded to his Britannic majefty. The fhips of war loft by the
French on this occafion were the Prudent of 74 guns, Entreprenant 74, Capricieux 64, Celebre 64, Bienfaifant 64, Apollo
50; Chevre, Biche and Fidelle frigates funk at the harbour's
mouth; Diana of 36 taken by the Boreas; Echo of 26 taken
by the Juno.

We now return to Europe. The fpirited minifter who, at
this time, held the reins of government; whofe fucceffive expeditions were diftinct gradations in a regular plan of operation;
whofe invafions on the coaft of France were principally intended to divide the forces of the enemy: this active minifter, I fay,
determined once more to invade the coaft of Normandy. · Part
of the troops which, fince the laft expedition, had been encamped on the ifle of Wight, were fent to Germany. The
duke of Marlborough and Lord George Sackville were likewife
ordered upon that fervice. The remainder of the troops now
commanded by Lieutenant-general Bligh, embarked on board
the fleet under Commodore Howe, and failed from St. Helen's on
the firft day of Auguft. On the 6th, in the evening the fleet
came to an anchor in the bay of Cherburg, and a few fhells
were thrown into the town that night. Next morning, about
feven o'clock, the fleet got under way, and at nine brought up
in the bay of Maris, two leagues weft of the town, where the
general refolved to land his troops. The governor of Cherburg, fince his late alarm, had thrown up feveral intrenchments, and planted fome batteries along the coaft. Behind
thefe works there appeared about two thoufand regular troops.
On the 7th, at two in the afternoon, the grenadiers and guards
commanded by General Drury, in flat-bottom boats, landed,
without oppofition, under cover of an inceffant fire from the
fleet. Having formed his troops on the beach, he marched immediately towards a party of the enemy, received their fire, and

VOL. IV.                              Q                              then

A. D.
1758.
then attacked them with fuch refolution, that they foon fled in the utmoft confufion, and with confiderable lofs. They left behind them two pieces of brafs cannon. Of the Englifh, about twenty were killed or wounded.

The remainder of the infantry being difembarked, General Bligh marched to the village of Erville, and there pitched his tents for the night. The ground which he had chofen for his encampment was fo inadequate, in point of extent, to the number of troops, that the tents were crowded together as clofe as they could ftand, without order or regularity. If the French commander had not been as ignorant in his profeffion as his enemy, the Britifh army would, in this fituation, have been furrounded and deftroyed, or taken: two or three thoufand men, judicioufly commanded, were fufficient. But, either for want of fkill, or ftrength, or refolution, the Englifh army was fuffered to fleep in perfect fecurity, and the fucceeding dawn did not difcover a fingle French foldier in fight of the camp. On reconnoitring the neareft fort, called Quirqueville, it was found defolate; fo that the light-horfe were now difembarked without the leaft interruption, and the army proceeded, in two columns, towards Cherburg, which they entered without firing or receiving a fingle fhot, the town and all the forts being entirely abandoned by the troops. The inhabitants, in confidence of a promife of protection, contained in a manifefto publifhed by General Bligh, remained in the town, and received their hoftile vifitors with politenefs and hofpitality. I am forry to record, to the difgrace of Englifh difcipline, that their confidence was abufed. The proper means of reftraining the licentious brutality of the common foldiers were neglected, till the juft complaints of the fufferers reminded the general of his duty.

General Bligh now proceeded, according to his inftructions, to demolifh the harbour and bafon, which had been conftructed by Lewis XV. at a vaft expence, and were intended as an afylum for men of war. It appeared, however, from the unfinifhed ftate of the fortifications, that the importance of Cherburg had of late dwindled in the eftimation of the French miniftry. Whilft the engineers were thus employed, the light horfe were fent to fcour the country, and to reconnoitre a French camp at Walloign, about twelve miles from Cherburg. In thefe excurfions they frequently fkirmifhed with the enemy, and in one of

thefe

these rencounters Lindsay, a captain of the British light-horse, A. D. was unfortunately killed. He was a very active and gallant 1758. officer. The great business of demolition being finished, on the 16th of August, at three in the morning, the army evacuated Cherburgh, marched down to Fort Galet, and there embarked without molestation.

In our estimate of the utility of this enterprize, we are to remember, that the primary object was, by keeping the French coast in perpetual alarm, to oblige them to retain an army for their own security, which would otherwise have marched to Germany. Exclusive of this consideration, the expedition to Cherburg was, by no means, unimportant. Twenty-seven ships were burnt in the harbour. A hundred and seventy-three pieces of iron ordnance and three mortars were rendered useless; and twenty-two brass cannon and two mortars were sent to England. These cannon were afterwards exposed, for some time, in Hyde Park, and then drawn through the city in pompous procession, amidst the joyful acclamations of the people, the oldest of whom had never beheld a similar triumph.

Thus far the operations of this terrific, itinerant army were successful. But the general's commission did not end with the destruction of the forts and harbour of Cherburg. By his secret instructions he was ordered to keep the coast of France in continual alarm; to make descents, and attack any place that might be found practicable, between the east point of Normandy and Morlaix. In compliance with these instructions, the fleet weighed anchor on the 18th of August, and steered towards St. Malo, with a design to make a second attack upon that nest of privateers. But they were obliged, by contrary winds, to run for the English coast. They came to an anchor in Weymouth road on the 23d; they sailed from thence on the 25th, but were obliged to put back the same evening. The next attempt proved more successful. The fleet, though not without difficulty, kept the sea, and, standing to the southward, soon made the coast of France; but it was the 4th of September before they came to an anchor in the bay of St. Lunaire, about two leagues west of St. Malo. Whilst the fleet was bringing up[u], the commodore, with Prince Edward, (afterwards

[u] Account of our last attempt on the coast of France, by an officer.

Q 2

duke

A. D.
1758.
duke of York,) who attended Mr. Howe in the capacity of midshipman, went off in their barge to reconnoitre the shore. Seeing no appearance of an enemy, the troops were disembarked, without opposition; but not entirely without misfortune. One of the flat-bottom boats being run down by the Brilliant, was overset, and five soldiers drowned. As soon as the troops were landed, Sir William Boothby, with 300 grenadiers, was detached with orders to destroy a hundred and fifty vessels in the harbour of Briac, near St. Malo. He executed his commission effectually; but the number of vessels in that harbour did not exceed fifteen.

The British army continued in their encampment near St. Lunaire four days, which were spent in deliberations concerning the practicability of an attack upon St. Malo. It was finally determined to be impracticable, and Mr. Howe having declared that it was impossible to re-embark the troops from the place where they had landed, it was resolved that the troops should march over-land, and that the fleet should, in the mean time, proceed to the bay of St. Cas, and there remain ready to receive them. The commodore weighed anchor, and stood to the westward. On Friday, the 8th, in the morning, general Bligh struck his tents, and began his march towards the village of Gildau, where he was told the river, which he must necessarily pass, was fordable at low water. The day's march, though short, proved fatiguing to the troops, on account of the heavy rain and bad roads; and, as the army marched in a single column, it was night before the rear came to their ground. When Colonel Clark, who marched at the head of the advanced guard, arrived at the village of Gildau, he saw a body of about three hundred peasants on the opposite bank of the river, apparently forming with an intention to oppose his passage. A few shot from two or three field-pieces immediately dispersed them. Orders were issued to prepare for passing the river at six o'clock next morning, and the army went to rest. Next morning, at six o'clock, the troops were ready to plunge into the river, when it appeared that the general had been so totally misinformed as to the time of fording, that it was now *high* instead of *low* water, and that it would be three in the afternoon before the troops could pass. Such a mistake, though apparently of no

great

great importance, as it difcovered the fallibility of the general's A. D
intelligence, was a bad omen. 1758

The army forded the river in two columns, without any other
moleftation than a volley or two of mufket-fhot from the oppofite village, by which Lord Frederic Cavendifh, and a few grenadiers were flightly wounded. They paffed the river, and
pitched their tents immediately. Why they marched no farther
that night, is difficult to imagine. On Sunday morning the army again decamped, and marched towards Mattingnon. When
the advanced guard approached the town, they faw a party of
French dragoons, and obferved that the hedges were lined by
foot which feemed to be regulars. This being reported to the
general, all the grenadiers were ordered to advance, and they
preffed forward with great eagernefs; but the enemy did not
think fit to wait for them. Having marched about four miles,
the army encamped to the fouthward of Mattingnon, after parading through the town by beat of drum. From this circumftance, it is evident that General Bligh had not the leaft idea
that a fuperior army was at this time within a few hours march
of his camp [x].

This evening a French foldier was brought into the camp,
who informed the general, that nine battalions of, foot two
fquadrons of dragoons, with five thoufand guardes de cofts,
were on their march from Breft, and that they were not above
two leagues diftant. He named the general officers, and the regiments. His intelligence, however, produced no other effect
than an order to the piquets of the Englifh army to be particularly vigilant. During the night, the advanced guard of the
enemy came fo near, as to exchange fome fhot with the out-
pofts. Neverthelefs, General Bligh continued fo totally unap-
prehenfive, that he ordered the ufual drums, preparatory to a
march, to beat next morning at three o'clock. The drums beat
accordingly, and the army marched, in a fingle column, towards
St. Cas, which is about a league from Mattingnon. If the
troops had marched in two columns, they would have reached

[x] " I recollect," fays the author of the account of this expedition, " that the
" language of this day, in the months of fome of our confiderable perfonages,
" was——" By G—d, a man might march through France with a fingle com-
" pany of grenadiers."

their

their ſhips in half the time.   When the head of the colum
reached the eminence, about half a mile from the ſea, they hau,
orders to halt, and the regiments formed the line as they advanced in ſucceſſion ;  but, before the grenadiers in the rear reached the ground, the youngeſt brigade was ordered to march
down to the beach.  Meanwhile the frigates which were intended to cover the embarkation, and the boats, were approaching
the land.   Before the grenadiers quitted the height, they ſaw
the enemy advancing in four columns.   The grenadiers marched deliberately down to the beach, and there reſted on their
arms, whilſt the battalions were conveyed to their tranſports
in the flat-bottom boats.

The rear of the Engliſh army had ſcarce quitted the height
before it was poſſeſſed by the enemy.   As ſoon as they began
to deſcend, Mr. Howe made a ſignal for his frigates to fire;
which order was executed with ſo much ſkill and dexterity, that
many of the French were killed, and their whole army thrown
into confuſion.  The Britiſh troops were now all embarked, except the grenadiers and four companies of the firſt regiment of
guards ;  in all about 1400 men.   The enemy continued to advance, and their cannon deſtroyed ſome of our boats.   General Drury, who was now the ſenior officer on ſhore, formed his
little army, and moſt imprudently advanced up the hill to meet
his enemy.   By this manœuvre he quitted a parapet of ſand
banks, and effectually ſilenced the frigates, which could not
now fire without deſtroying their friends.   This inconſiderable
body of Engliſh troops, with every diſadvantage of ſituation,
and commanded by a man of no experience or abilities, maintained their ground againſt ten times their number, till moſt of
them had entirely ſpent their ammunition.  Thus circumſtanced,
after making terrible havock in the enemies ranks, they yielded
to neceſſity, and retreated to their boats.  Unhappily, the boats
then in ſhore were inſufficient to receive half the number of
men which now crowded to the beach, and the boats were conſequently in an inſtant ſo overloaded, that moſt of them were
a-ground.   In this horrible ſituation, expoſed to the continual
fire of a numerous army, they remained for ſome time ;  till, at
laſt, the commodore himſelf leapt into his boat, and, rowing
to the ſhore, took one of the flat-boats in tow.   The reſt of
the

e fleet followed his example, and about 700 men were
ought on board. The other half were either fhot, taken prifoners, or drowned. Among the killed were Major-general
Drury, Lieutenant-colonel Wilkinfon, and Sir John Armitage,
a volunteer. Lord Frederick Cavendifh, Lieutenant-colonels
Pearfon and Lambert, and fixteen officers of inferior rank, were
taken prifoners. Four captains of men of war [y], who went on
fhore in order to expedite the embarkation of the troops, were
alfo obliged to furrender themfelves to the enemy. Eight feamen were killed, and feventeen wounded.

This terrible difafter was very juftly afcribed to a total want
of military knowledge, fagacity, and experience in the general,
who imprudently gave ear to thofe about him, who talked of
marching through France with a fingle company of Britifh grenadiers. His marching, in an enemy's country, in a fingle column, was extremely imprudent. His beating *the general* the
morning of his march from Mattingnon, was inexcufable; and
his dilatory proceedings on the fatal day of embarkation, admit
of no apology. But, though our lofs on this occafion was confiderable, the enemy had certainly no great caufe of triumph:
they had defeated a rear-guard of fourteen hundred men with
an army of at leaft fifteen thoufand, and their lofs in killed and
wounded was much greater than that of the Englifh [z]. This
check, however, was no proof that the minifter's plan of operation was improper. His defign was fully anfwered, and was
certainly attended with falutary confequences. Commodore
Howe returned to Spithead, and the troops were difembarked.

We are now to recollect, that, after the reduction of Senegal, an attempt was made upon the ifland of Goree; but without fuccefs, owing to the want of fufficient naval force. The
Britifh minifter, fenfible that his conqueft on the coaft of Africa
was incomplete without the reduction of this ifland, fent out a

[A. D. 1758.]

[y] *Viz.* Rowley, Maplefon, Pafton, and Elphinfton.

[z] In the account of this affair publifhed at Paris, by authority, they acknowledge 400 men killed and wounded, and make the number of Englifh prifoners
600. Now, as our entire lofs was only 700, the number of our killed muft have
been proportionably very fmall. The real number of our killed and wounded
was about 200. The French loft three times that number.

fmall

A. D.
1758.

small squadron of four ships of the line, two frigates, and two bomb-ketches, commanded by Commodore Keppel, with 600 land forces under Colonel Worge. This armament sailed from Cork on the 11th of November, and, after a tempestuous voyage, anchored in the road of Gorée, about a league from the island, on the 24th of December. Gorée is a barren island, not a mile in length, situated near Cape Verde. The Dutch took possession of it in the beginning of the last century. The French took it in 1677, and since that period it has remained in possession of their East-India company. On the south-west side there was a small fort called St. Michael, and another, less considerable, called St. Francis, near the opposite extremity. Besides these forts, there were several flight batteries along the shore, mounting in the whole a hundred cannon. The garrison, commanded by Monf. St. Jean, consisted of 300 regulars, and about the same number of negro inhabitants.

On the 28th, in the morning, the troops were ordered into the boats, ready for landing, if necessary; and, the ships being properly stationed on the west side of the island, a general cannonading began, which was answered by the enemy with great spirit, and with such success, that above a hundred of the English were killed or wounded. Nevertheless, the French garrison, though not one of them was killed, were so terrified by the fire from the ships, that the governor was obliged to surrender at discretion. A detachment of marines was landed to take possession of the island, and the British flag was hoisted on the castle of St. Michael.

Mr. Keppel, having taken his prisoners on board, and left a sufficient garrison under the command of Major Newton, touched at Senegal, and then returned to England. But this expedition, though successful, was not unattended by misfortunes. The Litchfield, of 50 guns, a transport, and a bomb-ketch, were on their outward passage separated from the fleet, and wrecked on the coast of Barbary, about nine leagues to the northward of Saffy. A hundred and thirty people, among which were several officers, were drowned. Captain Barton, with about two hundred and twenty, reached the inhospitable shore. They suffered great hardships, and were enslaved by the emperor of Morocco, our worthy ally, who held them in cap-

I                                        tivity

-tivity till they were ranfomed by the king of Great Britain.
Such is the faith of barbarian princes!

Our naval exploits in the Weft-Indies, in the courfe of this year, were not attended with any important confequences. There were performed, however, feveral gallant actions, which ought not to pafs unnoticed.  Captain Forreft of the Augufta, having failed from Port-Royal in Jamaica, cruifed off Cape Francis, a harbour in the ifland of St. Domingo; he was accompanied by the captains Suckling and Langdon, commanding the Dreadnought and Edinburgh. There lay at that time, at the Cape, a French fquadron of four fhips of the line and three ftout frigates, which the French commodore, piqued at feeing the coaft infulted by Forreft's little fquadron, reinforced with feveral ftore-fhips, which he mounted with cannon, and fupplied with feamen from the merchant-veffels, and with foldiers from the garrifon.  Thus prepared, he weighed anchor, and ftood out for fea. When Forreft perceived the approach of the French fhips, he called his two captains. " Gentlemen," faid he, " you " know our own ftrength, and fee that of the enemy. Shall we " give them battle?" Being anfwered in the affirmative, he bore down on the French fleet, and, between three and four in the afternoon, came to action. The French attacked with great impetuofity, and difplayed uncommon fpirit in the fight of their own coaft.  But, after an engagement of more than two hours, their commodore found his fhip fo much fhattered, that he was obliged to make a fignal for his frigates to tow him out of the line. The reft of the fquadron followed his example, and availed themfelves of the land breeze to efcape in the night from the three Britifh fhips, which were too much damaged in their fails and rigging to purfue their victory.

Captain Forreft fignalized his courage in this engagement; but he difplayed equal courage, and ftill more uncommon conduct and fagacity in a fubfequent adventure near the weftern coaft of Hifpaniola.  Having received intelligence, that there was a confiderable French fleet at Port au Prince, a harbour on that coaft, ready to fail for Europe, he proceeded from Jamaica to cruife between Hifpaniola and the little ifland Goave. He difguifed his fhip with tarpaulins, hoifted Dutch colours, and, in order to avoid difcovery, allowed feveral fmall veffels to pafs,

without giving them chace. The fecond day after his arrival in
thofe parts, he perceived a fleet of feven fail fteering to the
weftward. He kept from them to prevent fufpicion, but, at the
approach of night, purfued them with all the fail he could
crowd. About ten in the evening he came up with two veffels
of the chafe, one of which fired a gun, and the other fheered
off. The fhip which had fired no fooner difcovered her enemy,
than fhe fubmitted. Forreft manned her with thirty-five of his
own crew, and now perceiving eight fail to leeward, near the
harbour of Petit Goave, ordered them to ftand for that place,
and to intercept any veffels that attempted to reach it. He
himfelf, in the Augufta, failed directly for the French fleet,
and, coming up with them by day-break, engaged them all
by turns as he could bring his guns to bear. The Solide, the
Theodore, and the Marguerite, returned his fire; but, having
foon ftruck their colours, they were immediately fecured, and
then employed in taking the other veffels, of which none had
the fortune to efcape. The nine fail, which, by this well-conducted ftratagem, had fallen into the power of one fhip, and
that even in the fight of their own harbours, were fafely conducted to Jamaica, where the fale of their rich cargoes rewarded the merit of the captors.

While Forreft acquired wealth and glory by protecting the
trade of Jamaica, the vigilance of Captain Tyrrel fecured the
Englifh navigation to Antigua. In the month of March this
enterprifing and judicious commander demolifhed a fort on the
ifland of Martinico, and deftroyed four privateers riding under
its protection. In November of the fame year, he, in his
own fhip the Buckingham of fixty-four guns, accompanied by
the Weazle floop commanded by Captain Boles, difcovered, between the iflands of Guadaloupe and Montferrat, a fleet of nineteen fail under convoy of the Floriffant, a French man of war of
feventy-four guns, and two frigates, of which the largeft carried thirty-eight, and the other twenty-fix guns. Captain Tyrrel, regardlefs of the great inequality of force, immediately gave
chafe in the Buckingham; and the Weazle, running clofe to
the enemy, received a whole broadfide from the Floriffant.
Though fhe fuftained it without confiderable damage, Mr. Tyrrel ordered Captain Boles to keep aloof, as his veffel could not
                                        be

be suppofed to bear the fhock of heavy metal; and he alone A. D
prepared for the engagement. The Floriffant, inftead of lying to 1758
for his coming up, made a running fight with her ftern chace,
while the two frigates annoyed the Buckingham in her purfuit.
At length, however, fhe came within piftol-fhot of the Floriffant, and poured in a broadfide, which did great execution.
The falutation was returned with fpirit, and the battle became
clofe and obftinate. Mr. Tyrrel, being wounded, was obliged
to leave the deck, and the command devolved on the brave Mr.
Marfhall, his firft lieutenant, who fell in the arms of victory.
The fecond lieutenant took the command, and finally filenced
the enemy's fire. On board the Floriffant 180 men were flain,
and 300 wounded. She was fo much difabled in her hull, that
fhe could hardly be kept afloat. The largeft frigate received
equal damage. The Buckingham had only feven men killed,
and feventeen dangeroufly wounded: fhe had fuffered much,
however, in her mafts and rigging, which was the only circumftance that prevented her from adding profit to glory, by making prizes of the French fleet under fo powerful a convoy.

In the Eaft-Indies the French fquadron was commanded by
Mr. d'Aché, and the Englifh by Admiral Pocock, who had
fucceeded Admiral Watfon. The former was reinforced by a
confiderable armament under the command of General Lally,
an adventurer of Irifh extraction in the French fervice. The
Englifh admiral was alfo reinforced on the 24th of March by
four fhips of the line; and, being foon after apprized of Lally's
arrival, he hoifted his flag aboard the Yarmouth, a fhip of
fixty-four guns, and failed in queft of the enemy. He made the
height of Negapatam the 28th of March, and the day following
difcovered the enemy's fleet in the road of Fort St. David. It
confifted of eight fhips * of the line, and a frigate, which immediately ftood out to fea, and formed the line of battle. Pocock's

| * FRENCH. | | | Duke of Orleans, | — | 60 guns, |
|---|---|---|---|---|---|
| Zodiaque, | — | 74 guns, | Duke of Bourgogne, | — | 60 |
| Bien Aimé, | — | 74 | Condé, | — | 50 |
| Vengeance, | — | 64 | Moras, | — | 50 |
| St. Louis, | — | 64 | Sylphide, | — | 36 |

Squadron

A. D. squadron confifted only of feven fhips [b]; with which he formed
758. the line, and, bearing down upon Mr. d'Aché, began the engagement. The French commodore, having fuftained a warm
action for about two hours, in which one of his largeft fhips
was difabled, fheered off with his whole fleet. Being afterwards
joined with two more fhips of war, he again-formed the line of
battle to leeward. Admiral Pocock, though his own fhip and
feveral others were confiderably damaged, and, though three
of his captains [c] had mifbehaved in the engagement, prepared
again for the attack. But the manœuvres of the French fleet
feem to have been intended merely to amufe him; for they
neither fhowed lights, nor gave any fignal in the night, and next
morning the fmalleft trace of them could not be obferved.

Admiral Pocock made various attempts to bring the French
fquadron to a fecond engagement. Thefe, however, proved
ineffectual till the third of Auguft, when he perceived the enemy's fleet, confifting of eight fhips of the line and a frigate,
ftanding to fea off the road of Pondicherry. They would have
gladly eluded his purfuit, but he obtained the weather-gage, and
failed down upon them in order of battle. As it was now impoffible to efcape without coming to action, the French prepared
for the engagement, and fired on the Elifabeth, which happened to be within mufket-fhot of the fhip in their van. But this
fpirited attack was not feconded with equal perfeverance. In
little more than ten minutes after Admiral Pocock had difplayed
the fignal for battle, Mr. d'Aché fet his forefail, and bore
away, maintaining a running fight in a very irregular line for

| [b] ENGLISH. | | | Weymouth, | — | 60 guns, |
|---|---|---|---|---|---|
| Cumberland, | — | 66 guns, | Tyger, | — | 60 |
| Yarmouth, | — | 64 | Newcaftle, | — | 50 |
| Elifabeth, | — | 64 | Salifbury, | — | 50 |

[c] Captain Brereton of the Cumberland was one of the three who mifbehaved.
God forbid that we fhould particularife an individual with a view to infult his
misfortunes. A man may poffefs much probity, great good fenfe, and many
amiable qualities, without being born with that conftitutional courage, or endowed with that accurate circumfpection, which qualifies him for doing his duty
as a fea-officer. We name this gentleman as an example, that the character of
a naval commander, when once hurt by mifconduct, is feldom to be retrieved;
and we would, if poffible, perfuade men in power of the dangerous confequences
of again intrufting, with an honourable employment, thofe who, on any former
occafion, have fhowed themfelves undeferving of fo important a charge.

near

near an hour. The whole squadron immediately followed his example; and at two o'clock they cut away their boats, crowded sail, and put before the wind. They escaped by favour of the night into the road of Pondicherry; but their fleet was so much damaged, that, in the beginning of September, their commodore sailed for the isle of Bourbon in order to refit, thus leaving the English admiral (whose squadron had always been inferior to that of the French in number of ships and men as well as in weight of metal) sovereign of the Indian seas.

Having examined the naval successes of Great Britain in the different quarters of the world, we shall, for the reader's satisfaction, exhibit in one view the consequences of these glorious exploits. During the course of this year the French lost sixteen men of war [d], while the English lost no more than three [e]: the French lost forty-nine privateers and armed merchant-men, carrying 619 guns and 3824 men. The diminution of their commerce, and the dread of falling into the hands of the English, prevented many of their trading vessels from venturing to sea. Of these, however, they lost 104; and not less than 176 neutral vessels, laden with the rich produce of the French colonies, or with military and naval stores, to enable them to continue the war, rewarded the vigilance of the English navy. The loss of ships, on the part of Great Britain, amounted to three hundred and thirteen, a considerable number, but consisting chiefly of empty transports, and coasting or disarmed vessels, of little value or importance.

The capture of so many of the enemy's vessels, though it added much wealth and glory to those concerned in maritime affairs, was not the only, or even the principal, advantage which Great Britain derived from the spirited efforts of her seamen. The conquests acquired to the nation were still more important. Not to mention the taking of Fort Du Quesne, on the river

[d] These were the Foudroyant of 80 guns; the Esperance 74; the Alcide, Lys, Orpheus, Raisonable, of 64 each; the Arc-en-Ciel and Duc d'Aquitaine of 50 guns each; the Aquilon of 48; the Royal Chariot and Hermione of 36 each; the Melampé, Emerald, and Nymph, of 34; the Brune of 30; and the Galatea of 32.

[e] These were the Warwick of 60 guns; the Greenwich, 50, the Wincholsea, 24.

Ohio,

A. D. Ohio, a place of the utmost confequence, on account both of
1758. its ftrength and fituation; the acquifition of the ftrong fortrefs
of Louifbourg, with the iflands of Cape Breton and St. John;
the demolition of Frontenac, and the reduction of Senegal,
were events not more deftructive to the commerce and colonies
of France, than advantageous to thofe of Great Britain: even
the Britifh expeditions to the coaft of France, though conducted
with little prudence, brought glory and renown to the invaders,
and taught an ambitious people, that, while they were intent
on ravaging the territory of their neighbours, their own dominions were ftill within the reach of the Britifh thunder.

The repeated triumphs of the year had infpired the Englifh
with a warlike enthufiafm: they difcourfed about nothing but
new plans of conqueft; and every object appeared inconfiderable, compared with military glory. In this difpofition of the
nation, the king affembled the parliament the 23d day of November. The lord-keeper, who harrangued them in his name,
(the king being indifpofed), recapitulated the glorious events of
the war, and obferved, that, as it was uncommonly extenfive, it
muft likewife be uncommonly burdenfome; but that no higher
fupplies fhould be required, than fuch as were adequate to the
neceffary fervices. The nation were not at prefent of a temper
to refufe any reafonable demand. They voted, therefore, fixty
thoufand feamen, including fourteen thoufand eight hundred
and forty-five marines, for the fervice of the enfuing year; and
they granted for their maintenance the fum of three millions
one hundred and twenty thoufand pounds. Befides this, two
hundred thoufand pounds were voted towards the building and
repairing of fhips of war. Thefe fums together, how enormous
foever they may appear, amounted to little more than was annually expended in fubfidies to German princes, and pay to
German troops. Yet the former rendered the Englifh name
illuftrious in every quarter of the globe, while the advantages
of the latter ftill remain undifcovered.

1759. The operations of the year 1759 began in the Weft-Indies.
In the end of the preceding year, a fquadron of nine fhips of
the line, with one frigate and four bomb-ketches, as well as
fixty tranfports, containing fix regiments of foot, commanded
by General Hopfon, failed thither, with orders to attack and
                 reduce

reduce the French Caribbee iflands. The fleet was to be under A. D. the orders of Commodore Moore, who was already in thofe 1759. parts. Martinico, as the feat of government, and the centre of commerce, is the moft confiderable of thefe iflands. The principal towns are St. Pierre and Port-Royal, places ftrong by nature and art, and at that time defended by a numerous and well-difciplined militia, as well as by a confiderable body of regular troops. Port-Royal was the firft object of Englifh ambition. The fhips of war eafily drove the enemy from their batteries and entrenchments, and the troops landed without meeting any confiderable oppofition : but after they had effected their landing, they found it impoffible to convey the cannon to a fufficient vicinity for attacking the town. General Hopfon judged the difficulties on the land fide unfurmountable. Commodore Moore thought it impoffible to land the cannon nearer the town ; and, in confequence of thefe opinions, the forces were re-embarked, in order to proceed to St. Pierre. When they had arrived before that place, and examined its fituation, new difficulties arofe, which occafioned a council of war. The commodore had no doubt of being able to reduce the town, but, as the troops had fuffered greatly by difeafes, and the fhips might be fo much difabled in the attack, as to prevent them from availing themfelves of their fuccefs, and from undertaking any other expedition during that feafon, he advifed, that the armament fhould be brought before Gaudaloupe, the reduction of which would tend greatly to the benefit of the Englifh fugar iflands. Gaudaloupe falls little fhort of Martinico in the quantity and richnefs of its productions. It long continued, however, in a languifhing condition, the French having treated Martinico with the predilection of a partial mother for a favourite child, to the great prejudice of all her other colonies. But the fituation and natural advantages of Gaudaloupe abundantly juftified the opinion of Commodore Moore ; and if our minifters had underftood the value of fuch a conqueft, this ifland might have ftill continued a bright gem in the Britifh crown. The fleet arrived, on the 23d of January, before the town of Baffeterre, the capital of Guadaloupe, a place of confiderable extent, defended by a ftrong battery, which, in the opinion of the chief engineer, could not be reduced by the fhipping. But commodore

dore Moore entertained very different fentiments, and brought his fhips to bear on the town and citadel. The Lyon, a fhip of 60 guns, commanded by Captain Trelawney, began the engage-ment, againft a battery of ninety-guns: the reft of the fleet took their ftations a-breaft of the other batteries, and the ac-tion, in a little time, became general. The commodore, mean-while, fhifted his flag into the Woolwich frigate, and kept aloof without gun-fhot, that he might have a more diftinct view of the ftate of the battle; an expedient feldom practifed, though the propriety of it cannot admit of the fmalleft doubt. All the fea commanders behaved with extraordinary fpirit and refolution in the attack; particularly Captains Leflie, Burnet, Gayton, Je-kyl, Trelawney and Shuldam. The action had lafted from nine in the morning till five in the afternoon, when the fire of the citadel was filenced. The Burford and Berwick being driven to fea, Captain Shuldam in the Panther, was unfupported, and two batteries played on the Rippon Captain Jekyl, who filen-ced one of them, but could not prevent his veffel from running a-ground. The enemy, perceiving her difafter, affembled on the hill, lined the trenches, and poured in a fevere fire of mufquetry: they afterwards brought an eighteen pounder to bear, and, for two hours, raked her fore and aft with great effect: a box, containing nine hundred cartridges, blew up on the poop, and fet the fhip on fire. The captain hoifted a fignal of diftrefs, which brought Captain Leflie, in the Briftol, who ran in between the Rippon and the battery, and engaged with fuch impetuofity, as faved Captain Jekyl from deftruction, which otherwife was unavoidable. At feven in the evening, the large fhips having filenced the batteries to which they were oppofed, the four bombs began to play on the town, with fhells and carcaffes. In a fhort time the houfes were in flames, the magazines of gunpowder blew up with a terrible explofion, and the fugar, rum, and other combuftible materials compofing a continued and permanent line of fire, formed a fuitable back-ground to this terrible picture.

Notwithftanding the vivacity of the engagement, the lofs on the part of the Britifh was not very confiderable. Next day our fleet came to anchor in the road off Baffeterre, having inter-cepted feveral fhips, which had turned out and endeavoured

2                                                    to

to efcape. They found the hulls of feveral more veffels, which A. D the enemy had fet on fire, to prevent them from failing into 1759 their hands. The troops landed in the afternoon, without oppofition, took poffeffion of the town and citadel, and difplayed the Britifh colours on the walls. The country, however, was ftill far from being reduced : it abounded in mountains and narrow defiles, of difficult and dangerous accefs ; and although the governor, Monfieur D'Etreuil, poffeffed neither bravery nor conduct, the inhabitants of Guadaloupe were determined to defend their poffeffions to the laft extremities. It is foreign to our defign to enter into any detail of the operations by land, which were drawn out to an extraordinary length. The French were too prudent to hazard a general engagement with regular troops : they determined to weary them out, if poffible, by maintaining a kind of petty war, in detached parties, in which the Britifh were haraffed by a hard duty, and fuffered greatly by difeafes in an unhealthy climate, ill-fupplied with thofe conveniencies to which they were accuftomed. In this manner the war continued from the 24th of January till the firft of May, when the inhabitants of Guadaloupe thought proper to capitulate. Their example was followed, a few days afterwards, by thofe of Defirade, Santos, and Petite-terre, three fmall iflands in that neighbourhood ; and, on the 26th of May, the ifland of Marie-Galante likewife furrendered, which left the French no footing in the Leeward Iflands.

Thefe conquefts being happily finifhed, part of the troops were fent in the tranfports to England. They failed the 3d of July from the harbour of Baffeterre ; and next day Commodore Moore's fquadron was joined by two fhips of the line, which rendered him greatly fuperior to Mr. de Bompart, the French commodore, who lay in the harbour of Martinico. At this time Vice-admiral Cotes commanded in the Jamaica ftation ; but neither he nor Moore could bring Mr. de Bompart to an engagement : fo that the naval tranfactions in the Weft-Indies, during the remainder of the year, confifted folely in the taking of feveral rich prizes and armed fhips of the enemy, by cruifers detached from the Englifh fquadrons.

The reduction of Guadaloupe and the neighbouring iflands, afforded an aufpicious omen for the fuccefs of the Britifh opera-

A. D. tions in North America. Thefe were carried on in the year
1759. 1759, on the moft extenfive fcale. The fplendour of military
triumph, and the difplay of extraordinary genius in the art of
war, eclipfed, in fome meafure, the glory of the navy. But if
we confider the conduct of the war with attention, we fhall
find, that our admirals had a principal fhare in the happy confequences which refulted even from our military expeditions.
The hearty and powerful co-operation of the navy facilitated
every enterprife; but the nation, fond of novelty, and tranfported with their fucceffes by land, to which they were lefs accuftomed, conferred the moft exalted honours on their generals,
while they hardly beftowed due praife on their naval commanders. About the middle of February, a fquadron of twenty-one
fail f of the line failed from England, under the command of the
Admirals Saunders and Holmes, two gentlemen of approved
honour and bravery. By the 21ft of April they were in fight
of Louifbourg; but, the harbour being blocked up with ice,
they were obliged to bear away for Halifax. From hence they
detached Rear-admiral Durel, with a fmall fquadron to the ifle
of Courdres, in the river St. Laurence, in hopes that he might
intercept a fleet of French tranfports and victuallers deftined
for Quebec. He accordingly took two ftore-fhips; but, before
he reached his ftation, feventeen fail of tranfports had already
got to the capital of Canada. Meanwhile Admiral Saunders
arrived at Louifbourg, and took on board eight thoufand troops,
under the command of General Wolfe, whofe name is fo illuftrious in the memoirs of the prefent year. With this armament
it was intended, that the general fhould proceed up the river
St. Lawrence, and undertake the fiege of Quebec. The reduc-

| f The Neptune, | — | 90 guns, | The Alcide, | — | 64 guns, |
|---|---|---|---|---|---|
| Royal William, | — | 80 | Devonfhire, | — | 64 |
| Princefs Amelia, | — | 80 | Captain, | — | 64 |
| Dublin, | — | 74 | Stirling Caftle, | — | 64 |
| Shrewfbury, | — | 74 | Prince of Orange, | — | 60 |
| Northumberland, | — | 70 | Medway, | — | 60 |
| Oxford, | — | 70 | Pembroke, | — | 60 |
| Somerfet; | — | 70 | Bedford, | — | 60 |
| Vanguard, | — | 70 | Centurion, | — | 54 |
| Terrible, | — | 64 | Sutherland, | — | 50 |
| Trident, | — | 64 | | | |

tion of this wealthy and populous city, which gave an opening A. D to the poſſeſſion of all Canada, was the object to which all the 1759 other operations of the Engliſh in North America were ſubſer-vient, and which they were deſigned to aſſiſt. For this purpoſe General Amherſt, who commanded an army of regulars and provincials, amounting to twelve thouſand men, was order-ed to reduce Ticonderoga and Crown-point, croſs the lake Champlain, and proceed along the river Richlieu, to the banks of the St. Lawrence, to effect a junction with the armament under Wolfe and Saunders. For the ſame purpoſe, General Prideaux, who commanded the provincials of New York, with a large body of the Indians of the Five Nations, collected by the influence of Sir William Johnſon, was commiſſioned to inveſt the French fort erected near the Fall of Niagara, and, having ſeized that important paſs, to embark on the lake Ontario, fall down the river St. Lawrence, and co-operate with the united armies. This ſcheme, however, was too refined and complica-ted to be put in execution. The operations began by the taking of Crown-point and Ticonderoga; the Engliſh ſtandard was alſo diſplayed at Niagara. But theſe events were not of the ſmalleſt importance in effecting the conqueſt of Quebec; nor did the troops engaged in them afford any aſſiſtance to the northern armament. This, of itſelf, under ſuch commanders as Wolfe and Saunders, ſeconded by the happy ſtar of Britain, which every where prevailed in the preſent year, was ſufficient to perform far more than had been expected, and to overcome obſtacles of art and nature, that, at firſt ſight, appeared unſur-mountable.

Admiral Saunders arrived the latter end of June, with his whole embarkation, at the iſle of Orleans, a few leagues from Quebec. As he had diſcovered ſome excellent charts of the river St. Lawrence in veſſels taken from the enemy, he expe-rienced none of thoſe difficulties with which the navigation of this immenſe ſtream is ſaid to be attended. The iſland of Or-leans extends quite up to the baſon of Quebec, and its moſt weſterly point advances to a high promontory on the continent, called Point Levi. Both theſe were at preſent occupied by the French, but not with ſuch powerful guards as their importance required. The firſt operation of General Wolfe's troops was to

diſlodge

diſlodge the enemy, and to ſecure theſe poſts, without the command of which the fleet could not have lain in ſafety in the
harbour of Quebec.   This city now appeared full to view, at
once a tempting and diſcouraging ſight :   no place is more favoured
voured by nature, and there is none of which nature ſeems
more to have conſulted the defence: it conſiſts of an upper and
lower town, the former built on a lofty rock, which runs with
a bold and ſteep front along the weſtern banks of the river St·
Lawrence :   at the termination of this ridge, the river St.
Charles, from the north-weſt, and the St. Lawrence, join their
waves, which renders the ground on which Quebec ſtands a
ſort of peninſula.   On the ſide of St. Lawrence is a bank of
ſand, which prevents the approach of large veſſels to the town;
an enemy, therefore, who attacks it, muſt either traverſe the
precipice which I have mentioned, or croſs the river St. Charles.
If he attempts the former, he muſt overcome a dangerous rock,
defended by the whole force of the beſieged, which the importance of the poſt would draw thither.   The difficulty of approaching the place, by Charles river, is not leſs conſiderable,
as all the country to the northward, for more than five miles,
is rough, broken, and unequal, full of rivulets and gullies, and
ſo continues to the river of Montmorenci, which flows by the
foot of a ſteep and woody hill.   Between the two rivers the
French army was poſted, their camp ſtrongly fortified, and
their forces, amounting to twelve thouſand men, commanded
by Mr. Montcalm, a general of tried bravery and conduct.
General Wolfe, having ſeized the weſt point of the iſle of Orleans, and that of Levi, erected batteries on the high grounds,
which fired continually on the town.   Admiral Saunders was
ſtationed in the north channel of the iſle of Orleans, oppoſite to
the Falls of Montmorenci, while Admiral Holmes proceeded up
the river St. Lawrence, beyond Quebec, which not only diverted the enemy's attention from the quarter on which the attack
was intended, but prevented their attempts againſt the batteries
already erected by the Engliſh.   But, notwithſtanding this advantageous poſition, to undertake the ſiege of a city ſkilfully
fortified, well ſupplied with proviſions and ammunition, and defended by an army far ſuperior to that of the beſiegers, was a
deſign ſo bold and adventurous, that even the ſanguine temper
of

of General Wolfe began to despair of its success: yet, what- A. D.
ever it was possible to perform, he was determined to at- 1759.
tempt.   He caused the troops, therefore, to be transported
over the north channel of the river St. Lawrence to the north-
east of Montmorenci, with a view, after he had crossed the latter, of moving towards the enemy's flanks, and enticing them
to an engagement.   But his endeavours in this way proved ineffectual, Mr. Montcalm having chosen his situation with too
much judgment to abandon it imprudently.   Meanwhile the
fleet had been exposed to the most imminent danger. A violent
storm had caused several transports to run foul of each other;
many boats foundered, and some large ships lost their anchors.
The enemy, taking advantage of the confusion produced by
this disaster, sent down seven fire-ships from Quebec at midnight, which must have been attended with the most fatal consequences to the whole expedition, had not the English sailors
resolutely boarded these instruments of destruction, run them
fast a-ground, and prevented them from doing the smallest damage to the British squadron.

The general, despairing of being able to decoy the enemy to
an engagement, and sensible that the approach of winter would
put an end to all military operations in that northern climate,
came at last to the resolution of forcing the French entrenchments.   The best dispositions were made for this purpose both
by sea and land; but the design was disappointed by an accident
which could neither be foreseen nor prevented: the English
grenadiers, who led the attack, had orders to form themselves
on the beach; but, instead of attending to this necessary in-
junction, they rushed with an impetuous ardour towards the
enemy's entrenchments in the most tumultuous confusion: they
were met by a violent and steady fire, which prevented them
from being able to form, and obliged them to take shelter behind a redoubt, which the French had abandoned on their approach.   There they were forced to continue till night came on,
when it was necessary to make a retreat, which could not be
effected without considerable loss.

This check is said to have had a strong effect on the mind and
health of General Wolfe, who saw all his own measures mis-
carry, while those of other commanders in North America,
during

A. D. during the same year, had been attended with extraordinary suc-
1759. cefs. About this time he sent home a letter, couched in terms
of despondency, but which displayed a spirit that would continue
the campaign to the last possible moment. As it seemed neceffary to abandon all farther prospects of gaining any advantage
on the side of Montmorenci, Admiral Holmes's squadron, which
had returned to assist in the late unsuccessful attack, was again
ordered to move up the river for several days successively. This
had a better effect than before; for, though Montcalm kept his
situation, he detached Mr. de Bougainville with 1500 men to
watch the motions of the English admiral. Admiral Saunders,
who still remained in his first position, was ordered to make a
feint with every appearance of reality, as if the troops had intended to land below the town, and attack the French entrenchments on the Beauport shore. While the enemy were amused
by these movements, the general embarked his troops aboard the
transports the 12th July at one in the morning, and proceeded
three leagues farther up the river than the intended place of landing: then he put them into boats, and fell down silently with the
tide, unobserved by the French centinels posted along the shore:
the ships of war followed them, and, by a well-conducted navigation, arrived exactly, at the time concerted, to cover their
landing. When they were put on shore, a hill appeared before them extremely high and steep, having a little winding
path, so narrow that two men could not go abreast, and even
this strongly entrenched and defended by a captain's guard.
This small body was speedily dislodged by the English light infantry; after which the whole army ascended the hill, and at
day-break appeared regularly formed in order of battle.

Montcalm could hardly believe the advices that were brought
him, so impregnable did he imagine the city to be on this side:
but his own observation soon convinced him of the English
movements, and that the high town might be attacked by their
army, while the low town might be destroyed by their fleet.
It was thus become necessary, notwithstanding all his disinclina-
tion to such a measure, to decide the fate of Quebec by the
event of a battle: accordingly he quitted Beauport, passed the
river St. Charles, and formed his troops opposite to the English
army. The success of this engagement, conducted with the
most

most deliberate wisdom, united with the most heroic bravery, put A. D. Great Britain in possession of the capital of French America; but 1759. not without the loss of the brave General Wolfe, who expired in the arms of victory. It is foreign to my design to describe the judicious disposition, animated behaviour, and steady persevering courage of the British troops: these were the immediate cause of the reduction of Quebec; but the matter could not have been brought to this issue, had not the marine co-operated with an unanimity, ardour, and perseverance, that can never be enough celebrated. When the English entered the place, they found the fortifications in tolerable order, but the houses almost totally demolished. 5000 men were left to defend the garrison, and the remainder returned to England with the fleet, which sailed soon, lest it should be locked up by the frost in the river St. Lawrence.

If we turn our attention to the affairs of the East-Indies, we shall find the British arms equally triumphant. The French were unsuccessful in all their attempts by land, particularly in the siege of Madrass: they had still, however, a considerable superiority of land-forces in India, and they had strained every nerve to enable the fleet under Mr. d'Aché to cope with that of Admiral Pocock. The former was augmented to eleven [g] sail of the line, besides frigates and store-ships, an armament hitherto unknown in the Indian seas. The English commander no sooner had intelligence of their arrival in those parts than he sailed to the coast of Coromandel, and determined, by the most unremitted exertions of vigilance, to pursue, and give them battle. This resolution shews the ardour and spirit of the English navy at this period, as their enemies had a superiority of 192 guns, 2365 men, besides a great advantage in the size of their ships [b]. In the morning of the second of September the French fleet were descried from the mast-head: Admiral Pocock immediately threw out the signal for a general chase; but, the wind abating, he could not approach near enough to engage, though

[g] These were;

| | Guns. | Men. | | | Guns. | Men. |
|---|---|---|---|---|---|---|
| The Zodiaque, | 74 | 660 | The Illustre, | — | 64 | 600 |
| Minotaur, | 74 | 660 | The Fortune, | — | 64 | 600 |
| The Comte of Provence, | 74 | 660 | The Avenger, | — | 64 | 500 |
| The Centaur, | 70 | 660 | The Duke of Orleans, | — | 60 | 500 |
| The Active, | 64 | 600 | The St. Louis, | — | 60 | 500 |
| | | | The Duke of Bourgogne, | — | 60 | 500 |

[b] See a list of the English vessels, p. 132.

he

A. D.
759.

he crowded all the fail he could carry: during feveral days his endeavours to bring the French fleet to an engagement, which they always declined, were equally fruitlefs. At length they totally difappeared, and the admiral ftood for Pondicherry, on a fuppofition that they intended to fail thither. His conjecture was well founded; for on the eighth day of September he obferved them ftanding to the fouthward, and on the tenth, about two in the afternoon, Mr. d'Aché, feeing no poffibility to efcape, made the fignal for battle. The cannonading began without farther delay, and both fquadrons engaged with equal impetuofity: but the French directing their cannon at the mafts and rigging, while the Englifh fired only at the hulls of the fhips, the former fuftained fuch a lofs of men, and found their veffels in fo fhattered a condition, that they were glad to fheer off, with all their canvas fet. The lofs on the fide of the Englifh was not inconfiderable, there being in the whole 569 men killed and wounded: but that on the fide of the French muft have been far greater, as their fhips could hardly keep the fea, and they were obliged to make the beft of their way to the ifland of Mauritius, in order to be refitted. Soon after this engagement Admiral Cornifh arrived from England with four fhips of the line, and confirmed the dominion of the Englifh over the Indian feas.

The French, being equally unfuccefsful in Afia, Africa, and America, fought in vain to repair their misfortunes: no fooner was a fleet put to fea than it was either taken or deftroyed: they were active to no purpofe; for, while they built and armed veffels with the greateft fpeed and diligence, they only laboured for the Englifh, whofe fleet was continually augmented by captures from the enemy. But neither the lofs of their poffeffions, nor the deftruction of their fleets, nor the complaints of twenty millions of people exhaufted by oppreffion, could check the fatal ambition of the French court. The miniftry feemed to derive courage from defpair, and the greater misfortunes they fuftained, the more daring were the projects which they had in agitation. All their ports were now filled with preparations for an invafion of Great Britain. Men of war, tranfports, and flat-bottomed boats, were got ready with the utmoft diligence: they talked of a triple embarkation. Mr. Thurot,

t                                                                who,

who, from being a captain of a merchant veſſel, had ſucceſſively A. D become a commander of a privateer, and now a commodore in 1759 the French ſervice, commanded a ſquadron, of men of war and ſeveral tranſports at Dunkirk, which, it was believed, were in_ tended againſt Scotland. The deſign againſt England was to be carried on from Havre de Grace and ſome other ports of Normandy, where a great number of flat-bottomed boats had been prepared for the purpoſe of tranſporting troops. The third embarkation, deſtined againſt Ireland, was to be made at Vannes in the Lower Brittany. The land-forces were commanded by the Duc d'Aguillon, while a powerful ſquadron under Mr. de Conflans was to cover and ſecure their landing. In order to counteract theſe machinations, the Engliſh miniſtry ordered a ſquadron under Commodore Boyce to be ſtationed before Dunkirk: Admiral Hawke was ſent with a large fleet to block up the harbour of Breſt, while a ſmaller fleet kept a watch upon that of Vannes. As to Havre, from which the danger ſeemed moſt imminent, Rear-admiral Rodney was deſpatched, with orders immediately to proceed to the bombardment of that place. He accordingly anchored in the road of Havre in the beginning of July, and made a diſpoſition to execute his inſtructions. The bomb-ketches were placed in the narrow channel of the river leading to Honfleur; and, having begun the bombardment, continued to throw their ſhells for above two days without intermiſſion. The town was ſet on fire in ſeveral places, the boats overſet or reduced to aſhes, and, at the expence of nineteen hundred ſhells and eleven hundred carcaſſes, the French preparations at Havre were totally deſtroyed.

While the danger threatening England from the northern coaſt of France was thus happily removed, the honour of the Britiſh flag was effectually maintained by the gallant Admiral Boſcawen, who commanded in the Mediterranean. The French had aſſembled there a conſiderable armament ⁱ under the com-

| ⁱ It conſiſted of the following ſhips: | | Le Modeſta, | — | 64 guns, |
|---|---|---|---|---|
| L'Ocean, | — 80 gens, | Le Lion, | — | 64 |
| Le Redoubtable, | —, 74 | Le Triton, | — | 64 |
| Le Centaur, | — 74 | Le Fier, | — | 50 |
| Le Souverain, | — 74 | L'Oriflamme, | — | 50 |
| Le Guerrier, | — 64 | La Chimere, | — | 26 |
| Le Temeraire, | — 74 | La Minerve, | — | 24 |
| Le Fantaſque, | — 64 | La Gracieuſe, | — | 24 |

mand of Mr. de la Clue, which fome believed to be deſtined for America, while others conjectured, that it was deſigned to reinforce the ſquadron at Breſt, and to co-operate with it in the intended deſcent on the Engliſh coaſt.   At preſent Mr. de la Clue continued to lie in the harbour of Toulon, before which Admiral Boſcawen took his ſtation with fourteen ſhips of the line ᵏ, beſides frigates and fire-ſhips.

Boſcawen, having in vain diſplayed the Britiſh flag in ſight of Toulon, and tried every other art to bring the enemy to an engagement, ordered three ſhips of the line, commanded by the Captains Smith, Barker, and Harland, to advance and burn two French veſſels lying cloſe to the mouth of the harbour.   They prepared for executing their orders with the utmoſt alacrity, but met with a warm reception from ſeveral batteries, which had not been before perceived; and, the wind unfortunately ſubſiding into a calm, they ſuſtained ſuch conſiderable damage as made it convenient for the Engliſh admiral to put into Gibraltar to refit his ſhattered ſhips.   Mr. de la Clue ſeized this opportunity of ſailing, in hopes of paſſing the Gut of Gibraltar unmoleſted during the abſence of the Engliſh fleet. But Boſcawen had previouſly detached two frigates, of which one cruiſed off Malaga, and the other hovered between Eſtepona and the fortreſs of Ceuta, in order to obſerve the motions of the enemy. On the 17th day of Auguſt the Gibraltar frigate made the ſignal at the maſt-head for the enemy being in ſight; upon which the Engliſh admiral without delay hove up his anchors, and put to ſea.   At day-light he deſcried ſeven large ſhips, part of Mr. de la Clue's ſquadron, from which five ſhips of the line and three frigates had been ſeparated in the night. Having made the ſignal to chace, and to engage in line of battle a-head, his foremoſt ſhips came up with the rear of the enemy about half after two.   The Admiral himſelf did not wait to return the fire of the

ᵏ Theſe were;

| | | | | | |
|---|---|---|---|---|---|
| The Namur, | —— | 90 guns, | The Intrepid, | —— | 64 guns, |
| Prince, | —— | 90 | Edgar, | —— | 64 |
| Newark, | —— | 80 | America, | —— | 64 |
| Culloden, | —— | 74 | St. Alban's, | —— | 60 |
| Warſpight, | —— | 74 | Jerſey, | —— | 60 |
| Conqueror, | —— | 74 | Portland, | —— | 60 |
| Swiftſure, | —— | 70 | Guernſey, | —— | 50 |

ſternmoſt,

sternmost, but employed every effort to come up with the Ocean, A. D which Mr. de la Clue commanded in person; and about four 1759 o'clock he ran athwart her hawse, and poured into her a furious broadside, which was returned with equal vivacity. This dispute, however, was not of long continuance; for the French admiral being wounded in the engagement, and the next in command perceiving that Boscawen's vessel had lost her mizenmast and top-sail yards, went off with all the sail he could carry. Mr. Boscawen shifted his flag from the Namur to the Newark, and joined some other ships in attacking the Centaur, which was obliged to strike. The pursuit continued all night, and Mr. de la Clue, finding himself at day-break on the coast of Portugal, determined rather to burn his ships than allow them to fall into the hands of the victors. When he reached the Portuguese shore, he put his ship under the protection of the Fort Almadana, to which the English paid no regard. He himself landed with part of his men; but the Count de Carne, who succeeded to the command of the Ocean, having received a broadside from the America, struck his colours, and the English took possession of this noble prize, deemed the best ship in the French navy. Meanwhile Captain Bentley brought off the Temeraire, little damaged, and having on board all her officers and men; while Rear-admiral Broderic burnt the Redoubtable, and took the Modeste. The scattered remains of the French fleet got with difficulty into the harbour of Cadiz, where they were soon after blocked up. Nothing was wanting to complete the glory of this victory; for it was obtained with the loss of only fifty-six men killed, and 196 wounded, and not one officer lost in the action.

After the memorable naval engagement off Cape Lagos, the French met with a disaster by land equally calamitous. The important battle of Minden deprived them of all hopes of again getting possession of Hanover, or of putting their affairs in such a situation in Germany as might afford them the prospect of any other than an ignominious peace. They were under the unhappy necessity, therefore, of trying a last effort on an element which had hitherto been extremely unpropitious to all their designs. Their sole hopes now centered in their fleets at Brest and Dunkirk, the former of which was blocked up by Admiral Hawke, and the latter by Commodore Boyce. They still expected, how-

A. D.
1759.

ever, that the winter ftorms would compel the Englifh fleets to take refuge in their own harbours, and thus afford them an opportunity to crofs the fea unoppofed, and to execute the object of their deftination againft the Britifh coafts. In this expectation they were not wholly difappointed : on the 12th of October a violent gale of wind, which gathered into an irrefiftible ftorm, drove the Englifh fquadrons off the French coaft. Thurot, a French adventurer, availed himfelf of this accident to obtain his releafe from Dunkirk, without being difcovered by Commodore Boyce, who, upon the firft information of his departure, failed immediately in purfuit of him : but Thurot had the good fortune or dexterity to elude his vigilance, by entering the port of Guttenburgh in Sweden, where he was laid up till after Chriftmas by the feverity of the weather and want of neceffaries to enable his fhips and men to keep the feas.

Admiral Hawke's fquadron had taken refuge, during the violence of the ftorm, in the harbour of Torbay. When its fury began to fubfide, the French Admiral Conflans perceiving no enemy on the coaft, immediately put to fea. But the fame day that *he* failed from Breft, the Englifh admiral failed from Torbay. The two fquadrons [1] were the moft powerful of any employed

| ENGLISH FLEET. | | Guns. | Men. |
|---|---|---|---|
| Royal George, | — | 100 | 880 |
| Union, | — | 90 | 770 |
| Duke, | — | 90 | 750 |
| Namur, | — | 90 | 780 |
| Mars, | — | 74 | 600 |
| Warfpight, | — | 74 | 600 |
| Hercules, | — | 74 | 600 |
| Torbay, | — | 72 | 700 |
| Magnanime, | — | 74 | 700 |
| Refolution, | — | 74 | 600 |
| Hero, | — | 74 | 600 |
| Swiftfure, | — | 70 | 520 |
| Dorfethire, | — | 70 | 520 |
| Burford, | — | 70 | 520 |
| Chichefter, | — | 70 | 520 |
| Temple, | — | 70 | 520 |
| Revenge, | — | 64 | 480 |
| Effex, | — | 64 | 480 |

| | | Guns. | Men. |
|---|---|---|---|
| Kingfton, | — | 60 | 400 |
| Intrepid, | — | 60 | 420 |
| Montague, | — | 60 | 420 |
| Dunkirk, | — | 60 | 420 |
| Defiance, | — | 60 | 420 |

| FRENCH FLEET. | | Guns. | Men. |
|---|---|---|---|
| Le Soleil Royal, | — | 80 | 1200 |
| Le Tonnant | — | 80 | 1000 |
| Le Formidable, | — | 80 | 1000 |
| L'Orient, | — | 80 | 1000 |
| L'Intrepide, | — | 74 | 815 |
| Le Glorieux, | — | 74 | 815 |
| Le Thefée, | — | 74 | 815 |
| L'Heros, | — | 74 | 815 |
| Le Robufte, | — | 74 | 815 |
| Le Magnifique, | — | 74 | 815 |
| Le Jufte, | — | 70 | 800 |

Le

ployed in the courfe of the war, and worthy to be entrufted A. D. with the fate of the two leading kingdoms in Europe. Their 1759 forces were nearly equal, the Englifh being, by fome veffels, more numerous, but having no fuperiority in number of men, or weight of metal.

Sir Edward Hawke directed his courfe for Quiberon-bay on the coaft of Bretagne, which he conjectured would be the rendezvous of the French fquadron, but here fortune oppofed his well-concerted meafures; for a ftrong gale fprung up in an eafterly point, and drove the Englifh fleet a great way to the weftward: at length, however, the weather became more favourable, and carried them in directly to the fhore. The Maidftone and Coventry frigates, who had orders to keep a-head of the fquadron, difcovered the enemy's fleet in the morning of the 20th of November. They were bearing to the northward between the ifland of Belleifle and the main land of France. Sir Edward Hawke threw out a fignal for feven of his fhips, that were neareft, to chace, in order to detain the French fleet until they themfelves could be reinforced with the reft of the fquadron, which were ordered to form into a line of battle a-head, as they chaced, that no time might be loft in the purfuit. Thefe manœuvres indicated the utmoft refolution and intrepidity; for at this time the waves rolled mountains high, the weather grew more and more tempeftuous, and the fea, on this treacherous coaft, was indented with fand and fhoals, fhallows and rocks, as unknown to the Englifh pilots as they were familiar to thofe of the enemy. But Sir Edward Hawke, animated by the innate fortitude of his own heart and the warm love of his country, difregarded every danger and obftacle that ftood in the way of his obtaining the important ftake which now depended. Mr. de Conflans might have hazarded a fair battle on the open fea without the imputation of temerity; but he thought proper to attempt

| | Guns. | Men. | | | Guns. | Men. |
|---|---|---|---|---|---|---|
| Le Superbe, | — | 70 | 800 | Le Solitaire, | — | 64 | 750 |
| Le Dauphin, | — | 70 | 800 | Le Brilliant, | — | 64 | 750 |
| Le Dragon, | — | 64 | 750 | L'Eveille, | — | 64 | 750 |
| Le Northumberland, | 64 | 750 | Le Bizarre, | — | 64 | 750 |
| Le Sphinx, | — | 64 | 750 | L'Inflexible, | — | 64 | 750 |

The French had five frigates, and ten joined Hawke between Ufhant and Belleifle.

a more

A. D. a more artful game, which, however, he did not play with the
1759. addrefs which his fituation required. As he was unwilling to rifk
a fair engagement, he could have no other view but to draw
the Englifh fquadron among the rocks and fhoals, that, at a
proper time, he might take advantage of any difafter that befel
them : but, fluctuating between a refolution to fight and an inclination to fly, he allowed the Britifh fhips to come up with
him, and then crowded his fail when it was too late to efcape.
At half an hour after two the van of the Englifh fleet began
the engagement with the rear of the enemy. The Formidable,
commanded by the French rear-admiral Mr. du Verger, behaved with uncommon refolution, and returned many broadfides
poured into her by the Englifh fhips as they paffed to bear
down on the van of the French. Sir Edward Hawke referved
his fire, and ordered his mafter to carry him along-fide of the
French admiral. The pilot obferved, that he could not obey
his orders without the moft imminent rifk of running upon a
fhoal : the brave admiral replied, " You have done your duty
" in pointing out the danger; now you are to obey my com-
" mands, and lay me along-fide the Soleil Royal." While the
pilot was preparing to gratify his defire, the Thesée, a French
fhip of feventy guns, generoufly interpofed itfelf between the
two admirals, and received the fire which Hawke had deftined
for a greater occafion. In returning this fire, the Thesée
foundered, in confequence of a high fea that entered her lower-
deck ports : the Superbe fhared the fame fate ; the Heros
ftruck her colours, and the formidable did the fame about four
in the afternoon. Darknefs coming on, the enemy fled towards
their own coaft. Seven fhips of the line hove their guns overboard, and took refuge in the river Villaine : about as many
more, in a moft fhattered and miferable condition, efcaped to
other ports. The wind blowing with redoubled violence on a
lee fhore, Sir Edward made the fignal for anchoring to the
weftward of the fmall ifland Dumet, where he continued all
night in a very dangerous riding, continually alarmed by hearing guns of diftrefs. When morning appeared, he found the
French admiral had run his fhip on fhore, where fhe was foon
after fet on fire by her own men. Thus concluded this memorable action, in which the Englifh fuftained little lofs but
what

what was occafioned by the weather. The Effex and Refolu- A. D.
tion unfortunately ran on a fand-bank called Lefour, where 1759.
they were irrecoverably loft, in fpite of all the affiftance that
could be given; but moft of their men and fome part of their
ftores were faved. In the whole fleet no more than one lieutenant and thirty-nine feamen and marines were killed, and two
hundred and two wounded. The lofs of the French in men
muft have been prodigious. All the officers on board the Formidable were killed before fhe ftruck. They had, befides, four
of the beft fhips in their navy deftroyed, one taken, and the
whole of their formidable armament, the laft hope of the
French marine, fhattered, difarmed, and diftreffed.

It would be unjuft to pafs over a circumftance which charac-
terizes the fpirit that diftinguifhed the Englifh navy at this
happy period. Admiral Saunders happened to arrive from his
glorious Quebec expedition a little after Hawke had failed.
Notwithftanding the length of the voyage, and the feverity of
the duty in which he had been fo long employed, he loft not a
moment in fetting fail, with a view to partake the danger and
honour of the approaching engagement. Fortune did not favour
the generofity of his intentions. He was too late to give affiftance; but fuch a refolution was alone equal to a victory.

Under fuch commanders it was impoflible that the Englifh
fhould not maintain the afcendant over their enemies. Accordingly, in the words of a celebrated writer, who ought not on
this fubject to be fufpected of partiality, " the Englifh had ne-
" ver fuch a fuperiority at fea as at this time. But," continues
he, " they at all times had the advantage over the French.
" The naval force of France they deftroyed in the war of 1741;
" they humbled that of Lewis XIV. in the war of the Spanifh
" fucceffion; they triumphed at fea in the reigns of Louis XIII.
" and Henry IV. and ftill more in the unhappy times of the
" league. Henry VIII. of England had the fame advantage
" over Francis I. If we examine into paft times, we fhall
" find, that the fleets of Charles VI. and Philip de Valois
" could not withftand thofe of the Kings Henry V. and Edward
" III. of England. What can be the reafon of this continual
" fuperiority ? Is it not that the fea, which the French can
" live

" live well enough without, is effentially neceffary to the Eng-
" lifh, and that nations always fucceed beft in thofe things for
" which they have an abfolute occafion ? Is is not alfo becaufe
" the capital of England is a fea-port, and that Paris knows
" only the boats of the Seine ? Is it that the Englifh climate
" produces men of a more fteady refolution, and of a more
" vigorous conftitution, than that of France, as it produces
" the beft horfes and dogs for hunting ?" Fearful leaft he had
gone too far in fuggefting a reafon which is doubtlefs the true
one, he returns to his natural fcepticifm, and concludes in a
flattering ftrain ; " but from Bayonne even to the coafts of Pi-
" cardy and Flanders, France has men of an indefatigable la-
" bour ; and Normandy alone formerly fubdued England [m]."

The events above related compofe the principal operations of
the Britifh navy during the prefent year. But befides the actions
of whole fquadrons, there were a great many captures made
by fingle fhips, attended with circumftances highly honourable
and advantageous. The Favourite of twenty guns, commanded
by Captain Edwards, carried into Gibraltar a French fhip of
twenty-four guns, laden with the rich productions of St. Domingo, valued at 40,000 l. A French privateer belonging to
Granville, having on board two hundred men, and mounted
with twenty cannon, was taken by the Montague, Captain Parker, who foon after made prize of a fmaller veffel from Dunkirk, mounted with eight guns, and having on board fixty men.
About the fame period, that is in the month of February, Captain Graves of the Unicorn brought in the Moras privateer of
St. Malo, carrying two hundred men and two and twenty guns.
The Veftal, Captain Hood, belonging to Admiral Holmes's
fquadron in the Weft-Indies, engaged a French frigate called
the Bellona, greatly fuperior to the Veftal in men and weight
of metal, and, after an obftinate engagement, which lafted
above two hours, took her, and brought her fafely into port.
The Englifh frigates the Southampton and Melampe, commanded by the Captains Gilchrift and Hotham, defcried in the evening of the 28th of March, as they were cruifing to the northward, the Danaé, a French fhip of forty guns and three hun-

---

[m] Voltaire, Siecle de Louis Quinze.

dred

dred and thirty men. The Melampe came up with her in the night a confiderable time before the Southampton, and with admirable gallantry maintained the combat againft a fhip of double her own force. As they fought in the dark, Captain Gilchrift was obliged to ly by until he could diftinguifh the one. from the other. At day-break he bore down on the Danaé with his ufual valour, and, after a brifk engagement, in which fhe had forty men killed and many more wounded, compelled her to furrender. This victory, however, was clouded by a misfortune which happened to the brave Gilchrift. He received a wound in the fhoulder, which, though it did not deprive him of life, rendered him incapable of future fervice. On the 4th of April another remarkable exploit was achieved by his majefty's fhip Achilles, commanded by the honourable Captain Barrington. The Achilles, which mounted fixty guns, encountered, to the weftward of Cape Finifterre, a French fhip of equal force, called the Count de St. Florentin, under the command of the Sieur de Montay. After a clofe engagement of two hours, during which the French captain was flain, and one hundred and fixteen of his men killed or wounded, the Count de St. Florentin ftruck her colours. She was fo much damaged that it was very difficult to bring her into Falmouth. The Achilles had but twenty-five men killed or wounded, and had fuftained no hurt but in her mafts and rigging. On the 27th of March Captain Faulkner of his majefty's fhip the Windfor, mounting fixty guns, difcovered off the rock of Lifbon four large fhips to leeward, and gave them chace. As he approached they formed the line of battle a-head, at the diftance of about a cable's length afunder. He clofed with the fternmoft fhip, which fuftained his fire about an hour; and then, upon a fignal given, the other three edged off, and the fhip engaged ftruck her colours. She proved to be the Duke de Chartres, pierced for fixty guns, but having only twenty-four, with a complement of three hundred men, about thirty of whom were killed in the action. She belonged, as well as the other three, that efcaped, to the Eaft-India company, was loaded with fixty tons of gunpowder, and an hundred and fifty tons of cordage, with a large quantity of other naval ftores. The Windfor had, in this engagement, but one man killed and eighteen wounded.

A. D.
1759.
About the same time Captain Hughs of his majesty's frigate the Tamer, took and carried into Plymouth two privateers, called le Chasseur and le Conquerant, the one from Cherburgh and the other from Dunkirk. A third, called the Despatch, from Morlaix, was brought into Penzance by the Diligence sloop; while the Basque from Bayonne, furnished with two and twenty guns, fell into the hands of Captain Parker of the Brilliant. Captain Atrobus of the Surprize took the Vieux, a privateer of Bourdeaux; and a fifth from Dunkirk, struck to Captain Knight of the Liverpool. In the month of May a French frigate called the Arethusa, mounted with two and thirty guns, and commanded by the marquis of Vandreuil, submitted to two English frigates, the Venus and the Thames, commanded by the Captains Harrison and Colby. The engagement was warm; the loss on the side of the English inconsiderable. The enemy had sixty men killed and wounded. In the beginning of June an armed ship, belonging to Dunkirk, was brought into the Downs by Captain Angel of the Stag; and a privateer of force, called the Countess de la Serre, was subdued and taken, after an obstinate engagement, by his majesty's ship the Adventure, commanded by Captain Moore. In the beginning of October the Florissant, a French ship of 74 guns, was engaged near the chops of the channel by Captain Porter of the Hercules. The English vessel having lost one of her top-masts and rigging, the Forissant took advantage of this misfortune to sheer off, and escaped behind the isle of Oleron.

While the English cruizers were attended with continual success in Europe, several armed-ships of the enemy and rich prizes were taken in the West-Indies. About the same time that the Velour from St. Domingo, carrying twenty guns and above one hundred men, and loaded with a rich cargo, was taken by the Favourite sloop of war, commanded by Captain Edwards, two French frigates and two Dutch ships, laden with French commodities, fell into the possession of cruizers detached from Admiral Coates's squadron stationed at Jamaica. Captain Collingwood, commanding his majesty's ship the Crescent, off St. Christopher's attacked two French frigates, the Amethyste and Berkeley: the former escaped, but the latter was conveyed into the harbour of Basseterre.

These

These particular losses, combined with the general destruction A. D of the French squadrons by Boscawen, Hawke, Saunders, and 1759 Pocock, in a great measure ruined the French navy. In the course of the year the English had enriched their marine with twenty-seven ships of the line, and thirty-one frigates of French construction. They had destroyed eight ships of the line and four frigates, whereas the English navy had lost, during all the various operations of the present year, no more than seven men of war and five frigates. In reviewing the captures of merchantmen, the balance is not so much in our favour. Notwithstanding the courage and vigilance of the English cruizers, the French privateers swarmed to such a degree, that in the course of the present year they took 210 British vessels, chiefly, however, coasters and small craft, that did not chuse to confine themselves and wait for a convoy. On the other hand, we took 165 merchant vessels from the enemy; of which, as it appears from some examples above given, many contained very valuable cargoes.

While the naval power of France was falling to its ruin, her commerce was cut off in its source by the taking of Guadaloupe and Quebec. The French government, broken by repeated calamities, and exhausted by exorbitant subsidies to its German allies, was reduced to the lowest ebb of fortune. The monarch, however, still found a resource in the loyalty and attachment of his people. They acquiesced in the bankruptcy of public credit, when the court stopped payment of the interest on twelve different branches of the national debt; they declared against every suggestion of accommodation that was not advantageous and honourable, and they sent in large quantities of plate to be melted down and coined into specie, for the support of the war.

The liberal supplies granted by the British parliament, which met in November, formed a striking contrast with the indigence of our rivals. For the service of the ensuing year they voted seventy-three thousand seamen, including eighteen thousand three hundred and fifty-five marines; and they allotted three millions six hundred and forty thousand pounds for their maintenance. The sums destined to other purposes were no less ample; the whole amounted to fifteen millions five hundred and three thousand five hundred and sixty-four pounds. Of this

U 2

immense

immenfe fupply not lefs than two millions three hundred and forty-four thoufand four hundred and eighty-fix pounds were paid to foreigners, for fupporting the war in Germany, exclufive of the money expended by twenty thoufand Britifh troops in that country, and the charge of tranfporting them, with the expence of pontage, waggons, and other contingencies, and the exorbitant article of forage, which alone amounted, in the courfe of the laft campaign, to one million two hundred thoufand pounds.

The comparative expence of our naval preparations, and of the German war, affected, with equal aftonifhment and concern, many difinterefted and difpaffionate men, whofe imaginations were lefs heated than thofe of the bulk of the people with the enthufiaftic ardour of victory. Amidft the triumphs of glory and fuccefs concealed murmurs were heard, which, in a free nation, were fpeedily re-echoed with increafed force. Men formed themfelves into parties according to their different notions upon this fubject, and the difpute between the naval and continental fchemes came to be the common topic, not only of public affemblies but of private converfation. The abettors of the naval intereft afferted, that the infular fituation of Great Britain, as well as the continued experience of many ages, clearly pointed out the courfe which England ought to purfue in her wars with France. They pretended not that the former kingdom ought never, in any cafe, to take part in the difputes of the continent; but this, they thought, ought always to be as an auxiliary only. She might even engage with fuccefs in a continental war againft France, provided fhe had a concurrence in her favour of the neighbouring powers of the continent. This was the grand principle of King William, and the foundation of that alliance, at the head of which, in defence of the liberties of Europe, he acted the greateft part that can be allotted to man. It was on the fame principle that, in conjunction with the powers of the empire, we carried on the war with fo much honour and fuccefs againft France, under the duke of Marlborough. But to engage in a continental war with that kingdom, not only unaffifted but oppofed by the greateft part of thofe ftates with which we were then combined, is an attempt never to be juftified by any comparative calculation of

the

the populoufnefs, the revenues, or the general ftrength of the A: D
two nations. They afferted ftill farther, that the theatre we 1759
had chofen for that war was the moft unfortunate that could
poffibly be imagined. Germany has at all times proved the
firmeft bulwark againft French ambition. What, therefore
could France herfelf more heartily defire than to fee the fwords
of the Germans turned againft each other, and England co-
operate with all her power in embittering the hoftilities which
have already defolated that country. In carrying on a war
there, France has many advantages : fhe fupports her armies in
a great meafure by pillaging thofe whom, in every view, it is
her intereft to weaken : fhe is not very remote from her own
frontiers, from which her armies may be recruited and fupplied
without great expence : even when unfuccefsful, fhe is brought
ftill nearer her own territories, fupports her troops with ftill
greater facility, and exhaufts ftill lefs the natural wealth of her
people. If fhe was obliged to take refuge at home, would the
Englifh continue fo frantic as to follow her into her own dominions ? To Great Britain, on the other hand, every thing is
unfavourable in fuch a war. The utmoft fuccefs with which
her arms can be attended, will only carry the Englifh to a
greater diftance from their refources ; and, by going a certain
length, the tranfport of provifion, artillery, ammunition, and
the infinite impediments of a large army, muft become altogether impracticable. Upon this plan, victory itfelf cannot fave
us, and all our fuccefles will only ferve to accumulate new di-
ftrefles, new difficulties, and new charges. As to the king of
Pruffia, what does he give us in return for the immenfe fubfidies
which are paid him ? Inftead of affifting our armies, is he able to
defend himfelf ? Befides, he is the worft ally we could have
chofen, on account of his long and intimate connection with
our enemies, and the general lightnefs of his faith in deferting
every engagement which forms an obftacle to his ambition. He
is looked upon as the protector of the proteftant religion : but
has he not defolated the firft proteftant electorate ? has he not
divided the reformed ftates of Germany, and turned their
fwords againft each other ? And do not his writings fufficiently
teftify not only his indifference to the proteftant caufe, but his
total difregard to all religion whatever ? Had England kept
herfelf

herfelf clear of the inextricable labyrinth of German politics, fhe might, without exhaufting her own vigor by attacking France on her ftrong fide, have been before this time, in poffeffion of all the French colonies together : even had the French, therefore got poffeffion of Hanover, (which could not have fuffered more by this event than it has already done in the courfe of the war,) England, while her own power was entire, and while fhe held all the commercial refources of France in her hands, muft not only have recovered the Hanoverian dominions to their lawful fovereign, but have procured full indemnification to them for what they had fuffered in our quarrel.

The advocates for continental meafures were obliged to acknowledge the exorbitant expence of a German war; but they affirmed, that, if it had coft England much, it had coft France ftill more, as the number of French troops to be paid exceeds the difference between French and Englifh pay. They obferved, that her fubfidies to German princes greatly exceeded ours, although fhe had not derived fo much advantage from all her allies together as England had done from the victory of the king of Pruffia at Rofbach : that the German war had brought the finances of France to that deplorable condition which all Europe had witneffed : that her chief ftrength and attention, being engaged in this quarter, were in a great meafure withdrawn from her navy, her commerce, and her colonies; which had enabled England to deprive her of the beft part of her colonies, to render her commerce equally precarious and unprofitable, and to give fuch a blow to her navy as, perhaps, fhe might never be able to recover. But had England, inftead of exhaufting the French refources by diverting their efforts to Germany, allowed that country to receive laws from her rival, the continental war would have foon terminated, and France, ftrengthened by victory, by conqueft, and by alliance, would have preferved the whole force and revenue of her mighty monarchy entire, to act againft Great Britain.

Thefe reafonings will be interefting as long as the great fyftem of European politics continues in any meafure the fame, and as long as the meafures of the Britifh court are liable to be warped by the fame motives as formerly. I would therefore obferve, that taking for granted the facts alledged by the partizans of our
German

German allies, (many of which require proof), and suppofing A. D. that France had expended even more than Great Britain in pro- 1759. fecuting the German war, the principal queftion would ftill be undecided. It would be proper ftill farther to inquire, whether England or France could maintain the fame number of troops, and make the fame efforts in Germany, at the fmalleft expence? whether, on the plan of a continental war alone, the revenues and refources of France or England will be foooneft exhaufted? and which of the two kingdoms could, with the fmalleft trouble and expence, augment its navy, and profecute fucceſsful enterprifes in diftant parts of the world? Thefe queries need only be propofed; their folution is obvious, and it fhows, in the fulleft light, the impropriety of England's carrying the war into the continent of Europe, while France poffeffed any fpecies of foreign commerce, or a fingle foot of land in Afia, Africa, or America.

But notwithftanding the force of evidence, and the clamour of party, the court remained firm in its firft refolution. The continental fyftem prevailed more than ever; and although the fupplies granted for maintaining the navy were liberal beyond example, yet, the ftrength and attention of the nation being diverted to a different channel, our marine enterprifes appeared to languifh at a time when paft fuccefs ought to have caufed them to be pufhed with the utmoft vigour, and fewer exploits were achieved at fea in 1760 than are recorded in the memoirs of the preceding year.

The Britifh navy at this time amounted to 120 fhips of the 1760 line, befides frigates, fire-fhips, floops, bombs, and tenders. Of thefe capital fhips feventeen were ftationed in the Eaft-Indies, twenty for the defence of the Weft-India iflands, twelve in North America, ten in the Mediterranean, and fixty-one either on the coaft of France, in the harbours of England, or cruizing in the Englifh feas for the protection of commerce. Confidering thefe mighty preparations, it is remarkable, that the return of the little fquadron commanded by Thurot (which, as was already mentioned, had taken refuge the preceding year in the harbour of Gottenburg in Sweden) fhould have caufed a general alarm over the three kingdoms. This inconfiderable armament originally confifted of five frigates, on board of which

were

A. D. were 1270 land-foldiers. They had failed from Gottenburg to
1760. Bergen in Norway, and during that voyage had suffered fo
much by ftorms, that they were obliged to fend back one of
their largeft veffels to France. It was not till the fifth of December that they were able to fail directly for the place of their
deftination, which was the northern coaft of Ireland. In this
voyage their ill fortune continued to purfue them. For near
three months they were obliged to ply off and on among the
weftern ifles of Scotland, during which time they fuffered every
poffible hardfhip: their men thinned and difheartened, fuffering
by famine and difeafe, one fhip irrecoverably loft, and the remaining three fo fhattered, that they were obliged to put into
the ifle of Ilay. Here this enterprifing adventurer, though op-
preffed with misfortune, and fteeled by fuch hardfhips as too
often extinguifh every generous principle of humanity, behaved
with the utmoft juftice and moderation, paying handfomely for
the cattle and provifions which he had occafion to ufe, and
treating the natives with unufual courtefy and kindnefs.

As foon as the weather permitted, Thurot quitted this ifland,
and purfued his deftination to the bay of Carrickfergus in Ireland, where, on the 21ft of February, he effected a defcent with
600 men. They advanced without oppofition to the town,
which they found as well guarded as the nature of the place,
which was entirely open, and the circumftances of Colonel Jennings, who commanded only four companies of raw undifciplined men, would allow. A vigorous defence was made, until
the ammunition of the Englifh failed; and then Colonel Jennings
retired to the caftle of Carrickfergus, which, however, was in
all refpects untenable, being unprovided in provifions and ammunition, and having a breach in the wall of near fifty feet wide:
neverthelefs, they repulfed the affailants in their firft attack,
having fupplied the want of fhot with ftones and rubbifh. At
length the colonel furrendered, on condition that his troops
fhould be ranfomed by exchanging them for an equal number of
French prifoners; that the caftle of Carrickfergus fhould not be
demolifhed, nor the town burned or plundered. This laft circumftance, however, was not ftrictly obferved. The magiftrates
of Carrickfergus refufed fuch fupplies of wine and provifions as
the French officers demanded, and thus, by their own impru-

dence,

dence, caused the town to be subjected to a contribution, which, A. D however, was not immoderate. Thurot, having by this time 1760 got notice of the defeat of Conflans's expedition, and hearing that a confiderable body of regular troops were affembled, and preparing to march to the affiftance of the inhabitants of Carrickfergus, embarked, and fet fail for France, after gaining great reputation by the exploits of a fquadron, which deferves to be confidered as little better than a wreck of the grand enterprife againft the Britifh coafts.

But this gallant adventurer had not left the bay of Carrickfergus many hours, when he perceived, near the coaft of the ifle of Man, three fail that bore down on him. Thefe were Englifh frigates, the Æolus of thirty-fix guns, commanded by Captain Elliot, the Pallas and Brilliant, each of thirty-two guns, under the command of the Captains Clements and Logie, who had been defpatched by the duke of Bedford, lord-lieutenant of Ireland, in queft of the French fquadron. At nine in the morning of the 28th of February, Captain Elliot came up with the Belleifle, commanded by Thurot, which was fuperior to the Æolus in ftrength of men, number of guns, and weight of metal; but both fhip and men were in a bad condition. The engagement was hardly begun, when the Pallas and Brilliant attacked the other two fhips of the enemy. The action was maintained with great fpirit on both fides for an hour and a half, when Captain Elliot's lieutenant boarded the Belleifle, who immediately ftruck her colours, the gallant Thurot having fallen in the action. The Englifh took poffeffion of their prizes, and conveyed them into the bay of Ramfay in the Ifle of Man. In this engagement three hundred of the French were flain, or difabled; whereas our lofs did not exceed forty killed and wounded. The name of Thurot had become fo terrible to all the fea-ports of Britain and Ireland, that the fervice performed on this occafion was deemed effential to the quiet and fecurity of thefe kingdoms. The thanks of the houfe of commons of Ireland were voted to the conquerors of Thurot as well as to lieutenant-colonel Jennings, the commanding officer at Carrickfergus; and the defeat and capture of this petty fquadron was celebrated with the moft hearty and univerfal rejoicings. Such was the fate of the laft branch of the grand armament which had so long been the hope of France, and the terror of Great Britain.

In North America the affairs of the French had taken such a turn as afforded them a happy prospect of future success. While the operations of the war there were intrusted to the land-forces alone, England was unfortunate, and France triumphant : but no sooner did our squadrons appear on the coast, than every thing returned to its former situation, and Britain was as victorious as before. The garrison left for the defence of Quebec amounted originally to 5000 men, a number much too small, considering both the nature of the place, and the number of French forces which still remained in Canada. The fortifications of Quebec were weak and incomplete, without any kind of outworks; and the town had been reduced, during the late siege, almost to a ruin. Mr. Levi had collected at Montreal 6000 experienced militia of Canada, with 300 Indians, besides ten battalions of regular troops, amounting to about 5000 men more. With this force he took the field on the 17th of April; and while his provisions and ammunition fell down the river St. Lawrence under a convoy of six frigates, the French army arrived in ten days march at the heights of Abraham, three miles distant from Quebec. General Murray, who commanded the garrison, had it in his option either to remain within the city, or to march out and try his fortune in the field. As his troops were habituated to victory, and provided with a fine train of artillery, he was unwilling to keep them shut up in a place which appeared to him scarcely tenable. He determined, therefore, to lead them against the enemy; a resolution, which, considering the immense inequality of numbers, (for, although the garrison originally consisted of 5000, he had not now above 3000 effective men), favoured more of youthful temerity than of military discretion. At first, however, fortune seemed to favour his designs. The English army, having marched out of the city, and descended from the heights of Abraham, attacked the enemy's van with such impetuosity, that it was obliged to give way, and to fall back on the main body. This advantage brought them full on the main army of the French, which by this time had formed in columns. The fire became so hot, that it stopped the progress of our troops; and the French,

**wheeling**

wheeled to right and left, formed a femicircle which threatened to furround them, and to cut off their retreat. Near a third
of the Englifh army were now killed or wounded, and nothing
could be thought of in this fituation but to make proper movements to fecure their return to Quebec. This they effected
without lofing many men in the purfuit; and the fevere misfortune, occafioned by their own temerity, roufed the governor
and troops to the moft ftrenuous efforts in defence of the place.
The French loft no time in improving their victory. They
opened the trenches on the very night of the battle: but, being deficient in artillery, they had performed nothing of confequence before the 15th of May, when the befieged were reinforced by the arrival of the Britifh fleet. Then the enemy
underftood what it was to be inferior at fea; for, had a French
fquadron got the ftart of the Englifh in failing up the river,
Quebec muft have reverted to its former owners.

On the 9th of May, to the great joy of the garrifon, an
Englifh frigate anchored in the bay, and told them that Lord
Colville who had failed from Halifax with the fleet under his
command, on the 22d of April, was then in the river St. Lawrence. He had been retarded in his paffage by thick fogs and
contrary winds. About the fame time Commodore Swanton,
arriving with a fmall reinforcement from England, and hearing
that Quebec was befieged, failed up the St. Lawrence with all
expedition. On the 15th he anchored at Point Levi, and early
next morning ordered Captain Schomberg of the Diana, and
Captain Deane of the Loweftoffe to flip their cables, and attack
the French fleet, confifting of two frigates, two armed fhips,
and a confiderable number of fmaller veffels. They were no
fooner in motion than the French fhips fled in the utmoft diforder. One of their frigates was driven on the rocks above Cape
Diamond; the other ran afhore, and was burned at Point au
Tremble, about ten leagues above the town, and all that remained were taken or deftroyed.

Mr. Levi had the mortification to behold, from the heights of
Abraham, this action, which at one ftroke put an end to all the
hopes he had conceived from his late victory. He was perfuaded that thefe frigates, by the boldnefs of their manner, preceded a confiderable reinforcement, and he therefore raifed the

fiege

siege in the utmost precipitation, leaving behind him a great quantity of baggage, tents, stores, magazines of provisions and ammunition, with thirty-four pieces of battering cannon, ten field-pieces, six mortars, and a great number of scaling-ladders, intrenching tools, and other implements necessary in a siege.

This event, which was entirely owing to the seasonable assistance of the fleet, was equally important in itself and in its consequences. While it secured the possession of Quebec, it gave an opportunity to General Murray to march to the assistance of General Amherst, who was employed in the siege of Montreal, the second place in Canada for extent, commerce, and strength. Here the whole remaining force of the French in North America was collected under the command of Mr. Vaudreuil, an enterprising and artful general, who neglected no means of protracting the siege. At length he was obliged to yield to the united armies, and on the 8th of September, 1760, surrendered his garrison to be sent to France, on condition that they should not serve in the present war, and yielded up the inhabitants of his government as subjects to the king of Great Britain.

The French had not neglected to send relief to a place, which was the last object of their hopes for regaining possession of Canada. They had despatched three frigates, with twenty ships of burden, containing a reinforcement of troops and military stores for the garrison of Montreal. But when the commander of this expedition understood, that the fleet under Lord Colville had anticipated his arrival in the river St. Lawrence, he attempted to land his whole embarkation in the bay of Chaleurs, that they might endeavour, if possible, to join the principal army by land. But here they were discovered by Captain Byron with three of his majesty's ships; their armament was taken or destroyed, and their whole design disconcerted. Thus, by the bravery of our troops, and the uncommon spirit, vigilance, and activity of our navy, every attempt of the enemy was frustrated, and the quiet possession of all Canada confirmed to Great Britain.

In the East-Indies the British arms were attended with equal success. After raising the siege of Fort St. George in February 1759, the English army possessed themselves of the important town and fortress of Conjeveram, as well as of the city Masulipatam,

patam, both on the Coromandel coaft. This coaft joins to the A. D
rich province of Bengal, where the French intereft had been 1760
totally ruined by the conduct and gallantry of Colonel Clive.

Encouraged by thefe advantages, a body of 1200 men, Europeans and Seapoys, advanced farther, and attempted to diflodge
an army of French and their confederate Indians, encamped under the cannon of a fort near Wandewafh. They were repelled
with the lofs of between three and four hundred killed and
wounded. But Colonel Coote, at the head of the principal body
of Englifh troops on that coaft, compenfated for this difafter by
invefting and taking Wandewafh in three days. Soon after, he
obtained a complete victory over General Lally, who commanded an army twice as numerous as that of the Englifh, and confifting of 2200 Europeans and 10,000 blacks. After this decifive engagement, which, excepting the battle of Plaiffy, was
more important in its confequences than any fought in India
during the war, Colonel Coote undertook the fiege of Chilliput,
which furrendered in two days. He then profecuted his march
to Arcot the capital of the province, the fort of which being
filenced, the garrifon furrendered themfelves prifoners of war.
After the reduction of Arcot all the inferior places, fuch as Per-
macoil and Allumparva, fubmitted. The important fettlement
of Carrical was reduced by the fea and land forces, commanded
by Rear-admiral Cornifh and Major Monfon; and Colonel
Coote formed the blockade of Pondicherry by land, while the
harbour was befet by the Englifh fquadron. This town was the
only important fettlement which now remained to our enemies
in India.

During all this time Admiral Pocock had, with his ufual
fkill and intrepidity, feconded the efforts of the troops. He had
more than once compelled Mr. d'Aché, the greateft admiral
that France could boaft of, and who alone fupported the declining reputation of her marine, to take fhelter under the walls
of Pondicherry. Pocock had reduced the French fhips to a
very fhattered condition, and killed a great many of their men;
but, what fhews the fingular talents of both admirals, they had
fought three pitched battles in the courfe of eighteen months,
without the lofs of a fhip on either fide.

The

A. D.  The Britifh fquadrons in the Weft-Indies were commanded
1760. by Admiral Holmes on the Jamaica ftation and Sir James Douglas in the Leeward iflands.   The active vigilance of thefe
commanders not only enabled them to protect the iflands from
infult or invafion, but prompted them to annoy the enemy.
Rear-admiral Holmes, having in the month of October received
intelligence, that five French frigates were equipped at Cape
François on the ifland of Hifpaniola, in order to convoy a fleet
of merchantmen to Europe, he ftationed the fhips under his
command in fuch a manner as gave them an opportunity to
intercept this fleet.  The principal French fhip was the Sirenne,
commanded by Commodore M'Cartie, an Irifh officer of confiderable reputation.   After two fharp engagements fhe ftruck
to the Boreas, while the other four frigates bore away, with all
the fail they could crowd, for the weft end of Tortuga, to fhelter themfelves in Port au Prince.   They were purfued by the
Lively and Hampfhire; the former obliged one of the French
frigates to fubmit, after a warm engagement of an hour and a
half.  The Hampfhire ftood for the other three, and, running
between the Duke of Choifeul and the Prince Edward, engaged
them both at the fame time.   The firft, having the advantage
of the wind, made her retreat into Port au Paix: the other ran
afhore about two leagues to leeward, and ftruck her colours.  At
the approach of the Hampfhire, the enemy fet her on fire, and
fhe blew up.  The Fleur de Lys, that had run into Frefh-water
bay, a little to leeward of Port au Prince, fhared the fame fate;
and thus by the gallantry of the Captains Norbury, Uvedale, and
Maitland, and the prudent difpofition of Admiral Holmes, two
large frigates of the enemy were taken, and three deftroyed.

Immediately after this event, advice being received by Admiral
Holmes, that the enemy's privateers fwarmed about the ifland
of Cuba, he ordered the boats of the Trent and Boreas to be
manned, that they might proceed, under the direction of the
Lieutenants Millar and Stuart, to the harbour of Cumberland in
that ifland.  There they met with the Vainqueur of ten guns,
fixteen fwivels, and ninety men, the Mackau of fix fwivels and
fifteen men, and the Guefpe of eight guns and eighty-five men.
The boats, after furmounting many difficulties, rowed up to the
Vainqueur, boarded and took poffeffion of her under a clofe fire.
                                                            The

The Mackau was taken without refiftance; but, before they A. D. could reach the Guelpe, the enemy fet her on fire, by which 1760. fhe was deftroyed.

The fame enterprifing courage diftinguifhed the officers of the fquadron commanded by Sir James Douglas off the Leeward Iflands. The Captains Obrien and Taylor, cruifing near the Grenades, were informed that the Virgin, once a Britifh floop, with three French privateers, had taken refuge under the guns of three forts on one of thefe iflands. They failed thither in order to attack them; and their enterprize was crowned with fuccefs. Having demolifhed the forts, they took the four fhips after a warm engagement, which lafted feveral hours. They next entered another harbour on the fame ifland, where they had intelligence of three more fhips; they demolifhed the fort on this harbour, and carried off the three prizes. In returning to Antigua they fell in with thirteen victuallers, who immediately furrendered. At the fame time eight privateers were taken by the fhips which Commodore Douglas employed in cruifing round the ifland of Guadaloupe.

While the Englifh were carried forward with a continual tide of profperity in diftant parts of the world, no action of importance was achieved in the Britifh feas by the naval force of that kingdom. Admiral Rodney ftill maintained his ftation off the coaft of Havre de Grace, to obferve the French movements towards the mouth of the Seine. The Admirals Bofcawen and Hawke alternately commanded the powerful fquadron which ftill remained in the bay of Quiberon, to interrupt the navigation of the enemy, to watch and detain the French veffels which had run into the mouth of the river Villaine after the defeat of Conflans; and to divert the efforts of the French from other quarters, by employing a great number of their forces on that part of the coaft.

Meanwhile a numerous body of forces were affembled, and a great number of tranfports collected at Portfmouth. The troops were actually embarked with a good train of artillery; generals were nominated to the command of the enterprize; and the eyes of the whole nation were fixed upon this armament, which had been prepared at an immenfe expence, and the deftination of which remained a profound fecret. But, to

the

A. D. the aftonifhment of all thofe who were not admitted behind the
1760. curtain, the whole fummer was fpent in idlenefs and inaction,
and upon the death of the late king, in the month of October
following, the enterprize was entirely laid afide.

The feeming inutility of thefe mighty preparations occafioned
loud clamours in the nation. Thefe were ftill farther increafed
by the inactivity of the powerful fquadrons in the Britifh feas.
It was faid, that with either of thefe, or with the armament
prepared at Portfmouth, we might have reduced the ifland of
Martinico in the Weft-Indies, Mauritius on the coaft of Africa,
or Minorca in the Mediterranean, all of which were objects
equally important to our power and commerce. It was afked
what advantage we derived from thofe fquadrons which were
fo well provided in all neceffaries by the liberality of the fupplies,
but which were condemned to inactivity, or employed in ufelefs
parade? This queftion, however, was not unanfwerable. The
armament at Portfmouth might be intended to intimidate the
French into propofals of peace; to alarm the coaft of Bretagne,
and thereby make a diverfion in favour of Germany; or to
tranfport troops into Flanders, in order to effect a junction
with the hereditary prince of Brunfwick, who, at the head of
20,000 men, had croffed the Rhine, and was at firft as fuccefsful as finally unfortunate in that daring expedition.

Nor were the fquadrons on the French coaft altogether unneceffary. While Admiral Rodney hovered near the mouth of the
Seine he perceived, on the 5th of July at noon-day, five large
flat-bottomed boats, with their colours flying, as if they had
fet the Englifh fquadron at defiance. Thefe boats were defpatched, by way of experiment, to try whether it were poffible
for veffels of this newly invented conftruction to efcape the vigilance and efforts of an Englifh fleet. The French had prepared above an hundred of them, which then lay at Caen in
Normandy. The ten which now failed ftood backwards and
forwards on the fhoals, intending to amufe Mr. Rodney till
night, and then to proceed under cover of darknefs. He perceived their drift, and gave directions that his fmall veffels fhould
be ready to fail in the night for the mouth of the river Orne, in
order to cut off the enemy's retreat, while he himfelf with the
larger fhips ftood for the fteep coaft of Port Baffin. The dif-

position was judicious, and attended with succefs. The flat-
bottomed boats, having no way to escape, ran ashore at Port
Baffin, where the admiral destroyed them, together with the
small fort which had been erected for the defence of this harbour. Each of these vessels was one hundred feet in length,
and capable of containing four hundred men. The disaster
which befel them taught the French minister of the marine not
to build any further hopes upon such aukward machines. The
remainder were ordered to be unloaded at Caen, and sent to
Rouen to be laid up as useless.

This was not the only service which Rodney's squadron performed. In the month of November Captain Ourry of the
Acteon chased a large privateer, and drove her on shore between Cape Barfleur and La Hogue; and his cutters scoured
the coast, and took or destroyed forty vessels of considerable
burden, which carried on a great fishing near Dieppe.

Besides the purposes above mentioned, which were answered
by Admiral Boscawen's fleet, it effectually prevented any vessels
from sailing from the harbours of Breft or Rochfort, with the
design to reinforce the French in North America, which might
have protracted the war there to another campaign. The enterprizing spirit of this English admiral, impatient of continuing
so long in a state of inaction, how advantageous soever to the
interests of his country, prompted him to employ his men in
the execution of some actual service. He exercised them, therefore, in taking a small island near the river Vannes, which he
ordered them to cultivate and plant with vegetables for the use
of the seamen infected with scorbutic disorders, arising from
the constant use of salt provisions, from the sea air, and from a
want of proper exercise.

Sir Edward Hawke, who relieved Mr. Boscawen in September, pursued the same plan. Sensible of the inconveniencies to
which a fleet on that station is exposed for want of fresh water,
which must be carried to them by transports hired on purpose,
he detached Lord Howe in the Magnanime, with the ships Frederick and Bedford, to reduce the little island Dumet, which
abounded in that great necessary of life. This island, about
three miles in length and two in breadth, was defended by a
small fort mounted with nine cannon, and garrisoned with one

A. D. company of the regiment of Bourbon, who furrendered with
1700. little or no refiftance after the fhips had begun the attack.

We have not interrupted the hiftory of the Britifh fquadrons
by relating the exploits of particular cruizers, feveral of which
conferred the higheft honour on the Englifh navy. On the 2d
of April Captain Skinner of the Biddeford, and Captain Kennedy of the Flamborough, both frigates, having failed from Lifbon, fell in with two large French frigates, convoy to a fleet of
merchant fhips, which the Englifh captains immediately determined to engage, notwithftanding the great inferiority of their
ftrength. The enemy did not decline the battle, which began
about half an hour after fix in the evening, and raged with
great fury till eleven. By this time the Flamborough had loft
fight of the Biddeford, and the frigate with which the former
was engaged bore away with all the fail fhe could carry. Captain Kennedy purfued her till noon the next day, when he entirely loft fight of her; by which means fhe got into Lifbon
with the lofs of feveral men befides the lieutenant of marines,
and confiderably damaged in her hull and rigging. In three
days he was joined by the Biddeford, who, after a moft fevere
conflict, had compelled her antagonift to fly, and had chafed
her till fhe was out of fight. Soon after the action began,
Captain Skinner, while ftanding upon the arm-cheft to infpect
the feveral pofts, and to animate his men by his example, was
unfortunately killed. He was an officer equally brave and
bountiful, and as much beloved for his gentlenefs and humanity
as refpected for his fkill and courage by thofe who ferved under
him. The command devolved upon the honourable Lieutenant
Knollis, who maintained the battle with great fpirit, even after
he was wounded, till a fecond fhot through his body deprived him of life. Notwithftanding thefe difafters, the crew of
the Biddeford, though deprived of their officers, their main-
top-maft fhot away, the fhip difabled in her rigging, and the
enemy's fire which continued exceedingly hot, difcovered no
figns of fear, or of difinclination to the fervice. The mafter
of the fhip now affumed the command, and every man aboard
acted as if on his perfonal bravery alone the fortune of the
engagement had depended. While the mafter kept the quarter-
deck, and took care of the pofts there, the purfer was ftationed

on

on the main-deck, and kept up a brisk and well-directed fire. A. D.
Numbers of the wounded men returned with cheerfulness to 1760.
their posts, after the surgeon had dressed their wounds. Their
cool determined valour prevailed over a ship double their own
in strength. The enemy's fire began to slacken, one gun becoming silent after another, till the enemy did not discharge
four guns in a quarter of an hour. It was believed they were going to strike; but it proved, that they were preparing for flight;
for a little after, about ten at night, the engagement having
lasted three hours, they bore away with all the sail they could
crowd. The Biddeford took the opportunity to pour a broadside into her enemy, and a volley of small arms nearly at the
same instant. But, when she attempted to chase, the sailors
found they had no command of their ship, the rigging being
cut to pieces, and the masts and yards shattered and disabled.

The spirit of enterprize, a consciousness of their own superiority, and a contempt of the French, seem to have been communicated to the meanest seaman of Great Britain at this happy
period. As an example of this kind, the bravery of five Irish-
men and a boy, belonging to the crew of a ship from Water-
ford, has been much celebrated. The ship, in her return from
Bilboa, being taken by a French privateer off Ushant, the captors removed all the hands but these five men and a boy, who
were left to assist nine Frenchmen in navigating the vessel. These
daring Hibernians immediately formed a plan of insurrection,
which they executed with success. Four of the French mariners
being below deck, three aloft among the rigging, one at the
helm, and another walking the deck, Brian, who headed the
enterprize, tripped up the heels of the French steersman, seized
his pistol, and discharged it at him who walked the deck; but,
missing the mark, he knocked him down with the butt-end of
the piece. At the same time hallooing to his confederates below, they assailed the enemy with their broad swords, and, soon
compelling them to submit, came upon deck, and shut the
hatches. The Irish being now in possession of the quarter-deck,
the French who were aloft called for quarter, and surrendered
without opposition. As neither Brian nor any of his associates
could read or write, or knew the least principle of navigation,
they steered the ship northward at a venture, and the first land

they

A. D.  they made was the neighbourhood of Youghall in the county
1760.  of Cork.

The captures from the French, within the courfe of this year,
confifted of royal fhips of war, privateers, and armed merchantmen. The royal fhips were fix, mounting in all 176 guns.
The privateers and armed merchantmen amounted to 110,
which carried 848 carriage-guns, 240 fwivels, and 6389 men.
The Englifh navy fuffered little from the French during this period, but fuftained great damage from the weather. The Conqueror, a new fhip of the line, was loft in the channel off the
ifland of St. Nicholas; the crew and guns were faved. The
Lyme of twenty guns foundered in the Cattegate in Norway,
and fifty of the men perifhed. In the Weft Indies a tender, belonging to the Dublin commanded by commodore Sir James
Douglas, was loft in a gale of wind, with 100 chofen mariners.
But thefe loffes, great as they were, feemed inconfiderable, compared to that of the Ramillies, a magnificent fhip of the fecond
rate, belonging to the fquadron which Admiral Bofcawen commanded on the coaft of France, In the beginning of February
a feries of ftormy weather obliged the admiral to return from
the bay of Quiberon to Plymouth, where he arrived with much
difficulty. The Ramillies, having overfhot the entrance to the
found, and being embayed near a point called the Bolt-head,
about four leagues higher up the channel, was dafhed in pieces
among the rocks, after her anchors and cables had given way.
All her officers and men, (one midfhipman and twenty-five of
the feamen excepted), amounting to 700, perifhed.

The number of merchant veffels taken by the French amounted to above 300, chiefly, however, coafters and colliers of very
inconfiderable value. Nor would it have been at all furprifing
if the French had taken not only more numerous but more valuable prizes. While their own commerce was in a great meafure deftroyed, and they had no merchant fhips at fea but fome
coafters, and a few veffels, under convoy from the Weft Indies,
the trading fleets of England covered the ocean. Every year her
commerce was augmenting; the money which the war carried
out was returned by the produce of her induftry; the finking
fund amounted annually to above three millions, and, in the
year

year 1760, 8000 veſſels were employed by the traders of Great
Britain.

But, notwithſtanding this happy flow of proſperity, if we compare the naval and military tranſactions of the preſent year with thoſe of the preceding, they will appear extremely inconſiderable. Excepting the reduction of Montreal, which was a natural conſequence of our prior conqueſts in Canada, no additional acquiſitions of great conſequence had been made by the Britiſh arms. The Engliſh ſtrength and wealth were employed in the war of Germany ; but our operations, undertaken upon national principles, and tending to the intereſt of Great Britain, began gradually to languiſh. It was hoped, therefore, that after a general war of five years, carried on upon a larger ſcale, and attended with greater expence, and more ſurpriſing revolutions of fortune, than any war of equal duration that had ever taken place among the nations of Europe, it was now full time to give tranquillity to the four quarters of the globe, all of which had been ſhaken by our commotions. The poſture of affairs was now much altered from what had taken place during the firſt periods of hoſtility. The ambition of France, which had inflamed the fuel of diſſention, had been crowned with ſucceſs in the beginning of the war. Admiral Byng behaved diſgracefully in the Mediterranean, Minorca was taken, and the battle of Haſtembeck ſeemed to decide the fate of the electorate of Hanover. The duke of Cumberland was ſhut up at Cloſterſeven, and the Canadians obtained conſiderable advantages over the Engliſh in North America. But now all was changed. The French had not reaped the fruits which they expected from their ſucceſs in Germany, and had been obliged to abandon ſome part of their conqueſts; their intereſt was totally ruined in North America; in the Eaſt Indies, where they had formerly ſo many flouriſhing ſettlements, they were confined to one town; and the principal ſource of their wealth was cut off by the loſs of Guadaloupe, Goree, and Senegal, and the deſtruction of their commerce and ſhipping. The misfortunes which France had already experienced in carrying on a naval war againſt Great Britain, induced her, as early as the year 1758, to ſignify her pacific intentions to the Engliſh miniſtry, who declined liſtening at that time to any propoſals of negotiation. In the following

year

A. D. year the court of London was not so decisively bent on continu-
1760. ing the war; but it was not till 1761 that they began to think se-
riously of laying down their victorious arms. Had France been
equally sincere in the wishes for accommodation which she publicly professed, matters might then have been amicably adjusted.
But she had by this time discovered an after game, which remained for her to play, notwithstanding all her bad fortune.
She had alarmed the pride and jealousy of the court of Spain,
whose rich and extensive American possessions seemed now to
lie at the mercy of the English colonies, and whose honour was
deeply wounded in the disgrace inflicted on the first prince of
the house of Bourbon. If the whole strength of the Spanish monarchy, augmented by continual accessions during a long peace,
could be drawn into the vortex of hostility, France expected to
be able still to retrieve her affairs. While she publicly declared
for peace, her secret hopes were all centered in war; she treated of friendship with a spirit of enmity; and, the false principles
upon which she negotiated being discovered by the penetration
of the British ministry, these allowed not the prospect of a treaty to amuse them into a neglect of the naval and military operations which had been previously concerted.

The parliament which assembled the 18th of November,
1760, had voted 70,000 seamen for the service of the ensuing
year, including 18355 marines, and a sum not exceeding four
pounds monthly *per* man for their maintenance, the whole
amounting to 3,640,000 pounds. No material alteration was
made in the disposition of the several squadrons which consti-
tuted the navy of Great Britain. That in the bay of Quiberon
was commanded by Sir Edward Hawke and Sir Charles Hardy.
Admiral Saunders was stationed in the Mediterranean. The
Rear-admirals Stevens and Cornish commanded in the East-Indies, Rear-admiral Holmes at Jamaica, Sir James Douglas at
the Leeward islands, and Lord Colville at Halifax in Nova
Scotia. Besides these, single ships cruised in different parts, in
order to protect the British merchantmen, and squadrons were
occasionally equipped under various commanders.

1761.    The scene of action, in the year 1761, opened in the East-
Indies. After the defeat of the French near Wandewash, the
taking of the city Arcot, and the reduction of the fortresses of
Chilliput

Chilliput and Carrical, the French were blocked up in Pondicherry, a town of near four miles in circuit, elegantly built, strongly fortified, and defended by the whole force which remained to the enemy on the coaft of Coromandel. The periodical rains which fall on that coaft rendered a regular fiege impracticable; fo that the blockade, which had been commenced by the fleet under Admiral Stevens and the land forces under Colonel Coote, was continued with the beft difpofition, and the moft extraordinary patience, for full feven months. On the 26th of November, 1760, four batteries were raifed, at fome diftance, to enfilade the ftreets of Pondicherry, whilft others were advanced nearer, in order to play upon the works. The works of the befiegers fuffered much from ftorms, which ruined the batteries and approaches: but thefe were repaired with great alacrity, and the enemy was reduced to the moft extreme diftrefs. They lived on camels, elephants, dogs, and cats. Even this wretched provifion was fo fcarce, that it was purchafed at an immenfe price: five pounds had been paid for the flefh of a dog.

In the midft of this diftrefs their hopes were fuddenly revived by a dreadful misfortune which happened to the Englifh fleet. On the firft of January, 1761, one of thofe terrible tempefts, fo deftructive and fo frequent in the Indian feas, obliged Admiral Stevens to flip his cables and put to fea. The reft of the Britifh fquadron were driven from before the walls of Pondicherry. The duke of Aquitaine and the Sunderland foundered in the ftorm, and their crews perifhed. The Newcaftle, the Queenborough, and Protector fire-fhip, were driven on fhore and deftroyed; but the men were happily faved, together with the guns, ftores, and provifions. Many other fhips fuftained confiderable damage. This unexpected difafter elevated to the higheft pitch the fpirits of the garrifon, and general Lally, feeing the port clear, loft not a moment to fend an exprefs to the French agent in the neighbouring neutral fettlements, in order to obtain a fupply of provifions. This letter was intercepted by Admiral Stevens, and is publifhed in the appendix *; as it difcovers the fingular character of this daring adventurer. As the

___

* Appendix, N° VIII.

admiral

A. D. 1761. admiral imagined, that Lally had made the same solicitations by other messengers, he immediately despatched letters to the Dutch and Danish settlements, mentioning the good condition of the greater part of his fleet, and assuring them that he would make prize of such vessels as he found infringing the neutrality by attempting to supply the enemy. He was sufficiently in a condition to make good his threats; for, in four days after the storm, he had, with incredible diligence and celerity, repaired the damage of his ships, and appeared before Pondicherry with eleven sail of the line and two frigates, all fit for service. The siege was now carried on with redoubled ardour. By the 15th of January a battery was raised within point blank; a breach was effected in the curtain; the west face and flank of the northwest bastion were ruined, and the guns of the enemy entirely silenced. The principal of the Jesuits came out with two civilians, and proposed terms of capitulation in the name of the inhabitants. General Lally disdained to capitulate, but sent out a paper, full of invectives against the English for breach of treaties relative to India : the obstinacy of the governor made the proposal of the inhabitants be disregarded; so that the city of Pondicherry, with a garrison of near 2000 European soldiers, a vast quantity of military stores, and great riches, was, without any formal surrender, abandoned to the discretion of the besiegers.

After the reduction of Pondicherry on the coast of Coromandel, a body of English forces was embarked for an expedition against Mahie, a settlement on the coast of Malabar, which the French had lately fortified at a very considerable expence. The place was attacked with so much vigour, that the French governor thought proper to surrender it about the beginning of February, by which means the English obtained the command of the whole peninsula of India, the most extensive as well as the most profitable sphere of commerce in the world.

These important successes had not, since the commencement of the war, been chequered by any considerable misfortune attending the British arms in the east. We must not, however, omit to mention the achievements of the Count d'Estaing, who in the year 1759 had made himself master of the English fort of Gombroon in the Gulf of Persia, and taken two frigates, with

2

three

three other veſſels belonging to the company. He performed A. D. this with four ſhips under Dutch colours, one of which carried 1761. ſixty-four guns, and another twenty-two, with a land force of 150 Europeans, and about 200 Caffres. In the ſucceeding year the fort of Natal on the coaſt of Africa ſurrendered to him at diſcretion, and he found two ſhips in the road. He afterwards ſailed to Sumatra, where the Engliſh carried on a great trade in pepper, and, before the end of the following April, reduced, Tapponapoli and Bencoolen or Marlborough fort, which laſt, though in a good ſtate of defence, was ingloriouſly abandoned by the Engliſh garriſon, after they had burnt a veſſel richly loaded, (the Denham Indiaman), that lay in the harbour. The activity and enterprize of Mr. d'Eſtaing would deſerve commendation, if his character had not been ſtrongly marked with perfidy and cruelty. He had ſurrendered himſelf at the ſiege of Madraſs, and had engaged not to ſerve againſt the Engliſh until he ſhould be regularly exchanged; ſo that, when he attacked Gambroon, he was a priſoner on parole. When he became maſter of that place, he paid no regard to the terms on which it had ſurrendered. He promiſed to prevent thefts and diſorders; but the houſes were ſet on fire, and the factory given up to the licentious pillage of the Arabs.

After the expulſion of the French from North America, the Engliſh found in the Cherokees a cruel and barbarous and not an unwarlike enemy. They defended themſelves with a ſavage heroiſm againſt the ſuperior arts of a civilized nation, nor could they be reduced to the neceſſity of accepting a peace from their conquerors, until the Engliſh had penetrated with great courage and perſeverance into their country, deſtroyed fifteen of their towns or villages, and burnt or cut down the greateſt part of their harveſt.

While the continent of North America was thus reduced to a ſtate of undiſturbed obedience, the Britiſh ſquadrons were ſtill carrying on their conqueſts in the Weſt-Indies. On the fourth of June Sir James Douglas ſailed from Guadaloupe with the Dublin, Belliqueux, Sunderland, and Montague, four ſhips of he line, and a conſiderable body of land forces under the command of Lord Rollo, deſtined for an expedition againſt the iſland of Dominica. This iſland, though one of thoſe called neutral,

A. D. had been occupied and fortified by the French.  Its extent is
1761. about ten leagues in length, and eight in breadth; it is well
watered by rivers plentifully supplied with fish; produces abundant pasture for cattle, and is very fruitful in coffee, cocoa, tobacco, and cotton.  It is situated within ten leagues of Martinico, the capital of the French sugar-islands, which, in case of
an invasion, it could easily supply with men and provisions; a
circumstance which rendered it of great importance to France,
and an object worthy the ambition of the British ministry.

The armament under Lord-Rollo and Sir James Douglas arrived within a league of Roseau, the capital of Dominica, on
the sixth of June; and, the fleet having anchored, a lieutenant
of the navy, accompanied by a land-officer, was immediately
despatched with a manifesto, signed by the commodore and general, requiring the inhabitants of the neutral island of Dominica to surrender, and take the oaths of allegiance to his majesty King George.  The manifesto being read to the people of
Roseau, some of the principal inhabitants set off in a boat, and
went on board the English fleet.  Their behaviour and conversation discovered no dislike to the British government: on the
contrary, they seemed very well pleased that his majesty's forces
had come to take possession of the island.  But, when they were
put on shore in the afternoon, they, as well as the rest of the
inhabitants, were encouraged by the French governor, Mr.
Longprice, to stand on the defensive, and to declare they would
not tamely surrender, while they had arms in their hands.  As
soon as this determination was known, the ships anchored
as near as possible to the shore, and the necessary dispositions
were made for landing the troops.  This was effected, about
five in the evening, under cover of the shipping.  They formed
quickly on the beach; and, while the main division took possession of the town, the corps of grenadiers, consisting of the
companies of the fourth and twenty-second regiments, seized a
flanking battery, and part of the adjoining entrenchment, which
had been abandoned.  But the enemy continued to annoy the
British troops by their musquetry from behind bushes and trees,
and by their cannon fired from a battery which overlooked the
town.  By this means the troops might have suffered greatly
during the night; the enemy, perhaps, might have been reinforced

forced before morning, and, fortified in a ſtrong poſt with four A. L
entrenchments on a ſteep hill, might have been enabled to make 1761
a vigorous defence. Lord Rollo, therefore, judged it beſt to
order them to be immediately diſlodged by the grenadiers ſupported by the battalions; which ſervice was performed with
ſo much order and rapidity, that, before night, the French
were driven ſucceſſively from all their entrenchments, and the
battery above them, where Colonel Melvill immediately took
poſt with his grenadiers. Lord Rollo continued at their advanced poſt during the night, having eſtabliſhed a communication,
by proper guards, with the reſt of the troops who poſſeſſed the
town. Next day he eſtabliſhed his head-quarters at Roſeau,
where he received the ſubmiſſion of the inhabitants, who came
to lay down their arms, and take the oaths of allegiance to his
Britannic majeſty.

While this important conqueſt was acquired by the aſſiſtance
of part of the ſquadron belonging to the Leeward iſlands, the
remainder were employed in protecting the Britiſh traders, and
ſcouring thoſe ſeas of the Martinico privateers, of which they
took a great number. Nor was the ſquadron ſtationed off Jamaica leſs vigilant, or leſs alert: Rear-admiral Holmes, who
commanded there, planned his cruiſes with judgment, and executed them with ſucceſs. Having received intelligence in the
beginning of June, that ſeveral ſhips of war belonging to the
enemy had ſailed from Port Louis, he immediately made ſuch a
diſpoſition of his ſquadron as was moſt likely to intercept them.
He himſelf in the Hampſhire fell in with the St. Anne, and
chaſed her to leeward down upon the Centaur. The French
captain, perceiving this laſt ſhip, and dreading the danger of
being between two fires, hauled up between them, and ran cloſe
in ſhore, until he was becalmed about a league to the northward of Donna-Maria bay. The Centaur chaſed, and got up
along-ſide; upon which the Frenchman, who had fired his ſtern
chace, ſtruck his colours, and ſurrendered a very fine ſhip,
pierced for ſixty-four guns, loaded with coffee, ſugar, and indigo, and manned with near 400 ſailors and marines.

Earlier in the ſame year the French were foiled in an attempt
to regain a footing on the coaſt of Africa. They were too ſenſible of the advantages attending the lucrative trade of this coaſt,

Z 2

A. D. to remain satisfied under a total exclusion from it. In order to
761. recover some part of what they had lost, they sent two frigates
to surprize James-fort at the mouth of the Gambia. The little
garrison there, received them with such resolution, that one
frigate was forced on shore, and lost; and the other sailed
off, after having sustained considerable damage. There had
been two more frigates appointed by the French to act on this
service. But these had been intercepted by Sir Edward Hawke's
squadron, stationed in the bay of Quiberon.

This unimportant capture, and that of a few merchantmen of
little value, did not justify to the nation the inactivity in which
the British squadron on the coast of France had been allowed
to remain. Something of greater consequence was expected
from such a powerful armament under the direction of such
naval commanders as Sir Edward Hawke and Sir Charles Hardy.
But in the month of March, to the general surprize and indignation of the public, the two admirals returned to Spithead,
and another squadron, with a great body of land-forces on
board, was afterwards sent to occupy their station. This squadron consisted of the Sandwich, ninety guns; the Valiant, Temeraire, Torbay, Dragon, and Swiftsure, seventy-four guns
each; the Prince of Orange, seventy guns; the Hampton-court
and Essex, sixty-four guns each; the Achilles, sixty-guns; and
several frigates, bomb-ketches and fire-ships, with upwards of
an hundred transports, carrying 9000 soldiers under the command of Major-general Hodgson. The expedition was intended against Belleisle, the reduction of which, it was imagined,
would be attended with inconsiderable difficulties and many advantages. This island is between twelve and thirteen leagues in
circumference, and the largest of all the European islands belonging to the French king. It contains only one city, called
La Palais, three country towns, 103 villages, and about 5000
inhabitants, who live by the natural fertility of the soil, and
the curing and vending of pilchards. There are three harbours
in this island, Palais, Lauzion, and Goulfard, every one of
which labours under some considerable defect. But, although
the harbours are bad, small privateers might issue from thence
greatly to the molestation of the French coasting trade, and the
fleet of England might ride, between these harbours and the
continent of France, in a well-protected road. The real advantages,

tages, however, arising from this conquest, were not the only A. D
inducements to undertake it. Nothing could wound more cruel- 1761
ly the pride of France than the acquisition of what might be
regarded as a part of her coast ; and, at the same time, the jealoufy of Spain would be lefs alarmed by our advantages in this
quarter, than by thofe which we might obtain by pufhing our
conquefts in the Weft-Indies.

The fleet failed from Spithead on the 29th of March in three
divifions, commanded by Commodore Keppel, Sir Thomas
Stanhope, and Captain Barton. On the 6th of April a wefterly
wind enabled them to approach the coaft of France, and the
commodore detached feveral frigates, with orders to ftation
themfelves in fuch a manner as might intercept the enemy's
communication with the continent. Next morning the fleet
paffed along the fouthern fhore of the ifland, and came to an
anchor in the great road, about 12 o'clock at noon. The commanders agreed, that the defcent ought to be made on the
fouth-eaft extremity of the ifland, near the Point Lomaria. But, in order to amufe the enemy, a feint was made
to attack the citadel of Palais, while two large fhips conveyed
the troops to the intended landing-place, and filenced a battery
which the enemy had there erected. The flat-bottomed boats
were now approaching the fhore, and about 260 had actually
landed under the command of Major Purcel and Captain Ofborne, when the enemy, fuddenly appearing on the heights,
poured in fuch a fevere fire as threw them into the utmoft confufion, and intimidated the reft of the troops from landing.
Captain Ofborne, at the head of 60 grenadiers, advanced with
great intrepidity fo near as to exchange feveral thrufts with the
French officer. But the handful of men which he commanded
were foon overpowered by numbers. He himfelf, as well as
Major Purcel and two fea-officers, were fhot, and the attempt
ended with the lofs of above 500 killed, wounded, or taken
prifoners. This difcouraging check was fucceeded by tempeftuous weather, which did confiderable damage to the large veffels,
and ftaved or overfet twenty flat-bottomed boats.

Thefe difafters did not difpirit the Englifh commanders. They
determined to examine the whole coaft, in order to find a place
more favourable for another attack. As foon as the weather
afforded

afforded them the profpect of making a fecond trial, they pitch‑
ed on a place near the above-mentioned point of Lomaria,
where the exceffive fteepnefs and difficulty of the rocks had
rendered the enemy lefs attentive than elfewhere. On the 22d
of April, in the morning, the troops were difpofed in flat-bottomed boats, and rowed towards different parts of the ifland;
which diftracted the French operations, and obliged them to
divide their forces. Meanwhile Captain Paterfon, at the head
of Beauclerk's grenadiers, and Captain Murray, with a detach‑
ment of marines, landed near Lomaria, mounted the precipice
with aftonifhing intrepidity, and fuftained the whole fire of
the enemy, until they were reinforced by the approach of the
greateft part of the Englifh troops. The French then retired
before the bayonets of the Britifh foldiers, leaving many of
their wounded companions and feveral field-pieces. Nor was
the action without lofs on our fide. Forty men were killed, and
many more wounded, among whom were Colonel Mackenzie
and Captain Murray of the marines, and Captain Paterfon of
Beauclerk's grenadiers, who loft his arm in the engagement.

The whole army being now landed, Mr. de St. Croix ordered all his out-pofts to repair to a camp under the walls of the
town of Palais, where he determined to make a vigorous defence, his forces, when joined by the militia of the ifland,
amounting to four thoufand men fit for fervice. On the 23d of
April the Englifh troops were formed into columns, and began
their march towards the capital of the ifland. Next day General
Hodgfon ordered a detachment of light horfe to take poft at
Sauzon; and, on the 25th, a corps of infantry took poffeffion
of a village called Bordilla; and the whole army intrenched itfelf in that neighbourhood. The tempeftuous weather rendering it impoffible to bring on fhore the artillery and implements
neceffary in a fiege, the French governor feized this opportunity
to erect fix redoubts for defending the avenues of Palais, the
citadel of which had been planned and fortified with admirable
fkill by the celebrated Vauban. General Hodgfon, compelled
by neceffity to defer his military operations, publifhed a manifefto, addreffed to the inhabitants, offering them the free enjoyment of their religious and civil rights, provided they would
fubmit themfelves to the protection of the Englifh government;

an

an affurance which had confiderable effect on the natives, but A. D produced no alteration on the refolution of the governor, who, 1761 when fummoned to furrender, declared he was determined to defend the place to the laft extremity. About the latter end of April fome mortars being brought up, began to play upon the town, and the befiegers broke ground on the 2d of May. The day after, in the evening, the enemy attacked the trenches with great vigour, and threw the piquets on the left in confufion. Notwithftanding the efforts of General Crawford, who performed every thing that could be expected from the bravery and conduct of an experienced officer, the works of the befiegers were deftroyed, feveral hundreds of their men were killed, and the general with his two aid-du-camps fell into the hands of the enemy. The French did not attempt to pufh the advantage any farther, by attacking the piquets on the right, who had prepared to give them a warm reception. They retired after their firft fuccefs, and allowed the Britifh to repair the damage which they had fuftained. This was done in lefs than twenty-four hours, and a redoubt was alfo begun on the right of the works to prevent a fecond furprize.

From this time the fiege was carried on with the utmoft vigour; and the befieged gave fuch continual proofs of their courage and activity, as confirmed the reputation of Mr. de St. Croix for a gallant officer, confummate in the art of war. The engineers being unanimoufly of opinion, that the works could not be properly advanced, until the French redoubts fhould be taken, the general made the difpofition for that purpofe on the 13th. The attack began at day-break, with four pieces of cannon and thirty cohorns, which poured a terrible fire into the redoubt on the right of the enemy's flank. This opened a way for a detachment of marines, fuftained by part of Loudon's regiment, to advance to the parapet, and with fixed bayonets, to drive the French from the works, and take poffeffion of the poft. The other redoubts were fucceffively reduced by the fame detachment reinforced by Colvill's regiment, and the enemy were compelled, after great flaughter, to take fhelter in the citadel. Such was the ardour of the affailants, that they entered the ftreets of Palais pell-mell with the fugitives; and

having

A. D.
1761.
having taken poſſeſſion of the town, they releaſed the Engliſh priſoners above-mentioned.

The defence being now confined entirely to the citadel, which could have no communication either with the reſt of the iſland or with the continent of France, it was evident that the place muſt ſoon be obliged to ſurrender for want of proviſions. But Mr. de St. Croix determined to ſell it as dearly as poſſible, and to maintain his own honour at leaſt, if he could not the poſſeſſion of the citadel of Palais. On the part of the Engliſh nothing was neglected. Parallels were finiſhed, barricadoes made, batteries conſtructed, an inceſſant fire from mortars and artillery was maintained day and night, from the 13th of May till the 25th. Then the fire of the enemy began to abate; by the end of May a breach was made in the citadel; and, notwithſtanding the indefatigable induſtry of the governor in repairing the damage, the fire of the beſiegers increaſed to ſuch a degree that the breach became practicable by the 7th of June, and the place was apparently no longer tenable. Then Mr. de St. Croix capitulated upon terms [b] not unworthy of his noble defence, and the garriſon marched out with the honours of war.

Thus was the whole iſland of Belleiſle reduced under the Engliſh government after a defence of two months, in the courſe of which we loſt eighteen hundred men killed and wounded. The loſs moſt regretted was that of Sir William Williams, a young gentleman of great talents and expectations, who had already made a diſtinguiſhed figure in parliament. He was the third gentleman of faſhion, whom, in this war, the love of glory had brought to an honourable death in hoſtile expeditions againſt the coaſt of France.

Having particularized the ſucceſsful operations of the Britiſh ſquadrons in the taking of Belleiſle, Dominica and Pondicherry, as well as in defeating the projects which the French meditated againſt our ſettlements on the coaſt of Africa, we ſhall mention the exploits performed by ſingle cruizers in the courſe of the year, many of which confer the higheſt honour on the Britiſh flag. Captain Elphinſtone, commander of the Richmond frigate of 32 guns and 220 men, ſtationed on the coaſt of Flanders, being inform-

b See Appendix, Nᵒ IX.

i

ed

ed that a French frigate called the Felicité had made prize of
an Englifh merchantmen, failed in queft of the enemy; and
coming in fight of her, about eleven at night on the 23d, a fevere engagement began next day, about ten in the morning,
near Gravefande, which is but eight miles diftant from the
Hague. The vicinity of the place induced the young prince of
Orange, as well as the ambaffadors of England and France, to
fet out, in order to view the combat, in the iffue of which, as
the fhips were exactly of equal force, the honour of the two
nations was materially interefted. About noon both fhips ran
afhore, along fide of each other; and in this fituation the fight
continued with great obftinacy, till the French abandoned their
quarters, their fhip being much damaged, the captain flain, and
above 100 men killed or wounded. The Richmond foon floated, without fuftaining any confiderable hurt, having obtained
the victory at the expence of three men killed, and thirteen
wounded. The French ambaffador loudly exclaimed againft
this attack as a violation of the Dutch neutrality, and demanded fignal reparation for the infult and injury which his countrymen had fuftained. But the Dutch at that time did not think
it convenient to urge their remonftrances with vehemence,
and they were anfwered in fuch a manner by the Britifh ambaffador as prevented any difficulties arifing between the two
courts.

On the 23d of the fame month Captain Hood, commanding
the Minerva frigate of 32 guns and 220 men, cruifing in the
chops of the channel, defcried a large fhip of two decks fteering
to the weftward. This was the Warwick of 60 guns taken
from the Englifh, the moft boafted capture the enemy had
made in the courfe of the war. She had formerly carried 60,
but was now mounted with only 36 guns, and commanded by
Mr. le Verger de Belair. Her crew amounted to about 300
men, including a company of foldiers intended as a reinforcement to the garrifon of Pondicherry. Notwithftanding her fuperiority, Captain Hood gave chace, and, the wind blowing a frefh
eafterly gale, he came up with her at 20 minutes paft ten. His
attack was warmly returned; the fire on both fides was terrible.
Several mafts of both fhips were fhot away, and they fell foul
of one another, while the fea ran very high; fo that the crews
were greatly incumbered by their broken mafts and fhattered

A. D.
1761.
rigging. The high sea separated them, and the Warwick fell to leeward. About a quarter after eleven the Minerva's bowsprit was carried away, and the fore-mast soon followed it. This misfortune made Captain Hood almost despair of coming up with the enemy, who had got three leagues to leeward. However, he cleared his ship with incredible activity, and, bearing down, renewed the attack about four o'clock. In three quarters of an hour the enemy struck, having thirteen men killed and thirty-five wounded. The loss of men was equal on board the Minerva, and all her masts were destroyed : nevertheless, her prize was conveyed in triumph to Spithead. On the 8th of the same month Captain Hood had taken the Ecureil privateer belonging to Bayonne, of 14 guns and 122 men.

On the 13th of March another French ship called the Entreprenant, built for 44 guns, but mounted with 26, having 200 men on board and a rich cargo, bound for St. Domingo, was encountered near the Land's-end by the Vengeance frigate commanded by Captain Nightingale. The Vengeance was mounted with 26 guns, nine and four pounders, and carried 200 men. There was a great disparity in the size of the ships and in the weight of metal. But the English captain, as usual, gave chace, and got up with the enemy at five o'clock in the afternoon. The action was maintained on both sides with uncommon fury, and continued for near an hour, during which time the Vengeance being set on fire, the Entreprenant ran her bowsprit upon the taffaril of the English frigate, with an intention to board her. In this design, however, the French miscarried through the skill and activity of Captain Nightingale, who found means to clear himself, and stood to leeward, in order to repair his rigging. The ship was no sooner in proper condition than he ranged close up again to the enemy, whose fire was still directed against the rigging of the English frigate, which, after this second attack had lasted above an hour, being again disabled, allowed the enemy to sheer off, and bear away. But the English a second time repaired their damage, wore ship, ran up within pistol-shot, and began a third attack more furious than any of the preceding. The engagement continued an hour and an half before the Entreprenant called for quarter. She had 15 men killed, and 24 wounded,

wounded. The Vengeance had an equal number wounded, but only six men killed.

These losses did not complete the misfortunes of the French navy, during the present year, in the British seas. In April a French frigate called the Comete, of 32 guns and 250 men, just sailed from Brest, was taken by Captain Deane of the Bedford man of war, and conveyed safely into Portsmouth. About the same time Captain Bograve of the Albany sloop of 16 guns and 125 men, came up with the Pheasant frigate, of equal force, after a chace of 28 hours. The French captain, having thrown his guns overboard, struck as soon as the Albany came along-side of him, and the prize was carried into Spithead. In the course of the same month a large East-India ship, fitted out from France, with 28 guns and 350 men, fell in with the Hero and the Venus, commanded by the Captains Fortescue and Harrison, and, being taken without opposition, was carried into Plymouth.

The same spirit of enterprize and activity distinguished the cruizers belonging to the squadron commanded by Vice-admiral Saunders in the Mediterranean. In the beginning of April the Oriflamme, a French ship of 40 guns, being off Cape Tres Foreas, was descried by the Isis of 50 guns, commanded by Captain Wheeler. The English captain gave chace, and came up with the enemy about six in the evening; but the Frenchman, having the advantage of the wind, maintained a running fight till half past ten, during which Captain Wheeler unfortunately was shot. The command devolved on Lieutenant Cunningham, who perceiving it to be the enemy's intention to reach, if possible, the neutral coast of Spain, ordered his men to board her, which was done with great bravery; and, her commander in a short time submitting, she was brought into the bay of Gibraltar. The number of her killed and wounded amounted to 45: the loss of the Isis did not exceed four killed, and nine wounded. The next action in those seas was much more destructive to the British sailors. The Thunderer, Captain Proby, in company with the Modeste, Thetis, and Favourite sloop, cruized off the coast of Spain, with a view to intercept the Achilles and Bouffon, two French ships of war, which lay in the harbour of Cadiz. These were descried on the 16th of July by the

A a 2    British

Britiſh ſhips, which gave them chaſe. The Thunderer came up
with the Achilles about midnight, and, after a ſhort but warm
action of half an hour, obliged the enemy to ſtrike. The French
had, on this occaſion, fired their guns with more effect than
uſual; for in the Engliſh ſhip 40 men were killed, and upwards
of 100 wounded: among the latter was the captain. The Thetis purſued the Bouffon, but could not bring her to an engagement till ſeven next morning. The engagement was maintained
on both ſides with great impetuoſity for the ſpace of half an
hour, when the Modeſte ranging up, and thus putting the
French ſhip between two fires, compelled her to ſubmit. The
victors carried their prizes, which had been much damaged in
their rigging, and ſuffered great loſs in their crews, into the bay
of Gibraltar.

These advantageous captures were preludes to one of the moſt
remarkable and glorious actions that diſtinguiſhed the whole
war. On the 10th of Auguſt Captain Faulkner of the Bellona,
a ſhip of the line, and Captain Logie of the Brilliant, a frigate of
30 guns, ſailed from the river Tagus for England, and on the
14th diſcovered three ſail ſtanding in for the land, one of the
line of battle, and two frigates. Theſe veſſels had no ſooner
deſcried Captain Faulkner, than they bore down upon him until
within the diſtance of ſeven miles, when ſeeing the Bellona and
the Brilliant through the magnifying medium of a hazy atmo-
ſphere, they concluded they were both two-decked ſhips, and,
dreading the iſſue of an engagement, reſolved to avoid it by flight.
The Engliſh captains, judging them to be enemies by their crowd-
ing ſail to eſcape, immediately chaſed, which continued all night.
At five in the morning they approached ſo near as to diſcern the
Courageux, a 74 gun ſhip, and two frigates of 36 guns, the Ma-
licieuſe and the Hermione. The French captain now perceived,
that one of the Engliſh veſſels was a frigate; and the Bellona,
being one of the beſt-conſtructed ſhips in the Engliſh navy, lay
ſo fluſh in the water, that ſhe appeared at a diſtance conſider-
ably ſmaller than ſhe really was. The Frenchman, therefore,
no longer declined the engagement, but hoiſted a red enſign in
the mizen-ſhrouds as a ſignal for his two frigates to cloſe with
and attack the Brilliant. At the ſame time he took in his ſtud-
ding ſails, wore ſhip, and ſtood for the Bellona, while Captain

Faulkner

Faulkner advanced with an eafy fail, manned his quarters, and A. I made every neceffary difpofition for an obftinate engagement.  176

Both commanders had a fair opportunity to meafure their ftrength and abilities. The wind was gentle, the fea calm; the fhips were of equal rates, their guns and weight of metal the fame. The Courageux had 700 men; the Bellona 550. While the veffels came up with each other, the fire was fufpended on both fides till they were within piftol-fhot. The engagement then began with a dreadful fire of mufquets and artillery. In lefs than ten minutes all the Bellona's braces, fhrouds, and rigging, were tore and fhattered, and her mizen-maft went by the board, with the men on the round top, who faved their lives with much difficulty, by clambering into the port-holes. Captain Faulkner, apprehenfive that the enemy would feize the opportunity of his being difabled, to fheer off, gave orders for immediate boarding; but the Courageux, by falling athwart the bow of her enemy, rendered this altogether impracticable. In this pofition the Englifh fhip might be raked fore and aft with great execution. The haul-yards, and moft of the other ropes by which fhe could be worked, were already fhot away. But Captain Faulkner made ufe of the ftudding fails with fuch dexterity as to wear the fhip quite round; and his officers and men, perceiving this change of pofition, flew to the guns on the other fide, now oppofed to the enemy, from which they poured a terrible difcharge, which continued twenty minutes without intermiffion or abatement. The fire became fo intolerable that the French hauled down their enfign, and called for quarter. The damage done to the rigging of the Bellona was confiderable; but fhe had fuffered very little in the hull, and the number of the killed and wounded did not exceed forty. The Courageux, on the other hand, appeared like a wreck on the water. Nothing was feen but her foremaft and bowfprit; her decks were torn up in feveral places, and large breaches were made in her fides. Above 220 of her men were killed, and half that number of wounded were brought on fhore at Lifbon, to which place the prize was conveyed.

During the action between the larger fhips, Captain Logie of the Brilliant had difplayed the moft fignal courage and addrefs. He could not attempt to board, or expect to make prize of two

fhips,

A. D.
1761.
ships, each of which was of equal strength with his own. But
he so managed his attack and defence as to keep the two French
frigates continually employed, and to prevent either of them
from giving the smallest assistance to the Courageux. Finally,
he obliged them both to sheer off, and to consult their safety by
flight, after they had suffered considerably in their masts and
rigging.

In all the engagements which we have described the advantage was continually on the side of the English. The French
neither managed their ships with that facility, nor fought their
guns with that dexterity and skill, which appeared in all the
operations of their opponents. Their aukwardness in working
ship may be ascribed to inexperience; but their inferiority in
managing their guns, it is impossible to refer to any such cause.
The French sailors are regularly taught the practical part of
gunnery, an advantage which the English, in general, have little opportunity to acquire. But even here the British seamen
shewed themselves, on every occasion, superior to the enemy;
a superiority owing, not to their education or discipline, but to
that bravery and resolution which never forsake them in the moment of danger, but allow them to remain in full possession of
their faculties at a time when the French are rendered incapable,
through fear, of any vigorous exertion either of mind or body.

In the course of the year 1761 the French lost 117 privateers
and armed merchantmen, which mounted 698 carriage-guns
and 239 swivels, and carried 5576 men, exclusive of four Indiamen, of which the cargoes were valued at near 400,000
pounds, and many unarmed merchant-ships. Their royal navy
was deprived of six ships of the line and eight frigates, which
together carried 636 guns and 6240 men. In the course of the
same year the English lost 814 merchantmen, a proportion of
three to one, which arose from the inattention of the English
vessels to the orders of the convoys sent to protect them, from
the immense numbers of them which covered the seas, and from
the enemy's venturing the whole remains of their strength in
privateers fitted out in order to interrupt our commercial navigation. Among all the vessels that were taken we find but one of
any considerable value, the Ajax East-Indiaman, Captain Lindsey from Bengal, valued at 200,000 pounds. Excepting the
Warwick,

Warwick, which was retaken, the royal navy loft but one fmall A. L
veffel, the Speedwell cutter of eight guns; and the captain was 1761
honourably acquitted by a court-martial, who were unanimoufly
of opinion, that the faid cutter, being taken in the harbour of
Vigo, was an illegal capture. There is a circumftance which
fhews, in a clearer light than the number of captures, the general refult of the naval advantages obtained by Great Britain.
Notwithftanding the various exchanges made by cartel fhips in
the courfe of the year, we ftill retained in our poffeffion upwards
of 25,000 French prifoners; whereas the number of Englifh
prifoners in France did not exceed 1200.

Notwithftanding many fpirited exertions of the Englifh navy 1762
in the year 1761, it is obvious, that the naval as well as the military operations of Great Britain had continued gradually to
languifh during the courfe of two years. The French, like ruined gamefters, had little more to lofe, and the fmallnefs of the
ftake produced a degree of phlegm and indifference in the victors, which deprived them of their wonted activity. Befides
this, all their external glory could not alleviate their domeftic
fufferings. Great Britain groaned under a burden of an hundred
millions, without enjoying any other confolation than that of
feeing her opponent as much indebted, and more exhaufted,
than herfelf. Had the parties, therefore, been left to their own
ftrength and refources, there would fpeedily have been an end
of the conteft. But France, by a dexterity of negotiation, of
which there is hardly an example in hiftory, acquired, at the
end of a moft ruinous war, fuch a powerful and hearty affiftance as afforded her the faireft hopes of retrieving all her mif-
fortunes. We have already hinted at the partiality of Spain in
the caufe of our enemies, and the motives of her uneafinefs at
the unexampled fuccefs of the Britifh arms. Thefe were heightened by the intrigues of the French ambaffador at the court of
Madrid; fo that while our artful and ambitious rival was negotiating a treaty at London, and feemed defirous of procuring
the bleffings of peace by the moft humiliating conceffions, her
minifter at the Spanifh court was employed in fuch meafures as,
inftead of extinguifhing the flames of war, tended to fpread
them more widely, and to make them rage with redoubled
fury. Every conceffion on the part of France was a new incen-
tive

A. D. tive to the animofity of Spain.   When the negotiation of the
1762. peace, therefore, feemed neareft to a conclufion, it was precifely
at that time the fartheft removed from an happy iffue; for then
was the moment for Spain to interpofe, and, at one explofion,
to blow up the whole bafis of the treaty.   Along with a very
agreeable plan for an accommodation, Mr. Buffy, the French
agent at London, delivered a private memorial, fignifying, that,
in order to eftablifh the peace upon the moft folid foundation,
it might be proper to invite the king of Spain to guaranty and
confirm it; and for this purpofe it would be neceffary finally
to adjuft the differences which fubfifted between the crowns of
Spain and England.   He condefcended on three points which
had been difputed between thefe crowns, the reftitution of the
captures which had been made on the Spanifh flag, the privilege
of the Spanifh nation to fifh on the banks of Newfoundland,
and the demolition of the Englifh fettlements made in the bay
of Honduras.

When thefe unexpected propofals were made, the manly fpirit of Mr. Pitt rejected, with the utmoft fcorn, the idea of negotiating the difputes of his nation with Spain, a power with
which we were actually at peace, through the medium of an
enemy humbled and almoft at our feet.   He called on the Spanifh ambaffador to difavow this extraordinary memorial, which
was equally infolent and irregular, as matters of fuch high moment, relating to the interefts of Spain, ought not to have been
propofed by a French agent, commiffioned to negotiate a particular and diftinct bufinefs, when the Spaniards had an ambaffador refiding in London, from whom no intimation of thefe matters had been previoufly received.   But the Spaniard, when thus
called upon, inftead of difavowing, openly acknowledged and
juftified the ftep taken by Mr. de Buffy.   He declared, that the
kings of France and of Spain were united not only by the ties
of blood but by a mutual intereft.   He magnified the humanity
and greatnefs of mind which his moft Chriftian majefty demon-
ftrated in the propofition which had fo unjuftly given offence.
He infifted much on the fincere defire of peace, the only motive
which influenced the conduct of the two monarchs, and concluded haughtily, that, if his mafter had been governed by
any other principles, " his Catholic majefty, giving full fcope to

2

" his

" his greatnefs, would have fpoken from himfelf, and as be-
" came his dignity."

Mr. Pitt had penetration enough to fee through the veil that
covered this hoftile declaration. He perceived, that there was a
perfect union of affections, interefts, and councils between the
two courts; that Spain muft inevitably coincide with all the
meafures of France; and that, if fhe deferred to declare war, it
was only for her own convenience, and efpecially becaufe fhe
waited the arrival of her flota from America. Totally poffeffed
with this idea, the minifter determined to act with a magnanimity becoming the dignity of his nation.

Great Britain was fingularly circumftanced at this period of
time. She had carried on a continental war againft France,
Auftria, the Empire, Ruffia, in a word, all the great northern
powers on the continent. She had deftroyed the marine, the
commerce, and the colonies of France. The interference of
Spain alone was wanting to fet her at war with all the great
powers of Europe; and Spain is precifely that country againft
which fhe can at all times contend, with the faireft profpect of
advantage and honour. That extenfive monarchy, though vigorous at the extremities, is exhaufted at the heart; her refources
lie at a great diftance; and whatever power commands the
ocean, may command the wealth and commerce of Spain.

The fituation of Great Britain, as well as the character of the
minifter, foared above the timid policy which commonly prevails
in modern courts. There was not only a great man, but a great
occafion, which is often wanting to a great man to difplay the
full force of his mind. Mr. Pitt afferted, with the magnanimous
patriotifm of an ancient Roman, that, defpifing ufelefs ceremonies and infignificant forms, we ought to confider the evafions
of the Spanifh court as a refufal of fatisfaction, and that refufal
as a fufficient declaration of war; we ought therefore, from prudence as well as from fpirit, to fecure to ourfelves the firft blow
by interrupting the Spanifh refources in their arrival to Europe,
and by the fame early and effective meafures, which had reduced France to a dependence on Spain, difable Spain from giving
affiftance to France. This procedure was fuited to the offended
majefty of the Britifh empire, and would teach Spain and every
other power the danger of prefuming to dictate in our affairs, or

A. D. to intermeddle with a menacing mediation, as infidious as it was
1762. audacious. He would allow our enemies, whether fecret or declared, no time to think and recollect themfelves.

The fentiments of Mr. Pitt fhocked the delicacy of his colleagues in adminiftration. They talked of the chimerical heroifm
of unneceffarily entering on a war, and of feeking new enemies, while no mention was made of new allies, nor indeed of
any new refource whatfoever. To plunge into fuch meafures
could not fail to alarm and fcandalize all Europe. The Spanifh
king's partiality in favour of France was ftill doubtful; but, had
we *real caufe* not only for fufpicion but complaint, the law of
nations and of reafon requires, that recourfe fhould be had to
expoftulation, and demands of fatisfaction. If thefe failed of
fuccefs, then is the time to take up arms, after employing the
forms univerfally acknowledged among civilized nations as neceffary to diftinguifh lawful war from lawlefs violence and oppreffion. This unfeafonable oppofition tranfported the minifter
beyond the bounds of moderation. He affirmed, " That this
" was the time for humbling the whole houfe of Bourbon; that,
" if this opportunity were let flip, it might never be recovered,
" and, if he could not prevail in this inftance, he was refolved
" to fit no longer in that council; that being called to the mi-
" niftry by the voice of the people, to whom he was account-
" able for his conduct, he would not remain in a fituation which
" made him refponfible for meafures which he was not permit-
" ted to guide." Accordingly he refigned the feals the 9th
of October, and his colleagues continued to negotiate by means
of Lord Briftol, ambaffador at the court of Madrid, for near
two months longer. Mr. Wall, the prime minifter of Spain,
was repeatedly folicited, in moderate and inoffenfive terms, to
difclofe the nature of the treaty, which, as the French induftri-
oufly circulated, had taken place among all the different branches of the houfe of Bourbon. As often as the queftion was pre-
pofed, it was artfully avoided. At length, Lord Briftol being
inftructed to make the demand with greater force, Mr. Wall
entered into a long and bitter complaint againft England, accufed
her of infolence and ambition, of a boundlefs defire of conqueft
and dominion, and of having fhewn to the world, by the haughtinefs of her late proceedings, that fhe intended to drive the
French

French from all their poſſeſſions in the new world that ſhe A. D
might have an eaſier taſk in ſeizing the Spaniſh dominions in 176?
thoſe parts; that he would be the man to adviſe the king of
Spain not to ſuffer his territories to be invaded, without arming
his ſubjects in their defence. As to the queſtion which had been
ſo often put to him, he gave no other reply, but that the king
his maſter had thought proper to renew his family compacts;
and then, as if he had gone farther than he was authoriſed, he
ſuddenly changed the diſcourſe, and continued his declamatory
invective againſt Great Britain. This was the happy effect of
the meaſures of the Engliſh miniſtry, whoſe forbearance and
good breeding were repaid by inſult and reproach. At length
their patience forſook them; they perceived that longer moderation would be conſtrued into fear, and they ſent orders to Lord
Briſtol to renew his inſtances concerning the treaty. with becoming firmneſs, while at the ſame time he ſignified, that a re-
fuſal to diſcloſe its contents, or to diſavow an intention to take
part with our enemies, would be conſidered as an aggreſſion on
the part of Spain, and an abſolute declaration of war. The demand was made in the preciſe terms of the order, and then the
pride of Spain tore aſunder that veil which her policy had ſo
long thought proper to aſſume. Her flota was by this time ſafe
in the harbour of Cadiz. She was now ſecure as to her intereſt,
and could give full ſcope to her reſentment. Mr. Wall, therefore, replied to the Engliſh requiſition in theſe memorable
words: " That the ſpirit of haughtineſs and diſcord, which
" dictated this inconſiderate demand of the Engliſh miniſtry,
" and which, for the misfortune of mankind, ſtill reigns ſo
" much in the Britiſh government, is what has made the decla-
" ration of war; that in that moment the war was declared,
" when the king's dignity was attacked; and that the Engliſh
" ambaſſador might return how and when he thought proper."
    The earl of Briſtol quitted Madrid the 17th of December;
and ſoon after the Spaniſh ambaſſador left London. Europe
was thus plunged into a new war by the very means which had
been uſed to draw her out of an old one. A mere punctilio, if
we can poſſibly believe Mr. Wall, was the motive which weighed with his maſter and himſelf, and prompted their humane
magnanimity to involve one half of Europe in diſcord and miſe-

A. D. ry. But whoever diligently attends to the measures of the Spa-
1762. nish court from the memorial presented by Mr. de Bussy to the
final answer of Mr. Wall, will perceive that their motives to
hostility were of a nature more serious and important. The insult offered to the king's honour in the question proposed by
Lord Bristol, might have been easily done away. Spain might
have required England to disavow the proceedings of her ambassador, a request which, upon sufficient security of the pacific
intentions of the former, the latter would readily have granted.
But the insult to the king's honour was held out as a pretence
for coming to a rupture at a time which seemed to suit the interests of Spain. The real cause of the war was her partiality
for the French, her uneasiness at seeing the eldest branch of
the house of Bourbon reduced to extremity, and her jealousy
of the growing power of England, whose renown offended her
pride, and whose naval greatness threatened the safety of her
distant dominions. It appeared, however, to Mr. Wall, to be
below the dignity of the Spanish monarch to avow reasons of
disgust, in which fear seemed to have any share. He therefore
directed the count de Fuentes his ambassador at London, to
carry on the farce, and, before he left the English court, to
publish a paper or manifesto, in which he assigns, as the only
cause of the rupture, the insulting manner in which the affairs
of Spain had been treated during Mr. Pitt's administration. He
declares to the British king, to the English nation, and to the
whole universe, that the horrors of war, into which the Spaniards and English are going to plunge themselves, must be attributed only to the immeasurable ambition of him who held
the reins of the government, and who appears still to hold them,
although by another hand; that, if the respect due to royal
majesty had been regarded, explanations might have been had
without any difficulty: the ministers of Spain might have said
frankly to those of England what the count de Fuentes, by the
king's express orders, declares publicly, viz. that the much-
talked-of treaty is only a convention between the members of
the family of Bourbon, wherein there is nothing that has the
least relation to the present war; that there is an article for the
mutual guaranty of the dominions of the two sovereigns, but it is
specified therein, that that guaranty is not to be understood

but

but of the dominions which fhall remain to France after the
prefent war fhall be ended.

This extraordinary paper, which may be called the king of
Spain's declaration of war againft the Right Honourable William
Pitt, Efq; was evidently intended for the ignoble purpofe of
fowing diffentions among the fubjects of Great Britain. It was
anfwered in every article with the utmoft moderation, perfpicui-
ty, and force, in a memorial publifhed by Lord Egremont, who
fucceeded Mr. Pitt as fecretary for the fouthern department. It
is obvious, that the Spanifh manifefto, whilft it pretends to fet
forth the purport of a treaty dated the 15th of Auguft, does not
deny the exiftence of any other treaty, which might more offen-
fively concern the interefts of Great Britain; nor does it fay the
leaft word that can explain the intentions of Spain, or the farther engagements that fhe may have contracted with France.

When the terms of this famous treaty came to be difclofed, it
was found to contain articles fufficient to alarm not only Great
Britain, againft whofe interefts it was particularly levelled, but
all the other powers of Europe. It was rather an act of incor-
poration, than of alliance among the kings of France, Spain,
the two Sicilies, the duke of Parma, and all the branches of the
Bourbon houfe. It contained ftipulations hitherto unheard of
in any treaty. By the 23d and 24th articles the fubjects of the
feveral branches of that auguft family are admitted to a mutual
naturalization, and to a general participation of reciprocal privileges and immunities. They appear, by the 26th article, to
difclofe to one another their alliances and negociations. By the
17th and 18th they formally engage not to make, or even to
liften to any propofal of peace from their common enemies, but
by mutual confent, being determined in time of peace, as well
as in time of war, to confider the interefts of France and Spain
as the fame, to compenfate their feveral loffes and advantages,
and to act as if the two monarchies formed only one and the
fame power. There are but two reftrictions to the extent of
this fcheme. The direct trade to America forms an exception
to the abfolute community of interefts, and in the 8th article it
is provided, that France fhall not be entitled to the affiftance of
Spain, when fhe is involved in a war in confequence of her
engagements by the treaty of Weftphalia, unlefs fome maritime
power

A. D.
1762. power take part in thofe wars. This article plainly points at the object againſt which the whole treaty was more immediately directed. It indicates, that the direct and immediate tendency of the whole is to affect England, and infinuates to the other powers of Europe, that their connection with England is the circumſtance which is to provoke the refentment, and call forth the activity of Spain.

· Excepting theſe two reſtrictions, the family-compact produced that entire union between the French and Spaniſh monarchies, which was ſo much dreaded on the death of Charles II. and which it was the great object of the treaty of partition, and the war of the grand alliance, to prevent. France acquired by negotiation and intrigue what ſhe could never acquire by force of arms, and, at the cloſe of an unfortunate war, obtained an advantage greater than any ſhe could have expected from the moſt fortunate iſſue of her affairs.

England was never placed in a more critical ſituation. She had to contend not only againſt all the great continental powers, but againſt the principal naval ſtrength of Europe. When war was declared in January 1762, the Spaniards had at Ferrol 11 ſhips of the line ready to ſail, and their whole fleet amounted to 100 ſhips of war [c].

The French, upon the concluſion of the family-compact [d], felt themſelves animated with new vigour. The ſhattered remains of their navy became of confideration when united with that of Spain. The ſpirits of the people, long funk in deſpondency, revived, and great exertions were made to put their fleet once more on a refpectable footing. The government tried every re-

[c] LIST of the SPANISH FLEET.

| | | | | | |
|---|---|---|---|---|---|
| 1 Ship of | — | 86 guns. | 1 Ship of | — | 50 guns. |
| 1 | — | 84 | 3 | — | 30 |
| 2 | — | 80 | 7 | — | 26 |
| 1 | — | 76 | 3 | — | 24 |
| 1 | — | 74 | 8 | — | 22 |
| 7 | — | 70 | 5 | — | 20 |
| 29 | — | 68 | 5 | — | 18 |
| 1 | — | 64 | 4 | — | 16 |
| 1 | — | 62 | BOMBKETCHES. | | |
| 8 | — | 60 | 4 of | — | 16 guns. |
| 2 | — | 58 | 1 | — | 14 |

Four fire ſhips.

[d] See Appendix No X.

source; private merchants contributed the last farthing for A. I equipping privateers, and several communities engaged to fit 176: out men of war at their own expence.

Great Britain enjoyed peculiar and sufficient advantages to excite her activity, and to balance the combination of all her enemies. The uniform tenor of success on our side made the people believe themselves invincible; and this belief, combined with the solid experience acquired in such a variety of services, and so many sharp conflicts by sea and land, inspired an enthusiasm of disciplined valour, which indeed rendered it almost impossible to resist them. The prospect of a Spanish war, while it held forth the hopes of immense plunder, conspired with the prevailing propensities, and roused to the most vigorous exertions of public and private strength. Nor had the parliament, which met the 3d of November, 1761, been wanting in liberality to second the generous ardour of the nation. They went through the estimates with diligence, and granted such liberal supplies as greatly exceeded those of all former years. 70,000 seamen, including 19,061 marines, were voted for the service of the year 1762; the land forces were maintained at the number of 67,676, besides the militia of England, the two regiments of fencible men in North Britain, the provincial troops in North. America, and 67,177 German auxiliaries to support the war of Westphalia. For the payment of the sea and land forces, of subsidies to our German allies, and of the deficiencies of the grants of former sessions, they voted the sum of 18,617,895 l. 2 s. 8 d. of which 12,000,000 were borrowed on remote funds, at four *per cent. per ann.* with an addition of 1 *per cent. per ann.* for 99 years.

When war was declared against Spain, his majesty granted a commission, impowering the admiralty to issue letters of marque, for privateers to act against the subjects of that kingdom. At the same time he communicated the measure which the treaty between Spain and France had compelled him to take, in a speech to both houses of parliament. Such ample supplies were already granted, that no farther demand was made on this account; and so immensely had the power of England increased in the course of three reigns, that an union, the suspicion of which had alarmed all Europe in the time of the grand alliance, was beheld without the smallest symptom of fear or despondency.

The

A. D. The king of Great Britain difdained not only to take any illibe-
1762. ral advantages of his enemies, but even to retort their wrongs.
Although his Catholic majefty detained the Britifh fhips in his
ports, and laid reftraints on the Britifh fubjects within his dominions, the fubjects of Spain were left at entire liberty, and
the merchantmen which had arrived in Englifh harbours, before they had been apprized of the declaration of war, were allowed to depart in fafety.   This magnanimity became the dignity of the Britifh nation.   It is the part of fear to fnatch at
every pitiful advantage.   But had Britain defcended fo low, it
would have been unworthy of the grand fcene of action and
glory, which was now ready to open in remote parts of the earth.
   The failure of the expedition againft Martinico in 1759 did
not difcourage our adminiftration from making this ifland the
object of another attempt.   Martinico ftill furnifhed a confiderable refource to the declining commerce of France.   It is the
largeft of all the Caribbee iflands, advantageoufly fituated between Barbadoes and Guadaloupe, and to windward of Antigua
and St. Chriftophers.   It extends 20 leagues in length, and is
about 130 miles in circumference, indented by a great number
of creeks and harbours, diverfified with hill and dale, fhaded
with wood, watered by many ftreams, and produces a very confiderable quantity of fugar, indigo, coffee, cotton, ginger, aloes,
and pimento.   Here the governor-general of all the French
iflands in the Weft-Indies refides, and here is eftablifhed the fovereign council, whofe jurifdiction extends over the French An-
tilles, and even to the fettlements of that crown in the iflands of
St. Domingo and Tortuga.   In a word, Martinico is the moft
populous and flourifhing of all the French fettlements acrofs the
Atlantic.   Its towns and harbours are ftrongly fortified; the
country itfelf is rendered extremely difficult of accefs by woods,
rivers, rocks, and ravines; defended by a body of regular
troops, befides a difciplined militia confifting of 10,000 white
natives, and four times that number of negroes, whom they can
arm in cafes of emergency.   The acquifition of Martinico would,
in cafe of a peace, furnifh us with a place of the utmoft importance, either to retain or to exchange; and, if Spain was unchange-
ably determined on a war, it would put us on a refpectable footing in that part of the world where the Spaniards are moft vul-

                          x                              nerable,

merable, and where, every wound affecting the vitals of the state, they feel with quickeſt ſenſibility.

The plan for proſecuting this important conqueſt had been laid down by Mr. Pitt ; the preparations had been made, the officers appointed, and every neceſſary order given for carrying the whole deſign into execution. Upon a change of adminiſtration the project was not abandoned. As every thing, which had been the object of war in North America was by this time completely acquired, it was eaſy to draw a conſiderable part of the army from that quarter. A draught of eleven battalions was ordered from New York, and alſo to aſſemble the different bodies of troops that were ſcattered among the Leeward iſlands. Rear-admiral Rodney ſailed from England in October, and took on board his tranſports four battalions at Belleiſle. The general rendezvous was in the iſland of Barbadoes, where the united armaments from England and North America amounting to eighteen battalions and as many ſhips of the line, beſides frigates, bombs, and fire-ſhips, arrived in the month of December. The land-forces alone fell little ſhort of 12,000 men, and, taking the military and naval together, it was ſuch an armament as had never been before ſeen in that part of the world. The fleet proceeded from Barbadoes the fifth day of January, and on the eight anchored in St. Anne's bay on the eaſtern coaſt of Martinico, after the ſhips had ſilenced ſome batteries which the enemy had erected on that part of the iſland. In the courſe of this ſervice the Raiſonable, a ſhip of the line, was, by the ignorance of the pilot, run upon a reef of rocks, from which ſhe could not be diſengaged ; but the crew were ſaved as well as the ſtores and artillery. General Monkton, who commanded the land-forces, judged this an improper place for a diſembarkation, and therefore detached the brigadiers Haviland and Grant under a ſtrong convoy to the bay of Petite Anſe, where a battery was cannonaded and taken by the ſeamen and marines. The detachment then effected a landing, and marched to the ground oppoſite to Pigeon Iſland, which commands the harbour of Fort-Royal ; but, the roads being found impaſſable for artillery, General Monkton thought it improper to land the main body there, and proceeded to a creek called Cas Navires, where the whole forces were diſembarked on the

A. D. 16th, without the lofs of a man, the fleet having been station-
1762. ed fo properly, and directing their fire with fuch effect, that
the enemy was obliged in a fhort time to abandon the batteries
erected to defend this inlet.

When the landing was effected, the difficulties were far from
being at an end. The inhabitants of Martinico feemed determined to defend the ifland to the laft extremity. Every pafs was
guarded and fortified. The detachment, which had firft landed, were attacked in the night by a body of grenadiers, freebooters, negroes, and mulattoes; but thefe met with fo warm
a reception, that they were compelled, after fuftaining confiderable lofs, to retire with precipitation.

The general determined to attack the town and citadel of
Fort-Royal although his march thither was incumbered with
difficulties and dangers, there being many ravines and gullies,
very deep, and difficult of accefs, well covered with batteries and
redoubts, and defended by the flaves as well as natives in arms.
Befides the difficulties of the approach, the town and citadel
are overlooked, and commanded by two very confiderable emi-
nences called Morne Tortuefon and Morne Garnier. Whilft
the enemy kept poffeffion of thefe, it was impoffible to attack
the town. They were protected like the other high grounds in
this ifland by natural ravines, ftrengthened by every contrivance
of art. The Morne Tortuefon was firft to be attacked. To favour this operation, a body of regular troops and marines were ordered to advance on the right, along the fea-fide, towards the
town, in order to take the redoubts which lay in the lower
grounds. A thoufand failors in flat-bottomed boats rowed clofe
to the fhore to affift them. On the left, towards the country,
a corps of light infantry, properly fupported, was to get round
the enemy's left, whilft the attack in the centre was made by
the Britifh grenadiers, and the main body of the army, under the fire of batteries which had been erected on the oppofite fide with great labour and perfeverance, the cannon
having been dragged upwards of three miles by the feamen,
acrofs the enemy's line of fire, to which they expofed themfelves with amazing indifference.

The attack, which was planned with fo much judgment, was
executed with equal fpirit and refolution. The Britifh troops
fucceeded

succeeded in every quarter. The enemy were succeffively driven A. I
from poft to poft: fome fled into the town; others mounted to 176
Morne Garnier; while the Englifh ftandard was difplayed at
Morne Tortuefon. But nothing decifive could be effected againft
the town until the French were driven from the former eminence. It was three days before proper difpofitions could be
made for this purpofe. During this interval the enemy's whole
force fallied out of the town, or defcended from the hill, and
attacked the Englifh in their advanced pofts. But they were repelled with fingular bravery; and, the ardour of the Britifh
troops hurrying them forward, they improved a defenfive advantage into an attack, paffed the ravines, mingled with the
enemy, fcaled the hill, feized the batteries, and pofted themfelves on the fummit of Morne Garnier.

All the fituations which commanded the town and citadel
were now fecured, and the Englifh, in the morning of the 28th,
began to play their artillery; which the governor no fooner obferved than he ordered the chamade to be beat, and furrendered
the place by capitulation. On the 4th of February the gates
were delivered up to the Englifh, and next morning the garrifon,
to the number of 800, marched out with the honours of war.
On the 7th Pigeon Ifland, which was ftrongly fortified, and
counted one of the beft defences of the harbour, furrendered at
the firft fummons, and obtained a capitulation fimilar to that of
the citadel. Deputations were fent from different quarters of
the ifland by the inhabitants, defiring the fame terms. But the
governor-general, Mr. de la Touche, retired with his forces to
St. Pierre the capital, which he meant to defend with uncommon vigour. It is probable, however, that, when he arrived
there, his opinion was altered by the advice of the inhabitants.
They faw the Englifh mafters of all the reft of the ifland; they
reflected on the favourable capitulation which the ifland of Guadaloupe had obtained, and the good faith with which the terms
of this capitulation had been obferved. Although they changed
mafters, they changed neither laws nor religion; their property
was more fecure than under the ancient government, their commerce more free and unreftrained, and they were furnifhed with
all neceffaries from the dominions of Great Britain; whereas
formerly they depended for fubfiftence upon the moft precarious

and

and hazardous methods of fupply. Thefe confiderations had great weight with the inhabitants of St. Pierre, who perfuaded the governor to fend two deputies with propofals of capitulation. On the 14th the terms were fettled, and the agreement figned. On the 16th the Englifh commander took poffeffion of St. Pierre, and all the pofts in that neighbourhood, while the governor-general, the lieutenant-governor, the ftaff-officers, and about 320 grenadiers were embarked in tranfports to be conveyed to France. Thefe fignal fucceffes were obtained at the fmall expence of 400 men, including a few officers killed and wounded in the different attacks. Fourteen French privateers were found in the harbour of Port-Royal, and a much greater number, from other parts of the ifland, were delivered up to Admiral Rodney, in confequence of the capitulation with the inhabitants, who in all other refpects were very favourably treated [e].

The furrender of Martinico, which was the feat of government, the principal mart of trade, and the centre of all the French force in the Caribbees, naturally drew on the furrender of all the dependent iflands. While General Monkton was regulating the capitulation of St. Pierre, Commodore Swanton failed with a fmall fquadron to the fertile ifland of Granada, which was given up without oppofition. St. Lucia and St. Vincent, the right to which had fo long been difputed between the two nations, followed its example. By thefe acquifitions the Englifh colonies at Antigua, St. Chriftopher's, and Nevis, as well as the fhips trading to thefe iflands, were fecured againft the hoftilities of the enemy; the commerce of Great Britain acquired an annual addition to the amount of at leaft a million fterling, and the Britifh nation became undifturbed poffeffors of that chain of innumerable iflands, which forms an immenfe bow, extending from the eaftern point of Hifpaniola almoft to the continent of South America.

The confequences of this important conqueft were ftill more important than the conqueft itfelf. It opened a way for humbling effectually the pride of Spain. In the courfe of a few months, more decifive ftrokes were ftruck againft that haughty monarchy than during ten years of the former Spanifh war. In

[e] See Appendix, No XL.

that

that war Great Britain acquired wealth and honour; but in this A. I
she displayed such a scene of national glory as Europe had never 176:
before beheld. As these events, however, did not immediately follow upon the reduction of Martinico, it is proper here to
pause, and to contemplate the effects of that formidable alliance
concluded in the 1761, among the different members of the
house of Bourbon.

The kings of France and Spain imagined they had acquired
such an ascendant over all their neighbours by forming this
league, that they might henceforth neglect with impunity the
observance of those rules which the most ambitious and despotic
princes commonly prescribe to themselves in the execution of
their boldest designs. This evidently appeared in their conduct
towards Portugal, the ancient and natural ally of Great Britain.
Portugal possessed gold without possessing industry or ingenuity.
England furnished the Portuguese with all the conveniencies of
life, and received specie in return. The balance of trade was
supposed to bring annually into Great Britain about a million
sterling. This commercial connection was strengthened by the
strongest political ties. The two kingdoms were so situated,
that they had little to fear from one another, while they might
mutually impart many reciprocal advantages. The harbours of
Portugal afforded protection as well as supplies to the English
fleet, while the English fleet defended the lucrative commerce of
the Portuguese with their American colonies. The natural and
inveterate antipathy between Spain and Portugal made it neceffary for the latter to look out for some powerful distant ally.
None is so advantageous in that view as England, which in her
turn might derive great advantages from Portugal, in profecu-
ting a war against any of the southern powers of Europe.

The united monarchs, unwilling to trust the issue of the war
to hostilities committed against England on her own element,
determined to wound her through the sides of this ally. They
were strongly invited to this measure by the present unhappy circumstances of Portugal. That kingdom was altogether unprovided in the means of defence. The military spirit, by which
the Portuguese had formerly distinguished themselves, was totally extinct. The nobles were overwhelmed in ignorance,
bigotry, and oppression spiritual as well as temporal. There
was

was neither skill, discipline, nor order among the troops, nor indeed any appearance of a regular army, and the frontier places were ill fortified, worse garrisoned, and almost entirely destitute of ammunition and artillery. In this condition Portugal received a fatal blow from an earthquake in 1756. The wealthy and flourishing city of Lisbon was levelled with the ground, near 30,000 of the inhabitants were buried in her ruins, and those who remained with the court itself were reduced to the utmost distress and misery. As if this earthquake, which had overturned their capital, had also shaken and distracted the frame of their government, and the temper of their minds, the most dreadful distempers broke out in the state. A series of horrid crimes and cruel punishments succeeded to this national calamity. Two of the most noble and wealthy families of Portugal, having engaged themselves in a sacrilegious attempt on the life of their sovereign, were cut off at once, with little distinction of age or sex, by a bloody and dreadful exertion of justice. Many others, who were accused or suspected, suffered death, or exile, or imprisonment. Among these, and partly from the same causes, one of the most considerable religious orders for wealth, influence, and policy, was stripped of its possessions, and entirely driven out of the country.

This being the unfortunate situation of Portugal, the house of Bourbon hoped that kingdom would be an easy conquest, notwithstanding all the succours it could possibly receive; which would not only be a great loss to the commerce of Great Britain, and a considerable inconvenience to her in carrying on the war, but would afford a valuable deposite, to be exchanged at the peace, for the further acquisitions England might make at the expence of France or Spain. Full of these ideas, his Catholic majesty gave orders for providing magazines and artillery, and for strengthening his fortified places on the side of Portugal. The Spanish army, supplied with able engineers from France, overspread the Portuguese frontiers; the commerce of corn between the two kingdoms was prohibited, and every thing threatened a sudden invasion. In the midst of these hostile preparations the French and Spanish ministers presented a joint memorial to the court of Lisbon, the purport of which was to persuade his most Faithful majesty to desert his antient alliance,

and

and to co-operate with the two crowns againſt Great Britain. A. D
The memorial inſiſted largely on the tyranny which Great Bri- 1762
tain exerted upon all powers, eſpecially the maritime; and upon Portugal among the reſt; on the particular inſult which had
been offered to her juriſdiction by Admiral Boſcawen's attack on
Mr. de la Clue's ſquadron in a Portugueſe harbour. The memorial concluded with a declaration, that as ſoon as his moſt
Faithful majeſty had taken his reſolution, which they doubted
not would be favourable, that the king of Spain would march
his troops into Portugal, in order to garriſon the harbours and
defend them againſt the hoſtile attempts of the Engliſh. An
anſwer was required in four days, and any delay beyond that
time was to be conſidered as a negative.

Such inſolent propoſals were never made to an independent
kingdom. His Portugueſe majeſty anſwered in a moderate and
humble ſtrain, but with becoming firmneſs. He took notice of
the misfortunes of his country, which prevented her from
taking part in an offenſive war; he offered his mediation between the contending parties, but was reſolved at all events to
preſerve his faith to England inviolate; which ought not, he
obſerved, to give the ſmalleſt offence, as his alliance with that
crown was antient and merely defenſive. This anſwer drew on
a reply, in which the miniſters of the united kingdoms denied
that the alliance between England and Portugal was purely defenſive, and for this unheard-of reaſon, " That the defenſive
" alliance was converted into an offenſive one by the ſituation
" of the Portugueſe dominions, and the nature of the Engliſh
" power. The Engliſh ſquadrons," ſaid they, " cannot in all
" ſeaſons keep the ſea, nor cruiſe on the principal coaſts for
" cutting off the French and Spaniſh navigation, without the
" ports and the aſſiſtance of Portugal; that theſe iſlanders
" could not inſult all maritime Europe, if the whole riches of
" Portugal did not paſs into their hands; which furniſhes them
" with the means to make war, and renders the alliance be-
" tween the two courts truly and properly offenſive." They
conclude moſt inſultingly, " That the king of Portugal ought
" to be glad of the neceſſity which they laid upon him to make
" uſe of his reaſon, in order to take the road of his glory and
" of the common intereſt." The king replied with ſufficient
ſpirit;

A. D. fpirit; the two minifters took leave and retired the 27th of
1762. April; and; immediately after, war was declared by France
and Spain againft Portugal.

The advantages which Portugal poffeffed in herfelf for ba-
lancing this powerful combination, confifted principally in the
nature of the country, which is fo extremely barren and uncultivated as to make it very difficult for any confiderable army
to fubfift in it. The badnefs of the roads, and the number
and fteepnefs of the mountains, made it no lefs difficult to advance by rapid marches, and to improve the advantages of the
campaign with proper expedition. Add to this, that towards
the frontiers of Spain the only roads are narrow and difficult
defiles, which may be maintained by a fmall body of forces
againft a very powerful invafion. But, notwithftanding thefe
circumftances, the whole hopes of Portugal centered in the affiftance from England. The greater her own weaknefs, the
more confpicuous were the magnanimity and refources of Great
Britain, who, at the clofe of fo expenfive and ruinous a war,
made fuch aftonifhing efforts in protecting her allies. She fent
a fquadron of ten fhips of the line to Lifbon f, befides frigates.
With thefe fhe fent officers, troops, artillery, military ftores,
provifions and money; every thing that could enable the Portuguefe to exert their natural ftrength, and every thing which
could fupply that ftrength where it was deficient.

The Spaniards could entertain no hopes of depriving the
Englifh of the ufe of the Portuguefe ports by attacking them
by fea; fo that they repofed their whole confidence in the bravery and good fortune of their troops. It belongs not to our defign to give a particular account of the military operations in
this effeminate country, which could hardly furnifh out a faint
image of war. The inacceffible and difficult nature of the

---

f Lift of Sir Edward Hawke's fquadron which failed from St. Helen's for Lifbon, June 25th.

| | | | | |
|---|---|---|---|---|
| Royal George, | — | 100 guns. | Naffau, | — | 64 guns. |
| Princefs Amelia, | — | 80 —— | Effex, | — | 64 —— |
| Prince, | — | 90 —— | Achilles, | — | 60 —— |
| Ocean, | — | 90 —— | Launcefton, | — | 40 —— |
| Magnanime, | — | 74 —— | Æolus, | — | 32 —— |
| Prince of Orange, | — | 70 —— | Tartar, | — | 28 —— |
| Lancafter, | — | 66 —— | | | |

country, joined to the spirit and activity of the British troops, A. D were sufficient to defend the Portuguese dominions with very 1762 feeble efforts on the part of the natives. After a campaign of about five months the Spaniards had got possession of no advanced posts in which they could maintain themselves during the winter. The heavy rains, which begin to fall in October, and the want of provisions for men and horse in an enemy's country, made them fall back to the frontiers of Spain, where every thing had been provided for them in great abundance.

Thus did the arms of Great Britain save Portugal, by undertaking to defend her cause within her own territories. The same power protected this useful ally not only against present but future dangers, by the operations carried on in remote parts of the earth, where the success of the British squadrons compelled the house of Bourbon to accept terms of accommodation, in which the interests of Portugal were not neglected.

While the English troops were employed in taking possession of Martinico and the dependent islands, a French fleet appeared to windward of the former, and sent an officer on shore to obtain information. They continued cruising to windward for two days, and even approached within cannon-shot of Trinity, as if they had intended to make a descent; but afterwards they changed their course, and bore away for the harbours of Dominica. Admiral Rodney, being informed of their arrival in those parts, got under sail with his squadron, and beat up to windward in quest of the enemy; they did not wait his approach, but made haste to take refuge in their own harbours. While Rodney's fleet commanded the Caribbees, Lord Colville's squadron was stationed at Halifax in Nova Scotia, in order to protect the coast of North America, and the new conquests in the gulf and river of St Lawrence. Sir Charles Saunders was reinforced in such a manner as enabled him to give law in the Mediterranean, and either to prevent a junction of the French and Spanish fleets, or, if that should be found impracticable, to give them battle when joined. For the defence of the British coast, and in order to answer the emergencies of war, a powerful squadron was kept in readiness at Spithead; another rode at anchor in the Downs, under the command of Admiral Moore; and from these two

A. D.  were occasionally detached into the channel, and all round the
1762. island, a number of light cruisers, which acted with such vigilance and activity, that not a ship could venture from any of
the French sea-ports without running the most imminent risque
of being taken ; and scarce a day passed in which some privateer of the enemy, either French or Spanish, was not brought
into the harbours of Great Britain.    Rear-admiral Cornish had
the direction of the fleet in the East Indies, Admiral Pocock
who had acquired so much glory there, being called to a more
dangerous and important command, the consequences of which
we are now going to relate.    The whole of these squadrons
combined with detached cruisers in different parts, amounted to
more than 240 ships of war ; a force which, considering the
disciplined valour and naval experience of our seamen, was fit
to contend against the maritime strength of the whole world
united.

The rupture with Spain, which was rendered incurable by the
invasion of Portugal, brought on the execution of a plan which
had been long in agitation, upon the presumed probability of
such an event.    It is said that Admiral Knowles was the first
who laid before his Royal Highness the duke of Cumberland a
scheme for the reduction of the island of Cuba, in which the
whole trade and navigation of the Spanish West Indies centers,
and without which it cannot be carried on.    The duke approved
of the plan, and recommended it to the ministry.    But after
they had considered the draughts and plan, which his royal highness put into their hands, Lord Anson, the first lord of the admiralty, produced his own, which had been made out upon
more accurate information ; and after maturely considering both
plans, Lord Anson's was adopted.    However, the duke of Cumberland had so much merit in this affair, that he was permitted
to appoint his favourite Lord Albemarle commander in chief of
the land forces, and his brothers, major-general and commodore
Keppel, to important commands in an expedition which, it was
imagined, would be equally lucrative and honourable.

Nothing indeed could be so proper at this time as an attempt
against the Spanish West Indies.    The French were now expelled from every place in North America, except their settlement
                                                              of

of Louisiana, which was deemed of little importance.    They A. D.
had lost their West India islands; so that hardly any thing re- 1762
mained to be done in that part of the world but an expedition
against those of Spain.    But it shewed great wisdom in the British administration, who determined on this measure, that they
fixed their eyes at once on the capital object.    The failure of
an armament in a subordinate attempt is a bad preparative for a
greater; as the former, even though successful, is far from
being decisive.    The plan of the war of 1740, in which we
began with smaller attempts, and so proceeded to more considerable, was mean and ignoble, because the success in the first
of those attempts did nothing to insure success in the second;
nor were both together of any consequence in deciding the fortune of the war.    But the plan now adopted was great and just;
for by beginning with the Havanna we aspired at a conquest,
which being obtained, would enable us to terminate the war
with honour, as it entirely intercepted the enemy's resources;
and if we chose to prosecute our advantage, the acquisition of
the Havanna might put us in possession of the whole Spanish
America.

The fleet destined to extend the British empire in the west,
sailed from Portsmouth the 5th of March, under the command
of Admiral Pocock, whose valour and conduct had contributed
so much towards that sovereignty which his country possessed in
the East Indies. They sailed for the island of Hispaniola, where
they were happily met at Cape Nicholas, the north-west point
of the island, by a detachment from the fleet at the Caribbees,
under the command of that gallant and able officer Sir James
Douglas.    The junction happened on the 27th of May; and
the united squadrons consisted of 19 sail of the line, 18 smaller
ships of war, and about 150 transports, having on board above
10,000 land forces and marines.    A supply of 4000 men had
been ordered from New York, which, it was supposed, would
arrive time enough to bear part in their military operations.

There were two choices before the admiral for his course to
the Havanna.    The first and most obvious was the common
way to keep to the south of Cuba, and fall into the tract of the
galleons.    But this, though by much the safest, would prove

by

by far the moſt tedious paſſage ; and delays, above all things, were dangerous, as the fleet had been ſo late in ſailing from England, that it would be extremely difficult to arrive before the hurricane ſeaſon, which would put an end to all naval and military operations. He therefore reſolved to run along the northern ſhore of the iſland of Cuba, purſuing his courſe from eaſt to weſt, through a narrow paſſage not leſs than 700 miles in length, called the Old Straits of Bahama. This paſſage, through almoſt the whole of its extent, is bounded on the right and left, by the moſt dangerous ſands and ſhoals, which has cauſed the navigation to be avoided by ſingle and ſmall veſſels. There was no pilot in the fleet whoſe experience could be depended on to conduct them ſafely through it. The admiral, however, being provided with a good chart of Lord Anſon's, reſolved to truſt to his own vigilance and ſagacity to carry through thoſe ſtraits a fleet of near 200 ſail. So bold an attempt had never been before made ; but the ſucceſs of the expedition depending entirely on diſpatch, made it prudent to hazard it. At the ſame time no precaution was omitted, which could remove the imputation of temerity. A veſſel was ſent to reconnoitre the paſſage, and make ſoundings : ſome frigates followed ; floops and boats were ſtationed on the right and left, on the ſhallows, with well-adapted ſignals both for the day and the night. The fleet moved in ſeven diviſions, and being favoured with a fair wind and good weather, got through this perilous paſſage on the 5th of June without accident or interruption.

Two days before the accompliſhment of this hazardous navigation, the Echo and Alarm frigates, which had been ordered a-head of the fleet, deſcried four veſſels which proved to be the Thetis, a Spaniſh frigate of 18 guns and 65 men, and the Phœnix of 22 guns and 175 men, and two brigs, bound to Suga in the Straits, for a cargo of timber for the uſe of the ſhips at the Havanna. The Engliſh frigates gave them chace, and obliged them to ſtrike in three quarters of an hour. This, though a ſmall ſucceſs, was an auſpicious beginning of the expedition againſt the Havanna. This place, the object of their long voyage and of ſo many anxious hopes and fears, was now before
them.

them. Though St. Jago, fituated on the fouth-eaft fide of the island be denominated the capital of Cuba, yet the Havanna is fuperior to it in wealth, fize, and importance. The harbour upon which it ftands is, in every refpect, one of the beft in the world. It is entered by a narrow paffage, upwards of half a mile in length, which afterwards expands into a large bafon, fufficient to contain 1000 fail of the largeft fhips, having almoft throughout fix fathoms water, and perfectly fecured from every wind. In this bay the rich fleets from the feveral parts of the Spanifh Weft Indies affemble, in order to fet out together on their voyage to Europe. Great care had been taken to fortify a place which, befides being extremely populous, wealthy, and flourifhing in itfelf, is the centre of the richeft commerce of the world. The entrance into the harbour is fecured on one fide by the Moro fort, built upon a projecting point of land, all of folid mafon-work, having a ditch 70 feet deep from the edge of the counterfcarp, and more than 40 feet of that depth funk in the rock: on the other it is defended by a fort called the Puntal, which joins the town. The Havanna itfelf, which is fituated to the weft of the harbour, and oppofite to the Moro fort, is furrounded by a good rampart, flanked with baftions, and ftrengthened by a ditch.

The Spaniards, fenfible that, upon a rupture with Great Britain, their Weft Indies were the faireft mark for the attack of the enemy, maintained a powerful fleet in thofe parts, and had actually a confiderable fquadron of fhips of the line in the harbour of the Havanna[s]. But fo little confidence did they repofe in their fhipping for refifting the efforts of the Englifh armament, that the only ufe which they made of it was to fink three of their largeft veffels behind an immenfe boom which they had thrown acrofs the mouth of the harbour. Their chief

[s] Lift of Spanifh fhips at the Havanna:

| | | | | | |
|---|---|---|---|---|---|
| Tiger, | — | 70 guns. | Afia, | — | 64 guns |
| Reyna, | — | 70 — | America, | — | 6 — |
| Soverano, | — | 70 — | Europa, | — | 60 — |
| Infante, | — | 70 — | Conqueftador, | — | 60 — |
| Neptune, | — | 70 — | San Genaro, | — | 60 — |
| Aquilon, | — | 70 — | San Antonio, | — | 60 — |

hope

hope was in the ftrength of the place, and the difficulties attending all military operations which are drawn out to any confiderable length in this unhealthy climate. Thefe circumftances encouraged Don Juan de Prado, governor of the Havanna, to determine on a vigorous defence. He was affifted by the activity of the Marquis del Real, commodore of the fleet, and by the counfels and experience of the viceroy of Peru, and the governor of Carthagena, who happened to be then in the place on their way to their refpective governments.

On the 7th of June all things were in readinefs for landing ; and, in order to effect this with the leaft inconvenience, the admiral, with the greateft part of the fleet, bore away to the weftward, that the enemy's attention might be drawn towards this quarter, while the earl of Albemarle and the whole army were landed, under the direction of Commodore Keppel, between the rivers Bocanao and Coxemar, about fix miles to the eaftward of the Moro-caftle. A body of Spaniards appeared on the fhore ; but, fome floops being ordered to fcour the beach and the woods with their cannon, the troops paffed the river Coxemar in great order, without the fmalleft oppofition. The firft attempt was to drive the enemy from a fmall redoubt on the top of the hill Cavannos which overlooked the Moro. This was effected on the 10th, and at the fame time three bombketches, being anchored on the fhore, began to throw fhells into the town, under cover of the fhips Stirling-caftle and Echo.

The principal body of the army, deftined to act againft the Moro, was divided into two corps, one of which, commanded by General Elliot, advanced a confiderable way into the country, towards the fouth-eaft of the harbour in order to cover the fiege, and to fecure the parties employed in watering and procuring provifions. The other, conducted by General Keppel, was immediately employed in the attack on the fort, and a detachment headed by Colonel Howe, was encamped to the weftward of the town, partly with a view to cut off the communication between it and the country, and partly to make a diverfion in favour of the grand operation.

The feamen having landed fafcines, ftores, and artillery with great expedition, the engineers, under the direction of Mr. Mackellar,

kellár, whofe abilities were equally diftinguifhed at Louifbourgh A. D
and the Havanna, began to erect batteries of bombs and cannon, 1762,
while a body of poineers were employed in cutting parallels, and
forming a line with fafcines to fecure the troops from the fire
of the enemy. The hardfhips fuftained in this fervice are almoft
inexpreffible. The thinnefs of the earth made it extremely difficult to cover the approaches. It was neceffary to cut roads for
communication through thick woods. The artillery was to be
dragged a great way over a rough rocky fhore. During this
fatigue the fupplies of provifion were not plentiful, and water
was to be brought from a great diftance. Many men dropped
down dead with heat, thirft, and fatigue. But the fpirit and
ardour of the troops, the unanimity and conduct of the commanders by fea and land, overcame every difficulty. On the
29th, 2000 chofen Spaniards, with a numerous body of Negroes and Mulattoes, landed in two divifions, to the right and
left of the Moro, with an intention to deftroy the works of the
befiegers. They were repulfed by the piquets and advanced
pofts with great bravery, and compelled to retreat in confufion,
leaving behind them 200 of their number killed or taken.

The cannonading began, on the 1ft of July, from two
batteries bearing twelve cannons, fix large mortars, three
fmall ones, and twenty-fix royals. The enemy had feventeen
pieces of artillery on the front attacked. The fire was for a
confiderable time pretty near on an equality, and kept up with
great vivacity on both fides. At length that of the enemy began
to fail. Their attention was divided in confequence of an attack
made upon the north-eaft face by three fhips of the line, the
Cambridge, Dragon, and Marlborough, commanded by the
Captains Gooftrey, Hervey, and Barnet. Thefe fhips, having
laid their broadfides againft the fort, kept up one of the warmeft firings ever feen, for feven hours, without intermiffion. But
the Moro, fituated upon a high hill, had great advantages, and
the fire from the oppofite fort of Puntall galled them exceedingly. They were obliged to retire in a very fhattered condition,
after lofing above 100 men, among whom was captain Gooftrey
of the Marlborough, a brave and experienced officer.

When

When the Spaniards were releafed from the fire of the fhips, they redoubled their activity againft the batteries, and on both fides a conftant unremitted fire was kept up for feveral days. During this fharp and doubtful contention the merlons of the grand battery unfortunately took fire on the 3d of July. The flames became too powerful for oppofition, and the labour of 600 men, for feventeen days, was deftroyed in a few hours. This ftroke was felt the more feverely, becaufe the other hard-fhips of the fiege were become fcarcely fupportable. Sicknefs had reduced the army to almoft half its number. Three thoufand feamen were at one time unfit for fervice, and near double that number of foldiers. The fcarcity of water, and the total want of wholefome provifions, exafperated the difeafe. The army was ready to perifh by thefe calamities; and, if the hurricane feafon came on before the place were reduced, the deftruction of the fleet was inevitable.

The unconquered fpirit of the commanders could hardly maintain the languifhing activity of the troops, when Sir James Douglas who had parted from the admiral, in order to fteer his courfe for Jamaica, arrived with the fleet from that ifland, carrying many conveniences for the fiege. This favourable circumftance with the hopes of a confiderable reinforcement from New York, which arrived a few days afterwards, reftored the vigour of the men, and rouzed them to every effort. New batteries arofe in the place of the old, the fire of which foon became equal, and afterwards fuperior to that of the enemy; the cannon of the fort was filenced, the upper works demolifhed, and a lodgement at length made in the covered way. Notwithftanding this advantage, the immenfe ditch cut in the folid rock formed an obftacle that was very difficult to furmount. To fill it up was impoffible, and the work of mining would have been impracticable, if fortunately a thin ridge of rock had not been left to cover the extremity of the ditch, which would otherwife have been open to the fea. On this narrow ridge the miners paffed wholly uncovered, and with very little lofs made a lodgment at the foot of the wall. While they formed a mine for throwing the counterfcarp into the ditch, another fap was carried on along the glacis. In the night of the 21ft a ferjeant and twelve men fcaled

led

led the wall by furprife; but, the garrifon being alarmed before A. D any additional troops could fuftain them, they were obliged to 1762 retreat.

The governor of the Moro now plainly faw, that the place muft be fpeedily reduced, unlefs fome bold meafure were tried for its immediate relief. Accordingly, next day at four in the morning, he ordered a fally to be made from the town by 1500 men, compofed chiefly of the country militia and negroes, divided into three detachments, who attacked the befiegers in as many different places. Meanwhile a warm fire was kept up from the fort of Puntall, and the fhipping in the harbour. But the Englifh guards, though furprifed, defended themfelves with great refolution, the pofts attacked were fpeedily reinforced, and the enemy were driven precipitately down the hill, without being able to deftroy any part of our approaches. The Englifh loft fifty men killed or wounded, and the Spaniards had 400 killed or taken prifoners.

On the 30th of the month, about two in the morning, a floating battery was towed into the harbour, and fired with grape-fhot and fmall arms into the ditch, though without any great interruption to the miners; and the clofe fire of the covering party foon compelled the enemy to retire. This was the laft effort for the relief of the Moro: for on that day the mines did their work. A part of the wall was blown up, and fell into the ditch, leaving a breach which, though very narrow and difficult, the engineer judged practicable. Orders were immediately given for the affault. Lieutenant-colonel Stuart commanded the attack. The troops, hoping to fee an end of all their hardfhips, entered on this moft dangerous fervice with the greateft refolution. The enemy who were drawn up to receive them, when they had paffed the breach, were terrified at the determined valour which appeared in their countenances, and fled on all fides. In vain Don Lewis de Velafco the governor, whofe bravery and conduct had excited during the whole fiege the admiration of his enemies, endeavoured, with romantic courage, to defend the colours of Spain. He fell, as well as his fecond the Marquis Gonfales, while attempting to no purpofe to rally his troops. About 400 of the garrifon laid down their arms, and were

VOL. IV. E e made

A. D.
762.
made prisoners: as many were slaughtered on the spot; others ran to the boats, and were drowned in attempting to escape to the town.

The Moro-fort thus came into the possession of the English after a vigorous struggle of 40 days from the commencement of the operations against it. This advantage was not immediately followed by the surrender of the Havanna. The governor seemed still determined to defend that place, the fire of which was immediately turned against the fortress which had been lost, while a ship of the line was sent down into the harbour, in order to batter it with more effect. Meanwhile Lord Albemarle ordered a line of batteries to be erected along the hill of the Cevannos, which commanded almost the whole eastern side of the city. Batteries were likewise erected on the western side of the town, which had hitherto been only guarded. When these preparations were perfectly ready to take effect, his lordship, by message, represented to the governor the irresistible force of the attack which he was ready to make on the place, but which, in order to prevent unnecessary effusion of blood, he was willing to suspend, that the Spaniards might have time to capitulate. This representation was made on the 10th of August, but to no purpose, the governor returning for answer, that he was determined to defend the place, committed to him, to the last extremity. Next morning at day-break, forty-five cannon and eight mortars, erected on the batteries at Cevannos, began to play against the town and the Puntall with such continued and irresistible fury, that this fortress was silenced before ten. In another hour the north bastion was almost disabled. About two in the afternoon white flags were displayed from every quarter of the town, and in a little time after a flag of truce arrived at the head quarters with proposals of capitulation. The established religion and the ancient laws were to be preserved, and private property was secured to the inhabitants. The garrison, which was reduced to 700 men, were to have the honours of war, and to be conveyed to Old Spain, together with the Spanish commodore, the governor of the Havanna, the viceroy of Peru, and the governor of Carthagena. The Spaniards struggled hard to save twelve ships of the line which lay in the harbour;

bour; but this was a capital point, and wholly inadmiſſible. A. D
They likewiſe made powerful attempts to have the harbour de- ː762
clared neutral during the war; but this would have deſtroyed,
in a great meaſure, the importance of the conqueſt. It was de-
bated for two days, when hoſtilities were on the point of being
renewed; which made the enemy recede from their demand,
and the Engliſh took poſſeſſion of the place the 14th of Auguſt[b].

The acquiſition of the Havanna united in itſelf all the advantages that can be obtained in war. The enemy loſt a whole
fleet; they were deprived of a wealthy eſtabliſhment commanding a rich and extenſive territory; and they ceded a port which
commanded the only paſſage by which their ſhips could conveniently ſail from the bay of Mexico to Europe. While this port
is in the hands of an enemy, who are maſters at ſea, the court
of Madrid can receive no ſupplies of treaſure from the Weſt
Indies, except by beating up to windward from Carthagena,
which would expoſe them to infinite trouble as well as danger
from the Engliſh ſquadrons, or by ſurrounding Cape Horn, or
paſſing through the Straits of Magellan from the South-ſea, a
voyage of intolerable length, and ſubject to equal inconveniencies. The reduction of the Havanna, while it diſtreſſed the
enemy in the moſt eſſential manner by ſtopping the ſources of
their wealth, opened an eaſy avenue to the conquerors for
reaching their American treaſures. In no former war had Great
Britain acquired ſuch immenſe ſums at the expence of her enemies. Her ſucceſs in the Eaſt Indies is ſaid to have brought into
England near ſix millions ſince the commencement of hoſtilities;
and, in the conqueſt now made, ſhe obtained, beſides an immenſe quantity of artillery, ſmall arms, ammunition, and warlike ſtores, about three millions ſterling in ſilver, tobacco, and
valuable merchandiſe, collected, on account of the king of Spain,
in the magazines of the Havanna. In this calculation of national
profit we muſt not omit the capture of the Hermione, a regiſter
ſhip, the value of which fell little ſhort of a million ſterling. If
it had not been for theſe extraordinary pecuniary ſupplies, with
which the war was attended, it would have been difficult to

ⁱ See Appendix, N° XII.

E e 2

carry

A. D carry it on to fuch an amazing extent. The money which was
1762. brought into the kingdom invigorated commerce, and urged the
hand of induftry. The remittances for foreign fubfidies were in
a great meafure paid by bills on merchants fettled abroad, who
had received the value of thefe draughts in the produce of Britifh manufactures. The trade of England increafed gradually
every year, and fuch a fcene of national profperity, during the
courfe of a long, expenfive, and bloody war, was never exhibited by any people in the world.

In the expedition againft the Havanna, the fpirit, unanimity,
and perfeverance of the army and navy were eminently confpicuous. Never indeed was there a period of fuch cordial co-
operation between the land and fea forces, or fuch a punctual
attention to orders. One captain only, of the name of Campbell, having neglected to perform his duty in leading the fquadron which attacked the Moro, was obliged to quit the fervice.

As it is our plan to give an account of the more important
enterprizes, which fucceeded through the co-operation of the
navy, before we proceed to relate the exploits purely naval
which diftinguifh the year 1762, we muft now carry the
reader's attention to the expedition againft the Philippine iflands,
which is one of the beft conducted, moft fplendid, and moft important of all the fucceffes which adorn the annals of this glorious war  The defign of this expedition, which, if fuccefsful,
would give as fevere a wound to the interefts of Spain in the
Eaft-Indies, as fhe had received, by the taking of the Havanna,
on the fide of America, was fuggefted by the following accident.
After the memorable defence of Madrafs in 1759, Colonel Draper's bad ftate of health obliged him to leave that country. He
embarked in company with the honourable Captain Howe, then
commander of the Winchelfea, for Canton in China, a place with
which the inhabitants of the Philippines carry on a confiderable
traffic. Here the colonel employed himfelf in acquiring a minute
knowledge of the prefent ftate of the Spaniards in thefe iflands,
and difcovered that, confiding in their remote diftance from
Europe, they were perfuaded, that no attempt againft them
would ever be deemed practicable. This had lulled them into
                                                        fuch

fuch a perfect fecurity, that they had totally neglected the keeping up of a regular military force for their own defence.

Colonel Draper communicated his ideas on this fubject to
Lord Anfon and Lord Egremont, upon the firft rumours of a
war with Spain. His information met with that attention which
it deferved. He was defired to give a memorial in writing, explaining his plan at full length, and affured, that, if a Spanifh
war became unavoidable, the undertaking fhould be recommended to his majefty.

The motives to the execution of this enterprize were many
and powerful. The Philippines or Manillas form a principal
divifion of that immenfe Indian Archipelago, which confifts of
above 1,200 iflands, extending from the nineteenth degree of
north latitude, almoft in a continued chain, to the fhores of New
Guinea and the great fouthern continent. The Philippines,
which form the northernmoft clufter of thefe iflands, are, fome
of them, among the largeft, and all of them, naturally, among
the richeft iflands in the world. They were added to the Spanifh monarchy, in its meridian glory, under Philip II. and,
being happily fituated for commerce, they were ufed as the centre of communication for the Afiatic and American trade. They
may receive European goods by the way of the Cape of Good
Hope, and connecting the traffic of China, Japan, and the
Spice-iflands with that of Europe and America, unite all the
extenfive dominions of Spain in one commercial chain with the
richeft countries upon earth.

The principal ifland of the Philippines is called Manilla or
Luconia, extending 300 miles in length, and 90, at a medium,
in breadth. The foil is cultivated by the natives with uncommon induftry for this part of the world; the Chinefe, who, after the Tartar conqueft in the laft century, fled here in great
numbers, are the artizans, and the Spaniards enjoy the government, and beft part of the commerce. The reft of the Philippine iflands, as far as the Spanifh power prevails in them, are
under the government of Luconia, the capital of which is Manilla, fituated on the fouth-eaft of the ifland, and lying upon a
very fair and fpacious harbour. Here the large veffels or galleons annually arrive, and from this place they fail for Acapulco

A. D.  pulco in America, loaded with money or goods to the value of
1762.  near a million ſterling. In the war of 1739, the taking one of
theſe galleons was conſidered as the moſt brilliant ſucceſs which
attended the Britiſh ſquadrons. But now they were to aim at an
higher object; not at a particular cargo, but at the principal
mart of commerce which ſupplied this cargo; and which, when
put in our poſſeſſion, would enable us to deſtroy the intercourſe
of any other European ſtate with the empires of China and Japan, while it procured the higheſt reſpect for the Britiſh flag all
over thoſe wealthy and extenſive regions.

The grandeur of this deſign was ſufficient to rouze the moſt
vigorous efforts of adminiſtration. But the additional weight
of Spain, in the ſcale of the enemies of Great Britain, required
all the exertions of her ſtrength nearer home. It was impoſſible, therefore, to ſpare ſhips or troops for undertaking a conqueſt ſo diſtant and precarious, however advantageous and
ſplendid. But, fortunately, the preceding events of this glorious war naturally paved the way for thoſe which were to follow. The ſucceſs of one expedition not only ſuggeſted the idea,
but facilitated the execution of another. By the fortune of our
arms in the eaſt, we were become arbiters of the great peninſula of India; the French were expelled; the Dutch humbled;
and there was nothing in thoſe parts to reſiſt the Britiſh force,
or even to afford employment to all the troops that were kept
on foot. Nothing, therefore, was demanded from Great Britain, but a light frigate to carry Colonel Draper to Madraſs,
where alone ſuitable preparations might be made for this important enterpriſe. He arrived there the latter end of June, 1762,
and was appointed brigadier-general and commander in chief of
the land-forces to be employed in the expedition. The ſquadron
commanded by Vice-admiral Corniſh, a brave and able officer,
conſiſted of ſeveral ſhips of the line[i], beſides frigates. The
troops allotted for this expedition conſiſted of one regiment,

i Theſe were the Norfolk, Panther, America, Seaford frigate, Eliſabeth,
Grafton, Argo frigate, Lenox, Weymouth, Seahorſe frigate. The Falmouth
was left at the requeſt of the preſident and council of Madraſs, to convoy the
Eſſex Indiaman which had on board the treaſure for the China cargoes; but ſhe
arrived time enough to have her ſhare in the expedition.

with

with a company of the royal artillery, reinforced with 600 fe- A. D.
poys, one company of Caffres, one of Topazes, one of pioneers, 1762.
with several hundreds of unarmed Lascars, for the use of the
engineers and the park of artillery. The admiral supplied a
fine battalion of 550 seamen, and 270 marines. The whole
force amounted to no more than 2300 effective men; an inconsiderable number, but of tried valour, inured to toil and hard-
ship, and rendered equal by their disciplined bravery to the
strength of a great army. The 79th regiment, which was the
only regular body of troops employed on this service, had been
the first who checked the progress of the French in India; their
valour had given the happy turn to the war under Colonel
Coote; they were inured to the climate, and accustomed to
victory; and their arms were worthy to extend the glory of
Great Britain to the remotest verge of Asia.

The enterprise was no sooner resolved upon, than the admiral detached Captain Grant of the Seahorse to the entrance of
the Chinese sea, with instructions to intercept all vessels bound
for Manilla, that the enemy, who were even ignorant of the
declaration of war, might receive no intelligence of any design
formed against them. The success of the enterprise depended
much on expedition, not only in order to prevent the enemy
from being rouzed from their security, but in order to take advantage of the wind; for if the north-west Monsoon should set
in with any violence before the fleet were well advanced on their
voyage, the whole design would be defeated. Accordingly no
time was lost. In the space of three weeks the troops were
embodied and formed, and the stores got ready and shipped,
notwithstanding a raging and perpetual surf, which in those climates is one of the greatest difficulties in any expedition, greatly embarrassing the embarkation, and rendering still more hazardous the debarkation of troops, especially in the face of an
enemy.

The fleet sailed in two divisions the beginning of August, and
on the 19th arrived at Malacca; a place formerly considered as
the key of the Indian commerce, and still the centre of a very
considerable trade. The Dutch, to whom it now belonged, although they looked with no very favourable eye on the progress

of

A. D. of the English in thofe eaftern regions, were afraid to difcover
1762. any fymptom of jealoufy. The English fleet ufed Malacca as
a port of their own, and fupplied themfelves not only with refrefhments, but with every neceffary not already provided for
the fiege of Manilla. In 39 days from Malacca they came in
fight of Luconia; the weather having in general proved favourable, although the fquadron was once feparated in a ftorm.

The next in command to the vice-admiral was Commodore
Tiddeman; and the battalion of feamen and marines was under
the Captains Collins, Pitchford, and Ourry, who behaved during the whole fervice with equal gallantry and conduct. The
officers fubordinate to Brigadier-general Draper were the Lieutenant-colonels Monfon and Scott, Major Barker who commanded
the artillery, and Major Moore. Mr. Drake, and fome other
gentlemen in the Eaft-India company's fervice, were appointed
to take care of the interefts of their conftituents, according to
a convention made with the prefident and council of Madrafs,
by which the Eaft-India company were to have a third part of
the booty or ranfom, and to be invefted with the government of
the conquered country. The land and fea forces agreed by
common confent to participate in the diftribution of their feveral captures, according to the rules eftablifhed in the navy. The
character of the commanders, as well as thefe wife precautions,
prevented the leaft difagreement from arifing between the army
and marine, either in the conduct of the enterprife, or in the
divifion of the fruits of their fuccefs.

The admiral having founded the coaft, difcovered a convenient place for landing the troops, about two miles to the fouthward of Manilla. On the 24th of September, the proper difpofitions being made, and the three frigates Argo, Seahorfe,
and Seaford, moored very near the fhore, to cover the defcent;
three divifions of the forces were put on board the boats of the
fleet, conducted by the Captains Parker, Kempenfield, and Brereton, and landed at the church and village of Malata. This
was not performed without great difficulty, on account of a violent furf, which dafhed many of the boats to pieces. At the
fame time the enemy began to affemble in great numbers,
both horfe and infantry, to oppofe the defcent, but the Captains

2                                           King,

King, Grant, and Peighin, who commanded the covering fri- A. D
gates, maintained such a warm fire of cannon to the right and 1762
left that they soon dispersed, and the general disembarked his
troops without the loss of a single man. The days which immediately succeeded their landing were spent in seizing the most
advantageous posts, in securing the communication with the navy, and in reconnoitring the roads and approaches to the town.
They found it defended by some good works, constructed in a
regular manner, and garrisoned by about 800 Spanish troops.
The English forces were too few to invest the place, so as to
prevent it from being supplied with provisions from the country, or from receiving assistance from the natives, a fierce and
daring people, who, though unacquainted with the use of fire
arms and the regular discipline of war, were like all the inhabitants of the Indian isles, extremely formidable on account of
their martial spirit, native intrepidity, and contempt of death.
The governor of the place was a churchman and archbishop,
who stiled himself Captain-general of the Philippines; and,
however ill qualified by his profession for the defence of a town
attacked, seemed well fitted for this task by his spirit and resolution.

The day after the troops landed the enemy abandoned a small
fort called the Pulverista, which proved an excellent place of
arms for covering the landing of the stores and artillery. Colonel Monson, with an advanced party of 200 men, occupied
the church of the Hermita, about 900 yards from the city.
The head quarters were fixed in the curate's house, and secured
by the seventy-ninth regiment, as a post of the utmost importance, both from its strength, and the commodious cover it afforded from the rains which had deluged the country, and rendered it impossible to encamp. The marines were left at the
Malata, in the neighbourhood of the Pulverista, to preserve tho
communication with the fleets, and guard the stores and artillery, which, on account of the surf, were not landed without
great danger and fatigue. The battalion of seamen were stationed between the seventy-ninth regiment and the marines; and
a body of men was advanced within 300 yards of the town, and
possessed themselves of the church of St. Jago, which they

maintained, notwithſtanding its being expoſed to the fire of the enemy.

Before batteries could be erected, the enemy, on the 26th of September, attempted a ſally with about 400 men. They were commanded by the Chevalier de Fayette, and having two field-pieces, advanced to the right of the Engliſh advanced poſts, and began to cannonade. But Colonel Monſon at the head of the picquets, reinforced by a ſmall body of ſeamen, ſoon drove them back into the town. Their retreat was ſo precipitate that they left one of their field-pieces on the glacis.

It was imagined that the evidence of their inferiority in this ſlight encounter would be an inducement to the governor to endeavour at obtaining advantageous terms by an early ſurrender. A ſummons was ſent to him for this purpoſe; to which he returned ſuch an anſwer as ſhowed we had nothing to expect but what we were able to command. Indeed, had the valour of the garriſon correſponded to the ſpirited declaration of the governor, the town would have had nothing to apprehend from an enemy, whoſe numbers obliged them to confine their operations to one corner of the place, leaving two thirds of it open to all manner of ſupplies. The front, to which the attack was directed, was defended by the baſtions of St. Diego and St. Andrew; a ravelin which covered the royal gate, a wet ditch, covered way and glacis. The baſtions were in good order, mounted with a great number of fine braſs cannon; but the ditch had never been completed, the covered way was out of repair, and the glacis was too low.

While the works were going forward with great rapidity, ſome ſtraggling ſeamen were murdered by the ſavages, which induced the governor to ſend out a flag of truce to apologiſe for this barbarity, and at the ſame time to requeſt the releaſe of his nephew, who had been lately taken in the bay by the boats of the fleet. His demand was complied with, and lieutenant Fryar was ſent under a flag of truce, to conduct the priſoner to town. At that time a detachment of the garriſon, intermixed with a body of Indians, ſallied out to attack one of the poſts of the beſiegers; when the ſavages, ignorant of the law of nations, and diſregarding the ſacred character of an officer under a ſafe conduct,

conduct, affaulted Mr. Fryar with the moft brutal fury, mang- A. D
ling his body in a moft fhocking manner, and mortally wound- 1762.
ing the Spanifh gentleman, who endeavoured to protect his conductor. In their attack they were foon repelled by the Britifh
party who defended the poft; their favage cruelty had exafperated the troops, and whenever they fell into the hands of the
Englifh foldiers, they found no mercy.

Meanwhile the indefatigable vigour and unconquerable fpirit
of our foldiers and feamen had raifed three batteries for cannon
and mortars, which played on the town with confiderable effect.
The navy which had hitherto affifted no otherwife than in covering the landing, and in furnifhing men and ftores, began
now to take a direct part in the fiege. On the 29th the admiral
ordered the Elifabeth and the Falmouth to lie as near the town
as the depth of water would allow, and to enfilade the enemy's
front in order to fecond the operations of the army. Although
the fhallows kept them at too great a diftance to have all the
effect which could have been wifhed, their fire did not fail to
produce great confufion and terror among the inhabitants, and
to add very confiderably to the fatigue of the garrifon.

The operations of the befiegers were for fome days retarded
by an event which threatened to deftroy at once all the effects
of their induftry and courage. During the firft days of October a
deluge of rain poured down, accompanied by a mighty ftorm
of wind. The fquadron was in the greateft danger, and all
communication with it and the army entirely cut off. The
South-fea Caftle ftore-fhip, which had lately arrived, and contained the greateft part of the tools and neceffaries for profe-
cuting the fiege, was driven on fhore. The governor, or arch-
bifhop of the place, added to the advantage of thefe appearances in his favour, by calling in the aid of his ecclefiaftical
character. He gave out, that the angel of the Lord was gone
forth to deftroy the Englifh, like the hoft of Sennacherib of
old; and this miferable fuperftition did not fail to raife the fpirits of a fearful and cowardly garrifon.

The circumftances of this ftorm, by an extraordinary fpecies
of good fortune, became favourable to the befiegers. The
South-fea Caftle, by being driven on fhore without any confi-

derable damage, gave an eafy and ready accefs to all the ftores and provifions which fhe contained. In the fituation in which fhe lay on fhore, her cannon became a protection to the rear of the Englifh camp; and, by enfilading the whole beach to the fouthward, fhe kept in awe a body of Indians who threatened an attack on the Pulverifta and the magazine of the befiegers at the Malata. At the fame time the confidence which the enemy derived from the natural helps arifing from the ftorm, and in the fupernatural ones added by their fuperftition, rendered them more remifs and languid in their defence; while the roaring of the fea, occafioned by the great furf, prevented them from hearing the noife of the Englifh workmen, who were bufy in the night in completing the feveral batteries, in finifhing a parallel and communication from thefe to the advanced poft at the church, on the left of which they eftablifhed a fpacious place of arms. All this was accomplifhed on the 3d, and, the battery being opened againft the left face of St. Diego's baftion, the fire was fo well directed by the fkill of Major Barker, that in a few hours twelve pieces of cannon, mounted on the face of the baftion, were totally filenced, and the enemy obliged to retire. In lefs than two days all their other defences were greatly impaired.

The Spaniards, feeing their fortifications no longer tenable, projected a fally difpofed in two attacks upon the two moft important pofts of the Englifh. The firft was to be made upon the cantonment of feamen, who were known to have had the moft confiderable part in the management of the artillery during the whole fiege. The fecond was to be made on the church of St. Jago, which had been of fo much confequence in protecting the befiegers in their approaches, and which covered a flank of the army.

In the middle of the night preceding the 4th of October, 1000 Indians marched out upon the firft attack. They were much encouraged by the inceffant rains, which they hoped had rendered the fire-arms ufelefs; while their own arms, confifting only of bows and lances, could fuffer nothing from fuch accidents. Their approach was favoured by a great number of thick bufhes, growing on the fide of a rivulet, through which they

paffed

paffed in the night, without being perceived by the patroles. A. D When they arrived at the quarter of the feamen, they began the 1762 work of deftruction with a more than hoftile fury. The Englifh, though furprifed, maintained their ground with fteadinefs, and repelled the mad rage of the favages with manly perfevering courage. Prudently fatisfied with this advantage, they remained firm in their pofts till day-break, when two picquets of the feventy-ninth regiment arrived to their affiftance. The Indians, notwithftanding the weaknefs of their armour, advanced in the moft refolute manner to the attack, fought with incredible ferocity, when repulfed, returned with redoubled fury to the muzzles of the Englifh mufquets, and died like wild beafts gnawing their bayonets. At length, however, they were obliged to retreat before the difciplined valour of the Englifh, having loft 300 men in this daring and unequal attack.

The bad fuccefs of the firft attempt did not difcourage thofe who were ordered on the fecond. This began juft as the former had been defeated, and appeared at firft more favourable to the hopes of the Spaniards. The Sepoys, who defended the church of St. Jago, were far from poffeffing the firmnefs of the Englifh failors, and, being diflodged without difficulty, retired in confufion from their poft. The enemy, who confifted not only of Indians but of a ftrong detachment from the Spanifh garrifon, immediately feized the church, climbed to the top, and from thence poured down a violent fire on our people, who maintained themfelves with patience and refolution, until a detachment with ten field-pieces came to their relief. Then the Spaniards were compelled to give way, leaving 70 of their number dead on the fpot. Nor were we freed from thefe refolute attacks without confiderable lofs. This, with the former action, coft the befiegers above forty men, including Captain Strahan of the feventy-ninth regiment, and Lieutenant Porter of the Norfolk, two gallant officers who fell univerfally regretted.

This was the laft effort of the garrifon in its own defence. The unruly fpirit of the Indians, impatient of repulfe, and difcouraged by repeated defeats, led them to return home. The fire of the garrifon grew faint, and all the outworks of the enemy were now in a ruinous condition. The operations of the befiegers,

A. D. fiegers, on the other hand, were fo well directed, and carried
1762. on with fuch vigour, that on the 5th the breach appeared practicable. It was expected, that the garrifon would demand a capitulation, when no law of honour, becaufe there was no profpect of fuccefs, required a farther defence. But the befiegers
had to do with the fullen obftinacy of Spaniards, who neglected
all opportunities of obtaining favourable terms, and without
taking proper meafures for defending the breach.

The Englifh general, not finding any defire of capitulation in
the enemy, prepared without delay, and with the moft judicious
arrangements for the ftorm. On the 6th, at four in the morning, the troops deftined for this fervice filed off from their quarters in fmall bodies to avoid fufpicion, and, gradually affembling
at the church of St. Jago, concealed themfelves in the place of
arms, and on the parallel between the church and the battery.
Meanwhile Major Barker maintained a clofe fire upon every part
of the enemy's works, from which we might apprehend any moleftation. At day-break a large body of Spaniards were feen
formed on the baftion of St. Andrew, as if they had received
intimation of the intended affault, and had refolved to annoy the
affailants from the retired flanks of the baftion, where they had
ftill two cannon fit for fervice. But the explofion of fome fhells
thrown among them by the befiegers had fo good an effect,
that it made them difperfe and retire in confufion.

The Britifh troops took immediate advantage of this event,
and directed by the fignal of a general difcharge from the artillery and mortars, rufhed on to the affault under cover of a thick
fmoke which blew directly on the town. Lieutenant Ruffel, at
the head of fixty volunteers from different corps, led the way.
They were fupported by the grenadiers of the feventy-ninth regiment. A body of pioneers, to clear the breach, and, if neceffary, to make lodgements, followed; a battalion of feamen advanced next, fupported by two grand divifions of the feventy-
ninth regiment; and the troops of the Eaft-India company formed the rear. Difpofed in this excellent order, the affailants, to
the number of 2000 men, mounted the breach with amazing
fpirit and activity. The Spaniards retired fo fuddenly that it was
imagined they depended entirely on their mines. Captain Ste-
venfon was ordered to examine the ground, which removed all

apprehenfion

apprehenfion from this danger; and the Englifh troops penetra- A. D
ted into the town without meeting with any oppofition until they 1762
came to the royal gate, where there was a guard-houfe defended by 100 Spaniards and Indians. Here Major More was tranf-
fixed with an arrow, and about twenty of our men fell. The
guard refufed quarter, and were cut to pieces. In proceeding
forward the troops were galled with fhot from the galleries of
lofty houfes furrounding the great fquare. But the Spanifh foldiers every where gave way before them. Three hundred perifhed in endeavouring to efcape by paffing a deep and rapid river. The governor and principal magiftrates imprudently retreated to the citadel, which was by no means a tenable poft:
and, as the Englifh general had no offer of capitulation either on
the part of the garrifon or inhabitants, it was impoffible to prevent fome of the calamities which ufually happen to cities taken
by ftorm, from the cruel rapacious licenfe of the common foldiers. Thofe who had retired into the citadel, dreading to be
expofed to equal fufferings, furrendered at difcretion. The
marquis of Villa Medina, with the reft of the Spanifh officers,
were admitted as prifoners of war on their parole of honour;
and all the Indians were difmiffed in fafety. At the fame time
Admiral Cornifh and General Draper, influenced by a generofity
familiar to our commanders, though able to command every
thing by force, admitted the inhabitants to a capitulation, by
which they enjoyed their liberties, lives, properties, and the adminiftration of their domeftic government. In confequence of
this agreement the town and port of Cavité, with the iflands and
forts depending upon Manilla, were furrendered to his Britannic
majefty; and four millions of dollars were promifed as a ranfom
for faving the houfes and effects of the inhabitants ᵏ. The admiral
took poffeffion of feveral large fhips, with a vaft quantity of military and naval ftores; and the Englifh found here every refrefhment to recruit the men, and every neceffary to refit the
fquadron. The Eaft-India company were entitled to one third
of the ranfom, and the conqueft according to agreement was
delivered up to Dawfon Drake, Efq; and the other individuals
appointed to receive them in behalf of that company.

ᵏ As this ranfom was never paid, commanders in future will do well to take
hoftages.

This

This important acquisition was rendered complete by another fortunate event. During the siege Admiral Cornish received intelligence by the capture of an advice ship, that the galleon from Acapulco was arrived at the straits which form the entrance into the Archipelago of the Philippines. This intelligence was not to be neglected, as so rich a prize would greatly enhance the value of the conquest, and not a little compensate the disadvantage of a repulse. Two ships of war, the Panther a ship of the line, Captain Parker, and the Argo frigate Captain King, were immediately despatched in quest of the galleon. After twenty-six days cruising they descried on the 30th of October, being off the island Capul, a sail standing northward. The Panther being driven by the current among the Narangor, was obliged to anchor; but the Argo coming up with the chace, engaged her for near two hours, during which the English frigate was roughly handled, and even obliged to desist, until his damage could be repaired. The current flackening, Captain Parker was enabled to get under sail, and about nine next morning came up with the enemy, who after having been cannonaded near two hours at a very small distance, struck her colours. The English captain was not a little surprised to learn when the Spanish officers came on board, that instead of the Sancta Philippina, which was expected from Acapulco, he had taken the Sanctissima Trinidad, which was bound for that port. This vessel had left Manilla the first of August, and had sailed 300 leagues to the eastward of the Embocadero; but meeting with a hard gale of wind, and being dismasted, was obliged to put back and refit. In the first engagement with the Argo this galleon mounted only six guns, though she was pierced for sixty. In her engagement with the Panther, she mounted but thirteen. The English captains had both been surprised to find so obstinate a resistance, with so little activity of opposition. But their wonder ceased when they examined the galleon with attention. She was a huge vessel that lay like a mountain on the water, and her sides so excessively thick that the shot had made no impression upon any part, except her upper works. She had 800 men on board; and the value of her cargo was registered at one million and a

I

half

half of dollars; that which was unregistered in order to be A. D smuggled amounted to full as much; so that this capture was a 1762 valuable addition to the conquest, and a fresh wound to the enemy.

At no period of time had the Spanish monarchy suffered such mortifying disasters as in the course of this war; of which there was no conquest more advantageous in itself, or more honourably atchieved, than that of the Philippines. The British forces effected their landing before Manilla on the 24th of September; their battery of cannon was not completed until the 3d of October, and on the 6th they were masters of the city. In this short time, notwithstanding the tempestuous season of the year which prevented the communication between the land and sea forces, a territory was acquired consisting of fourteen considerable islands, which from their extent, fertility, and convenience of commerce, furnished the materials of a great kingdom. The conquest of the Havanna had in a great measure interrupted the communication between the wealthy American colonies of the Spaniards and Europe. The reduction of the Philippines now excluded them from Asia. The two together secured all the avenues of the Spanish trade, and cut off all intercourse between the parts of their vast but unconnected empire. Never indeed were any people more to be pitied than the Spaniards. They were plunged precipitately into a war against every principle of sound policy and caution, merely to gratify the private inclinations of their sovereign, in favour of the interests of his family, which stood in direct opposition to those of his people. Unfortunately for the happiness of mankind the former interests will always be preferred under the government of an absolute prince. Whatever conclusions, therefore, may be drawn, at any future period, in favour of the pacific intentions of the Spaniards, from the national advantages that would result from a pacific conduct, ought not to have great weight on the councils or measures of Great Britain. We ought in this case to distrust appearances. The advantage, at least the supposed advantage of a king of Spain and of his subjects, are not always the same. The national advantage is most obvious to strangers, but that of the king will prevail in the cabinet; and Spain will undertake another

A. D. war againſt Great Britain, though more ruinous than the for-
1762. mer, whenever the intereſts or honour of the houſe of Bourbon
demand her aſſiſtance. We may be permitted another obſervation at this particular time [k]. The ſucceſs of the laſt war
againſt Spain, than which none more brilliant is recorded in
hiſtory, depended in a great meaſure on the rapidity with which
all our meaſures were carried into execution. The garriſon at
the Havanna was in no ſtate of defence ; the inhabitants of
Manilla were unacquainted with the declaration of war. The
dominions of Spain from which ſhe draws her principal reſour-
ces, lying at an immenſe diſtance from the capital and one another, renders it more neceſſary for her than for any other
power to temporize, until ſhe can inſpire with activity all the
parts of her extenſive but disjointed empire. For this reaſon
Great Britain cannot be too much on her guard to watch the
firſt ſymptom of approaching hoſtility. To take the advantage
of the firſt ſtroke, without waiting for the formal declaration
of war, may expoſe her to the cenſure of minute politicians ;
but to wait patiently till ſhe herſelf receives it, will render her
the ſcorn of her enemies.

The reduction of the Manillas will be handed down as a memorable event to the lateſt poſterity. Another expedition,
which was much celebrated at the time, and which adorned the
luſtre of the Britiſh arms in the courſe of this autumn, was the
recovery of the iſland of St. John in Newfoundland. About
the latter end of May, intelligence was received by the admiralty
that a French ſquadron under the command of M. de Ternay had
ſailed from Breſt under cover of a fog. The deſtination of this
ſquadron being uncertain, Sir Edward Hawke, with the duke of
York as rear-admiral, were immediately ordered from Spithead
with ſeven ſhips of the line, and two frigates, in hopes that
they might fall in with the enemy. They viſited the coaſt of
France ; and, after cruiſing for ſome time in the chops of the
Channel for the protection of our trade, returned to Portſmouth,
not having ſeen M. de Ternay's fleet. It was deſcried, however, on the 11th of May, about fifty leagues to the north-

[k] October, 1778.

ward.

ward of the Lizard by Captain Rowley, who had failed with A. D three ships of war, the Superbe of 74 guns, the Gofport of 44, 1762 and the Danaé of 38, as convoy to a fleet of merchantmen bound to the Eaft and Weft Indies, and the continent of Ame-rica. Captain Rowley no fooner perceived them than he made a difpofition for battle, though greatly inferior in ftrength. The French fhips bore down upon him; when he hoifted Britifh colours, and fired at the neareft, when fhe was within little more than random fhot. The enemy immediately hoifted Eng-lifh colours, and tacked to the northward. He gave them chace till three in the afternoon, when they were fcarcely in fight; and, having no hope of bringing them to action, he difconti-nued the purfuit, and rejoined his convoy.

The French fquadron confifted of the Robufte of 74 guns, the Eveille of 64, the Garonne of 44, and the Licorne of 30, carrying 1500 foldiers under the command of the Count d'Hau-fonville. They fteered their courfe for Newfoundland, and on the 24th of June entered the bay of Bulls, where the troops were landed without oppofition. Having taken poffeffion of an inconfiderable Englifh fettlement in this bay, they fteered for the town of St. John's, which, being defended by no more than fixty-three men, furrendered upon capitulation. This little garrifon were made prifoners of war, together with the officers and crew of his majefty's floop the Gramont, which was in the harbour. The French likewife took feveral merchant-veffels, deftroyed the ftages erected for curing cod, and every thing elfe belonging to the fifhery. They afterwards began to repair the fortifications of the town, of which they had determined to keep poffeffion.

When the news of this lofs reached England, the antimini-fterial party employed it as a fubject of reproach againft the king's fervants. Their abufe, though mean, illiberal, and vul-gar, was not altogether ill-founded. Mr. Pitt's advice for guarding Newfoundland from any fuch attempt, had been ne-glected by the miniftry, who, while on this occafion they re-prefented the lofs of a place cold, barren, and inhofpitable, as of very little confequence, did not delay to prepare an arma-ment for regaining the poffeffion of it.

But

But their preparations for this purpose were rendered unnecessary by the vigilant celerity of Lord Colville and Sir Jeffery Amherst, who commanded by sea and land in North America. The former, upon receiving advice of the progress of the French in Newfoundland, immediately sailed thither from Halifax, and blocked up the harbour of St. John's with one ship of the line and one frigate only, even while M. de Ternay lay at anchor in it, with a superior squadron. On the 11th day of September his lordship was joined by Colonel Amherst, whom his brother Sir Jeffery had detached from New York, with orders to touch at Louisbourg, and take on board some troops, which, with those embarked at Halifax, amounted to about 800 men, chiefly Highlanders and light infantry. The light infantry landed, after a short resistance, at Torbay, about seven miles to the northward of St. John's, it not being possible to land at Kitty-vitty, where the enemy had stopped up the narrow entrance, by sinking shallops in the channel. The French had continued to annoy the boats, as the troops landed; until the light infantry obliged the enemy to retreat. The French afterwards took to the woods, through which the British had to march for four miles. They wounded several of our men with their bush fire, which was very troublesome till Captain M'Donald's company of light infantry rushed in upon them, took some prisoners, and dispersed the rest. The British forces advanced to the strong post of Kitty-vitty which they took sword in hand. This advantage secured their communication with the ships for landing the stores and artillery. The enemy posted on a hill on the other side of the river fired upon our men; but a detachment was sent to drive them from this eminence, from which they retreated with precipitation, leaving several prisoners behind. The French were still in possession of two very high and steep hills, the one in the neighbourhood of our advanced posts, and the other in the neighbourhood of St. John's, and commanding all the intermediate space. It was necessary to dislodge them; which was performed by Captain M'Donald with great bravery and resolution, at the head of his own and the provincial light infantry. With this corps he passed the sentries and advanced guard unobserved, and was not discovered till the main body of the French

saw

saw him climbing up the rocks, and almost at the top, which he A. D gained; having received the enemy's fire, he poured in his own 1762 with such vivacity that the French gave way. The gallant captain received a mortal wound; his lieutenant with four men were killed, and eighteen wounded.

On the 16th Colonel Amherst proceeded vigorously in his preparations to attack the town of St. John's. The breast-work and unfinished battery which commanded the harbour being taken, the entrance of the channel was cleared, and the stores and artillery were landed without difficulty. This was fortunately performed before a violent gale of wind, which happened immediately after, and drove Lord Colville to a considerable distance from the coast. In his absence M. de Ternay took advantage of a thick fog, to slip his cables and to make his escape, leaving the garrison of St. John's to defend itself. His ships were seen at a great distance by the British squadron; but his conduct was so unlike that of Englishmen in abandoning a place intrusted to his protection, that it was not imagined the ships which they descried could be those of M. Ternay.

On the 17th at night the colonel opened a battery, with one eight-inch mortar, seven cohorns, and six royals. The enemy, at the same time, began a brisk fire from the fort, and threw several shells. In the morning of the 18th the Count d' Haufonville, who had declared two days before, in a letter to Colonel Amherst, that he would not surrender the fort until it were totally destroyed, thought proper to alter his resolution, and to demand a capitulation. The garrison surrendered prisoners of war, on condition of being conveyed to Brest with the first opportunity; which condition was immediately fulfilled by Lord Colville, who had, by this time, returned into the harbour. Thus the town and fort of St. John's with all the other places which the French had taken on this coast were recovered by the indefatigable labour and persevering bravery of a handful of men, without the loss of above twenty soldiers in this important service.

In the retaking of St. John's as well as in the reduction of the Havanna and the Philippines, the fleet and army co-operated with singular harmony and success. As they underwent the same

fame fatigue, and were expofed to fimilar dangers, they ﹖
entitled to an equal fhare of glory as well as of reward. Bu﹖
is obvious that the vaft fuperiority of the Englifh feamen to ﹖﹖
French and Spanifh, and their firm hardinefs in performu﹖
fome branches of fervice which no land troops in the worl﹖
would have dared to attempt, was the principal caufe of that
uniform and uninterrupted train of good fortune which crownea
the Britifh arms. The manly firmnefs and perfevering refolution
of our feamen, directed by the experienced valour and active
vigilance of our naval commanders, overcame obftacles of art
and nature which appeared at firft fight unfurmountable. Every
meafure was taken at that critical moment which was moft favourable to its fuccefs; no advantage was left unimproved, no
error unrepaired. The whole plan of every expedition, as well
as its fubordinate parts, was conducted with heroic bravery,
and guided by confummate wifdom.

Nor was the merit of the fleet lefs confpicuous in thofe attempts which were more immediately directed againft the naval
ftrength and refources of the enemy In the courfe of the year
we meet with feveral actions at fea, which would adorn the annals of any country. We fhall relate them in the order of time
in which they happened.

Had the enemy's defigns fucceeded, we fhould have had few
exploits to boaft of near the coaft of France. In the month of
December of the year 1761, they attempted to burn at once all
the Britifh fhips of war that lay at anchor in the road of Bafque.
They prepared three fire-fhips, which being chained together,
were towed out of the port, and fet on fire with a ftrong breeze
that blew directly on the Englifh fquadron. This attempt, however, was made with hurry and trepidation, and the wind lucki-
ly fhifting drove them clear of the fhips they were intended to
deftroy. They were confumed to no purpofe, after blowing up
with a terrible explofion, and every perfon on board perifhing.
On the 7th of March, his majefty's fhip Milford fell in with a
Spanifh letter of marque in her paffage to St. Domingo.    She
had been a privateer of Bayonne, and pierced for 20 guns, but
carried at prefent only 16 fix-pounders, ten fwivels, and 94 men,
and had a valuable cargo on board.    The engagement was hot
and

…defperate.   Captain Man of the Milford foon received a A. D
…rtal wound.   Mr. Day the firft lieutenant, taking the com- 1762
…nd of the fhip, was immediately fhot through the head.  The
…efence of the king's fhip devolving on Lieutenant Nafh, this
fficer received feveral wounds in his hands and face.  The
engagement continued almoft for twenty-four hours, when the
enemy ftruck, both fhips being miferably fhattered.

About the fame time his Majefty's fhip Fowey, of 24 guns,
nine pounders, and 135 men, commanded by Captain Mead,
fell in with La Ventura, a Spanifh frigate of 26 guns, 12 pounders, and 300 men, carrying money to pay the Spanifh troops
at Porto-Rico and St. Domingo.  Thefe frigates engaged about
feven leagues from Cape Tiberone.  The fight continued an hour
and an half, when their mutual damages obliged them both at
the fame time to fheer off and repair.  This done, Captain Mead
at ten o'clock of the night bore down a fecond time on the enemy; but after exchanging a broadfide without any vifible effect,
it being too dark to form any fatisfactory notion of the diftance
and motion of the Spanifh veffel, he made fail to windward,
keeping a proper look-out, that he might not lofe fight of her,
but be able to renew the attack with advantage by day-light.
Accordingly in the dawn of the morning, the Fowey, keeping
her men at their quarters, ran up as clofe to the Ventura as it
was poffible without falling on board of her.  The engagement,
renewed for the third time, was more bloody and defperate than
before.   It lafted with extraordinary courage and conduct on
both fides till half an hour paft eight, when the Spanifh frigate
having received feveral fhot between wind and water, and being
reduced almoft to a wreck, was compelled to ftrike her colours.
She had near 50 men killed; and both fhips were fo much difabled that neither of them had tackles left to hoift out a boat,
nor indeed a boat that could fwim.  Captain Mead, who is
known by his ufeful invention for cleaning a fhip's bottom at
fea, had occafion for all his ingenuity on this occafion.   He
contrived by nailing tarpaulins over the fhot-holes of a fmall
boat, to bring the Spanifh officers on board the Fowey.  His
gallantry was the more confpicuous on this occafion, as the
fhip's mafter was drunk and unfit to give the leaft affiftance
during

A. D.    But their preparations for this purpofe were rendered unne-
1762. ceffary by the vigilant celerity of Lord Colville and Sir Jeffery
Amherft, who commanded by fea and land in North America.
The former, upon receiving advice of the progrefs of the French
in Newfoundland, immediately failed thither from Halifax, and
blocked up the harbour of St. John's with one fhip of the line
and one frigate only, even while M. de Ternay lay at anchor
in it, with a fuperior fquadron. On the 11th day of September
his lordfhip was joined by Colonel Amherft, whom his brother
Sir Jeffery had detached from New York, with orders to touch
at Louifbourg, and take on board fome troops, which, with
thofe embarked at Halifax, amounted to about 800 men, chiefly Highlanders and light infantry. The light infantry landed,
after a fhort refiftance, at Torbay, about feven miles to the
northward of St. John's, it not being poffible to land at Kitty-
vitty, where the enemy had ftopped up the narrow entrance, by
finking fhallops in the channel. The French had continued to
annoy the boats, as the troops landed; until the light infantry
obliged the enemy to retreat. The French afterwards took to
the woods, through which the Britifh had to march for four
miles. They wounded feveral of our men with their bufh fire,
which was very troublefome till Captain M'Donald's company of
light infantry rufhed in upon them, took fome prifoners, and
difperfed the reft. The Britifh forces advanced to the ftrong
poft of Kitty-vitty which they took fword in hand. This advantage fecured their communication with the fhips for landing the
ftores and artillery. The enemy pofted on a hill on the other
fide of the river fired upon our men; but a detachment was fent
to drive them from this eminence, from which they retreated
with precipitation, leaving feveral prifoners behind. The French
were ftill in poffeffion of two very high and fteep hills, the one
in the neighbourhood of our advanced pofts, and the other in
the neighbourhood of St. John's, and commanding all the intermediate fpace. It was neceffary to diflodge them; which was
performed by Captain M'Donald with great bravery and refolution, at the head of his own and the provincial light infantry.
With this corps he paffed the fentries and advanced guard unob-
ferved, and was not difcovered till the main body of the French
                                                            faw

saw him climbing up the rocks, and almoſt at the top, which he A. D gained; having received the enemy's fire, he poured in his own 1762 with ſuch vivacity that the French gave way. The gallant captain received a mortal wound; his lieutenant with four men were killed, and eighteen wounded.

On the 16th Colonel Amherſt proceeded vigorouſly in his preparations to attack the town of St. John's. The breaſt-work and unfiniſhed battery which commanded the harbour being taken, the entrance of the channel was cleared, and the ſtores and artillery were landed without difficulty. This was fortunately performed before a violent gale of wind, which happened immediately after, and drove Lord Colville to a conſiderable diſtance from the coaſt. In his abſence M. de Ternay took advantage of a thick fog, to ſlip his cables and to make his eſcape, leaving the garriſon of St. John's to defend itſelf. His ſhips were ſeen at a great diſtance by the Britiſh ſquadron; but his conduct was ſo unlike that of Engliſhmen in abandoning a place intruſted to his protection, that it was not imagined the ſhips which they deſcried could be thoſe of M. Ternay.

On the 17th at night the colonel opened a battery, with one eight-inch mortar, ſeven cohorns, and ſix royals. The enemy, at the ſame time, began a briſk fire from the fort, and threw ſeveral ſhells. In the morning of the 18th the Count d' Hauſonville, who had declared two days before, in a letter to Colonel Amherſt, that he would not ſurrender the fort until it were totally deſtroyed, thought proper to alter his reſolution, and to demand a capitulation. The garriſon ſurrendered priſoners of war, on condition of being conveyed to Breſt with the firſt opportunity; which condition was immediately fulfilled by Lord Colville, who had, by this time, returned into the harbour. Thus the town and fort of St. John's with all the other places which the French had taken on this coaſt were recovered by the indefatigable labour and perſevering bravery of a handful of men, without the loſs of above twenty ſoldiers in this important ſervice.

In the retaking of St. John's as well as in the reduction of the Havanna and the Philippines, the fleet and army co-operated with ſingular harmony and ſucceſs. As they underwent the

ſame

A. D. during the action.  The gunner, too, happened to be wounded
762. in the beginning of the engagement; and a lieutenant, with 24
men, were on fhore.

On the 3d of April, after this wreck was carried into Port-
Royal in Jamaica, the Huffar frigate, Captain Carket, attacked
four fhips, lying under a fort in Tiberone bay; one of which
carrying 16 guns fhe burnt, funk another of 14 guns, cut out
one of 16 and another of 12, and carried them into Jamaica.
In this defperate enterprize the Huffar had but one man killed
and 12 wounded; whereas the French had 17 killed and 35
wounded.  But moft of the crews of the enemy's fhips efcaped
afhore in their boats during the engagement.

On the 21ft of May two Britifh frigates, cruifing off Cape
St. Vincent, made prize of the Hermione, a Spanifh regifter-
fhip, bound from Lima to Cadiz, loaded with fuch a quantity
of treafure and valuable effects as enriched all the captors. The
Hermione had but 28 guns, and furrendered with little or no
refiftance; fhe was indeed in no fituation to make a proper defence, the officers on board not being acquainted with the declaration of war between the two kingdoms.  This fhip carried
2,600,000 hard dollars; and her whole cargo was valued at a
million fterling, which is more than had ever been before taken
in one bottom.  The lofs of fuch an immenfe treafure at the
beginning of a war which required the greateft expence, muft
have been a heavy blow to the ambition of the court of Madrid.
The prize was brought from Gibraltar to England, and the gold
and filver being conveyed in covered waggons to London, was
carried in proceffion to the bank, amidft the acclamations of
the people, who confidered this as an aufpicious omen of fuccefs in the war againft Spain.

In the beginning of April Captain Outry of the Acteon, in
the latitude of Tobago, took a large Spanifh regifter-fhip, bound
for Lagueira, laden with artillery, ftores, and ammunition. In
September, a fleet of 25 fail of French merchant-fhips, richly
laden with fugar, coffee, and indigo, took their departure from
Cape Francis for Europe, under convoy of four frigates.  Five
of thefe veffels were furprized and taken in the night by fome
privateers of New York and Jamaica.  Next day it was their

2                                      misfortune

misfortune to fall in with Commodore Keppel, who made prize A. D
of their whole fleet and convoy, which were carried into the 1762
harbour of Port-royal in Jamaica.

. Nor were the Britilh cruisers lefs fuccefsful on the coafts of
Europe. In the beginning of April Captain Gambier of the Burford arrived at Plymouth with a large Eaft-India-man which
had failed from the ifle of Bourbon with a valuable cargo, and
been taken by one of Admiral Pocock's fquadron in the chops
of the channel. About the end of Auguft Captain Hotham of
the Æolus chaced two Spanifh fhips into the bay of Aviles, in
the neighbourhood of Cape Pinas; and on the 2d day of September, ftanding into the bay, came to an anchor in fuch a
fituation as to bring his guns to bear not only upon one of the
fhips, but alfo upon a fmall battery fituated on an eminence.
After a fhort but warm conteft both the battery and fhip were
abandoned; but before Captain Hotham could take poffeffion
of his prize, fhe ran aground, and bulging, was burned by the
captors. On the 20th of September he took a veffel of confiderable value belonging to Bourdeaux. In the beginning of
November Captain Ruthven of the Terpfichore took a French
fhip of 20 guns bound from Bourdeaux to Cape Francis. The
Action, in which the captain was wounded, was fharp and obftinate. On the ninth of the fame month the enemy loft the
Oifeau, a frigate of 26 guns, commanded by the Chevalier de
Modene, who fell in with Captain Tonyn of the king's fhip
the Brune, about feven leagues from Carthagena. The engagement was maintained with great fpirit on both fides; but
at length the chevalier was obliged to fubmit, having loft about
30 men, including all his officers, excepting three, who with
himfelf were wounded in the action.

A continuation of fuccefs had infpired the Englifh with an enthufiafm of valour as well as of magnanimity. Of the firft we
have an example in an exploit of the Brilliant and Duke of York
privateers; and of the latter in the behaviour of Captain Clark
of the Sheernefs frigate. Thefe privateers entered a fmall port
near Cape Finifterre, defended by a battery at the entrance. In
two hours time they beat the Spaniards from the fort, hoifted
Englifh colours, and fpiked up the cannon. They might have
laid the town in afhes, but were fatisfied with burning two fhips,

A. D. and bringing off four more which were loaded with wine for
1762. the use of the Spanish fleet at Ferrol. The Minerva, a French
frigate, had, in company with four other ships of war, given
chace to the Sheerness commanded by Captain Clark, who took
refuge in the harbour of Villa Franca, and there anchored, the
wind blowing fresh. He was immediately followed by the Captain of the Minerva, who, actuated by an idle spirit of vanity
and insolence, resolved to lie between him and the shore, and
ran his ship upon the rocks which bound the eastern side of the
harbour. Being himself ignorant of the art of seamanship, and
ill assisted by a crew little acquainted with such emergencies,
his ship was in a short time dashed in pieces; and a considerable
number of his people perished, notwithstanding all the assistance
he could receive from his consorts. On this melancholy occasion Captain Clark, forgetting they were enemies, and that this
very calamity was occasioned by their resentment against him
and his country, exerted himself vigorously for their relief. He
could not have done more if his friends had been in danger.
By this generous assistance the greatest part of the crew and all
the officers were saved.

The same firm and resolute spirit, and the same enterprizing
gallantry, appeared in every branch of the English marine.
Even the packets performed exploits which would have done
honour to ships of war of any other country. The Hampden,
of eight carriage guns and 30 men, sailing between Faro and
Gibraltar, was attacked by 11 privateers, which bore down in
order of battle. The commodore was a barcolongo of eight
guns and 60 men; the second was a xebeque of the same number of guns and men; five of a lesser size followed a little a-stern;
other four carrying 30 men each, with one gun in the prow,
brought up the rear. The engagement began at eleven in the
forenoon in sight of Gibraltar, and continued till half past
one, when that mighty squadron were ordered by the commander in chief to haul their wind, and to return from whence they
came. The Hampden proceeded to Gibraltar, with her sails
and rigging greatly damaged, but without any other considerable
loss. The Harriot packet, in her passage from New York to
Falmouth, discovered equal gallantry, having twice repulsed a

French

French privateer of more than double her force. The captain A. D was rewarded with a purfe of an hundred guineas, and promo- 1762 ted to the command of a Lifbon packet.

It would be tedious to relate every naval exploit of the year 1762, in the courfe of which our men of war and privateers fought and took 120 confiderable prizes, carrying 844 guns and near 6000 men. Neither French nor Spaniards had force at fea which was fit to annoy our trade in any great degree, and they were deterred from rifking their lives and properties on board of privateers, by the rough treatment which thefe commonly met with from the Englifh frigates or armed merchant-men. Since the Spaniards, through the ambition of the court, had been precipitated into this fatal war, they had loft 12 fhips of the line befides frigates ; and the French had been deprived of a marine fufficient to conftitute the ftrength of a great kingdom. Their whole lofs amounted to 18 fhips of the line and 36 frigates taken ; fourteen fhips of the line and thirteen frigates deftroyed. On the other hand the French took two and deftroyed three Englifh frigates ; and thirteen Britifh fhips of the line, with fourteen frigates, were loft by accident. But not one capital Englifh fhip fell into the hands of the enemy.

The profpect of rich plunder, which always attends a Spanifh war, had revived the fpirit of privateering, after it was in a great meafure extinguifhed by the repeated difafters of the French, which had left them fcarcely any thing more to lofe by fea. Some attempts were made in this way, which feem bold and daring beyond the fpirit and abilities of private perfons. The expedition againft Buenos Ayres in particular, though it ended unfortunately by a fatal accident againft which human prudence is too weak to provide, deferves, on account of the boldnefs and magnitude of the defign, to be recorded among the memorable naval exploits of the year. It was the laft act of hoftility between the Englifh and Spaniards, and concluded in a manner the moft proper for difpofing brave and generous nations to a mutual forgivenefs of injuries, and a fincere defire of accommodation.

The attempt againft this Spanifh fettlement was undertaken by fome private adventurers, after we had made ourfelves ma-

fters

fters of the Havanna, and taken meafures for the conqueft of the Philippines.   Government thought proper to encourage their defign, not fo much from any lucrative motive as on account of the fituation of Buenos Ayres, which of all the Spanifh colonies lies the moft conveniently for molefting the poffeffions of our Portuguefe allies, and which, if we fhould be fo fortunate as to get it into our power, would afford a ftation well adapted for enterprizes againft the trade and the dominions of Spain in the South Seas. The embarkation was made from the Tagus, and confifted of the Lord Clive and Ambufcade privateers, the former of which was equal in force to a fhip of 50 guns.   They were reinforced by a Portuguefe frigate, and fome fmall armed veffels and ftore-fhips, and had on board 500 foldiers, partly Englifh, partly Portuguefe.   The expedition was under the command of Captain Macnamara, an adventurer of fpirit and experience, who had been many years a captain in the Eaft-India company's fervice, and had embarked his whole fortune in the prefent enterprife.

The armament failed from Lifbon the 30th of Auguft, 1762, from which place to the mouth of the Plata the voyage proved favourable.   But when they had entered that vaft river the 2d of November, difficulties and obftructions began to encounter them on every fide.   A violent gale of wind, attended with thunder and lightning, attacked them at their entrance.   When the tempeft ceafed, they found that the river was fhoaly, and of fo difficult navigation that they muft meet with no fmall obftructions in making their way to Buenos Ayres.   The Spaniards were not here, as in other places, unacquainted with the declaration of war.   They were well prepared for making a vigorous refiftance, and had begun, fome weeks before, to act on the offenfive by taking the Portuguefe fettlement of Nova Colonia.

This unexpected intelligence and the difficulties of the voyage to Buenos Ayres determined the adventurers to abandon for fome time this firft defign, and to begin with the recovery of Nova Colonia. An Englifh pilot who knew the place and river, and whom they accidently met with on board a Portuguefe veffel, encouraged them to the attempt, undertaking to carry the
commodore's

commodore's ship into the harbour, and within pistol-shot of A. D the enemy's principal battery.

On the 1st of January, 1763, he made good his promise. The English ships arrived before Nova Colonia in good order, and the men in high spirits. They adorned their vessels with all the pomp and parade of a naval triumph. Their colours were fully displayed; the soldiers drest in new red uniforms, and disposed upon the poop and upon the tops, made a gallant appearance. In this manner they advanced to the attack the 6th of January, with horns sounding and drums beating, and every movement expressive of hope and victory.

The Lord Clive made the signal for engaging, and soon after anchored under the eastmost battery of the place, while the Ambuscade was exposed to a warm fire from the middle and west batteries, as well as from two Spanish frigates. But the plan of engagement was not exactly followed; the Portuguese frigate on which they had great dependence, having anchored at such a distance that none of her shot reached the shore. The Spaniards pointed their guns well, and stood to them with firmness. But the ships having rectified several mistakes in their first disposition, began a most fierce cannonading, which lasted from eleven in the forenoon till three in the afternoon, when the enemy's fire began visibly to abate, and their men to retire to the eastmost battery as the place of greatest security. Against this the fire of the English was directed with redoubled violence; and they had hopes every minute of seeing the Spanish colours struck. But when they were on the point of attaining the object of all their desires, the commodore's ship, by some accident which has never been accounted for, unfortunately took fire. In a moment she was all in a blaze; and the same instant discovered the flames and the impossibility of extinguishing them. There was to be seen a most dreadful spectacle. The sides of the vessel were immediately crowded with naked men, who but a few minutes before reckoned themselves in the assured prospect of wealth and conquest. Some clung to the sails and rigging until the violence of the flames obliged them to forego their hold; others precipitated themselves into the sea; many died by their own hands; and several of still more determined

courage

courage went to the lower guns in the midft of all this fcene of confufion and horror, and kept up a conftant fire on the enemy, till they were driven by the flames to perifh in another element. The commodore perifhed; and of 340 men, only 78 efcaped.

None of the other veffels durft approach the Clive for fear of fharing her fate. The Ambufcade, which had fuffered greatly from the enemy's fire, efcaped to the Portuguefe fettlement of Rio de Janeiro. Such of the Lord Clive's crew as, by uncommon dexterity in fwimming, reached the fhore, were humanely received by the Spaniards, whofe refentment was extinguifhed in the calamity of their enemies. The Englifh came to them naked; they clothed them decently; they were deftitute of every neceffary; they fupplied abundantly all their wants, received them into their houfes, and treated them rather like their deareft friends than enemies come to expel them from their poffeffions.

The war thus clofed with an action the fitteft that can be imagined to difpofe the minds of men to humanity, gentlenefs, and benevolence, and to prepare them for receiving with approbation the meafures which had been taken for giving peace [1] to the four quarters of the world.

[1] Concluded at Paris the 10th of February, 1763. See Appendix, No. XIII. for the articles of this treaty of peace.

LIVES

# L I V E S

## OF THE

# A D M I R A L S,

### INCLUDING A NEW AND ACCURATE

# N A V A L   H I S T O R Y.

## C H A P.   XXIV.

The Naval History of GREAT-BRITAIN, from the
end of the War in 1763 to the year 1779.

AS the war of 1755 had been undertaken in order to A. D
protect the British colonies in America against the en- 1763
croachments of the French, so the security of these
colonies seems to have been the principal object in the treaty of
peace, of which the terms were, doubtless, more advantageous
to the English settlements in America than to the island of Great
Britain. The unexampled success of the war enabled England
to dictate the conditions of peace. She had it in her option to
retain the West-India islands of Martinico, Guadaloupe, Ma-
riegalante, and Desiderade, the possession of which would have
brought the most important advantages to her commerce, or by
ceding these islands, to secure the American settlements on the
north

A. D. north by the acquisition of Canada. She preferred the interest
1763. of her colonies. It was no less in her power to retain the important conquests she had made from Spain, as to obtain an
equivalent for these conquests by stipulating such commercial
advantages as would' have added immense wealth to Great Britain, or to defend her American colonies in the south by acquiring the forts of St. Augustine and Pensacola, and the extensive
country of Florida. In this instance, also, the interest of America prevailed. The colonies were secured from every hostile
attack, and, at the price of British blood and treasure and every
national advantage, were placed in such a situation as no longer
required the protection of Great Britain. From that moment
they may be said to have obtained independence, when their
condition enabled them to assume it.

It has long been observed, that England generally loses by
negotiation the advantages which she has acquired by force of
arms. If this observation be well founded, the circumstance,
perhaps, does not so much arise from the unskilfulness of her
ministers as from the nature of the English constitution. In a
free country there are a great many little interests, all of which
must be considered by a minister, and some of which may be
allowed, at certain times, in consequence of a particular combination of circumstances, to prevail over the general interest of
the community. At the time that the public attention was employed in considering the proposed terms of peace, the conduct
of the West-India interest in parliament was extremely remarkable. The popular lord-mayor of London assumed the lead
among those colonists, who composed a powerful and complete
body in the house of commons. These gentlemen, while the
peace was in agitation, spared neither pains nor expence to persuade the English nation, that it was far more eligible to retain
Canada than the West-India islands. The reason for their being so anxious to spread this opinion, was, because the possession
of the French West Indies would have annihilated their own
importance; whereas the possession of Canada could not detract any thing from the value of Jamaica, Antigua, and the
other islands, in which their property consisted. It is said that
the late minister had, against his own sentiments, purchased

their friendſhip by complying with their deſires in this particular; A. D. and their clamorous efforts to render their own voice that of the 1763. public, had, doubtleſs, a conſiderable influence with the miniſters who negotiated the peace. But this was not all. The Engliſh had not yet learned to ſeparate their own intereſts from thoſe of America; and thoſe who then held the helm of affairs were fooliſhly dazzled with the notion of acquiring an extenſive and undiſturbed empire acroſs the Atlantic. When the Weſt-India patriots obſerved them determined in this deſign, and that the retaining of Canada and the ceſſion of the iſlands was a point irrevocable in the negotiation, they joined heartily in oppoſing the whole ſyſtem of the peace. The odium of this meaſure was thrown entirely on adminiſtration; but the clamour of pretended patriots and the ambition of courtiers had united in bringing about an event which has been one conſiderable ſource of the ſubſequent calamities which have befallen Great Britain.

The parliament which met in the year 1763 approved of the peace, and voted 16,000 men to be employed for the ſea ſervice for 1764, including 4287 marines. The king in his ſpeech had recommended keeping the fleet on a reſpectable footing; the ordinary of the navy amounted to 368,598 l. and 200,000 l. was voted towards the building and repairs of his majeſty's ſhips for 1764. Nothing could be more proper than theſe preparations, which inſured the performance of the articles of the general peace on the part of France and Spain; all of which, excepting the liquidation of the Canada bills, and the Manilla ranſom, were fulfilled with great punctuality.

Notwithſtanding the pacific intentions of the French and Spaniſh courts, ſome occurrences unavoidably happened in diſtant parts which were employed as arguments by the oppoſers of the peace for again embroiling Great Britain with both theſe kingdoms. The firſt event of this kind was a miſunderſtanding between the Engliſh and French commanders in America. This afforded matter for popular declamation; but, when the facts were fully explained, it appeared that the differences had entirely ariſen from the commander of an Engliſh frigate having, purſuant to his orders from England, obliged a French ſhip to keep within the bounds of navigation preſcribed by treaty. This mat-

A. D.  ter was hardly explained to the satisfaction of the public, when
1763.  a sloop of war arrived at Portsmouth from Newfoundland,
which represented the French fleet on that coast as extremely
formidable. It was asserted that the French, in direct opposition
to the treaty of peace, intended to fortify St. Peter's, and that
the British squadron in those parts, commanded by Mr. Palliser,
was by no means in a condition to prevent this measure. Upon
this intelligence, the party in opposition pronounced a French
war to be unavoidable, unless we were disposed to sacrifice all
our late conquests. Meanwhile Mr. Palliser dispatched a sloop
to the French governor at St. Peter's to inquire into the truth of
the reports which prevailed, and to know if he had mounted
cannon and erected works on that island. The governor answered by assurances that there was no more than one four-
pounder mounted, without a plat-form, and with no other intention than to make signals, and to answer those which were
made by the fishermen ; that the guard had never exceeded 50
men ; and that no works or buildings whatever had been erected contrary to the treaty. The suspicions had arisen from the
equivocal conduct of a captain of a French ship of 50 guns,
which, as it appeared by the commodore's letters, was the only
large vessel the French had in those parts. This ship, with one
frigate of 26 guns, and another of inferior force, formed their
whole strength, and Mr. Palliser was assured that none of those
vessels had ever attempted, or would ever attempt to enter into
any of the harbours on the coast of Newfoundland.

The clamour which was excited by the conduct of a French
squadron at Turk's island, was supported on a better foundation.
This place is the most considerable of a number of small islands
which go under the same name on the coast of Spanish Hispaniola.   It is only four miles in length, has not any good harbour, and is so barren and uncomfortable a spot that it is impossible for any settlement to subsist upon it.   But as the coast
abounds with various kinds of fish, especially turtle, and affords
great quantities of salt, the Bermudians and other British
subjects resorted thither in order to fish, and to gather salt
in the dry season. Two hundred of them were employed in
this manner in the month of June, when a French ship of 74
guns,

guns, with a fnow, floop, and xebeque, arrived from Cap A. L.
François. Having landed on Turk's ifland, they laid hold of the 176
Englifh, plundered and burnt their cabins, detained their perfons for fome days as prifoners, and when difmiffed, ordered
them never to return into thofe parts.   Mr. Lyttleton the governor of Jamaica was no fooner informed of thofe hoftilities
than he fent notice of them to the miniftry, who gave fuch inftructions as the occafion required to Lord Hertford, then ambaffador in France.   Meanwhile an account of the whole tranfaction was laid before the public ; and it was generally thought
that the French intended to attempt a fettlement on Turk's ifl-
and.   The oppofition reprefented the attack upon the Eng ifh
falt-gathers as a premeditated plan of the French politics, which
was to be executed by the treacherous D'Eftaign then governor
of St. Domingo, for expelling the Britifh fubjects not only from
thefe wretched iflands, but from all their other poffeffions in the
Weft Indies.   They infifted that the paft hoftilities and prefent
intentions of the French were a juftifiable ground for a new
war.   But this clamour was effectually filenced by the declaration of the French court in anfwer to the demands of the Britifh ambaffador.   It difavowed the proceedings of the French
fubjects in the Weft Indies, difclaimed all intention of acquiring or conquering Turk's ifland, ordered the Count d'Eftaign
to caufe thefe iflands to be immediately abandoned, and every
thing therein to be reftored to the condition in which it was
before the late violent proceedings.   Full reparation alfo was
ordered to be made to the Britifh fubjects for the lofs of their
property and other injuries, according to an eftimation to be
immediately fettled by the governors of Jamaica and St. Domingo.

The ufual remiffnefs of the court of Spain in giving inftructions to their governors in diftant parts, concerning the obfervation of treaties negotiated in Europe, had almoft occafioned a
rupture betwixt England and that kingdom, which, however,
terminated in a manner equally honourable for Great Britain.
On the 22d of February 1764, an order came from Don Jofeph  1764
Rofado, governor of Baccabar, commanding the Englifh fettlers
in the bay of Honduras to retire from every other place, and to
confine themfelves to the banks of the river Balis.  The Englifh

A D in thofe parts are under the protection of the governor of Ja-
1764. maica; to whom they formed a petition, fetting forth, "That
"   the Spanifh orders had occafioned a total ftagnation of bufi-
"   nefs; that the commanders of fhips who had hitherto fup-
"   plied the petitioners with provifions, feeing no probability of
"   being paid for what they had already furnifhed, declined be-
"   ing longer concerned in that commerce; and that having no
"   plantations of their own, and being cut off from the only
"   fupply in which they could confide, they faw no poffible
"   means of preferving themfelves and their families from fa-
"   mine." In confequence of this petition Governor Lyttleton
fent an agent from Jamaica to inquire into the true ftate of the
grievances complained of, and to ufe his beft endeavours to redrefs them. Upon inquiry it was found, that the order of the
Spanifh governor of Baccabar was in confequence of a letter of
the 29th of December 1763, written by Mr. d'Eftines, captain-
general of Jucatan, who had arrived at Campeachy on the 7th
of the fame month. This letter injoined the neceffity of confi-
ning the logwood cutters to particular diftricts, in order to prevent the Spaniards from being impofed on by pretenders to the
rights of Britifh fubjects. Accordingly the Englifh were limited
to 20 leagues up the fouth fide of the new river: in the river
Balis, and four leagues to the fouthward of its mouth, they
were not to be interrupted; but if difcovered beyond thefe limits, their negroes were feized, their property confifcated, and
their own perfons arrefted.

    While proper meafures were ufed in America for removing
thefe grievances, and for keeping the Spaniards to the 17th ar-
-ticle of the treaty, which afcertained the right of the Englifh to
cut logwood in the bay of Campeachy, the earl of Rochford,
then ambaffador at Madrid, had inftructions to complain of the
conduct of Mr. d'Eftines. To his memorial, which was dictated in the moft fpirited terms, the Spanifh minifter replied,
"   That he had no advices from that governor relative to the
"   fubject of the complaint; but that it was certainly his Catho-
"   lic Majefty's intention to abide by the 17th article of the laft
"   treaty of peace; that he had already given pofitive orders to
"   his governor of Jucatan for that purpofe; that thefe orders
                                          "  fhould

" fhould be renewed, and the Englifh no longer interrupted in
" cutting logwood in the ftipulated places."

This anfwer, though in appearance fufficiently explicit, did not fatisfy the antiminifterial party in Great Britain. They affirmed that the reply of his Catholic majefty's minifter was difingenuous, becaufe it ftipulated no fatisfaction to the fufferers, nor any punifhment on the offending party; and they called out for an immediate declaration of war againft Spain. Partly, perhaps, in order to quiet the violence of their clamours, the earl of Rochford was ordered to make frefh remonftrances. Thefe occafioned the fending of new orders to the governor of Jucatan, in which his proceedings with regard to the Britifh fubjects in the bay of Honduras are difapproved by his Catholic majefty; he is commanded to repair their injuries, to give them no difquiet in future under any pretence whatever; it being the defire of the king of Spain to preferve peace with Great Britain, and to give the greateft proofs of his friendfhip to the Britifh nation.

The pacific intentions of France and Spain, which had been fufficiently difcovered in every tranfaction fince the conclufion of the treaty, was entirely owing to the known ftrength of the Britifh navy in thofe parts where the natural enemies of this kingdom are moft vulnerable. The American feas were covered with Englifh fhips of war, which in a great meafure interrupted the illicit commerce between the Britifh colonies and the French and Spanifh fettlements. This occafioned affecting reprefentations to be fent from acrofs the Atlantic. The colonifts complained that all the Britifh fhips of war were now converted into guarda-coftas, and their commanders into fo many cuftom-houfe officers, who feized every foreign fhip carrying gold and filver to be exchanged for Britifh commodities; and they afferted that, if this refource by which they were fupplied with fpecie from France and Spain was cut off, it would be impoffible for them to make their remittances to England.

The univerfality of thefe complaints engaged the miniftry to mitigate the rigour of the orders which they had fent out at the conclufion of the peace to the Weft-India governors, and commanders of fhips, for annoying the contraband trade of the
colonies

A. D. colonies with France and Spain. The navy of Great Britain
1764. was thus delivered from a fervice, which was in fome meafure
unworthy of that dignity and fplendour by which it had been
diftinguifhed; and a few veffels were henceforth employed in an
undertaking which was more fuitable to the naval greatnefs of
this ifland.

It had long been a queftion with the learned, whether the
unexplored part of the fouthern hemifphere contained another
continent, or whether fo great a part of the globe exhibited only
an immenfe expanfe of water. The former opinion feemed to
be rendered probable by analogical reafoning concerning the
geography of the earth, and received fome additional ftrength
from the various difcoveries of new lands in thofe remote parts,
by the feveral commercial powers who held poffeffions in America. The Englifh, Portuguefe, Dutch, and French navigators
had diftinguifhed themfelves, for above two centuries, in this
immenfe field of enterprize; and, although they failed in all
their attempts to determine the main queftion, they met with
fuch a variety of new objects as gave rife to other queftions,
and excited frefh curiofity. Soon after the acceffion of his prefent majefty to the throne, a defign was formed of fending out
veffels for examining with particular attention the wonders of
the fouthern hemifphere, and for confirming what was true and
detecting what was falfe in the various and contradictory accounts of former navigators. In the year 1764, the kingdom
being then in a ftate of profound peace, the Dolphin and the
Tamer, the former a fhip of war of the fixth rate, and the latter a floop mounting fixteen guns, were defpatched for this purpofe, under the command of Commodore Byron, whofe inftructions, dated the 17th of June in that year, explain the nature
and object of the expedition. " Whereas nothing can redound
" more to the honour of this nation as a maritime power, to
" the dignity of the crown of Great Britain, and to the ad-
" vancement of the trade and navigation thereof, than to make
" difcoveries of countries hitherto unknown; and whereas there
" is reafon to believe that lands and iflands of great extent,
" hitherto unvifited by any European power, may be found in
" the Atlantic Ocean, between the Cape of Good Hope and
　　　　　　　　　　　　　　　　　　　　　　" the

" the Magellanic Streights, within the latitude convenient for
" navigation, and in climates adapted to the produce of commo-
" dities useful in commerce; and whereas his majesty's islands
" called Pepy's island and Falkland islands, lying within the
" said tract, notwithstanding their having been first discovered
" and visited by British navigators, have never yet been so suf-
" ficiently surveyed, as that an accurate judgment may be form-
" ed of their coasts and product, his majesty taking the premi-
" ses into consideration, and conceiving no conjuncture so proper
" for an enterprize of this nature as a time of profound peace,
" which his kingdoms at present happily enjoy, has thought fit
" that it should now be undertaken." Captain Byron, pursuant
to these instructions, sailed from the Downs on the 21st of
June; and having visited the Falkland islands, passed through
the Straits of Magellan into the Pacific Ocean, where he discovered the islands of Disappointment, George, Prince of Wales,
Danger, York island, and Byron island. He returned to England in the month of May in the year 1766—having determined
in the course of this long navigation many doubtful points, the
result of which is highly interesting to the public, and may be
of great importance to future navigators.

Commodore Byron came in sight of Cape Frio on the coast
of Brazil on the 11th of September, and anchored the day following in the great road of Rio de Janeiro. This city is governed
by the viceroy of Brazil, who received the English officers with
a ceremonious politeness. The people aboard the commodore's
ship, having been supplied with fresh provisions and greens every,
day, were very healthy; but there being many sick aboard the
Tamer, a place was appointed for them on shore, where they
soon recovered. On the 16th of October both ships weighed
anchor, and the crews were impatient to get to sea, in order to
avoid the excessive heats which prevail on that coast. They
were obliged, however, to remain five days above the bar,
waiting for the land breeze; nor was it without much difficulty
they got out at last, on account of the narrowness of the entrance between the two first forts, which renders the passage so
dangerous that the ships must have been lost, had they followed
the advice of the Portuguese pilot. During the delay at Rio de

A. D.
1764.
Janeiro feveral Englifh failors were decoyed by the Portuguefe to leave their refpective fhips. This is a common practice on the coaft of Brazil, efpecially at Rio de Janeiro, where the Portuguefe, carrying on a great trade, fpare no pains, nor labour, nor deceit to entice foreign feamen to enter into their fervice.

The commodore, having loft fight of the coaft of Brazil on the 22d of October, called all hands upon deck, and informed them that he was not, as they imagined, bound immediately to the Eaft Indies, but upon certain difcoveries, which it was thought might be of great importance to our country, in confideration of which the lords commiffioners of the admiralty had been pleafed to promife them double pay, and feveral other advantages, if during the voyage they fhould behave themfelves to his fatisfaction. They all expreffed the greateft joy upon the occafion; affured him they would undergo with cheerfulnefs every difficulty and danger in the fervice of their country, and obey his orders with the utmoft zeal. The commodore continued to fteer his courfe towards the fouth; and on the 11th November found himfelf in the latitude, 42 degrees 34 minutes fouth; longitude, 58 degrees 17 minutes weft. While he was in the latitude of 35 degrees 50 minutes, he found the weather as cold as it is in the fame feafon in England, although the month of November is a fpring month in the fouthern hemifphere, anfwering to the month of May in Europe; and they were 20 degrees nearer the line than we are in Britain; fo much colder is it towards the fouthern regions of the earth. The people on the forecaftle were frequently deceived with the appearance of land On the 12th November they called out at once, " Land right a-head." The commodore looked forward under the forefail, and faw what at firft appeared to be an ifland, rifing in two rude craggy hills. He fent officers to the maft-head who called out that they faw land a great way to the windward. As they continued their navigation, the land ftill kept the fame appearance, and the hills looked blue, as they generally do at a diftance. Many of the feamen faid they faw the fea break upon the fandy beaches; but having fteered for above an hour, what they had taken for land vanifhed at once, and, to their great aftonifhment, appeared to have been a fog

2

bank.

bank. After this extraordinary difappointment the commodore A. D
fhaped his courfe for Cape Blanco, which he difcovered on the 1764
17th, but after two days failing was ftill at a lofs for Port Defire, no defcription being more confufed than that which Sir
John Narborough had given of that harbour. On the 20th he
difcovered an ifland, which correfponded with Narborough's
defcription of Penguin ifland; and in the evening faw a remarkable rock, rifing from the water's edge like a fteeple, on the
fouth fide of the entrance of Port Defire. This rock is an excellent land-mark for the harbour, which is otherwife very difficult to find. During his ftay at this place, which was till the
5th of December, the commodore ordered every part of it to
be founded, and found that there is no danger but what may be
feen at low water. He difcovered feveral wells of frefh water
at a fmall diftance from the beach, and found great quantities
of guanicoes and wild fowl. Here is alfo fuch plenty of excellent mufcles, that a boat may be loaded with them every trip
at low water; and in fome parts of the coaft there are bufhes
which might produce a tolerable fupply of fuel. On the whole,
Port Defire would be a very convenient place for fhips to touch
at, if it were not for the rapidity of the current.

Having unmoored on the 5th December, they proceeded in
fearch of Pepy's ifland, which is faid in Cowley's voyage to ly
in 47 degrees fouth latitude. But they fought for it during feveral days in vain, and were at length obliged by hard weather
to fteer for the Cape Virgin Mary, the north entrance of the
Streights of Magellan. On the 20th they ran clofe in fhore to
this cape, there being a long fpit of fand running to the fouthward. In the evening they brought up clofe to this fpit of fand,
having feen many guanicoes feeding in the vallies, and a great
fmoke all the afternoon. At this place the Dolphin anchored;
but the Tamer, not being able to fetch the anchoring ground,
kept under way all night. However, both veffels anchored next
morning two miles from the fhore. This was the coaft of Patagonia, which, according to very early accounts was faid to
be inhabited by a race of giants; but the veracity of thefe accounts had become doubtful, from the contradictory affertions
of many later navigators who had been on that coaft, and had

A. D. never met with any men of an extraordinary stature. This cir-
1764. cumstance naturally engaged the commodore's attention. When
his ship, therefore, had come to an anchor, he saw exactly
what had happened to the crew of the Wager, as mentioned in
the account written by Mr. Bulkeley of her voyage. A great
number of horsemen rode backwards and forwards directly
abreast of the ship, waving in their hands something white as an
invitation for them to come on shore. The commodore, being
extremely desirous to know what these people were, ordered
out his twelve-oared boat, and went towards the beach with
Mr. Marshal his second lieutenant, and a party of men well
armed, Mr. Cumming his first lieutenant following in the six-
oared cutter. When they came within a short distance of the
shore, they saw above 500 people, some on foot, but the greater part on horseback, who continued waving and hallooing,
as invitations to land. They appeared to be entirely unarmed;
but the commodore made signs to them to remove to a little
distance, with which they immediately complied. The English
then landed, and were drawn up on the beach, where the commodore ordered them to continue, while he alone went forward
towards the Indians, who retired as he approached. He therefore again made signals that one of them should come near,
which one of them who appeared to be a chief immediately complied with. He was of a gigantic stature, and seemed to realize
in part the tales of Polyphemus of old. He had the skin of a
wild beast thrown over his shoulders, and his face was painted so
as to make a most hideous appearance. The commodore did not
measure him, but supposes his height to have been about seven
feet. With this frightful Colossus he marched forward to join
the rest, who still continued at a distance, as they had been desired. Mr. Byron made signs for them to sit down, which they
readily obeyed. There were among them several women proportionably large, and few of the men seemed less than the chief
who had first come forward. They received with much pleasure the trinkets which were distributed among them, and behaved in a most regular and orderly manner, no one testifying
the least impatience or displeasure, that his neighbour was served
before him, or that his present was better than his own. They
made

made figns for the commodore to go along with them, and of- A. D
fered him one of their horfes; but he made them underftand 1764
that he muft return to his fhip, at which they expreffed great
concern. During the pantomimical conference, an old man often laid his head down upon the ftones, and fhutting his eyes for
about half a minute, firft pointed to his mouth, and afterwards
to the hills, meaning probably, that if the ftrangers could ftay
all night, he would bring them fome provifions. Thefe people
are not only tall, but well proportioned: except the fkins which
they wore with the hair inwards, moft of them were naked, a
few only having on their legs a kind of boot, with a fhort
pointed ftick faftened to each heel, which ferved as a fpur.
When the commodore, and fome of his people who had by
this time come up, thought proper to leave them, not one of
them offered to follow, but continued to remain in the fame
pofition in which they had been placed. They had a great
number of dogs, with which they probably hunt the wild animals which ferve them for food. Their horfes were not large,
nor in good cafe, yet they appeared to be nimble and well broken. The bridle was a leathern thong, with a fmall piece of
wood that ferved for a bit, and the faddles refemble the pads,
which are ufed among the country people in England. The
women rode aftride, and both men and women without ftir-
rups; yet they galloped fearlefsly over the fpit upon which the
Englifh landed, the ftones of which were large, loofe and flip-
pery.

Mr. Byron, having quitted this part of the coaft, and being
in latitude 51 degrees fouth, and longitude 63 degrees 22 minutes weft, obferved on the 14th of January a low flat ifland,
full of high tufts of grafs refembling bufhes. He continued
his courfe along the fhore of this ifland about fix leagues, and
then faw another ifland low and rocky. On the former he
difcovered one of the fineft harbours in the world, which he
named Port Egmont in honour of the earl, who prefided at
the board of admiralty. The mouth of this harbour is fouth-
eaft, diftant feven miles from the rocky ifland, which is a good
mark to know it by. In every part of Port Egmont, where
the whole navy of England might ride in perfect fafety, there

K k 2 is

is great plenty of frefh water; and geefe, ducks, fnipes and other birds are fo numerous, that the fhip's company grew tired of them. Here are wild celery and wood forrel in the greateft abundance, befides many other refrefhments, which are in the higheft degree falutary to thofe who have contracted fcorbutic diforders during a long voyage. Nor is there any want of muf-cles, clams, cockles and limpets; the feals and penguins are innumerable, and it is impoflible to walk on the beach without firft driving them away. The coaft, alfo, abounds with ani-mals of a more dangerous kind. There are fea lions of an enormous fize; and a very fierce quadruped refembling a wolf. The fangs of this creature are remarkably long and fharp; and it is fo fierce as to run againft every animal that it fees. It is not eafy to guefs how this quadruped fhould have got to thefe iflands, which are diftant at leaft one hundred leagues from the continent. The firft navigator who vifited thofe parts is fuppo-fed to be Captain Davies, the affociate of Cavendifh, in 1592. In 1594, Sir Richard Hawkins faw land, fuppofed to be the fame, and, in honour of his miftrefs Queen Elifabeth, called them Hawkins's Maiden Land. Long afterwards they were feen by fome French fhips from St. Maloes; and Frezier, probably for that reafon, called them the Malouins, a name which has fince been adopted by the Spaniards. Commodore Byron thinks there is little reafon to doubt they are the fame called Pepy's Iflands by Cowley; and he took poffeffion of Port Egmont and all the neighbouring iflands for his majefty King George the Third, by the name of Falkland Iflands.

Commodore Byron having examined thofe parts with a de-gree of attention that had never been before beftowed on them, made fail for Port Defire, and on the 6th of February faw land, and ftood in for the port. During the run from Falkland Iflands to this place, the number of whales about the fhip was fo great as to render the navigation dangerous. On the 14th he put to fea, in order to go through the Streights of Magel-lan, and to examine with attention the principal bays and har-bours formed by the coaft on each fide. He entered the Streight the 17th of February, and quitted it the 9th of April, having employed feven weeks and two days in the voyage,

which

which was attended with incredible difficulties and dangers. A. D These, however, were to be afcribed entirely to his entering 1764 the Streight near the time of the equinox, when the worſt weather was to be expected: but at a proper ſeaſon of the year, not only a ſingle veſſel but a whole ſquadron might paſs the Streight in leſs than three weeks.    One great advantage of this paſſage above the doubling Cape Horn, is the facility with which fiſh is almoſt every where to be procured, with wild celery, ſcurvy graſs, berries, and many other vegetables.

Having cleared the Streight, he purſued his courſe to the weſtward, and on the 9th of May, being in latitude 26 degrees 46 minutes ſouth, longitude 94 degrees 45 minutes weſt, determined to ſteer a north-weſt courſe until he got the trade wind, and then to ſtand to the weſtward till he ſhould fall in with Solomon's iſlands, if any ſuch there were, or make ſome new diſcovery.    On the 31ſt there was a great number of birds about the ſhip, which made him conclude that land was at no great diſtance.    But none was diſcovered till the 7th of June, in latitude 14 degrees 5 minutes ſouth, longitude 144 degrees 58 minutes weſt. Then a ſmall iſland was obſerved at the diſtance of ſome leagues.    In a very ſhort time another iſland was diſcovered to windward, much larger than the firſt.    The ſhip ſtood for the ſmall iſland, which had a moſt beautiful appearance, being ſurrounded with a beach of the fineſt white ſand, and within covered with tall trees, which extended their ſhade to a great diſtance. It ſeemed to be about five miles in circumference, and from each end of it a ſpit runs into the ſea, upon which the ſurge broke with great violence.    The natives appeared on the beach with ſpears in their hands, at leaſt ſixteen feet long.    They made large fires, probably for ſignals, as the ſame appeared immediately after on the larger iſland.    The commodore ſailed round this iſland, but, to the great regret and diſappointment of the ſhip's company, no anchoring-place could be found within leſs than a cable's length of the ſhore, which was ſurrounded cloſe to the beach with a ſteep coral rock. The ſailors, diſtreſſed with the ſcurvy, ſaw cocoa nuts in great abundance, the milk of which is perhaps the beſt antiſcorbutic in the world. They had reaſon to believe that there were limes;

bananas,

A. D. bananas, and other fruits which are generally found between
764. the tropics; and, to increafe their mortification, they faw the
fhells of many turtles fcattered about the fhore. Having viewed this forbidden paradife with fenfations of inexpreffible diftrefs, they wrought up to the other ifland, which was difcovered to be equally inacceffible. They perceived feveral other
low iflands, or rather peninfulas, moft of them being joined one
to the other by a neck of land very narrow, and almoft level
with the furface of the water. Here the cocoa trees are eafily
difcovered, being higher than any other part of the furface.
A boat being fent to found the lee fide of thefe iflands for an anchoring place, the Indians ran down in great numbers to the
fhore, armed with long fpears and clubs, and making ufe of
many threatening geftures. A gun was fired over their heads,
which made them fly to the woods; but the boat returned
without being able to difcover any foundings clofe in with the
furf, which broke very high upon the fhore. The commodore
thus finding it impoffible to obtain any refrefhment here, named this clufter of ifles the Iflands of Difappointment, and continued his voyage to the weftward.

Land was again difcovered in lefs than twenty-four hours, at
the diftance of fix leagues. In the morning of the 10th of
June, being within three miles of the fhore, they perceived it
to be a long low ifland, with a white beach, of a pleafant appearance, full of cocoa-nut and other trees. It was furrounded with a rock of red coral, and the natives behaved in the
fame hoftile manner as thofe of the Iflands of Difappointment.
No anchoring place was to be found, nor was it poffible to eftablifh any friendly intercourfe with the Indians. When the
veffel came to the weftermoft point of this ifland the failors obferved another about four leagues diftant. They vifited every
part of its coaft, but could find no foundings. The boats having approached very near the fhore, made figns to the natives,
who appeared in great numbers, that they wanted water. The
Indians readily underftood them, and directed them to run
down farther along the fhore. Some of them fwam off to our
boats, carrying cocoa nuts, and water in the fhells. The principal object of the boats was to obtain fome pearls; and the
men,

men, to aſſiſt them in explaining their meaning, had taken with A. D
them ſome of the pearl-oyſter ſhells, which they had found in 1764
great numbers upon the coaſt. But all their endeavours to
make themſelves underſtood by the Indians were ineffectual;
and, as no anchorage could be found for the ſhips, the commodore proceeded to the weſtward, having named theſe iſlands,
which are ſituated in latitude 14 degrees 41 minutes ſouth, longitude 149 degrees 15 minutes weſt, King George's iſlands.

On the day following, that is, the 13th of June, about three
o'clock in the afternoon, land was again diſcovered, bearing
S. S. W. diſtant about ſix leagues. The commodore ſtood
for it, and found it to be a low and very narrow iſland, lying
eaſt and weſt, with a very green and pleaſant appearance, but
a dreadful ſurf breaking on every part of it. It abounds with
inhabitants, is about twenty leagues in length, and lies in latitude 15 degrees ſouth, and the weſtermoſt point of it in longitude 151 degrees 53 minutes weſt. To this place, which was
every where inacceſſible, the commodore gave the name of the
Prince of Wales iſland.

From the weſtern extremity of this iſland he ſteered towards
the north-weſt, and on the 16th ſaw vaſt flocks of birds,
which always took their flight to the ſouthward when evening
came on. This appearance, as well as the obſervation that all
the little iſlands, which had been diſcovered, were full of inhabitants, made it probable, that there was a continent, or at
leaſt ſome larger iſlands to the ſouthward. But the ſickneſs of
the ſhip's crew made it impoſſible for them to purſue their diſco-
veries in that direction. On the 21ſt of June they were in latitude 12 degrees 33 minutes ſouth, longitude 167 degrees 47 minutes weſt, and next morning diſcovered a moſt dangerous reef
of breakers, at the diſtance of a league. Land was ſeen a little
afterwards from the maſt-head, having the appearance of three
iſlands, with rocks and broken ground between them. The
ſouth-eaſt of theſe iſlands is about three leagues in length between the extreme points, from both which a reef runs out,
upon which the ſea breaks to a tremendous height. The iſlands
themſelves had a more fertile and beautiful appearance than any
before diſcovered, and, like the reſt, ſwarmed with people,
whoſe

A. D.
1764.

whofe habitations were feen ftanding in clufters all along the coaft, which is unfortunately furrounded in fuch a manner by rocks and breakers, that it cannot be approached without the moft imminent danger. The commodore, therefore, named thefe the Iflands of Danger. They ly in latitude 10 degrees 15 minutes fouth, longitude 169 degrees 28 minutes weft.

He fteered from thence N. W. by W. and on the 24th difcovered another ifland bearing S. S. W. diftant about feven or eight leagues. It appeared, upon approaching nearer to it, to be low, and covered with wood, among which were cocoa-nut trees in great abundance. It is near thirty miles in circumference; a dreadful fea breaks upon almoft every part of the coaft, where no anchorage is to be found. The commodore fent out the boats with orders to land, if poffible, and procure fome refrefhments for the fick. They brought off about 200 cocoa nuts, which, to perfons afflicted with the fcurvy, were an ineftimable treafure. They reported, that there was no fign of the ifland's ever being inhabited. They found thoufands of fea-fowl fitting upon their nefts, which were built in high trees; and thefe birds were fo tame, that they fuffered themfelves to be knocked down, without taking to flight. The commodore was at firft inclined to believe that this ifland was the fame that in the Neptune François is called Maluita, and laid down about a degree to the eaftward of the great ifland of St. Elifabeth, the principal of the Solomon's iflands; but, being afterwards convinced of the contrary, he called it the Duke of York's ifland.

He continued his courfe till the 29th, in the track of Solomon's iflands, but found no reafon to believe that any fuch exifted in the fituation affigned them by the French. He difcovered, however, on the 2d of July, an ifland bearing north, diftant about fix leagues. Next morning it was found to be low and flat, of a delightful appearance, and full of wood, among which the cocoa-nut tree was very confpicuous. It is extremely populous, and the natives, in more than fixty canoes, put off from the fhore and made towards the fhip, which lay by to receive them. "After thefe Indians," fays the commodore, "had gazed at us fome time, one of them fuddenly jumped "out of his proa, fwam to the fhip, and ran up the fide like a

I
"cat;

" cat ; as foon as he had ftepped over the gunwale, he fat A.D
" down upon it, and burft into a violent fit of laughter; then 1764
" ftarted up, and ran all over the fhip, attempting to fteal
" whatever he could lay his hands upon, but without fuccefs,
" for being ftark naked it was impoffible for him to conceal his
" booty for a moment. Our feamen put on him a jacket and
" trowfers, which produced great merriment, for he had all
" the geftures of a monkey newly dreffed ; we alfo gave him
" bread, which he eat with a voracious appetite, and after ha-
" ving played a thoufand antic tricks, he leaped overboard,
" jacket and trowfers and all, and fwam back to his proa.
" After this feveral others fwam to the fhip, ran up the fide to
" the gun-room ports, and having crept in, fnatched up what
" eyer lay in their reach, and immediately leaped again into the
" fea, and fwam away at a great rate, though fome of them,
" having both hands full, held up their arms quite out of the
" water to prevent their plunder from being fpoiled. Thefe
" people are tall, well proportioned and clean limbed ; their
" fkin is a bright copper colour, their features extremely good,
" and there is a mixture of intrepidity and cheerfulnefs in their
" countenances that is very ftriking. They had long black
" hair, which fome of them wore tied up behind in a great
" bunch, others in three knots ; fome of them had long beards,
" fome only whifkers, and fome nothing more than a fmall
" tuft at the point of the chin. They were all of them ft..rk
" naked, except their ornaments, which confifted of fhells,
" very prettily difpofed and ftrung together, and were worn
" round their necks, wrifts, and waifts. One of thefe men,
" who appeared to be a perfon of fome confequence, had a
" ftring of human teeth about his waift, which was probably a
" trophy of his military courage, for he would not. part with
" it in exchange for any thing that I could offer him. Some
" of them were unarmed, but others had one of the moft
" dangerous weapons I had ever feen. It was a kind of fpear
" very broad at the end, and ftuck full of fhark's teeth, which
" are as fharp as a lancet at the fides, for about three feet of
" its length. We fhowed them fome cocoa nuts, and made
" figns that we wanted more ; but inftead of giving any inti-

" mation that they could fupply us, they endeavoured to take away thofe we had." The commodore fent out boats to found, and they reported that there was ground at the depth of thirty fathom within two cables length of the fhore ; but as the bottom was coral rock, and the foundings much too near the breakers for a fhip to lie in fafety, he was obliged to make fail, without procuring any refrefhments. This ifland, to which his officers gave the name of Byron's Ifland, lies in latitude 1 degree 18 minutes fouth, longitude 173 degrees 46 minutes eaft. Here ended the difcoveries made by the Dolphin. She afterwards fhaped her courfe for the ifle of Tinian, which, to her great regret and difappointment, appeared to be no longer that delightful place of which the elegant author of Anfon's voyage has given fo luxuriant a defcription. From thence fhe proceeded to Batavia, and having doubled the Cape of Good Hope, proceeded on her return to England. She came to anchor in the Downs on the 9th of May, 1766, having been juft nine weeks in coming from the Cape, and fomewhat more than two and twenty months upon the voyage round the world.

We have not interrupted the courfe of Commodore Byron's difcoveries, by relating the tranfactions of the year 1765, which if not the ultimate caufe, were the immediate occafion of thofe difturbances that gradually proceeded to fuch a degree of violence, as required the moft vigorous exertions of the naval ftrength of this kingdom. The parliament, which affembled towards the clofe of the year 1764, voted 16,000 men to be employed in the fea fervice for the year 1765, including 4287 marines ; and a fum not exceeding 4 l. per man per month for their maintenance. The fhips ftationed in the Britifh feas had no call to exert their activity; but thofe on the coaft of America were employed in the fame fervice which had been attended with fuch bad effects the preceding year. The trade of America with Great Britain had increafed, during the laft years, and after the conclufion of the war, beyond the hopes and fpeculations of the moft fanguine politicians. The Americans bought annually to the amount of three millions of Britifh commodities. Their trade, however, was not confined to the mother country. It fwelled out on every fide ; and having fil- led

led all its proper channels to the brim, overflowed with a rich A. D abundance. In short, the contraband trade kept pace with the 1764 regular, and was its moſt natural effect. This, doubtleſs, was an evil; but being connected with the cauſe of our proſperity, it was an evil that ought to have been treated with the greateſt delicacy and addreſs. Unfortunately for the intereſts of the Britiſh empire on both ſides of the Atlantic, a gentleman now preſided in the treaſury, who had beheld with peculiar jealouſy the increaſe of this contraband trade. Mr Grenville, when firſt lord of the admiralty, and not ſtrictly called upon in his official line, had preſented a very ſtrong memorial to the lords of the treaſury, heavily complaining of the growth of the illicit trade in America. We have already hinted at the bad conſequences ariſing from the attempt to put an entire ſtop to the commerce between the Britiſh and Spaniſh colonies. Theſe were ſeen and acknowledged even by adminiſtration. A law was made therefore, the 5th of April 1764, which rendered legal, in ſome reſpects, the intercourſe between the different eſtabliſhments in the new world. But the ſame law loaded this commerce with very heavy impoſitions, and ordered the money ariſing from theſe to be paid in ſpecie into the Britiſh exchequer. While it was thought expedient to fit out armed cutters, under the command of ſea officers, to prevent ſmuggling in the Britiſh ſeas, the naval commanders on the coaſts of America were employed in rendering effectual the late commercial regulations. Theſe gentlemen could not be ſuppoſed to become acquainted with all the forms which this buſineſs required. They were unacquainted with the caſes in which ſhips were liable to penalties; nor did they better underſtand thoſe caſes in which they were even exempted from detention. Hurried on by the natural violence of their diſpoſitions, and acting with that irregular vivacity and contempt of formal rules, which they had exerted with ſuch advantage and glory in defence of their country againſt the common enemy, they ruined the intereſts of trade, while they diſappointed the expectations of the treaſury. The commerce between Britiſh ſubjects was the firſt that ſuffered, notwithſtanding that vaſt number and intricacy of bonds, clearances, cockets, regiſters, &c. which had been e-

ſtabliſhed

A. D ſtabliſhed to protect it. The trade carried on between the Bri-
1764. tiſh and Spaniſh colonies, which was ſo extremely advantageous
to the former, was nearly annihilated. The new-made cuſtom-
houſe officers ſeized, indiſcriminately, all veſſels carrying on that
trade, whether belonging to fellow-ſubjects or foreigners, which
the ordinary cuſtomhouſe-officers, ſtationed on them, had always permitted to paſs unnoticed. Beſides the general traffic
between the Engliſh, French, and Spaniſh Americans, there
was a particular and moſt advantageous trade carried on between North America and the French Weſt-Indies. It conſiſted chiefly in an exchange of ſuch commodities as muſt otherwiſe have remained a drug, if not an incumbrance, on the hands
of the poſſeſſors. The balance was paid in ſpecie to North
America, which, together with the balance of the Spaniſh
trade, enabled them to make their remittances to Great Britain.
This intercourſe between North America and the French Weſt-
India iſlands, was conſidered as ſo neceſſary to the former, that
it was permitted to be maintained during the firſt years of the
war; directly, by means of flags of truce; indirectly, through
the Dutch and Daniſh iſlands; and, at length, through the
Spaniſh port of Monti Chriſti in the iſland of Hiſpaniola.
When the Engliſh, towards the concluſion of the war, had obtained the moſt diſtinguiſhed advantages, and in a manner laid
ſiege to all the French Weſt-India iſlands, government determined to put a ſtop to this intercourſe, not ſo much in the light
of a contraband trade, as in that of a treaſonable practice,
without which it would be impoſſible for theſe valuable iſlands
to hold out againſt our attempts to reduce them. When the
war concluded, the arguments of treaſon ceaſed, and this intercourſe again returned to its former flouriſhing condition. But,
upon the eſtabliſhment of the new revenue laws, it ſunk under
the ſame blow which deſtroyed the general commercial intercourſe of the new world.

Before the eſtabliſhing of theſe laws produced any conſiderable effect in Great Britain, it was attended with very fatal conſequences to the ſituation and circumſtances, as well as to the
temper and diſpoſition of the coloniſts. Immediately on a ſtop
being put to their trade, they came to a reſolution not to buy

any

ay clothing they could poffibly live without, that was not of A. D heir own manufacturing. Not having the ufual returns to 1764 make to Great Britain for the woollen goods which they ufually purchafed from her, they adopted a plan of retrenchment dictated by neceffity, and gave up all hopes of being clothed in the finery of their mother country. The refolution taken with regard to this article was rendered general by a vote of the houfe of commons, which followed the law impofing new duties upon their foreign trade : " That towards farther defraying the " neceffary expences of protecting the colonies, it may be pro- " per to charge certain ftamp-duties upon them." When this determination of the Britifh legiflature was known in America, the inhabitants entered into affociations, not only to abide by their former refolution taken in confequence of the interruption of their trade by the naval cuftom-houfe officers, but to encourage as much as poffible all kinds of manufacture within themfelves. Thefe meafures were defpifed by the miniftry, who concluded that becaufe the wool of the colonies is not fo good as that of Great Britain, it would be impoffible for them not to depend upon her for that article; and becaufe the other commodities which they purchafed from this country were fuch as it would be extremely inconvenient for them to want, they muft be foon difgufted with an agreement, entered into in a moment of refentment, which muft be more diftreffing to themfelves than injurious to the mother country. But the firm perfeverance of the colonies in adhering to the principles of their affociation, proved the weaknefs of this reafoning. They were ready to fubmit to every other hardfhip rather than yield to what they deemed an infringement of their liberties.

In confequence of this general difpofition of perfons of all ranks in thefe colonies, great evils began to be felt, and ftill greater to be apprehended. A temporary interruption of commercial intercourfe between England and America immediately took place which could not fail to be extremely prejudicial to the former. The numerous body employed in preparing, buying, or tranfporting goods to the American market, were deprived of employment. While individuals were reduced to beggary, the revenue fuffered in proportion by the want of the export and

import

import duties. Yet neither thefe evils, nor the fear of totally alienating America from the interefts of Great Britain, deterred the miniftry from paffing that law, the bare fufpicion of which had occafioned fuch difguft. The ftamp-act made its way through both houfes, and received the royal affent by commiffion, the 22d of March, 1765.

The news of this unfortunate event firft reached the province of New-England, which of all the Englifh colonies has ever had the ftrongeft bent towards republican licentioufnefs. The fullen obftinacy and hatred which already poffeffed them, were converted, by this frefh inftance of what their leaders taught them to deem little better than tyranny, into the moft violent fury, which every where broke out into action. The fhips in the harbour hoifted their colours half-maft high, in token of the deepeft mourning; the bells rang muffled; the populace treated the act with the moft licentious contempt; many of the better fort gradually mixed in thefe tumults, and the affemblies not only of New England, but of all the confiderable provinces, which had by this time caught the flame, inftead of barely conniving at the people's afferting their independence by tumultuous acts, proceeded to avow it themfelves in the moft expreffive terms, grounding it on the fame arguments which their friends on this fide the water had already ufed to prove it. The hiftory of what follows is that of the difgrace of Great Britain. The miniftry, whether unwilling or unable to fupport by force of arms the law which they had thought proper to enact, refigned their places. Their fucceffors yielded to the ftorm, inftead of refifting it, while refiftance could yet be effectual. They obtained a momentary popularity by repealing the ftamp-act, which had been fo offenfive to the colonies, and fo hurtful to a confiderable part of the trading intereft of Great Britain. But the factious, turbulent fpirit which had taken poffeffion of the former, was far from being mollified by the lenient conceffions in their favour, and the great confideration fhewn to their circumftances by their legiflature. The miniftry, whofe debility or moderation had tended to confirm them in their difregard to the authority of parliament, did not long continue in office. But the effects of their adminiftration were permanent. The colonifts were no longer fatisfied in committing private acts of out-

rage;

rage; they did not content themselves with showing difrespect A. D
to their governors and other servants of the crown; but open- 1765
ly set at defiance the power of the whole legiflative body. Even
the affembly of New York, a province where the ideas of legal
fubordination had been long and firmly eftablished, voted in
direct oppofition to an act of laft feffion for providing the troops
with neceffaries in their quarters, and paffed an act of affembly
by which thefe provinces were regulated in a mode totally inconfiftent with that prefcribed by parliament.

Adminiftration combated this rebellious ufurpation of power
by another act of the legiflature, incapacitating the affembly of
New York for all legal functions, till they had in every refpect
complied with the Britifh regulations refpecting the troops. At
the fame time they oppofed the licentious fpirit of the other
provinces by new revenue laws, which, as no vigorous means
were ufed to enforce them, were as nugatory as the former.
The Rockingham adminiftration repealed the ftamp-act, but 1766
afferted the right of taxation; their fucceffors (the Duke of
Grafton was now at the head of the treafury) exercifed this
right, by laying duties on the importation of glafs, paper, and 1767
fome other commodities, into the colonies. The officers appointed to collect this revenue were every where treated like
criminals; and the authority of Great Britain was totally difregarded. Befides the tumultuous riots which happened in
particular parts, the general temper and conduct of the whole
people became every day more licentious. That republican fpirit, which is as inconfiftent with the genuine principles of the
Britifh conftitution as it is agreeable to the wild doctrines and
levelling principles in which the inhabitants of Bofton had been
nurfed, began firft openly to difplay itfelf in that capital. Having adopted refolutions of a nature the moft violent and factious, the affembly there fent a circular letter, figned by the
fpeaker, the 11th of February, 1768, to all the other affem- 1768
blies of North America. In this they expatiated largely on the
natural rights of men and the tyranny of the Britifh legiflature,
and they fummoned the colonies to unite in one common caufe
for maintaining their privileges inviolate. This letter was anfwered by many of the provinces in a fimilar tone; and the flame of
rebellion

A. D. rebellion began to fpread over the whole North American con-
768. tinent.

One vigorous meafure gave it a confiderable check in the
place where it had firft broke out. Two regiments were ordered from Ireland to fupport the authority of parliament over the
inhabitants of Bofton, and feveral detachments from different
parts of the continent rendezvoufed at Halifax for the fame
purpofe. Upon the firft rumour of thefe movements, the Boftonians were as much alarmed as if they had been on the point
of fuffering all the horrors of invafion from a cruel foreign
enemy. The affembly, or convention, which on many occafions
had treated not only their governor, but even the parliament of
Great Britain with the moft indecent afperity of expreffion,
drew up a memorial in terms of great moderation, difclaiming
all pretence to any authority whatever, and advifing and recommending it to the people to pay the greateft deference to government, and to wait with patience the refult of his majefty's
wifdom and clemency for a redrefs of their grievances. If
the moft unhappy infatuation had not prevailed over the councils of Great Britain, the fudden change produced by this appearance of vigour, might have opened the eyes of adminiftration, and taught them that coercive meafures alone could reduce
the Americans to a fenfe of their duty. But inftead of pufhing
the advantage which they had obtained, in order to deftroy the
very feeds of rebellion, the firft deceitful appearance of tranquillity made them relax their feverity; the Americans had
time to recollect themfelves and to recover from their panic;
and the important moment was again loft of eftablifhing, without great effufion of blood, the fovereignty of parliament over
the whole Britifh empire.

While fo little attention was beftowed on preferving the dominions of which we were already in poffeffion, continual efforts were made for extending the limits of our territories by
frefh difcoveries. In Auguft, 1766, the Dolphin in which
Commodore Byron had circumnavigated the world, was again
fent out under the command of Captain Wallis, with the Swallow, commanded by Captain Carteret. They proceeded together to the weft end of the Streights of Magellan, and fepara-

2                      ted

ted in the great fouthern ocean. Captain Wallis directed his A. D. courfe more wefterly than any navigator before him had done 1768. in fo high a latitude; but he met with no land till he came within the tropic, where he difcovered the iflands Whitfunday, Queen Charlotte, Egmont, Duke of Gloucefter, Duke of Cumberland, Maitea, Otaheite, Eimeo, Tapanamou, Howe, Scilly, Bofcawen, Keppel, and Wallis, and returned to England in May 1768. Captain Carteret kept a different route, in which he difcovered the iflands Ofnaburgh, Gloucefter, Queen Charlotte, Carteret, Gower, and the Streight between New Britain and New Ireland, and returned in March 1769.

Captain Wallis, having cleared the Streights of Magellan the 12th of April, 1767, proceeded weftward, but did not fall in with any undifcovered land till the 6th of June. A few days before, the failors had obferved feveral gannets, which, with the uncertainty of the weather, inclined them to believe that land was not far diftant. This belief was confirmed by their feeing a great many birds on the 5th; and the day after, being in latitude 19 degrees fouth, and longitude 137 weft, they faw plainly from the deck a low ifland, at about five or fix leagues diftance. When they were within a few miles of this ifland they faw another, bearing north-weft by weft. The captain fent his boats manned and armed to the fhore of the former, which returned in a few hours, bringing with them feveral cocoa nuts and a confiderable quantity of fcurvy grafs. The crews reported, that they had feen none of the inhabitants, but had vifited feveral huts, or rather fheds, confifting only of a roof, neatly thatched with cocoa-nut and palm leaves, fupported upon pofts, and open all around. They had found no anchorage, and the furf was fo high that it was with difficulty they had got on fhore, the whole ifland being furrounded with a reef of rocks, which rendered it extremely difficult of accefs. The captain, therefore, finding it anfwered no purpofe to continue longer at this ifland, which, being difcovered on Whitfuneve, he called Whitfun-ifland, ftood away for the other, diftant about four leagues. When the fhip came under the lee of the latter, the boats were immediately difpatched, but could find no foundings till within half a cable's length of the fhore.

A. D. They landed, however, and found the ifland fandy and level,
768. full of trees, but without underwood, and abounding with fcurvy grafs, and wells of excellent water. As the boats approached the fhore, the Indians thronged down towards the beach,
and put themfelves upon their defence with long pikes, as if to
difpute the landing. The boats crew then lay upon their oars,
and made figns of friendfhip, fhewing at the fame time feveral
ftrings of beads, ribbands, knives, and other trinkets. The
Indians ftill made figns for them to depart, but at the fame
time eyed the trinkets with fuch a wifhful curiofity, as left room
to expect that it might be poffible to eftablifh an intercourfe.
This, however, was not effected, but the boats landed, and
the fhip was fupplied with water and other neceffary refrefhments. Captain Wallis took poffeffion of the ifland in the
name of George the Third, and named it Charlotte's ifland in
honour of her majefty. It is about fix miles long, and one
broad, and lies in latitude 19 degrees 18 minutes fouth, longitude 138 degrees 4 minutes weft. The fame day that they left
this place they difcovered another ifland, bearing eaft by north,
diftant fifteen miles. Here the fea breaks over a reef of rock,
running from eaft to weft, and forms itfelf into a lagoon in the
middle of the ifland, which is low, covered with trees, but
without any huts or inhabitants. The Indians belonging to
Charlotte ifland had fled thither in their canoes when the Englifh landed on their coaft; and feeing their enemies, as they
imagined, purfuing them to this place, they left their women
and children on the beach, and advanced with pikes and fire-
brands, making a great noife, and dancing in a ftrange manner.
The foil of this ifland was fandy, there is no verdure under the
trees, the fhore every where rocky, and no anchorage. The
captain therefore left a place where there was no profpect of
obtaining any refrefhment, having firft named it Egmont ifland
in honour of the firft lord of the admiralty. It lies in latitude
19 degrees 20 minutes fouth, longitude 138 degrees 30 minutes
weft.

On the 11th of June, about mid-day, they faw an ifland,
bearing weft fouth-weft, and ftood for it. At four in the afternoon they were within a quarter of a mile of the fhore, but
could

could find no foundings, the ifland being furrounded by rocks, A. D. on which the fea breaks very high. As to appearance, foil, and 1768. inhabitants, it differed little from the iflands which they had juft left. The captain named it Gloucefter ifland, in honour of his royal highnefs the duke of that name. It lies in latitude 19 degrees 11 minutes fouth, longitude 140 degrees 4 minutes weft.

In failing weftward the captain difcovered two other fmall iflands, the firft of which he named after the duke of Cumberland, and the fecond after Prince William Henry. Thefe, however, had nothing to recommend them above thofe already mentioned; fo that he continued to proceed weftward, in hopes of finding higher land, where the fhip might come to an anchor, and fuch refrefhments as they ftood in need of be procured. On the 17th he difcovered high land, with frequent fires, which proved it to be inhabited. This alfo was an ifland, nearly circular, above two miles in diameter. There was no anchorage to be found, but the inhabitants appeared more numerous than the fmallnefs of the place could fupport, which gave hopes that there were lands of greater extent not far diftant, which might be lefs difficult of accefs. The captain having named this ifland, which lies in latitude 17 degrees 51 minutes fouth, longitude 147 degrees 30 minutes weft, Ofnaburgh, in honour of Prince Frederick, bore away to the fouth-weft; and the fame day difcovered very high land in the weft-fouth-weft. This was the famous ifland of O-Taheite, which Captain Wallis named King George the Third's ifland. It confifts of two principal divifions, which are united by a narrow neck of land. The circumference of both is about forty leagues, lying in latitude 17 degrees 46 minutes fouth, and longitude 149 degrees 13 minutes weft. The Dolphin happened to approach this coaft the 18th of June, during a thick fog; and the crew were much furprifed, when it cleared away, to find themfelves in the middle of fome hundreds of canoes. The Indians, who affembled to the number of many thoufands, behaved at firft in a friendly manner; one of them holding up a branch of the plantain tree as a token of peace. But afterwards, having furrounded the fhip with a number of canoes loaded with ftones, they began, on a fignal

M m 2                                                    given,

A. D. given, to throw them with great violence, which obliged the
1768. captain to order fome guns to be fired. The terror of the fire-
arms foon made them defift from hoftilities; and an intercourfe
was eftablifhed by which the Englifh procured hogs, fowls,
bread, fruit, apples, bananas, and cocoa nuts, in exchange for
nails, hatchets, and various trinkets, which the Indians held in
great value. The Dolphin lay off this ifland from the 24th of
June to the 27th of July; during which the Englifh examined
the interior parts as well as the coaft, which they found to be
luxuriantly fertile and extremely populous. The inhabitants are
well lodged, and clothed with a ftuff made of the macerated
fibres of a fhrub which grows in great abundance in their country. They are of the ordinary European fize, a tawny complexion, the men well made, and the women handfome　Captain Wallis could not difcover what were their religious fentiments, or whether they entertained any ideas of fuperior and
invifible powers. But, having become fomewhat acquainted
with them, he found them not only juft in their dealings, but
generous and humane, and fo extremely fufceptible of attachment, that feveral of them, efpecially the queen of the ifland,
were exceedingly afflicted when their vifitants were obliged to
depart.

After leaving this ifland, which has been examined with more
attention in later voyages, the captain fteered his courfe for Tinian. In his way thither he fell in with feveral fmall iflands,
none of which afforded good anchorage. The principal of
them is Bofcawen's ifland, lying in latitude 15 degrees 50 minutes fouth, longitude 175 degrees weft; Keppel's ifle, in latitude 15 degrees 55 minutes fouth, longitude 175 degrees 3 minutes weft; and Wallis's ifle, in latitude 13 degrees 18 minutes
fouth, longitude 177 degrees weft. The boats, in examining
the laft, found that in two or three places there is anchorage in
eighteen, fourteen, and twelve fathom, upon fand and coral,
without a reef of rocks which furrounded the ifland. There is
alfo a breach in this reef, about fixty fathom broad; and a fhip,
if preffed with neceffity, might anchor here in eight fathom,
but it is not fafe to moor with a greater length than half a cable. The plans of all thefe iflands were delivered by the captain

tain on his return into the hands of the admiralty, with their A. D
longitudes and latitudes so accurately laid down, that succeed- 1768
ing navigators had no difficulty in finding them.

Captain Caterct, as we have already mentioned, separated
from his companion after passing the Streights of Magellan, and
steered a course considerably nearer to the equator. On the
26th of July, 1767, being in latitude 10 degrees south, longitude 167 degrees west, he was in hopes of falling in with some
of the islands called Solomon's Islands, this being the latitude
in which the southernmost of them is laid down. What increased
this expectation was the seeing a number of sea birds, which
often hovered about the ship; but the captain was not so fortunate as to meet with any land; and as he sailed over the southern limits of that part of the ocean in which Solomon's Islands
are said to ly, and Commodore Byron, in the voyage formerly
described, had traversed the northern without finding them,
there is reason to conclude, that, if there be any such islands,
their situation in all our charts is erroneously laid down.

Captain Cateret continued his voyage, nearly in the same parallel, towards the west; but did not discover land till the 12th
of August, when he fell in with a cluster of islands, of which
he counted seven. Having ancored at about three cables
length from the shore, he soon observed some of the natives,
who were black, with woolly heads, and stark naked. A boat
was despatched in search of a watering place, at which the natives disappeared; and the boat returned with an account that
there was a fine run of fresh water abreast of the ship, and close
to the beach, but that the whole country in that part being almost an impenetrable forest, the watering would be very dangerous if the natives should endeavour to prevent it; that there
were no esculent vegetables for the refreshment of the sick, nor
any habitations as far as the country had been examined, which
was wild, foresty and mountainous. The captain therefore
tried some other places, where the sailors saw hogs, poultry,
cocoa-nut trees, plantains, bananas, and a great variety of other
vegetable productions, as they sailed along the shore. Unfortunately, however, an unhappy dispute arose between the boat's
crew and the natives, who defended themselves bravely with

bows

A. D.
1768.

bows and arrows, which they fired in regular platoons.   This
prevented all friendly intercourse; and the ship's company were
so much weakened by disease, that they could not hope to obtain what they wanted by force.   The captain gave the general
name of Queen Charlotte Islands to the whole cluster, and af-
signed particular names to the most remarkable.   That which
he called Howe's lies in latitude 11 degrees 10 minutes south,
longitude 164 degrees 43 minutes east.   Egmont Island lies in
latitude 10 degrees 40 minutes south, longitude 164 degrees
49 minutes east.   The east side of these two islands, which ly
exactly in a line with each other, including the passage between
them of four miles, extend about eleven leagues; both of them
appear to be fertile, and afford a very agreeable prospect, being
covered with tall trees of a beautiful verdure.   Lord Howe's
Island, though more flat and even than the other, is notwithstanding high land.   At the distance of about thirteen leagues
from the north-east point of Egmont Island is another of a
stupendous height, and a conical figure, the top of which is
shaped like a funnel, emitting smoke, though no flame.
This he called Volcano Island.   To a low flat land, which,
when Howe and Egmont Islands were right a-head, bore
north-west, he gave the name of Keppel's Island.   It lies in
latitude 10 degrees 15 minutes south, longitude 165 degrees
4 minutes east.   The largest of two others to the south-east he
called Lord Edgecumb's Island, the small one Perry's Island;
the other islands, of which there are several, he did not particularly name.

As all hopes of obtaining refreshment in those parts were at
an end, and the ship was not in a condition of pursuing her
voyage to the southward, the captain gave orders to steer north,
hoping to refresh at the country which Dampier has named
Nova Britannia.   Accordingly he sailed from Egmont Island
the 18th of August, with a fresh trade wind; and on the 20th
discovered a flat low land, in latitude 7 degrees 56 minutes
south, longitude 153 degrees 56 minutes east, which he called
Gower's Island.   Here, to the great mortification of all on
board, no anchorage could be found, but some cocoa nuts were
purchased from the natives, who approached the ship in their
canoes.

canoes. They were in every respect the same sort of people A. D
that had been met with in the neighbouring places. The night 1768
was exceedingly dark, and by day-break a current had set the
ship considerably to the southward of the island, and in sight
of two others, situated nearly east and west of each other.
That to the east is much the smallest, and was named Simpson's
Island. The other is lofty, has a stately appearance, lies in latitude 8 degrees 26 minutes south, longitude 159 degrees 14 minutes east, and its length from east to west is above six leagues.
It was named by the officers Caterer's Island, in honour of their
commander. A boat was sent on shore, which the natives endeavoured to cut off, and hostilities having thus commenced,
the English seized their canoe, in which they found an hundred
cocoa nuts. The canoe was large enough to carry eight or ten
men, neatly built, adorned with shell-work and figures rudely
painted. The people were armed with bows and arrows, and
spears pointed with flints. By some signs which they made, it
appeared that they were not wholly unacquainted with the use
of fire-arms. Like the inhabitants of the neighbouring islands
they were quite naked, and equally dextrous at swimming and
managing their canoes. In the following days the ship found
no soundings at the small islands which she fell in with, and
which the captain supposes to be those called Ohang Java, discovered by Tasman. They are nine in number, and to the
north ly two others which are mentioned by no preceding navigator, and which the captain named Sir Charles Hardy and
Winchelsea Islands. The former lies in latitude 40 degrees 50
minutes south, longitude 154 degrees east; the latter is distant
about ten leagues, in the direction of south by east.

On the 26th of August they saw another large island to the
northward, which was supposed to be St. John's island, discovered by Schouten, and soon after they saw high land to the
westward, which proved to be Nova Britannia. The next day
a north-westerly current sent them into a deep bay or gulf,
which has been distinguished by Dampier by the name of St.
George's bay. From this place they sailed to a little cove at
several miles distance, to which they gave the name of English
Cove. Here they found wood and water in great plenty, also
                                                          rock

A. D. rock oyfters and cockles of a very large fize. Higher on the
1768. fhore they procured cocoa nuts, and the upper part of the tree
that bears them, which is called the cabbage. This cabbage is
a white, crifp, juicy fubftance, which, ufed raw, taftes fomewhat like a chefnut, but, when boiled, is fuperior to the beft
parfnip. For each of thefe cabbages they were obliged to cut
down a tree, by which means they deftroyed, in the parent
ftock, a great deal of cocoas, which are the moft powerful
antifcorbutic in the world. The fhip's company, who were extremely afflicted with the diforder, recovered faft, and had an
opportunity of examining the neighbourhood, where the country is high and mountainous, but covered with trees of various
kinds, fome of which are of an enormous growth, and proba-
bably would be ufeful for many purpofes. Among others they
found the nutmeg tree in great plenty, though the nuts were
not then ripe, and appeared not to be of the beft kind, owing
perhaps to their growing wild, and being overfhadowed by
taller trees. The different kinds of palm, with the beetle nut
tree, various fpecies of the aloe, canes, bamboos, and rattans,
grow with wild luxuriance. The woods abound with pigeons,
doves, rooks, parrots, and a large bird with black plumage,
that makes a noife fomewhat like the barking of a dog. The
people fent out to examine the country fell in with feveral habitations of the natives, which appeared by the fhells that were
fcattered about them, and the fires half confumed, to have been
but very lately deferted. From the meannefs of thefe hovels,
it appeared that the inhabitants ftood low even in the fcale of
favage life.

    Englifh Cove lies a few miles from Wallis Ifland, which is di-
ftant about three leagues from Cape St. George, the latitude of
which is 5 degrees fouth, and its longitude 152 degrees 19 minutes eaft, about two thoufand five hundred leagues due weft
from the continent of America. The captain weighed anchor
the 7th of September, having taken poffeffion of this country,
with all its iflands, bays, ports and harbours, for his majefty
King George the Third. This was performed by nailing upon a
high tree a piece of board, faced with lead, on which was engraved the Englifh union flag, with the name of the fhip and

                           her

her commander, the name of the cove, and the time of her A. D
coming in and failing out of it. A boat had been fent out fe- 1768
veral times to examine the harbours of the coaft, and from one
of thefe expeditions returned with a load of cocoa nuts, which
fhe procured in a fine fmall harbour about four leagues weft-
north-weft from Englifh Cove. Of this harbour the captain
received fo agreeable accounts that he thought proper to vifit it,
and found that it was formed by two iflands and the main.
The largeft, which is to the north-weft, he called Cocoa-nut
Ifland, and the fmaller, which is to the fouth-eaft, he called
Leigh's Ifland. His officers named the harbour in honour of
their captain; it is by far the beft ftation they had fallen in with
during their long run from the Streights of Magellan. The
captain would have continued here a fufficient time to give his
people all the refreshments they wanted, if the lives of all on
board, in their prefent unhealthy condition, the quantity of
fhips provifions, and the fhattered ftate of the veffel, had not
depended upon their getting to Batavia while the monfoon
continued to blow from the eaftward.

He weighed anchor the 9th, but was again driven by winds
and currents into St. George's bay, which, contrary to what
had been fuppofed, he found inftead of a bay to be a channel
between two iflands. This channel he found to be divided by
a pretty large ifland, which he named in honour of the duke of
York, and feveral fmall ones lying fcattered around it. The
land of the Duke of York's Ifland lies level, and has a delightful appearance; the centre is covered with lofty woods, and
near the fhore are the houfes of the natives, extremely numerous, built among groves of cocoa-nut trees, the whole forming
a profpect the moft beautiful and romantic that can be imagined.
The largeft of the two iflands that are divided by the channel
or ftreight, which is about eight leagues broad, the captain left
in poffeffion of its ancient name of New Britain. It lies on the
fouth fide, and there is upon it fome high land, and three remarkable hills clofe to each other, which he called the Mother
and Daughters. To the northern ifland he gave the name of
New Ireland, and to the ftreight that of St. George's Channel.
Continuing to fteer along the coaft of New Ireland, he difco-

vered a large island, with a pleasant appearance, very populous, which he named in honour of the Earl of Sandwich. It lies in latitude 2 degrees 53 minutes south, longitude 149 degrees 17 minutes east. All the time the ship lay off this island there was an incessant noise like the beating of a drum ; and ten canoes put off from New Ireland, with about an hundred and fifty men on board. The people are black and woolly headed, but have not the flat noses and thick lips of the Africans. None of them would come on board, but conveyed such trifles as they exchanged for the nails and iron offered them by the English, upon the end of a long stick. The canoes were long, narrow, and neatly made : one of them could not be less than ninety feet ; formed, however, of a single tree, rowed by three and thirty men, and without any appearance of sails. These negroes, though stark naked, except a few ornaments of shells upon their arms and legs, had their heads and beards abundantly covered with white powder.

The western extremity of New Ireland the captain named Cape Byron. It lies in latitude 2 degrees 30 minutes south, longitude 149 degrees 2 minutes east. Over against the coast of New Ireland, to the westward of Cape Byron, lies a fine large island, covered with trees, to which he gave the name of New Hanover. To the westward of New Hanover he discovered, at the distance of eight leagues, seven small islands, which were named the Duke of Portland's Islands ; the middle of which lies in latitude 2 degrees 29 minutes south, longitude 148 degrees 27 minutes east. The ship was now clear of the streight, whose length from Cape St George to Cape Bryon is above eighty leagues. The necessity which pushed Captain Carteret on this discovery may be very advantageous to future navigators, as St. George's Channel is a much better and shorter passage than round all the land and islands to the northward ; and refreshments of various kinds may be procured from the natives inhabiting the opposite coasts of the channel, or the islands that lie near them, for beads, ribbands, looking-glasses, and especially iron tools and cutlery ware, of which they are immoderately fond.

The

The captain proceeded weftward the 15th of September, and A. D the fame day difcovered an ifland of confiderable extent, with 1708 many others lying to the fouthward. From thefe many canoes, crowded with Indians, paddled to the fhip: they made various figns, which were repeated, to fhow that whatever they meant the fame was meant to them. In order to invite them on board, the fhips company held up whatever trifles they thought would give them pleafure; but they had no fooner come within reach of the people on deck, than they threw their lances at them with great force. It was neceffary to reprefs their fury by firing fmall fhot, with which one of them was killed, and the canoes rowed off with great expedition. In failing along, many other canoes appeared, and behaved in the fame hoftile manner. From one, in which a man was killed by the fhot of a mufket, the reft precipitately leaped into the fea, which afforded an opportunity of feizing the canoe, which was full fifty feet long though one of the fmalleft that had come out, and filled with fifh, turtle, yams, and cocoa nuts. The fhip being difengaged from this fierce and unfriendly people, purfued her courfe along the other iflands, which are between twenty and thirty in number, and of confiderable extent; one in particular would alone make a large kingdom. The captain, not having had an obfervation of the fun for feveral days, and there being ftrong currents, could not exactly afcertain their fituation, but he judged the middle of the largeft to lie in latitude 2 degrees 18 minutes fouth, longitude 146 degrees 44 minutes eaft, at the diftance of five and thirty leagues from New Hanover. He called them Admiralty Iflands, and, if his fhip had been in better condition, and provided with proper articles for the Indian trade, he would have examined them with particular attention, efpecially as their appearance is very inviting, being clothed with a beautiful verdure, the woods lofty and luxuriant, interfperfed with fpots cleared for plantation, groves of cocoa-nut trees, and houfes of the natives, who feem to be very numerous. With thefe iflands it would be eafy to eftablifh a commercial intercourfe, as the fuperiority of our fire arms would foon perfuade the natives that all conteft is vain; and the traffic would be advantageous on both fides, as the Indians might be fupplied with many arti-

cles

cles which they are greatly in want of, and the Englifh might
in all probability be fupplied with the valuable fpiceries produced in the Moluccas ; for the Admiralty Iflands lie in the fame
degree of latitude, and the nutmeg tree was found on the coaft
of New Ireland, a foil comparatively barren and rocky.

Having paffed thefe iflands the fhip continued her courfe weft
by north with a fine eaftern breeze, and on the 19th difcovered two fmall iflands, both low land, level and green. The neareft the captain called Durour's Ifland. Its latitude is about 1 degree 14 minutes fouth, its longitude 143 degrees 21 minutes
eaft. At no great diftance is the other, which was called Mat-
ty's Ifland, and two others, ftill fmaller, lying to the fouth-
weft, were called Stephen's Iflands. All thefe have a beautiful
green appearance, are covered with trees, and replenifhed with
inhabitants. On the 25th of September the fhip fell in again
with land, which proved to be three iflands, the largeft lying
fifty miles north of the line, and in longitude 137 degrees 51
minutes eaft. Several canoes foon came off, filled with the natives, who, after making figns of peace, came on board without the leaft appearance of fear or diftruft. They fold their
cocoa nuts with great pleafure for fmall pieces of iron. They
are of the Indian copper colour, their features pleafing, their
teeth remarkably white and even, of the common ftature, nimble,
vigorous and active in a furprifing degree. They are not, like
the other people on all the iflands that had been vifited, quite
naked, though they had only a flight covering for the waift,
which confifted of a narrow piece of fine matting. They offered to leave a certain number of their people as pledges, if
the failors would go on fhore, to which they ftrongly urged
them ; and one of them would by no means leave the fhip when
fhe purfued her courfe ; the captain carried him to Celebes,
where, being taken ill at fea, he unfortunately died. The iflands from which he had been taken were remarkably fmall and
low, the largeft being no more than five miles in compafs. The
captain gave them the name of Freewill Iflands, from the fo-
ciable and benevolent difpofition of the natives.

The remaining route of Captain Carteret to the coaft of Min-
danao, and from thence to the ifland of Celebes, had been
explored

explored by Dampier and other navigators. But the captain has A. D
rectified several miltakes which his predecessors had fallen into, 1768.
particularly in the account of the Streight of Macaſſar. He
made the entrance of this ſtreight the 14th of November, and
anchored before the town of Macaſſar the 15th of December.
In the neighbourhood of this place he obtained permiſſion, after
much altercation and many threats uſed with the Dutch governor, to continue a conſiderable time, until the crew were a
little recovered from their languor and debility, and the ſhip put
in a condition to undertake her voyage to Batavia. This voyage
being ſucceſsfully performed, the captain doubled the Cape of
Good Hope, and had a pleaſant paſſage to the iſland of
St. Helena. He left this place the 24th of January, 1769, to
proſecute his voyage to England; and after a month's navigation diſcovered a ſhip to leeward, in the ſouth-weſt quarter,
which hoiſted French colours. When this ſhip was near
enough to hail the Swallow, Captain Carteret was ſurpriſed to
hear the Frenchman mention his own name as well as that of
his ſhip, inquiring after his health, and telling him, that, after
the return of the Dolphin to Europe, it was believed he had
ſuffered ſhipwreck in the Streights of Magellan, and that two
ſhips had been ſent out in queſt of him. The captain aſked in
his turn who it was that was ſo well acquainted with all theſe
particulars, and how this knowledge had been acquired. The
Frenchman anſwered, that the ſhip was in the ſervice of their
Eaſt-India company, commanded by Mr. Bougainville, returning from the iſle of France, who had got an account of the
voyage of the Dolphin and Swallow from the French gazette at
the Cape of Good Hope. An offer was then made of ſupplying the Swallow with refreſhments, which was a mere verbal
civility, as the ſhip had immediately ſailed from the ſame places
at which Mr. Bougainville himſelf had been ſupplied; and it
was aſked if Captain Carteret had any letters to ſend to France.
As he happened to have ſeveral, which he had received from
French gentlemen at the Cape, this furniſhed an occaſion to
Mr. Bougainville to ſend his boat on board, which was preciſe-
ly what he deſired. A young officer, dreſſed in a waiſtcoat and
trowſers, but whoſe rank Captain Carteret ſoon found to be

superior

A. D.
768.
superior to his appearance, came down to the cabin; and being asked several questions by Captain Carteret, to which he replied with great readiness and ingenuity, contrived to introduce inquiries concerning the Streights of Magellan, the hardships which the Swallow had suffered in her voyage, and other topics equally interesting. These questions the captain endeavoured to elude as long as it was possible; but the queries of the young Frenchman becoming too particular and troublesome, having desired to know on what side the equator the Swallow had crossed the south seas, the captain rose up abruptly with some marks of displeasure. His visitor was going to make an apology, to prevent which Captain Carteret desired him to present his compliments to Mr. Bougainville, and, in return for his obliging civilities, present him with one of the arrows with which the Indians had wounded some of the English.

When the captain came on deck he was asked by his lieutenant whether the Frenchman had entertained him with an account of his voyage. This led him to explain the general purport of their conversation, upon which the lieutenant observed, that the boat's crew had not kept their secret as well as their officer, but given sufficient intimation, that they had been round the world, mentioning the different places they had touched at, and many particulars of their voyage. This disingenuous artifice of Mr. Bougainville, to draw Captain Carteret into a breach of his obligation to secrecy, was unworthy of that spirit of enterprize which led him to undertake so dangerous a navigation, which he has related with so much elegance.

According to his own account, he sailed from France in November 1766, in the frigate La Boudeuse; and, having spent some time on the coast of Brazil and at Falkland islands, got into the southern ocean, by the Streights of Magellan, in January 1768. In this ocean he discovered the four Facardines, the Isle of Lanciers, Harpe Island, Thrumb-Cap, and Bow Island. About twenty leagues farther to the west he discovered four other islands, and afterwards fell in with Otaheite, Isles of Navigators, and Forlorn Hope, which to him were new discoveries. He then pass'd through between the Hebrides; discovered the Shoal of Diana, the land of Cape Deliverance; several small

islands

islands to the north; passed the coast of New Ireland; touched A. D
at Batavia, and arrived in France in March 1769, about the  1768
same time that Captain Carteret arrived in England.

The admiralty did not wait for his arrival to fit out another
expedition, which was attended with circumstances peculiarly
interesting. The brilliant discoveries of Captain Wallis, who
returned to England in May 1768, inspired the most sanguine
hopes of completing the great purpose for which all these
voyages had been undertaken. Many southern lands were already
discovered, which heightened the probability of finding at
length the great *Terra Australis incognita*, which had been so
long sought for in vain. Among the countries which Wallis
had discovered and explored was the island of Otaheite, the
situation of which appeared extremely proper for answering a
particular purpose, which the admiralty had in their view in the
present expedition, besides the general design of discovering
unknown lands. The year 1769 was rendered remarkable by
the transit of the planet Venus over the disk of the sun; a
phænomenon of the greatest importance to the sciences of
astronomy, geography, and navigation, and which every where
engaged the attention of the learned in those branches of knowledge. In the beginning of the year 1768 the Royal Society
presented a memorial to his majesty, setting forth the advantages
to be derived from accurate observations of this transit in different parts of the world, particularly from a set of such observations made in a southern latitude, between the 140th and 180th
degrees of longitude, west from the Royal Observatory at Greenwich; but that the society were in no condition to defray the
expence necessary for equipping vessels to convey the observers
to their destined stations. In consequence of this memorial the
admiralty were directed by his majesty to provide proper vessels
for the purpose. Accordingly the Endeavour bark, which had
been built for the coal trade, was purchased and fitted out for
the southern voyage, and the command of her entrusted to
Lieutenant (now Captain) Cook, himself a distinguished member of the Royal Society, and appointed by his associates, in conjunction with Mr. Charles Green the astronomer, to make the
requisite observations on the transit.

Captain

A. D.    Captain Cook failed from Deptford the 30th of July, 1768,
1768. with inftructions to proceed directly to Otaheite, and, after the
aftronomical obfervations fhould be completed, to profecute the
defign of making difcoveries in the Pacific ocean, by proceeding
fouthward to the latitude of 40 degrees, and, if he did not find
land, to continue his voyage to the weft, between the latitudes
of 40 degrees and 35 degrees fouth, till he fell in with New Zealand, which he was directed to explore, and thence to return
to England by fuch route as he fhould judge moft convenient.

In executing thefe inftructions, Mr. Cook endeavoured to
make a direct courfe to Otaheite, and in part fucceeded; but
when he came within the tropic he fell in with feveral iflands,
which had not been before difcovered. He remained three
months at Otaheite, and then vifited many neighbouring iflands,
till then unknown. On the 6th of October, 1769, he fell in
with the eaft fide of New Zealand, and continued exploring
the coaft of this country till the 31ft of March, 1770. He
then proceeded to New Holland, and furveyed its eaftern coafts,
which had not been before vifited; and, paffing between its
northern extremity and New Guinea, afterwards touched at the
ifland of Savu, Batavia, the Cape of Good Hope, and St. Helena, and arrived in England on the 12th of July, 1771.

Befides the aftronomical purpofes which were anfwered by
this voyage, and the important difcoveries of new lands, made
in the courfe of the longeft navigation hitherto undertaken, the
expedition of Captain Cook was diftinguifhed by another circumftance particularly interefting to the lovers of philofophy.
The expedition was adorned by the prefence of Mr. Banks, a
man of letters as well as of fortune, who was accompanied by
Dr. Solander, an accomplifhed difciple of Linnæus. Both thefe
gentlemen were remarkable for an extenfive and accurate knowledge of natural hiftory; and, being otherwife men of liberal
education and principles, they were led to make various obfervations, not only on the natural curiofities and productions, but
on the manners, policy, religion, and language of the feveral
countries which they vifited. Seldom have men of fuch talents
poffeffed that fpirit of daring enterprize which prompts to the
difcovery and examination of unknown lands. Seldom have

2                                          diftant

distant countries been visited and described by philosophers; for A. D.
avarice and ambition, and not the thirst of knowledge, have ge- 1769.
nerally excited to such undertakings men of a bold and hardy,
but of a narrow and illiberal spirit. The ingenious observations
made during the course of the present voyage tend to fill up the
picture of which former navigators had only sketched the out-
lines.

The reception which Captain Cook and his companions met
with from the Portuguese at Rio de Janeiro, where he put in the
13th of November in order to purchase provisions and necessaries, was most unworthy of the design in which they were engaged. That ignorant superstitious people could form no idea
of the object of their voyage. The purpose of making philo-
sophical discoveries they treated with the utmost contempt, and
watched the persons of the English travellers with all the jealous severity of fear and ignorance. Mr. Cook continued his
voyage to the Streights of Le Maire, which separate Staten
Island from Terra del Fuego. He arrived at the entrance of
the Streights the 14th of January, which is near the middle of
summer in those parts. As the weather was calm Mr. Banks
was desirous of examining the coast of the main land, and af-
cending a mountain which appeared at a little distance in search
of plants. This was effected; but so excessive is the cold in
the southern hemisphere, that, at a degree of latitude which in
the summer months is temperate in Europe, all those who undertook this expedition were in danger of being frozen to death;
and several of Mr. Banks's attendants actually perished.

In this miserable climate the inhabitants appeared to be the
most destitute and forlorn of all human beings. They have no
dwelling but a wretched hovel of sticks and grass, which not
only admits the wind, but the snow and the rain. They are
destitute of every convenience that is furnished by the rudest art,
having no implement even to dress their food. They have no
other clothing than the skin of the guanicoe or seal, which is
thrown over their shoulders, drawn over their feet, and worn
round the waists of the women as a succedaneum for a fig-leaf.
Shell-fish seems to be their only food, which being in no great
plenty in any particular place, obliges them to wander perpetu-

A. D.
769.
ally in fmall hordes over thofe dreary and inhofpitable regions, which appear fo ill fitted to be the habitations of men. Yet thefe favage tribes are, perhaps, only miferable in the imaginations of thofe who furvey them, and who, placing themfelves in their fituation, conceive what exquifite fufferings they would feel if reduced to the fame manner of life. The wandering inhabitants of Terra del Fuego are contented with their lot. Though deprived of whatever is comfortable, they are ftudious to adorn their perfons. Their faces are painted in various forms; the region of the eye generally white, and the reft of the face diverfified with ftreaks of red and black.

The captain fell in with the ifland of Terra del Fuego about twenty leagues to the weftward of the Streight of Le Maire. The Streight itfelf is about five leagues long and as many broad; and has a bay in the middle of it, which affords good anchorage, as well as excellent wood and water. The doubling of Cape Horn has been fo much dreaded, that, in the general opinion, it is more eligible to pafs through the Streights of Magellan; but Captain Cook's experience feems to prove the contrary; for he was no more than thirty-three days in coming round the land of Terra del Fuego, from the eaft entrance of the Streight of Le Maire; whereas Captain Wallis employed above three months in getting through the Streights of Magellan in the fame feafon of the year.

Captain Cook, continuing his voyage in a north-wefterly direction, obferved the latitude, on the 24th of March, 1769, to be 22 degrees 11 minutes fouth, and longitude 127 degrees 55 minutes weft. Some of the people, who were upon the watch in the night, reported that they faw a log of wood pafs by the fhip, and that the fea, which was rather rough, became fuddenly as fmooth as a mill-pool. However, they fell in with no land till the 4th of April, when an ifland of an oval form appeared at the diftance of a few leagues. They approached it on the north fide within a mile, but found no bottom with 130 fathom of line. The whole is covered with trees, efpecially palms and cocoa-nut trees; among the groves of which the natives were feen walking in great numbers. The captain named this Lagoon Ifland. It is fituated in latitude 18 degrees 47 minutes
fouth,

fouth, and longitude 139 degrees 28 minutes weft. In purfuing his voyage weftward he fell in with feveral other inconfiderable iflands at no great diftance from the former. Thefe were Thrumb-Cap, The Groups, Bird Ifland, and Maitea, to which Captain Wallis had given the name of Ofnaburgh.

On the 11th of April land was feen a-head, which was known by its fituation to be Otaheite, the fame which is defcribed in the voyage of Captain Wallis, to which he gave the name of King George the Third's Ifland. When the fhip came near to the fhore, it was immediately furrounded by the natives in their canoes, who offered cocoa nuts, fruit refembling apples, bread fruit, and fome fmall fifhes, in exchange for beads and other trifles. Soon after arrived other canoes, in which were fome of thofe Indians who had maintained a good deal of intercourfe with the crew of Captain Wallis's fhip, and who were immediately known to Mr. Gore, the fecond lieutenant, who had gone round the world with that captain. One of thefe antient acquaintance came on board, and as foon as the fhip was properly fecured, went on fhore with the captain and the other gentlemen. They were all received with many marks of friendfhip by the hofpitable Indians, and a treaty was ratified between them by exchanging the green branches of a tree, which was the fymbol of peace among many ancient and powerful nations. The fhip continued on the coaft of Otaheite three months, trading with the natives, and examining the ifland. The ordinary rate of traffic was a fpike nail for a fmall pig, and a fmaller nail for a fowl; a hatchet for a hog; and twenty cocoa nuts, or bread fruit, for a middling fized nail. Looking-glaffes, knives, and beads, are excellent articles of commerce, and for thefe every thing may be obtained which the natives can beftow. During the whole time that the Englifh continued here, they lived in the moft friendly intercourfe with the Indians; and confidered the ifland not as before in a curfory manner, but with a critical attention.

Though Otaheite lies within the tropic of Capricorn, it is one of the moft healthy and delightful fpots in the world. The heat is not troublefome, and the air is fo pure that frefh meat will keep very well for two days, and fifh one day. The winds

generally

A. D. 769.

generally blow from the divisions between east and south; the tide rises but little, and being governed by the winds is extremely uncertain. The coast is of a bold elevation, rises like an amphitheatre, and the mountains every where covered with wood, present to the view the most captivating prospect. The stones all over this island appear to have been burnt; and there are other marks of violent concussions and subterraneous fires, by which the face of nature has been altered in this and the neighbouring isles. The exterior ranges of hills are sometimes barren, and contain a great quantity of yellowish clay, mixed with iron ore; but this excepted, there are no other indications of metals, or valuable minerals of any kind.

The soil of Otaheite is a rich black mold, producing spontaneously a great variety of the most excellent fruits; sugar canes, which the inhabitants eat raw; ginger, turmeric, and a great number of other excellent roots, which are unknown in other climates. The trees are the greatest curiosity of Otaheite. The Chinese paper-mulberry tree is that of which the natives make their cloth. The trunk of the bread-fruit tree, which furnishes nourishment to the whole island, is six feet in the girth, and about twenty feet to the branches. There is a species of the fig, the branches of which bending down, take fresh root in the earth, and thus form a congeries of trunks, united by a common vegetation, which have the appearance of one stock of astonishing magnitude. Another tree, covered with a dark-green foliage, bears golden apples, which resemble the anana or pine-apple in juiciness and flavour. The most beautiful tree in the world received the name of Barringtonia; the natives call it Huddoo; it had a great abundance of flowers, larger than lilies, and perfectly white, excepting the tips of their numerous chives, which were of a bright crimson. The fruit, which is a large nut, has the property of various plants of tropical climates, of intoxicating fish, so that they come to the surface of the water, and suffer themselves to be taken by hand. There is a great variety of excellent fish, which, as they form the principal object of luxury, the catching of them is the main occupation of the natives. There are no venomous reptiles or troublesome insects, but ants and mosquitos. Besides poultry

exactly

exactly like thofe of Europe, there are wild ducks; beautiful A. D green turtle doves; large pigeons of a deep blue plumage; par- 1769 roquets valued for their red falkers, and often feen tame in the houfes of the natives. There are no quadrupeds in the ifland, but hogs, dogs, and rats; all which are extremely numerous.

The perfons of the inhabitants being examined with particular attention, there was no occafion to alter the idea which captain Wallis had given of them. Captain Cook rather feems to heighten the panegyric; and Mr. Bougainville affirms, that were a painter to delineate an Hercules or a Mars, it would be impoffible to difcover more advantageous models. The women of the lower ranks are of a fmaller ftature than the reft, which is attributed to their early and promifcuous intercourfe with men; for the better fort, who do not gratify their paffions in the fame unbridled manner, are above the middle ftature of the Europeans. The men of confequence in the ifland wear the nails of their fingers long, which they confider as a very honourable diftinction, fince only fuch people as have no occafion to work can fuffer them to grow to that length. The women always cut their hair fhort round their heads. Both men and women have the hinder part of their thighs and loins marked with black lines in various directions, by ftriking the teeth of an inftrument fomewhat like a comb through the fkin, and rubbing into the punctures a kind of pafte made of foot and oil, which leaves an indelible ftain. This cuftom, which is called tattowing, is common to all perfons beyond the age of twelve years; and the legs of people of fuperior rank and authority are checquered with the fame decorations. Both fexes are not only decently but gracefully clothed with the ftuff above-mentioned. The drefs of the better fort of women confifts of feveral pieces; one is wrapped round the waift, fo as to hang down in the form of a petticoat, and being of a thin pliable texture, difplays an elegant figure to the greateft advantage. " The women of Ota-
" heite," fays Mr. de Bougainville, " have features as agree-
" able as thofe of the Europeans; and are unrivalled in the
" fymmetry and beautiful proportion of their limbs. The men
" who live much on the water are of a redder complexion than
" thofe who chiefly refide on fhore. Some have their hair
" brown,

A. D. " brown, red or flaxen, in which they are exceptions to all-the
769. " natives of Asia, Africa, and America, who have their hair
" universally black."

Their houses are nothing more than a roof, scarcely four feet from the ground, raised on three rows of pillars, one row on each side, and one in the middle. The covering consists of palm leaves, the pillars of wood, and the floor is strowed with hay or covered with mats. These simple habitations contain no other furniture except a few blocks of wood, which serve them as pillows, and their ordinary apparel is made use of instead of blankets and sheets. The size of the house is proportioned to the number which constitutes the family, and is seldom occupied except during the hours of repose. In these dormitories it is the established rule for the master and mistress to sleep in the middle, round them the married people, in the next circle the unmarried women, and the servants at the extremity of the shed, or in fair weather in the open air.

They are quite unacquainted with the method of boiling water, as they have no vessels among them that will bear the heat of the fire. Their meat is always broiled or roasted. They use shells for carving, but eat with their fingers. Some attempted the use of the knife and fork, in imitation of the English, but we are told by Mr. Hawkesworth, that they could not guide these implements; by the mere force of habit, the hand came always to the mouth, while the food at the end of the fork went to the ear. Their general drink is water, or the milk of the cocoa nut. They have a plant called ava ava, of an intoxicating quality, which the men make use of sparingly; the women never; and they testified aversion for the strong liquors which were offered them. They eat alone, or at least only in company with a guest that happens to come in; and the men and women never sit down together to a meal. Persons of rank are constantly fed by their inferiors, frequently their women, and this custom is so strongly confirmed, that a chief who dined on board the Endeavour would have returned without his meat, if one of the servants had not fed him. The origin of these singular customs has not been explained. The idea of cleanliness to which these people are so strongly attached, that
they

they perform their ablutions several times every day, may per- A. D haps account for the great men's requiring to be fed. But that 1769 a people remarkably fond of society, and particularly that of their women, should exclude its pleasures from the table, where among all other nations, whether civil or savage, they have been principally enjoyed, is truly inexplicable. Captain Cook imagined this strange singularity among the inhabitants of Otaheite must have arisen from some superstitious opinion; but they constantly affirmed the contrary. They ate alone, they said, because it was right; but why it was right to eat alone they never attempted to explain.

These islanders, who ly on the ground, and inhabit huts exposed to all the inclemencies of the weather, are remarkably healthy and vigorous, and generally attain to old age, without feeling the inconveniencies of this melancholy period of life. Mr. de Bougainville describes an old man, whom they saw on their landing, who had no other character of old age, than that remarkable one which is imprinted on a fine figure. His head was adorned with white hair, and a long white beard; all his body was nervous and fleshy; he had neither wrinkles, nor showed any other token of decrepitude. This venerable man seemed displeased at the arrival of these strangers, retired without making any return to the courtesies which they paid him, and instead of taking part in the raptures which the multitude expressed, his thoughtful and suspicious air seemed to indicate a fear, that the society of a new race of men might disturb the uninterrupted happiness which he had so long enjoyed. They are utterly destitute of medical knowledge, which they hold in contempt; but they are good proficients in surgery, the operations of which they often experience to be useful. One of the English seamen, when on shore, ran a large splinter into his foot, which his companion, after giving him exquisite pain, vainly attempted to extract with his pen-knife. An old Indian who happened to be present, called a man from the other side of the river, who, having examined the lacerated foot, fetched a shell from the beach, which he broke to a point with his teeth; with which instrument he laid open the wound, and ex-
                                                            tracted

A. D.
769.

tracted the fplinter; whilft this operation was performing, the old man went a little way into the wood, and returned with fome gum, which he applied to the wound, upon a piece of the cloth that was wrapped round him, and in two days time it was perfectly healed. This gum was produced by the apple tree; the furgeon of the fhip procured fome of it, and ufed it as a vulnerary balfam with great fuccefs.

The language of the inhabitants of Otaheite is foft and melodious, abounding with vowels, which renders its pronunciation eafily acquired. It is almoft totally without inflexion either of nouns or verbs; but a fufficient acquaintance with it has not been attained to determine whether it is copious or otherwife. It was impoffible to teach the Indians to pronounce the Englifh names of their guefts, but they did not fail to come as near to it as poffible, the giving of the name being an indifpenfable ceremony, which they never omitted when they introduced a new acquaintance. They converted the Englifh names into words refembling Spanifh or Italian; Cook they called Toote; Hicks Hete; Mr. Gore, Toarro; Dr. Solander, Torano; Parkinfon, Patini; Mr. Monkhoufe, a midfhipman, they called Matté, which fignifies in their language dead, becaufe he commanded a party that killed a man for ftealing a mufket. The neareft imitation they could reach of King George, was by calling him Kihiargo. They are not deftitute of genius for the fciences, though they have no opportunity of cultivating them. A map of Otaheite, engraved for Captain Cook's firft voyage, was taken out and laid before Tuahow the high admiral, without informing him any thing of what it was. He prefently difcovered its meaning, and was overjoyed to fee a reprefention of his own country. Thefe people have a remarkable fagacity in foretelling the weather, particularly the quarter from whence the wind will blow. In their long voyages they fteer by the fun in the day, and in the night by the ftars; all of which they diftinguifh feparately by names; and know in what part of the heavens they will appear in any of the months, during which they are vifible in their horizon; nor are they lefs acquainted with the periods of their annual appearance. They reckon time by moons, thirteen of which compofed the year. They divide the day and

I

the

the night, each into fix parts. They judge of the time of the
day by the height of the fun. It is faid, that the higheft number for which they have names is 200. They exprefs the diftance from one place to another by the time it would take to
run over it. They entertain no notion of the baneful influence
of comets, but they confider thofe meteors which are called
fhooting ftars, as evil genii.

The government of the inhabitants of Otaheite is compared
by Dr. Hakefworth to the early ftate of every nation in Europe under the feudal fyftem. There is a king or fovereign in
each of the two peninfulas into which the ifland is divided;
with the lands of the different diftricts, whofe poffeffions are
cultivated by their vaffals and villeins. The king poffeffes far
lefs authority over the whole fociety, than each chieftain poffeffes in his own diftrict, and the nobles are nearer on a footing
with their fovereign than the lower ranks are with the nobles.
Intermarriages are not permitted between the nobles and the
vulgar; every advantage and honour is confined to the former;
and even fuch articles of food as are reckoned delicacies, pork,
fifh and fowl, are only to be ufed by the nobility. Of thefe
there are different orders, as in all the feudal kingdoms. There
are different liveries, fo to fpeak, to diftinguifh thefe orders;
and the rank of every individual is afcertained by the height at
which their fervants wear their fafhes. Like the ancient no ili-
ty of Europe, they enjoy the right of private war; and each
nobleman, at the head of his vaffals, repels injuries, and main-
tains his rights, by the decifion of arms. Their influence, indeed, over their followers is moft powerful. They have intelligence of every event; they receive notice of every crime that
is committed; they beftow reward, inflict punifhment, and their
decifions are fubmitted to with the moft paffive and unreferved
obedience. Otaheite, therefore, affords in miniature, the picture of two feudal kingdoms, for the whole inhabitants, including women and children, do not exceed 6000. One circumftance alone, as it is related by Dr. Hawkefworth, is peculiar
to this people. The child of the prince, or of the baron, fuc-
ceeds to the titles and honours of his father as foon as it is
born; fo that a baron who was yefterday diftinguifhed by epi-

thets of honour, and approached with the ceremony of lower-
ing the garments and uncovering the upper part of the body, is
to-day, if his wife be delivered of a son, reduced to the rank
of a private person; all marks of respect being transferred to
the child, though the father still continues to possess and admi-
nister the estate. If this circumstance be authentic, it furnishes a
remarkable distinction between the government of Otaheite and
that of the feudal nations of Europe. In these, force generally
prevailed over right. The weakness of age and sex often excluded from the succession those who were naturally entitled to
it. The estate of a child or of a woman was often acquired
by a distant collateral relation; even the destination of royalty
proceeded not in a regular line, the uncle often usurping the
rights of a son, the brother those of a daughter.

The religion of these islanders is not the circumstance which
first attracts the attention of travellers. Captain Wallis, who
first visited and described them, is inclined to believe, that they
had not any religious worship or belief. But subsequent accounts
inform us of their religious tenets, which are as superstitious
and absurd as those of other pagan nations. They admit that
great and primitive truth, that all is derived originally from one
first cause. But they suppose the Supreme Being to have im-
pregnated a rock, which brought forth the year; which daughter, embraced by the father, produced the thirteen months;
which, in conjunction with each other, produced the days. In
the same manner were the stars and all the other objects of nature created, so that the idea of generation runs through the
whole; an idea impressed with peculiar force on the imagination
of these Indians, who of all men are particularly the most ad-
dicted to the sexual pleasures. They believe the existence of
the soul after death, and of a greater or less degree of happiness to be then enjoyed; but they are said to have no conception of a state of punishment or reward hereafter. The share
of happiness in a future life, they imagine, will be proportioned
not to the merit but to the rank of individuals; the nobles enjoying the first distinction of felicity, while their vassals and
villeins must be satisfied, even in the region of spirits, with a
subordinate lot. This religious tenet is evidently derived from
their

their political ufages. The priefthood, as in many antient A. D countries, is hereditary. The priefts are profeffedly the men of 1769 fcience, but their knowledge is altogether frivolous, confifting in being converfant in the names and rank of the fubordinate divinities, and the opinions concerning the origin of the uni-verfe, handed down from one generation to another, by real tradition, in detached fentences, and in a phrafeology unintel-ligible to thofe who do not belong to the facred families.

The general manners and character of the people are fuch as naturally refult from the limited ftate of fociety in which they live, and the faint gradations of improvement to which they have attained. Their paffions, like thofe of children, are vio-lent, but tranfitory. They pafs fuddenly, yet without an ap-parent caufe, from an excefs of grief to the tranfports of joy. Their propenfity to particular friendfhips, like that of all rude people, is ftrong: and their fidelity inviolable. When the Eng-lifh vifited them for the fecond time, every Indian chofe his friend. With a difpofition naturally generous, they difcovered a fingular propenfity to theft. Of this there are innumerable examples in all the accounts which are related of them. But perhaps it has not been fufficiently attended to, that their incli-nation to this vice might depend lefs on the depravity of their moral principles, than on their limited notions of property. Even after they had experienced the power of their new vifi-tants, they continued to pilfer as affiduoufly as before; and perfons who, in other refpects, difplayed no fmall elevation of character, had a particular predilection for riches acquired by ftealth.

Another trait of their character, which had been in fome meafure miftaken by the firft travellers into their country, is the licentioufnefs of their amours. Mr. de Bougainville and Dr. Hawkefworth affert, that there were no women in the ifland who had the fmalleft pretenfions to chaftity. This affertion, however, Captain Cook difcovered to be too general. The women of rank, that is, all the female noblefle, are not devoid of honour; although they do not imagine their inferiors ought to be condem-ned for yielding to promifcuous love. But, notwithftanding the exception which the captain has difcovered, it muft be acknowledged, that their manners in this particular are such as could scarcely escape observation and censure. When the Dolphin first arrived on the coast, a great number of women appeared on the beach, and were very importunate with the men in the boat to come on shore. They stripped themselves naked, and endeavoured to allure them by many wanton gestures; and when they found, that notwithstanding all their endeavours to detain them, the boat was putting off, they pelted them with apples and bananas, shouting and showing every possible sign of derision and contempt. After this, canoes, with a number of women, came close by the side of the ship, where the same wanton gestures were repeated. A regular traffic being established on shore, it was settled that a river should separate the natives and the strangers, and that a few only of the former should cross at a time, for the purpose of trading. Several young women were then permitted to cross the river, who, though they were not averse to the granting of personal favours, were tenacious of making the most of them. An iron nail was commonly the price of beauty; and in proportion to the charms of the damsel was the size of the nail which she received. The men scrupled not to promote this kind of dealing, for fathers and brothers would bring their daughters and sisters, for the purpose of prostitution to the sailors. When they presented the girl, they showed a stick of the size of the nail which was demanded for her, and he who came up to the price was entitled to the merchandize.

From the unbridled licentiousness of the inhabitants of this island, the French gave it the name of the new Cythera. When Mr. de Bougainville arrived on this shore, he was received with the same lascivious compliments which had been lavished on the English. "It was very difficult," says that officer, "with such seducing incitements, to keep at their work 500 "young French sailors, who had been deprived of the sight of "women for six months." Notwithstanding the endeavours used to keep the crew in order, the captain's cook found means to escape on shore. He had no sooner singled out a fair one, than he was immediately encircled with a large party of natives, who stripped him of his clothes from head to foot, and with
great

great tumult and violent exclamations, examined every part of A. D his body very minutely. When their curiofity had been fully 1765 gratified they reftored his clothes, and handing the girl to him, fignified by figns fufficiently expreffive, that fhe was very much at his fervice. But by this time the ardour of the Frenchman had fubfided, and every tumultuous paffion was abforbed in that of fear He entreated them, as the only favour they could be-ftow, to convey him on board, and he reached the fhip more dead than alive.

When Captain Cook lay off this fhore the women of Ota-heite had fo totally divefted themfelves of all apprehenfions of ill treatment from the Englifh failors, that great numbers of the lower clafs remained on board the fhip, after the numerous tribe of vifitants had returned on fhore in the evening. They ventured, without fcruple, to pafs the night on board, having ftudied the difpofition of Britifh feamen fo well as to know that they ran no rifk by confiding in them, but, on the contrary, might make fure of every bead, nail and hatchet that their lovers could mufter. The evening, therefore, was as completely de-dicated to mirth and pleafure, as if the fhip had been at Spit-head inftead of Otaheite. Before it was perfectly dark the women affembled on the forecaftle, and one of them blowing a flute with her noftrils, all of them danced a variety of dances ufual in their country, moft of which were little confiftent with European ideas of delicacy. Even the better fort are not entire-ly exempted from the national weaknefs. A chief named O-tai came on board, accompanied by his wife and two fifters; one of whom, named Morarai was a moft graceful figure, with the moft delicate and beautiful *contours* of the hands and all above the zone; an ineffable fmile fat on her countenance; her admi-ration at feeing the new objects aboard the fhip difplayed itfelf in the livelieft expreffions; nor was fhe fatisfied with looking round the decks, but defcended into the officers cabins, attend-ed by a gentleman of the fhip. Having curioufly examined every part, Morarai took a particular fancy to a pair of fheets which fhe faw fpread on one of the beds, and made a number of fruitlefs attempts to obtain them from her conductor, to whom they belonged. He propofed a fpecial favour as the condition.

condition. She hefitated fome time, and at laft, with feeming reluctance, confented. But, when the yielding nymph was about to furrender, the fhip ftruck violently on the reef, and the affrighted lover, more fenfible to danger than to his fair miftrefs, quitted her unrifled charms, and flew upon deck. Repeated fhrieks made the condition of the fhip more alarming; every perfon on board exerted himfelf to the utmoft on this emergency; at length they brought her again to float. When the danger was over, the officer bethought himfelf of his abandoned fair one; but, on vifiting his cabin, he found her gone, and his bed ftripped of its fheets. Moraria, however, had conducted the theft with fuch dexterity, as would have rendered it not only excufable but praife-worthy among the Spartans; having appeared on deck, and continued a confiderable time, without exciting any miftruft of her acquifition. Four days after this adventure, the fame officer, accompanied by feveral others, ftrolling about the country, came to the fpot where O-tai and his fair fifter refided. He thought it to no purpofe to inquire after his loft bed-linen, but chofe rather to renew his folicitations to the lady. Beads, nails, and various trifles were prefented to her, which fhe readily accepted, but remained inflexible to the paffionate addreffes of her lover. She was already in poffeffion of the fheets, which were the only wealth of fufficient value in her eyes to induce her to admit the tranfient embraces of a ftranger; though fhe was accufed by her countrywomen of admitting tow-taws, or men of the loweft rank, to her bed at night; and thus impofing on her brother, who would have been highly offended at the proftitution, not of her perfon, but of her dignity.

Though it be evident that the general character of the natives of Otaheite is extremely deficient in point of modefty, yet many of their cuftoms, perhaps, are more immodeft in appearance than in reality. The ufual way of expreffing their refpect to ftrangers is by uncovering themfelves to the middle; and a ceremony of a fimilar kind, but expreffive only of refpect, was ufed by Oorattao, a woman of rank, who vifited Mr. Banks. After laying down feveral plantain leaves, a man brought a large bundle of cloth, of the manufacture of that country, which

which having opened, he spread it piece by piece upon the A. D ground, in the space between Mr. Banks and his visitants. 1769 There were in all nine pieces; but, having spread three pieces one upon another, the lady came forward, and, stepping upon them, took up her garments all round her to the waist; she then turned about three times with great composure and deliberation, and with an air of perfect innocence and simplicity; which having done, she dropped the veil: when other three pieces were spread, she repeated the same ceremony; and so the third time, when the last three pieces were laid out; after which the cloth was again rolled up, and delivered to Mr. Banks, as a present from the lady, who, with her attending friend, came up, saluted him, and received such presents in return as he thought proper to offer them. Examples of this kind would lead us to believe, that the indecency of the natives of Otaheite, like that of most nations who have made small advancements in the arts of social life, proceeds less from a natural propensity to voluptuous excess, than from their imperfect notions of propriety. As what has appeared in them a strong inclination to the vice of stealing, arises, probably in some degree, from their limited ideas of property, so the apparent licentiousness of their manners, with regard to the fair sex, may proceed from a want of those cultivated notions of delicacy which prevail in polished countries. They see nothing indecent in the unreserved intercourse of the sexes; among them Venus is the goddess of hospitality; her worship is celebrated without mystery; and every passion is gratified before witnesses, without any more signs of shame than appears in other countries when people associate at a meal. Yet it must not be dissembled, that some of their customs discover a certain refinement in sensual pleasure, which is the characteristic of a degree of depravity that could hardly be expected in their simple state *.

We return from this digression, in which we have endeavoured to reduce into a small compass the various accounts of Wallis, Cooke, Foster, and Bougainville, concerning the manners and character of a people, whose discovery is one of the most

* Hawkesw. II. 125. Bougainville, 230, &c.

brilliant

brilliant that has been made by modern navigation. The island, indeed, is more interesting to the philosopher than to the merchant, as it produces nothing that can be converted into an article of distant traffic, and can be useful only in affording refreshments to shipping, in their voyages through these seas. Captain Cook took his leave of Otaheite the 13th of July, 1769, having carried with him Tupia, one of the natives; who informed him that four of the neighbouring islands lay at the distance of less than two days fail. The names of these were Ulietea, Hyaheine, Otaha, and Bolabola. The first is about twenty-one leagues in circuit. Its productions are the same as those of Otaheite, nor is there any thing to distinguish the appearance and manners of its inhabitants from those of that island. The same may be said of the other three, as well as of the small islands of Tubai and Maurua; to all of which, as they lie contiguous to each other, Captain Cook gave the name of the Society islands, but did not think it necessary to distinguish them separately by any other names than those by which they are known to the natives. They are situated between the latitudes of 16 degrees 10 minutes, and 10 degrees 55 minutes south, and between the longitudes of 150 degrees 17 minutes, and 152 degrees west, from the meridian of Greenwich. Ulietea and Otaha lie at the distance of two miles from each other, and are both inclosed within one reef of coral rocks, so that there is no passage for shipping between them. Ulietea affords a great many good harbours both on the east and west side; the entrances into them, indeed, are but narrow; but, when a ship is once in, nothing can hurt her. The northernmost, on the west side, in which the ship lay, is called Ohamaneno; the channel leading into it is about a quarter of a mile wide, and lies between two low sandy islands. This harbour, though small, is preferable to the others, because it is situated in the most fertile part of the island, and where fresh water is easily to be got. Otaha also affords two good harbours, one on the east side and the other on the west. The island of Bolabola lies north-west and by west from Otaha, distant about four leagues. It is surrounded by a reef of rocks, and several small islands, in compass together about eight leagues. This island is rendered re-

markable by a high craggy hill, which appears to be almost A. D
perpendicular, and terminates at the top in two peaks, one 1769
higher than the other. The captain did not take time to examine the harbours, but understood that Bolabola is not deficient
in this particular. The island of Houaheine is situated in the
latitude of 16 degrees 43 minutes south, and longitude 150 degrees 52 minutes west, distant from Otaheite about thirty-one
leagues, and about seven leagues in compass. The harbour,
which is called by the natives Owalle, lies on the west side,
under the northernmost high land. The climate is more forward that that of Otaheite, and the country abounds with provisions. The inhabitants of all these islands treated the English with the most courteous hospitality ; and testified great sor-
row at the departure of their guests, which, however, did not
take place till Captain Cook had, with the usual formality, taken possession of their territories in the name of his majesty
King George.

The captain left these shores the 9th of August, 1769, and
met with nothing remarkable in his course till the 13th about
noon, when he saw land bearing south-east, which Tupia told
him was an island called Oheteroa. It is situated in the latitude
of 22 degrees 27 minutes south, and in the longitude of 150
degrees 47 minutes west, about thirteen miles in circuit, and
the land rather high than low, but neither populous nor fertile
in proportion to the other islands which had been discovered in
those seas. The chief produce seems to be a tree of which they
make their weapons, called in their language Etoa ; many plantations of it were seen along the shore, which is not surrounded,
like the neighbouring islands, by a reef. The ship, or boats,
made the whole circuit of Oheteroa, and found there was neither harbour nor anchorage about it ; and the hostile disposition
of the natives rendering it impossible to land without bloodshed, the captain determined not to attempt it, having no motive that could justify the risk of life.

Tupia mentioned several islands lying at different distances
and in different directions from this, between the south and the
north-west ; and that, at the distance of three days sail, there
was an island called Mancoa, or Bird Island. But so many discoveries of this kind had already been made, that the captain

purpofed to fpend no more time in fearch of iflands, only in examining thofe which he happened to fall in with during his
courfe, and to proceed fouthward in fearch of a continent.
After a navigation of above fix weeks land was difcovered,
which became the fubject of much eager converfation, it being
generally believed to be the Terra Auftralis Incognita. It was
indeed the coaft of New Zealand, which, ever fince it had been
difcovered by the Dutch navigator Tafman, in 1642, has paffed
with moft geographers for a part of the great fouthern continent. But Captain Cook difcovered that New Zealand confifted
of two iflansd, divided by a ftreight which is called after his
name, and fituated between the latitudes of 34 degrees 22 minutes and 47 degrees 25 minutes fouth, and between the longitudes of 166 degrees and 180 degrees eaft. This indefatigable
navigator employed almoft fix months in fully exploring the
coafts of both iflands, of which he diftinguifhed the feveral
bays, rivers, capes, &c by particular names. The firft place
where he anchored, on the northernmoft ifland, he called Po-
verty Bay, becaufe he found in it no refrefhments, nor any thing
except wood neceffary for a fhip. From hence he proceeded
fouthward, almoft to the forty-firft degree of latitude; and then
reverfing his courfe, failed to the north-eaftern point of land,
and the broadeft part of the whole ifland. He afterwards anchored in a port, fituated in latitude 56 degrees 54 minutes fouth,
and in longitude 184 degrees 4 minutes weft, which, as he here
made an obfervation of the tranfit of Mercury over the fun, he
called Mercury Bay. The river which empties itfelf into the
head of this bay he called the Thames, on account of its refemblance to the Englifh river of that name. The banks of this
river are reprefented as the moft eligible place in thofe iflands
for fettling a colony. More to the north-weft is the Bay of
Iflands, fo named from the great number of little iflands that
line its fhores, forming feveral harbours equally fafe and commodious, where there is depth and room for any number of
fhipping. Captain Cook, in doubling the northern extremity
of New Zealand, met with a gale of wind, which, for its
ftrength and continuance was fuch as he had never experienced
before. He was three weeks in making ten leagues, and five

weeks

weeks in making fifty. Having doubled the cape he proceeded A. I
along the weſtern ſhore, which is extremely barren, conſiſting 1765
of banks of white ſand, and which he therefore called the De-
ſert Coaſt. The ſouthern part of this coaſt bends towards the
weſt, and is diſtinguiſhed by a remarkably high peak of a moſt
majeſtic appearance, covered with perennial ſnow. This peak,
which received the name of Mount Egmont, is ſurrounded by a
flat country of a pleaſant appearance, cloathed with wood and
verdure. Having coaſted this ſhore, the captain entered the
Streight which divides the northern from the ſouthern iſland.
The latter underwent a very accurate ſurvey. On the eaſtern
coaſt he diſcovered a ſmall iſland of a circular form, in the latitude of 43 degrees 44 minutes ſouth, which he called Banks's
Iſland. Proceeding ſouthward he found the extremity of the
land almoſt ſeparated from the reſt, it being joined by a long
and narrow iſthmus. The ſouth-eaſt ſide is of very dangerous
navigation, on account of the ridges of rocks which riſe for
many leagues out of the ſea. But the weſtern extremity affords a
commodious bay, with many harbours and coves ſcattered on
different parts of it, where good anchorage may be found. On
the ſhore, the ſoil is a deep black mold, formed of decayed vegetables. The trees gradually diminiſh in height and circumference, in receding from the ſhore, contrary to what is obſerved in other parts of the world. The captain having left the
above-mentioned bay, (which he called Duſky Bay), proceeded
along the weſtern coaſt, and entered Cook's Streights by the
ſouth-weſt point of land, behind which he anchored in a fine
harbour, which he named Admiralty Bay. A little more to the
eaſtward is Queen Charlotte's Sound, the entrance of which
lies in latitude 41 degrees ſouth, longitude 175 degrees 25 minutes eaſt. This ſound is three leagues broad at its mouth, and
contains a collection of the fineſt harbours in the world. There
are a great number of ſmall iſlands lying at the entrance, and
the land about it is ſo high as to be ſeen at the diſtance of twenty leagues. Here the ſailors caught near three hundred weight
of fiſh, and found wood and water in abundance. The captain
ordered the water-caſks to be filled in this neighbourhood, and
prepared to leave New Zealand on the 30th of March, having

circum-

A. D.
769.
circumnavigated the whole coaft, and made frequent excurfions into the interior parts of the country.

Thefe iflands produce no quadrupeds but dogs and rats; there are few fpecies of birds, and of thefe none, except perhaps the gannet, is the fame with thofe of Europe. For this fcarcity of animals upon the land, the fea makes an abundant recompence; every creek fwarming with fifh, equally wholefome and delicious. The fhip feldom anchored in any ftation, or with a light gale paffed any place, which did not afford enough of fifh with hook and line to ferve the whole fhip's company; the feine feldom failed of producing a ftill more ample fupply; and the variety of fpecies was equal to the plenty. There are mackarel of many kinds, one of which is exactly the fame as we have in England; and the other fpecies of fifh unknown to the European feas, were diftinguifhed by the names of thofe kinds to which they bear the neareft refemblance, and they do honour to the comparifon. Among the vegetable productions of New Zealand, the trees claim a principal place; there being forefts of vaft extent, full of the ftraighteft, the cleaneft, and the largeft timber, any where to be feen. The trees here, however, are too hard and too heavy to be made into mafts; but for every other purpofe they feem to be exceedingly fit, on account of their fize, their grain, and their apparent durability. There are few eatable vegetables in new Zealand, except wild celery, and a kind of creffes, which grow in great abundance upon all parts of the fea-fhore. Of the efculent plants raifed by cultivation, there are only yams, fweet potatoes, and cocoas. Gourds are cultivated by the natives for the fake of the fruit, which furnifhes them with veffels for various ufes. There is a plant that ferves the inhabitants inftead of hemp and flax, which excels all that are put to the fame purpofes in other countries. Of this plant there are two forts; the leaves of both refemble thofe of flags, but their flowers are fmaller, and their clufters more numerous; on one kind they are yellow, on the other a deep red. Of the leaves of thefe plants, with very little preparation, they make all their common apparel, as well as their ftrings, lines and cordage for every purpofe, which are fo much ftronger than any thing we

can

can make with hemp, that they will not bear a comparison. A. D.
Of the leaves of this plant, without any other preparation than 1769.
that of splitting them into proper breadths, and tying the
stripes together, they make their fishing nets, some of which
are of an enormous size.

From the populousness of the sea-coasts, it was at first imagined, that the natives of New Zealand were extremely numerous. But it was afterwards found, that the interior parts were
entirely destitute of inhabitants, or very thinly peopled; for the
principal food of the New Zealanders consisting in fish, they
are afraid to remove to a great distance from the chief source of
their subsistence. The flesh of dogs, and the few vegetables
above-mentioned, are the only succedaneum they have to support life; so that when the dry stock fails in the season when few
fish are caught, the distress is dreadful; and this calamity, which
too often happens, accounts for a practice prevalent in New Zealand of fortifying every village with the utmost care, and the
horrid custom of eating those who are killed in battle. The
New Zealanders rather exceed the European size; are stout,
well limbed and fleshy; exceedingly active and vigorous; and
discover great manual dexterity in all the arts to which they ap-
ply. Their colour resembles the brown hue of the Spaniards;
the women have not a feminine delicacy in their appearance,
but their voice is remarkably soft; and by this they are principally distinguished, the dress of both sexes being the same. This
dress is to a stranger the most uncouth that can be imagined.
It is made of the leaves of the hemp plant, split into three or
four slips, interwoven with each other into a kind of stuff between netting and cloth, with all the ends, which are eight or
nine inches long, hanging out on the upper side. Of this singular cloth two pieces serve for a complete dress; one of them
is tied over their shoulders with a string, and reaches as low as
the knees; to the end of this string is fastened a bodkin of bone,
which is easily passed through any two parts of this upper garment to keep them together. The other pieces of cloth, or
lower garment, is wrapped round the waist, and reaches nearly
to the ground. When they have only the upper garment on,
(for the lower is not so constantly worn), and sit upon their
hams,

A. D.
1769

hams, they bear a refemblance to a thatched houfe; but however ugly their drefs, it is a proper defence againft the inclemencies of the weather to men who often fleep in the open
air.

Thefe people being inured to war, and accuftomed to confider every ftranger as an enemy, were always difpofed to attack
the Englifh until they were intimidated by their manifeft fuperiority. But when they were convinced of the power of fire-
arms, and obferved the clemency of their enemies in forbearing
to make ufe of thefe dreadful weapons, except in their own defence, they became at once friendly and affectionate; and when
an intercourfe was eftablifhed, were rarely detected in any act
of difhonefty. They excel the inhabitants of Otaheite as much
in modefty, as they fall fhort of them in the cleanlinefs of their
perfons, and the convenience of their habitations. The women,
however, were not impregnable; but the terms and manner of
compliance were as decent as thofe in marriage among us, and
according to their notions, the agreement was as innocent. The
confent of friends was neceffary to obtain the perfonal favours
of a young woman, and by the influence of a proper prefent
this confent might generally be obtained.

The ingenuity of thefe people appears principally in the conftruction and management of their canoes, and in whatever relates to war or fifhing. The larger canoes are 68 feet long, 5
feet broad, and 3 and a half feet deep; each fide confifting of
one entire plank, 63 feet long, fitted and lafhed to the bottom
with great dexterity and ftrength. They have no defenfive armour; although they have a great variety of thofe which are
fitted for deftruction. The principal of thefe are fpears, darts,
battle-axes, and the patoo-patoo, which is faftened to their
wrifts by a ftrong ftrap, left it fhould be wrenched from them,
and which the principal people generally wear fticking to their
girdles, confidering it as a military ornament, and part of their
drefs, like the poniard of the Afiatic, and the fword of the
European. Tillage, weaving, and the other arts of peace feem
to be beft known and moft practifed in the northern part of this
country. They have an inftrument which ferves at once for
fpade and plough. The ground is rendered as fmooth as in a
garden;

garden, and every root has its small hillock, ranged in a regular A. I quincunx by lines, which were seen with the pegs remaining in 1770 the ground. The religion, government and language of the New Zealanders bear a remarkable resemblance to those of the natives of Otaheite. Tupia understood their discourse, and was perfectly understood by them. This similarity of dialogue proves a common origin; but which of the two countries was first peopled; whether they were peopled from one another, or both from some more ancient mother-land; and what this land is— are questions which in all probability will never be resolved.

Captain Cook sailed from New Zealand the 31st of March, 1770, and made the coast of New Holland the 19th of April. It was in latitude 37 degrees 58 minutes south, and longitude 210 degrees 39 minutes west, when he first discovered land. The southernmost point of land in sight at this time was judged to lie in latitude 38 degrees, longitude 211 degrees 7 minutes, beyond which, although the weather was very clear, nothing could be observed. The great body of Van Diemen's Land, however, ought, according to the maps, to have borne due south; but the captain not having seen it, does not determine whether it joins the point now discovered or not. Standing to the northward he observed a bay, which seemed to be well sheltered from all winds, and into which he determined to go with the ship. There he anchored in the afternoon under the south shore, about two miles within the entrance, in six fathom water, the south point bearing south-east, and the north point east. This place was a-breast of a small village, consisting of about six or eight houses; and, while the sailors were preparing to hoist out the boat, they saw an old woman, followed by three children, come out of a wood. She was loaded with firewood, and each of the children had also its little burden. She often looked at the ship, but expressed neither fear nor surprise. Some canoes returned from the fishing; the men landed, and the old woman having kindled a fire, they began to dress their dinner, to all appearance wholly unconcerned about the ship. They were all stark naked, the woman herself being destitute even of a fig leaf. It was natural to imagine that these savages, who seemed to pay no regard to the ship's coming into the bay,

would

A. D.
1770.
would have paid as little attention to the people's coming on
shore.  But, as soon as the boat approached the rocks, two of
the men came down upon them to defend their coast, and the
rest ran away.  Each of the two champions was armed with a
lance about ten feet long, and a short stick, which he seemed
to handle as if it was a machine to assist him in throwing his
lance.  They called out in a loud harsh tone, and in a language
which none of those in the boat, although Tupia was of the
party, understood a single word.  The courage of these Indians was remarkable, as they were but two against forty in the
boat ; which the captain ordered to ly on her oars, while he
endeavoured to obtain the good-will of his opponents by throwing them nails, beads, and other trifles, which they took up,
and seemed to be well pleased with.  When he made signs to
them that the ship wanted water, they waved with their hands,
which he interpreted as an invitation to land.  But this was not
their meaning ; for, when the boat began to advance, they renewed their opposition.  One appeared to be a youth of nineteen
or twenty, and the other a man of middle age ; both of such
determined obstinacy that it was necessary to fire a musket between them.  Upon the report the youngest dropped a bundle
of lances upon the rock, but recollecting himself in an instant,
he snatched them up again with great haste, and threw a stone
at the boat.  A second musket was fired, which struck the oldest on the legs, who immediately ran to one of the houses, distant about an hundred yards, and returned with a shield or tar-
get for his defence.  A third musket was fired before they be-
took themselves to flight, and left the boat master of the shore.
Here there was abundance of water, and such a variety of
plants, that the captain gave it the name of Botany bay.  It
lies in latitude 34 degrees south, and longitude 152 degrees 37
minutes east.  The country in general is level, low, and woody.
There are two kinds of trees, larger than the English oak ;
one of them yields a reddish gum like *sanguis draconis*, and the
wood is heavy, hard, and dark-coloured.  The woods abound
with birds of an exquisite beauty, particularly of the parrot
kind ; and crows exactly the same with those in England.
About the head of the harbour, where there are large flats of

sand

fand and mud, there is great plenty of water-fowl; and on the A. D banks themfelves are vaft quantities of oyfters, mufcles, and 1770 cockles, which feem to be the principal fubfiftence of the inhabitants.

The captain having left this place, where he could eftablifh no intercourfe with the natives, proceeded northwards in order to examine the eaftern coaft of New Holland, and to diftinguifh by name the more remarkable places that he met with in his voyage. Having paffed what he called Hervey's Bay, diftinguifhed by Mangrove trees, he anchored in Buftard Bay, in latitude 24 degrees 4 minutes fouth, longitude 151 degrees 42 minutes eaft. He gave it that name from the great numbers of birds of the buftard fpecies, as large as turkeys, one of which weighed feventeen pounds and a half, and was the moft delicate bird that had been met with during the whole voyage. Here are oyfters in great numbers, and of various kinds; among others the hammer oyfter, and abundance of fmall pearl oyfters. And Captain Cook fays, that, if in deep water there is equal plenty of fuch oyfters at their full growth, a pearl fifhery might be eftablifhed to very great advantage. Proceeding about two degrees farther north, he anchored again in Thirfty Sound. From the great variation in the needle, when brought on fhore, and from feveral other obfervations at this place, it feems probable that iron ore abounds in the hills. Along the whole coaft the fea conceals fhoals, which fuddenly project from the fhore, and rocks that rife abruptly like a pyramid from the bottom.

Off Cape Tribulation, which lies in latitude 16 degrees 6 minutes fouth, and longitude 146 degrees 39 minutes eaft, our intrepid and hitherto fuccefsful adventurers were expofed to the moft imminent danger. On the 10th of June, at eleven o'clock at night, the fhip fuddenly ftruck againft a coral rock, and became immoveable except by the heaving of the furge, which, beating her againft the craggs of the rock on which fhe lay, caufed fo violent a concuffion that it was with the utmoft difficulty any one on board could ftand on his legs. At the dawn of day land appeared at eight leagues diftance, without any ifland in the intermediate fpace upon which they might be fet on fhore by the boats, and afterwards proceed to the main, if the fhip fhould go to pieces: the wind, however, died away, till it became a dead calm, by which the ship escaped instant, and otherwise inevitable, destruction.  At eleven in the forenoon it was high water, but so much shorter was the day-tide than that of the night, that, notwithstanding the ship had been lightened near fifty tons, she did not float by a foot and a half.  Thus disappointed, they proceeded to lighten her still more, by throwing overboard every thing that could possibly be spared.  The water now began to rush in so fast, that two pumps could scarcely keep her free.  At five in the afternoon the tide again began to rise, and with it the leak increased so fast that it was necessary to man two more pumps, of which one only could be wrought.  Three of the pumps, however, being kept going, the ship righted at nine; but by this time the leak had gained so considerably, that it was imagined she must go to the bottom as soon as she ceased to be supported by the rock.  The floating of the ship therefore was anticipated, not as an earnest of deliverance, but as a forerunner of destruction.  The boats were not capable of carrying all on shore, where, should any of the crew be able to arrive, their fate would be still more melancholy than that of those who perished in the shipwreck.  Banished on a coast where even nets and fire-arms could scarcely furnish the means of subsistence, and possessing the means of no effectual defence against the natives, they must speedily fall a prey to indigence or ferocity, or languish during the remainder of life in a desolate wilderness, without the hope of any domestic comfort, and cut off from the society of men.  To those only who have waited in such a suspence, death has approached in his wildest terrors.  While every one was reading his own sensation in the countenance of his companions the ship floated, and was heaved into deep water.  It was no small consolation to find that she did not now admit more water than she had done upon the rock.  By the gaining of the leak upon the pumps there were no less than three feet nine inches water in the hold; and the men having endured excessive fatigue of body, and agitation of mind, for more than twenty-four hours, and having but little hope of succeeding at last, began to flag, when this favourable circumstance again animated their vigour, and made them exert the most extraordinary efforts.  But none of them could work at the pumps above five or six minutes together, and then, being totally exhausted,

hausted, they threw themselves down upon the deck, though a A. D
stream of water was running over it from the pumps several 1770
inches deep. When those who succeeded them had worked
their spell, and were exhausted in their turn, they threw themselves down in the same manner, and the others starting up
renewed their labour. At eleven o'clock a breeze from the sea
springing up, the ship was got under sail, and stood for the land.
The exact situation of the leak could not be discovered, and
therefore it was impossible to stop it within, and it was as
impossible to continue that degree of labour, by which the
pumps had been made to work. In this situation a happy
expedient was adopted. It is called fothering the ship, and
is done by taking a large studding-sail, on which a quantity
of oakum and wool, chopped small and mixed together, was
stitched down in handfuls as lightly as possible; over this the
dung of sheep and other filth was spread; and the sail, thus
prepared, was hauled under the ship's bottom by ropes, which
kept it extended. When it came under the leak, the suction
which carried in the water, carried in with it the oakum and
wool from the surface of the sail, which in other parts the water was not sufficiently agitated to wash off. This contrivance
succeeded so happily, that one pump was able to reduce the
water from the leak: and so susceptible are mankind of sudden
joy whenever so partially relieved from imminent danger, that
scarcely greater transport could have been felt, if they had been
arrived into a safe harbour, than this favourable alteration occasioned. At six in the evening the ship was brought to an anchor for the night in seventeen fathom water, at the distance of
seven leagues from the shore, and one from the ledge of rocks
upon which she had struck. The next morning she came to an
anchor within two miles of the shore, no harbour having been
discovered. But the day following was most propitious by the
discovery of a harbour to leeward, most excellently adapted to
the purpose for which it was wanted; and, what was no less
fortunate than remarkable, in the whole course of the voyage
no place had been seen which would have afforded the same
relief to the ship in the situation she then was. Three whole
days intervened before a favourable wind arose to carry them
into their destined haven, in which time they found leisure and in-

clination

clination to reflect, that there was nothing but a lock of wool between them and deſtruction. At length theſe buffeted adventurers ſet their impatient feet on land, after giving the ſtrongeſt proof of a manly, inflexible firmneſs; for, ſays Captain Cook, " Upon this occaſion I muſt obſerve, both in juſtice and grati- " tude to the ſhip's company and the gentlemen on board, that " although in the midſt of our diſtreſs, every one ſeemed to " have a juſt ſenſe of his danger, yet no paſſionate exclamations " or frantic geſtures were heard or ſeen; every one appeared " to have the moſt perfect poſſeſſion of his mind, and every " one exerted himſelf to the utmoſt with a quiet and patient " perſeverance, equally diſtant from the tumultuous voice of " terror, and the gloomy inactivity of deſpair *." Their change of ſituation was now viſible in every countenance, for it was moſt ſenſibly felt in every breaſt. They had ſailed three hundred and ſixty leagues, with a man continually in the chains heaving the lead, which perhaps never happened to any other veſſel. They had been three months entangled among ſhoals and rocks that every moment threatened them with deſtruction; frequently paſſing the night at anchor, within hearing of the ſurge that broke over them; ſometimes driving towards it even while their anchors were out, and knowing that if by any accident, to which an almoſt continual tempeſt expoſed them, they ſhould not hold, every perſon on board muſt inevitably periſh.

The harbour which afforded them relief in this extreme emergency, they named after their veſſel Endeavour River. It lies in latitude 15 degrees 26 minutes ſouth, and its longitude by obſervation is 214 degrees 42 minutes 30 ſeconds weſt. It is only a ſmall bar harbour, or creek, which runs in a winding channel three or four leagues inland, and at the head of which there is a ſmall brook of freſh water. There is not depth of water for ſhipping above a mile within the bar, and at this diſtance only on the north ſide, where the bank is ſo ſteep for near a quarter of a mile, that a ſhip may ly afloat at low water, ſo near the ſhore as to reach it with a ſtep, and the ſituation is extremely convenient for heaving down; but at low water the depth upon the bar is not more than nine or ten feet, nor more

* Hawkeſworth, vol. III,

than

than 17 or 18 at the height of the tide; the difference between A. D
high and low water, at spring tides, being about 9 feet.    At 1770
the time of new and full moon it is high water between nine
and ten o'clock.    This part of the coast is so barricaded with
shoals as to make the harbour exceedingly difficult of access; the
safest approach is from the southward, keeping the main land
close upon the board all the way; and the situation of the harbour may always be found by the latitude, which has been very
accurately laid down.

The captain having refitted at this place, where the principal
refreshment to be procured was turtle, and a plant called, in
the West Indies, Indian kale, set sail the beginning of August,
to examine the northern extremity of the country.    The rocks
and shoals off this coast are more dangerous, perhaps, than in
any part of the globe; for here are reefs of coral rising like an
immense wall, almost perpendicularly out of the sea; always
overflowed at high water, and at low water, in many places,
dry.    The enormous waves of the vast southern ocean meeting
with so abrupt a resistance break with inconceivable violence,
in a surf which no rocks or storms in the northern hemisphere
can produce.    The danger of navigating the unknown parts of
this ocean was greatly increased to our adventurers, by their
having a crazy ship, and being short of provisions and every
other necessary.    " Yet," says Captain Cook, " the distinction
" of the first discoverers made us cheerfully encounter every
" danger, and submit to every inconvenience; and we chose
" rather to incur the censure of imprudence and temerity, which
" the idle and voluptuous so liberally bestow upon unsuccessful
" fortitude and perseverance, than leave a country which we
" had discovered, unexplored, and give colour to a charge of
" timidity and irresolution *."

The captain resolved to keep the main land on board in his
future route to the northward; because, if he had gone without
the reef, it might have carried him so far from the coast as to
prevent his being able to determine whether this country joined
to New Guinea.    This was a question which former navigators
had left undecided, and which Captain Cook was determined to

* Hawkef. vol. III.

decide.

A. D. decide. In the execution of this enterprize, he braved such
1770. dangers as would have appalled the resolution of any man whose
spirit for discovery had not extinguished all regard to personal
safety. He found the two countries to be divided by a narrow
sea, or streight, the north-east entrance of which lies in the
latitude of 10 degrees 39 minutes south, and in the longitude of
218 degrees 36 minutes west. It is formed by the northern
extremity of New Holland, and a congeries of islands, which,
it is probable, extend all the way to New Guinea. These islands
differ very much in height and circuit, and many of them seemed to be well clothed with herbage and wood, and well peopled
with inhabitants.

To this channel or passage the captain gave the name of Endeavour Streights. Its length from north-east to south-west is
ten leagues, and its breadth five leagues, except at the north-east
entrance, where it is less than two miles, being contracted by
the islands which ly there. On one of these islands the captain
took possession of the eastern coast of New Holland, from the
latitude of 38 degrees to 10 degrees 30 minutes south, in the
name of his majesty King George the Third, and distinguished
that immense extent of country by the appellation of New South
Wales. The ascertaining of the division between New Holland
and New Guinea was the last discovery made by Captain Cook
in this voyage. He was now arrived in seas which had been already navigated, and where every coast had been laid down by
Dutch or Spanish navigators. Instead, therefore, of following
this judicious and enterprising adventurer in his navigation to the
isle of Java, and his voyage homeward, it is proper to look
back, and consider the information that may be derived from
his discoveries relative to New Holland.

This immense island, for such is the title by which it seems to
be improperly distinguished, exceeds in magnitude the habitable
parts of the continent of Europe; extending from 10 degrees
to 44 degrees south, between 110 degrees and 154 degrees east.
It received the name of Holland from its having been chiefly
explored by Dutch navigators. The land first discovered in those
parts was called Eeendraght, or Concord Land, from the name
of the ship which made the discovery in 1616. Two years
after,

after, another part of this coast was discovered by Zeachen, who gave it the name of Arnheim and Diemen, though a different part from what received the name of Diemen's Land from Tasman ; the latter being the southern extremity of the island, whereas the former lies in 15 degrees south. Van Meitz, Carpenter, and Dampier discovered different parts of the coast ; but our information derived from all these adventurers was nothing in comparison of what we have received from Captain Cook.

The whole eastern coast of New Holland is well watered by brooks and springs, but there are no great rivers. The face of the country, every where bleak and barren, is considerably less so towards the south, where the trees are taller and the herbage richer ; but no underwood is any where to be seen. There are but two sorts of timber trees, the gum tree and the pine ; the esculent plants are few, but there are a variety of such as gratify the curiosity of the botanist. The species of birds are numerous, and many of exquisite beauty. Venomous serpents abound, and great variety of reptiles, most of which are harmless. The greatest natural curiosity in this country is the ant, of which there are several sorts. One is green, and builds its nest upon trees, by bending down the leaves, and gluing the points of them together, so as to form a purse. The viscus used for this purpose is an animal juice, which nature has enabled them to elaborate. Thousands of these busy insects were seen using all their strength to hold the leaves in a proper position, while other industrious multitudes were employed within, in applying the gluten. " To satisfy ourselves," says Captain Cook, " that the
" leaves were bent and held down by these diminutive artificers,
" we disturbed them in their work, and as soon as they were
" driven from their station, the leaves in which they were em-
" ployed sprung up with a force much greater than we could
" have thought them able to conquer by any combination of
" their strength. But though we gratified our curiosity at their
" expence, the injury did not pass unrevenged, for thousands
" immediately threw themselves upon as, and gave us intolera-
" ble pain with their stings, especially those which took posses-
" sion of our necks and our hair, from which they were not
" easily driven." There is another species, possessing no power

of

of tormenting, and refembling the white ants of the Eaft Indies. Thefe conftruct nefts upon the branches of trees three or four times as big as a man's head; the materials of which are formed of fmall parts of vegetables kneaded together, with a glutinous matter, with which nature has furnifhed them. Upon breaking the outfide cruft of this dwelling, innumerable cells, furnifhed with inhabitants, appear in a great variety of winding directions, all communicating with each other, and with feveral apertures which lead to other nefts upon the fame tree. They have alfo another houfe built upon the ground, generally at the root of a tree; and formed like an irregularly fided cone, fometimes more than fix feet high, and nearly as much in diameter. The outfide of thefe is compofed of well tempered clay, about two inches thick, and within are the cells, which have no opening outward. Between thefe two dwellings, one of which is their fummer, and the other their winter refidence, there is a communication by a large avenue, or covered way, leading to the ground by a fubterraneous paffage. The fifh here are of kinds unknown to Europe, except the fhell-fifh and the mullet. Upon the fhoals and reef are the fineft green turtle in the world, and oyfters of various kinds, particularly the rock oyfter, and the pearl oyfter. In the rivulets and falt creeks are alligators.

This extenfive country is very thinly inhabited, and that by men in the loweft ftage of favage life. On the coaft the natives never appeared in larger companies than thirty together, and the ground being entirely uncultivated, they drew their principal fubfiftence from the fea. It is probable that the inland parts of the country are totally deftitute of inhabitants. The only tribe with which any intercourfe was eftablifhed, confifted of 21 perfons, 12 men, 7 women, a boy and a girl. The men are middle fized, clean limbed, and remarkably vigorous and nimble. Their countenances are expreffive; their voice foft and effeminate; their bodies encrufted with dirt, which makes them appear almoft as black as negroes. They crop their black hair, and keep their beards fhort by finging them. The women were never feen but at a diftance, for when the men croffed the river to the fhip they left them behind. Neither fex have any confcious fenfe of indecency in difcovering the whole body. They recei-

ved

ved the things that were given them, but were infenfible to all A. I
the figns that were made that fomething was expected in return. 177
Many of the trinkets that had been given them were afterwards
found thrown negligently away in the woods, like the play-
things of children, which pleafe only when they are new. The
bodies of many were marked with large fcars, inflicted with
fome blunt inftrument, and which they fignified by figns to have
been memorials of grief for the dead. There was no appearance of a town or village in the whole ifland; their houfes
were framed without art or induftry; fome of them only fufficient for a man to ftand upright in, but not large enough for
him to extend his length in any direction. They are built with
pliable rods, about the thicknefs of a man's finger, in the form
of an oven, and covered with palm leaves and bark. The door is
a large hole. Under thefe houfes or fheds they fleep, coiled up
with their heels to their head, in which pofition one of the
houfes will hold three or four perfons. Towards the north of
the ifland thefe houfes were made ftill flighter; one fide being
entirely open, and none of them above four feet deep. Thefe
hovels were fet up occafionally by a wandering hord, in any
place that would furnifh them for a time with fubfiftence, and
left behind them when they removed to another fpot. When
they mean to continue only a night or two at a place, they fleep
without any fhelter except the bufhes and grafs, the latter of
which is here near two feet high. They have a fmall bag, about
the fize of a moderate cabbage net, which the men carry upon
their back by a ftring that paffes over their heads. It generally
contains a lump of paint and rofin, fome fifh-hooks and lines,
fhells of which their hooks are made, a few points of darts,
and ornaments of fhells and bones, with which they adorn their
wrifts and nofes. This is the whole inventory of the richeft
man among them. They are unacquainted with the ufe of nets
in fifhing. Their fifh-hooks are neatly made, and fome of them
extremely fmall. For ftriking turtle they have a peg of wood,
about a foot long, and well bearded; this fits into a focket at
the end of a ftaff of light wood, as thick as a man's wrift, and
eight feet long. To the ftaff is tied one end of a loofe line,
about four fathoms long, the other end of which is faftened to

the peg. To strike the turtle the peg is fixed into the socket; and when it has entered his body, and is retained there by the barb, the staff flies off, and serves for a float to chase their victim in the water. It assists also to tire him, till they can overtake him with their canoes, and haul him ashore. Their lines are made of the fibres of a vegetable, and are from the thickness of half an inch to the fineness of an hair. They bake their provisions by the help of hot stones, like the inhabitants of the South-sea islands. They produce fire with great facility, and spread it in a wonderful manner. For this purpose they take two pieces of dry soft wood. The one is flat, the other a stick with an obtuse point at one end. This they press upon the other, and turn it nimbly by holding it between both hands as we do a chocolate mill. By this method they get fire in less than two minutes, and from the smallest spark increase it with great speed and dexterity. " We have often seen," says Captain Cook, " one of them run along the shore, to all appearance with no- " thing in his hand, who stooping down for a moment, at the " distance of every fifty or an hundred yards, left fire behind " him, as we could see, first by the smoke, and then by the " flame among the drift wood, and other litter that was scat- " tered along the place. We had the curiosity to examine one " of the planters of fire when he set off, and we saw him " wrap up a small spark in dry grass, which, when he had run " a little way, having been fanned by the air which his motion " produced, began to blaze. He then laid it down in a place " convenient for his purpose, inclosing a spark of it in another " quantity of grass, and so continued his course." Their weapons are spears or lances; some have four prongs pointed with bone and barbed. To the northward the lance has but one point; the shaft is made of cane, straight and light, from eight to fourteen feet long, consisting of several joints, where the pieces are let into each other and bound together. The points of these darts are either of hard heavy wood, or bones of fish: those of wood are sometimes armed with sharp pieces of broken shells stuck in, and at the junctures covered with rosin. The canoes to the northward are not made of bark, but of the trunk of a tree hollowed by fire; and none of them carry more than

four

four people. The only tools feen among them are the adze, A. I wretchedly made of ſtone; ſome ſmall pieces of ſtone in the 177 ſhape of a wedge; a wooden mallet, and ſome awkward inſtruments, or rather fragments of ſhells and coral. The uncultivated ſtate of the inhabitants of New Holland; their total ignorance of agriculture, and the arts moſt neceſſary to human life, accounts for their being found in very ſmall numbers together. They could not live in large ſocieties without being expoſed to periſh for want of the neceſſaries of life. But it is hard to ſay how there comes to be ſo very few of theſe little wandering communities in a country of ſuch amazing extent; and whether they are thinned by civil broils, excited by the horrid appetite of devouring each other, that prevails in New Zealand, or that their population is prevented by any other cauſes, cannot be aſcertained. Though their country is at ſo little diſtance from New Guinea, they have never in all probability viſited that iſland. If they had, the cocoa nuts, bread fruits, plantains, and other vegetables, which abound there, would naturally have been tranſplanted to New Holland. But no traces of them are to be found; and the miſerable inhabitants, deſtitute of all neceſſaries but what they procure by fiſhing, unacquainted with the uſe of clothes to defend them againſt the rigour of the elements, and unprepared to live in ſuch numbers together, as might enable them to obtain the ſmalleſt degree of knowledge even in the rude arts of uncultivated life, are reduced to the loweſt condition in which the human ſpecies have ever been diſcovered in any part of the globe. Yet men ſunk in this humiliating ſtate preſent us with the rudiments of all the arts and paſſions which diſtinguiſh the greateſt and moſt poliſhed nations. Their contrivances for fiſhing prove them capable to attain the higheſt pitch of mechanical ingenuity. Their regard to ſeparate property ſhows them as fuſceptible of avarice as they are ſenſible to the dictates of juſtice; and their attempts, however awkward, to adorn their perſons, indicate a deſire to pleaſe, and to render themſelves mutually agreeable. One advantage of theſe voyages into diſtant lands is to furniſh materials for the hiſtory of man. They prove, beyond the poſſibility of diſpute, the elevation and dig-

nity

nity of his nature; for, how unfortunate foever his external circumftances, he difcovers himfelf, by the plaineft marks, to poffefs the feeds of all thofe various attainments which diftinguifh the heroes and fages of the moft enlightened periods.

It is equally agreeable to the writer and reader to dwell on the brilliant and ufeful difcoveries of Britifh navigators in diftant parts; and it is extremely mortifying to be obliged to return from this pleafing theme, to record the unhappy meafures of the Britifh adminiftratiou, which have involved the navy, the army, and the whole empire in circumftances not lefs difgraceful than calamitous and afflicting. It would not, however, be agreeable to the truth of hiftory entirely to afcribe the diftreffing fcenes which followed, to the negligence and incapacity of minifters. Notorious as thefe have appeared, the fituation and behaviour of the nation at large feemed to forebode fome fatal calamity. Intoxicated with more than expected profperity, the people, at the clofe of the late war, were feized with an extravagant degree of giddy infolence, which made them defpife the reft of mankind. In an overgrown and wealthy capital, where every capricious abfurdity is apt to be carried to the moft vicious excefs, the vulgar were taught to fpurn at regularity, fubordination, and law. From refentment, envy, and the worft paffions incident to the human frame, the meaneft of mankind were capable of throwing the nation into confufion; of heaping an oppreffive weight of popular odium on the fervants of the crown; and, however defective their dexterity, yet working with fuch fturdy engines as the ignorant prejudices of a licentious rabble, they were able to divide the one half of the ifland againft the other. Our enemies faw with pleafure the effect of their wretched cabals, which were not more defpicable in themfelves than deftructive in their confequences: France and Spain learned with inexpreffible joy the refpectable employment of the Britifh parliament in the never-ending debates concerning the expulfion of Mr Wilkes; in which, in their opinion, the queftion was, to decide whether an out-law, a bankrupt, and an impious blafphemer, fhould be appointed to defend the laws, the property and religion of England. They were charmed with the petitions and remonftrances of the city of London, and were glad to find

find the English ministers too much employed in an altercation A. D. with the magistrates of the metropolis, and in quieting the un- 1770. happy riots which clamorous incendiaries had excited among the people at home, to engage in vigorous measures for re-establishing their authority in America.

The conduct of administration, with regard to this country, was beyond any thing that their most sanguine wishes could have hoped. Contradictory instructions given to the governors; taxes imposed and repealed again and again; assemblies called and dissolved, and allowed to sit again without disavowing the measures which had occasioned their former dissolution; troops sent, driven out, with many alternate proposals of violence and submission; treasons charged, adopted by parliament, not proved, nor attempted to be proved, neither detected nor punished.— The administration of Lord North, who, already chancellor of the exchequer, was in the beginning of 1770 appointed first lord of the treasury, did not announce any alteration in the hesitating, ambiguous conduct which had been hitherto maintained. The first measure which he adopted relative to America was to bring in a bill for a repeal of part of an act passed in the seventh of his present majesty, establishing duties on paper, painters colours, glass, and tea. The duties on the other articles were abolished; that on tea only was continued. The motives assigned for the bringing in this bill, were the dangerous combinations which these duties had given birth to beyond the Atlantic, and the dissatisfaction which they had created at home, among the merchants trading to the colonies. It did not fail to be remarked on this occasion, that while the minister condemned these duties in the gross, and the law upon which they were founded as so absurd and preposterous that it was astonishing how it could originate in a British house of commons, he yet, notwithstanding this decisive declaration, proposed a repeal of but part of the law, and still continued the duty on tea, lest he should be thought to give way to American ideas, and to take away the impositions, as having been contrary to the rights of the colonies. Another inconsistence, not less glaring, and of still more importance, was the declaring the law of taxation, while no vigorous step was taken to enforce it.

Great

Great Britain, difturbed by factious riots at home, and threatened with a rebellion in America, was to be infulted by the unprovoked hoftility of foreign powers. Our unhappy inteftine divifions, which had gradually fpread from the convulfions in the capital to the remoteft parts of the empire, had fo filled the hands and engaged the thoughts of government, that little attention either had or could for fome time paft have been given to our foreign interefts. Thus convulfed at home, and in a ftate of contention with our colonies, already productive of the moft alarming appearances, it was not to be fuppofed, from the known fyftems of policy eftablifhed and practifed among rival ftates, that fuch evident opportunities of advantage would be overlooked by the natural and ever-watchful enemies of Great Britain. The ftate of France, indeed, being nearly as unfortunate as our own, prevented that kingdom from exprefling her fecret animofity. But the principles of the family compact actuated every member of the houfe of Bourbon; and a ftroke was at this time aimed by Spain which affected the honour of the Britifh flag, and tarnifhed the recent glory of the nation.

The firft difcovery, the fituation and the importance of Falkland iflands, have already been defcribed. Gold and filver being almoft the only objects which excited the attention of the firft difcoverers and conquerors of the new world, thefe iflands producing nothing of this kind were neglected for almoft two centuries. Experience, and the extenfion of commerce, have at length fhewn the probability that the fouthern parts of the new world afford other commodities, which may be turned to as great advantage by induftrious nations as mines of gold and filver. In particular it is thought, that the greateft and moft advantageous fifhery in the world might be eftablifhed there; and navigators fay, that an hundred whales are to be met with in the high fouthern latitudes, for one that is to be found on the coaft of Greenland. Befides this motive, which was alone fufficient to excite the enterprize of a commercial nation, Lord Anfon's voyage fully explained the advantages that would refult to England, in time of war, from having a friendly port and place of refrefhment confiderably more to the fouth, and much nearer Cape Horn than the Brazils. The jealous and difagreeable

able character of the American Portuguese; which rendered it A. D desireable to avoid all dependence on such insidious and contemp- 1770 tible allies; the great length of the voyage, by which the vigour and health of the men, as well as water and other provisions, were exhausted before they arrived at the place of action; were the principal inducements mentioned by Lord Anson for carrying this measure into execution. He pointed out the place most proper for forming the establishment, and, when at the head of the admiralty, made preparations for sending frigates to make discoveries in those seas, and particularly to examine the condition and circumstances of the above-mentioned islands. But this project was not so cautiously conducted as to escape the vigilance of the court of Spain, who made such representations on this subject to the British ministry that the scheme was for the present laid aside, and continued dormant till the conclusion of the last war, when it was again revived by the earl of Egmont, who then presided in the admiralty. Accordingly Commodore Byron was sent out in the year 1764, the success of whose expedition we have already related. About the same time Mr. Bougainville sailed into those seas to make discoveries for the crown of France, and touched at Falkland's Islands. But, in a requisition of the court of Spain, the French easily sold or ceded all right to any property in what is called the Magellanica regions; with which sale or disposition it appears that Great Britain was not acquainted, nor even with any settlements ever formed there by the French.

In the year 1769 there was an English frigate and a sloop upon that station; and Captain Hunt of the Tamer frigate, cruising off Falkland's Islands, fell in with a Spanish schooner belonging to Port Solidad taking a survey of them. The English captain, according to the orders which he had received, desired the Spaniard to depart from that coast, as belonging to his Britannic majesty. The schooner departed, but returned in two days after, and brought on board an officer with letters and a present from Don Philip Ruez Puenta, the Spanish governor of Port Solidad. These letters were couched in terms of apparent civility. Don Ruez affected to disbelieve the report of the captain of the schooner, and attributed Captain Hunt's being in those feas to chance or ftrefs of weather. He offered him upon that prefumption every refrefhment, and all acts of kindnefs in his power; but if the improbable account which he had received fhould happen to be true, he warned the Englifh captain of his danger, reminded him of the violation of treaties, and the fole dominion of the king of Spain in thofe feas, and at the fame time authorized the Spanifh officer to order the Englifh fubjects immediately to depart.

Captain Hunt, in anfwer to the Spanifh officer with whom the governor had defired him to correfpond, afferted the fole dominion of his Britannic majefty, as well by right of difcovery as fettlement, and warned the Spaniards in his name, and by his orders, to depart the iflands, and allowed them fix months from the date of the letter to prepare for their departure. The Spanifh officer made a formal proteft, as well upon the grounds already mentioned as upon Captain Hunt's refufing to allow him to vifit the fettlement, and his threatening to fire into the Spanifh fchooner upon her attempting to enter the harbour; he alfo protefted againft the captain's going to Solidad which he had propofed in an amicable manner, and declared that it fhould be confidered as an infult.

About two months after this tranfaction, two Spanifh frigates of confiderable force, with troops on board for the new fettlement, arrived at Port Egmont, the principal place in Falkland's Iflands, under pretence of wanting water. The commander in chief wrote a letter to Captain Hunt, in which he expreffed great aftonifhment at feeing an Englifh flag flying, and a kind of fettlement formed; charged him with a violation of the laft peace, and protefted againft the meafure in all its parts, at the fame time declaring he would abftain from any other manner of proceeding until he had acquainted his Catholic majefty with this difagreeable tranfaction. Captain Hunt, as before, founded his poffeffion on the claim of right, juftified his conduct by the orders of his fovereign, and again warned the Spaniards to depart totally from thofe iflands.

The Spanifh frigates having continued eight days at Port Egmont, during which time they were fupplied with water, and treated with great civility by our people, departed feemingly

z

without any hostile intention. But Captain Hunt, dreading the consequences which soon followed, thought proper to return as soon as possible to England, to give an account of what had passed to the admiralty. He was succeeded at Port Egmont by the Favourite sloop, Captain Maltby, which, with the Swift, Captain Farmer, each of 16 guns, formed the whole force upon that station. Even this was unfortunately lessened, the Swift being overset in the Streights of Magellan where she had gone to make discoveries. The people, except three, were happily saved, by the fortitude and constancy of a few of their number, who, in an open cutter, undertook a voyage of three weeks in the most boisterous seas in the world. They arrived at Port Egmont, and brought the Favourite to the relief of their distressed companions.

It was not long after this dreadful danger and unexpected deliverance, when a Spanish frigate came into the same port, under pretence that she had been fifty-three days from Buenos Ayres, and was distressed for water: but three days after, her consorts, consisting of four other frigates, also arrived, and it soon appeared that they had been only 26 days at sea, had parted from the first in a gale of wind, and, instead of being in their way to Port Solidad, were now arrived at their place of destination. These five frigates carried 134 pieces of cannon, and had on board between 16 and 1700 men, including soldiers and marines; besides which, they had brought with them a train of artillery, and other materials sufficient to have invested a regular fortification.

A Spanish broad pendant was immediately hoisted on the arrival of the four last frigates, and as no doubt of their intentions now remained, Captain Farmer ordered most of the officers and men who had belonged to the Swift to come on shore to the defence of the settlement, while Captain Maltby began to bring the Favourite near to the Cove. Upon the first motion of the Favourite one of the Spanish frigates sent an officer on board to acquaint the captain, that if he weighed they would fire into his vessel. He, however, got under sail, regardless of this menace: the frigate fired two shot, which fell to leeward of him; and three of the Spanish vessels got under way, and worked to windward as he did.

The whole strength of the English in the island consisted in a wooden block-house, which had not even a port-hole in it, and only four pieces of cannon, which were sunk in the mud, to defend it. From the first appearance of the Spanish force, Captain Farmer had been active in clearing the stores out of the block-house, and in endeavouring to make it as defensible as its nature would permit. He raised the cannon, cleared the platform, and cut out port-holes. In the mean time letters were sent from the Spanish commodore to both the captains separately, requesting them in the politest terms to consider his great power, and their own defenceless situation; and that they would, by quitting the place, prevent his being under the disagreeable necessity to proceed to hostilities. These were followed by another the next day in which he offered, if they would quietly, and with good-will, abandon Port Egmont, he would peaceably put his troops on shore, and treat them with all the consideration which the harmony subsisting between the two powers required; that he would allow them to carry away all their property, and give them a receipt for any part of it they might chuse to leave behind, in order that the matter might be amicably adjusted between their respective courts. If contrary to expectation, they should endeavour to maintain the settlement, he would then proceed to the accomplishment of his orders; and in that case threatened them with an attack by sea and land, expatiating in a pompous style on the spirit and brilliancy which they would experience in his military and naval forces. He concluded by requiring a categorical answer in fifteen minutes after the receipt of his letter.

To this arbitrary summons the British officers replied, that words are not always deemed hostilities, and that it was impossible for them to believe he should venture in a time of profound peace, and when by his own acknowledgment the most perfect harmony subsisted between the two courts, to commit an act of the most fatal tendency. That the king of Great Britain was able to defend the honour of his flag, and to protect the security of his dominions in all parts of the world: and, had even

a

a shorter time than fifteen minutes been allowed them to deli- A. D
berate, it could not alter their determined resolution to defend 1770
the charge entrusted to them to the utmost of their abilities.

Previous to the designed attack the Spanish commodore desired that some of our officers might be sent to view the number
and condition of the troops and artillery which he intended to
land in order to persuade the English captains of the inefficacy
of their obstinate resistance to his commands. This was complied with; but without shaking the British resolution. The
Spanish frigates then warped in close to the shore, and moored
head and stern opposite to the block-house and battery. The
same evening, the 9th of June, Captain Maltby came on shore
with fifty of the Favourite's men, who brought with them two
six-pounders, ten swivels, and a quantity of small arms and
ammunition, The next morning a part of the Spanish troops
and artillery landed, about half a mile to the northward of our
people; and when they had advanced half way from the place
of their landing, the rest of the boats, with the remainder of
the troops and artillery, put off from one of the Spanish frigates, and rowed right in for the Cove, being covered by the
fire of the frigates, whose shot went over the block-house,

The English fired some shot; but seeing the impossibility of
defending the settlement, and the Spaniards having now broke
through all the limits of peace and amity, so that their hostility
could neither be denied nor explained away, our officers with
great address having brought the affair to that point which they
desired, determined with equal propriety to save the valuable
lives of their people who must have been unavoidably cut off
in this unequal contest. Accordingly they hung out a flag of
truce, and demanded articles of capitulation.

The substance of these articles, concluded between the English captains on one hand, and Don John Ignatio Madariaga,
major-general of the royal navy of Spain, on the other, was,
that the British subjects should be allowed to depart in the Favourite, and to take with them such of their stores as they
thought proper; that an inventory should be made of the remainder, which were to be deposited in the hands of the governor of Solidad, who became answerable for them; that the

A D. Englifh flag fhould continue flying on fhore and on board the
1770. floop; but that they were to exercife no jurifdiction except over
their own people; nor to appear under arms until the time of embarkation, to which they were to march out with drums beating
and colours flying. There was a reftriction with regard to the
time of their departure, until the governor of Solidad or his
deputy, fhould arrive to make the inventories, and to take charge
of the ftores. For the better fecurity of this limitation a new
and wanton infult was offered to the Britifh flag, the Favourite's
rudder being forcibly taken away, and kept on fhore during the
time of their detention. The account of the violent tranfactions of the Spaniards at Falkland's Iflands, previous to this
open and unprovoked hoftility, was brought to England by Captain Hunt early in the month of June. The nation heard the
news with indignation and refentment; efpecially as they had
already much reafon to complain of the ungenerous conduct of
the Spaniards in detaining fome thoufands of Englifh prifoners,
feized under pretence of carrying on an illicit trade by the Spanifh guarda coftas. The neceffity of putting ourfelves in a
refpectable condition of defence was infifted on by the moft popular members in both houfes. Their partizans clamoured a-
gainft the tamenefs of adminiftration, and maintained the neceffi-
fity of an immediate declaration of war, in order to difappoint
the perfidious defigns of our ancient and inveterate enemies.

The malignant nature of thefe defigns, it was faid, appeared
too evidently in a dreadful national calamity, which happened
about this time, in the conflagration at Portfmouth. An event
fo prejudicial to our maritime ftrength, attended with fuch critical circumftances, was confidered as a part of a great and fettled plan for the reduction of our power and opulence. The
fire which happened about the fame time in Peterfburgh, and
which was alfo accompanied by fome alarming particulars, did
not leffen the fufpicion on this occafion; and the reward of a
thoufand pounds offered by government, in the Gazette, for
the difcovery of thofe who had occafioned the fire in the dock-
yard at Portfmouth, added a new caufe of jealoufy and diftruft.

The

The lofs fuftained by the fire was fuppofed, according to the A. D. firft loofe calculations, to amount to half a million, but by later 1770. and more accurate eftimates, is made to be only 150,000 l. which is comparatively nothing to the dreadful confequences that muft have enfued, without a fpeedy and effectual affiftance, The quantity of ftores confumed was fupplied with great expedition from the other docks; the public buildings and workhoufes were foon reftored; and the lofs thus rendered of very little confequence to our marine in general.

Notwithftanding the alarm occafioned by thefe tranfactions in the nation, the miniftry made little preparation for war. Some fhips indeed were put into commiffion, and there was greater buftle in the dock-yards than in the time of profound tranquillity. It was not, however, till the latter part of Auguft, that houfes were opened at the ports for manning fixteen fail of the line, and prefs-warrants were not iffued till near a month after. Much about this time the Favourite returned with our people from Falkland's Iflands; but notwithftanding the melancholy ftory which they told, to the difgrace of the Englifh name, fuch was the licentioufnefs and depravity of the times, that even the manning of the navy met with great difficulties. The legality of prefs-warrants was publicly called in queftion, and the opinions of counfel applied to on the fubject. In the city of London, upon the election of Alderman Crofby to the mayoralty, that magiftrate totally refufed to back the prefs-warrants, and afferted, that the confiderable bounty granted by the city was intended to prevent fuch violences. Alderman Wilkes had before difcharged an impreffed man. Such tranfactions will tranfmit in proper colours to pofterity the names of thofe patriotic magiftrates, who did their utmoft to impede the public fervice, when the fecurity of the Britifh dominions and the dignity of the crown were at ftake.

When the parliament was affembled the 13th of November, 1770, the fpeech from the throne took notice that an immediate demand had been made from the court of Spain of fuch fatisfaction as there was a right to expect for the injury received; and at the fame time declared, that the preparations for war fhould not be difcontinued, until full reparation fhould be obtained.

A. D.
1770.
obtained.  The addreffes of both houfes of parliament were
fpirited, and the ftrongeft and moft unreferved affurances were
given, that every degree of requifite fupport fhould be cheerfully
granted.  At the fame time that the bleffings of peace were acknowledged, the fulleft confidence was placed in his majefty,
that he would never be induced, by a miftaken tendernefs for
the prefent eafe of the people, to facrifice their more effential and
more lafting interefts.  So early as the 29th of November 40,000
men were voted for the fea fervice; extenfive grants were afterwards paffed for the ordinary and fupport of the navy; the
land forces for home fervice were augmented from about 17,000
to above 23,000 effective men; a new battalion was added to
the ordnance, and a fmall addition made to the pay of the fub-
altern officers belonging to that corps.

As the feffion advanced, the profpect of peace feemed gradually to diminifh.  The negotiation and the tranquil intentions
of Spain, which had been alledged by the miniftry in anfwer to
the clamours for immediate war, were no longer heard of, and
a ftate of hoftility with that country feemed to be confidered as
the probable iffue of this affair.  In fact, the negotiation was
for a confiderable time interrupted, and only renewed through
the mediation of France, and finally concluded at the earneft
defire of that court, and the terror infpired into the Spaniards
by the vigour of the Britifh preparations.

About a fortnight before the arrival of our people from
Falkland's Iflands, a letter was received at the office of Lord
Weymouth, fecretary of ftate for the fouthern department,
from Mr. Harris our minifter at Madrid, acquainting government, that a fhip had arrived from Buenos Ayres, with an account of the intended expedition, its force, and the time fixed
for its failing.  At the fame time Prince Mafferano, the Spanifh
ambaffador, acquainted his lordfhip, that he had good reafon to
believe the governor of Buenos Ayres had taken it upon him to
make ufe of force, in difpoffeffing our people of Port Egmont;
and that he was directed to make this communication to prevent the bad confequences of its coming through other hands;
at the fame time expreffing his wifhes, that whatever the tranfactions at Port Egmont may have been, in confequence of a

ftep

step taken by the governor, without any particular instruction from his Catholic majesty, they might not be productive of measures dangerous to the good understanding between the two crowns.

Lord Weymouth replied, that if force had been used it was difficult to see how the fatal consequences could be avoided; that the instructions given to the British officers at Falkland's Islands were of the most pacific nature; but that still the circumstance of Mr. Buccarelli, the governor of Buenos Ayres, having acted without orders, left an opening for conciliation, provided the ambassador would disavow the conduct of that gentleman. Prince Masserano, however, declared, that he had no instructions to that purpose, but deprecated all resolutions and measures that might involve the two crowns in a war.

Upon a second conference with the ambassador, Lord Weymouth demanded, in his majesty's name, as a specific condition of preserving the harmony between the courts, a disavowal of the proceedings at Port Egmont, and that the affairs of that settlement should be restored to the precise state in which they were previous to these proceedings. He at the same time sent instructions to Mr. Harris, to inform Mr. Grimaldi the Spanish minister of state of what had passed here, and of the proposed satisfaction, which alone could put it in his majesty's power to suspend his preparations for hostility. Mr. Grimaldi at first expressed himself in very vague terms. He had reason to foresee that some disagreeable event would happen in the South seas, from the notorious disapprobation of the court of Spain to any British establishments in those parts. He could not blame the conduct of Mr. Buccarelli, as it was founded upon the laws of America. At the same time he wished to have prevented this conduct, and had actually, upon the first surmise of the design, despatched a vessel from the Groyne, to hinder it from being put in execution; that the Spanish nation had so little to get and so much to lose by a war, that nothing but the last extremity could reduce them to so violent a measure; and that the king his master wished only to act consistently with his own honour and the welfare of his people, and that so far as our demand was compatible with those two points, there was no doubt of

its

its being agreed to. In a subsequent meeting he assured the British envoy, that his Catholic majesty was determined to do every thing in his power to terminate this affair in an amicable manner : that instructions for this purpose had been transmitted to Prince Masserano at the court of London, differing from the requisition of that court in terms only, and not essentially, so that he had no doubt the proposals which they contained would readily be adopted.

Prince Masserano, accordingly, proposed a convention to Lord Weymouth, in which the king of Spain disavowed any particular orders given to Mr. Buccarelli, at the same time that his majesty allowed that governor had acted agreeably to his general instructions, and to the oath which his office obliged him to take. He further stipulated the restitution of Falkland's Islands without prejudice to his Catholic majesty's right; and he expected that the king of Great Britain would disavow Captain Hunt's menace, which, he said, gave immediate occasion to the steps taken by Mr. Buccarelli. To this it was answered, that when his Britannic majesty's moderation condescended to demand redress for the injury which his crown had received, he could not possibly accept as a convention that satisfaction to which he had so just a title without entering into any engagement in order to procure it. That the idea of his majesty's becoming a contracting party upon this occasion, is entirely foreign to the case; for having received an injury, and demanded the most moderate reparation of that injury his honour can permit him to accept, that reparation loses its value if it is to be conditional, and to be obtained by any stipulation whatsoever on the part of his majesty.

Upon this answer Prince Masserano told Lord Weymouth, that he had no power to proceed in this affair, except by convention, without farther instructions from Madrid. While the ambassador sent for these, Lord Weymouth despatched an express to Mr. Harris, to lay before the Spanish minister the unexpected obstacles that had arisen in this affair, and to demand a direct answer to the object of his first requisition. For several days, however, no answer was returned; but at length Mr. Grimaldi intimated, that the king his master had sent instructions to Prince

Masserano,

Maſſerano, by which he was empowered to treat again, and to A. D grant every reaſonable ſatisfaction for the ſuppoſed inſult; that 1770 his Catholic majeſty was willing to come into any method regarding the manner of giving the ſatisfaction that ſhould appear the moſt eligible to the king of Great Britain, expecting, however, that, as he went ſuch a length to ſave his honour, his own ſhould alſo be conſidered, ſo far as it did not interfere with the ſatisfaction that was to be offered.

Nothing could appear to be more ſatisfactory than theſe pretended inſtructions given to Prince Maſſerano. Mr. Grimaldi's anſwer was given the 7th November, and was received in London the 19th; but it ſoon appeared that the conduct of Prince Maſſerano did not at all accord with the pacific intentions and conciliatory ſentiments profeſſed at Madrid. The earl of Rochford, who ſucceeded Lord Weymouth in office, wrote a letter to Mr. Harris, dated the 21ſt December, in which he informed him, that all negotiations with the Spaniſh ambaſſador had for ſome time been at an end, the anſwer to the king's demand being totally inadmiſſible; and that, it being inconſiſtent with his majeſty's honour to make any farther propoſal to the court of Spain, he was deſired to withdraw from Madrid with all convenient ſpeed.

Thus was the negotiation entirely broken off. How it came again to be renewed ſeems to have been better known in all the coffeehouſes of Europe than to the Engliſh ſecretaries of ſtate. No document relative to its renewal has ever been laid before parliament or the public, but it is reaſonable, from the duplicity and deſign diſcovered by Spain in the whole tranſaction, to look for the motives of conciliation in every other quarter, rather than in the pacific or friendly diſpoſitions of the court of Madrid.

The family compact, by which the different branches of the houſe of Bourbon engaged to employ their whole force in the mutual ſupport and aſſiſtance of each other, was propoſed, and carried into execution by the wiſdom and addreſs of the duke of Choiſeul. That able miniſter little imagined a compliance with the terms of this formidable union might become extremely inconvenient to France, for the intereſt of which it had principally

A. D.
1770.

been formed. It did not occur to him, that the haughty spirit of Spain, exasperated by the disgraceful wounds received in the war with Great Britain, would prompt her to take the first opportunity of seeking revenge; while France, exhausted in her resources; without money or credit; convulsed by the most violent dissentions between the first orders of the state, while the people were ripe for sedition from the want of the first necessaries of life, might be in no condition to afford Spain that assistance which had been stipulated between them. The credit of the duke who had contrived the family compact, long considered as a masterpiece of policy, but now found to be attended with consequences in every view disgraceful to France, began to decline: he was soon after removed from his employment, and obliged to retire. Other councils prevailed, more agreeable to the pacific dispositions of an aged prince, who had nothing farther in view but to end his days in the bosom of ease and tranquillity.

The interval that passed between the breaking off of the negotiation between Great Britain and Spain, with the transactions of which the public has never been informed by authority, was probably filled up by listening to the mediation of France, which disarmed the ardent hostility of her southern ally, and persuaded her, much against her own inclination, to propose an accommodation, in form at least, less offensive to the dignity of Great Britain. It was not till the first day of the meeting of parliament, January 22d, 1771, after the Christmas recess, that, instead of a *convention*, a *declaration* was proposed and signed by Prince Masserano, and accepted by the earl of Rochford. By the former the ambassador, in name of his master, disavows the violence used at Port Egmont, and stipulates that every thing shall be restored there precisely to the same state in which it was before the reduction; but at the same time declares, that this restoration is not in any wise to affect the question of the prior right of sovereignty of those islands; and, by the acceptance, the performance of these stipulations is to be considered as a satisfaction for the injury done to the crown of Great Britain *. This transaction was immediately announced to both

1771.

* Appendix, N° XIV.

houses.

houfes. While the friends of adminiftration propofed an addrefs A. D
of thanks to his majefty for having fupported the honour of the 1771
crown of Great Britain by a firm and unvaried adherence to his
juft demand of fatisfaction, and for not having too haftily engaged the nation in the hazards and burdens of war, the gentlemen in oppofition affirmed, that the whole tranfaction was
equally unfafe and difgraceful ; that inftead of having provided
a reparation for former hoftilities, or a fecurity againft future,
it contained in itfelf the genuine feeds of perpetual hoftility and
war : that it is as difhonourable to the crown itfelf as to the
nation, and admitting the fafhionable language, that the dignity
of the former, and the reparation to it, are the only objects of
confideration, it will be found as fhamefully deficient in this
refpect as in every other. Thus, by this infamous accommodation, the honour of the crown of England had not been put on
the fame footing with that of inferior kingdoms. The French
king, for a fmall violation of territorial right in the purfuit of
an outlawed fmuggler, had thought it neceffary to fend an ambaffador extraordinary to the king of Sardinia to apologize for
it in the moft folemn and public manner. When the Englifh
fleet under Admiral Bofcawen deftroyed fome French fhips on
the coaft of Portugal, Great Britain fent an ambaffador extraordinary to the court of Lifbon, to make reparation in honour;
but when the Spaniards infult the Britifh flag, and commit the
moft outrageous acts of hoftility on Britifh fubjects, they propofe a declaration, in which the right to employ the fame violence again is maintained and defended : for, though the court
of Spain had difavowed the act of hoftility as proceeding from
particular inftructions, fhe continued to juftify it under her general inftructions to her governors, under the oath by them taken, and under the eftablifhed laws of America; and that this
juftification of an act of violence under general orders, eftablifhed laws and oaths of office, is far more dangerous and injurious to this kingdom than the particular enterprize which has
been difavowed, as it moft evidently fuppofes, that the governors
of the Spanifh American provinces are not only authorized, but
required, to raife forces by fea and land, and to invade our
poffeffions in thofe parts, in the midft of profound peace. Ma-

A. D. ny other objections of equal weight were urged against the ac-
771. ceptance of the Spanish declaration, in a strong, animated, elo-
quent, and argumentative protest of the house of peers, which
will remain to all posterity to their immortal honour *.

The tame measures of government, however, were adopted
by a great majority. During the recess of parliament, September 16, 1771, Spain fulfilled her engagements contained in the
declaration, by the restoration of Port Egmont, which was delivered up to Captain Scott; who was sent thither with a small
squadron for that purpose. Ministry seemed to think all was
secured by an amicable termination of this dispute; and parliament was not called till after the Christmas holidays, 21st Ja-
772. nuary, 1772. The late meeting of this assembly, which indicated that no urgent business required an early attendance, and
the pacific declaration from the throne, were sufficient to lull
the nation into the most perfect security. What, therefore, must
have been their surprise and indignation, when a motion was
made so early as the 29th of January, that 25,000 seamen should
be voted for the service of the ensuing year. It was urged, in
support of this motion, that, the French having sent a considerable fleet to the East Indies, we were obliged upon that account
to augment our naval force there, as the propriety of our being
always superior to them in that part of the world was so evident
as not to admit of an argument: that a larger squadron was
now employed for the protection of Jamaica and our other West-
India islands, than in former years of peace; as the importance of our valuable possessions in that quarter, the probability
of the Spaniards making their first attempt upon them in case of
a war, and the considerable fleet which they kept in those seas,
rendered an augmentation of our maritime strength on that station a matter of the most evident necessity: that the war between the Turks and Russians made it also necessary to employ
a greater number of ships for the protection of our commerce
in the Mediterranean and Archipelago than had been customary
in times of general peace. Besides these general reasons for
augmentation, much stress was laid upon the great reform with
regard to the guard-ships, it being acknowledged, that for se-

* Appendix, Nº XV.

veral years paſt theſe ſhips had been exceedingly neglected, and A. D confidered merely as jobs; ſo that at the time of the late ex-1772 pected war there were neither ſhips nor men fit for ſervice: but that now things were ſo much altered for the better, that twenty of the beſt ſhips in the navy were kept upon that duty, and were in ſuch complete condition, and ſo nearly manned, that a ſlight preſs would at any time enable them in a very few days to put to ſea: That the reſt of the fleet was alſo in good condition, and in about a year we ſhould have near eighty ſhips of the line at home fit for ſervice, beſides thoſe that were upon foreign duty. Many pointed and ſevere ſarcaſms were levelled at the miniſtry for accompanying a ſpeech, which breathed nothing but effuſions of peace, with all the actual preparations for war. Some gentlemen in oppoſition declared for the motion, upon the avowed principle that the ſupplies demanded were not in any degree to be confidered as a peace eſtabliſhment; while the greater part of theſe gentlemen arraigned the adding to the burdens of a nation already ſinking under the weight of an overgrown and monſtrous public debt. They obſerved that our peace eſtabliſhment was every year increaſing, and that arguments ſimilar to thoſe at preſent alledged could never be wanting to oppoſe any diminution of it: that already it was nearly double to what it had been at the acceſſion of George the Firſt; laſt year we had ſuſtained all the inconveniencies of a war without any of its advantages; and it ſeemed to be the intention of government to perſiſt for ever in the ſame ruinous meaſures. Theſe obſervations were at preſent regarded as the clamours of party; and the events which followed fully juſtified the neceſſity of keeping the navy on a reſpectable footing.

The progreſs of the Ruſſians in the Mediterranean rendered it neceſſary for both France and Spain to ſtand on their guard, and to watch the growing greatneſs of theſe new and formidable allies of Great Britain. But, in the beginning of the year 1773, there were more extraordinary preparations in the French 177; and Spaniſh ports than any apprehenſion of this kind could account for. Thoſe preparations were carried on with the utmoſt vigour and induſtry, not only in the ports of the Mediterranean, but in thoſe of the ocean, and afforded room for ſuſpecting

the

A. D. the moft hoftile intentions. Strong remonftrances on this fub-
1773. ject were made on the part of Great Britain at the courts of
Paris and Madrid, accompanied with a declaration, that, if fuch
meafures were continued, his Britannic majefty would be under
a neceffity of fending fuch a fleet of obfervation into the Mediterranean, as fhould effectually fruftrate any attempts that
might be made againft the Ruffians. In the mean time a powerful fleet was equipped, and ordered to rendezvous at Spithead,
and thofe warlike preparations were for fome time continued on
all fides. The rapidity with which Great Britain affembled fuch
a naval force as was fufficient to contend with that of all her
enemies united, and the magnificence and military pomp with
which her mighty preparations were difplayed *, reftrained the
hoftile difpofitions which had begun to prevail at Paris and Madrid, and prevented the profecution of meafures which muft
have involved all Europe in their confequences. The vigorous
exertions on this occafion were like a flafh of lightning, which
for a moment brightened the gloom of night that fat fo thick
and heavy on the Britifh councils. But after this tranfient flafh
the darknefs returned more intenfe and horrible than before.

The conduct of adminiftration will be an enigma to pofterity. Poffeffed of a naval force that made the greateft princes of
Europe tremble, they have been fo far from quieting the diffen-
fions which prevailed in America, that they have totally aliena-
ted from Great Britain thofe flourifhing and wealthy provinces,
and reduced their country to that ftate of defpair in which we
now live. Two roads were open before them, either of which
might have been followed, if not with equal glory, yet with an
equally affured profpect of fuccefs. By difregarding the clamours of an interefted oppofition, and making ufe of the power
in their hands, they might, while all Europe were filent in our
prefence, have inflicted whatever punifhment became neceffary
to reduce the rebellious provinces to an humble fenfe of their
duty. But this method was fo far from being adopted, that a
firft lord of the treafury talked of compelling the Americans to

* See Appendix, No XVI.

submit

submit to taxes without bloodshed; and a first lord of the admiralty, upon the appearance of measures which indicated vigour, voted a reduction of 4000 seamen; assuring the house, that the low establishment proposed would be fully sufficient for conquering the Americans; of whose power and courage he spoke with the utmost contempt, affirming that they were not disciplined nor capable of discipline, and that formed of such materials, and so indisposed to action, the numbers of which such boasts had been made, would only facilitate their defeat.

Another road, which might have been pursued with universal applause, would have been to abandon that odious measure of taxing a free people without their own consent. Had that been done, the weight of opposition would have been removed at once, and the Americans, if they still continued refractory, might have been compelled by force of arms to acknowledge the supremacy of the mother country without one sympathizing voice in Europe to condole with them for the rigours of a punishment which they had justly drawn on their own heads. But neither of these methods being adopted, the ministry hesitated between peace and war; and their tame, equivocal, temporising conduct brought the Americans to a maturity of resistance and rebellion, the effects of which we should now proceed to describe and deplore, if, in deducing a chronological account of the naval transactions of Great Britain, there were not some intervening events, which deserve to be particularly related.

These are the discoveries which continued to be made by our navigators in the years 1773, 1774, and 1775. They were not, as of late years, confined entirely to the southern ocean. While Captain Cook was employed in exploring this part of the globe, the honourable Constantine Phipps, now Lord Mulgrave, was sent to examine how far navigation was practicable towards the north pole. This was done in consequence of an application to Lord Sandwich, first lord of the admiralty, from the Royal Society. His lordship laid the request of the Society before the king, who ordered the Racehorse, and Carcass, bombs, to be fitted out for the expedition. The command of the former was given to Captain Phipps, and of the latter to Captain Lutwidge. The idea of a passage to the East Indies by the

A. D. the north pole, was fuggefted as early as the year 1527, by
1773. Robert Thorne, a merchant of Briftol, who addreffed a paper
to Henry the Eighth on that fubject; but Henry, as ufual, was
involved in a multiplicity of affairs, which prevented him from
giving any attention to this application. In the reign of Queen
Elifabeth Sir Hugh Willoughby made the attempt with three
fhips, *anno* 1553. He proceeded to the latitude of 75 degrees
north, but being obliged to winter in Lapland, he and all his
company perifhed miferably. Three years afterwards Captain
Burroughs failed on the fame defign, and advanced to 78 degrees north. To him fucceeded Captains Jackman and Pell
in 1580, in two fhips; the latter of whom, with his fhip, was
loft. The Dutch began to purfue the fame difcovery in 1595,
and fucceffive voyages were made, which tended rather to
prove the impracticability of failing to high northern latitudes,
than the probability of finding the paffage, which was the object of thefe daring enterprifes. In 1607 Henry Hudfon was
equipped by a company of London merchants, to difcover a
paffage by the north pole to Japan and China. He penetrated
to 80 degrees 23 minutes north, and was then ftopped by the
ice. Two years after another fhip was fent out by the Ruffia
Company of merchants in London; the fhip was commanded
by Jonas Poole, who could not with his utmoft endeavours advance farther than 79 degrees 5 minutes north. In the year
1614 another voyage was undertaken, in which Baffin and
Fotherby were employed, but without fuccefs; and next year
Fotherby, in a pinnace of 20 tons, with ten men, was equally
unfuccefsful. John Wood, with a frigate and a pink, failed
in 1676, but returned without effecting any thing. Moft
of thefe voyages having been fitted out by private adventurers, for the double purpofe of difcovery and prefent advantage,
it was natural to fuppofe, that the attention of the navigators had
been diverted from the more remote and lefs profitable object
of the two, and that they had not profecuted the chief purpofe
of difcovery with all the care that could have been wifhed.
"But," fays Captain Phipps, " I am happy in an opportunity
" of doing juftice to the memory of thefe men, which, with-
" out having traced their fteps, and experienced their difficul-
" ties, it would have been impoffible to have done. They ap-

" pear

" pear to have encountered dangers, which at that period muſt A. L

" have been particularly alarming from their novelty, with the 1773

" greateſt fortitude and perſeverance, as well as to have ſhewn

" a degree of diligence and ſkill, not only in the ordinary and

" practical, but in the more ſcientific parts of their profeſſion,

" which might have done honour to modern ſeamen, with all

" their advantages of later improvements. This, when com-

" pared with the ſtate of navigation, even within theſe forty

" years, by the moſt eminent foreign authors, affords the moſt

" flattering and ſatisfactory proof of the very early exiſtence

" of that decided ſuperiority in naval affairs, which has carried

" the power of this country to the height it has now attained."

The captain ſailed in February 1773, and after paſſing the iſlands of Shetland, the firſt land he made was Spitzbergen, in latitude 77 degrees, 59 minutes, 11 ſeconds north, and longitude 9 degrees, 13 minutes eaſt. The coaſt appeared to be neither habitable nor acceſſible, but formed of high black rocks, without the leaſt marks of vegetation, moſtly bare and pointed, in ſome places covered with ſnow, and toweiing above the clouds. The vallies between the high cliffs were filled with ſnow or ice. " This proſpect," ſays Captain Phipps, " would have

" ſuggeſted the idea of perpetual winter, had not the mildneſs

" of the weather, the ſmooth water, bright ſun-ſhine, and con-

" ſtant day-light, given a cheerfulneſs and a novelty to the

" whole of this ſtriking and romantic ſcene. The height of one

" mountain ſeen here was found to be 1503 yards. The har-

" bour of Smeerenberg, lying in latitude 79 degrees, 44 mi-

" nutes north, longitude 9 degrees, 50 minutes, 45 ſeconds eaſt,

" has good anchorage in fifteen fathoms. Cloſe to this harbour

" is an iſland, called Amſterdam Iſland, where the Dutch uſed

" formerly to boil their whale-blubber, and the remains of ſome

" conveniencies erected by them for that purpoſe are ſtill viſible.

" They attempted once to form an eſtabliſhment here, and left

" ſome people, who all periſhed in the winter. The Dutch

" ſhips ſtill reſort to this place for the latter ſeaſon of the whale-

" fiſhery. The moſt remarkable views which theſe dreary re-

" gions preſent, are what are called the ice-bergs. Theſe are

" large bodies of ice, filling the vallies between the high moun-

" tains. Their face towards the sea is nearly perpendicular, and
" of a very lively green colour.  One was about 300 feet high,
" with a cascade of water issuing out of it.  Large pieces fre-
" quently break off from the ice-bergs, and fall with great noise
" into the water."

Captain Phipps has been very accurate in describing the few
animals which these inhospitable regions produce, and was at
pains to examine the vegetable and mineral productions.  He
proceeded afterwards to Moffen Island in latitude 80 degrees
north, longitude 12 degrees, 20 minutes east, which is of a
round form, about two miles in diameter, with a lake in the
middle, frozen with eternal ice.  At the Seven Islands which lie
in latitude 81 degrees, 21 minutes north, the two ships became suddenly fast in the ice on the 31st of July.  These islands
and north-east land, with the frozen sea formed almost a bason,
having but about four points open for the ice to drift out in case
of a change of wind.  The passage by which the ships had come
in to the westward became close, and a strong current set in to
the east, by which they were carried still farther from their
course.  The labour of the whole ship's company to cut away
the ice proved ineffectual; their utmost efforts for a whole day
could not move the ships above 300 yards to the westward
through the ice, whilst the current had at the same time driven
them far to the north-east and eastward.  Appearances remained thus threatening for four or five days, the safety of the crew
seemed all that could possibly be effected.  As it had been foreseen that one or both of the ships might be sacrificed in the prosecution of the voyage, the boats for each ship were calculated,
in number and size, to be fit in any emergency to transport the
whole crew.  Driven to this state of danger and suspense, on the
6th of August the boats were hoisted out, and every possible
method taken to render them secure and comfortable; but the
next day the wind blew eastwardly, and the ships were moved
about a mile to the westward.  But still they run not so far
west by a great way as when they were first beset with the ice;
however, on the 9th of August, the current had visibly changed,
and run to the westward, by which both the ships had been
carried considerably in that direction.  On the 10th a brisk wind

at

at north-north-east accomplished their deliverance, and freed A. D them from the dreadful prospect of perishing, as many former 1773 adventurers had done in those polar regions. Having found it impracticable to penetrate any farther towards the north, they returned to the harbour of Smeerenberg; having, in the prosecution of this voyage, reached 81 degrees 36 minutes north latitude, and between the latitudes of 79 degrees 50 minutes, and 81 degrees, traversed 17 degrees and a half of longitude, that is from 2 degrees east to 19 degrees 30 minutes east."

While Lord Mulgrave was employed in ascertaining the limits of navigation towards the north, Captain Cook was indefatigable in examining the respective dominions of land and ocean in the southern hemisphere. Notwithstanding the various voyages, in which this part of the globe had been traversed in the many different directions, all tending to render the existence of a southern continent more improbable, the fact was not yet brought to a clear and demonstrative evidence. To determine this point was the main object of the present voyage, on which Captain Cook sailed in the Resolution, accompanied by Captain Fourneaux in the adventure, the 2d of April, 1772. The ships in which they embarked were the most proper that could be contrived for such a dangerous undertaking; Captain Cook in the clear, simple, and manly narrative which he has published of his proceedings, having proved beyond the possibility of doubt, that north-country vessels, or such as are built for the coal trade, are the fittest for pursuing with success the discovery of remote countries. To the nature of his ships, which were of this safe and commodious construction, rather than to his own nautical skill and abilities, he modestly ascribes the singular felicity of his voyage, which was far beyond the experience or hopes of former navigators.

Besides the advantages arising from the form of the vessels, and the skill of the commander, the provision of every sort exceeded all that had been known on any former occasion. Every circumstance and situation that could be foreseen or apprehended was provided for with unexampled liberality. A considerable sum of money was allotted by parliament to encourage

A. D.
773·

two gentlemen, eminent in natural hiftory, to facrifice their time, and encounter the toils and dangers of fuch a voyage. With the fame generous fpirit for the improvement of knowledge, a landfcape-painter of merit, and two able aftronomers, were alfo engaged. Nor was any attention omitted which could be deemed neceffary for the fubfiftence, fecurity, health, or comfort of all the voyagers.

Having failed with fo many circumftances in their favour, they reached the Cape of Good Hope without meeting with any remarkable occurrence, and departed from thence the 22d of November, 1772. They returned to the fame place the 22d of March, 1775, having failed no lefs than 20,000 leagues in two years and four months; an extent of voyage nearly equal to three times the equatorial circumference of the earth, and which it is highly probable, never was traverfed by any other fhip in an equal period of time. When we take into computation the voyage to and from the Cape to England, the whole time confumed is above three years, during which they experienced every variety of climate from 52 degrees north latitude to 71 degrees fouth, and were continually expofed to all the hardfhips and fatigue infeparable from a feafaring life; and yet what is moft extraordinary, the numerous fhip's company on board the Refolution, preferved a more uninterupted ftate of good health, than perhaps they could have enjoyed on fhore in the moft temperate climate of the earth. In that long and various courfe, of 118 perfons only four were loft; and of that four only one fell a victim to ficknefs: a fact unparalleled in the hiftory of navigation.

In the moft healthy climates no bills of mortality have produced fuch an inftance amongft an equal number of men during a like period. When, therefore, we confider the numbers of brave feamen who perifhed by marine difeafes under Anfon and other navigators, the greateft praife is due to Captain Cook for his judicious management in preferving the health of the men under his command. The chief prefervative againft the fcurvy, ufed by this judicious commander, was fweet wort, which was given not only to thofe who were afflicted with that diftemper, but likewife to thofe who were thought likely to take it. Portable

foup

foup and four krout were alfo ufed with fuccefs in preferving A. D
the health of the feamen. The fhip's company were kept in 1773.
conftant exercife, and their cleanlinefs contributed not a little
to their health. The fhip was frequently purified by fires, a
practice much recommended by Captain Cook. Frefh water
was alfo an object of particular attention. Not fatisfied with
having plenty of that neceffary article, he would always have
the pureft, and therefore, whenever an opportunity offered, he
emptied what he had taken in a few days before, and filled
his cafks anew. As a teftimony of regard for thefe important improvements for preferving the health of feamen, the
Royal Society was pleafed to beftow Sir Godfrey Copley's medal
upon Captain Cook.

The firft cruize from the Cape of Good Hope, November 22d,
1772, was employed in afcertaining the great queftion concerning the *Terra Auftralis incognita*. The two fhips failed in company, and the 10th of December following, being in latitude 50
degrees 40 minutes fouth, faw the firft ice. The mafs was
about 50 feet high, and half a mile in circuit, flat at top, and
its fides rofe in a perpendicular direction, againft which the fea
broke exceedingly high. From this time the icy mountains began to be very frequent, exhibiting a view as pleafing to the eye
as terrible to reflection; " for," fays the captain, " were a
" fhip to get againft the weather-fide of one of thefe maffes of
" ice, when the fea runs high, fhe would be dafhed to pieces in
" a moment." On the 14th, being in latitude 54 degrees 50
minutes fouth, 21 degrees 34 minutes eaft, they were ftopped,
in their route to the fouthward, by an immenfe field of low
ice, to which no end could be feen to the fouth, eaft or weft.
In different parts were hills of ice, like thofe that had been before found floating in the fea; and the fhip's company were often
amufed with the flattering profpect of land, which turned out to
be fog-banks. A boat was here hoifted out to try the direction
of the current, and Mr. Wales the aftronomer, accompanied by
Mr. Fofter the naturalift, took the opportunity of going in her
to make experiments on the temperature of the fea at different
depths. A thick fog came on, which blackened into fuch a degree of obfcurity, that they entirely loft fight of both the fhips.

In

In a four-oared boat, in an immense ocean, far from any hospitable shore, surrounded with ice, and destitute of provisions, their
situation was as frightful as any that can well be imagined. In
this dreadful suspense, they determined to ly still, hoping that,
provided they preserved their place, the sloops would not abandon them. The most delightful music they ever heard was the
jingling of the bell of the Adventure, which took them on board.
The ships then changed their course to the eastward, where the
large islands of ice were hourly seen in all directions; so that they
became as familiar to those on board as the clouds and the sea.
A strong reflection of white on the skirts of the sky was a certain indication of these islands; although the ice itself is not entirely white, but often tinged, especially near the surface of the
sea, with a beautiful berylline blue. This colour sometimes appeared 20 or 30 feet above the surface, and was most probably
produced by some particles of sea-water dashed against the mass
in tempestuous weather. Different shades of white were frequently observed in the larger islands, lying above each other in
strata of a foot high, which confirms Captain Cook's opinion
concerning the formation and increase of these masses, by heavy
falls of snow at different intervals. The 26th the islands still
surrounded them, behind one of which, in the evening, the
setting sun tinged its edges with gold, and brought upon the
whole mass a beautiful suffusion of purple. " Although," says
Captain Cook, " this was the middle of summer with us, I
" much question if the day was colder in any part of England.
" The mercury in Fahrenheit's thermometer constantly kept
" below the freezing point. The shooting at penguins afford-
" ed great sport but little profit, the birds diving so frequently
" in the water, and continuing so long under it, that the fow-
" lers were generally obliged to give over the pursuit. Their
" thick glossy plumage turned off the small shot, and it was
" necessary to attack them with ball."

Having hitherto met with no land, Captain Cook determined,
January 2d, 1773, to go in search of Cape Circumcision, which
is laid down by Bouvet in 58 degrees 53 minutes south, 10
degrees 6 minutes east; but as he saw no appearance of it in that
situation, although the weather was very clear, he supposed it

to have been nothing but fields and mountains of ice. January A. D
9th, three boats were hoisted out, and in a few hours took up as 1773
much ice as yielded fifteen tons of good fresh water. The salt
which adhered to the ice was so trifling as not to be tasted, and
entirely drained off by lying a short time on the deck. Crantz
some years ago advanced in his history of Greenland, that
those great masses of ice in the northern seas dissolved into fresh
water, from which he inferred, that they owed their origin to
the vast rivers of those hyperborean regions; but it was reserved
to Captain Cook to establish the doctrine, that the freezing of sea
water into ice, not only deprives it of all its salt particles, but
that it will thaw into soft, potable, and most wholesome water.
He has also proved by experience, that the bad qualities which
for so many ages have been attributed to melted snow and ice-
water are destitute of all foundation. This happy discovery of
deriving the greatest advantage from the ice mountains, which
seem to threaten our navigators with nothing less than destruction, enabled them to persevere in their voyage for a length
of time that would have been otherwise impossible, and contributed to that unparalleled degree of health, which they so fortunately enjoyed.

January 17th, they crossed the Antarctic circle in longitude 39
degrees 35 minutes east, which had till then remained impenetrable to all former navigators. The ice-islands became more and
more numerous; and in longitude 67 degrees 15 minutes south, an
immense field of congelation extended to the southward as far as
the eye could reach, which obliged Captain Cook to put about,
and stand north-east by north. Here were seen many whales
playing about the ice, and various flocks of brown and white
pintadoes, which were named Antarctic peterels, because they
seemed to be natives of that region. January 31st, two islands of
ice were seen in latitude 50 degrees 50 minutes south, one of
which appeared to be falling to pieces by the crackling noise it
made; and this was the last ice seen until they returned again
to the southward. In the neighbourhood of this latitude they
fell in with the islands discovered by Messrs. Thirguelen, St.
Allouard and Marion, French navigators, all of which were
islands of inconsiderable extent, high, rocky, destitute of trees,

and

A. D. and almoſt entirely barren.   It was ſuppoſed that the French
773. had diſcovered the north cape of a great ſouthern continent;
but though that land was not found by Captain Cook, his long
navigation proves, that their diſcovery, if not an ice field, could
only be a ſmall iſland.

The Reſolution loſt ſight of the Adventure the 8th of February, and the two ſloops continued ſeparate for the reſt of
the cruiſe, but afterwards met in Queen Charlotte's Sound in
New Zealand.   They proceeded together to Otaheite, and
other iſlands within the tropics, and again ſeparated near to
Cook's Streights, and never more joined during the voyage.
Captain Furneaux returned a ſecond time to the place of rendezvous at Queen Charlotte's Sound, but his conſort having left
that place a conſiderable time before his arrival, he, after re-
freſhing his crew, ſet ſail for England, which he reached in
July 1774.

The Reſolution continuing her voyage, in 58 degrees ſouth,
Captain Cook obſerved for the firſt time, on February 17th, the
Aurora Auſtralis, a phænomenon which had never before been
taken notice of by any navigator in the ſouthern hemiſphere.
It conſiſted of white columns of a clear white light, ſhooting up
from the horizon to the eaſtward, almoſt to the zenith, and
ſpreading gradually over the whole ſouthern part of the ſky.
Theſe columns differed from the ſouthern lights in being always of a whitiſh colour.   The ſky was generally clear when
they appeared, and the air ſharp and cold, the thermometer
ſtanding at the freezing point.   In March 26th, Captain Cook
made the coaſt of New Zealand, and anchored in Duſky Bay,
after having been one hundred and ſeventeen days at ſea, without
having once ſeen any land, in which time they had ſailed three
thouſand ſix hundred and ſixty leagues.

The captain continued during the following months, which
are the winter ſeaſon in that climate, to viſit his old friends at
Otaheite, the Society and Friendly Iſlands: and after examining a ſpace of more than 40 degrees of longitude between the
tropics, he returned to Queen Charlotte's Sound.   There he
changed the fair-weather rigging of his ſhip for ſuch as might
reſiſt the ſtorms and rigours of the high ſouthern latitudes, and

ſet

set sail the 27th November to explore the unknown parts of the Pacific Ocean. On December 6th he reached the 51st degree 32 minutes south latitude, and the 180th degree east longitude, consequently the point of the antipodes of London. December 15th, in 66 degrees south, and 159 degrees west, the farther course to the southward was interrupted by the ice-islands, among which they were almost embayed, which obliged them to tack to the north, and soon after they got clear of all the ice, but not without receiving several knocks from the larger pieces, which would have destroyed any vessel less carefully prepared to resist those repeated shocks. They crossed the Antarctic circle a second time on December the 20th, in the longitude of 147 degrees 46 minutes west. The next morning they saw innumerable ice-islands, high and rugged, their tops formed into various peaks, which distinguished them from those hitherto observed, which were commonly flat at the top. Many of those now seen were between two and three hundred feet in height, and between two and three miles in circuit, with perpendicular cliffs or sides, astonishing to behold. Most of their winged companions had now left them, except the grey albatrosses, and instead of the other birds, they were visited by a few Antarctic peterels, two of which were shot. From the appearance of the former, Captain Cook says, " we may with " reason conjecture that there is land to the south." December the 22d, they had penetrated to 67 degrees 31 minutes south, being the highest latitude they had yet reached. The longitude was 142 degrees 54 minutes west. They celebrated Christmas day the 25th with great festivity, the sailors feasting on a double portion of pudding, and regaling themselves with the brandy which they had saved from their allowance several months before, being solicitous to get very drunk. The sight of an immense number of ice-islands, among which the ship drifted at the mercy of the current, every moment in danger of being dashed in pieces, could not deter them from indulging in their favourite amusement ; as long as they had brandy left, they would persist to keep Christmas, though the elements had conspired together for their destruction.

A. D.  January 3d, 1774, being in latitude 56 degrees south, and lon-
1774. gitude 140 degrees 31 minutes west, the wind obliged them to
steer more to the north-east than they would have chosen, by
which they left unexamined a space of 40 degrees of longitude, and
20 degrees of latitude; which, however, was afterwards explored
on the return of the Resolution next year, and likewise by Captain
Furneaux in the Adventure much about this time.  The wind
increased so much on January the 15th, that it was very doubtful whether our navigators would return to give an account of
their voyage.  At nine at night a huge mountainous wave struck
the ship on the beam and filled the deck with a deluge of water, which poured into the cabin extinguished the lights, and
left the gentlemen there in doubt whether they were not entirely overwhelmed, and sinking into the abyss.  They passed
for a third time the Antarctic circle on January 26th, in longitude 109 degrees west, when they found the mildest sun-shine
that had been experienced in the frigid zone.  This led them to
entertain hopes of penetrating as far towards the south pole as
other navigators had done towards the north; but the next day
they discovered a solid ice-field before them of immense extent,
bearing from east to west.  A bed of fragments floated all round
this field, which seemed to be raised several feet high above the
level of the water.  Whilst in this situation, they observed the
southern part of the horizon illuminated by the rays of light reflected from the ice to an amazing height.  Ninety-seven ice-
island were counted within the field, beside these on the outside;
many of them were large, and looked like a ridge of mountains, rising one above another till they were lost in the clouds.
The outer or northern edge of this immense field was composed
of loose or broken ice close packed together; so that it was not
possible for any thing to enter it.  Captain Cook, however, is
of opinion, that there must be land to the south behind this ice;
but adds, " It can afford no better retreat for birds, or any
" other animals, than the ice itself, with which it must be en-
" tirely covered.  I who was ambitious not only of going far-
" ther than any body had gone before, but as far as it was
" possible for man to go, was not sorry at meeting with this in-
" terruption; as it in some measure relieved us, and shortened
" the

" the dangers and hardſhips inſeparable from the navigation A. D
" of the ſouthern polar regions.  Since then we could not 1774
" proceed farther to the ſouth, no other reaſon need be aſſign-
" ed for my tacking and ſtanding back to the north, being at
" this time in the latitude of 71 degrees, 10 minutes ſouth,
" and longitude 106 degrees, 54 minutes weſt."

Captain Cook then went in ſearch of the land, ſaid to have
been diſcovered by Juan Fernandez about a century ago, in latitude 38 degrees, and laid down by Mr. Dalrymple in 90 degrees
weſt, but no ſuch land was found in this ſituation : if there is any
land in the neighbourhood, it can be nothing but a ſmall iſland.
The captain then proceeded to the Marqueſas iſlands diſcovered
by Mendana in 1595, and viſited a ſecond time during this voyage
the Queen of tropical iſlands, Otaheite ; where, having refreſh-
ed, he ſailed for the new Hebrides, which though diſcovered as
early as 1606 by that great navigator Quiros, had never been
ſufficiently explored.  Captain Cook, beſides aſcertaining the
extent and ſituation of the Iſlands of this Archipelago, which
had been barely ſeen by others, added the knowledge of ſeveral
before unknown, which entitled him to give the whole the appellation which they now bear.  They are ſituated in the direction of north-north weſt and ſouth-ſouth eaſt, between the
latitudes of 14 degrees, 29 minutes, and 20 degrees, 4 minutes
ſouth, and between the longitudes of 166 degrees, 41 minutes,
and 170 degrees, 21 minutes eaſt, extending 125 leagues.  Of
all theſe iſlands Tierra del Eſpiritu Santo is the moſt weſterly
and the largeſt, being twenty-two leagues in length, and twelve
in breadth.  The lands, eſpecially on the weſt ſide, are exceedingly high and mountainous, generally covered with wood,
and the vallies uncommonly luxuriant, watered by ſtreams and
chequered with plantations. On the weſt ſide is a large and ſafe
bay, the two points which form its entrance lying at the
diſtance of ten leagues from each other.  The inhabitants are
of a ſtout make, dark colour, with woolly hair ; though almoſt
naked, their perſons are adorned with ſhells and feathers ; round
their middle they wear a narrow belt, from which is hung a
matted belt which covers them behind and before as low as the
knees.  They had no other arms but ſpears with two or three

Y y 2                                prongs,

A. D. prongs, which feemed rather intended for attacking fifh than
774· men. The fecond day after the fhip arrived on their coaft they
were with much difficulty prevailed on to approach near
enough to receive fome prefents, of which nails were accepted
with the greateft pleafure. They faftened a branch of the pepper plant to the rope by which the nails were let down, which
was the only return they made for the generofity of the ftrangers. Their language bears fome refemblance to that of the
Friendly Iflands.

Mallicollo is the moft confiderable ifland next to Efpiritu Santo, being 18 leagues in length, and 8 at its greateft breadth. It
is not only fertile, but appears to have been very anciently inhabited, as the natives called it by nearly the fame name which
Quiros had received 160 years ago. The people here are defcribed as the moft ugly and ill-proportioned that can well be
imagined, and differing in almoft every refpect from the other
iflanders in the South-fea. They are of a dark colour, and diminutive fize, long heads, monkey faces, their hair black and
curly, but not fo foft or woolly as that of a negroe. The men
go quite naked; and what increafes their natural deformity is
a rope as thick as a man's finger tied round the belly, cutting
a deep notch acrofs the body, which feems divided into two
parts by this tight and unnatural ligature. Moft other nations
invent fome kind of covering from motives of fhame, but here
a roll of cloth, continually faftened to the belt, rather difplays
than conceals, and is the oppofite of modefty. They are armed with fpears, bows and arrows; but are of a more pacific difpofition than moft other favages, having ventured to the fhip
without much invitation, and received with much complacence
the prefents offered them, for which they made a fuitable return. When they returned on fhore the found of finging and
beating their drums was heard all night. Mr. Fofter fuppofes
there may be 50,000 inhabitants on this extenfive ifland, which
contains more than 60 fquare miles, covered for the moft part
with a continued foreft, of which a few infulated fpots only are
cleared, which are loft in the extenfive wild like fmall iflands
in the Pacific Ocean.

Very

Very few women were seen, but thofe few were no lefs ugly A. D
than the men ; of a fmall ftature, their heads, faces, and fhoul- 1774
ders painted red.   Their food confifts principally of vegetables,
which they cultivate with much care ; hogs and fowls abound,
and by means of their canoes they draw a confiderable fupply
of fifh from the ocean.   When the Refolution was about to
depart, Captain Cook fays, " the natives came off in canoes,
" making exchanges with ftill greater confidence than before,
" and giving fuch extraordinary proofs of their honefty as fur-
" prifed us.   As the fhip at firft had frefh way through the
" water, feveral of the canoes dropped aftern after they had
" received goods, and before they had time to deliver theirs
" in return ; inftead of taking advantage of this, as our friends
" at the Society Iflands would have done, they ufed their ut-
" moft efforts to get up with us, and deliver what they had
" already been paid for ; one man in particular followed us a
" confiderable time, and did not reach us till it was calm, and
" the thing was forgotten ; as foon as he came along-fide he
" held up the article, which feveral on board were ready to
" buy, but he refufed to part with it till he faw the perfon to
" whom he had before fold it ; this perfon not knowing the
" man again, offered him fomething in return, which he con-
" ftantly refufed, and fhowing him what had been given before,
" at length made him fenfible of the nice point of honour by
" which he was actuated."   Befides excelling all their neighbours
in probity, they appeared the moft intelligent of any nation that
had been feen in the South-fea.   They readily underftood the
meaning conveyed by figns and geftures, and in a few minutes
taught the gentlemen of the fhip feveral words in their language,
which is wholly diftinct from that general tongue of which fo
many dialects are fpoken at the Society Iflands, the Marquefas,
Friendly Ifles, Eafter Ifland and New Zealand. They were not
only affiduous in teaching, but had great curiofity to learn the
language of the ftrangers, which they pronounced with fuch
accuracy, and retained with fuch force of recollection, as led
their inftructors to admire their extenfive faculties and quick
apprehenfion ; fo that what they wanted in perfon or beauty

was

was amply compenſated to them in acuteneſs of underſtanding, and probity of heart.

Captain Cook continued ſixteen days at another iſland called Tanna, diſtinguiſhed by a furious volcano, which was ſeen burning at a great diſtance at ſea. The ſoil of this iſland is compoſed of decayed vegetables intermixed with the aſhes of the volcano, and the country is in general ſo covered with trees, ſhrubs, and plants, as to choak up the bread-fruit and cocoa nuts. The natives are not numerous, but ſtronger and better proportioned than the Mallicolleſe. Not one ſingle corpulent man was ſeen here; all are active and full of ſpirit. Their features are large, the noſe broad, but the eyes full and generally agreeable. They ſeem to excel in the uſe of arms, yet they are not fond of labour; they never would put a hand to aſſiſt in any work the ſhip's company was carrying on, which the Indians of other iſlands uſed to delight in : here they throw all the laborious drudgery on the women, many of whom were ſeen carrying a child on their backs, and a bundle under their arm, and a fellow ſtrutting before them with only a club or a ſpear. The plantations conſiſt of yams, bananas, eddoes, and ſugar canes, all which, being very low, permit the eye to take in a great extent of country. There are plenty of hogs, but very few domeſtic fowls. Rats of the ſame ſpecies common in the other iſlands were ſeen running about in great numbers. They particularly frequent the fields of ſugar canes, where they make deſtructive depredations.

Captain Cook continued ſurveying theſe iſlands during the month of Auguſt 1774; from which he ſet ſail the 1ſt September, and having ſtood to ſouth-weſt all night, next day no more land was to be ſeen. On the 4th of September, being in the latitude of 19 degrees, 14 minutes ſouth, and the longitude of 165 degrees eaſt, land was diſcovered bearing ſouth-ſouth-weſt, for which he continued to ſteer till five in the evening. The ſhip had hardly got to an anchor on the 5th before it was ſurrounded by a great number of canoes, carrying the natives, moſt of whom were unarmed. They were prevailed on to receive ſome preſents, lowered down to them by a rope, in return for which they tied two fiſh that ſtunk intolerably. Theſe

mutual

mutual exchanges brought on a degree of confidence; several A. D.
came on board, and stayed dinner, but could not be persuaded 1774
to eat any thing but yams. They were curious in examining
every part of the ship, which they viewed with uncommon attention. They were fond of spike-nails, and pieces of coloured
cloth, especially red. After dinner the captain went on shore
with two armed boats, carrying with him one of the natives,
who had conceived an attachment for him. They landed on a
sandy beach before a vast number of people, who had assembled
merely from curiosity. The captain made presents to all those
his friend pointed out, who were either old men, or such as
seemed to be persons of some note: he offered to make presents
to some women who stood behind the crowd, but his friend restrained him from this act of complaisance. A chief, named
Teabooma, then made a speech consisting of short sentences,
to each of which two or three old men answered by nodding
their heads and giving a kind of grunt, significant of approbation. The speech was made on account of the strangers, to
whom it seemed to be very favourable. The captain having then
inquired by signs for fresh water, some pointed to the east, and
others to the west. His friend undertook to conduct him to it
in the boats; and having rowed about two miles up the coast to
the east, where the shore was mostly covered with mangrove
trees, they entered by a narrow creek, which led to a little
straggling village, near which was abundance of fresh water.
The ground near this village was finely cultivated, being laid
out in plantations of sugar cane, plantains, yams, and other
roots, and watered by little rills, artfully conducted from the
main stream which flowed from the hills. Here were some cocoa-nut trees, which did not seem burdened with fruit: the
crowing of cocks was heard, but none of them were seen. In
proceeding up the creek, Mr. Foster shot a duck, which was
the first use these people saw of fire-arms. The captain's friend
was at much pains to explain to his countrymen how it had
been killed. " The day being far spent," says the captain, " and
" the tide not permitting us to stay longer in the creek, we took
" leave of the people, and got on board a little after sun-set.
" From this little excursion I found we were to expect nothing
" from

" from thefe people but the privilege of vifiting their country
" undifturbed : for it was eafy to fee they had little more than
" good nature to beftow. In this they exceeded all the nations
" we had yet met; and, although it did not fatisfy the demands
" of nature, it at once pleafed, and left our minds at eafe."

The captain continued the greateft part of the month in examining this ifland, to which he gave the name of New Caledonia. It is the largeft of all the tropical iflands in thofe parts,
and, excepting New Holland and New Zealand, is the largeft
that has been difcovered in the fouth Pacific Ocean. It extends
from 19 degrees, 37 minutes, to 22 degrees, 30 minutes fouth
latitude, and from 163 degrees, 37 minutes, to 167 degrees, 14
minutes eaft longitude, being twelve degrees diftant from New
Holland, and the country bearing a ftrong refemblance to thofe
parts of New South Wales that lie under the fame parallel of
latitude. The whole coaft feems to be furrounded by reefs and
fhoals which render the accefs to it very dangerous, but at the
fame time guard the coafts againft the violence of the wind and
fea, caufe them to abound with fifh, and fecure an eafy and fafe
navigation for canoes. Thefe Indians are ftout, tall, and in general well proportioned; their beards and hair black and ftrongly frizzled, fo as to be almoft woolly in fome individuals. They
are remarkably courteous and friendly; but their appearance is
very indecent, every Caledonian being, like the natives of Tanna and Mallicollo, an ambulant ftatue of the Roman garden-god.
Yet there was not a fingle inftance of the women permitting
any improper familiarities. They fometimes indeed mixed in
the crowd, and amufed themfelves with encouraging the propofals of the feamen, beckoning them to come along the bufhes;
but, as foon as the failors followed, they gave them the flip,
running away with great agility, and laughing very heartily at
their ridiculous difappointment.

Their houfes or huts are circular as a bee-hive, and full as
clofe and warm. The entrance is by a fquare hole, big enough
to admit a man bent double; the fide-walls four feet and a half
high; the roof more lofty, peaked at the top, and fupporting
a poft of wood ornamented with carving or fhells. They commonly erect feveral huts in the neighbourhood of each other,

under

under a clufter of thick fig-trees, whofe foliage is impervious to A. D the rays of the fun. The fhip did not continue long enough 1774 on this coaft for the captain to acquire any cert in knowledge concerning the language, government, and religion of the na-tives. They are governed by chiefs, like the inhabitants of the New Hebrides, and pay a great degree of deference to old age. No circumftance was obferved in their behaviour which denoted the fmalleft fuperftition of any kind.

After leaving New Caledonia, the Refolution, fteering fouth-ward, fell in with an uninhabited ifland the 10th October, 1774, which the captain named Norfolk Ifle, in honour of the noble family of Howard. It lies in latitude 29 degrees 2 minutes fouth, longitude 168 degrees 16 minutes eaft. It is about three miles long, very fteep, covered with cyprefs trees, abounding in a red porous lava, which indicates that this ifland had been a volcano. The productions of New Zealand are here combined with thofe of the New Hebrides and Caledonia; for the cyprefs of the one, as well as the cabbage palm of the other, flourifh in great perfection, the former yielding timber for the carpen-ter, and the latter affording a moft palatable and wholefome re-frefhment. The fifh caught here, together with the birds and vegetables, enabled the fhip's company to fare fumptuoufly every day during their ftay. Here is likewife the valuable flax plant of New Zealand; all which circumftances, if the ifland were a little larger, would render it an unexceptionable place for an European fettlement.

The greateft defect of Norfolk ifland, as well as of all thofe lately vifited, is the fcarcity of animal food, with which, how-ever, they might eafily be ftored in great abundance. But this circumftance obliged the captain to fail again for New Zealand, where he came to an anchor in Queen Charlotte's Sound the 19th October, 1774. Here he continued till the 10th of No-vember, when, having already fatisfied himfelf of the non-exift-ence of an undifcovered continent in the Pacific Ocean, he pro-ceeded to examine the Magellanic regions, and, by exploring the unknown parts of the Atlantic and Indian oceans, to complete the furvey of the fouthern hemifphere. The firft object of this cruife was to difcover an extenfive coaft laid down by Mr. Dalrymple,

A. D. between 40 and 53 degrees weft longitude, and in the latitude of 1774 54 and 58 degrees fouth, in which he places the bay of St. Se-baftian.    But no fuch coaft was to be found; and as Captain Furneaux in the Adventure paffed acrofs that part where the eaftern and weftern fhores are laid down, it appears that no fuch land exifts in the fituation affigned to it in the Englifh or French charts.    On January 14th, 1775, land was difcovered in lati-tude 53 degrees 56 minutes fouth, longitude 39 degrees 24 mi-nutes weft; the mountains appeared of an immenfe height, co-vered with fnow and ice to the water's edge.    Towards the fouth feveral low lands were feen, which appeared to have fome verdure upon them, and were therefore called the Green Iflands. This land, which was at firft fuppofed to be part of a great con-tinent, was found at length to be an ifland of 70 leagues in cir-cuit, between the latitudes of 53 degrees 57 minutes and 54 degrees 57 minutes fouth, and the longitudes of 38 degrees 13 minutes and 35 degrees 34 minutes weft.    It is not eafy to con-ceive any thing more difmal than the face of nature in this ifland. Though it was in the midft of the fummer of that climate, the ifland feemed in a manner walled round with ice, and muft have been nearly inacceffible in any other feafon.    Captain Cook landed in a bay on the northern fide, which he called Poffeffion Bay, becaufe here he took poffeffion for his majefty of this dreary manfion of fterility under the name of Southern Geor-gia.    The head of the bay, as well as two places on each fide, were terminated by perpendicular cliffs of great height, fuch as are found in the harbour of Spitzbergen in the northern hemi-fphere.    Pieces were continually breaking off, and floating out to fea; and a great fall happened while the fhip was in the bay, which made a noife like cannon.    The other parts of the country were not lefs favage and horrible.    The wild rocks raifed their lofty fummits till they were loft in the clouds, and the vallies lay involved in fnow, affording no trees nor fhrubs, nor the leaft figns of vegetation.    Captain Cook examined alfo the fouthern parts of this ifland, which afforded nothing but a ftrong-bladed grafs growing in tufts, wild burnet, and a plant of the moffy kind fpringing from the rocks.    Seals, fea-lions, and penguins were the only appearances of animated nature in
this

this land of defolation, which the captain left on the 26th of
January, intending to fteer eaft-fouth-eaft until he arrived in 60
degrees latitude, beyond which he meant not to proceed, unlefs
he difcovered certain figns of falling in with land. In the profecution of this defign he met with nothing but thick fogs and
continual iflands of ice, the unintermitting afpect of which at
length tired even this perfevering adventurer. Many on board
were at this time afflicted with fevere rheumatic pains and colds,
and fome were fuddenly taken with fainting fits, fince their un-
wholefome, juicelefs food could not fupply the wafte of animal
fpirits. When the hope of reaching a milder climate diffufed a
general fatisfaction, another frozen country rofe to their view
the 31ft January. Captain Cook gave the name of Sandwich
Land to this difcovery, which may poffibly be the northern
point of a continent; for he is of opinion, that there is a tract
of land near the pole, which is the fource of moft of the ice
that is fpread over this vaft fouthern ocean. He likewife thinks
that it extends fartheft to the north, oppofite the fouthern Atlantic and Indian oceans, becaufe ice was always found more to
the north in thofe feas than in the fouthern Pacific, which he
imagines would not happen unlefs there was land of confiderable extent to the fouth. But the danger of exploring thefe unknown regions of winter is fo great that he concludes, feemingly on good grounds, that no man will ever venture farther than
he has done. The moft fouthern extremity that was feen lies
in latitude 59 degrees 30 minutes fouth, longitude 27 degrees
30 minutes weft. To this he gave the name of Southern Thule,
beyond which nothing, perhaps, will ever be difcovered. It is
impoffible to conceive any profpect more inexpreffibly horrid
than the appearance of this country; a country doomed by nature never to feel the genial warmth of the fun's rays, and
where all life and vegetation are for ever fhut up in eternal froft.
This forbidden coaft admitted of no anchorage; every place
that looked like a harbour being blocked up with ice. Captain
Cook having thus fully accomplifhed the defign of his voyage,
proceeded northward, and arrived at the Cape of Good Hope
as above mentioned.

Z z 2

Before

A. D.
1775

Before we conclude the hiftory of this voyage, it muft not be omitted that Captain Cook, when he returned to Otaheite, April 1774, had an opportunity of examining with more accuracy than had been hitherto done, the naval force of this ifland. Having gone by appointment to the diftrict called Opparee, to pay a vifit to Otoo the king, he obferved a number of large canoes in motion; all of which, to the number of three hundred and thirty, drew up in regular order, completely manned and equipped. The veffels were decorated with flags and ftreamers, fo that the whole made a more fplendid appearance than could have been expected in thofe feas. Their inftruments of war were clubs, fpears, and ftones; the canoes were ranged clofe along fide of each other with their heads afhore, and the ftem to the fea; the admiral's veffel being nearly in the centre. Befides the veffels of war, there were an hundred and feventy fail of fmaller double canoes, all with a little houfe upon them, and rigged with maft and fail, which the war canoes had not. The former muft have been intended for tranfports and victuallers, for in the war canoes there was no fort of provifions whatever. In all the three hundred and thirty veffels the captain gueffed there might be feven thoufand feven hundred and fixty men, a number which, he fays, appears incredible, efpecially as he was told the whole belonged to two diftricts, the ifland being divided into more than forty. In this computation, however, he allowed but forty men, troops and rowers, to each of the larger canoes, and eight to each of the fmaller; an eftimate which all his officers agreed rather to fall fhort of, than to exceed the truth. The fleet was going out to attack the inhabitants of Eimeo, who had ventured to provoke the Otaheiteans to a naval engagement. The captain was obliged to depart before he faw the conclufion of this affair; but the marine ftrength which he witneffed led him to important reflections concerning the populoufnefs of Otaheite. " It had been obferved," he fays, " that the number of war canoes belonging to the diftricts of " Attahourou and Ahopata was an hundred and fixty; to Tet- " taha forty, and to Matavai ten; and that this diftrict did " not equip one fourth part of that number. If we fuppofe " every diftrict in the ifland, of which there are forty-three, to
" raife

" raife and equip the fame number of war canoes as Tettaha, A. D
" we fhall find, by this eftimate, that the whole ifland can 1774
" raife and equip 1720 war canoes, and 68,000 able feamen;
" allowing forty men to each canoe. And, as thefe cannot
" amount to above one third part of the number of both fexes,
" children included, the whole ifland cannot contain lefs than
" 204,000 inhabitants; a number which at firft fight exceed-
" ed my belief. But, when I came to reflect on the vaft
" fwarms which appeared wherever we came, I was convinced
" that this eftimate was not much, if at all, too great. There
" cannot be a greater proof of the richnefs and fertility of Ota-
" heite, (not forty leagues in circuit), than its fupporting fuch
" a number of inhabitants." We now return from defcribing
the difcoveries of this enterprifing and judicious commander,
to relate the fequel of our domeftic misfortunes.

It has been already obferved, that although the miniftry had
given way to the refractory fpirit of the colonies in many other
inftances, yet the odious and ill-judged tax on tea imported into
America was ftill fupported by the force of an act of parliament. This regulation, which had been much objected to at
home, was univerfally obnoxious on the other fide of the Atlantic. The Americans forefaw, that if the tea was once landed,
and in the hands of confignees appointed by the Eaft-India company, which had lately fallen under the direction of government, it would be impoffible to prevent its fale and confump-
tion; and they therefore confidered the duty on this commo-
dity as a meafure calculated to deceive them into a general
compliance with the revenue laws, and thereby to open a door
to unlimited taxation. Befides, all the dealers both legal and
clandeftine, who, as tea is an article of fuch general confump-
tion in America, were extremely powerful, faw their trade at
once taken out of their hands. Views of private intereft thus
confpiring with motives of public zeal, the fpirit of oppofition
univerfally diffufed itfelf throughout the colonies, who determined to prevent the landing of the tea by every means in their
power.

Meanwhile the tea fhips had failed from England, October,
1773, with the following deftinations: For Bofton, New York,
and Philadelphia, three fhips, each loaded with 600 chefts of
tea;

A. D. tea; for Charleſtown and Rhode-Iſland, two ſhips, loaded with
1774. 200 cheſts each; the whole amounting to 2200 cheſts. As the
time of this arrival approached, the people aſſembled in different places in great bodies in order to concert meaſures for preventing this dangerous importation. The conſignees appointed
for vending the tea by the Eaſt-India company, were compelled, in moſt places, at the riſk of their lives and properties, to
relinquiſh their employments. Committees were appointed by
the people to propoſe teſts, and to puniſh thoſe who refuſed
ſubſcribing whatever was propoſed, as enemies to their country. In the tumultuary aſſemblies held on theſe occaſions innumerable reſolutions were paſſed derogatory to the legiſlative
power of Great Britain. Inflammatory hand-bills and other
ſeditious papers were publiſhed at New York, Charleſtown, and
Philadelphia; but Boſton, which had ſo long taken the lead in
rebellion, was the ſcene of the firſt outrage. The ſhips laden
with tea having arrived in that port, were boarded (18th December, 1773) by a number of armed men, under the diſguiſe
of Mohawk Indians, who in a few hours diſcharged the valuable cargoes into the ſea. Charleſtown in South Carolina followed this pernicious example. At New York alone the tea
was landed under the cannon of a man of war.

When the American diſpatches arrived, March 7, 1774, and
brought advice of the outrages committed againſt the tea-ſhips
at Boſton, his majeſty ſent a meſſage to both houſes, in which
they are informed, that in conſequence of the unwarrantable
practices carried on in North America, and particularly of the
violent proceedings at the town and Port of Boſton, with a view
of obſtructing the commerce of this kingdom, and upon grounds
and pretences immediately ſubverſive of its conſtitution, it was
thought fit to lay the whole matter before parliament; that they
may enable his majeſty to take ſuch meaſures as may be moſt
likely to put an immediate ſtop to thoſe diſorders, and conſider
what farther regulations may be neceſſary for ſecuring the execution of the laws, and the juſt dependence of the colonies upon
the crown and parliament of Great Britain. The miniſter who
delivered this meſſage allowed, that the deſtruction of the tea at
Boſton might have been prevented by calling in the aſſiſtance of
the

the naval force which lay in the harbour; but as the leading A. D.
men in that city had always made great complaints of the in-1774.
terposition of the army and navy, and charged all disturbances
of every sort to their account, this assistance had with great
prudence been declined; the Bostonians were left to the free
exercise of their own judgment, and the result had given the
lie to all their former professions.

The message and declaration seemed to be at variance with
each other. In the former his majesty desires the parliament to
impower him to stop the course of disorders, which the minister allows might have been prevented by the exertion of that
force with which he was already entrusted. But it seems that
government had not as yet been sufficiently persuaded of the evil
intentions of the inhabitants of Boston, and wished to give them
a farther opportunity of displaying the most extensive depravity
of their political characters. This being now evident to every
unprejudiced mind, the minister opened his plan for the restoration of peace, order, justice, and commerce in the Massachuset's
Bay. He stated, that the opposition to the authority of parliament had always originated in that colony, which had been insti-
gated to a rebellious conduct by the irregular and seditious proceedings of the town of Boston. That therefore, for the purpose of a thorough reformation, it became necessary to begin with
that town, which by a late unparalleled outrage had led the way
to the destruction of commerce in all parts of America. That,
had such an insult been offered to British property in a foreign
port, the nation would have been entitled to demand satisfaction.
He proposed, therefore, that the town of Boston should be obliged to pay for the tea which had been destroyed, and to give
security in future, that trade may be safely carried on, property
protected, laws obeyed, and duties regularly paid. For this purpose, he said, it would be necessary to take away from Boston the
privilege of a port until his majesty should be satisfied in these
particulars. Upon these arguments leave was given to bring in
a bill (March 14th) "for the immediate removal of the officers
" concerned in collecting the customs from the town of Boston
" in the province of the Massachuset's Bay in North America,
" and to discontinue the landing and discharging, lading and
" shipping

A. D. 1774. " fhipping of goods, wares, and merchandife at the faid town " of Bofton, or within the harbour thereof." This bill paffed in the houfe of commons the 25th of March; and, after being carried up to the lords, received the royal affent the 31ft of March.

This law forms the æra at which has been dated the decifive refolution of parliament to proceed to extremities with the province of Maffachufet's Bay. Befides the fhips of war already in America, the Prefton, Admiral Graves, with the Royal Oak, Worcefter, and Egmont, were ordered to repair with all convenient fpeed to Bofton. But at the fame time that thefe refolutions were taken, General Gage was appointed governor of the obnoxious colony, a gentleman who had long refided there, and was well acquainted with the inhabitants, with whom he had formed the moft intimate connections. This to many afforded a proof that the miniftry had fallen back into their former irrefolution; and the Boftonians threatened on the one hand with an act which deprived them of their ordinary means of fubfiftence, and foothed on the other by the appointment of a governor moft agreeable to their wifhes, maintained their wonted fpirit, and continued to defy the equivocal, temporizing timidity of the mother country. They ventured to hold a town-meeting, at which they refolved to invite the other colonies to ftop all imports and exports to and from Great Britain, Ireland, and the Weft Indies, until the Bofton port bill fhould be repealed. They artfully connected the fafety of the liberties of North America with the punifhment of one rebellious city, and, expatiating on the injuftice and cruelty of the odious bill, appealed from it to God and the world. The governor arrived the middle of May, and was received at Bofton with the ufual honours. He laid nothing before the provincial affembly but what the ordinary bufinefs required; but gave them notice of their removal to the town of Salem on the firft of June, in purfuance of the late act of parliament.

Meanwhile the Bofton port bill, as well as the refolutions taken at the town-meeting, were defpatched to every part of the continent. Thefe, like the Fury's torch, fet the countries every where in a flame through which they paffed. At New York the

1

[populace

populace had copies of the bill printed upon mourning paper, A. D
which they cried about the streets, under the title of a barbarous, 1774
cruel, bloody, and inhuman murder. The house of burgesses in
Virginia appointed the first of June, the day on which the Boston bill was to have effect, to be set apart for fasting, prayer,
and humiliation; an example which was followed by almost
every province of North America. Even the inhabitants of Salem, who derived evident advantage from the degradation of a
neighbouring town, declared, that they must be dead to every
idea of justice, and lost to all the feelings of humanity, if they
could indulge one thought to seize on wealth, and raise their
fortunes on the ruins of their suffering neighbours.

Thus the Boston port bill, unassisted by these active exertions
of the military or naval power of Great Britain which might
have rendered it an object of terror, raised a flame from one
end to the other of the continent of America, and united all the
old colonies in one common cause. They all agreed in determining not to submit to the payment of any internal taxes that were
not imposed by their own assemblies, and to suspend all commerce with the mother country, until the American grievances in
general, and those of Massachuset's Bay in particular, were fully
redressed. Nor were they less unanimous in entering into a general agreement, which was formed at Boston under the name
of a solemn league and covenant, for mutually supporting each
other, and maintaining what they deemed the rights of freemen,
inviolate. They soon after appointed deputies from each province to attend a General Congress, which should contain the
united voice and wisdom of America, and which they agreed
should be held at Philadelphia the 5th of September, 1774.
Among the first acts of this assembly was a declaration, in
which they acknowledge their dependence, but insist on their
privileges. They cheerfully consent to the operation of such
acts of the British legislature as are confined to the regulation of
their external commerce, for the purpose of securing the commercial advantages of the whole empire to the mother country:
but they insist, that the foundation of the English constitution
and of all free government, is a right in the people to participate
in their legislative council, and as the colonies are not, and from

A. D. various caufes cannot be reprefented in the Britifh parliament,
1774. they are entitled to a free and exclufive legiflation in their feveral provincial affemblies, in all cafes of taxation and internal policy. They recommend to the feveral provinces the continuance
of the meafures which they had already adopted, for eftablifhing a powerful national militia, and for raifing money to pay
thofe brave troops who would at every hazard defend the privileges of America.

The General Congrefs gave a confiftence to the defigns of
twelve colonies differing in religion, manners and forms of government, and infected with all the local prejudices and aver-
fions incident to neighbouring ftates. The ftrength which all
derived from this formidable union might have been fufficient
to alarm Great Britain; but the miniftry, inftead of fleets and
armies, continued ftill to fight the Americans with acts of parliament. For this purpofe the firft lord of the treafury moved,
1775. 10th February, 1775, for leave to bring in a bill to reftore the
trade and commerce of the province of Maffachufet's Bay and
New Hampfhire, as well as of the colonies of Connecticut and
Rhode Ifland; and to prohibit thefe provinces from carrying on
any fifhery on the banks of Newfoundland, and other places
therein mentioned. Upon the third reading of this bill a motion was made for an amendment, that the colonies of New
Jerfey, Pennfylvania, Maryland, Virginia, and South Carolina,
fhould be included in the fame reftrictions with the New England provinces. This amendment, however, was over-ruled;
although it could hardly be denied that thefe provinces had rendered themfelves equally culpable with thofe of New England.
Nearly about the fame time, parliament voted an augmentation
of 4383 foldiers, and 2000 feamen; and it was intended that
the troops at Bofton fhould amount to full ten thoufand, a number deemed more than fufficient for quelling the prefent difturb-
ance. While the nation feemed in general heartily to concur in
thofe vigorous meafures, they were not a little aftonifhed at the
famous conciliatory motion made by Lord North, containing
the following refolution: " That when the governor, council
" and affembly of any colony fhould be willing to contribute
" their proportion to the common defence, and for the fupport
" "

" of the civil government, fuch proportion to be raifed under
" the authority of the affembly of that province, it will be pro-
" per to forbear impofing or levying any tax, duty or affeffment
" from the faid province, excepting only fuch duties as it may
" be expedient to impofe for the regulation of commerce."
This propofition was confidered by many of thofe who fupported the general meafures of government, as a dereliction of thofe
rights which they had hitherto contended to be effential to the
Britifh legiflature ; while the oppofition afferted, that it would
be received with the fame indignation by the Americans, as
every other meafure intended to difunite their interefts.

This law which occafioned great difcontents in England, met
not with the fmalleft regard in America. While the parliament were employed in enacting it, the ill humour that prevailed among the troops and inhabitants at Bofton, broke out
into action. It is ftill undecided which party commenced hoftilities ; but the fkirmifhes at Lexington and Concord, proved
the bravery of the Provincials far fuperior to the ideas generally entertained of it. The blood fhed on thefe occafions excited
the greateft indignation in the other colonies, and they prepared for war with as much eagernefs and defpatch, as if an enemy
had already appeared in their own territories. In fome places
the magazines were feized, in others the treafury, and without
waiting for any account or advice, a ftop was almoft every
where put at the fame time to the exportation of provifions.
The governor and forces at Bofton, as well as the inhabitants,
continued clofely blocked up by land ; while they were excluded from all fupplies of frefh provifions, which the neighbouring
countries could have afforded them by fea. As the military
ftores began to be exhaufted without the poffibility of receiving
any fpeedy fupply, the governor thought proper to enter into a
capitulation with the Boftonians, by which, upon condition of
delivering up their arms, they were allowed to depart with all
their other effects. Though all the poor and helplefs were fent
out, and many others obtained paffports both then, and at
different times afterwards, yet the greater part of the inhab-
tants were upon different grounds obliged to remain in the city,
which breach of faith, as the Americans termed it, on the part

of General Gage, is deſcribed with great indignation in all their ſubſequent publications.

The Continental Congreſs met at Philadelphia May 10th, 1775, and adopted ſuch meaſures as confirmed the people in their warlike reſolutions. They provided for the array and ſupport of an army, named generals, eſtabliſhed a paper currency, for the realizing the value of which the " Twelve United Co" lonies" became ſecurities ; ſoon after Georgia acceded to the Congreſs, from which time they were diſtinguiſhed by the name of the " Thirteen United Colonies." It was ſaid, that in the whole extent of North America, from Nova Scotia to Florida, near 200,000 men were training to arms under the auſpices of the Congreſs. This aſſembly took meaſures not only for defending themſelves, but for diſtreſſing their enemies. They ſtrictly prohibited the ſupplying of the Britiſh fiſheries with any kind of proviſion ; and, to render this order effectual, ſtopt all exportation to thoſe colonies and iſlands which ſtill retained their obedience. This prohibition occaſioned no ſmall diſtreſs to the people at Newfoundland, and to all thoſe employed in the fiſheries ; inſomuch that, to prevent an abſolute famine, ſeveral ſhips were under a neceſſity of returning light from that ſtation, to carry out cargoes of proviſions from Ireland.

In the mean time ſeveral private perſons, belonging to the back parts of Connecticut, Maſſachuſet's, and New York, without any public command, or participation that has hitherto been diſcovered, undertook an expedition of the utmoſt importance, and which threatened to deprive Great Britain of every ſingle poſſeſſion which ſhe held in North America. This was the ſurpriſe of Ticonderago, Crown-Point, and other fortreſſes, ſituated upon the lakes, and commanding the paſſes between the ancient Engliſh colonies and Canada. Theſe adventurers, amounting in the whole to about 240 men, ſeized Ticonderago and Crown-Point, in which they found above 200 pieces of cannon, beſides mortars, howitzers, and large quantities of various ſtores ; they alſo took two veſſels, which gave them the command of Lake Champlain, and materials ready prepared at Ticonderago for the equipping of others.

Although the troops at Boſton were greatly reinforced by the arrival of the generals Howe, Burgoyne, and Clinton, a

conſiderable

considerable body of marines, and several regiments from Ireland, they continued patiently to submit to all the inconveni-
ences of a blockade; nor did they receive any considerable af-
sistance from the great number of ships of war which almost
surrounded the peninsula. The Congress published a resolution,
June 8th, importing the compact between the crown and the
people of Massachuset's Bay to be dissolved. This was followed by a proclamation of General Gage, (June 12th), by
which a pardon was offered, in the king's name, to all those
who should forthwith lay down their arms, and punishment de-
nounced against those who obstinately persisted in disobedience.
They were to be treated as rebels and traitors; and, as the regular course of justice was stopped, martial law was to take
place until the rules of civil equity were restored to their due
efficacy.

The Provincials, considering this proclamation as an immediate prelude to hostility, determined to be before-hand with
their enemies. Having made the necessary preparations for
seizing the port of Charlestown, they sent a number of men,
with the greatest privacy in the night, to throw up works upon
Bunker's Hill. This was effected with such extraordinary order and silence, and such incredible dispatch, that none of the
ships of war, which covered the shore, heard the noise of the
workmen, who by the morning had made a small but strong
redoubt, considerable entrenchments, and a breast-work, that
was in some parts cannon proof. The sight of these works
was the first thing that alarmed the Lively man of war, and her
guns called the town, camp, and fleet to behold a sight, which
seemed little less than a prodigy. A heavy and continual fire
of cannon, howitzers, and mortars, was from this time carried
on against the works, from the ship, and floating batteries, as
well as from the top of Cop's Hill in Boston. About noon
General Gage caused a considerable body of troops to be embarked under the command of Major-general Howe, and Brigadier-general Pigot, to drive the Provincials from their works.
These troops, consisting of ten companies of grenadiers, as many of light infantry, and the 5th, 38th, 43d, and 52d battalions,
with a proper train of artillery, were landed and drawn up
without

A. D. without oppofition, under the fire of the fhips of war.   The
1775. two generals found the enemy fo numerous, and in fuch a poſture of defence, that they thought it neceſſary to ſend back for
a reinforcement before they commenced the attack; they were
accordingly joined by two companies of light infantry and grenadiers, by the 47th regiment, and by the firſt battalion of
marines, amounting in the whole to ſomething more than 2000
men.

The attack began by a moſt fevere fire of cannon and howitzers, under which the troops advanced ſlowly towards the
enemy, to afford an opportunity to the artillery to ruin the
works, and to throw the Provincials into confuſion.   Thefe,
however, ſuſtained the aſſault with a firmnefs that would have
done honour to regular troops, and detached a body of men to
Charleſtown which covered their right flank.   General Pigot,
who commanded the right wing, was thus obliged to engage
at the faine time with the lines and with thoſe in the houfes.
During this conflict Charleſtown was fet on fire; whether by
the troops, or by carcaſſes thrown from the ſhips, is uncertain,
but that large and beautiful town, which, being the firſt ſettle-
ment in the colony, was confidered as the mother of Boſton,
was in one day burnt to the ground.   The Provincials did not
return a ſhot until the king's forces had approached almoſt to
the works, where a moſt dreadful fire took place, by which
above a thouſand of our braveſt men and officers fell.   In this
action, one of the hotteſt ever known, (confidering the number
engaged), our troops were thrown into fome diforder; but in
this critical moment General Clinton, who arrived from Boſton
during the engagement, rallied them by a happy manœuvre,
and brought them inſtantaneouſly to the charge.   They attacked the works with fixed bayonets and irrefiftible bravery, and
carried them in every quarter.   The Provincials fought defpe-
rately, but being, as they affirm, deftitute of bayonets, and their
powder expended, they were obliged to retreat over Charleſtown
neck, which was enfiladed by the guns of the Glafgow man of
war, and of two floating batteries.   The king's troops took
five pieces of cannon, but no prifoners except thirty, who were
ſo feverely wounded that they could not efcape.

The

The poffeffion of part of the peninfula of Charleftown, and A. D of Bunker's Hill, which was immediately fortified, enlarged the 1775 quarters of the troops, who had been much incommoded by the ftreightnefs in which they were confined in Bofton; but this advantage was counterbalanced by the great additional duty which they were now obliged to perform. Befides, the Provincials loft no time in throwing up works upon another hill oppofite to Bunker's, on the fide of Charleftown neck which was ftill in their poffeffion. The troops were thus as clofely invefted in this peninfula as they had been in Bofton. Their fituation was irkfome and degrading, being furrounded and infulted by an enemy whom they had been taught to defpife, and cut off from all thofe refrefhments of which they ftood in the greateft need.

The refentment occafioned by their fufferings probably engaged them to continue a great cannonade upon the works of the provincials, which could have little other effect than to inure them to that fort of fervice in which they were employed. A regiment of light cavalry, which arrived from Ireland, increafed the wants of the garrifon, without being of the fmalleft ufe, as the cavalry were never able to fet foot without the fortifications. The hay which grew upon the iflands in the bay, as well as the fheep and cattle which they contained, became an object of great attention to the king's troops; but the Provincials having prepared a number of whaling boats, and being mafters of the fhore and inlets of the bay, were, notwithftanding the number of the fhips of war and armed veffels, too fuccefsful in burning, deftroying, and carrying away thofe effential articles of fupply. Thefe enterprifes brought on feveral fkirmifhes, and the enemy grew at length fo daring that they burnt the light-houfe fituated on an ifland at the entrance of the harbour, though a man of war lay within a mile of them at the time; and fome carpenters being afterwards fent, under the protection of a fmall party of marines, to erect a temporary light-houfe, they killed or carried off the whole detachment. From this time a fort of predatory war commenced between the king's fhips and the inhabitants on different parts of the coaft. The former, being refufed the fupplies of provifions and neceffaries which they wanted for
themfelves

themfelves or the army, endeavoured to obtain them by force and in thefe attempts were frequently oppofed, and fometime repulfed with lofs by the country people. The feizing of fhips, in conformity to the new laws for reftraining the commerce of the New-England provinces, was alfo a continual fource of animofity and violence, the proprietors hazarding all dangers in defending or recovering their veffels. Thefe contefts drew the vengeance of the men of war upon feveral of the fmall towns upon the fea coafts, fome of which underwent a fevere chaftifement.

The parliament, which met in October 1775, feemed more firmly determined, than on any former occafion, to purfue what were called vigorous meafures by the majority, and which the oppofition diftinguifhed by the epithets of cruel, bloody, and unjuft. The American petitions addreffed to the crown were rejected with contempt or indignation; and it was determined to carry on the war with a fpirit that fhould aftonifh all Europe, and to employ fuch fleets and armies in the enfuing year as had never before entered the new world. A motion was made from the admiralty, in the committe of fupply, that 28,000 feamen, including 6665 marines, fhould be voted for the fervice of the year 1776. This was accompanied with a general outline of the fervices to which the navy fhould be applied; particularly, that the fleet on the North-American ftation fhould amount to 78 fail. This would, doubtlefs, employ the greateft part of the feamen propofed; and happily the affairs of Europe did not require any confiderable exertion of our naval ftrength. The profeffions of the neighbouring courts were pacific and friendly; and, what was of more weight than profeffions, their preparations were nowife alarming. At any rate our guard-fhips were fo numerous and fo well appointed, that they might on the fhorteft notice be rendered fuperior to any force that our rivals could affemble. The motion for the augmentation was paffed; though not without fevere animadverfion from the moft diftinguifhed of our naval commanders, who arraigned in the plaineft terms the prefent government and conduct of our naval affairs, and infifted that the eftablifhment now propofed, though too

2

great

reat for peace, was by no means adequate to the demands of a war.

On the day following, (8th November), the minifter of the war department, having laid the eftimates for the land fervice before the committee of fupply, fhewed that our whole military force would amount to 55,000 men, of which upwards of 25,000 would be employed in America. On this occafion alfo many gentlemen affirmed, that the propofed force was totally unequal to the purpofe of conquering America by force of arms, the meafure upon which the miniftry feemed now abfolutely determined. This was fupported by the opinion of a great general officer who had been long in adminiftration; the other military gentlemen were called upon to declare their diffent if they thought otherwife, but they all continued filent.

A few days afterwards, the firft lord of the treafury brought in the famous prohibitory bill, totally interdicting all trade and intercourfe with the Thirteen United Colonies. All property of Americans, whether of fhips or goods, on the high feas or in harbour, are declared forfeited to the captors, being the officers and crews of his majefty's fhips of war; and feveral claufes were inferted in the bill to facilitate and leffen the expence of the condemning of prizes, and the recovery of prize-money. But, in order to foften thefe harfh meafures, the bill enabled the crown to appoint commiffioners, who, befides the power of granting pardons to individuals, were authorized to inquire into general grievances, and empowered to determine whether any part, or the whole of a colony, were returned to that ftate of obedience which entitled them to be received within the king's peace and protection, in which cafe the reftrictions of the prefent bill were to ceafe in their favour.

After all the boafted preparations for hoftility, the feeming contradiction in this bill was thought by many to fupport the confiftent character of adminiftration. It was ftill the fame alternative of war and peace; peace offered by Great Britain who had received the injury, and not by her enemies, on whom fhe pretended to be ready to wreak the whole weight of her vengeance. This mixed fyftem of war and conciliation was reprefented as highly improper at the prefent juncture. The meafure

A. D. adopted, whether of peace or war, should be clear, simple and
1775. decided, not involved in doubt, perplexity and darkness. If
war is resolved, and it is determined to compel America to sub-
miſſion, let the means of coercion be such as will, to a moral
certainty, inſure ſuccefs. Our fleets and armies muſt command
terms, which will in vain be ſolicited by our commiſſioners.

While theſe preparations and debates occupied the Britiſh ſe-
nate, the deſigns of the Americans gradually became more daring. Their ſuccefsful expedition to the lakes, with the reduction of Ticonderago and Crown Point, had opened the gates of
Canada; and the Congreſs came to the bold reſolution of ſend-
ing a force to invade and conquer that loyal colony. The Generals Schuyler and Montgomery, with two regiments of New
York militia, a body of New-England men, amounting in the
whole to three thouſand, were appointed to this ſervice. A
number of batteaux, or flat-boats were built at Ticonderago
and Crown Point, to convey the forces along Lake Champlain
to the river Sorel, which forms the entrance into Canada.
Having proceeded to the iſle Aux Noix, they propoſed to attack
the fort St. John's, in which they were retarded by a want of
ammunition ſufficient for carrying on the ſiege. Their commander Montgomery, who was well qualified for any military
ſervice, turned his thoughts to the reduction of the little Fort
Chamblée, which lies farther up the country, and was in a very
defenſible condition. · Here he found conſiderable ſtores, and
120 barrels of powder, which enabled him to puſh with vigour
the ſiege of St. John's. General Carleton, the governor of the
province, then at Montreal, was equally indefatigable in his endeavours to raiſe a force ſufficient for its relief. With the utmoſt difficulty he had got together about a thouſand men, compoſed principally of Canadians, with a few regulars and ſome
Engliſh officers and volunteers. With theſe he intended a junction with Colonel M'Lean, who had raiſed a regiment under the
name of Royal Highland Emigrants, conſiſting of the native
mountaineers of Scotland, who had lately arrived in America,
and who, in conſequence of the troubles, had not obtained ſettlements. But the deſigns of General Carleton were defeated
by a party of Provincials, who encountered him at Longueil,
and

and easily repulsed the Canadians. Another party pushed A. D M'Lean towards the mouth of the Sorel, where the Canadians, 1775 by whom he was attended, hearing of the general's defeat, immediately abandoned him to a man, and he was compelled, at the head of his few Scotch emigrants, to take refuge in Quebec. Meanwhile Montgomery obtained possession of St. John's, 3d November, 1775, where he found a considerable quantity of artillery, and many useful stores; the garrison, commanded by Major Preston, surrendered prisoners of war, and were sent up the lakes to those interior parts of the colonies, which were best adapted to provide for their reception and security.

Upon M'Lean's retreat to Quebec, the party who had reduced him to that necessity immediately erected batteries near the junction of the St. Lawrence and the Sorel, in order to prevent the escape of the armed vessels, which General Carleton had at Montreal, to the defence of Quebec. Montgomery meanwhile laid siege to Montreal, of which he got possession the 13th November; and Carleton's armament being pursued, attacked and driven from their anchors up the river by the Provincials, he himself narrowly escaped in a dark night, in a boat with muffled paddles, and after many dangers arrived at Quebec. His naval force, consisting of eleven armed vessels, fell into the hands of the Provincials.

The city of Quebec was at this time in a state of great weakness, as well as internal discontent and disorder. Besides this, Colonel Arnold appeared unexpectedly with a body of New-Englanders at Point Levi, opposite to the town. The river fortunately separated them from the place, otherwise it seems probable that they might have become masters of it in the first surprize and confusion. Several days elapsed before they effected a passage in boats furnished them by the Canadians, notwithstanding the vigilance of the English frigates in the river. The inhabitants of Quebec, however, had by this time leisure to unite for defending their city. When Montgomery, therefore, who with the utmost expedition had pushed forward to join Arnold, attempted on the 31st of December to carry the place by escalade, he met with the most vigorous and unexpected resistance. He himself was slain, Arnold wounded, and a considerable body of the Provincials taken prisoners of war. The

3 B 2

remainder

A. D. remainder did not again venture on any similar attack, but were
1775. satisfied with converting the siege into a blockade, and found
means effectually to prevent any supplies of provisions or necessaries from being carried into Quebec.

While the provincials obtained these important advantages in
Canada, the Virginians obliged their governor, Lord Dunmore,
to provide for his safety by embarking on board the Fowey man
of war. All connection between Great Britain and that colony
was dissolved July 18th. The governor in vain emancipated the
slaves, a measure which he had so often threatened, that its execution was rendered ineffectual. He determined, however, to
do every thing in his power to regain possession of some part of
the country which he had governed. Being joined by such
persons as were obnoxious on account of their loyalty, and supported by the frigates on the station, he endeavoured to establish such a marine force as might enable him, by means of the
noble rivers, which render the most valuable parts of Virginia
accessible by water, to be always at hand, and to profit by every
favourable occasion that offered. But his spirited endeavours to
redeem the colony were attended only with disappointment;
and his armament, too feeble for any essential service, was distinguished barely by acts of depredation. The unfortunate
town of Norfolk, having refused to supply his majesty's ships
with provisions, was attacked by a violent cannonade from the
Liverpool frigate, three sloops of war, and the governor's armed ship the Dunmore; and the first of January was signalized
with burning it to the ground. In South Carolina Lord William Campbell, the governor, after less vigorous exertions, was
obliged to retire from Charlestown on board a ship of war in
the river; and Governor Martin of North Carolina saved himself by the same expedient. The fleet of England served as a
peaceable asylum to the expelled magistrates of revolting provinces, while its army was ingloriously cooped up in Quebec
and Boston.

The Provincials were not less active in the cabinet than in the
field. November 13, 1775, the inhabitants of Massachuset's
Bay published letters of marque and reprisal, and established
courts of admiralty for trying and condemning British ships.
The General Congress, (December the 6th), having previously
agreed

agreed on articles of confederation and perpetual union, anfwer- A. D
ed with much acrimony the royal proclamation of Auguft 23d 1775
for fuppreffing rebellion and fedition, and declared, that whatever punifhment fhould be inflicted upon any perfons in the
power of their enemies, for defending the caufe of America,
the fame fhould be retaliated on the Britifh fubjects who fell
into their hands.

. In this ftate of obftinacy or firmnefs on the fide of the Americans, the diftreffed army at Bofton looked with impatience towards thefe kingdoms for the arrival of the expected reinforcements. The delays and misfortunes which the tranfports experienced in their voyage, and the fight of many veffels laden with
the neceffaries and comforts of life taken in the harbour, heightened the mortification and fufferings of thofe brave troops, who
were kept, by the feverity of the feafon, and the ftrength of the
enemy, in a total inaction during the whole winter. The American cruizers and privateers, though yet poor and contemptible, being for the greater part no better than whale-boats, grew
daily more numerous and fuccefsful againft the victuallers and
ftore-fhips; and among a multitude of other prizes, took an ord-
nance-fhip from Woolwich, containing a large mortar upon a
new conftruction, feveral pieces of fine brafs cannon, a great
number of fmall arms, with abundance of ammunition and all
manner of tools, utenfils, and machines neceffary for camps and
fieges. This important prize, which gave a new colour to the
military operations of the Provincials, was taken by a fmall privateer, which excited juft indignation againft the management
of our naval affairs, for hazarding a cargo of fuch value in a defencelefs veffel.

When news of the prohibiting act reached the Congrefs, they
fent orders to General Wafhington to bring affairs at Bofton to
as fpeedy a decifion as poffible, in order to difengage his army,
and to give them an opportunity to oppofe the new dangers with
which they were threatened. Wafhington, therefore, opened a
new battery, at a place called Phipp's Farm, on the night of the
2d of March, from whence a fevere canonade and bombard- 1776
ment was carried on againft the town. This attack was continued till the 5th, when the army, to their incredible furprize,
beheld fome confiderable works upon the heights of Dorchefter-
point, from which a 24 pound and a bomb battery were foon
                                                        after

L. D. after opened. The fituation of the king's troops was now ex-
776. tremely critical, it being neceffary either to abandon the town
which began to blaze on every fide, or to diflodge the enemy
and deftroy the new works. The latter, however, General
Howe, who had fucceeded General Gage in the command, judged to be impracticable, fo that nothing remained but to abandon Bofton, and to convey the troops, artillery, and ftores on
board the fhips. The embarkation rather refembled the emigra-
tion of a nation, than the breaking up of a camp; 1500 of the
inhabitants, whofe attachment to the royal caufe had rendered
them obnoxious to their countrymen, encumbered the tranfports
with their families and effects. This inconvenience, joined to
fcarcity of provifions and ill fuccefs, bred much difcontent. The
troops confidered themfelves as abandoned, having received no
advices from England fince the preceding October. Mutual jea-
loufies prevailed between the army and navy; each attributing
to the other, part of this uneafinefs which itfelf felt. The intended voyage to Halifax, at all times dangerous, was dreadfully
fo at this tempeftuous equinoctial feafon, and the multitude of
fhips, which amounted to 150 fail, increafed the difficulty and
apprehenfion. At the fame time the king's forces were under
the neceffity of leaving a confiderable quantity of artillery and
ftores behind. The cannon upon Bunker's Hill, and at Bofton
Neck, could not be carried off. Attempts were made to render
them unferviceable; but the hurry which then prevailed, prevented them from having any great effect. Some mortars and
pieces of cannon which were thrown into the water, were afterwards weighed up by the inhabitants of Bofton, who, the 17th
of March, received General Wafhington's army with drums beating, colours flying, and all the fplendour of military triumph.

It was above a week after this time before the weather permitted the fleet to get entirely clear of the harbour and road;
but this delay was amply compenfated by the voyage to Halifax,
which was fhorter and more fuccefsful than could have been
expected. Several fhips of war were left behind to protect the
veffels which fhould arrive from England; but the great extent
of the bay, with its numerous iflands and creeks, allowed fuch
advantages to the provincial armed boats and privateers, that
they

they took a great many of thofe veffels, which were ftill in ignorance that the town had changed mafters.

On the fide of Canada, General Carleton conducted his operations with more fuccefs. All the attempts of the Provincials to take Quebec by ftorm were rendered abortive; nor did they fucceed better in endeavouring by fire-fhips and otherwife to burn the veffels in the harbour. Such was the conftancy and vigilance of Governor Carleton, Brigadier M'Lean, and the activity of the garrifon, that the Americans intended to raife the fiege, which was prevented from being carried fuccefsfully into execution by the fpirit and vigour of the officers and crews of the Ifis * man of war and two frigates, which were the firft that had failed from England with fuccours, and which, having forced their way through the ice, arrived at Quebec before the paffage was deemed practicable. The unexpected appearance of the fhips threw the befiegers into the utmoft confternation, and the command which they obtained of the river cut off all communication between the different detachments of the enemy. General Carleton loft no time in feizing the advantages which the prefent fituation afforded. May 6th, he marched out at the head of the garrifon, and attacked the rebel camp, which he found in the utmoft confufion. Upon the appearance of our troops they fled on all fides, abandoning their artillery, military ftores, and all their implements for carrying on the fiege. During this tranfaction our fmaller fhips of war proceeded up the river with great expedition, and took feveral fmall veffels belonging to the enemy, as well as the Gafpee floop of war, which had, a few months before, unfortunately fallen into their hands.

The fuccefs at Quebec tended greatly to facilitate the reconqueft of Canada, and the invafion of the back part of the colonies by the way of the lakes, which was the firft of the three principal objects propofed in the conduct of the Britifh forces in

---

* This expedition was planned and executed by that excellent officer Captain Charles Douglas, (fince created a Baronet of Great Britain): he commanded the Ifis, and brought her and the other fhips of the fquadron, fo early as the 5th of May, up the river St. Laurence to Quebec, through large fields of floating ice, overcoming almoft unfurmountable obftacles. He alfo had the merit of planning the expedition on the lakes, afterwards executed with great fpirit by Captain Thomas Pringle under Sir Charles Douglas's directions. Without this early and fuccefsful expedition, Canada ran the rifk of being fubdued by the rebel troops commanded by General Arnold.

the

A. D. the enfuing campaign. The fecond was the making a ftrong
1779. impreffion on the fouthern colonies, which it was hoped would
at leaft have been attended with the recovery of one of them.
The third was the grand expedition againft the city and province
of New York.

It had for fome time been the fate of the fleets, tranfports, and
victuallers which failed from England to meet with fuch difficulties, delays, and fo many untoward circumftances, as in a great
degree fruftrated the end of their deftination. Sir Peter Parker's
fquadron which failed from Portfmouth at the clofe of the year,
did not arrive at Cape Fear till the beginning of May, where
they were detained by various caufes till the end of the month.
There they found General Clinton, who had already been at New
York, and from thence proceeded to Virginia, where he had
feen Lord Dunmore, and, finding that no fervice could be effected at either place with his fmall force, came thither to wait for
them.    After this junction, the fleet and army were both fufficiently powerful to attempt fome enterprize of importance *.
Charleftown in South Carolina was the place deftined for their
attack. The fleet anchored off the bar the beginning of June ;
but the paffing this obftacle was a matter of no fmall difficulty,
efpecially to the two large fhips, which notwithftanding the taking out of their guns, and the ufing every other means to lighten them as much as poffible, both ftruck the ground. When
this difficulty was overcome, our fleet attacked a fort lately erected upon the fouth-weft point of Sullivan's ifland, and commanding the paffage to Charleftown. The troops commanded by General Clinton, Lord Cornwallis, and Brigadier-general Vaughan,
were landed on Long-Ifland which lies to the eaftward of Sullivan's.   The Carolinians had pofted fome forces with artillery
at the north-eaftern extremity of the latter, at the diftance of
two miles from the fort, where they threw up works to prevent
the paffage of the royal army over the beach.   General Lee was

---

* Sir Peter Parker's fquadron confifted of the

| Briftol, | 50 guns, | Sir Pet. Parker |
| Experiment, | 50 —— | Capt. Scott |
| Solebay, | 28 —— | —— Symonds |
| Acteon, | 28 —— | —— Atkins |
| Active, | 28 —— | —— Williams |

| Syren, | 28 guns, | Capt. Furneaux |
| Sphinx, | 20 —— | —— Hunt |
| Friendfhip, | 22 —— | —— Hope |
| Ranger floop | | |
| Thunder bomb | | |
| St. Lawrence fchooner. | | |

encamped

encamped with a large body of troops on the continent, at the back and to the northward of the iſland, with which he held a communication open by a bridge of boats, and could by that means at any time march the whole, or any part of his force, to ſupport the poſt oppoſed to our paſſage from Long-Iſland This iſland is a naked burning ſand, where the troops ſuffered much from their expoſure to the intenſe heat of the ſun; and both fleet and army were much diſtreſſed through the badneſs of the water, and the defect or unwholeſomeneſs of the proviſions.

Theſe inconveniencies rendered deſpatch of the utmoſt importance; but it was not till the 28th of June that, every thing being ſettled between the commanders by ſea and land, the Thunder bomb took her ſtation, covered by an armed ſhip, and began the attack by throwing ſhells at the fort. The Briſtol, Solebay, Experiment, and Active, ſoon after brought up, and began a moſt furious and inceſſant cannonade. The Sphinx, Syren, and Actæon, were ordered to the weſtward, between the end of the iſland and Charleſtown, partly with a view to enfilade the works of the fort, and, if poſſible, to cut off all communication between the iſland and the continent, and partly to interrupt all attempts by means of fire-ſhips, or otherwiſe, to prevent the grand attack. But this deſign was rendered unſucceſsful by the ſtrange unſkilfulneſs of the pilot, who entangled the frigates in the ſhoals called the Middle Grounds, where they all ſtuck faſt; and though two of them were ſpeedily diſengaged, it was then too late to execute the intended ſervice. The Actæon could not be got off, and was burnt by the officers and crew the next morning, to prevent her materials and ſtores from falling into the hands of the enemy. Amidſt the dreadful roar of artillery and continued thunder from the ſhips, the garriſon of the fort ſtuck with the greateſt firmneſs and conſtancy to their guns, fired deliberately and ſlowly, and took a cool and effective aim. The ſhips ſuffered accordingly; and never did our marine, in an engagement of the ſame nature with any foreign enemy, experience ſo rude an encounter. The ſprings of the Briſtol's cable being cut by the ſhot, ſhe lay for ſome time ſo much expoſed to the enemy's fire, that ſhe was

A. D.
1776.
moft dreadfully raked. The brave Captain Morris, after receiving fuch a number of wounds as would have fufficiently juftified a gallant man in retiring from his ftation, ftill difdained, with a noble intrepidity, to quit his ftation, until his arm being fhot off, he was carried away in a condition which did not afford a poffibility of recovery. It is faid that the quarter-deck of the Briftol was at one time cleared of every perfon but the commodore, who ftood alone, a fpectacle of daring, intrepid firmnefs, which has never been exceeded, feldom equalled. The others on that deck were either killed, or carried down to have their wounds dreffed. The fortifications being extremely ftrong, and their lownefs preferving them from the weight of our fhot, the fire from the fhips produced not all the effect which was hoped or expected. The fort, indeed, feemed for a fhort time to be filenced, but this proceeded only from a want of powder, which was foon fupplied from the continent. The land forces all this while continued inactive; and night at length put an end to the attack of the fleet. Sir Peter Parker finding all hope of fuccefs at an end, and the tide of ebb nearly fpent, called off his fhattered veffels, after an engagement of above ten hours. The Briftol had 111, and the Experiment 79 men killed and wounded; and both fhips had received fo much damage that the Provincials conceived ftrong hopes, that they could never be got over the bar. The frigates, though not lefs diligent in the performance of their duty, being lefs pointed at than the great fhips, did not fuffer a proportionable lofs.

During thefe tranfactions the General Congrefs took an opportunity of preparing the people for the declaration of independency, by a circular manifefto to the feveral colonies, ftating the caufes which rendered it expedient to put an end to all authority under the crown, and to take the powers of government into their own hand. The caufes affigned were, the contempt of their petitions for redrefs of grievances, the prohibitory bill, by which they were excluded from the protection of the crown, and the intended exertion of all the force of Great Britain, aided by foreign mercenaries, for their deftruction. The colonies of Maryland and Pennfylvania at firft teftified a difinclination to the eftablifhment of a new government. Their deputies, however,

ever, were at length inftructed to coincide in this meafure, and A. D.
on the 4th of July, 1776, the Thirteen United Provinces de- 1776
clared themfelves free and independent ftates, abjuring all allegiance to the Britifh crown, and all political connection with
their mother country. A few weeks after this declaration, Lord
Vifcount Howe arrived at Halifax at the head of a powerful
fquadron, and fuch a number of land forces as had never before appeared in the new world. Befides the national troops
there were 13,000 Heffians and Waldeckers, commanded by
able officers of their own country. The whole, compofed of
the new reinforcements and the troops formerly in America,
amounted to an army of 35,000 men; which was fuperior in
number, difcipline, and provifions of every kind, to any force
the Americans could bring into the field. General Howe had
left Halifax a fortnight before his brother's arrival; the latter
being impatient of remaining in a place where nothing effential to
the fervice could be performed, and where provifions began to
grow fcarce, had embarked his troops on board the fleet commanded by Admiral Shuldam, and failed to Sandy Hook, the
firft land that is met with in approaching New York from the
fea. On his paffage he was met by fix tranfports with Highland
troops on board, who had been feparated from feveral of their
companions in the voyage. It appeared foon after that moft of
the miffing fhips, with above 450 foldiers and feveral officers,
had been taken by the American cruifers. The general found
every part of the ifland of New York ftrongly fortified, defended by a numerous artillery, and guarded by a confiderable army.
The extent of Long Ifland did not admit of its being fo ftrongly fortified or fo well guarded; it was, however, in a powerful
ftate of defence, having an encampment of confiderable force
on the end of the ifland near New York, and feveral works
thrown up on the moft acceffible parts of the coaft, as well as
at the ftrongeft internal paffes. Staten Ifland, which was of lefs
value and importance, was lefs powerfully defended; and on
this the general landed without oppofition. Here he was met
by Governor Tryon, who, like the other gentlemen invefted
with chief authority in North America, had been obliged to

efcape on fhip-board. Some hundreds of well-affected inhabitants from the neighbouring parts alfo joined the royal ftandard.

Lord Howe did not arrive at Staten Ifland till the 14th of
July, when he fent to the continent a circular letter fetting
forth the powers with which he and his brother were invefted
by the late act of parliament for granting general or particular
pardons to all thofe who, in the tumult and difafter of the
times, might have deviated from their juft allegiance, and who
were willing, by a fpeedy return to their duty, to reap the bene-
fits of the royal favour. Thefe letters were treated with as
little refpect as every other propofition of a fimilar kind, the
Americans contemning the idea of granting pardons to thofe who
were not fenfible of any guilt. Meanwhile the Britifh armament was joined by the fleet commanded by Sir Peter Parker,
as well as by fome regiments from Florida and the Weft Indies.
The greateft part of the forces being now united, an attack
againft Long Ifland was determined, as being more eafy of execution than againft the ifland of New York, and as the former abounded more with thofe fupplies which fo great a body
of men as were now affembled by fea and land demanded.

The neceffary meafures being taken by the fleet for covering
the defcent, the army was landed without oppofition on the
fouth-weft end of the ifland. Soon after this was effected, General Clinton, in the night of the 26th of Auguft, at the head
of the van of the army confifting of the light infantry, grenadiers, light horfe, referve under Lord Cornwallis, with fourteen
field-pieces, advanced towards the enemy's encampment, and
feized an important pafs which they had left unguarded. The
way being thus happily open, the whole army paffed the hills
without noife or impediment, and defcended by the town of
Bedford into the level country. The engagement was begun early in the morning, while the fhips made feveral motions on the left, and attacked a battery at Red Hook, which
perplexed the enemy, and called off their attention from
their right and rear where the main attack was intended. Nothing could exceed the fpirit and alacrity fhewn by all the different corps of which the Britifh army was compofed. They
made the enemy retreat on every fide, purfued them with great
flaughter,

flaughter, and fuch was the ambition between the Britifh and
foreign troops, that it was with difficulty General Howe could
reftrain their impetuofity in breaking through the American
lines, and cutting to pieces or taking prifoners all thofe who had
efcaped the danger of the battle and the purfuit. The victors
encamped in the front of the enemy's work on the evening after the engagement, and on the 28th, at night, broke ground in
form at 600 yards diftance from a redoubt which covered the
enemy's left.

During the battle General Wafhington had paffed over from
New York, and faw with great mortification the unhappy fate
of his braveft troops. The remainder were as much inferior in
number and difcipline to the Britifh army, as their inconfiderable
batteries were unequal to the affault of the royal artillery. No
hopes of fafety remained but in a retreat, which might well have
appeared impracticable in the face of fuch a commanding force
by land, and a fleet at fea which only waited a favourable wind
to enter the Eaft River, which would effectually cut off all communication between the iflands. This arduous tafk, however,
was undertaken and carried into execution by the fingular ability of General Wafhington. In the night of the 29th the Provincial troops were withdrawn from the camp and their different works, and with their baggage, ftores, and artillery, conveyed to the water fide, embarked, and paffed over a long ferry
to New York. This was conducted with fuch wonderful
filence and order, that our army did not perceive the leaft motion, and were furprifed in the morning at finding the lines
abandoned, and feeing the laft of the rear-guard in the boats
and out of danger. By this fuccefsful manœuvre General
Wafhington not only faved the troops on Long Ifland from
captivity, but fortified the courage and ftrength of his army at
New York, and enabled the Americans to continue the war
with unabating ardour. Yet this meafure he could not have
effected, had the Englifh general allowed his troops to force the
enemy's lines, had the fhips of war been ftationed in the Eaft
River, or had the vigilance of the Britifh foldiers watched and
intercepted the movements of the Provincials.

After

After the fuccefs attending the fuperior bravery of the Englifh in the engagement, and that attending the fuperior wifdom of Wafhington in the retreat, the commiffioners renewed their propofals of conciliation, which were ftill as fruitlefs as before. Laying afide, therefore, their pacific character, they again had recourfe to their military. The Britifh troops were impatient to meet the enemy, who had efcaped fo unexpectedly from their hands. A river only divided them, along the banks of which they erected batteries, while a fleet of 300 fail, including tranf-ports, hovered round the ifland of New York, and threatened deftruction on every fide. The fmall iflands between the oppo-fite fhores were perpetual objects of conteft, until by dint of a well-ferved artillery, and the aid of the fhips, thofe were fecu-red which were moft neceffary to their future operations. At length, every thing being prepared for a defcent, the men of war made feveral movements up the North River, in order to draw the attention of the enemy to that quarter of the ifland. Other parts feemed equally threatened, and increafed the uncer-tainty of the real object of the attack. While the rebels were in this ftate of perplexity, the firft divifion of the army, under the command of General Clinton, embarked at the head of Newtoun Bay, which runs pretty deep into Long Ifland, and where they were entirely out of view of the enemy. Being co-vered by five fhips of war upon their entrance into Eaft River, they proceeded to Kepp's Bay, where, being lefs expected than in fome other places, the preparation for defence was not fo confiderable. The works, however, were not weak, nor de-ftitute of troops, but the fire from the fhips was fo inceffant and well directed that they were foon abandoned, and the army landed without farther oppofition. The enemy immediately quitted the city of New York, and retired towards the north, where their principal ftrength lay, particularly at King's Bridge, by which their communication with the continent of New York was kept open. General Howe thought the works here too ftrong to be attacked with any profpect of fuccefs, and there-fore determined either to bring the rebels to an engagement on equal terms, or to inclofe them in their fortreffes. While he made what appeared to be the proper difpofitions for this pur-

pofe,

pose, with a fleet and army sufficient to cover and surround the A. D. whole island, General Washington, by a most judicious manœu- 1776. vre, formed his troops into a line of small detached encampments, which occupied every high and strong ground on the land opposite to King's Bridge. He left a garrison to defend the lines there, and Fort Washington; which, after a vigorous resistance, fell into the hands of the British forces. But general Howe could not bring Washington to an engagement, who availed himself of his skill and address while he fled before a superior force, retreating from one post to another, but always occupying more advantageous ground than his pursuers.

The British commander thus disappointed in his design of making any vigorous impression on the main body of the enemy, detached, on the 18th of November, Lord Cornwallis to take Fort Lee, and to advance farther into the Jerseys. The garrison of 2000 men abandoned the place the night before his Lordship's arrival, leaving their artillery, stores, tents, and every thing else behind. Our troops afterwards over-ran the greater part of the two Jerseys, the enemy flying every where before them; and at length extended their winter cantonements from New Brunswic to the Delaware. In the beginning of December General Clinton, with two brigades of British, and two of Hessian troops, with a squadron of ships of war commanded by Sir Peter Parker, were sent to make an attack upon Rhode Island, in which they succeeded beyond expectation. The general took possession of the island without the loss of a man; while the naval commander blocked up the principal marine force of the enemy, commanded by Hopkins, the admiral of the Congress, who then lay in the harbour of Providence..

On the side of Canada we left General Carleton driving the rebels towards the Lakes Champlain and St. George, of which they had formerly obtained possession, as well as of the important fortress of Ticonderago. If the British troops could recover these, and advance as far as Albany, before the severity of the winter set in, they might pour destruction into the heart of the middle or northern colonies, as General Washington could not attempt to hold any post in New York or the Jerseys against such a superior force as already opposed him in front, and ge-

neral

neral Carleton's army at his back. Notwithſtanding the moſt unremitting induſtry in preparing this northern expedition, it was not until the month of October that the Engliſh fleet was in a condition to ſeek the enemy on Lake Champlain. The ſhip Inflexible, which may be conſidered as admiral, had been re-conſtructed at St. John's, from which ſhe ſailed in twenty-eight days after laying her keel, and mounted 18 twelve pounders. One ſchooner mounted 14, and another 12 ſix pounders. A flat-bottomed radeau carried 6 twelve pounders, beſides howitzers; and a gondola 7 nine pounders. Twenty ſmaller veſſels, under the denomination of gun-boats, carried braſs field-pieces from nine to twenty-four pounders, or were armed with howitzers. Several long-boats were furniſhed in the ſame manner, and an equal number of long-boats acted as tenders. All theſe appertained to war; and there were beſides an immenſe number of tranſports and victuallers deſtined for the ſervice and conveyance of the army. The armament was conducted by Captain Pringle, and navigated by above 700 prime ſeamen, of whom 200 were volunteers from the tranſports, who after having rivalled thoſe belonging to the ſhips of war in all the toil of preparation, now boldly and freely partook with them in the danger of the expedition. The fleet of the enemy was not of equal force, and amounted to only fifteen veſſels of different kinds, conſiſting of two ſchooners, one ſloop, one cutter, three gallies, and eight gondolas. The principal ſchooner mounted 12 ſix and four pounders. They were commanded by Benedict Arnold, who was now to ſupport upon a new element the glory which he had acquired by his atchievements as a general.

The Britiſh armament proceeding up the lake the 11th of October, 1776, diſcovered the enemy drawn up with great judgment, in order to defend the paſſage between the iſland of Valicour and the weſtern main. A warm action enſued, and was vigorouſly ſupported on both ſides for ſeveral hours. The wind being unfavourable, the ſhip Inflexible and ſome other veſſels of force could not be worked up to the enemy, ſo that the weight of the action fell on the ſchooner Carleton and the gun-boats. As the whole could not be engaged, Captain Pringle, with the approbation of the general, withdrew his advanced

veſſels

veffels at the approach of night, and brought the whole fleet to A. I
anchor in a line, as near as poffible to the enemy, in order to 1776
prevent their retreat.

Arnold being now fenfible of his inferiority, took the opportunity which the darknefs of the night afforded to fet fail, unperceived, hoping to obtain fhelter and protection at Crown
Point. Fortune feemed at firft favourable to his purpofe, for
he had entirely loft fight of the enemy before next morning.
The chace, however, being continued both on that and the fucceeding day, the wind, and other circumftances peculiar to the
navigation of the lake, which had been at firft advantageous to
the Americans, became at length otherwife, fo that on the 13th
at noon they were overtaken, and brought to action a few
leagues fhort of Crown Point. The engagement lafted two hours,
during which thofe veffels of the enemy that were moft a-head
pufhed on with the greateft fpeed, and, paffing Crown Point,
efcaped to Ticonderago ; while two gallies, and five gondolas,
which remained with Arnold, made a defperate refiftance. But
their obftinate valour was at length obliged to yield to the fuperiority of force, fkill, and weight of metal by which it was
affailed. The Wafhington galley with Waterburg, a brigadier-
general and the fecond in command, aboard, ftruck, and was
taken. But Arnold determined that his people fhould not become prifoners, nor his veffel a prey to the Englifh. With
equal refolution and dexterity he run the Congrefs galley, in
which himfelf was, with the five gondolas, on fhore, in fuch a
manner as to land his men fafely and blow up the veffels, in
fpite of every effort that was ufed to prevent both. Not fatisfied with this fubftantial advantage, which in his fituation was
more than could have been expected from an experienced commander, he inflexibly perfifted in maintaining a dangerous point
of honour, by keeping his flag flying, and not quitting his gal--
ley till fhe was in flames, left the Englifh fhould have boarded
and ftruck it ; an attention which greatly raifed his repution in
America.

Thus was Lake Champlain recovered, and the enemy's force
nearly deftroyed, a galley and three fmall veffels being all that
efcaped to Ticonderago. The Provincials, upon the rout of

A. D. their fleet, set fire to the houses at Crown Point, and retired to
1776. their main body. Carleton took possession of the ruins, and being joined by his whole army, pushed on towards the enemy.
But the post of Ticonderago was too strongly fortified to be
taken without great loss of blood; and the benefit arising from
success could not be considerable, as the season was too far advanced to think of crossing Lake George, and of exposing the
army to the perils of a winter campaign, in the inhospitable wilds
to the southward. General Carleton, therefore, reimbarked the
army without making any attack upon this place, and returning to Canada, cantoned his troops there for the winter.

The Americans seem to have been guilty of an unpardonable
blunder in not maintaining a more powerful squadron on the
lakes, which laid open the heart of their country. But besides
the want of timber, artillery, and other materials necessary for
such an equipment, the carpenters, and all others concerned in
the business of shipping, were fully engaged in the sea-ports in
the construction and fitting out of privateers. To this the force
of the rebels was principally bent; and the interest of individuals which was more immediately concerned in the success of
particular cruizers, than in supporting the marine strength of
the nation, gave redoubled vigour to all the operations of the
former.

The West Indies, which in the want of food, and of staves
the article next in necessity to food, experienced the first melancholy effects of the American war, also suffered the most
from the Provincial privateers. The fleet which sailed from
Jamaica in August, 1776, being scattered by bad weather, fell
a prey to the activity of their cruizers, who had seized the proper
station for intercepting their passage. Nor was the trade from the
other islands more fortunate. So that though the Americans did
not begin their depredations till late in the year, the British loss
in captures, exclusive of transports and government store-ships,
was estimated considerably higher than a million sterling. Some
blame was thrown on the convoy, and much indignation felt
that the superintendence of our naval affairs, on which the glory
and security of the nation depend, should be entrusted to hands
unworthy to hold it. Such a sacred deposit required, it was
thought, not only pure but steady hands; the duties of the important

portant office to which it belongs calling for unremitting vigi- A. D
lance and activity, and being totally incompatible with a life of 1776
licentious and degrading pleafure. Religious men were not
furprized, that under fuch an inaufpicious influence the dignity of the nation fhould fuffer a total eclipfe, while the American cruizers fwarmed in the European feas, and replenifhed the
ports of France and Spain with prizes taken from the Englifh.
Thefe prizes were fold in Europe without any colour of difguife,
at the fame time that French fhips in the Weft Indies took
American commiffions, and carried on with impunity a fuccefsful war on Britifh trade and navigation.

Meanwhile the time of the meeting of parliament approached, when it was expected that the line of conduct neceffary for a
total conqueft, or happy conciliation with the colonies, would
be clearly pointed out and explained. The great armaments
which were continually increafing in the French and Spanifh
ports, and many other fufpicious appearances during the recefs,
rendered it neceffary to put into commiffion fixteen additional
fhips of the line, and to increafe the bounty to feamen for entering the fervice to five pounds *per* man. The expences of the
navy for the year 1777, including the ordinary at 400,005 l.
and the building and repairing of fhips which was voted at
465,500 l. amounted to no no lefs than 3,205,505 l. exclufive
of 4000 l. which was afterwards voted to Greenwich Hofpital.
The fupplies for the land-fervice fell little fhort of three millions,
although the extraordinaries of the preceding year which exceeded 1,200,000 l. were not yet provided for. In whatever
manner adminiftration might employ the force by fea and land,
the nation had provided for the fupport of both, with fuch liberal magnificence as equalled the fupplies during the laft war,
when the fleets and armies of Britain oppofed and defeated the
united efforts of the greateft powers in Europe. Soon after the 1777,
Chriftmafs recefs a bill was paffed, enabling the admiralty to
grant letters of marque and reprifal to the owners or captains
of private merchant-fhips, to take and make prize of all veffels
with their effects belonging to any of the inhabitants of the
Thirteen United Colonies. All the powers of the kingdom

3 D 2

were

A. D. were thus called forth, affording, as it would seem, a force in-
1777. finitely more than sufficient, had it been properly directed, to
crush this aspiring rebellion.

But unfortunately the star of America still maintained the
ascendant. The British troops whom we left in apparent security in their cantonments were assailed on all sides, in the
middle of winter, by General Washington, who remedied the
deficiency of his force by the manner of applying it, and by attacking unexpectedly and separately those bodies which he
could not venture to encounter if united. By some well-concerted and spirited actions this American Fabius, after a retreat
which would have done honour to the judgment of the most
circumspect of all the Romans, not only saved Philadelphia and
delivered Pennsylvania from danger, but recovered the greatest
part of the Jerseys, and obliged an army greatly superior in
number as well as in discipline to act upon the defensive, and
for several months to remain within very narrow and inconvenient limits.

The British nation, how much soever they were afflicted with
those misfortunes, still expected that notwithstanding this war
of posts, surprizes, and detachments, which had been successf-
fully carried on by the Americans during the winter, the regular forces would prevail in the end. They waited, therefore,
with much impatience for the approach of spring, when the
mighty armaments which they had raised with so high expectation of victory, might be brought into action. When the time
at length arrived, with equal astonishment and indignation, they
learned that from some improvidence or inattention, unac-
counted for at home, the army was restrained from taking the
field for want of tents and field equipage. The months of
March and April, therefore, instead of being employed in such
decisive enterprizes as might terminate the war, were confined
to some subordinate expeditions in which the naval superiority
of Britain was crowned with success. The Provincials had
erected mills and established magazines in a rough and mountainous tract called the Manour of Courtland, to which a place
called Peek's Kill, lying fifty miles up Hudson's river from
New York, served as a kind of port. Courtland Manour was
too strong to be attacked with any prospect of success; but
Peek's Kill lay within the reach of the navy. On the 23d of
March,

March, Colonel Bird was fent with 300 men under the conduct A. D of a frigate and other armed veffels, up the North River to de-1777 ftroy the works of the enemy at this place. Upon the approach of the Britifh armament, the Americans thinking themfelves unequal to the defence of the port, and being convinced that there was not time to remove any thing but their perfons and arms, fet fire to the barracks and principal ftorehoufes, and then retired to a ftrong pafs about two miles diftance, commanding the entrance into the mountains, and covering a road which led to fome of the mills and other depofits. The Britifh troops landed and compleated the conflagration, which had already gone too far to allow any thing to be faved. All the magazines were thus deftroyed, and the troops, having performed this fervice, returned after taking feveral fmall craft laden with provifions. Another expedition of a fimilar kind was undertaken againft the town of Danbury on the borders of Connecticut, and attended with equal fuccefs.

Thefe petty advantages were nothing, compared to the infinite benefit which the Americans derived from the delay of the Britifh army in taking the field. The Provincials were greatly augmented by reinforcements from all quarters to the Jerfeys. Thofe who fhuddered at a winter's campaign grew bold in fummer; and the certainty of a future winter had no greater effect than diftant evils ufually have. When General Howe paffed over from New York to the Jerfeys the middle of June, he found Wafhington's army, which fix weeks before had been nothing to his own in point of force, greatly increafed, and ftationed in fuch advantageous and inacceffible pofts as defied every affault. All his attempts to bring Wafhington to an engagement, or to make him quit his defenfive plan of conducting the war, proved abortive; and it appeared the height of temerity to attempt advancing to the Delaware, through fo ftrong a country entirely hoftile, and with fuch an enemy in his rear. Nothing remained, therefore, for General Howe but to avail himfelf of the immenfe naval force which co-operated with the army, and which in a country like America, interfected by great navigable rivers, gave him an opportunity of tranfporting his forces to the moft vulnerable parts of the rebellious provinces. The Americans had no force to refift the navigation, and it was impoffible for them to

know

A. D. know where the storm would fall, or to make provision against
1777. it. General Howe, accordingly, passed over with the army to
Staten Island, from which it was intended that the embarkation
should take place.

For the success of this grand expedition nothing was more requisite than despatch; yet, notwithstanding the assistance afforded by the crews of 300 vessels, it was not till the 23d of July
that the fleet and army were ready to depart from Sandy Hook.
The force embarked consisted of thirty-six British and Hessian
battalions, including the light infantry and grenadiers, with a
powerful artillery, a New-York corps called the Queen's Ran-
gers, and a regiment of light horse. Seventeen battalions with
a regiment of light horse, and the remainder of the New-York
corps, were left for the protection of that and the neighbouring
islands; and Rhode Island was occupied by seven battalions.

Philadelphia, the original feat of the General Congress, but
from which that body had retired to Baltimore, was the object
of these mighty preparations. The weather being unfavourable,
it cost the fleet a week to gain the Capes of the Delaware. The
information which the commanders received there of the measures taken by the enemy for rendering the navigation of that
river impracticable, engaged them to alter their design of proceeding by that way, and to undertake the passage by Chesapeak
Bay to Maryland, the southern boundary of which is at no
great distance from Philadelphia. The middle of August was
passed before they entered this bay, after which, with a favourable wind, they gained the river Elk near its extremity through
a most intricate and dangerous navigation. Having proceeded
up this river as far as it was possible for large vessels, the army
were relieved from their tiresome confinement on board the transports, which was rendered doubly disagreeable by the heat of
the season, and landed without opposition at Elk Ferry on the
25th of August. Whilst one part of the army advanced to the
head of the Elk, the other continued at the landing-place to
protect and forward the artillery, stores, and necessary provisions.

Meanwhile General Washington returned with his army from
the Jerseys to the defence of Philadelphia. Their force, including the militia, amounted to 13,000 men, which was still
          considerably

considerably inferior in number to the royal army. General A. D Howe, after publishing such proclamations as he thought necef- 1777 fary for quieting the minds of the inhabitants, and inducing them to return to the protection of the crown, began on the 3d of September to purfue his courfe to Philadelphia. Washington loft no opportunity of haraffing him in his march, by every poffible means which did not involve the neceffity of rifquing a general engagement. But feveral confiderable actions took place between the troops both before and after General Howe had entered Philadelphia, of which the army became poffeffed the 26th of September. In thefe actions victory always inclined to the fide of the king's troops, who fhewed as much ardour in the attack as Wafhington difcovered wifdom in the retreat, and in avoiding a general engagement. The Provincials had great difadvantage in the ufe of the bayonet, with which inftrument they were ill provided, and which they knew little how to manage. And when this circumftance is confidered, it will not appear furprifing that the difproportion between their number of flain and that of the king's troops fhould in every action have been confiderable.

When the Britifh troops had taken poffeffion of Philadelphia, their firft employment was to erect batteries which might command the river, and protect the city from any infult by water. This was fo neceffary a meafure, that the very day of the arrival of the forces, the American frigate Delaware, of 32 guns, anchored within 500 yards of the unfinifhed batteries, and being feconded by another frigate, with fome fmaller veffels, commenced a heavy cannonade, which lafted for feveral hours. Upon the falling of the tide, however, the Delaware grounded, and was taken; and the batteries newly erected were played with fuch effect againft the other veffels, that they were fortunate to be able to retire.

Meanwhile Lord Howe being apprized of the determined progrefs of the army to Philadelphia, took the moft fpeedy and effectual meafures to convey the fleet and tranfports round to the Delaware, in order to fupply the army with the neceffary ftores and provifions, as well as to concur in the active operations of the campaign. After a dangerous and intricate voyage, the

A. D. the fleet arrived in the weſtern or Pennſylvania ſhore, where
777. they drew up and anchored.   The paſſage to Philadelphia,
however, was ſtill impracticable, for the Americans had conſtructed great and numerous works with wonderful labour and
induſtry to interrupt the navigation of the river.   The principal
of theſe were the ſtrong batteries on a low and marſhy iſland,
or rather an accumulation of mud and ſand at the junction of
the Delaware and Schuylkill; a conſiderable fort or redoubt at
a place called Red Bank on the oppoſite ſhore of New Jerſey;
and in the deep navigable channel between theſe forts there had
been ſunk ſeveral ranges of frames or machines, which from
reſemblance of conſtruction were called chevaux de frize.
Theſe were compoſed of tranſverſe beams, firmly united, and
of ſuch weight and ſtrength as rendered it equally difficult to
penetrate or remove them.   About three miles lower down the
river they had ſunk other machines of a ſimilar form, and
erected new batteries on ſhore on the Jerſey ſide to co-operate
in the defence.   Both were farther ſupported by ſeveral gallies
mounting heavy cannon, together with two floating batteries, a
number of armed veſſels and ſmall craft of various kinds, and
ſome fire-ſhips.

The firſt thing requiſite for opening the channel was to get
the command of the ſhore.   Accordingly, upon the repreſenta-
tion of Captain Hammond of the Roebuck, which, with ſome
other ſhips of war, had arrived in the Delaware before Lord
Howe, the general detached two regiments to diſlodge the enemy from Billingsfort, the principal place of ſtrength on the
Jerſey ſhore.   This ſervice was ſucceſsfully performed; and Captain Hammond, after a vigorous conteſt with the marine force
of the enemy, was able with much labour to weigh up as much
of the chevaux de frize as opened a narrow and difficult paſſage
through this lower barrier.

It was not attempted to remove the upper barrier, which was
much the ſtronger, until the arrival of Lord Howe, who concerted meaſures for this purpoſe with the general.   The latter
ordered batteries to be erected on the Pennſylvania ſhore, to
aſſiſt in diſlodging the enemy from Mud Iſland.   He alſo detached, (22d October), a ſtrong body of Heſſians to attack the
redoubt

redoubt at Red Bank; while Lord Howe ordered the men of A. D war and frigates to approach Mud Island, which was the main 1777 object of the affault. The operations by land and fea were equally unfuccefsful. The Heffians were repulfed with great flaughter by the garrifon at Red Bank, as well as by the floating batteries of the enemy. The fhips could not bring their fire to bear with any confiderable effect upon the ifland. The extraordinary obftructions with which the Americans had interrupted the free courfe of the river, had even affected its bed, and wrought fome alteration on its known and natural channel. By this means the Augufta man of war of 64 guns, and Merlin floop were grounded fo faft at fome diftance from the chevaux de frize, that there was no poffibility of getting them off. In this fituation, though the fkill of the officers, feconded by the activity of the crews, prevented the effect of four fire-fhips fent to deftroy the Augufta, fhe unfortunately took fire in the engagement, which obliged the others to retire at a diftance from the expected explofion. The Merlin alfo was deftroyed, but few lives were loft.

These untoward events did not prevent a fecond trial on the 15th November to perform the neceffary work of opening the communication of the river. While the enemy left nothing undone to ftrengthen their defences, the Britifh fleet were inceffantly employed in conveying heavy artillery and ftores up the river to a fmall moraffy ifland, where they erected batteries which greatly incommoded the American works on Mud Ifland. At length every thing being prepared for an affault, the Ifis and Somerfet men of war paffed up the eaft channel, in order to attack the enemy's works in front; feveral frigates drew up againft a newly erected fort near Manto Creek; and two armed veffels, mounted with 24 pounders, made their way through a narrow channel on the weftern fide, in order to enfilade the principal works. The fire from the fhips was terrible, and returned during the whole day with equal vivacity. Towards the evening the fire of the fort began to abate, and at length was totally filenced. The enemy perceiving that meafures were taking for forcing their works on the following morning, fet fire to every thing that could be deftroyed, and efcaped under fa-

A. D.
777.
vour of the night. The forts on the main land did not afterwards make much refiftance, and, as well as that on the ifland,
afforded a confiderable quantity of artillery and military ftores
to the victors.

The American fhipping having now loft all protection on
either fide of the river, feveral of their gallies, and other armed
veffels, took the advantage of a favourable night to pafs the
batteries of Philadelphia, and fly to places of fecurity farther up
the river. This was no fooner difcovered than the Delaware
frigate, now lying at Philadelphia, was manned and fent in purfuit of them; and other meafures were taken which rendered
their efcape impoffible. Thus environed, the crews abandoned
and fet fire to their veffels, which were all confumed to the
number of feventeen, including the two floating batteries and
fire-fhips: with all thefe advantages, the advanced feafon of the
year and other impediments rendered the clearing of the river
in any confiderable degree impracticable; fo that the making
fuch a channel as afforded a paffage for tranfports and veffels of
eafy burden, with provifions and neceffaries for the army, was
all that could be effected by the fleet; while the whole fuccefs
of the army amounted only to their fecuring good winter quarters at Philadelphia.

If the confequences of victory were little calculated to remove the uneafinefs which began to be felt in England, as to
the nature and refult of the American war, the effects of defeat
in the army of the north, intended to co-operate with the grand
expedition, occafioned the moft gloomy apprehenfions. It had
been refolved in the cabinet, where all the future operations of
the campaign had been fettled with a painful and minute accuracy, that, while General Howe made a fevere impreffion on the
heart of America, the extremities fhould alfo feel the cruel effects of hoftility. General Carleton, who had fucceeded fo
well in this attempt in the former campaign, and to whofe unremitting activity, directed by experienced wifdom, the nation
are indebted for the prefervation of Canada, was fuperfeded in
the command, which was beftowed by government on General
Burgoyne. With an army of above feven thoufand regular
troops, provided in a manner the moft complete, and furnifhed
with

with the fineſt train of artillery ever ſeen in the new world, A. D.
that general proceeded to Canada, when, being joined by the 1777.
provincial militia of the country, he took meaſures according to
his inſtructions for being reinforced by a powerful band of ſavages. About the middle of June he met the Indians in Congreſs on the banks of Lake Champlain, where he ſaid every
thing that appeared moſt effectual for raiſing the valour, and
bridling the ferocity of our new allies. Soon after he publiſhed
a manifeſto to the inhabitants of the northern provinces, ſetting
forth the magnitude of his preparations, and denouncing againſt
the rebellious all the calamities and outrages of war, arrayed in
the moſt terrific forms. Encouragement and employment were
aſſured to thoſe who, with a diſpoſition and ability ſuited to the
purpoſe, ſhould cheerfully aſſiſt in redeeming their country
from ſlavery, and in re-eſtabliſhing legal government. Protection and ſecurity, clogged with conditions, reſtricted by our
circumſtances, and rather obſcurely and imperfectly expreſſed,
were held out to the peaceable and induſtrious, who continued
in their habitations.

After theſe previous ſteps, which the general judged neceſſary, it was intended, that the army, in concert with the naval
force on the lakes, ſhould proceed to the ſiege of Ticonderago,
and, after ſecuring that important fortreſs, advance ſouthward
on the frontiers of the provinces, where they would at length
join the force conducted by Sir Henry Clinton, and Commodore Hotham, which, advancing northward from New York,
deſtroyed the works, towns, and country of the enemy on both
ſides of the river. At firſt every thing ſucceeded with General
Burgoyne that could gratify the moſt ſanguine hopes of thoſe
who employed him. Ticonderago was taken, the remainder of
the rebel ſquadron on Lake George was purſued and defeated,
and the enemy every where fled before the victorious troops,
whom they had neither ſtrength nor ſpirit to withſtand. The
firſt impreſſions of deſpair produced on the minds of the rebels
had time to wear off by the delays of the march, in a country
ſo impracticable, that in ſome places it was hardly poſſible to
advance a mile in a day. The New-England governments, the
moſt immediately threatened, had time to recollect themſelves,

and

A. D. and to take every meafure that feemed moft neceffary for their
1777. defence. Arnold, who alternately acted the part of a general
and commodore, with equal fkill and bravery, was fent to reinforce the declining courage of the American troops, and carried with him a confiderable train of artillery. The terror excited by the favages, who were guilty of various enormities too
fhocking to be defcribed, produced at length an effect directly
contrary to what had been expected. The inhabitants of the
open and frontier country were obliged to take up arms to defend themfelves againft this barbarous race; and, when the regular army of the Provincials feemed to be nearly wafted, a new
one and more formidable was poured forth from the woods,
mountains, and marfhes, which in this part are thickly fown
with plantations and villages. General Gates, an officer of
tried ardour, and of a regular military education, took the command of this force, in which he co-operated with Arnold with
the moft fingular unanimity. The confequence is well known,
and will be long remembered. Burgoyne had gone too far to
retreat to Canada, nor could he proceed to Albany, without
forcing his way through the rebel army. After a number of
fkirmifhes, marches, and two bloody engagements, he entered
into the convention of Saratoga the 17th October, by which
the Britifh troops laid down their arms, and engaged never to
affift more in attempting to fubdue America.

During the operation of the caufes which led to this humiliating tranfaction, Sir Henry Clinton conducted his expedition
up the North River with uncommon fuccefs. Having embarked 3000 men for that expedition, accompanied by a fuitable
naval force, confifting of frigates, armed gallies, and fmaller
veffels, he attacked the forts of Montgomery and Clinton.
Several neceffary motions being made to mafk the real defign,
the troops were landed in two feparate divifions, at fuch a diftance as occafioned a confiderable and difficult march through
the mountains, which was conducted fo fkilfully, that they arrived at the forts, and began their refpective attacks at the fame
moment of time. The furprife and terror of the garrifon was
increafed by the appearance of the fhips of war, and the arrival
and near fire of the gallies, which approached fo clofe as to
                                                  ftrike

strike the walls with their oars. Both forts were carried by storm, and the flaughter of the enemy, occafioned by the obstinacy of their refiftance, was very confiderable. Thofe who efcaped fet fire to two fire-frigates and feveral other veffels, which, with their artillery and ftores, were confumed or funk. Another fort called Conftitution was in a day or two after, upon the approach of the combined naval and land forces, fet on fire and abandoned. The artillery taken in all the three amounted to 67 pieces of different fizes. A few days afterwards Continental Village, containing barracks for 1500 men, and confiderable ftores, was deftroyed. A large boom or chain, the expence of which was eftimated at L. 70,000, and which was confidered as an extraordinary proof of American induftry and fkill, was funk or carried away: and the whole lofs was the greateft which the enemy had hitherto fuftained. The navy continued to purfue the advantage. Sir James Wallace, with a flying fquadron of light frigates, and General Vaughan, with a confiderable detachment of troops, made various excurfions up the river, carrying terror and deftruction wherever they went. At the very time that General Burgoyne was negotiating conditions for his ruined army, the thriving town of Efopus, at no very great diftance, was reduced to afhes, and not a houfe left ftanding. The troops and veffels did not retire to New York until they had difmantled the forts, and left the river totally defencelefs. Thus it muft be confeffed that, amidft all our misfortunes, the navy carried on every operation in which they were concerned with their wonted fpirit and fuccefs.

When news of the various events which had marked and chequered this important year of the American war were brought to England, the nation were agitated by a tumult of paffions which it is not eafy to defcribe or analyfe. The boafted preparations which were to bring America at our feet, and which feemed capable, inftead of fubduing the rebels by open force, to look them into unconditional fubmiffion, produced none of the great effects which had been fo firmly expected. The armament conducted by the Howes had not been able to gain any decifive advantage over the force of the Provincials; the northern army, whether through the incapacity of the minifter,

A. D. nifter, or the rafhnefs of the general, had been delivered up or
1777. rather abandoned a miferable prey into the hands of our enemies.   Great part of the fhipping of the Americans had, indeed, been deftroyed; fome of their towns were in our poffeffion; their country had felt the calamities of war; their works
of defence, raifed with great art and induftry, had been weakened or demolifhed; but the fpirit of the people was ftill un-
fubdued, and their unremitting activity in a caufe which they
adored, animated by the firft gleams of fuccefs, would naturally
prompt them to more vigorous and daring efforts than they had
yet exerted.

Notwithftanding thefe fatal appearances, the Englifh miniftry
were fo entwined in the American war, that it was impoffible
for them conveniently to be difengaged from it: their meafures,
it feemed, could only be juftified by fuccefs, which, had it depended on the liberality of the fupplies, muft doubtlefs have been
obtained.   On the 27th of November, 1777, 60,000 feamen,
with 11,000 marines, were voted for the fervice of the enfuing
year.   The maintaining of thofe, with the building and repairing of fhips, the ordinary of the navy and half-pay, and the
difcharge of a million of debt, made the whole expence of the
fleet, for the year 1778, amount to above five millions fterling.
Yet this immenfe fum exceeded only by about half a million
the expence of the land forces; for, befides the national
troops, we had taken into pay about 25,000 Heffians, Hanove-
rians, Brunfwickers, and other Germans: and many corpora-
tions, as well as individuals, fubfcribed largely for raifing new
regiments to reinforce the ftanding military ftrength of the
country.   This meafure which, in any other war, would have
been univerfally approved as a mark of the higheft public fpirit,
was loudly condemned by oppofition, as furnifhing troops to
the king without confent of parliament; and the effect, produced on the public by the factious clamours againft the new levies, clearly fhowed the prevailing indifference, or rather difinclination to the continuance of a war, in which we had hitherto
met with little elfe but difappointments and difgrace.

Meanwhile the news of the defeat and furrender of General
Burgoyne's army were received in France the beginning of December,

cember, and began totally to change the views and behaviour of that court with regard to the Americans. The agents whom the Congress kept at Paris had hitherto been coolly received by the French ministry, though idolized by the levity or interestedness of the nation; but upon so favourable a turn in the affairs of their constituents, they renewed with more success their proposals for negociating a treaty, while the French king received the compliments of his nobility on the misfortune of the British troops, with as much complacence as if his own had obtained a signal victory. In consequence of these circumstances, so advantageous to the credit of the Americans, Monsieur Girard, royal syndic of Strasbourg, and secretary of his most Christian majesty's council of state, waited on the American agents by order of his majesty the 16th of December, and acquainted them, that, after long and full consideration of their affairs and propositions in council, his majesty was determined to acknowledge the independence of the Americans, and to make a treaty with them of amity and commerce. That in this treaty no advantage should be taken of their present situation to obtain terms which otherwise could not be convenient for them to agree to, his majesty desiring that the treaty once made should be durable, which could not be expected unless each nation found its interest in the continuance as well as in the commencement of it. It was therefore his intention to enter into such an agreement with them as they could not but approve, had their state been long established, and attained the fulness of strength and power. That his majesty was determined not only to acknowledge, but support their independence, even at the risque of a war; and, notwithstanding the expence and danger attending this measure, he expected no compensation on that account, as he pretended not to act wholly for their sakes, since, besides his real good-will to them and their cause, it was manifestly the interest of France that the power of England should be diminished, by separating America from it for ever. The only condition which he required, therefore, on the part of the Americans was, " That in no peace to be made with England " they should give up their independence, and return to the " obedience of that government." Upon this foundation the

treaty

A. D. treaty was drawn up and figned, and foon after difpatched
1778. receive the ratification of Congrefs.

It appears not from any thing laid before the public, that th
Britifh miniftry were officially informed of this important tranfaction. Above two months afterwards the firft lord of the
treafury, and the minifter for the fouthern department, declared they knew nothing for certain concerning any treaty between France and America. If this was really the cafe, the ambaffador at Paris fcarcely deferved thofe honourable and lucrative marks of royal approbation, which have been fince fo liberally beftowed on him; but if the fact is otherwife, and if we
may give entire credit to the defence of that nobleman when
called to account in the houfe of peers, it will be difficult to fave
the honour of minifters, whofe character and veracity is of lefs
importance to the public, than the humiliating and difgraceful
condition in which this once great and refpectable nation muft
appear in the eyes of Europe. In former times we fhould, inftead of diffembling the treaty, have demanded a full communication of all its contents; but, to ufe the words of an ingenious author, " when people are dejected by frequent loffes,
" torn by inteftine factions, or any other way internally di-
" ftreffed, their deliberations are confufed, their refolutions
" flow, and an apparent languor is vifible, when they attempt
" to carry their refolutions into execution."

However this queftion may be decided between the miniftry
at home, and their ambaffador at Paris, (for the tamenefs of
the public has not yet brought this affair to a full explanation),
it was generally believed that adminiftration knew of the propofed treaty between France and America, and that the plan of
conciliation propofed by Lord North the 17th of February,
was intended to counterwork the negotiations of our rivals.
The propofition of his lordfhip was for two acts of parliament:
the firft, a bill for enabling his majefty to appoint commiffioners
to treat, confent, and agree on the means of quieting the diforders
now fubfifting in certain of the colonies. The fecond, a bill
declaring the intention of parliament concerning the exercife of
the right of impofing taxes on the provinces of North America.
Both bills were paffed; and, notwithftanding the nice diftinctions

2                                                    which

Which are made in his lordship's speech, it appeared to common
underftandings that we gave up, by the latter bill, not only the
power of taxing America, but all that national pre-eminence
and fupremacy which had been fo pompoufly defcribed. We
thus renounced the original ground of the quarrel, and more
than America ever defired us to renounce; but fince the declaration of independency, and the conclufion of the treaty with
France, it was little to be doubted that our prefent conceffions
would be attended with no better fuccefs than our former pretenfions. In fact, the moderation of government, the unfea-
fonablenefs of which prevented its having any effect on the refolutions of the rebels, ferved only to damp the fpirits of thofe
who had entered moft heartily into all the meafures of government and coercion; and had not France, by throwing afide the
veil through which our minifters were ftill fond to view her,
rouzed the indignation and refentment of the Britifh nation,
the military ardour which had been fo happily excited would
have begun to fubfide, and the people would have again fallen
back into a lethargic languor and inactivity. But, on the 13th
of March, the marquis of Noailles, ambaffador from France,
delivered the following declaration, by order of his court, to
Lord Vifcount Weymouth; " That the United States of
America, who are in full poffeffion of independence, as pronounced by them on the 4th of July, 1776, having propofed
to the king to confolidate, by a formal convention, the connection begun to be eftablifhed between the nations, the refpective plenipotentiaries have figned a treaty of friendfhip and
commerce, defigned to ferve as a foundation for their mutual
good correfpondence. His majefty being determined to cultivate the good underftanding fubfifting between France and
Great Britain, by every means compatible with his dignity, and
the good of his fubjects, thinks it neceffary to make this proceeding known to the court of London, and to declare at the
fame time, that the contracting parties have paid great attention
not to ftipulate any exclufive advantages in favour of the French
nation; and that the United States have referved the liberty of
treating with every nation whatever, upon the fame footing of
equality. In making this communication, his moft Chriftian
majefty obferves, that the Britifh miniftry will find new proofs

VOL. IV.                           3 F                                    of

of his conftant and fincere difpofition for peace, and he therefore hopes they will take effectual meafures to prevent the commerce between France and America from being interrupted,
and to caufe all the ufages received between commercial nations
to be in this refpect obferved. In this juft confidence he thinks
it fuperfluous to acquaint them, that he has taken eventual
meafures, in concert with the United States of America, to
maintain the dignity of his flag, and effectually to protect the
lawful commerce of his fubjects." This declaration was immediately laid before the houfe of lords, with a meffage from the
king, fetting forth the perfidy of France, and contrafting it
with his own fteady adherence to the faith of treaties. The
meffage was anfwered by both lords and commons in a high
ftrain of indignation and refentment againft the reftlefs ambition of the French court. The Britifh ambaffador at Paris
was recalled, and the Marquis of Noailles left London. The
immediate confequences of thefe fteps were an embargo laid on
the fhipping in the French and Englifh ports ; the warmeft im-
prefs almoft ever known ; and the embodying and calling forth
the militia to the number of thirty thoufand men.

A war with France can never be unpopular in this country ;
and by bringing matters to fuch a point that the French appeared evidently to be the aggreffors, and wantonly to provoke
the hoftility of Great Britain, the miniftry, had this been their
own work, would have poffeffed the merit of ufing the fureft
means of rouzing the latent refentment and inherent antipathy
of the Englifh againft their natural enemies. The great body of
the people talked of nothing but violation of treaties, treachery,
war and vengeance. The new levies were carried on with redoubled vigour, efpecially in Scotland. A majority of both
houfes re-echoed the fentiments and language of the vulgar.
A few only ventured to think that France had done nothing inconfiftent with the univerfal practice of nations, and muft have
been deaf to every call of intereft, if fhe had not availed herfelf of the misfortunes or mifconduct of Great Britain to ag-
grandize her own power. Upon the fame principle that Queen
Elifabeth affifted with her troops and treafure the United States
of the Netherlands to throw off the yoke of a monarch then
formidable

formidable to all Europe, the French could not fail, in a more A. D
enlightened age, greedily to seize the occasion of supporting the 1778
independence of British America. If ever the French gave us
fair play, it was surely on the present occasion; they allowed us
to negotiate and to fight; to hesitate between war and peace,
and to throw away many precious years in armed truce and pacific hostility; and it astonished all Europe, not that they inter-
posed at length, but that they did not interpose sooner. Besides, as they had long assisted the Americans in an underhand
manner, the open avowal of this assistance was the greatest advantage that, in our present circumstances, we could possibly obtain.
It revived the decaying ardour of the nation, united every well-
wisher to his country in a common cause, and called forth the
most vigorous efforts, both public and private, that the hopes
of plunder, interest, resentment, and a sense of national honour
could inspire.

The effects of this spirit in augmenting our armaments by sea
and land were soon visible. If we may credit the words of those
who presided over the navy, in a short time we had, besides a
vast number of armed vessels and privateers, 228 ships of the
line, frigates and sloops in commission *. Of these, 50 ships of
the line were employed for the protection of Great Britain; the
whole number of vessels on the coast of America amounted (it
was said by men in office) to 130; Admiral Barrington was stationed at the Leeward Islands; Sir Peter Parker at Jamaica; the
men of war appointed to attend the Senegal fleet, were ordered
to remain on that coast for the protection of trade; and Admiral

* LIST of the SHIPS in commission.

| 1 ship of | 110 guns, | | 6 frigates of | 44 guns, |
|---|---|---|---|---|
| 10 — of | 90 — | | 3 —— of | 36 — |
| 2 — of | 80 — | | 28 —— of | 32 — |
| 32 — of | 74 — | | 25 —— of | 28 — |
| 1 — of | 70 — | | 26 —— of | 20 or 24 — |
| 22 — of | 64 — | | | |
| 4 — of | 60 — | | 88 frigates—55 sloops. | |
| 13 — of | 50 — | | | |
| | | | 85 ships of the line; | |
| 85 ships of the line. | | | 88 frigates; | |
| | | | 55 sloops; | |
| | | | 228 total. | |

3 F 2                                                Duff's

A. D. Duff's squadron in the Mediterranean was reinforced with several
1778. capital ships. Nor were the French flow in their preparations.
They had assembled a powerful squadron at Brest, and another at
Toulon; and their troops crowded the sea-ports, and covered
the northern parts of the kingdom *.

While these preparations were going forward in Europe, nothing decisive had happened in America. The king's army had
remained quiet in their winter quarters tolerably well supplied
with provisions; and General Washington's troops continued
hutted at Valley Forge, where it is said they suffered intolerable hardships. The greater part of the fleet remained at
Rhode Island, from which detachments were sent to cruise before the principal sea-ports of the continent, where, as well as
in the West Indies, they were successful in making a great number of captures. As the spring approached, and the navigation
of the Delaware became practicable, General Howe sent various
detachments to range the country round Philadelphia, in order
to open the communication for bringing in provisions and to
collect forage for the army. All these expeditions were successful; and on the 7th May Major Maitland was detached with the
second battalion of light infantry in flat-boats, protected by three
gallies and other armed vessels commanded by Captain Henry of
the navy, to destroy the American ships lying in the river between Philadelphia and Trenton; which was effected with great
success †. On the 25th of the same month was carried on a similar expedition from Rhode Island under the command of Lieutenant-colonel Campbell and Captain Clayton of the navy. They
destroyed 125 boats, collected by the rebels in Hickamanet river, together with a galley under repair, destined for an invasion of that island. Another detachment from the men of war
destroyed the rebel vessels in Warren Creek; and a third burnt
the saw-mills on a creek near Taunton river, employed in pre-

---

* Appendix. No XVII. List of French fleets.
† List of American ships burnt on the 8th and 9th of May.
    2 frigates, one for 32, the other for 28 guns;
    9 large ships;
    3 privateer sloops for 16 guns each;
    3 ditto for ten guns each;
    23 brigs, with a number of sloops and schooners.

paring materials to build boats and other fuitable craft for the purpofe of the before-mentioned invafion.

Thefe operations of the *petite guerre* clofed the military career of General Sir William Howe, who refigned the command to Sir Henry Clinton, and returned to England. The firft operation of the new commander was to evacuate Philadelphia, purfuant to the inftructions which he had received from the minifter. This meafure, though attended with great danger on account of the neighbourhood of Wafhington's army of 20,000 men, and though accompanied with a certain degree of difgrace necef-farily attached to the abandoning of a town, the poffeffion of which had been acquired at fuch an expence of blood and trea-fure, was yet deemed neceffary to enable his majefty's forces to refift the united efforts of the Americans and their new and powerful allies. On the 18th of June the army began their march, and proceeded to Gloucefter Point, and from thence croffed the Delaware in fafety through the excellent difpofition made by the admiral to fecure their paffage. They continued their march towards New York till the 28th, without any inter-ruption from the enemy, excepting what was occafioned by their having deftroyed every bridge on the road. Then the rebels began to approach nearer the royal army, not in order to rifk a general engagement, but to harafs their march, and if poffible to feize their baggage, which, as the country admitted of but one route, confifted of a train extending near twelve miles. The judicious difpofitions made by General Clinton, and the bravery of his troops, compelled the affailants to retire on every fide. The army marched without farther oppofition to Navefink, where they waited two days, in hopes that General Wafhington might be induced to take poft near Middletown, where he might have been attacked to advantage. But as he ftill declined affording an opportunity of coming to a general action, prepa-rations were made for paffing to Sandy-Hook Ifland by a bridge of flat boats, which by the extraordinary efforts of the navy was foon completed, and over which the whole army paffed in about two hours time on the 5th of July, the horfes and cattle having been previoufly tranfported. They were afterwards car-ried up to New York; while the fleet, the proceedings of which had

had been regulated by the motions of the army, anchored off Staten Ifland. This ftation was lefs difadvantageous than that of the Delaware, in cafe the French fleet at Toulon fhould efcape to America. This unfortunately had happened ; M. D'Eftaing having failed from Toulon the 13th of April with twelve fhips of the line befides frigates and ftore-fhips. The fact was known to the miniftry the 27th of the fame month ; but no effectual meafure had been taken in confequence of it. It was feveral days even before a council was called to take this important matter into confideration. The fucceeding month was fpent in naval reviews, and in parliamentary debates, in the courfe of which the minifters acknowledged that it was judged improper to detach any part of our fleet, until the internal fafety of Great Britain was fufficiently provided for. Meanwhile D'Eftaing's fquadron rode miftrefs of the fea, and purfuing their courfe to America, arrived on the coaft of Virginia the 5th of July. On the 8th they anchored at the entrance of the Delaware, and on the 11th arrived on the northern fhore of New Jerfey.

Lord Howe made no delay in taking the neceffary meafures to oppofe their attempts, until the expected reinforcement under the command of Admiral Byron fhould arrive from England. But nothing could be more blameable than the late departure, or more unfortunate than the tedious voyage of that admiral. He failed the 5th of June, and worked out of the channel againft a frefh wind at fouth-weft. Nothing very material happened till the 3d of July, when the fquadron was feparated in 49 degrees 4 minutes north latitude, and 26 degrees 48 minutes weft longitude from the Lizard, in a moft violent gale at north, accompanied with heavy rains. At eight o'clock next evening the ftorm abated, and of a fquadron of 14 veffels fhewed only the Princefs Royal, Invincible, Culloden, and Guadaloupe. On the 6th the Culloden was ordered to look out to the north-eaft quarter, and the Guadaloupe to the fouth-weft. The Guadaloupe joined again the next afternoon, and kept company till the 21ft, when fhe and the Invincible feparated in a thick fog on the banks of Newfoundland. On the 5th of Auguft the admiral fell in with the Culloden, after being feparated a month,

but

but she parted company again in the night of the 11th. The Princess Royal being thus left by herself, the admiral continued his best endeavours to get 'to Sandy Hook, but the prevailing wind being from the south-west to west, he made very slow progress.  On the 18th of August the crew of the Princess Royal perceived 12 sail of ships at anchor to leeward, distant about eight miles.  These were soon discovered to be part of D'Estaing's squadron, and, as the admiral could neither get into the road of Sandy Hook nor of New York, without passing through the midst of the enemy, he bore away for Halifax, where he arrived the 26th of August, and found the Culloden, which had reached that port before him.  The rest of the squadron afterwards dropped in gradually there, or into the harbour of New York, their crews very sickly, and their furniture much impaired.

Meanwhile D'Estaing's squadron had, on the afternoon of the 12th of July, come to anchor off Shrewsbury Inlet, about four miles from Sandy Hook.  They consisted of 12 sail of two-decked ships, and 3 frigates.  One of the large ships had 90 guns, one 80, six were of 74, three of 64, one of 50; the least of the frigates mounted 36 guns; and their complement in men was above 11,000.  To oppose this formidable squadron Lord Howe had only six sail of 64 gun ships, three of 50, two of 40*, with some frigates and sloops, for the most part poorly manned.  In this great disparity of force the spirit of British seamen blazed forth with more than its usual lustre.  A thousand volunteers from the transports presented themselves to man the fleet.  Such was their ardour, that many who had been detained as necessary for the watch in their respective ships,

* List of Lord Howe's fleet.

| Eagle, | of 64 guns, | Vice-admiral Howe, Captains Duncan and Curtis; |
|---|---|---|
| Trident, | 64 —— | Commodore Elliot, Captain Molloy; |
| Nonsuch, | 64 —— | Captain Griffiths; |
| St. Albans, | 64 —— | Fitzherbert; |
| Somerset, | 64 —— | Ourry; |
| Ardent, | 64 —— | Keppel; |
| Experiment, | 50 —— | Sir James Wallace; |
| Isis, | 50 —— | Raynor; |
| Preston, | 50 —— | Commodore Hotham; |
| Phoenix, | 40 —— | Captain Parker; |
| Roebuck, | 40 —— | Hammond. |

were

A. D. were found concealed in the boats which carried their more
1778. fortunate companions on board the feveral men of war. The
army were equally forward and impatient to fignalize their zeal
in a line of fervice, which, independent of the fpirit that animated them, would have been extremely difagreeable to men
unaccuftomed to a fea life. Though fcarcely recruited from
the fatigues of a long, toilfome, and dangerous march, they
were eager to caft lots to decide which fhould be appointed to
embark as marines. The mafters and mates of the merchantmen fhewed equal alacrity, feveral taking their ftations at the
guns with the common failors, others putting to fea in their
fmall fwift-failing fhallops, to alarm fuch fhips as might be
bound for the port, and to look out for the long-expected arrival of Byron's reinforcement. One of the name of Duncan,
with a fpirit of difinterefted patriotifm, that would have done
honour to the firft names of Greece or Rome in the moft brilliant period of thofe celebrated republics, wrote for leave to
convert his veffel, the whole hopes of his fortune, into a fire-
fhip, to be conducted by himfelf; rejecting all idea of any other
recompence than the honour of facrificing his life, fervices, and
expectations, to an ardent love of his country.

Lord Howe, encouraged by the noble enthufiafm of every
one who bore the name of Britain, and which could never have
been executed under a commander who was not univerfally beloved and refpected, loft not a moment in forming the difpofition of his fleet, with determined purpofe to refift the moft vigorous exertions of the enemy. While the French admiral
was employed in founding the bar, his lordfhip placed his fhips
in the ftrongeft fituation the channel within the Hook would
admit. He founded its feveral depths in perfon; he afcertained
the different fetting of the currents, communicated his difcoveries to the officers of the moft experience, and, after hearing
their feveral opinions, formed fuch plans of arrangement as
feemed beft adapted to counteract the enemy's defigns. He
lengthened his line, which was already formed of the Ifis,
Eagle, Somerfet, Trident, Nonfuch, and Ardent, by adding the
Leviathan ftorefhip, manned by volunteers for the occafion,
and fupplied with cannon from the train. One battery of two
howitzers, and another of three eighteen pounders, were erect-

I                ed

ed on the point, round which the enemy muft have paffed, to A. D
enter the channel.                                                1778

During thefe vigorous preparations the admiral had the
daily mortification to fee feveral of the Englifh traders fall into
the hands of the French. The Stanly armed brig, with five
prizes, unfortunately anchored in the middle of their fleet, the
darknefs of the night concealing their enfigns, and was boarded
before fhe difcovered her miftake. If fome traders and advice-
boats had not efcaped over the flats, the Hope, with a convoy
from Halifax, would likewife have been taken, and added to
the general lofs and indignation.

The French fquadron had maintained a conftant intercourfe
with the fhore by means of boats and fmall veffels; which was
obferved to ceafe on the 21ft of July. On the day following
they appeared under way. The wind was favourable for crof-
fing the bar, the fpring tides were at the higheft, and every circumftance concurred for attacking the Britifh fleet to the greateft advantage. The admiral, therefore, had reafon to expect one
of the hotteft actions ever fought between the two nations.
Had the Englifh men of war been defeated, the tranfports and
victuallers muft have been an eafy acquifition; and the army, of
courfe, compelled to furrender on any terms the enemy might
impofe. But D'Eftaing feems not to have poffeffed fufficient
courage to contend for fo great a ftake; and at three o'clock in
the afternoon he bore off to the fouthward, to the great mortification of our gallant feamen, who, confident of victory, only
longed for a battle.

Inftructions were immediately difpatched to the advice-boats
ftationed without on the flats, to follow and obferve the motions
of the French fleet. It was generally fuppofed that the enemy's defign was to force the port of New York, and that their
bearing to the fouthward was owing to the circumftances of
the weather. But advice was received, that they were feen on
the morning of the 23d, in the latitude of the Delaware. Soon
after this intelligence, the Englifh fleet received an unexpected
acceffion of force by the arrival of the Renown from the Weft
Indies; and fo extremely inferior were they in every refpect to
the enemy, that the addition of a fingle fifty gun fhip was a

A. D. matter of general exultation.  Such was the mortifying debility
1778 of the Britifh fleet, while the firft lord of the admiralty
triumphed in parliament in the fuperiority of Lord Howe's fquadron over that of M. D'Eftaing.

The Difpatch arrived from Halifax the 26th of July, which
brought no intelligence of Byron, but informed the admiral,
that the Raifonable and Centurion were both on their way to
New York.  Thefe, as well as the Cornwall, formed a moft
feafonable reinforcement.

It was now known for certain, that the French fleet had failed for Rhode Ifland.  On the 29th they had been feen off
Newport harbour;  the fame day two of their frigates had entered the Secconnet paffage;  next morning two line-of-battle
fhips had run up the Naraganfet paffage;  and the remainder of
the fquadron were at anchor without Brenton's Lodge, about
five miles from the town.  In this divided ftate of the enemy,
Lord Howe, notwithftanding the great inferiority of his force
even after the reinforcement, determined to fave the Britifh
garrifon at Rhode Ifland.  Two additional fire-fhips were conftructed by his orders, and all his fquadron was ready for fea
by the firft of Auguft.  The weather prevented, however, his
arrival at Rhode Ifland till the evening of the 9th.  By this
time D'Eftaing had entered the harbour under an eafy fail, cannonading the town and batteries as he paffed.  His fituation,
therefore, was much ftronger than that on which the Englifh
had depended at Sandy Hook.  The rebels alfo were poffeffed
of the left-hand fhore, the whole length of the harbour, which
gave them an opportunity not only to annoy the Britifh fleet
from the heights of Conanicut, near to which it muft have approached, but, during the attack againft D'Eftaing, to bring all
their guns to bear upon the Englifh fhips from the northern extremity of that ifland.

Next morning the wind blew directly out of the harbour,
and in a fhort time the French fquadron appeared ftanding out
to fea with all their fails on board.  Lord Howe immediately
made the fignal to get under way, and endeavoured by feveral
mafterly manœuvres to throw the enemy to leeward.  The
weather-gage was a matter of the utmoft importance, as, unlefs

he

he could obtain that, the fire-ships, in which were placed the A. D greateſt hopes in contending with ſuch a ſuperior force, could 1778 not be brought into action; and the frigates which had charge of them would likewiſe have been prevented from engaging. But the attention of the French was as great to preſerve this advantage, as the ſolicitude of the Engliſh to acquire it. Night put an end to the manœuvres on both ſides, and next morning preſented the two fleets in the ſame ſituation with regard to the weather, but at ſomewhat greater diſtance. The wind ſtill being to the eaſtward, blowing freſh, and there appearing no proſpect of change, Lord Howe, therefore, ordered the frigates which had the charge of the fire-ſhips to be informed, that, ſhould the enemy continue to preſerve the weather-gage, he would wait their approach with the ſquadron formed in a line of battle a-head, from the wind to the ſtarboard. At the ſame time he took a ſtep upon which no officer could have ventured, whoſe character for perſonal bravery was leſs fully eſtabliſhed. It is well known that a commander in chief, ſtationed in the line, cannot, after the action is commenced, obſerve the general conduct of the battle. His ſervices are then of no more avail than thoſe of any other officer, equally brave and expert in the management of a ſingle ſhip. But, as Lord Howe had on this occaſion to engage under ſo many diſadvantages, it was neceſſary to ſeek reſource in his ſuperior ſkill and activity, to be ready to profit of every fortuitous occurrence, and to compenſate for the inferiority of his force by his addreſs in applying it. He therefore ſhifted his flag on board the Apollo frigate, leaving the Eagle in the centre, and moved to a convenient diſtance to take a view of the whole line. Having by this gained a nearer view of the French fleet, and obſerved that they had placed their ſtrongeſt ſhips in the van, he ſtrengthened the rear of the Britiſh to receive their attack. About four o'clock the French admiral altered his bearing, and new-formed his line to engage to leeward. Lord Howe croſſed through the interſtices of the Engliſh line with the frigates and fire-ſhips, and in a few minutes after made a ſignal for his ſhips to ſhorten ſail, and cloſe to the centre. The engagement ſeemed now to be decided on by the commanders of both ſquadrons; but in a

ſhort

A. D.
1778.
short time the French again altered their courfe, and bearing to the fouthward were fpeedily, from the ftate of the weather, entirely out of fight.

The wind blew fo hard that it was neceffary for the Britifh to lie to all night to prevent the feparation of their fleet. But the gale increafed to fuch violence, that, notwithftanding this pre-caution, the Blue divifion was totally feparated from the reft; the centre and van with moft of the frigates ftill keeping toge-ther. The Apollo, in which the admiral was embarked, having loft her foremaft in the night, he fhifted his flag next day on board the Phœnix, Captain Hammond, then in company with the Centurion, Ardent, Richmond, Vigilant and Roebuck. The whole fleet was greatly difabled by the ftorm, their fails fhattered, their mafts fprung, and the fire-fhips rendered by the wet totally unfit for fervice. But, though the elements warred againft them, they failed not to affail their enemies wherever the opportunity offered. On the evening of the 13th, Captain Dawfon, in the Renown of fifty guns, fell in with the Langue-doc, carrying M. D'Eftaing, totally difmafted. Having run clofe under her lee, he gave her all his upper-deck guns; then ftanding off to windward, opened his lower ports, and, at half a cable's length, poured in three broadfides. The darknefs ob-liged him to lie to for the night, in the refolution of renewing the attack next morning: but at the firft dawn fix French fhips hove in fight, three of which remained with the wreck, and the other three gave him chace. The fame evening Commodore Hotham would have taken the Tonant, had it not been for the intervention of other French fhips. A circumftance of another kind prevented the Cæfar, a 74 gun fhip, from becoming a prize to the Ifis, after an action as brilliant as any on record in the hi-ftory of the Englifh navy. Captain Rayner of the Ifis, difcover-ing the force of his opponent, at firft endeavoured to efcape her; but fhe proved to be the fafteft failer. In a fhort time they were clofe on board each other, and engaged for an hour and a half within piftol-fhot. Notwithftanding the extraordinary difpro-portion of force, the addrefs and intrepidity of the Englifh captain was fo happily feconded by the ardour of his officers and men, that the Frenchman was forced to put before the wind. The Ifis

was

was incapable of purfuing him, being fo much fhattered in her A. D
mafts and rigging. Mr. Bougainville, the French captain, loft 1778
his arm, the firft lieutenant his leg, and they acknowledged
feventy men killed and wounded : whereas the Ifis had but one
man killed, and fourteen wounded. After thefe honourable
but partial engagements, the Englifh fhips failed for the general rendezvous, which the admiral had appointed at the Hook,
where they found their conforts almoft as much fhattered by
the ftorm, as they had been by the ftorm and the French fleet
together.

During the time requifite for repairing the difabled fhips, the
Experiment, being fent to explore the ftate of affairs at Newport, brought intelligence, the 23d of Auguft, that D'Eftaing's
fquadron had again returned to Rhode Ifland. Lieutenant
Stanhope arrived next day, having with great gallantry paffed
through the body of the French fleet in a whale-boat, conveying more complete information of the fituation of the enemy.
He had left them at anchor at the harbour's mouth, which it
was not probable they had entered, as the wind had all along
continued at eaft. The rebels, to the number of twenty thoufand, had advanced within fifteen hundred yards of our works.
From them, however, Sir Robert Pigot, who commanded the
Englifh garrifon, apprehended little danger ; but fhould the
French fleet come in, the governor ordered his meffenger to
fay it would make an alarming change.

Lord Howe loft not a moment, upon this information, to fet
fail for the relief of the place. But he was met at fea by the
Galatea with difpatches from General Pigot, acquainting him
that D'Eftaing had failed from his anchorage, and fteered in a
courfe for Bofton. His lordfhip, therefore, detached the Nau-
tilus, Sphinx, and Vigilant to Rhode Ifland, and proceeded with
the remainder of his fquadron in queft of the enemy. As it was
not probable that the French would attempt to navigate their
large fhips in their difabled ftate through the fouth channel,
within George's Bank, his lordfhip was in hopes that, by following that courfe, he might intercept their paffage to Bofton
Bay. But on entering that bay the 30th, he found to his great
mortification that the enemy had anticipated his arrival. The

next

A. D. next day he endeavoured to take advantage of a leading wind to
1778. view their pofition, but was prevented by the St. Albans running on fhore near the point of Cape Cod. He effected his purpofe, however, on the 1ft of September, and judging that no
attempt could be made againft them in their prefent fituation
with the fmalleft profpect of fuccefs, he ftood off to fea, in order to difengage his fhips from the navigation of the coaft, which
was extremely dangerous, the wind blowing frefh from the eaft,
and the appearance of the weather in other refpects unfavourable. When he arrived at Newport, he found that the meafures
which he had taken, had been effectual in relieving that important garrifon ; the rebel General Sullivan, on the unexpected
retreat of D'Eftaing, having retired from before the place after
uttering many bitter reproaches againft the brittle faith of his
new allies. Lord Howe afterwards returned to Sandy Hook,
and his health being infirm, furrendered the powers with which
he was intrufted to Rear-admiral Gambier, and fet fail for England, where he arrived the 25th of October.

The naval operations in Europe, though far lefs complicated,
were not more decifive than in America. The French, as early
as the month of May, had in the road of Breft nineteen fhips of
74 guns, three of 80, and fourteen frigates, commanded by the
Count D'Orvilliers, lieutenant-general of the marine. The duke
of Chartres, eldeft fon of the firft prince of the blood, commanded an eighty-gun fhip, and gave the fplendour of his name
to this formidable equipment. The Britifh fleet *, deftined to
act againft the main force of the enemy, was committed to Admiral Keppel, who failed from St. Helen's the 8th of June,
with unlimited difcretionary powers. Nothing particular hap-

---

* It confifted of the following fhips: The Victory of 100 guns, Admiral Keppel ; the Queen of 90 guns, Vice-admiral Harland ; the Ocean of 90 guns, Vice-
admiral Pallifer ; the Sandwich of 90 guns ; the Prince George of 90 guns ; the
Foudroyant, Shrewfbury, Egmont, Valiant, Courageux, Ramillies, Hector, Monarque, Elifabeth, Berwick, and Cumberland, of 74 guns each : the America,
Exeter, Stirling Caftle, Robufte, and Bienfaifant, of 64 guns each ; Arethufa
frigate of 30 guns ; Fox and Proferpine frigates ; the Alert and Meredith armed
cutters, and the Vulcan fire fhip ; in all 27 fail ; which were afterwards joined by
fome others. ——See Appendix, Nᵒ XXI. for a complete lift of the Britifh and
French fleets.

pened

pened until the 17th, when the English fleet being in line of A. I
battle, 25 miles diftant from the Lizard, they perceived two 177
fhips and two tenders furveying the fleet, and watching its motions. The fituation of the admiral was fomewhat embarraffing;
for by commencing hoftilities without exprefs orders, the whole
blame of the war might be laid upon him; but confidering that
it was neceffary to ftop thefe frigates, as well to obtain intelligence, as to prevent its being communicated, he immediately
directed the whole fleet to chace; and between five and fix in
the evening the Milford had got clofe along-fide the leeward fhip, which proved to be a large French frigate called
the Licorne, of 32 guns and 230 men. Her commander could
not be perfuaded by civil words to bring his veffel to the
Englifh fleet, fo that it was neceffary to fire a gun, which
made him prepare to obey the Englifh officer's requeft. The
other French fhip was purfued by the Arethufa and Alert cutter, and, at fome diftance aftern, the Valiant and Monarque.
Meanwhile the French frigate which had been overtaken by the
Milford, and was now attended by the America, changed her
courfe, and went upon a different tack, with a view to efcape.
One of the Englifh fhips attending her, fired a fhot acrofs her,
which was immediately followed by the French frigate's difchar-
ging a whole broadfide into the America, at the very moment
Lord Longford was upon the gunwale talking to the French captain in the moft civil ftrain. The latter then ftruck his colours;
and though his conduct merited the fire of the America, Lord
Longford's magnanimity difdained to take vengeance on an enemy whom he had entirely in his power. On the 19th the Valiant and Monarque who had chaced the other French fhip, were
feen making for the fleet with a difabled fhip in tow, which was
foon perceived to be the Arethufa with her main maft gone, and
much fhattered in other refpects. The Arethufa had, on the
night of the 17th, come up with her chace, which proved to be
the Belle Poule, a large French frigate with heavy metal. The
French captain peremptorily refufed to bring to, which obliged
Captain Marfhall of the Arethufa to fire a fhot, which was immediately returned by a whole broadfide from the French frigate. This brought on an engagement which lafted upwards of
two hours. The action was contefted with equal obftinacy on
both

A. D.
1778.

both fides.  The French frigate was fuperior in weight of metal, and in the number of men; advantages which fhe ftood in
need of: at length the Arethufa, being much fhattered in her
mafts, fails, and rigging, and there being little wind to govern
her, fhe could not prevent the French fhip from getting into a
fmall bay, where boats at day-light came out and towed her into fafety.   The Arethufa had eight men killed, and thirty-fix
wounded.  The French acknowledge forty flain, and forty-feven
wounded, on board the Belle Poule.   Captain Fairfax of the
Alert cutter was more fortunate, having taken, after a gallant
engagement, a French fchooner of ten carriage-guns and ten
fwivels that attended the Belle Poule.   And on the 18th the
Foudroyant, Courageux, and Robufte, had chaced and taken
the Pallas, a French frigate of 32 guns and 220 men.

From papers found on board the Pallas and Licorne French
frigates, the admiral difcovered that the enemy's fleet in Breft
water confifted of thirty-two fail of the line, and about a dozen
frigates; whereas his own confifted only of twenty of the former, and three of the latter.   In this perplexing fituation he
confidered the probable confequences of rifquing an engagement againft fuch odds, alfo the critical and hazardous fituation
the nation might be reduced to in cafe of a defeat, as the dock-
yards and whole fhipping in the ports of the channel would, in
that cafe, be at the mercy of the enemy; therefore, though he
forefaw that to come home without orders might be fatal to his
own reputation, yet he refolved to rifque that for the fafety of
his country, and accordingly returned to Spithead the 27th
June for a reinforcement.

At this juncture two fleets from the Weft Indies, with fome
fhips from the Levant, arrived, which afforded a fupply of feamen; by this feafonable relief the admiral was enabled to
fail again on the 9th July, with twenty-four fhips of the line,
and was joined on his way down the channel by fix more.  The
French king in the mean time had iffued orders for reprifals on
the fhips of Great Britain, affigning the capture of the frigates,
and our engagement with the Belle Poule, as the oftenfible reafons: thus nothing of war was wanting between the two nations but the ceremony of a proclamation.   The French fleet,
confifting of thirty-two fhips of the line, and a number of fri-

2

gates,

gates, had failed from Breft the 8th July; they were divided A. D into three fquadrons, under Count D'Orvilliers, (commander 1778 in chief), Count Duchaffault, and the Duke de Chartres, a prince of the blood, affifted by three other admirals *. On their departure from Breft, the Lively frigate, which had been cruifing to watch their motions, was captured, being fo much entangled amongft them that fhe could not efcape.

The Britifh fleet † was alfo divided into three fquadrons, commanded by Admiral Keppel, the Vice-admirals Sir Robert Harland and Sir Hugh Pallifer: Rear-admiral Campbell, from friendfhip to Admiral Keppel, condefcended to act as firft captain on board the Victory. The two fleets came in fight of each other in the afternoon of the 23d July, in the Bay of Bifcay, about 35 leagues to the weftward of Breft. At firft the French admiral, from his movements, feemed defirous to bring on an engagement, probably fuppofing the Britifh fleet to be nearly of equal force with what it was about four weeks before; but on coming nearer he difcovered his miftake, and from that moment he evidently determined to avoid an action. This plan he adhered to for the three following days, notwithftanding every effort ufed by the Britifh admiral to bring him to action; which the latter ardently wifhed for, before the Eaft and Weft India fleets, which were expected about this time, fhould arrive, finding it would be difficult to protect them effectually, as the French fleet overfpread many leagues of the ocean. All the advantage he could obtain in four days was to feparate two of the enemy's line of battle fhips, which returned to Breft, and could not afterwards rejoin their fleet: this placed both fleets upon an equality as to line of battle fhips. On the 24th the Britifh admiral threw out the fignal to chace to windward, which was continued the two following days, keeping at the fame time his fhips as much connected as the nature of a purfuit would admit, in order to feize the firft opportunity of bringing the enemy to a clofe engagement; but this proved ineffectual, the French cautioufly avoiding coming to action, and in their manœuvres fhowing great addrefs and nautical

---

* For a lift of the French fleet fee Appendix, N° XXI.
† See Appendix, N° XXI. for a lift of the Britifh fleet.

knowledge.

A. D.
1778.
knowledge. About four o'clock in the morning of the 27th July, the French were difcovered to windward about five miles diftance. Admiral Keppel finding fome of his fleet too much fcattered, made fignals to collect them together, ftill continuing to follow the enemy. About ten o'clock a heavy dark fquall came on, which continued near an hour; when it cleared up, the two fleets, by a fhift of wind, had neared each other, but on different tacks. About half paft eleven the fignal was hove out for a general engagement, at which time the fhips as they came up began firing. The French attacked at fome diftance the headmoft of Sir Robert Harland's divifion, which led the van. Their fire was warmly returned by almoft every fhip in the fleet, as they ranged along the line; and notwithftanding it had been extended by the chace, they were foon engaged, as the two fleets paffed each other. The cannonade was very heavy, and did confiderable execution on both fides. The enemy, as ufual, fired chiefly at the rigging, which crippled many of the Britifh fhips, while Mr. Keppel continued the old way of fighting, by firing principally at the hulls of the enemy's fhips with good fuccefs.

The action, for the fhort fpace it lafted, (about three hours), was very warm. The lofs on the fide of the Britifh was 133 killed, and 373 wounded; among the latter were four officers, none of whom died. The French concealed their lofs as much as poffible; they acknowledged, however, 150 killed, and about 600 wounded. From the manner of engaging it is probable they loft more men than the Britifh, perhaps double the number.

After the different fhips had repaired their damages, the commander in chief, about three o'clock in the afternoon, made the fignal to form the line of battle a-head. The red divifion, commanded by Sir Robert Harland, immediately obeyed; but the blue divifion never came into the line during the reft of the day, Sir Hugh Pallifer alledging, that his fhip the Formidable was fo much difabled that he could not obey the fignal.

Admiral Keppel's letter to the Admiralty prior to the engagement mentioned his being for feveral days in chace of the enemy, from which the public expected that, if an action fhould
happen,

happen, it would prove a decisive one : but, on reading the
Gazette account of this affair when it was over, and finding the
enemy had escaped with their whole fleet, not a ship being captured or destroyed, they were greatly chagrined and disappointed.

Both sides claimed the victory * in this undecisive action.
The French soon after the engagement, drew up in a line of
battle to leeward, and continued during the afternoon in that
position, with an intention, they assert, to renew the engagement ; but it is more probable, with a view, to bring off their
crippled ships in the night, which must have been abandoned
if they had fled sooner.

The French Gazette relates, that the English stole away in
the night, without showing any lights ; and in the morning, the
French having no expectation of being able to renew the action, and finding themselves unexpectedly off Ushant, (the effects of the winds and currents), while they supposed themselves near thirty leagues from any land, they took that opportunity of putting into Brest, in order to land their wounded
men.

Although the English, had no great reason to boast of victory, yet the French account is totally false ; for it appeared
by the evidence of witnesses upon oath, (in the subsequent
trials of Keppel and Pallifer), that the French, on purpose to deceive, stationed soon after it was dark three of their best sailing ships in a line, at considerable distances from each other,
with lights, in order to have the appearance of their whole
fleet. This finesse had the intended effect; their fleet stole away
in the night, and the three ships followed them at day-light
in the morning.

The British fleet was nearly in a line of battle all night, (excepting the Formidable and some other ships of Sir Hugh Pallifer's division); both Admiral Keppel, and Sir Robert Harland,
had distinguishing lights out, and also a light at their bowsprit end.
Sir Hugh Pallifer, not being in his station, had no lights, neither
in that situation would it have been proper, as it might have
misled some of the ships of his own and other divisions. The

---

* See Admiral Keppel's letter to the admiralty, giving an account of the
action. Appendix, No. XX.

men

men were on deck all night in every ſhip of the fleet, quarter-
ed at their guns, ready to renew the action in the morning,
expecting the French were alſo inclined to fight; but in this
they found themſelves miſtaken, their whole fleet being out of
fight, excepting the three ſhips above mentioned, which were
alſo at too great a diſtance to be overtaken.

Whether the want of ſucceſs in this engagement was owing
to any miſconduct in the commander in chief, to a miſunderſtanding between him and Sir Hugh Palliſer, or to ſome other
cauſe *, is perhaps not eaſy to determine †: but whatever reafons may be aſſigned for this, it is evident that a fair opportunity was loſt of ſtriking a blow againſt the maritime power of
France, which might have been deciſive.

The commander diſcovering in the morning that the French
had eſcaped, that many ſhips of his own fleet had ſuffered
greatly in their maſts and rigging, and that there was not the
leaſt proſpect of overtaking the enemy before they could reach
Breſt, he had no alternative but to bring the fleet home to be
repaired.  He arrived off Plymouth on the 31ſt of July.

Admiral Keppel put to ſea again with the ſame number of
ſhips and commanders, on the 22d of Auguſt.  The French
had left Breſt ſome days before, but inſtead of looking out for
the Britiſh fleet, they bore away for Cape Finiſterre, leaving
their trade at the mercy of our fleet and privateers.  Many of
their merchantmen accordingly fell into the hands of the Engliſh.  The Britiſh admiral continued cruizing in the bay till
the 28th of October, when he returned to Portſmouth, and
the French got to Breſt a few days after.

The Commiſſioners appointed to ſettle matters amicably with
the Americans had ſo little effect in ſuſpending the military or
naval operations acroſs the Atlantic, that it was not neceſſary
to interrupt the thread of our narration by giving an account of
their proceedings.  But as the propoſals which they were em-

---

* Some experienced ſeamen, attribute the miſcarriage on the 17th of July, to
the Britiſh fleet keeping the old way of fighting, by firing chiefly at the hulls of
the enemy; whereas if they had fired at the rigging and maſts, ſome of them
muſt have been much crippled, which would have forced the French admiral,
either to have ſubmitted to a general engagement, or to have abandoned the lame
ſhips.

† A Short account of Admiral Keppel's trial is ſubjoined.

powered to make, altered entirely the object of the war, it is A. D necessary to explain the purport of their commission, the means 1778 used for giving it effect, and the sentiments with which it was received. They sailed the 21st of April in his majesty's ship the Trident, and their arrival in America was notified the 9th of June, in a letter from Sir Henry Clinton to General Washington, intimating, that the Earl of Carlisle, William Eden, and George Johnston, three of the commissioners for restoring peace between Great Britain and America, were then at Philadelphia, and requesting a passport for their secretary Dr. Ferguson, with a letter from them to Congress. General Washington declined granting this request until the pleasure of Congress should be known; but while that assembly were deliberating on the expediency of the measure referred to them, an express arrived from the general, carrying a letter from the commissioners addressed to his excellency Henry Laurens the president, and other members of the Congress. This letter, after much debate, was read. It contained the powers with which the commissioners were furnished to suspend hostilities, to remove grievances, and to grant the requests which the colonies had frequently made on the subject of acts of parliament passed since the year 1763, and to settle a plan of policy for the future government of America, which should obtain force, when ratified by the parliament of Great Britain; the whole strain of the letter is highly respectful. The commissioners declare, it is their inclination " to establish " the powers of the legislatures in each particular state of Ame- " rica, to settle its revenue, its civil and military establishment, " and to allow it the exercise of a perfect freedom of legisla- " tion and internal government." They also declare themselves ready " to concur in measures towards extending every freedom " to trade that the respective interests of Great Britain and " America can require; to agree that no military force shall be " kept up in the different states of North America without the " consent of the General Congress, or particular assemblies; " and to concur in measures calculated to discharge the debts " of America, and raise the value and credit of the paper cir- " culation." To these advantageous and condescending propo-

fals

A. D. fals the Congrefs anfwered in terms of great haughtinefs. The
1778. commiffioners proceeded on a fuppofition, that the Americans
were fubjects of Great Britain, an idea utterly inadmiffible.
The commiffioners mentioned the infidious interpofition of
France, an expreffion fo difrefpectful to his moft Chriftian majefty, the good and great ally of the United States, that nothing
but an earneft defire to fpare the farther effufion of blood could
have perfuaded Congrefs to allow the reading of a paper drawn
up with fuch bold indecency of language. They obferve, however, that " they will be contented to enter upon a confidera-
" tion of a treaty of peace and commerce with Great Britain,
" not inconfiftent with treaties already fubfifting, when his
" Britannic majefty fhall demonftrate a fincere difpofition for
" that purpofe. The only folid proof of this difpofition will be
" an explicit acknowledgment of the independence of thefe
" ftates, or the withdrawing of his fleets and armies." Such
were the fruits of a negotiation, propofed with much triumph
by minifters, and accepted with great unanimity by parliament.
By the fame fatal mifconduct, or the fame unexampled misfortune, which had marked every ftep of the proceedings of the
Britifh adminiftration with regard to the colonies, the army had
orders to evacuate Philadelphia at the time of the arrival of the
commiffioners. At the moment that we held out terms of peace,
we difcovered our inability to continue the war with effect.
Such a remarkable coincidence naturally damped the hopes of
our negotiators as well as of all thofe who were ftill attached
to the interefts of the mother country. The Englifh general
had expected to receive a powerful reinforcement of troops;
he received commiffioners who had powers to negotiate away
the principal objects for which he fought. The commiffioners
expected to add weight and perfuafion to their propofals by
being feconded by the active operations of the army. They
were obliged to retire with that army, which now abandoned
its conquefts, and, inftead of afpiring at advantage, difcovered
great merit in being able to make a retreat without fuftaining
any irreparable lofs.

Thus it happened by a fatality unknown in any other age or
country, that the propofals of the commiffioners damped the
fpirits

spirits and checked the ardour of the troops, while the conduct A. D of the troops, however neceſſary and proper in itſelf, weakened, 1778 diſgraced, and vilified the propoſals of the commiſſioners. After this inauſpicious beginning, it could ſcarcely be expected that any future meaſures ſhould be attended with better ſucceſs. The commiſſioners, however, continued in America four months, publiſhing proclamations of grace and pardon to thoſe who deſpiſed their power; offering friendſhip and union to thoſe who avowed that they were not only divided from us for ever, but leagued with our worſt enemies; and endeavouring to treat with aſſemblies, or correſpond with private perſons, all which endeavours were rejected with marks of ineffable contempt. At length, after being expoſed to ſuch indignities as we do not recollect that the miniſters of any independent nation ever ſubmitted to among a civilized people, and after condeſcending to ſuch degrading language of their conſtituents, as was never held by the repreſentatives of any kingdom upon earth *, they determined to return home; previous to which they publiſhed a manifeſto dated at New York the 3d of October, 1778. This contained a recapitulation of the advantages which they were empowered to confer, with an appeal from the reſolutions of the Congreſs to the inhabitants at large, and a denunciation of a more deſtructive war than had hitherto been carried on, ſince, if the Britiſh colonies were to become an acceſſion to France, prudence would dictate to Great Britain the neceſſity of rendering that acceſſion of as little avail as poſſible to her enemy. Soon after the publication of this paper, which was not more effectual than the reſt of their proceedings, they ſet ſail for England.

The military and naval operations, it has been obſerved, were little interrupted by this extraordinary negotiation. The advanced ſeaſon of the year, however, prevented thoſe active and powerful exertions which alone could produce any deciſive effect; the ſpirits and vigour of the troops and ſeamen ſeemed

* As an example take the following memorable words of one of the commiſſioners in a letter to the preſident of the Congreſs : " If you ſhould follow the example of Great Britain in the hour of her inſolence, and ſend us back without " a hearing. I ſhould hope from private friendſhip, that I may be permitted to " ſee the country, and the worthy characters ſhe has exhibited."

gradually

A. D. gradually to languish, and their operations naturally degenera-
1778. ted into the *petite guerre*.   In those partial hostilities the king's
troops were generally successful. They destroyed several magazines belonging to the enemy; laid waste the possessions of some
of the most obstinate of the rebels; and demolished, by the assistance of the ships, some villages which were built for the reception of prize goods, and the accommodation of the sailors
belonging to the American privateers.   But no general engagement took place, nor was any thing decisive performed by the
English or French squadrons, both of which suffered greater injury from the weather than from the assaults of the enemy.
The surrender of Dominica by the English was in some measure
compensated by the taking of the islands of St. Pierre and
Miquelon, which were the only settlements the French possessed
in the northern parts of America. Thus every thing seemed to
tend to an equality; and we had the mortification to mourn
over our loss in the course of the war, without any prospect of
being soon able to repair it.   We had already lost two ships of
the line, thirteen frigates, and seven sloops of war*.   The

* List of English men of war taken or destroyed in the present war.

| Ships. | guns. | |
|---|---|---|
| Augusta, | 64 | burnt in the Delaware; |
| Somerset, | 64 | lost on the coast of New England; |
| Repulse, | 32 | lost off Bermudas; |
| Orpheus, Flora, Juno, Lark, each of | 32 | sunk or burnt at Rhode Island; |
| Minerva, | 32 | taken by the French in the West Indies; |
| Acteon, | 28 | burnt at Sullivan's Island; |
| Fox, | 28 | taken by the French off Brest. This ship had before been taken by the Americans, and retaken by the Flora; |
| Lively, | 20 | taken by the French off Brest; |
| Cerberus, | 28 | burnt at Rhode Island; |
| Mermaid, | 28 | run ashore by the French off Cape Henlopen; |
| Active, | 28 | taken by the French in the West Indies; |
| Syren, | 28 | destroyed by the Americans; |
| Drake, | 18 | taken by an American privateer; |
| Falcon, King's Fisher, | 18 | sunk or burnt at Rhode Island; |
| Pomona, | 18 | lost in the West Indies; |
| Merlin, | 14 | burnt in the Delaware; |
| Senegal, Thunder Bom | 14 | taken by the French off Rhode Island. |

1                                    merchant

merchant ships taken by the American privateers, were near a thousand in number, and valued at nearly two millions sterling. We had not taken one capital ship from the French, nor, excepting the Pallas and Licorne frigates, any man of war worth mentioning. After the naval force of the Americans seemed to be totally destroyed, it arose more than once from its ruins, and harassed our trade as much as before. The value of American captures, however, made by English vessels, exceeded, by several hundred thousand pounds, the loss which the British merchants had sustained; and when we take into the account the captures from the French, particularly the Modeste and Carnatic Indiamen, each of which was worth near half a million, the balance will appear to be considerably in favour of Great Britain. But, in estimating national advantages, we must not compensate the loss of English merchants by the gains of English seamen. The latter, being chiefly the profit of a few individuals, is not to be put in competition with the benefit of the great body of merchants and manufacturers; nor does it even indemnify the public for the damage and diminution which the navy itself has suffered by the misfortunes of the sea, and sustained from the efforts of the enemy.

In taking a general retrospect of the conduct of the war, in as far as the navy is concerned, it appears that the commanders in chief, as well as the captains of particular vessels, have for the most part acted with their usual bravery and wisdom. Whatever aspersions may be thrown on those who superintend the management of our marine, no dishonour has been fixed on the British flag, nor has the ancient glory of our seamen been tarnished. Hitherto, indeed, their spirited ardour and intrepidity have not produced the effects that usually result from them. But we are not to account for this, by supposing any diminution of those eminent qualities for which they have been long distinguished. The inauspicious and fatal influence which prevails in a high department has continued to give us one proof after another, that no people can be great without being virtuous. The iniquities of the ministers have been visited on the nation———.

*Quidquid delirant reges, plectuntur Achivi.*

A. D.   But that very circumſtance which has hitherto occaſioned our
1778.  perplexity and diſtreſs, the unhappy ſuperintendence of our naval affairs, is what ought at preſent to afford us juſt grounds of
conſolation. If our boundleſs ſupplies and powerful armaments
had been managed and directed by the wiſdom and virtue of
miniſters, and if, notwithſtanding this moſt favourable circumſtance, the exertion of our forces by ſea and land had been unable to maintain with honour the cauſe in which we are engaged, we ſhould have juſt reaſon to deſpair; becauſe it is plain,
that in ſuch a caſe we could not expect, by any alteration of
management, to defeat the malignant purpoſes of our natural and
inveterate enemies. But if our fleets and armies were condemned to reluctant inactivity at the beginning of the war; if while
we had the Americans only to contend with, we took no reſolutions becoming the dignity of a great nation; if while our
enemies prepared for hoſtility, by augmenting their troops and
equipping their ſquadrons, our own were allowed to rot, languiſh, and moulder away in a ſtate the moſt deplorable; if after
the meſſage delivered by the French ambaſſador, which was in
effect a declaration of war, had rouzed the ſpirit of the nation,
our miniſters ſtill remained profoundly ſunk in lethargic ſecurity, totally incapable of thoſe vigorous meaſures which their
ſituation required, and in every inſtance behind-hand with our
enemies; what could we poſſibly expect from ſuch a conduct
but misfortune, diſgrace, and complicated calamity? A French
fleet was equipped at Breſt, and another at Toulon. The deſtination of the latter appeared plainly to every body, not concerned in adminiſtration, to be for America. But the firſt lord
of the admiralty remained in doubtful ſuſpenſe. He knew not
what part of the empire might be attacked. He continued mo-
tionleſs himſelf, and received patiently the hoſtile aſſault; like
an unſkilful boxer, intending to cover the part on which he
had already received a blow, and then ſhifting his hand to another part juſt wounded, but poſſeſſing neither ſpirit nor addreſs
ſufficient to ward off the impending ſtroke. Even after D'E-
ſtaing's ſquadron had ſailed, the account of which we obtained
by the vigilance of a foreign reſident, without any thanks to the
court of admiralty, the important paſs of the Mediterranean

was

was left unguarded. It was still pretended, that the destination A. 1
of this fleet was uncertain : their sailing in an American di- 1778
rection might be a feint ; if a squadron should be detached
from our fleet in pursuit of them, they might perhaps return,
and form a junction with D'Orvilliers, which would give him a
decisive advantage over Admiral Keppel. Then the disgrace of
the nation burst forth with irresistible evidence. Notwithstanding the boasted declarations that our fleet was superior to the
united power of France and Spain, it happened that the fleet
of France alone commanded more than our respect. The immense sums voted for the navy supplies, for these three years
past, could not furnish us with ships to follow D'Estaing without leaving our own coast defenceless.

The consequence of this was, that while we employed several months in gleaning the old stores, that had lain for years
rotting in the different dock-yards, splicing and knotting cordage that had long been condemned as unserviceable, and patch-
ing up masts and yards from the remnants of a fleet once the
terror of the world, D'Estaing rode the waves in triumph, carrying protection and independence to America. If the fortune
of Lord Howe had not been equal to his activity, his fatigued
vessels, considerable part of which, from the nature of the service in which they were engaged, lay dispersed over the wide-
extended coast of North America, must have been attacked in
detail, and defeated by piece-meal. The admiral himself, with
the main force of his squadron, narrowly escaped destruction
in the Delaware ; for, had the French fleet arrived a few days
sooner, he would have been surprised in that river with two
ships of 64 guns, one of 50, two of 40, and a few frigates,
encumbered with a fleet of transports, victuallers, and private
traders, laden for the most part with the refugees from Philadelphia, who seized this last opportunity of transporting their
families and the wreck of their fortunes.

Thus was the main force of Great Britain on that side of the
Atlantic left to be the sport of contingencies. It was saved by
something that nearly resembles a miracle. Lord Howe resist-
ed until Byron's fleet, which had long been kept waving in the
harbour of Portsmouth, to the no small entertainment of the

A. D.
1778.

populace, at length arrived in America. But this fquadron had been equipped in fuch a manner as rendered it fitter for a naval review than for any effective fervice. It was unable to weather a fummer ftorm, and approached the coaft of America, having more need of protection than ability to yield affiftance. Among thefe and all the other multiplied errors which difgrace every part of our naval adminiftration, we find the great fource of our prefent calamities. If the fame adminiftration, or any thing like it, fhould continue, ftill greater misfortunes await us. But if we make a thorough reformation in this important department, we fhall foon fee that there is no reafon to defpair, until the whole mafs of citizens become as corrupt as thofe men who have brought difgrace and calamity upon their country.

Before concluding this chapter, we have thought proper to wait for the judgment of the court-martial concerning the conduct of Admiral Keppel in the action of the 27th of July. Though the period of this decifion extends beyond the limits affigned to the prefent work, yet as it tends to clear up an important tranfaction, the principal circumftances of which have been already related, we have thought it effential to the naval hiftory of the year 1778. Soon after the action, the periodical publications were filled, as ufual, with encomiums or fatires on the admiral, according to the various opinions, inclinations, or humours of the different writers, who chofe to celebrate or to arraign his character and conduct. As the admiral had little perfonal connection with the king's minifters, and belonged to a family which had been diftinguifhed by peculiar marks of friendfhip from the late Duke of Cumberland whom they followed in oppofition, it was evident that he owed the high command conferred on him to his profeffional abilities alone, without the fmalleft affiftance from court favour. Thofe who approved all the meafures of adminiftration were naturally, therefore, the loudeft in condemning his behaviour, while the antiminifterial party not only juftified his proceedings, but held him forth as an object deferving the warmeft gratitude and applaufe of his fellow-citizens. Various anonymous paragraphs were publifhed and anfwered. The panegyric of Sir Hugh Pallifer, vice-admiral of the Blue, occafioned a criticifm on

his

his conduct; it was said that he disobeyed orders by neglecting A. D
'to pay any attention to the admiral's signals, and thereby pre- 1778
vented the destruction of the whole French fleet. These invectives and recriminations might have passed on both sides
without any material consequence, and the propriety of Admiral Keppel's behaviour being blended with the prejudices of
party, would probably have remained a matter of doubt, until
the passions of contending factions subsiding, had left time for
listening to the impartiality of some future historian. But Sir
Hugh Palliser took a decisive step on the 4th of November; and
by giving his name to the public in a letter written for his own
justification, conveyed an indirect insinuation against his commander. In the beginning of December these imputations were
re-echoed in the House of Commons, which called up the admiral to vindicate his professional character. " If he was to go over
" the business of the 27th of July again, he would conduct him-
" self in the same manner. Every thing that could be done had
" been done; and he was happy to say, the British flag had not
" been tarnished in his hands. He felt himself perfectly easy
" on that head, and should never be ashamed of his conduct on
" the day alluded to. The oldest and most experienced officers
" in his Majesty's navy, in every engagement, saw something
" which they were before unacquainted with; and that day
" presented something new. He impeached no man of neglect
" of duty, because he was satisfied that the officer alluded to
" had manifested no want of courage, the quality most essential
" in a British seaman." He said " he was much surprized when
" an officer under his command had made an appeal to the
" public in a common newspaper, signed with his name, before
" any accusation had been made against him, and which tended
" to render him odious and despicable in the eyes of his coun-
" trymen." Sir Hugh Palliser declared " he was so conscious
" of not having been any hindrance to a reaction with the Brest
" fleet on the 27th of July, that he was equally indifferent with
" the honourable admiral how soon an inquiry were set on foot.
" He had discovered from what the admiral had just said, that
" the principal matter which weighed against him in the admi-
" ral's mind was the publication in the newspapers, which he
" had

A. D.
1778.
"had figned with his name, and by which he would abide. If
"it was imprudent, if it was wrong, the confequence was .
"himfelf. To fay any thing againft a friend was to a man of
"fenfibility the moft difagreeable thing in nature ; but where an
"officer's reputation was at ftake, the removing an unjuft ftig-
"ma was certainly the firft object. If there was any reafon of
"accufation, why not make it openly and fairly ? If not, why
"infinuate that he had been wanting in point of conduct, though
"a teftimony was given in favour of his courage ? This," he faid,
"was a language extremely different from that of the admiral's
"difpatch containing an account of the action, in which he in-
"formed the Admiralty-board of the fpirited and gallant conduct
"of all the officers under his command." Admiral Keppel acknowledged " he had given that approbation, and was ready to
"repeat it, and point the teftimony particularly as well as gene-
"rally. The vice-admiral had alluded to fignals, and faid that
"it was no fault of his that the fleet of France was not re-at-
"tacked. As to that he could only fay, that he prefumed every
"inferior officer was to obey the fignals of his commander ; and
"now when called upon to fpeak out, he would inform the
"houfe and the public, that the fignal for coming into the Vic-
"tory's wake was flying from three o'clock in the afternoon till
"eight in the evening unobeyed : at the fame time he did not
"charge the vice-admiral with actual difobedience. He doubt-
"ed not but, if an inquiry fhould be thought neceffary, that
"he would be able to juftify himfelf, becaufe he was fully per-
"fuaded of his perfonal bravery."

In confequence of this altercation, Sir Hugh Pallifer drew
up the following charge againft Admiral Keppel, which he exhibited at the Board of Admiralty on the 9th of December.

CHARGE of MISCONDUCT and NEGLECT of DUTY
againft the Honourable ADMIRAL KEPPEL, on the
27th and 28th of July, 1778, in divers inftances as under
mentioned.

" I. THAT on the morning of the 27th of July, 1778, having
" a fleet of thirty fhips of the line under his command, and being
"                                                                then

" then in the prefence of a French fleet of the like number of D. A
" fhips of the line, the faid admiral did not make the neceffary 1778
" preparations for fight, did not put his fleet into a line of bat-
" tle, or into any order proper either for receiving or attacking
" an enemy of fuch force; but on the contrary, although his
" fleet was already difperfed and in diforder, he, by making the
" fignal for feveral fhips of the vice-admiral of the Blue divifion
" to chace to windward, increafed the diforder of that part of
" his fleet, and the fhips were in confequence more fcattered
" than they had been before; and, whilft in this diforder, he
" advanced to the enemy, and made the fignal for battle.
" That the above conduct was the more unaccountable, as the
" enemy's fleet was not then in diforder, nor beaten, nor flying,
" but formed in a regular line of battle on that tack which ap-
" proached the Britifh fleet, all their motions plainly indicating
" a defign to give battle, and they edged down and attacked it
" whilft in diforder. By this unofficer-like conduct, a general
" engagement was not brought on, but the other flag-officers
" and captains were left to engage without order or regularity,
" from which great confufion enfued: fome of his fhips were
" prevented from getting into action at all; others were not
" near enough to the enemy; and fome, from the confufion,
" fired into others of the king's fhips, and did them confider-
" able damage: and the vice-admiral of the Blue was left alone
" to engage fingle and unfupported. In thefe inftances the
" faid Admiral Keppel negligently performed the duty impofed
" on him.

" II. That after the van and centre divifions of the Britifh
" fleet paffed the rear of the enemy, the admiral did not imme-
" diately tack and double upon the enemy with thefe two divi-
" fions, and continue the battle, nor did he collect them toge-
" ther at that time, and keep fo near the enemy as to renew
" the battle as foon as it might be proper: on the contrary, he
" ftood away beyond the enemy to a great diftance before he
" wore to ftand towards them again, leaving the vice-admiral
" of the Blue engaged with the enemy, and expofed to be cut
" off.

" III. That after the vice-admiral of the Blue had paffed the
" laft of the enemy's fhips, and immediately wore, and laid his

" own

" own ſhip's head towards the enemy again, being then in their
" wake and at a little diſtance only, and expecting the admiral
" to advance with all the ſhips to renew the fight, the admiral
" did not advance for that purpoſe, but ſhortened ſail, hauled
" down the ſignal for battle ; nor did he at that time, nor at
" any other time whilſt ſtanding towards the enemy, call the
" ſhips together in order to renew the attack, as he might have
" done, particularly the vice-admiral of the Red and his diviſion,
" which had received the leaſt damage, had been the longeſt
" out of action, were ready and fit to renew it, were then to
" windward, and could have bore down and fetched any part
" of the French fleet, if the ſignal for battle had not been haul-
" ed down, or if the ſaid Admiral Keppel had availed himſelf of
" the ſignal appointed by the 31ſt article of the fighting inſtruc-
" tions, by which he might have ordered thoſe to lead, who are
" to lead with the ſtarboard tacks on board, by a wind; which
" ſignal was applicable to the occaſion for renewing the engage-
" ment with advantage, after the French fleet had been beaten,
" their line broken, and in diſorder. In theſe inſtances he did
" not do the utmoſt in his power to take, ſink, burn, or deſtroy
" the French fleet that had attacked the Britiſh fleet.

" IV. That inſtead of advancing to renew the engagement,
" as in the preceding articles is alledged, and as he might and
" ought to have done, the admiral wore, and made ſail directly
" from the enemy, and thus he led the whole Britiſh fleet away
" from them, which gave them an opportunity to rally unmo-
" leſted, and to form again into a line of battle, and to ſtand
" after the Britiſh fleet. This was diſgraceful to the Britiſh flag;
" for it had the appearance of a flight, and gave the French
" admiral a pretence to claim the victory, and to publiſh to the
" world, that the Britiſh fleet ran away, and that he purſued
" it with the fleet of France, and offered it battle.

" V. That on the morning of the 28th of July, 1778, when
" it was perceived that only three of the French fleet remained
" near the Britiſh in the ſituation the whole had been in the
" night before, and that the reſt were to leeward at a greater
" diſtance, not in a line of battle but in a heap, the admiral did
" not cauſe the fleet to purſue the flying enemy, not even to

2                                              " chace

" chace the three ships that fled after the reft, but on the con- A. I
" trary he led the Britifh fleet another way directly from the 1778
" enemy. By thefe inftances of mifconduct and neglect a glo-
" rious opportunity was loft of doing a moft effential fervice to
" the ftate, and the honour of the Britifh navy was tarnifhed.

H. PALLISER."

THIS charge was fent to the Admiralty on the afternoon of
the 9th of December, and intimation thereof was given by that
board to Admiral Keppel the fame evening.

When the contents of the accufation were laid before the
public, the opinions of men, warped by a thoufand prejudices,
and fhaded by all the different gradations of knowledge and ignorance, were infinitely various, inconfiftent, oppofite, and contradictory. Thofe who only knew that we had neither taken
nor deftroyed any of the French fhips in the late engagement,
a circumftance which they could not hefitate in afcribing to the
mifconduct of our commanders, underftood, or fancied they underftood, the charges alledged againft the admiral. They wifhed
that the man who had tarnifhed the antient luftre of the Britifh
flag might be brought to condign punifhment; for never any
crifis was more alarming than the prefent, or more loudly demanded every exertion of difcipline and feverity, that fo thofe
who, fheltered under great examples, negligently or ignorantly
performed the fervice required of them, might be rouzed to a
fenfe of their duty or infufficiency, and either acquire fuch talents as were beneficial to the public, or decline the weight of a
command too heavy for their abilities.

This torrent of popular cenfure, which on another occafion
would have burft forth with irrefiftible fury, was effectually
checked by two circumftances, extremely honourable to the
admiral. His candid, open, liberal behaviour had endeared him
to the great body of Britifh feamen, who loved his manners, and
refpected his courage. He was known to have little connection
with the prefent miniftry, and efpecially to be no favourite with
the firft lord of the Admiralty. This was fufficient to occafion
a fufpicion that the minifters in general heartily concurred in
the accufation, partly to divert the public from melancholy reflections on our prefent deplorable condition, and partly to fhare

A. D. with others the blame which muſt otherwiſe have lain eſſ-
1778. tirely on their own ſhoulders. It was known that almoſt every
officer intruſted with a principal command had fallen under
their diſpleaſure; and although errors, doubtleſs, muſt have
been committed by our commanders in the courſe of the war,
yet a repeated ſeries of calamity could only be occaſioned by an
error at head-quarters, a defect of preparation, a want of vigour, ſkill, or integrity in thoſe who fitted out, planned, and
directed our naval and military expeditions.

The cauſe and reputation of Admiral Keppel were ſtill further ſupported by a memorial preſented to his Majeſty the 30th
of December, and ſigned by the firſt names in the Britiſh navy.
This paper, drawn up in the form of a petition, contained, in
elegant and nervous language, a ſevere remonſtrance againſt the
conduct not only of Sir Hugh Palliſer, but of the lords of the
Admiralty. The ſubſcribing admirals repreſented to the wiſdom and juſtice of his majeſty, that Sir Hugh Palliſer had with-
held the accuſation againſt his commander in chief, from the
twenty-ſeventh day of July to the ninth of December; that
the avowed motive of the accuſation was to recriminate againſt
charges conjectured by Sir Hugh Palliſer, but which in fact were
never made; that the commiſſioners of the Admiralty, without
conſidering theſe circumſtances, or giving any previous notice
to the party accuſed, had, on the ſame day on which the charge
was preferred, intimated their intention that a court-martial
ſhould be held on him, after forty years of meritorious ſervice,
in which the glory of the Britiſh flag had been maintained and
increaſed in various parts of the world. The conſequences of
ſuch meaſures are repreſented as dangerous to the honour of
his majeſty's officers, ſubverſive of the diſcipline of the navy,
and deſtructive to the public order of ſociety *.

This memorial occaſioned no alteration in the meaſures
adopted by the lords of the Admiralty, who iſſued their orders
to Sir Thomas Pye, admiral of the White ſquadron of his majeſty's fleet, to hold a court-martial at Portſmouth, the 7th of
January, for the trial of Admiral Keppel. The court accord-

* See Appendix, Nᶜ XVIII.

ingly

ingly was affembled, on the day appointed, with the ufual for- A. D
malities, and continued, by feveral adjournments, till the 11th 1779
of February. In the courfe of the evidence brought by the
profecutor, no one fact was proved that could give the fmalleft
fupport to a fingle article in the charge. Admiral Keppel, before bringing forward his witneffes, made a particular reply to
the various accufations of his adverfary; and in this reply fome
circumftances are incidentally mentioned, which place the adminiftration of the marine department in the fame light in which it
muft already have appeared to every one who confiders with attention the naval hiftory of the prefent period. In the month
of March 1778, the admiral was told that a fleet lay ready for
him to command. Having reached Portfmouth, he faw but fix
fhips ready, and " on viewing even thofe with a feaman's eye,
" he was not by any means pleafed with their condition." On
the 30th of June he failed with twenty fhips of the line. Thirty-two fhips of the line lay in Breft water, befides an incredible
number of frigates. " Was I to feek an engagement," fays the
admiral, " with a fuperior force? I never did, nor fhall I ever
" fear to engage a force fuperior to the one I then command-
" ed, or that I may hereafter command. But I well know
" what men and fhips can do, and if the fleet I commanded
" had been deftroyed, we muft have left the French mafters of
" the fea. To refit a fleet requires time. From the fituation
" of affairs, naval ftores are not very foon fupplied. Never
" did I experience fo deep a melancholy as when I found my-
" felf forced to turn my back on France! I quitted my ftation,
" and courage was never put to fo fevere a trial."

The admiral was permitted to fail a fecond time, without receiving official praife or blame for the part which he had acted.
Having taken two French frigates, he was fearful that a war
with France, and all its confequences, might be laid to his
charge. " This," he fays, " for any thing I can tell, may be
" treafured up to furnifh another matter for future accufation."
He was furprifed, on his return, to be threatened with the fate
of Admiral Byng, and ftill more furprifed to be charged with
cowardice. " I am exceedingly forry that the Admiralty have
" refufed me the liberty of producing my inftructions. In all

3 K 2 " former

" former courts-martial the inftru, and orders have been " fent with the charge to the members of the court. Although " on the 27th of July I fought and beat my enemy, and com- " pelled him to take fhelter by returning into port, yet the ef- " fort did by no means anfwer my wifhes. I rufhed on to re- " attack the enemy; and why I did not accomplifh my defign " will be feen in the evidence which I fhall produce."

When the admiral's witneffes were examined, it appeared, that if he had waited for forming the line of battle, and had not immediately taken advantage of a change of wind to clofe with the enemy, there could have been no engagement on the 27th of July. It was proved, that, having paffed the French fleet, he wore fhip in order to renew the engagement as foon as it was proper; as he could not have done it fooner, had the ftate of his own fhip admitted of it, without throwing the fhips aftern into the greateft confufion. The Englifh fleet at no time exhibited any figns of flying from the enemy; when the French after the engagement edged away, and made for fome of our. difabled fhips, it was neceffary to wear again, in order to pre- vent thofe fhips from falling into their hands. The three French fhips, which were feen on the morning of the 28th of July, could not have been purfued with the fmalleft profpect of fuc- cefs *. Thefe facts, which entirely deftroyed the charge againft Admiral Keppel, were eftablifhed by the witneffes on both fides. The evidence brought by the admiral, and particularly the teftimony of Admiral Campbell, Sir John Lindfay and Cap- tain Jarvis, proved, that the reafon why the Britifh fleet did not re-attack the French, was the difobedience of Sir Hugh Pallifer, vice-admiral of the Blue, who difregarded the admi- ral's fignal for forming the line, which continued flying from three o'clock in the afternoon till the evening. The court, having heard the profecutor's evidence and the prifoner's de- fence, unanimoufly proceeded to give fentence on the 11th of February in the following terms: " That it is their opinion " the charge againft Admiral Keppel is malicious and ill-found- " ed, it having appeared that the faid admiral, fo far from

* See Admiral Keppel's defence at large in the Appendix, N° XIX.

" having

" having by mifconduct and neglect of duty, on the days there-  A. I
" in alluded to, loft an opportunity of rendering effential fer-  1775
" vice to the ftate, and thereby tarnifhed the honour of the
" Britifh navy, behaved as became a judicious, brave, and ex-
" perienced officer." The prefident then delivered him his
fword, congratulating him on its being reftored with fo much
honour, and hoping ere long he would be called forth by his
fovereign to draw it again in the fervice of his country *.

Thus ended this celebrated trial, from which the public were
led to form a very different opinion of the action of the 27th
of July, from that which naturally prefented itfelf on reading
the admiral's public letter to the commiffioners of the marine
department. This letter, though it contained nothing directly
in oppofition to truth, (unlefs the general panegyric beftowed on
the fpirited conduct of Sir Robert Harland, Sir Hugh Pallifer,
and the captains of the fleet, be fuppofed to imply an acquittal
of every individual from the crime of difobedience), yet, by
concealing part of the truth, tended to miflead the judgment
of the public, and to give them both an inadequate and erro-
neous idea of the action. It feemed from the letter †, that the
admiral could have attacked the French fleet a fecond time that
afternoon while they were forming the line of battle; but it
appeared from the evidence, that this could not have been done,
nor the engagement renewed at any time that day, without
giving an evident advantage to the enemy, as Sir Hugh Pallifer's not coming into the admiral's wake agreeably to fignal,
left the Britifh fleet throughout the whole afternoon greatly inferior to that of France.

When the voice of party fpirit fhall be heard no more, the im-
partial voice of hiftory will afk Admiral Keppel, why he did not
make the particular fignal for each fhip in the Blue divifion feparately to come into his wake, when he faw Sir Hugh Pallifer
refufing to obey his fignal? By this means the engagement

* A few days after Admiral Keppel's acquittal both houfes of parliament
agreed unanimoufly in a vote of thanks for his gallant behaviour on the 27th of
July. That of the lords was fent by the lord chancellor, and that of the commons delivered to the admiral in his place by the fpeaker. The city of London
and Weft-India merchants followed this example.
† See Appendix, N° X X.

might

A. D.
1779.

might have been renewed, though the Formidable had continued in disobedience. However delicate a point it might be to criminate an officer who had behaved bravely, yet it will be allowed, that every degree of delicacy ought to have given place to the duty Mr. Keppel owed his country. The letter written after the action, inserted in the London Gazette, will be a sufficient warning to future commanders, not to bestow praise if they think censure is due. But if, on the one hand, Admiral Keppel was blameable in some particulars, Sir Hugh Palliser seems to have been culpable on the other. If the Formidable was so much crippled as was represented, why did not the vice-admiral shift his flag on board some other ship of his division? This, it might have been expected, would have naturally occurred to so brave a man as Sir Hugh Palliser. It is to be hoped, however, that when this officer is brought to a trial*, he will be able to explain his conduct; and that his not doing what he was ordered to do will appear to have arisen from some unknown circumstances, inferring at most an error in judgment, without any malignant purpose against his commander, or intention of tarnishing the naval honour of this kingdom †.

* Sir Hugh Palliser, about a fortnight after the trial, resigned his employments of lieutenant-general of the marines, one of the lords of the Admiralty, and governor of Scarborough-castle; he also vacated his seat in parliament, and retains nothing but his rank as vice-admiral of the Blue. Sir Hugh was tried by a court-martial in April 1779, by orders from the board of Admiralty, and acquitted.— Next year he was, on the death of Sir Charles Hardy, promoted to the government of Greenwich Hospital.

† The reduction of the French island of St. Lucia in the West Indies took place in the month of December, 1778; no advice was received in England of this event till March following, which was too late for its being inserted in the last edition of this work. This omission is now supplied in the Appendix, (N° XXII.) by an account of that important event, as transmitted to the Admiralty by the honourable Rear-admiral Barrington, who had the honour of commanding his Majesty's ships on that expedition.

APPEN-

# APPENDIX.

## No. I.   (P. 17.)

SAILING and FIGHTING INSTRUCTIONS *given to the Fleet on their sailing from Jamaica, by Edward Vernon, Esq; Vice-Admiral of the Blue, and Commander in Chief of all his Majesty's ships and vessels in the West Indies.*

### LINE OF BATTLE.

THE *Princess Amelia* to lead with the starboard, and the *Suffolk* with the larboard tacks on board.   But if I shall find it necessary, from the different motions of the enemy, to change our order of battle, to have those, who are now appointed to lead on the starboard tack, to continue to lead the fleet on the larboard tack on our going about; or those now to lead on the larboard tack, on the contrary to do the same, as the exigency of the service may require: I will, with my signal for tacking, hoist a Dutch jack on the flag-staff, under the Union-flag, the usual signal for tacking, when they are to continue to lead the fleet on their respective tacks accordingly.

*Rear-Admiral of the Blue, Sir* CHALONER OGLE.

| Frigates. | Ships of the Line. | Commanders. | Guns |
|---|---|---|---|
| | Princess Amelia, | Capt. Hemington, | 8c |
| Experiment. | Windsor, | Berkley, | 6c |
| Sheerness. | York, | Coates, | 6c |
| Vesuvius, fire-ship. | Norfolk, | Graves, | 8c |
| Terrible, bomb. | Russel, (the Admiral), | Norris, | 8c |
| Phaeton. | Shrewsbury, | Townsend, | 8c |
| Goodly. | Rippon, | Jolley, | 6c |
| | Litchfield, | Cleveland, | 5c |
| | Jersey, | Lawrence, | 6c |
| | Tilbury, | Long, | 6c |

*Vice*

*Vice-Admiral of the Blue*, VERNON.

| Frigates. | Ships of the Line. | Commanders. | Guns. |
|---|---|---|---|
| Squirrel. | Orford, | Capt. L. Aug. Fitzroy, | 70 |
| Shoreham. | Princefs Louifa, | Stapleton, | 60 |
| Eleanor. | Augufta, | Dennifon, | 60 |
| Seahorfe. | Worcefter, | Perry Mayne, | 60 |
| Strombolo. | Chichefter, | Robt. Trevor, | 80 |
| Succefs. | Pr. Caroline, (Admiral), | Watfon, | 80 |
| Vulcan. | Torbay, | Gafcoigne, | 80 |
| Cumberland. | Strafford, | Thos. Trevor, | 60 |
| Alderney Bomb. | Weymouth, | Knowles, | 60 |
| Pompey. | Deptford, | Moftyn, | 60 |
| Brig Tender. | Burford, | Griffin, | 70 |

*Commodore* LESTOCK'S *Divifion.*

| | Defiance, | Jn°. Trevor, | 60 |
|---|---|---|---|
| | Dunkirk, | Cooper, | 60 |
| Aftrea. | Lyon, | Cotterel, | 60 |
| Wolf Sloop. | Prince Frederic, | L. A. Beauclerc, | 70 |
| Ætna. | Boyne, (Commodore), | Colby, | 80 |
| Firebrand. | Hampton Court, | Dent, | 70 |
| Virgin Queen. | Falmouth, | Douglas, | 50 |
| | Montague, | Chambers, | 60 |
| | Suffolk, | Davers, | 70 |

### SIGNALS.

When the admiral would fpeak with the captain of any fhip undermentioned, he will raife a pendant, as againft the fhip's name, and of the colour fet above it ; if a lieutenant, the fame fignal with a weft of the enfign ; and if a boat without an officer, the weft will be hoifted but half-ftaff up.

*Memorandum:* When I would have any of the fire-fhips, bombs, or tenders, taken in tow, at the fame time that I make the fignal for the fhip that is to tow, and for the fhip that is to be towed, I will hoift up a flag, blue and white, at the flag-ftaff of the main top-maft head.

| Red. | White. | Blue. | Yellow. | | |
|---|---|---|---|---|---|
| Boyne | Prss Amelia | Chichester | Terrible | Main | Top-mast head. |
| Norfolk | Suffolk | Shrewsbury | Eleanor | Fore | |
| Worcester | Lyon | Defiance | Ætna | Mizen | |
| Tilbury | Squirrel | Torbay | Firebrand | Starb. | Main topsail yard-arm. |
| Windsor | Pris Louisa | Falmouth | Vesuvius | Larb. | |
| Burford | Pr. Frederic | Strafford | Phaeton | Starb. | Fore topsail yard-arm. |
| Montague | Orford | Weymouth | Strombolo | Larb. | |
| Shoreham | Augusta | Pss Caroline | Success | Sta.b | Mizen topsail yard-arm. |
| Hamptn Court | Dunkirk | Jersey | Vulcan | Larb. | |
| Litchfield | Ludl Castle | Deptford | Cumberland | Sta.b | Main yard-arm. |
| Experiment | Rippon | York | Alderney | Larb. | |
| Sea Horse | Sheerness | Ruffel | Brig. Tender | Starb. | Fore yard-arm. |
| Astrea | Wolf | | Virgin Queen | Larb. | |
| | | | Pompey | Starb. | cross jack yard-arm. |
| | | | Goodly | Larb. | |

When the ships are in line of battle, the frigates, fire-ships, bombs and tenders are to keep on the opposite side of the enemy. When I make the signal, in line of battle, for the van of the fleet to tack first, in order to gain the windward of the enemy then each ship is to tack in the headmost ship's wake, for losing no ground. For all other signals they are referred to the general printed sailing and fighting instructions, and such other additional instructions as you receive from me.

VERNON.

# No. II.   (P. 37.)

SHIPS *in* COMMISSION *in the year* 1741.

### FIRST RATES, 100 *guns.*

| | |
|---|---|
| Royal George, | Captain Allen. |
| Royal Sovereign, | Faulkener. |
| Victory, | Falkland. |

### SECOND RATES, 90 *guns.*

| | |
|---|---|
| Duke, | Commodore Brown. |
| St. George, | Captain Dilkes. |
| Marlborough, | Clinton. |
| Neptune, | Whorwood. |
| Sandwich, | Mead. |

### THIRD RATES, 80 *guns.*

| | |
|---|---|
| Princefs Amelia, | Captain Hemmington. |
| Boyne, | Leftock. |
| Princefs Caroline, | Griffin. |
| Chichefter, | Trevor. |
| Cumberland, | Steuart. |
| Lancafter, | Coyley. |
| Norfolk, | Graves. |
| Ruffel, | Norris. |
| Shrewfbury, | Townfend. |
| Somerfet, | Barnefley. |
| Torbay, | Gafcoigne. |

### 70 *guns.*

| | |
|---|---|
| Burford, | Captain Watfon. |
| Buckingham, | Young. |
| Prince Frederick, | Lord A. Beauclerc. |
| Grafton, | Rycault. |
| Elizabeth, | Durele. |
| Effex, | Robinfon. |
| Hampton Court, | Dent. |
| Ipfwich, | Martin. |
| Kent, | Mitchel. |

Lenox,

| | |
|---|---|
| Lenox, | Commodore Mayne. |
| Naſſau, | Captain Medley. |
| Prince of Orange, | Oſborne. |
| Norwich, | Herbert. |
| Orford, | Lord Auguſtus Fitzroy. |
| Suffolk. | Davies. |

### FOURTH RATES, 60 guns.

| | |
|---|---|
| Auguſta, | Captain Denniſon. |
| Centurion, | Anſon. |
| Dragon, | Barnard. |
| Deptford, | Moſtyn. |
| Dunkirk, | Cooper. |
| Jerſey, | Laurence. |
| Kingſton, | Richard Norris. |
| Princeſs Louiſa, | Stapleton. |
| Lion, | Cotterel. |
| Montague, | Chambers. |
| Pembroke, | Lee. |
| Plymouth, | Sir R. Butler. |
| Rupert, | Ambroſe. |
| Rippon, | Jolly. |
| Sunderland, | Byng. |
| Strafford, | Trevor. |
| Superb. | Hervey. |
| Tilbury, | Long. |
| Windſor, | Berkeley. |
| Warwick, | Toller. |
| Worceſter, | P. Mayne. |
| York, | Cotes. |

### 50 guns.

| | |
|---|---|
| Aſſiſtance, | Captain Cleland. |
| St. Albans, | Vincent. |
| Argyle, | Lingen. |
| Briſtol, | Young. |
| Chatham, | Strange. |
| Colcheſter, | Sir W. Hewit. |
| Cheſter, | Slaughter. |

3 L 2            Falkland,

| | |
|---|---|
| Falkland, | Oliphant, |
| Falmouth, | Douglas. |
| Gloucefter, | Michel. |
| Guernfey, | John Forbes. |
| Litchfield, | Knowles. |
| Newcaſtle, | Fox. |
| Orford, | Ruffel. |
| Portland, | Hawes. |
| Panther, | Cotes. |
| Ruby, | Frogmore. |
| Romney, | Smith. |
| Rochefter, | Allen. |
| Salifbury, | P. Ofborne. |
| Severn, | Legge. |
| Tiger, | Forbes. |
| Winchefter, | Lloyd. |

### FIFTH RATES, 40 *guns.*

| | |
|---|---|
| Anglefea, | Captain Reddifh. |
| Dover, | Burrifh. |
| Eltham, | Smith. |
| Hector, | Sir Y. Peyton. |
| Lark, | Lord G. Graham. |
| Liverpool, | Lord Banff. |
| Mary Galley, | John Durell. |
| Pearl, | Kidd. |
| Roebuck, | Crawford. |
| South-Sea Caftle, | Cuzack. |
| Torrington, | Knight. |

### SIXTH RATES, 20 *guns.*

| | |
|---|---|
| Alborough. | Captain Pocock. |
| Blandford, | Burrifh. |
| Biddeford, | Lord Forrefter. |
| Bridgewater, | Pet. |
| Deal-Caftle, | Weft. |
| Durfley Galley, | T. Smith. |
| Dolphin, | Holbourne. |

Experiment,

| | |
|---|---|
| Experiment, | Renton. |
| Flamborough, | Pearce. |
| Fox, | Masters. |
| Gibraltar, | W. Purvis. |
| Greyhound, | Balchen. |
| Garland. | Watson. |
| Kennington, | Peyton. |
| Lowestaffe, | Drummond. |
| Lyme, | Lord Mt. Bertie, |
| Lively, | Swaysland. |
| Phœnix, | Fanshawe. |
| Portmahon, | Pawlet. |
| Rose, | Frankland. |
| Rye, | Lushington. |
| Seahorse, | Limeburner. |
| Shoreham, | Boscawen. |
| Squirrel, | Warren. |
| Sheerness, | R. Maynard, |
| Success, | Thompson. |
| Scarborough, | Lisle. |
| Tartar Pink, | Townshend. |
| Winchelsea, | |
| Wager, | Chepe. |
| Royal Caroline, | Sir Charles Hardy. |

| | | | |
|---|---|---|---|
| Fire-ships, | 16 | Store ships, | 3 |
| Bomb sloops, | 6 | Yachts, | 6 |
| Sloops, | 15 | Smacks and Tenders, | 41 |

No. III.

## No. III.   (P. 48.)

BRITISH FLEET *in the Mediterranean, in the year* 1743.

VAN.   *Rear-admiral* ROWLEY.

| Frigates, &c. | Ships of the Line. | Commanders. | Guns. |
|---|---|---|---|
| | Stirling Caftle, | Cap$^t$ Cooper, | 70 |
| | Warwick, | Weft, | 60 |
| Oxford. | Naffau, | Lloyd, | 70 |
| Feverfham. | Cambridge, | Drummond, | 80 |
| Winchelfea. | Barfleur (Admiral), | De Langle, | 90 |
| | Princefs Caroline, | Ofborne, | 80 |
| | Berwick, | Hawke, | 70 |
| | Chichefter, | Dilkes, | 80 |
| | Kingfton, | Lovet, | 60 |

CENTER.   *Admiral* MATHEWS.

| | Dragon, | Cap$^t$ Watfon, | 60 |
|---|---|---|---|
| | Bedford, | Townfend, | 70 |
| Guernfey. | Princeffa, | Pit, | 74 |
| Chatham, | Norfolk, | Forbes, | 80 |
| Salifbury. | Namure (Admiral), | Ruffel, | 90 |
| Durfley Galley. | Marlborough, | Cornwall, | 90 |
| Ann Galley. | Dorfetfhire, | Burrifh, | 80 |
| | Effex, | Norris, | 70 |
| { | Rupert, | Ambrofe, | 60 |
| | Royal Oak, | Williams, | 70 |

REAR.   *Vice-admiral* LESTOCK.

| | Dunkirk, | Cap$^t$ Purvis, | 60 |
|---|---|---|---|
| | Somerfet, | Slaughter, | 80 |
| Nonfuch. | Torbay, | Gafcoigne, | 70 |
| Romney. | Neptune (Admiral), | Stepney, | 90 |
| Diamond. | Ruffel, | Long, | 80 |
| Mercury fire-fhip. | Buckingham, | Towrey, | 70 |
| | Boyne, | Frogmore, | 80 |
| | Elifabeth, | Lingen, | 70 |
| | Revenge, | Berkeley, | 70 |

COM-

## COMBINED FLEET.
### VAN. FRENCH.
*Commodore* GABARET.

| Frigates. | Ships of the Line. | Commanders. | Guns. |
|---|---|---|---|
| | Le Diamant, | Monf. de Maflie, | 50 |
| | Le Touloufe, | d'Aftrour, | 60 |
| | Le Serieux, | de Chylus, | 64 |
| L'Attalante. | L'Eole, | de Gravier, | 64 |
| Le Flore. | L'Efperance, (Comm^re), | Gabaret, | 74 |
| | Le St. Efprit, | de Piofin, | 74 |
| | Le Boreè, | de Marquife, | 64 |
| | L'Aguilon, | de Vandreuil, | 50 |

### CENTER. FRENCH.
*Admiral* DE COURT.

| | Le Tigre, | Monf. de Saurin, | 56 |
|---|---|---|---|
| | Le Trident, | de Caylus, | 64 |
| | Le Duc d'Orleans, | d'Orvey, | 74 |
| Le Zephire. | Le Terrible, (Adm^l), | de Court, | 74 |
| Le Volga. | Le Ferme, | de Sergue, | 74 |
| | Le Solide, | de Chateauneuf, | 64 |
| | Le Leopard, | de Galifet, | 64 |
| | L'Alcion, | de Lauce, | 56 |

### REAR. SPANISH.
*Admiral* NAVARRO.

| | Le Superbe, | Juan Valdez, | 60 |
|---|---|---|---|
| | Le Poder, | Rodriguez, | 60 |
| | Le S. Fernando, | de la Viga, | 60 |
| Two Frigates. | Le Conftant, | de Tortuga, | 70 |
| | L'Ifabella, | Pectathoui, | 70 |
| | Le R. Infanta, | Adm^l Navarro, | 114 |
| | Le Hercule, | Cofm. d'Alvarez, | 70 |
| | L'Amerique, | Fran. Patrouchi, | 70 |
| | Le Neptune, | Hen. Olivarez, | 60 |
| | L'Orient, | Joach. de Villena, | 60 |
| | Le Brillant, | Blaife de la Barrera, | 60 |
| | Le Retiro, | Juan Souriane, | 54 |

No.

## No. IV.   (P. 77.)

*Admiral* Bync's *Inſtructions from the Lords of the Admiralty.*

WHEREAS the King's pleaſure has been ſignified to us by Mr. Fox, one of his Majeſty's principal ſecretaries of ſtate, that, upon conſideration of the ſeveral advices which have been received relating to the ſuppoſed intention of the French to attack the iſland of Minorca, a ſquadron of ten ſhips of the line do forthwith ſail for the Mediterranean, under your command: and whereas we have appointed the ſhips named in the margin for this ſervice, you are hereby required and directed immediately to put to ſea with ſuch of them as are ready, (leaving orders for the reſt to follow you as ſoon as poſſible), and proceed with the utmoſt expedition to Gibraltar. Upon your arrival there, you are to inquire whether any French ſquadron is come through the Streights; and if there is, to inform yourſelf, as well as poſſible, of their number and force, and if any of them were tranſports. And as it is probable they may be deſtined for North America, and as his Majeſty's ſhips, named in the margin, are either at or going to Halifax, and are to cruiſe off Louiſbourg and the mouth of the Gulf of St. Lawrence, you are immediately to take the ſoldiers out of ſo many ſhips of your ſquadron, as, together with the ſhips at and going to Halifax, will make a force ſuperior to the French ſquadron, (replacing them with landmen or ordinary ſeamen from your other ſhips), and then detach them under the command of Rear-admiral Weſt, directing him to make the beſt of his way off Louiſbourg; and taking the afore-mentioned ſhips, which he may expect to find there, under his command, to cruiſe off the ſaid place, and the entrance of the Gulf of St. Lawrence; and uſe his utmoſt endeavours to intercept and ſeize the aforeſaid French ſhips, or any other ſhips belonging to the French, that may be bound to, or returning from that part of North America.

If, upon your arrival at Gibraltar, you ſhall not gain intelligence of a French ſquadron having paſſed the Streights; you are then to go on without a moment's leſs of time to Minorca:

or, if in confequence of fuch intelligence you fhall detach Rear-admiral Weft, as before directed, you are to ufe equal expedition in repairing thither with the fhips which fhall remain with you; and if you find any attack made upon that ifland by the French, you are to ufe all poffible means in your power for its relief. If you find no fuch attack made, you are to proceed off Toulon, and ftation your fquadron in the beft manner you fhall be able for preventing any fhip's getting out of that port; or for intercepting and feizing any that may get out; and you are to exert the utmoft vigilance therein, and in protecting Minorca and Gibraltar from any hoftile attempts.

You are alfo to be vigilant for protecting the trade of his Majefty's fubjects from being molefted, either by the French or by cruifers from Morocco, or any other of the Barbary ftates; and for that purpofe to appoint proper convoys and cruifers.

You are likewife to be as attentive as poffible to the intercepting and feizing as well fhips of war and privateers as merchant fhips belonging to the French, wherever they may be met with, within the limits of your command. But, in purfuance of the King's order in council, you are not to fuffer any of the fhips of your fquadron to take any French veffels out of any port belonging to the Ottoman empire, upon any pretence; nor to moleft, detain, or imprifon, the perfons of any of the fubjects of the Ottoman empire; and alfo, not to feize and detain any French fhip or veffel whatfoever, which they fhall meet with in the Levant feas, bound from one port to another in thofe feas, or to or from any ports of Egypt, having any effects of Turks on board.

Upon your arrival in the Mediterranean, you are to take under your command his Majefty's fhips and veffels named in the margin, which are at prefent there.

If any French fhip of war fhould fail from Toulon and efcape your fquadron, and proceed out of the Mediterranean, you are forthwith to fend, or repair yourfelf to England with a proportionable part of the fhips under your command; obferving that you are never to keep more fhips in the Mediterranean than fhall be neceffary for executing the fervice recommended to you.

To enable you to perform the above-mentioned fervices, you are to take care to keep the fhips and veffels under your command in conftant good condition, and to have them cleaned as often as fhall be requifite for that purpofe.

March 30,     (Signed)  *Anfon, Villiers, Rowley, Bofcawen,*
1756.                      *Bateman, Edgecombe, and J. Cleland.*

# No. V.   (P. 87.)

*State of the Royal Navy of Great Britain at the declaration of war againft France, in the year* 1756.

**Firft rates, 106 guns.**
Royal Ann,
Britannia,
Royal George,
Royal Sovereign,
Royal William.

**Second rates, 90 guns.**
Blenheim,
Duke,
St. George,
Namur,
Prince,
Ramillies,
Princefs Royal,
Union.

**Third rates, 80 guns.**
Barfleur,
Boyne,
Princefs Caroline,
Cambridge,
Cornwall,
Prince George,
Marlborough,
Neptune,
Newark,

Norfolk,
Ruffel.

**74 guns.**
Culloden,
Invincible,
Monarque,
Terrible,
Torbay,
Fougueux.

**70 guns.**
Bedford,
Berwick,
Buckingham,
Burford,
Captain,
Chichefter,
Dorfetfhire,
Edinburgh,
Elifabeth,
Effex,
Prince Frederick,
Grafton,
Hampton-Court,
Kent,
Lenox,

Monmouth,
Naffau,
Northumberland,
Royal Oak,
Orford,
Princeffa,
Revenge,
Stirling Caftle,
Suffolk,
Somerfet,
Vanguard,
Yarmouth,
Swiftfure,
Magnanime.

**66 guns.**
Princefs Amelia,
Cumberland,
Devonfhire,
Lancafter.

**64 guns.**
Ipfwich,
Intrepid,
Trident.

*Fourth*

*Fourth rates*, 60 *guns*.

| | | |
|---|---|---|
| St. Albans, | Affiftance, | Crown, |
| Anfon, | Antelope, | Diamond, |
| Augufta, | Briftol, | Dover, |
| Canterbury, | Centurion, | Eltham, |
| Defiance, | Chatham, | Prince Edward |
| Dragon, | Colchefter, | Expedition, |
| Dreadnought, | Chefter, | Enterprize, |
| Dunkirk, | Deptford, | Gofport, |
| Eagle, | Falkland, | Glory, |
| Exeter, | Falmouth, | Prince Henry, |
| Greenwich, | Gloucefter, | Humber, |
| Jerfey, | Guernfey, | Haftings, |
| Kingfton, | Hampfhire, | Hector, |
| Lion, | Harwich, | Jafon, |
| Medway, | Ifis, | Kinfale, |
| Princefs Louifa, | Litchfield, | Launcefton, |
| Princefs Mary, | Leopard, | Ludlow Caftle, |
| Prince of Orange, | Newcaftle, | Lark, |
| Montague, | Nonfuch, | Liverpool, |
| Nottingham, | Norwich, | Looe, |
| Pembroke, | Oxford, | Lynn, |
| Plymouth, | Portland, | Mary Galley, |
| Rupert, | Prefton, | Pearl, |
| Rippon, | Panther, | Penzance, |
| Strafford, | Ruby, | Pool, |
| Sunderland, | Rochefter, | Rainbow, |
| Superbe, | Salifbury, | Roebuck, |
| Tilbury, | Severn, | Romney, |
| Tiger, | Sutherland, | Saphire, |
| Vigilant, | Taviftock, | South-fea Caftle, |
| Windfor, | Winchefter. | Thetis, |
| Weymouth, | | Torrington, |
| Worcefter, | *Fifth rates*, 44 *guns*. | Woolwich. |
| York. | Adventure, | |
| | America, | *Sixth rates*, 24 *and* |
| | Anglefea, | 20 *guns*. |
| 50 *guns*. | Ambufcade, | Amazon, |
| Advice, | Chefterfield, | Alderney, |
| | 3 M 2 | Aldborough, |

Aldborough,
Arundel,
Bellona,
Biddiford,
Boston,
Bridgewater,
Blandford,
Centaur,
Deal Castle,
Durfley Galley,
Dolphin,
Experiment,
Flamborough,
Fowey,
Fox,
Gibraltar,
Greyhound,
Garland,
Glafgow,
Grand Turk,
Hind,
Invernefs,
Kennington,
Leoftoffe,
Lively,
Lys,
Lyme,
Margate,
Mercury,
Mermaid,
Nightingale,
Phœnix,
Port-Mahon,
Queenborough,
Renown,
Ranger,
Rofe,
Rye,

Sea-Horfe,
Shoreham,
Squirrel,
Seaford,
Sheernefs,
Syren,
Sphinx,
Surprize,
Succefs,
Scarborough,
Solebay,
Tartar,
Triton,
Unicorn,
Winchefter,
Wager,
Royal Caroline.

*Bombs.*

Firedrake,
Furnace,
Granado.

*Sloops.*

Albany,
Badger,
Baltimore,
Cruifer,
Defpatch,
Falcon,
Ferret,
Fly,
Fortune,
Grampus,
Happy,
Hazard,
Hornet,
Hound,

Jamaica,
King's Fifher,
Otter,
Peggy,
Peregrine,
Porcupine,
Ranger,
Raven,
Saltafh,
Savage,
Scorpion,
Shark,
Speedwell,
Swallow,
Swan,
Swift,
Trial,
Viper,
Vulture,
Wafp,
Weazle,
Wolf,

*Yachts.*

Catherine,
Charlotte,
Dorfet,
Fubbs,
Mary,
William and Mary,
Bolton,
Chatham,
Drake,
Portfmouth,
Queenborough;

Alfo feveral fire-
ships, hoys, &c.

No. VI.

## No. VI. (P. 87.)

*State of the Navy of France at the declaration of war against Great Britain in the year 1756.*

| Perrier de Salvert's squadron. | Guns. | | Guns. | | Guns. |
|---|---|---|---|---|---|
| | | Fier, | 50 | Licorne, | 30 |
| | Guns. | Hipopotame, | 50 | Sauvage, | 30 |
| Le Courageux, | 74 | Junon, | 46 | Concord, | 30 |
| Prothée, | 64 | Rose, | 30 | Amarante, | 12 |
| Amphion, | 50 | Pleide, | 26 | | |
| Aigle, | 50 | La Gracieuse, | 24 | *At Brest and Rochfort.* | |
| Fleur de Lys, | 30 | Nymphe, | 24 | Le Formidable, | 80 |
| Emeraude, | 28 | Topaze, | 24 | Entreprenant, | 74 |
| | | *Conflans's squadron.* | | | |
| *— At Brest.* | | Le Soleil, | 80 | *On a cruize.* | |
| Le Comet, | 30 | Bourgogne, | 80 | La Thetis, | 24 |
| Amethyste, | 30 | Tonnant, | 80 | Mutine, | 24 |
| Blonde, | 30 | Superbe, | 74 | Pomone, | 24 |
| Brune, | 30 | Defenseur, | 74 | Cumberland, | 24 |
| Zephyr, | 30 | Dauphin, | 74 | Galathé, | 24 |
| Hermione, | 26 | Juste, | 70 | Heroine, | 24 |
| Valeur, | 26 | Hardi, | 66 | Anemone, | 12 |
| Fidele, | 26 | Bienfaisant, | 64 | | |
| Friponne, | 26 | Inflexible, | 64 | *At Cape Briton and* | |
| | | Eveille, | 64 | *Martinico.* | |
| *Galissoniere's fleet.* | | Capricieux, | 64 | Le Prudent, | 74 |
| Le Foudroyant, | 80 | Arc-en-Ciel, | 50 | Aquilon, | 60 |
| Temeraire, | 74 | Diana, | 50 | Attalante, | 34 |
| Couronne, | 74 | | | Palmier, | 74 |
| Redoutable, | 74 | *For carrying troops* | | Bizarre, | 64 |
| Guerrier, | 74 | *to America under* | | Opiniatre, | 64 |
| Content, | 64 | *M. Beassier.* | | Active, | 64 |
| Triton, | 64 | Le Hero, | 74 | St. Michel, | 64 |
| Sage, | 64 | Illustre, | 64 | Alcion, | 54 |
| Lion, | 64 | Leopard, | 60 | Apollon, | 50 |
| Orphée | 64 | Sirene, | 30 | | |

| At Toulon. | Guns. | | Guns. | | Guns. |
|---|---|---|---|---|---|
| | | Floriffant, | 74 | Celebre, | 64 |
| Le Hector, | 74 | Northumberland, | 68 | Robufte, | 64 |
| Vaillant, | 64 | Dragon, | 74 | Solitaire, | 64 |
| Achille, | 64 | | | Terrible, | 64 |
| Hercule, | 64 | *In different docks.* | | Aigrette, | 30 |
| Oriflamme, | 50 | L'Ocean, | 80 | Veftable, | 30 |
| | | Centaure, | 70 | Minerva, | 24 |
| *Careening.* | | Diademe, | 74 | Oifeau, | 24 |
| L'Intrepide, | 74 | Zodiaque, | 74 | Protecteur, | 74 |
| Conquerant, | 74 | Monature, | 74 | Fantafque, | 64 |
| Magnifique, | 74 | Souverain, | 74 | Modefte, | 60 |
| Sceptre, | 74 | Glorieux, | 74 | Defiance, | 30 |
| Algougeux, | 74 | Not yet named, | 74 | Surprize, | 30 |
| Floride, | 74 | Belliqueux, | 64 | Warwick, | 50 |

## No. VII.    (P. 101.)

*Secret Inftructions to Sir John Mordaunt in the year* 1757.

GEORGE, R.

1ft, You fhall immediately, upon the receipt of thefe inftructions, repair to the Ifle of Wight, where we have appointed fhips to convey you, and the forces under your command, to the coaft of France; and, fo foon as the faid forces fhall be embarked, you fhall accordingly proceed, without lofs of time, under convoy of a fquadron of our fhips of war, to be commanded by our trufty and well-beloved Sir Edward Hawke, knight of the Bath, admiral of the Blue fquadron of our fleet; whom we have appointed commander in chief of our fhips to be employed in this expedition; the faid admiral, or the commander in chief of our faid fhips for the time being, being inftructed to co-operate with you, and be aiding and affifting in all fuch enterprifes, as, by thefe our inftructions, you fhall be directed to undertake for our fervice.

2d, Whereas we have determined, with the bleffing of God, to profecute the juft war in which we are engaged againft the French king, with the utmoft vigour; and it being highly expedient,

dient, and of urgent neceffity, to make fome expedition, that may caufe a diverfion, and engage the enemy to employ in their own defence, a confiderable part of their forces, deftined to invade and opprefs the liberty of the empire, and to fubvert the independency of Europe; and if poffible to make fome effectual impreffion on the enemy, which, by difturbing and fhaking the credit of their public loans, impairing the ftrength and refources of their navy, as well as difconcerting, and in part fruftrating their dangerous and extenfive operations of war, may reflect luftre on our arms, and add life and ftrength to the common caufe; and whereas we are perfuaded, that nothing, in the prefent fituation of affairs, can fo fpeedily and effectually annoy and diftrefs France, as a fuccefsful enterprize againft Rochfort; our will and pleafure is, that you do attempt, as far as it fhall be found practicable, a defcent, with the forces under your command, on the French coaft, at or near Rochfort, in order to attack, if practicable, and by a vigorous impreffion force that place; and to burn and deftroy, to the utmoft of your power, all docks, magazines, arfenals, and fhipping, that fhall be found there, and exert fuch other efforts, as you fhall judge moft proper for annoying the enemy.

3d, After the attempt on Rochfort fhall either have fucceeded or failed; and in cafe the circumftances of our forces and fleet fhall, with profpect of fuccefs, ftill admit of further operations, you are next to confider Port L'Orient and Bourdeaux, as the moft important objects of our arms, on the coaft of France; and our will and pleafure is, that you do proceed fucceffively to an attempt on both, or either of thofe places, as fhall be judged practicable; or on any other place that fhall be thought moft advifable, from Bourdeaux homeward to Havre, in order to carry and fpread, with as much rapidity as may be, a warm alarm along the maritime provinces of France.

4th, In cafe, by the bleffing of God upon our arms, you fhall make yourfelf mafter of any place on the coaft of France, our will and pleafure is, that you do not keep poffeffion thereof; but that, after demolifhing and deftroying, as far as may be, all works, defences, magazines, arfenals, fhipping, and naval ftores, you do proceed, fucceffively, on the ulterior

part

part of this expedition, according as any of them fhall be judged advifable, and may be performed with fuch time as fhall be confiftent with your return with the troops under your command, fo as to be in England at, or about, or as near as may be, the latter end of September, unlefs the circumftances of our forces and fleet fhall neceffarily require their return fooner; and you are to land the troops at Portfmouth, or fuch other of our ports as the exigency of the cafe may fuggeft.

5th, Whereas it is neceffary, that, upon certain occafions, you fhould have the affiftance of a council of war, we have thought fit to appoint fuch a council, which fhall confift of four of our principal land-officers, and of an equal number of our principal fea-commanders, including the commanders in chief of our land and fea forces, (except in cafes happening at land, relating to the carrying on any military operations, to be performed by our land forces only, in which cafes you may call a council of war, confifting of fuch officers of our land forces as you fhall think proper), and all fuch land and fea officers, in the feveral cafes before mentioned, are hereby refpectively directed, from time to time, to be aiding and affifting with their advice, fo often as they fhall be called together by you, or by the commander in chief of our fquadron, for that purpofe; and in all fuch councils of war, when affembled, the majority of voices fhall determine the refolutions thereof; and, in cafe the voices fhall happen to be equal, the prefident fhall have the cafting vote.

6th, And whereas the fuccefs of this expedition will very much depend upon an entire good underftanding between our land and fea officers, we do hereby ftrictly enjoin and require you, on your part, to maintain and cultivate fuch good underftanding and agreement; and to order that the foldiers under your command fhould man the fhips when there fhall be occafion for them, and when they can be fpared from the land fervice; as the commander in chief of our fquadron is inftructed on his part, to entertain and cultivate the fame good underftanding and agreement; and to order the failors and marines, and alfo the foldiers ferving as a part of the complements of our fhips, to affift our land forces, if judged expedient, by ta-

king poſt on ſhore, manning batteries, covering the boats, ſecuring the ſafe re-embarkation of the troops, and ſuch other
ſervice as may be conſiſtent with the ſafety of our fleet. And
in order to eſtabliſh the ſtricteſt union that may be between you
and the commander in chief of our ſhips, you are hereby required to communicate theſe inſtructions to him, and he will
be directed to communicate thoſe he ſhall receive to you.

7th, You ſhall, from time to time, and as you ſhall have opportunity, ſend conſtant accounts of your proceedings in the
execution of theſe our inſtructions, to one of our principal ſecretaries of ſtate, from whom you will receive ſuch further orders and directions as we may think proper to give you.

G. R.

## No. VIII. (P. 175.)

*Tranſlation of an intercepted letter from General Lally to Mr.
Raymond, French reſident at Pullicat, dated Pondicherry, the
2d January, 1761.*

Mr RAYMOND,

THE Engliſh ſquadron is no more, Sir; out of the twelve
ſhips they had in our road, ſeven are loſt, crews and all; the
four others diſmaſted; and it appears that there is no more than
one frigate that has eſcaped; therefore do not loſe an inſtant to
ſend us chelingoes upon chelingoes, loaded with rice: the
Dutch have nothing to fear now, beſides (according to the law
of nations) they are only to ſend us no proviſions themſelves,
and we are no more blocked up by ſea. The ſaving of Pondicherry hath been in your power once already; if you miſs the
preſent opportunity, it will be entirely your fault. Do not for-
get alſo ſome ſmall chelingoes; offer great rewards. I expect
ſeventeen thouſand Marattoes within theſe four days. In ſhort,
riſque all, attempt all, force all, and ſend us ſome rice, ſhould
it be but half a garſe at a time.

(Signed) LALLY.

part of this expedition, according as any of them fhall be judged advifable, and may be performed with fuch time as fhall be confiftent with your return with the troops under your command, fo as to be in England at, or about, or as near as may be, the latter end of September, unlefs the circumftances of our forces and fleet fhall neceffarily require their return fooner; and you are to land the troops at Portfmouth, or fuch other of our ports as the exigency of the cafe may fuggeft.

5*th*, Whereas it is neceffary, that, upon certain occafions, you fhould have the affiftance of a council of war, we have thought fit to appoint fuch a council, which fhall confift of four of our principal land-officers, and of an equal number of our principal fea-commanders, including the commanders in chief of our land and fea forces, (except in cafes happening at land, relating to the carrying on any military operations, to be performed by our land forces only, in which cafes you may call a council of war, confifting of fuch officers of our land forces as you fhall think proper), and all fuch land and fea officers, in the feveral cafes before mentioned, are hereby refpectively directed, from time to time, to be aiding and affifting with their advice, fo often as they fhall be called together by you, or by the commander in chief of our fquadron, for that purpofe; and in all fuch councils of war, when affembled, the majority of voices fhall determine the refolutions thereof; and, in cafe the voices fhall happen to be equal, the prefident fhall have the cafting vote.

6*th*, And whereas the fuccefs of this expedition will very much depend upon an entire good underftanding between our land and fea officers, we do hereby ftrictly enjoin and require you, on your part, to maintain and cultivate fuch good underftanding and agreement; and to order that the foldiers under your command fhould man the fhips when there fhall be occafion for them, and when they can be fpared from the land fervice; as the commander in chief of our fquadron is inftructed on his part, to entertain and cultivate the fame good underftanding and agreement; and to order the failors and marines, and alfo the foldiers ferving as a part of the complements of our fhips, to affift our land forces, if judged expedient, by ta-

king poft on fhore, manning batteries, covering the boats, fecuring the fafe re-embarkation of the troops, and fuch other
fervice as may be confiftent with the fafety of our fleet. And
in order to eftablifh the ftricteft union that may be between you
and the commander in chief of our fhips, you are hereby required to communicate thefe inftructions to him, and he will
be directed to communicate thofe he fhall receive to you.

 7*th*, You fhall, from time to time, and as you fhall have opportunity, fend conftant accounts of your proceedings in the
execution of thefe our inftructions, to one of our principal fecretaries of ftate, from whom you will receive fuch further orders and directions as we may think proper to give you.

G. R.

## No. VIII. (P. 175.)

*Tranflation of an intercepted letter from General Lally to Mr.
Raymond, French refident at Pullicat, dated Pondicherry, the
2d January, 1761.*

Mr Raymond,

 THE Englifh fquadron is no more, Sir; out of the twelve
fhips they had in our road, feven are loft, crews and all; the
four others difmafted; and it appears that there is no more than
one frigate that has efcaped; therefore do not lofe an inftant to
fend us chelingoes upon chelingoes, loaded with rice: the
Dutch have nothing to fear now, befides (according to the law
of nations) they are only to fend us no provifions themfelves,
and we are no more blocked up by fea. The faving of Pondicherry hath been in your power once already; if you mifs the
prefent opportunity, it will be entirely your fault. Do not for-
get alfo fome fmall chelingoes; offer great rewards. I expect
feventeen thoufand Marattoes within thefe four days. In fhort,
rifque all, attempt all, force all, and fend us fome rice, fhould
it be but half a garfe at a time.

(Signed) LALLY.

## No. IX.   (P. 184).

*Capitulation for the citadel of Belleifle, made June 7, 1761.*

*Preliminary article.* The Chevalier de St. Croix, brigadier in the king's army, and commandant of the citadel of Belleifle, proposes that the place fhall furrender on the 12th of June, in cafe no fuccours arrive before that time; and that, in the mean while, no works fhall be carried on on either fide, nor any act of hoftility, nor any communication between the Englifh befieging and the French befieged.———" Refufed."

I. The entire garrifon fhall march through the breach with the honours of war, drums beating, colours flying, lighted matches, and three pieces of cannon, with twelve rounds each. Each foldier fhall have fifteen rounds in his cartouch-box. All the officers, ferjeants, foldiers, and inhabitants, are to carry off their baggage: the women to go with their hufbands.——— " Granted. In favour of the gallant defence which the citadel " has made, under the orders of the Chevalier de St. Croix."

II. Two covered waggons fhall be provided, and the effects which they carry fhall be depofited in two covered boats, which are not to be vifited.——— " The covered waggons are refufed; " but care fhall be taken to tranfport all the baggage to the " continent by the fhorteft way."

III. Veffels fhall be furnifhed for carrying the French troops by the fhorteft way into the neareft ports of France, by the firft fair wind.——— " Granted."

IV. The French troops that are to embark are to be victualled in the fame proportion with the troops of his Britannic majefty; and the fame proportion of tunnage is to be allowed to the officers and foldiers which the Englifh troops have.——— " Granted."

V. When the troops fhall be embarked, a veffel is to be furnifhed for the Chevalier de St. Croix, brigadier in the king's army, to M. de la Ville, the king's lieutenant, to M. de la Garique, colonel of foot, with brevet of commandant in the abfence of the Chevalier de St. Croix, and to the field-officers,

including

Including thofe of the artillery and engineers; as alfo for the three pieces of cannon, as well as for the foldiers of the Cour-Royale, to be tranfported to Nantz, with their wives, fervants, and the baggage which they have in the citadel, which is not to be vifited. They are to be victualled in the fame proportion with the Englifh officers of the fame rank.——" Care fhall be " taken that all thofe who are mentioned in this article fhall be " tranfported, without lofs of time, to Nantz, with their bag- " gage and effects, as well as the three pieces of cannon granted " by the firft article."

VI. After the expiration of the term mentioned in the firft article, a gate of the citadel fhall be delivered up to the troops of his Britannic majefty, at which there fhall be kept a French guard of equal number, until the king's troops fhall march out to embark. Thofe guards fhall be ordered to permit no Englifh foldier to enter, nor no French foldier to go out.——" A gate " fhall be delivered to the troops of his Britannic majefty the " moment the capitulation is figned; and an equal number of " French troops fhall occupy the fame gate."

VII. A veffel fhall be furnifhed to the commiffaries of war, and to the treafurer, in which they may carry their baggage, with their fecretaries, clerks, and fervants, without being mo-lefted or vifited. They fhall be conducted, as well as the other troops, to the neareft port of France.—— " Granted."

VIII. Meff. de Taille, captain-general of the garde cofte, Lamp, major, two lieutenants of cannoneers of the garde cofte, and ninety bombardiers, cannoneers, ferjeants, and fufileers, gardes coftes of Belleifle, paid by the king, fhall have it in their choice to remain in the ifland, as well as all the other inhabi-tants, without being molefted either as to their perfons or goods. And if they have a mind to fell their goods, furni-ture, boats, nets, and, in general, any effects which belong to them, within fix months, and to pafs over to the continent, they fhall not be hindered; but, on the contrary, they fhall have proper affiftance and the neceffary paffports ——" They " fhall remain in the ifland under protection of the king of " Great Britain, as the other inhabitants; or fhall be tranfport- " ed to the continent, if they pleafe, with the garrifon."

3 N 2.        IX. M.

IX. M. Sarignon, clerk of the treasury of the French troops, the armourer, the Bourgeois cannoneers, the storekeepers, and all the workmen belonging to the engineers, may remain at Belleisle with their families, or go to the continent with the same privileges as above mentioned.———" Granted. To re-" main in the island, upon the same footing with the other " inhabitants, or to be transported with the garrison to the " continent, as they shall think proper."

X. The Roman-Catholic religion shall be exercised in the island with the same freedom as under a French government. The churches shall be preserved, and the rectors and other priests continued; and, in case of death, they shall be replaced by the bishop of Vannes. They shall be maintained in their functions, privileges, immunities, and revenues.———" All the " inhabitants, without distinction, shall enjoy the free exercise " of their religion. The other part of this article must necef-" sarily depend on the pleasure of his Britannic majesty."

XI. The officers and soldiers, who are in the hospitals of the town and citadel, shall be treated in the same manner as the garrison, and, after their recovery, they shall be furnished with vessels to carry them to France. In the mean while they shall be supplied with subsistence and remedies till their departure, according to the state which the comptroller and surgeons shall give in.———" Granted."

XII. After the term mentioned in the preliminary article is expired, orders shall be given that the commissaries of artillery, engineers, and provisions, shall make an inventory of what shall be found in the king's magazines, out of which bread, wine, and meat shall be furnished to subsist the French troops to the moment of their departure.———" They shall be furnished with " necessary subsistence till their departure, on the same footing " with the troops of his Britannic majesty."

XIII. Maj. Gen. Crawfurd, as well as all the English officers and soldiers who have been made prisoners since the 8th of April 1761 inclusive, shall be set at liberty after the signing of the capitulation, and shall be disengaged from their parole. The French officers of different ranks, volunteers, serjeants, and soldiers, who have been made prisoners since the 9th of

April,

April, shall also be set at liberty.———" The English officers
" and soldiers, prisoners of war in the citadel, are to be free
" the moment the capitulation is signed. The French officers
" and soldiers, who are prisoners of war, shall be exchanged
" according to the cartel of Sluys."

All the above articles shall be executed faithfully on both
sides, and such as may be doubtful shall be fairly interpreted.
———" Granted."

After the signature hostages shall be sent on both sides, for
the security of the articles of the capitulation.———" Granted."

" All the archives, registers, public papers, and writings,
" which have any relation to the government of this island,
" shall be faithfully given up to his Britannic majesty's commis-
" sary. Two days shall be allowed for the evacuation of the
" citadel; and the transports, necessary for the embarkation,
" shall be ready to receive the garrison and their effects. A
" French officer shall be ordered to deliver up all the warlike
" stores and provisions, and, in general, every thing which be-
" longs to his most Christian majesty, to an English commis-
" sary appointed for that purpose; and an officer shall be or-
" dered to shew us all the mines and souterains of the place."

         S. HODGSON.         A. KEPPEL.
        Le Chevalier de St. CROIX.

## No. X.    (P. 198.)

*A Lift of the Spanish Fleet as it stood at the breaking out of the war in 1762.*

| Ships. | Guns. | Ships. | Guns. |
|---|---|---|---|
| El Phœnix, | 80 | El Hercules, | 68 |
| El Rayo, | 80 | El Principe, | 68 |
| La Rayna, | 70 | El Victoriofo, | 68 |
| El Tigre, | 70 | El Terrible, | 68 |
| La Galicia, | 70 | El Allante, | 68 |
| El Infanto, | 70 | Africa, | 68 |
| La Princeffa, | 70 | El Firme, | 68 |
| El San Philippe, | 70 | El Aquilos, | 68 |
| El Oriente, | 68 | La Efpana, | 62 |
| El Levia, | 68 | Ferdinando, | 60 |
| El Aquilon, | 68 | Afia, | 60 |
| El Neptuno, | 68 | El Septentrion, | 60 |
| El Brillante, | 68 | El America, | 60 |
| El Gloriofo, | 68 | El Dragon, | 60 |
| El Guerriero, | 68 | La Europa, | 60 |
| El Vencedor, | 68 | La Caftella, | 60 |
| El Soberano, | 68 | El Campion, | 58 |
| El Hector, | 68 | El Tridente, | 58 |
| El Gallardo, | 68 | El Conqueftador, | 58 |
| El Magnanimo, | 68 | El Aftuto, | 58 |
| El Dichofo, | 68 | El Fuerte, | 50 |
| El Diligente, | 68 | Adventurero, | 30 |
| El Triumphante, | 68 | Andaluzio, | 30 |
| El Monarcho, | 68 | La Efmeralda, | 30 |
| El Serio, | 68 | La Pallas, | 26 |
| El Arrogante, | 68 | La Juno, | 26 |
| El Superbe, | 68 | La Eftrea, | 26 |
| El Ponderofo, | 68 | La Ventura, | 26 |
| El Contente, | 68 | La Venus, | 26 |
| | | L'Induftrie, | |

| Ships. | Guns. | Ships. | Guns. |
|---|---|---|---|
| L'Induftrie, | 26 | La Flora, | 20 |
| La Liebre, | 26 | El Diligente, | 20 |
| La Venganza, | 24 | El Jafon, | 20 |
| La Vittoria, | 24 | La Conception, | 20 |
| La Hermiona, | 24 | El Gabilan, | 20 |
| Galgo, | 22 | Gilano Xebeque, | 18 |
| La Dorada, | 22 | El Mercurio, | 18 |
| La Peria, | 22 | El Jupiter, | 18 |
| La Aquila, | 22 | El Vofante, | 18 |
| La Frecha, | 22 | El Cafador, | 18 |
| La Gazutta, | 22 | Marte, | 16 |
| El Catalan, | 22 | Liebre, | 16 |
| El Ibecinea, | 22 | El Majorquin, | 16 |

### Bomb-ketches.

| | | | |
|---|---|---|---|
| El Efterope, | 16 | El Pieramonte, | 16 |
| El Bronje, | 16 | El Bolcano, | 16 |

### Fire-fhips.

| | |
|---|---|
| El Valenciano, | El Botompago, |
| El Frueno, | El Bayo. |

### Addition made to the Spanifh navy during the war.

| | | | |
|---|---|---|---|
| El Monarco, | 86 | La Nouva Princeffa, | 84 |
| El Elephante, | 76 | El Vigorofo, | 74 |
| El Gujon, | 70 | El St. Geronimo, | 60 |
| El Diamante, | 64 | | |

No. XI.

## No. XI.    (P. 204.)

PAPERS relating to the conqueſt of MARTINICO.

*Articles of capitulation of the citadel of Fort Royal, in the iſland of Martinico, the 4th of February, 1762.*

*Article* I. THE commanding officer of the citadel ſhall march out at the head of the garriſon, compoſed of troops detached from the marine, the royal grenadiers, cannoniers, bombardiers and Swiſs ; the different detachments of the militia and freebooters, and the other volunteers, with the honours of war, and three rounds of ammunition each.——Anſwered, " The troops of his moſt Chriſtian Majeſty ſhall be embarked " and ſent to France, as ſoon as poſſible, at the expence of his " Britannic Majeſty ; but the troops belonging to the iſland " ſhall lay down their arms, and be priſoners of war, until the " fate of Martinico is determined."

II. That the officers and others ſhall preſerve their effects, have time to ſettle their affairs, and ſhall take their ſervants along with them.—" Granted "

III. That three days ſhall be granted for the evacuation of the place, at the end of which time the gate ſhall be given up to the troops of his Britannic Majeſty, whilſt the garriſon ſhall march out at nine to-morrow morning.——Anſwered, " The " gate of the fort ſhall be given up to the troops of his Bri- " tannic Majeſty this evening at five o'clock, and the French " garriſon ſhall march out at nine to-morrow morning."

              (Signed)      ROBERT MONKTON,

DE LIGNERY.                G. B. RODNEY.

*Capitulation demanded by the inhabitants of the island of Marti-
nico, represented by Messrs. D'Alesso, knight, Signior Defrag-
ny, La Pierre, captain of horse, and Feryre, captain of infantry, furnished with full powers from nine quarters of the
island.*

*Article* I. The inhabitants shall quit their posts with two
field-pieces, drums beating, colours flying, matches lighted,
and all the honours of war.———" The inhabitants shall march
" out of all their garrisons and posts with their arms; upon
" condition that they afterwards lay them down; and that all
" the forts, batteries, and military implements, be delivered to
" persons appointed to receive them."

II. The inhabitants shall have the free exercise of their religion, and the priests, nuns and friars, shall be preserved in their
cures and convents.———" Granted.".

III. The inhabitants shall not be obliged to take arms against
his most Christian Majesty, nor even against any other power.——
" They become subjects of his Britannic Majesty, and must
" take the oath of allegiance; but shall not be obliged to take
" arms against his most Christian Majesty, until a peace may
" determine the fate of the island."

" IV. The inhabitants shall be preserved in their privileges,
" rights, honours and exemptions.———" They are subjects of
" his Britannic Majesty, and shall enjoy their properties, and
" the same privileges as in the other of his Majesty's Leeward
" Islands."

V. The prisoners taken during the siege shall be restored on
both sides; the free mulattoes, as well as the negroes, shall be
restored as prisoners of war.———" The inhabitants and mu-
" lattoes will become British subjects, upon the submission of
" the whole island. The negroes taken in arms are deemed
" slaves."

VI. The subjects of Great Britain, who have taken refuge
in the island for crimes, or condemned to punishments, shall
have liberty of retiring.———" Refused."

VII. No others than the inhabitants of this island shall, till the peace, possess any estates, either by acquisition, agreement, or otherwise; but in case at the peace the country shall be ceded to the king of Great Britain, then it shall be permitted to the inhabitants, who shall not be willing to become his subjects, to sell their estates, and to retire to any place they think proper.———" All subjects of Great Britain may possess any lands or " houses by purchase. The remainder of this article granted, " provided they sell to British subjects."

VIII. The inhabitants and merchants shall enjoy all their privileges of commerce, as the subjects of Great Britain.——— " Granted; so that it does not affect the privileges of particu- " lar companies established in England, or the laws of the " kingdom, which prohibit the carrying on trade in other " than British bottoms."

    Signed by the above-mentioned deputies, and by *Robert Monkton* and *G. B. Rodney*, commanders of his Britannic Majesty's forces by sea and land, the 7th February, 1762.

On the 13th of February a similar capitulation was demanded for the whole island, and granted with the same restrictions.

No. XII.

## No. XII.   (P. 219.)

*Abstract of the articles of capitulation agreed upon between Sir George Pocock, knight of the Bath, and the earl of Albemarle, and the marquis of Real Transporte, commander in chief of the squadron of his Catholic majesty, and Don Juan de Prado, governor of the Havannah, for the surrender of the city, and all its dependencies, with all the Spanish ships in the harbour.*

### PRELIMINARY ARTICLE.

FORT La Punta and the land-gate shall be delivered to his Britannic majesty's troops to-morrow morning, the 13th of August, at twelve o'clock; at which time it is expected the following articles of capitulation shall be signed and ratified.

ARTICLE I. The garrison, consisting of the infantry, artillery-men, and dragoons, the different militia of the towns in the island, shall march out of the land-gate the 20th instant, provided in that time no relief arrives, so as to raise the siege, with all the military honours, arms shouldered, six field pieces of 12 pounders each, and as many rounds to each soldier; the regiments shall take out with them the military chests. And the governor shall have six covered waggons which are not to be examined upon any pretence whatever.—" The garrison shall " have the honours of war, and shall march out of the Punta " gate with two pieces of cannon, and six rounds for each gun. " The military chest refused. The governor will be allowed as " many boats as necessary to transport his baggage and effects " on board the ships destined for him. The military without " the town, as well as those within, to deliver up their arms " to the British commissary."

II. The marines, and the ships crews who have served on shore, shall obtain, on their going out, the same honours as the garrison of the city; and shall proceed with those honours on board the said ships, that they may, together with their commander in chief, Don Gutierres de Hevia, marquis del Real Transporte, sail in the said ships as soon as the port is open,

with

with all their money and effects, in order to proceed to some other port belonging to Spain, in doing which they will oblige themselves, that, during their navigation to their destined port, they shall not attack any vessels belonging to his Britannic majesty, his subjects or allies. Likewise liberty shall be granted to the marines and ships crews, with their officers, to go on board the said ships, and carry with them the effects and money in the city belonging to his Catholic majesty.———" The marquis " of Real Transporte, with his officers, sailors and marines, as " making part of the garrison, shall be treated in every respect " as the governor and regular troops. All ships in the Havan- " nah, and all money and effects belonging to his Catholic " majesty, shall be delivered up to persons appointed by Sir " George Pocock and the earl of Albemarle."

III. That the Roman Catholic religion shall be maintained and preserved in the same manner as it has hitherto been in all the dominions belonging to his Catholic majesty; and the different orders, colleges and universities remain in the full enjoyment of all their rights.——" Granted."

IV. That, in consideration that this port is situated by nature for the relief of those who navigate in those parts of Spanish and British America, that this port shall be allowed to be neutral to the subjects of his Catholic majesty; who are to be admitted in and out freely, to take in such refreshments as they may be in need of, as well as repairing their vessels, paying the current prices for every thing, and that they are not to be insulted nor interrupted in their navigation by any vessels belonging to his Britannic majesty, or his subjects or allies, from the capes Caloche, on the coast of Campeche, and that of St. Antonio to the westward of this island, nor from the Tortuga bank to this port; and from hence till they get into the latitude of 33 degrees north, till both their majesties agree to the contrary.——" Refused."

V. That the effects detained in this city belonging to the merchants of Cadiz, which have arrived here in the different register ships, and in which are interested all the European nations, a sufficient passport shall be granted to the supercargoes thereof, that they may freely remit the same with the register ships,

fhips, without running the rifque of being infulted in their paffage.——" Refufed."

VI. That thofe civil or other officers, who have had charge
of the management of the adminiftration and diftribution of the
royal treafure, or any other affair of a peculiar nature from
his Catholic majefty, they are to be left with the free ufe of
all thofe papers which concern the difcharge of their duty,
with free liberty to carry them to Spain for that purpofe; and
the fame fhall be underftood with the managers of the royal
company in this city.——" All public papers to be delivered to
" the fecretaries of the admiral and general for infpection,
" which fhall be returned to his Catholic majefty's officers, if
" not found neceffary for the government of the ifland."

       (Signed)  ALBEMARLE.
             G. POCOCK.

EL MARQUES DEL REAL TRANSPORTE.
JUAN DE PRADO.

No. XIII.

## No. XIII.    (P. 246.)

*Abſtraſt of the principal articles of the definitive treaty of peace and
friendſhip between his Britannic majeſty, the moſt Chriſtian king,
and the king of Spain; concluded at Paris the 10th day of February, 1763. To which the king of Portugal acceded on the
ſame day.*

BE it known to all thoſe to whom it ſhall or may in any
manner belong. It has pleaſed the Moſt High to diffuſe the
ſpirit of concord and union among the princes, whoſe diviſions
had ſpread troubles in the four quarters of the globe. For this
purpoſe the high contracting parties have named and appointed
their reſpective ambaſſadors, his ſacred majeſty the king of
Great Britain, John duke of Bedford; his ſacred majeſty the
moſt Chriſtian king, Gabriel de Choiſeul duke of Praſlin; his
ſacred majeſty the Catholic king, Don Jerome marquis of Grimaldi; his ſacred majeſty the moſt Faithful king, Martin de
Mello and Caſtro; who, having duly communicated to each
other their full powers, have agreed upon the articles, the tenor of which is as follows.

*Article* I. There ſhall be a Chriſtian, univerſal, and perpetual peace, as well by ſea as by land, and a ſincere and conſtant
friendſhip ſhall be re-eſtabliſhed between the before-mentioned
ſovereigns; and a general oblivion of every thing that may have
been done or committed before or ſince the commencement of
the æra that is juſt ended.

II. The former treaties concluded between the reſpective
kingdoms are hereby renewed and confirmed in the beſt form,
and ſerve as the baſis of the preſent definitive treaty.

III. The priſoners made on all ſides, and the hoſtages carried
away or given during the war, ſhall be reſtored without ranſom,
each crown reſpectively paying the advances made for the ſub-
ſiſtence and maintenance of their priſoners, by the ſovereign of
the country where they ſhall have been detained.

IV. His moſt Chriſtian majeſty renounces all pretenſions
which he has heretofore formed, or might form to Nova Scotia,

tia, or Acadia, in all its parts; and guarantees the whole of it,
with all its dependencies, to the king of Great Britain: more-
over, his moft Chriftian majefty cedes and guarantees to his
Britannic majefty, in full right, Canada, with all its dependencies, as well as the ifland of Cape Breton, and all the other
iflands and coafts in the Gulf and River of St. Lawrence, and in
general every thing that depends on the faid countries, lands,
iflands, and coafts, with the fovereignty, property, and poffeffion, and all rights acquired by treaty or otherwife, which the
crown of France has had till now over the faid places. His Britannic majefty, on his fide, agrees to grant the liberty of the
Catholic religion to the inhabitants of Canada.

V. The fubjects of France fhall have the liberty of fifhing and
drying on a part of the coafts of the ifland of Newfoundland,
fuch as it is fpecified in the 13th article of the treaty of Utrecht;
and his Britannic majefty confents to leave to the fubjects of the
moft Chriftian king the liberty of fifhing in the Gulf St. Lawrence, on condition that the fubjects of France do not exercife
the faid fifhery, but at the diftance of three leagues from all the
coafts belonging to Great Britain.

VI. The king of Great Britain cedes the iflands of St. Pierre
and Miquelon, in full right to his moft Chriftian majefty, to
ferve as fhelter to the French fifhermen; and his moft Chriftian
majefty engages not to fortify the faid iflands, to erect no buildings upon them but merely for the convenience of the fifhery,
and to keep upon them a guard of fifty men only for the police.

VII. In order to re-eftablifh peace on folid and durable foundations, and to remove for ever all fubject of difpute with regard
to the limits of the Britifh and French territories on the continent of America, it is agreed that, for the future, the confines
between the dominions of the refpective crowns in that part of
the world fhall be fixed irrevocably by a line drawn along the
middle of the Miffiffippi, from its fource to the river Iberville,
and from thence by a line drawn along the middle of this river,
and the lakes Maurepas and Pontchartrain to the fea; and for
this purpofe the moft Chriftian king cedes in full right the river
and port of the Mobile, and every thing which he poffeffed on
                                                          the

the left side of the river Mississippi, except the town of New Orleans, and the island in which it is situated.

VIII. The king of Great Britain shall restore to France the islands of Guadaloupe, of Marie-Galante, of Desirade, of Martinico, and Belleisle; and the fortresses of these islands shall be restored in the same condition they were in when they were conquered by the British arms.

IX. The most Christian king cedes and guarantees to his Britannic majesty the islands of Grenada and of the Grenadines; and the partition of the islands called neutral is agreed and fixed, so that those of St. Vincent, Dominica, and Tobago, shall remain in full right to Great Britain, and that of St. Lucia shall be delivered to France to enjoy the same likewise in full right.

X. His Britannic majesty restores to France the island of Goree; and his most Christian majesty cedes to Great Britain the river Senegal, with the forts and factories of St. Lewis, Podor, and Galam.

XI. In the East Indies, Great Britain shall restore to France the different factories which that crown possessed on the coast of Coromandel and Malabar, as also in Bengal, at the beginning of the year 1749. His most Christian majesty shall restore, on his side, all that he may have conquered in the East Indies during the present war.

XII. The island of Minorca shall be restored to his Britannic majesty as well as Fort St. Philippe; and the town and port of Dunkirk shall be put into the state fixed by the last treaty of Aix la Chapelle.

XIII. His Britannic majesty shall cause to be demolished all the fortifications which his subjects shall have erected in the Bay of Honduras; and his Catholic majesty shall not permit, on any pretence whatever, the British subjects to be disturbed in their occupation of cutting, loading, and carrying away logwood.

XIV. The king of Great Britain restores to Spain all the territory which he has conquered in the island of Cuba, with the fortress of the Havanna; and, in consequence of this restitution, his Catholic majesty cedes to Great Britain Florida, with Fort St. Augustine, and the bay of Pensacola, as well as all that

t                          Spain

Spain poſſeſſed on the continent of North America, to the eaſt and to the ſouth-eaſt of the river Miſſiſſippi.

XV. There is a reciprocal reſtoration, on all ſides, of the conqueſts made in Germany and Portugal.

XVI. The deciſion of the prizes, made in time of peace by the ſubjeĉts of Great Britain on the Spaniards, ſhall be referred to the courts of juſtice of the Admiralty of Great Britain, conformable to the rules eſtabliſhed among all nations; ſo that the validity of the ſaid prizes between the Britiſh and Spaniſh nations ſhall be decided and judged according to the law of nations, and according to treaties in the courts of juſtice of the nation who ſhall have made the capture.

## No. XIV.  (P. 338.)

*Abſtraĉt of the Declaration ſigned and delivered by Prince Maſſe-rano, ambaſſador extraordinary from his Catholic majeſty, dated the 22d January, 1771; which was the ſame day accepted by the earl of Rochford, one of his majeſty's principal ſecretaries of ſtate.*

HIS Britannic majeſty having complained of the violence which was committed on the 10th of June, 1770, at the iſland commonly called the Great Malouine, and by the Engliſh Falkland's Iſland, in obliging by force the commander and ſubjeĉts of his Britannic majeſty to evacuate the port by them called Egmont; a ſtep offenſive to the honour of his crown;—the prince de Maſſerano has received orders to declare, that his Catholic majeſty conſidering the deſire with which he is animated for peace, and for the maintenance of good harmony with his Britannic majeſty, and reflecting that this event might interrupt it, has ſeen with diſpleaſure this expedition tending to diſturb it; and in the perſuaſion, in which he is, of the reciprocity of ſentiments of his Britannic majeſty, and of its being far from his ſentiments to authorize any thing that might diſturb the good underſtanding between the two courts; his Catholic majeſty does diſavow the ſaid violent enterprize, and in conſequence, the Prince Maſſerano declares, that his Catholic majeſty engages to

give immediate orders that things fhall be reftored in the Great
Malouine, at the port called Egmont, precifely to the ftate in
which they were before the 10th of June, 1770: for which
purpofe his Catholic majefty will give orders to one of his officers to deliver up, to the officer authorized by his Britannic
majefty, the port and fort called Egmont, with all the artillery,
ftores, and effects of his Britannic majefty and his fubjects. The
prince de Mafferano declares at the fame time in the name of
the king his mafter, that the engagement to reftore the poffeffion of Port Egmont, cannot nor ought any ways to affect the
queftion of the prior right of fovereignty of the Malouine
Iflands, otherwife called Falkland's Iflands.

## No. XV.   (P. 340.)

*The Proteft of the Lords againft an addrefs to his Majefty to re-
turn thanks for his firm and fpirited conduct in demanding fatisfaction for the violent enterprize againft Falkland's Iflands.*

*DISSENTIENT,* I. Becaufe it is highly unfuitable to the
wifdom and gravity of this houfe, and to the refpect which we
owe to his majefty and ourfelves, to carry up to the throne an
addrefs, approving the acceptance of an imperfect inftrument,
which has neither been previoufly authorized by any fpecial full
powers produced by the Spanifh minifter, nor been as yet ratified by the king of Spain. If the ratification on the part of
Spain fhould be refufed, the addrefs of this houfe will appear
no better than an act of precipitate adulation to minifters;
which will juftly expofe the peerage of the kingdom to the indignation of their country, and to the derifion of all Europe.

II. Becaufe it is a direct infult on the feelings and underftanding of the people of Great Britain, to approve this declaration and acceptance, as a means of fecuring our own and the
general tranquillity, whilft the greateft preparations for war
are making both by fea and land.

III. Becaufe, from the declaration and correfpondence laid
before us, we are of opinion that the minifters merit the cenfure
                                                              of

of this house, rather than any degree of commendation, on account of several improper acts, and equally improper omissions, from the beginning to the close of this transaction : for it is afserted by the Spanish ministers that several discussions had passed which might give the British ministers reason to foresee the attack upon that settlement that was afterwards made by the forces of Spain. Captain Hunt also arriving from them gave them the same intimations ; yet so obstinately negligent and supine were his majesty's ministers, that they did not even make a single representation to the court of Spain ; which might have prevented the injury, and saved the enormous expence, and manifold hardships, which the nation has suffered in preparing to resent it.

IV. Because the negotiation entered into much too late, was from the commencement conducted on principles as disadvantageous to the wisdom of our public councils, as it was finally concluded in a manner disgraceful to the crown of Great Britain; for it appears that the court of Madrid did disavow the act of hostility, as proceeding from particular instructions, but justified it under her general instructions to her governors ; under the oath by them taken, and under the established laws of America.

V. Because nothing has been had or demanded as a reparation in damage for the enormous expence and other inconveniencies, arising from the unprovoked and confessed violence of the Spanish forces in the enterprize against Falkland's Island, and the long subsequent delay of justice.

VI. Because an unparalleled and most audacious insult has been offered to the honour of the British flag, by the detention of a ship of war of his majesty's, for twenty days after the surrender of Port Egmont, and by the indignity of forcibly taking away her rudder. No reparation in honour is demanded for this wanton insult, by which his majesty's reign is rendered the unhappy æra in which the honour of the British flag has suffered the first stain with entire impunity.

VII. Because the declaration by which his majesty is to obtain possession of Port Egmont, contains a reservation or condition of the question of the claim of prior right, being the firſt time ſuch a claim has ever authentically appeared in any public inſtrument concluded on by the two courts.

The above was ſigned by ſixteen peers.

## No. XVI. (P. 342).

*An account of the Naval Review at Portſmouth, in June* 1773.

EARLY in the morning on Tueſday the 22d inſtant, the king ſet out from Kew for Portſmouth, and being arrived at Portſea Bridge, between ten and eleven the ſame morning, was received by a royal ſalute of 21 guns. His majeſty then proceeded to the firſt barrier, when Major-general Parker, who commanded the garriſon during the royal reſidence at Portſmouth, delivered the keys to the king, who was pleaſed to return them. On his majeſty's entering the Grand-port Gate, he was ſaluted by a triple diſcharge of 232 pieces of cannon mounted on the ramparts of Portſmouth, at Blackhouſe Fort, and at South-Sea Caſtle. His majeſty proceeded through the town out of the Water-gate to the dock-yard, and arrived at the commiſſioner's houſe ten minutes before eleven o'clock, where he was received by the preſident of the council, and ſeveral other of the great officers of ſtate, the commiſſioners of the Admiralty, and the three admirals of the ſquadron at Spithead. The officers and workmen belonging to the yard, gave three cheers as his majeſty entered, and then returned to their ſeveral employments. After his majeſty had taken ſome refreſhment, he went to the governor's houſe, where he had a public levee, and then returning to the dock-yard, embarked at half an hour after one in a barge in which the royal ſtandard was immediately hoiſted. His majeſty then proceeded to Spithead, attended by the barge of the Board of Admiralty, with the flag of their office, the three admirals with their flags, and all the captains of the fleet with their pendants in their barges. As his majeſty paſſed the garriſon he was ſaluted by twenty-one guns from the Blockhouſe Fort, Saluting Platform and South-Sea Caſtle. When the royal ſtandard was ſeen by the fleet at Spithead, conſiſting of twenty ſhips of the line, two frigates, and three ſloops, moored in two lines abreaſt of each other,

other, the whole manned fhips, and faluted with twenty-one guns each.   The king went on board the Barfleur of 9e guns, where he was received by the Board of Admiralty, the captain being at the head of the accommodation ladder, and the fide manned by the lieutenants of the fhips.   As foon as his majefty paffed the guard of marines on the quarter-deck, the flag of the lord high admiral, which was then flying, was ftruck, and the royal ftandard hoifted at the main-top-maft head, the lord high admiral's flag at the fore-top-maft head, and the union flag at the mizen-top-maft head : on the right of which all the fhips, except the Barfleur, faluted with twenty-one guns each. The fhips being cleared as for action, and the officers and men at their refpective quarters, his majefty, after the nobility who came off upon this occafion, and the flag officers had paid their duty to him on the quarter deck, walked fore and aft on the lower gun-deck, and took a view of the whole.   His majefty then dined on board the Barfleur, and after dinner went into the Augufta yacht, and after making the circle of the fleet, failed into the harbour.   Similar ceremonies were repeated during the four following days, in which time the king made feveral naval promotions, knighted many admirals, and diftributed money to the failors and workmen.

No,

## No. XVII.  (P. 412.)

LIST of the FRENCH Fleet in 1778.

B. *fignifies Brefs*, T. *Toulon*, R. *Rochfort*, *and* L'O. *L'Orient.*

| Ships. | Guns. | Ships. | Guns. |
|---|---|---|---|
| B. La Bretagne, | 110 | T. Le Cæfar, | 74 |
| La Ville de Paris, | 90 | La Bourgogne, | 74 |
| Le St. Efprit, | 80 | Le Souverain, | 74 |
| La Couronne, | 80 | Le Deftin, | 74 |
| Le Duc de Burgogne, | 80 | L'Altier, | 64 |
| L'Orient, | 74 | Le Lion, | 64 |
| Le Magnifique, | 74 | Le Vaillant, | 64 |
| L'Intrepide, | 74 | B. La Pourvoyeure, | 40 |
| Le Sceptre, | 74 | La Confolante, | 40 |
| Le Palmier, | 74 | La Belle Poulle, | 32 |
| Le Defenfeur, | 74 | L' Amphitrite, | 32 |
| Le Diademe, | 74 | La Dedaigneufe, | 32 |
| Le Zodiaque, | 74 | La Tourterelle, | 32 |
| Le Minataure, | 74 | La Nymphe, | 32 |
| Le Robufte, | 74 | La Malicieufe, | 32 |
| Le Citoyen, | 74 | La Licorne, | 32 |
| Le Six Corps, | 74 | Le Zephir, | 32 |
| Le Diligent, | 74 | L'Aigrette, | 32 |
| Le Glorieux, | 74 | L'Oifeau, | 32 |
| Le Conquerant, | 74 | La Tolle, | 32 |
| T. Le Tonnant, | 80 | Le Dauphin, | 70 |
| Le Languedoc, | 80 | Le Northumberland, | 78 |
| L'Actif, | 74 | La Proteé, | 64 |
| Le Bien Aimé, | 74 | Le Sphinx, | 64 |
| Le Guerrier, | 74 | Le Vengeur, | 64 |
| L'Hector, | 74 | Le Solitaire, | 64 |
| Le Fendant, | 74 | L'Union, | 64 |
| Le Zelé, | 74 | Le Brilliant, | 64 |
| Le Protecteur, | 74 | L'Actionnaire, | 64 |
| Le Marfeillois, | 74 | L'Indien, | |

| Ships. | Guns. | Ships. | Guns. |
|---|---|---|---|
| B. L'Indien, | 64 | B. Le David, | 28 |
| Le Roland, | 64 | L'Elephant, | 26 |
| L'Alexandre, | 64 | La Fortune, | 24 |
| Le Bizarre, | 64 | La Seine, | 24 |
| Le Reflechi, | 64 | La Menagerie, | 22 |
| Le Triton, | 64 | L'Etoile, | 20 |
| La Provence, | 64 | La Tampane, | 20 |
| Le Fantafque, | 64 | La Porteufe, | 20 |
| Le Hardi, | 64 | L'Eclufe, | 20 |
| Le Caton, | 64 | La Bouffole, | 20 |
| L'Amphion, | 50 | Le Compas, | 20 |
| Le Fier, | 50 | L'Efturgeon, | 20 |
| R. L'Artefien, | 64 | La Danae, | 26 |
| Le Refolu, | 64 | La Mouche, | 26 |
| Le St. Michel, | 64 | L'Enjouée, | 26 |
| Le Bourdelois, | 50 | L'O. Le Triton, | 26 |
| L'Hippopotame, | 50 | T. La Cagnelle, | 26 |
| L'O. Le Flamand, | 60 | L'Atalante, | 26 |
| T. Le Sagittaire, | 50 | La Precieufe, | 26 |
| L'Imperieux, | 32 | La Sultane, | 26 |
| L'Envieux, | 32 | La Chimere, | 26 |
| La Terpfichore, | 32 | L'Engageante, | 26 |
| La Comete, | 30 | La Gracieux, | 26 |
| La Diligente, | 26 | La Pleiade, | 26 |
| B. Le Renomeé, | 30 | La Fine, | 26 |
| La Sibylle, | 30 | La Topaze, | 26 |
| L'Indifcrete, | 30 | L'Aurore, | 26 |
| La Senfible, | 28 | La Fiore, | 26 |
| La Legere, | 26 | La Mignone, | 26 |
| L'Infidelle, | 26 | L'Amelone, | 26 |
| La Sincere, | 26 | L'Aimable, | 26 |
| L'Inconftante, | 26 | R. L'Ecole, | 16 |
| La Bondeufe, | 26 | Le Courrier, | 16 |
| La Blanche, | 26 | La Nourrice, | 14 |
| La Thetis, | 24 | La Barbue, | 14 |
| L'Etourdi, | 20 | La Corifante, | 14 |
| La Couliffe, | 28 | Le Solomon, | 12 |

In.

In all 67 capital veffels, 49 frigates, befides a great number of advice-boats, prames, pinks, xebeques and bomb-ketches.

## No. XVIII. (P. 442.)

*On the 30th December, the Duke of Bolton delivered to his Maje-fty, in his clofet, at St. James's, the following Memorial of the Admirals.*

## To the KING.

WE the fubfcribing admirals of your Majefty's royal navy, having hitherto on all occafions ferved your Majefty with zeal and fidelity, and being defirous of devoting every action of our lives, and our lives themfelves to your Majefty's fervice, and the defence of our country, think ourfelves indifpenfibly bound by our duty to that fervice and that country, with all poffible humility, to reprefent to your wifdom and juftice,

That Sir Hugh Pallifer, vice-admiral of the Blue, lately fer-ving under the command of the honourable Auguftus Keppel, did prefer certain articles of accufation, containing feveral mat-ters of heinous offence againft his faid commander in chief, to the lords commiffioners for executing the office of lord high admiral of Great Britain, he the faid Sir Hugh Pallifer being himfelf a commiffioner in the faid commiffion. This accufation he the faid Sir Hugh Pallifer with-held from the twenty-feventh day of July laft, the time of the fuppofed offences committed, until the ninth day of this prefent December, and then brought forward for the purpofe of recrimination againft charges conjec-tured by him the faid Sir Hugh Pallifer, but which in fact were never made.

That the commiffioners of the Admiralty, near five months after the pretended offences aforefaid, did receive from their faid colleague in office, the charge made by him againft his faid commander, and without taking into confideration the relative fituation of the accufer and the party accufed, or attending to the avowed motives of the accufation, or the length of time of

with-

with-holding, or the occasion of making the same, and without any other deliberation whatever, did, on the very same day on which the charge was preferred, and without previous notice to the party accused of an intention of making a charge against him, give notice of their intending that a court-martial should be held on the said Admiral Keppel, after forty years of meritorious service, and a variety of actions in which he had exerted eminent courage and conduct, by which the honour and power of this nation, and the glory of the British flag, had been maintained and increased in various parts of the world.

We beg leave to express to your Majesty our concern at this proceeding, and to represent our apprehensions of the difficulties and discouragements which will inevitably arise to your service therefrom; and that it will not be easy for men, attentive to their honour, to serve your Majesty, particularly in situations of principal command, if the practice now stated to your Majesty be countenanced, or the principles upon which the same has been supported shall prevail with any lord high admiral, or with any commissioner for executing that office.

We are humbly of opinion, that a criminal charge against an officer (rising in importance according to the rank and command of that officer) which suspends his service to your Majesty, perhaps in the most critical exigencies of the public affairs, which calls his reputation into doubt and discussion, which puts him on trial for his life, profession and reputation, and which, in its consequences, may cause a fatal cessation in the naval exertions of the kingdom, to be a matter of the most serious nature, and never to be made by authority but on solid ground, and on mature deliberation. The honour of an officer is his most precious possession and best qualification; the public have an interest in it; and whilst those under whom we serve countenance accusation, it is often impossible perfectly to restore military fame by the mere acquittal of a court-martial. Imputations made by high authority remain long and affect deeply. The sphere of action of commanders in chief is large, and their business intricate, and subject to great variety of opinion; and before they are to be put on the judgment of others for acts done upon their discretion, the greatest discretion ought to be employed.

Whether the Board of Admiralty hath by law any such discretion, we, who are not of the profession of the law, cannot positively assert; but if we had conceived that this Board had no legal use of their reason in a point of such delicacy and importance, we should have known on what terms we served. But we never did imagine it possible, that we were to receive orders from, and be accountable to those who, by law, were reduced to become passive instruments to the possible malice, ignorance, or treason of any individual who might think fit to disarm his Majesty's navy of its best and highest officers. We conceive it disrespectful to the laws of our country to suppose them capable of such manifest injustice and absurdity.

We therefore humbly represent, in behalf of public order, as well as of the discipline of the navy, to your Majesty, the dangers of long concealed, and afterwards precipitately adopted charges, and of all recriminatory accusations of subordinate officers against their commanders in chief; and particularly the mischief and scandal of permitting men, who are at once in high civil office, and in subordinate military command, previous to their making such accusations, to attempt to corrupt the public judgment, by the publication of libels on their officers in a common news-paper, thereby exciting mutiny in your Majesty's navy, as well as prejudicing the minds of those who are to try the merits of the accusation against the said superior officer.

| | |
|---|---|
| HAWKE, | BRISTOL, |
| JOHN MOORE, | JAMES YOUNG, |
| BOLTON, | MATTHEW BARTON, |
| SAMUEL GRAVES, | FRANCIS GEARY, |
| HUGH PIGOT, | SHULDHAM, |
| ROBERT HARLAND. | CLARK GAYTON. |

No. XIX.

## No. XIX.　(P. 444.)

*January* 30, 1779.

*This morning, at half paſt ten o'clock, the court-martial were refumed, and Admiral Keppel delivered the following ſpeech:*

### The DEFENCE *of Admiral* KEPPEL.

SIR,

AFTER forty years ſpent in the ſervice of my country, little did I think of being brought to a court-martial to anſwer to charges of miſconduct, negligence in the performance of duty, and tarniſhing the honour of the Britiſh navy. Theſe charges, Sir, have been advanced by my accuſer. Whether he has ſucceeded in proving them or not the court will determine. Before he brought me to a trial, it would have been candid in him to have given vent to his thoughts, and not by a deceptious ſhew of kindneſs to lead me into the miſtake of ſuppofing a friend in the man who was my enemy in his heart, and was ſhortly to be my accuſer. Yet, Sir, after all my miſconduct; after ſo much negligence in the performance of duty, and after tarniſhing ſo deeply the honour of the Britiſh navy, my accuſer made no ſcruple to fail a ſecond time with the man who had been the betrayer of his country! Nay, during the time we were on ſhore, he correſponded with me on terms of friendſhip, and even in his letters he approved of what had been done, of the part which he now condemns, and of the very negligent miſconduct, which has ſince been ſo offenſive in his eyes!

Such behaviour, Sir, on the part of my accuſer, gave me little reaſon to apprehend an accuſation from him. Nor had I any reaſon to ſuppoſe that the ſtate would criminate me. When I returned, his majeſty received me with the greateſt applauſe. Even the firſt lord of the Admiralty gave his flattering teſtimony to the rectitude of my conduct, and ſeemed with vaſt ſincerity to applaud my zeal for the ſervice. Yet in the moment of approbation, it ſeems as if a ſcheme was concerting againſt my

life;

life; for, without any previous notice, five articles of a charge were exhibited against me by Sir Hugh Pallifer, who, moft unfortunately for his caufe, lay himfelf under an imputation of difobedience of orders, at the very time when he accufed me of negligence! This to be fure was a very ingenious mode of getting the ftart of me. An accufation exhibited againft a commander in chief might draw off the public attention from negléct of duty in an inferior officer. I could almoft wifh, in pity to my accufer, that appearances were not fo ftrong againft him. Before the trial commenced, I actually thought that my accufer might have fome tolerable reafons for his conduct. But from the evidence, even as adduced to account for the behaviour of the honourable gentleman in the afternoon of the 27th of July, from that evidence I fay, Sir, I find that I was miftaken. The trial has left my accufer without excufe, and he now cuts that fort of figure which, I truft in God, all accufers of innocence will ever exhibit!

I have obferved, Sir, that the opinions of officers of different ranks have been taken. I truft that the court will indulge me with the fame liberty, in the evidence for my defence. Some have refufed to give their opinions. I thought it ftrange, as plain fpeaking, and a full declaration, are the beft of evidences in a good caufe.

I would wifh, Sir, the court to confider, that in all great naval, as well as military operations, unlefs the defign be fully known, the feveral manœuvres may have a ftrange appearance. Mafters have been called to give their opinions on the higher departments of command. Higher authorities fhould have been taken. Such authorities are not fcarce, for I am happy to fay, there never was a country ferved by naval officers of more bravery, fkill and gallantry, than England can boaft at prefent. As to this court, I entreat you, gentlemen, who compofe it, to recollect, that you fit here as a court of honour, as well as a court of juftice, and I now ftand before you, not merely to fave my life, but for a purpofe of infinitely greater moment—to clear my fame.

My accufer, Sir, has not been a little miftaken in his notions of the duty of a commander in chief, or he would never have

accufed

accufed me in the manner he has done. During action fubordi-nate officers either are (or they ought to be) too attentive to their own duty to obferve the manœuvres of others. In general engagements it is fcarcely poffible for the fame objects to appear in the fame point of view to the commanders of two different fhips. The point of fight may be different. Clouds of fmoke may obftruct the view. Hence will arife the difference in the opinions of officers as to this or that manœuvre, without any intentional partiality. Whether I have conceived objects in ex-act correfpondence with the truth; whether I have viewed them unfkilfully, (or, as my accufer has been pleafed to term it, unofficer-like), thefe are matters which remain to be determined. I can only fay, that what Sir Hugh Pallifer has imputed to me as negligence, was the effect of deliberation and choice. I will add, that I was not confined in my powers when I failed; I had ample difcretion to act as I thought proper for the defence of the kingdom. I manœuvred; I fought; I returned; I did my beft. If my abilities were not equal to the tafk, I have the confolation to think, that I did not folicit, nor did I bargain for the command. More than two years ago, in the month of No-vember, 1776, I received a letter from the firft lord of the marine department, wherein he obferved, " That owing to mo-" tions of foreign courts, it might be neceffary to prepare a " fleet of obfervation." My reply to this letter was, " That " I was ready to receive any command from his majefty, and I " begged to have the honour of an audience." This requeft was complied with. I was clofetted, and I told the king, " that " I was willing to ferve him as long as my health would per-" mit." I heard no more until the month of March, 1778, at which time I had two or three audiences, and I told his maje-fty, that " I had no acquaintance with his minifters, but I " trufted to his protection and zeal for the public good." Here were no finifter views; no paltry gratifications; I had nothing, I felt nothing but an earneft defire to ferve my country. I even accepted the command in chief with reluctance. I was appre-henfive of not being fupported at home. I forefaw that the higher the command, the more liable was I to be ruined in my reputation. Even my misfortunes, if I had any, might be con-

ftrued

ftrued into crimes. During forty years fervice I have not received any particular mark of favour from the crown. I have only been honoured with the confidence of my fovereign in times of public danger. Neither my deficiencies nor my mifconduct were ever before brought forward to the public. And it is now fomewhat ftrange, that fo well acquainted as my accufer muft have been with my deficient abilities, it is ftrange, I fay, Sir, that he fhould be the very perfon who brought me the meffage to take the command upon me; nay, further, Sir, he brought me that meffage with great feeming pleafure! There was, or there was not reafon at that time to doubt my ability. If there was reafon, how could my accufer wifh me to accept a command for which I was difqualified? If there was not any reafon to doubt my profeffional abilities fixteen months ago, I have given no reafon why they fhould be fince called in queftion. When I returned from the expedition, I did not complain of any thing. I endeavoured to ftop all murmurings. I even trufted the firft lord of the admiralty in the fame manner as I would have done my moft intimate friend. This might be imprudent. It might be dangerous. But, Sir, I am by nature open and unguarded, and little did I expect that traps would artfully be laid to endeavour to catch me on the authority of my own words.

It was in the month of March, 1778, that I was told a fleet lay ready for me to command. When I reached Portfmouth I faw but fix fhips ready, and, on viewing even thofe with a feaman's eye, I was not by any means pleafed with their condition. Before I quitted Portfmouth, four or five more were ready, and I will do the perfons in office the juftice to fay, that from that time they ufed the utmoft diligence in getting the fleet ready for fervice. On the 30th of June I failed with twenty fhips of the line, and very fortunately fell in with the Belle Poule and other French frigates; and the letters and papers found on board them were of material fervice to the ftate. Captain Marfhall diftinguifhed himfelf with the greateft honour. I confefs that when I fell in with thofe frigates I was at a lofs how to act. On the one hand I conceived the incident to be favourable to my country, and on the other I was fearful that a war with France

and

and all its consequences might be laid to my charge. For any thing I can tell this may yet be the case. It may be treasured up to furnish another matter for future accusation. To this hour I have neither received official approbation or censure for my conduct. With twenty ships of the line I sailed. Thirty-two ships of the line lay in Brest water, besides an incredible number of frigates. Was I to seek an engagement with a superior force? I never did, nor shall I ever fear to engage a force superior to the one I then commanded, or that I may hereafter command. But I well know what men and ships can do, and if the fleet I commanded had been destroyed, we must have left the French masters of the sea. To refit a fleet requires time. From the situation of affairs, naval stores are not very soon supplied. Never did I experience so deep a melancholy as when I found myself forced to turn my back on France! I quitted my station, and courage was never put to so severe a trial.

I was permitted to sail a second time, without receiving official praise or blame for the part I had acted. These were discouraging circumstances. But they did not disturb my temper. My principal object was to get ready for sea with all possible haste. I was surprised on my return to be threatened with the fate of Admiral Byng, and I was still more surprised to be charged with cowardice.

With thirty ships of the line I sailed early in July. The French admiral sailed from Brest with thirty-two ships. I believe that, when the fleets came in sight of each other, the French were not a little surprised to see me so strong. I desire not to throw the slightest imputation on the courage of the French admiral. I believe him to be a brave man, and one who had some particular reasons for the line of conduct he pursued. I was determined, if possible, to bring the French to battle, as I had every reason to think, that their having avoided an engagement, when it was for four days in their power to attack me, was owing to their expecting some capital reinforcements. I therefore thought, that the sooner I could engage them the better, especially as I knew that the principal fleets of our trade were daily expected in the Channel, and if the French fleets had been permitted to disperse without an action, our East and

West

Weft India fleets might have been intercepted, the convoys might have been cut off, and the ftake of England might have been loft. I beg leave to mention, that, in the reign of King William, the gallant Admiral Ruffel was two months in fight of a French fleet, and he could not poffibly bring them to action. My being in fight of the French fleet four days before the engagement, will not therefore appear to be fo extraordinary as it has been reprefented. Had it not been for the favourable change of wind on the morning of the 27th of July, I could not have brought the French to action when I did.

I am exceedingly forry, Sir, that the Admiralty have refufed me the liberty of producing my inftructions. In all former court-martials the inftructions and orders have been fent with the charge to the members of the court. As it has been denied in this inftance, I muft, and do fubmit.

Although on the 27th of July I fought and beat my enemy, and compelled him to take fhelter by returning into port; yet the effort did by no means anfwer my wifhes. I rufhed on to re-attack the enemy. Why I did not accomplifh my defign will be feen in the evidence I fhall produce. I might, it is true, have chaced the three fhips which were vifible on the morning of the 28th of July, but with very little profpect of fuccefs. I therefore chofe to return to Plymouth with my fhattered fleet, to get ready for fea again, not, however, forgetting to leave two fhips of the line to cruife for the protection of our trading fleets, which, thank God, all arrived fafe.

On my return, Sir, I moft cautioufly avoided to utter a fyllable of complaint, becaufe it might have fufpended our naval operations, which at that time would have been highly dangerous. I could not think of attending to a court-martial, when greater objects were in view.

With refpect to the fecond edition of the Formidable's log-book, it appears to have been fabricated rather for the purpofe of exculpating the profecutor than to criminate me. I fhall therefore pafs it over, and permit the gentleman to make the moft of fuch an exculpation. I cannot, however, be fo civil to the alterations and additions in the log-book of the Robufte.

I                                                          Captain

Captain Hood's conduct muſt have ſtruck the court, as I believe it did every perſon, except the proſecutor, with aſtoniſhment.

A great ſtreſs, Sir, has been laid on my letter to the Admiralty.  There is a paſſage in it where I ſeemed to approve the conduct of every officer in the fleet.  The court will obſerve, that I was not in my letter to inform all Europe, that a vice-admiral under my command had been guilty of neglect, whilſt there remained a poſſibility of excuſe for his conduct.  As to court-martials, one very bad conſequence will, I am ſure, reſult from this trial: it will terrify a commander in chief from accepting a commiſſion, if he ſhould be liable to be brought to a trial by every ſubordinate officer.

As I have touched on my letters, I will juſt obſerve, Sir, that the moſt diſagreeable taſk I ever experienced was that of writing my letter of the 30th of July  However, if I writ ill, I am confident that I fought well; and the deſertion of the trade of France was evident from the numbers of rich captures which we made: a number far exceeding any thing ever known in ſo ſhort a period!  His majeſty noticed this in a ſpeech from the throne.

Mr. Preſident, I now deſire that the judge-advocate may be directed to read the charge, and I will anſwer the ſeveral accuſations.

*The* REPLIES *of Admiral* KEPPEL *to the* CHARGES *againſt him.*

*The firſt of the Charges, contained in the firſt article, is,*

" THAT on the morning of the 27th of July, 1778, having
" a fleet of thirty ſhips of the line under my command, and
" being then in the preſence of a French fleet of the like num-
" ber of ſhips of the line, I did not make the neceſſary prepa-
" rations for fight."

To this I anſwer, That I have never underſtood preparations for fight to have any other meaning in the language and under-ſtanding of ſeamen, than that each particular ſhip, under the di-rection and diſcipline of her own officers, when in purſuit of an enemy, be in every reſpect cleared and in readineſs for action; the contrary of which no admiral of a fleet, without a reaſonable cause; will presume: and as from the morning of the 24th, when the French fleet had got to windward, to the time of the action, the British fleet was in unremitting pursuit of them, it is still more difficult to conceive that any thing more is meant by this charge, than what is immediately after conveyed by the charge that follows it, *viz.* " That on the same morning of " the 27th I did not put my fleet into line of battle, or into " any order proper either for receiving or attacking an enemy " of such force."

By the second part of the charge I feel myself attacked in the exercise of that great and broad line of discretion, which every officer, commanding either fleets or armies, is often obliged, both in duty and conscience, to exercise to the best of his judgment; and which, depending on circumstances and situations infinitely various, cannot be reduced to any positive rule of discipline or practice :—a discretion which, I submit to the court, I was peculiarly called upon, by the strongest and best motives, to exercise, which I therefore did exercise, and which, in my public letter to the Board of Admiralty, I openly avowed to have exercised. I admit, that, on the morning of the 27th of July, I did not put my fleet into a line of battle, because I had it not in my choice to do so, consistently with the certainty, or even the probability, of either giving or being given battle, and because, if I had scrupulously adhered to that order, in which, if the election had been mine, I should have chosen to have received or attacked a willing enemy, I should have had no enemy either to receive or attack.

I shall therefore, in answer to this charge, submit to the court my reasons for determining to bring the enemy to battle at all events, and shall shew, that any other order than that in which my fleet was conducted, from my first seeing them to the moment of the action, was incompatible with such determination.

In order to this I must call the attention of the court to a retrospective view of the motions of the two fleets from their first coming in sight of each other.

On my first discovering the French fleet at one o'clock in the afternoon of the 23d of July, I made the necessary signals for forming my fleet in the order of battle, which I effected towards

the

the evening, and brought to by fignal, and lay till the morning, when perceiving that the French fleet had gained the wind during the night, and carried a preffed fail to preferve it, I difcontinued the fignal for the line, and made the general fignal to chace to windward, in hopes that they would join battle with me, rather than fuffer two of their capital fhips to be entirely feparated from them, and give me a chance of cutting off a third, which had carried away a top-maft in the night, and which, but for a fhift of wind, I muft have taken. In this, however, I was difappointed; for they fuffered two of them to go off altogether, and continued to make every ufe of the advantage of the wind.

This affiduous endeavour of the French admiral to avoid coming to action, which, from his having the wind, was always in his option, led me to believe that he expected a reinforcement. This reflection would alone have been fufficient to determine me to urge my purfuit, in as collected a body as the nature of fuch a purfuit would admit of, without the delay of the line, and to feize the firft opportunity of bringing on an engagement.

But I had other reafons no lefs urgent.

If by obftinately adhering to the line of battle, I had fuffered, as I inevitably muft, the French fleet to have been feparated from me; and if, by fuch feparation, the Englifh convoys from the Eaft and Weft Indies, then expected home, had been cut off, or the coaft of England had been infulted, what would have been my fituation!—Sheltered under the forms of difcipline, I might perhaps have efcaped punifhment, but I could not have efcaped cenfure. I fhould neither have efcaped the contempt of my fellow-citizens, nor the reproaches of my own confcience.

Moved by thefe important confiderations, fupported by the examples of Admiral Ruffel, and other great commanders, who, in fimilar fituations, had ever made ftrict orders give way to reafonable enterprize; and particularly encouraged by the remembrance of having myfelf ferved under that truly great officer, Lord Hawke, when, rejecting all rules and forms, he grafped at victory by an irregular attack, I determined not to lofe fight of the French fleet, by being out-failed from preferving the line of battle, but to keep my fleet as well collected as I could, and near enough to affift and act with each other, in cafe a change of wind, or other favourable circumftances, fhould enable me to force the French fleet to action.

Such were my feelings and reflections when the day broke on the morning of the 27th of July, at which time the fleet under my command was in the following pofition : Vice-admiral Sir Robert Harland was about four miles diftant, on the Victory's weather-quarter, with moft of the fhips of his own divifion, and fome of thofe belonging to the centre. Vice-admiral Sir Hugh Pallifer at about three miles diftant, a point before the lee-beam of the Victory, with his mainfail up, which obliged the fhips of his divifion to continue under an eafy fail.

The French fleet was as much to windward, and at as great a diftance as it had been the preceding morning, ftanding with a frefh wind at fouth-weft, clofe hauled on the larboard tack, to all appearance avoiding me with the fame induftry it ever had done.

At this time, therefore, I had no greater inducement to form the line, than I had the morning of the former day ; and I could not have formed it without greatly increafing my diftance from the French fleet, contrary to that plan of operation, which I have already fubmitted to the judgment of the court.

The Vice-admiral of the Blue next charges, " That although " my fleet was already difperfed and in diforder, I, by making " the fignal for feveral fhips in his divifion to chace to wind- " ward, increafed the diforder of that part of my fleet, and " that the fhips were in confequence more fcattered than they " had been the day before ; and that, whilft in this diforder, I " advanced to the enemy, and made the fignal for battle."

In this part of the charge there is a ftudious defign to mif- lead the underftanding, and, by leaving out times and interme- diate events, to make the tranfactions of half a day appear but as one moment. It is, indeed, impoffible to read it, without being poffeffed with the idea, that at half paft five in the morn- ing, when I made the fignal for fix of the fhips of the vice-ad- miral of the Blue's divifion to chace to windward, I was in the immediate profpect of clofing with an enemy, approaching me in a regular line, and all their motions plainly indicating a defign to give battle—inftead of which, both the fleets were on the

larboard

larboard tack, the enemy's fleet near three leagues, if not more, to windward, going off close by the wind with a preffed fail.—— My reafon, therefore, for making that fignal, at half paft five, was to colleft as many fhips to windward as I could, in order to ftrengthen the main body of the fleet, in cafe I fhould be able to get to action, and to fill up the interval between the Victory and the vice-admiral, which was occafioned by his being far to leeward; and it is plain that the Vice-admiral muft have himfelf underftood the object of the fignal, fince it has appeared in the courfe of the evidence, that on its being made, the Formidable fet her main-fail, and let the reefs out of her top-fail; and, indeed, the only reafon why it was not originally made for the whole divifion, was, that they muft have then chafed as a divifion, which would have retarded the beft going fhips by an attendance on the vice-admiral.

Things were in this fituation, when, at half paft nine, the French admiral tacked, and wore his whole fleet, and ftood to the fouthward, on the ftarboard tack, clofe hauled; but the wind immediately after they wore about, coming more foutherly, I continued to ftand on till a quarter paft ten, at which time I tacked the Britifh fleet together by fignal. Soon after we wore about, on the ftarboard tack, the wind came two points in our favour to the weftward, which enabled us to lie up for a part of them; but in a dark fquall that foon after came on, I loft fight of the enemy for above half an hour, and when it cleared away at eleven o'clock, I difcovered the French fleet had changed their pofition, and were endeavouring to form the line on the larboard tack, which finding they could not effect without coming within gun-fhot of the van of the Britifh fleet, they edged down, and fired on my headmoft fhips, as they approached them on the contrary tack, at a quarter after eleven, which was inftantly returned; and then, and not till then, I made the fignal for battle. All this happened in about half an hour, and muft have been owing to the enemy's falling to leeward in performing their evolution during the fquall, which we could not fee, and by that means produced this fudden and unexpected opportunity of engaging them, as they were near three leagues a-head of me when the fquall came on,

If,

If, therefore, by making the fignal for the line of battle, when the van of my fleet was thus fuddenly getting within reach of the enemy, and well connected with the centre, as my accufer himfelf has admitted, I had called back the vice-admiral of the Red, the French fleet might either have formed their line compleat, and have come down upon my fleet while in the confufion of getting into order of battle, or (what I had ftill greater reafon to apprehend) might have gone off to windward out of my reach altogether; for even as it was, the enemy's van, inftead of coming clofe to action, kept their wind, and paffed hardly within random fhot.

My accufer, next afferts, as an aggravation of his former charge,

" That the French fleet was in a regular line on that tack " which approached the Britifh fleet, all their motions plainly " indicating a defign to give battle."

Both which facts have already been contradicted by the teftimony of even his own witneffes: that the enemy's fleet was not in a regular line of battle, appeared by the French admiral being out of his ftation, far from the centre of his line, and next, or very near, to a fhip carrying a vice-admiral's flag, and from fome of their fhips being a-breaft of each other, and in one, as they paffed the Englifh fleet, with other apparent marks of irregularity. Indeed every motion of the French fleet, from about nine, when it went upon the ftarboard tack, till the moment of the action, and even during the action itfelf, I apprehend to be decifive againft the alledged indication of defigning battle; for if the French admiral had really defigned to come to action, I apprehend he never would have got his fleet on the contrary tack to that on which the Britifh fleet was coming up to him, but would have fhortened fail and waited for it, formed in the line on the fame tack; and even when he did tack towards the Britifh fleet, the alledged indication is again directly refuted, by the van of the French fleet hauling their wind again, inftead of bearing down into action, and by their hoifting no colours when they began to engage.

Notwithftanding thefe incontrovertible truths my accufer imputes it to me that a general engagement was not brought on;
but

but it is evident from the testimony of every witness he has called, that a general engagement was never in my choice; and that so far from its being prevented by my not having formed the line of battle, no engagement, either general or partial, could have been brought on if I had formed it; indeed it is a contradiction in terms to speak of a general engagement, where the fleet that has the wind, tacks to pass the fleet to leeward on the contrary tack.

Such was the manner, in which, after four days pursuit, I was at last enabled by a favourable shift of wind to close with the fleet of France; and if I am justifiable on principle in the exercise of that discretion which I have been submitting to your judgment, of bringing, at all events, an unwilling enemy to battle, I am certainly not called upon to descend to all the minutiæ of consequences resulting from such enterprize, even if such had ensued, as my accuser has asserted, but which his own witnesses have not only failed to establish, but absolutely refuted. It would be an insult on the understanding of the court, were I to offer any arguments, to shew that ships which engage without a line of battle, cannot so closely, uniformly and mutually support each other, as when circumstances admit of a line being formed; because it is self-evident, and is the basis of all the discipline and practice of lines of battle. But in the present case, notwithstanding I had no choice in making my disposition for an attack, nor any possibility of getting to battle otherwise than I did, which would be alone sufficient to repel any charge of consequent irregularity, or even confusion, yet it is not necessary for me to claim the protection of the circumstances under which I acted, because no irregularity or confusion either existed or has been proved; all the chacing ships, and the whole fleet, except a ship or two, got into battle, and into as close battle as the French fleet, which had the option by being to windward, chose to give them. The vice-admiral of the Blue himself, though in the rear, was out of action, in a short time after the Victory, and so far from being left to engage singly and unsupported, was passed during the action by three ships of his own division, and was obliged to back his mizen-top-sail to keep out of the fire of one of the

largest

largest ships in the fleet, which must have continued near him all the rest of the time he was passing the French line, as I shall prove she was within three cables length of the Formidable when the firing ceased.

### Answer to the Second Article.

The moment the Victory had passed the enemy's rear, my first object was to look round to the position of the fleet which the smoke had till then obscured from observation, in order to determine how a general engagement might best be brought on after the fleet should have passed each other.

I found that the vice-admiral of the Red, with part of his division, had tacked, and was standing towards the enemy with top gallant sails set, the very thing I am charged with not having directed him to do; but all the rest of the ships that had passed a-head of me were still on the starboard tack, some of them dropping to leeward, and seemingly employed in repairing their damages. The Victory herself was in no condition to tack, and I could not immediately wear and stand back on the ships coming up a stern of me, out of the action (had it been otherwise expedient) without throwing them into the utmost confusion. Sir John Ross, who very gallantly tried the experiment, having informed the court of the momentary necessity he was under of wearing back again to prevent the consequences I have mentioned, makes it unnecessary to enlarge on the probable effect of such a general manœuvre, with all the ships a-head. Indeed I only remark it as a strongly relative circumstance, appearing by the evidence of a very able and experienced officer, and by no means as a justification for having stood away to a great distance beyond the enemy before I wore, because the charge itself is grossly false. In fact, the Victory had very little way while her head was to the southward, and although her damages were considerable, was the first ship of the centre division that got round towards the enemy again, and some time before the rest were able to follow her, since, even as it was, not above three or four were able to close up with her on the larboard tack; so that, had it even been practicable to have wore sooner than I did, no good purpose could have been answered by it; hence I must have only wore the sooner back again to have collected the difabled fhips which would have been thereby left ftill farther a-ftern.

The Formidable was no otherwife left engaged with the enemy during this fhort interval than as being in the rear, which muft always neceffarily happen to fhips in that fituation, when fleets engage each other on contrary tacks, and no one witnefs has attempted to fpeak to the danger my accufer complains of, except his own captain, who, on being called upon to fix the time when fuch danger was apprehended, ftated it to be before the Formidable opened her fire, which renders the application of it as a confequence of the fecond charge too abfurd to demand a refutation.

### Anfwer to the third Article.

As foon as I had wore to ftand towards the enemy, I hauled down the fignal for battle, which I judged improper to be kept abroad till the fhips could recover their ftations, or at leaft get near enough to fupport each other in action. In order to call them together for that purpofe, I immediately made the fignal to form the line of battle a-head of all the centre and Red divifion, I embraced that opportunity of unbending her main top-fail, which was totally unferviceable, and, in doing which, the utmoft expedition was ufed, the fhips a-ftern of me doing all they could in the mean time to get into their ftation; fo that no time was loft by this neceffary operation.

The Formidable was a-head of the Victory during this period; it was her ftation in the line on that tack. Yet, at the very moment my accufer dares to charge me with not calling the fhips together to renew the attack, he himfelf, though his fhip was in a manageable condition, as appeared by the evidence of his own captain, and though he had wore, expecting, as he fays, the battle to be renewed, quitted his ftation in the front of that line of battle, the fignal for which was flying, paffed to leeward of me on the ftarboard tack while I was advancing to the enemy, and never came into the line during the reft of the day.

In this fituation I judged it neceffary that the vice-admiral of the Red, who was to windward, and paffing forward on my weather-bow, with fix or feven fhips of his divifion, fhould

lead on the larboard tack, in order to give time to the ships
which had come laſt out of action to repair their damages, and
get collected together; and the ſignal appointed by the 31ſt
article of the fighting inſtructions not being applicable, as the
French fleet was ſo nearly a-head of us, that by keeping cloſe
to the wind we could only have fetched them, I made the
Proſerpine's ſignal, in order to have diſpatched Captain Sutton
with a meſſage to Vice-admiral Sir Robert Harland, to lead the
fleet to the larboard tack; but, before he left the Victory with
the orders he had received, the French fleet wore and ſtood to
the ſouthward, forming their line on the ſtarboard tack, their
ſhips advancing regularly out of a collected body, which they
had got into from the operation of wearing, and not from any
diſorder or confuſion which really exiſted. I could have derived
no immediate advantage from it, not having a ſufficient force
collected to prevent their forming, by an attempt to renew the
attack. The Victory was at this time the neareſt ſhip to the
enemy, with no more than three or four of the centre diviſion,
in any ſituation to have ſupported her or each other in action.
The vice-admiral of the Blue was on the ſtarboard tack, ſtanding away from his ſtation, totally regardleſs of the ſignal that
was flying to form the line, and moſt of the other ſhips, except
the Red diviſion, whoſe poſition I have already ſtated, were far
a-ſtern, and five diſabled ſhips at a great diſtance on the lee
quarter. Moſt of theſe facts are already eſtabliſhed by the accuſer's own evidence. I ſhall prove and confirm them all by
the teſtimony of that part of the fleet, whoſe ſituations will enable them to ſpeak to them with certainty.

I truſt they will convince the court, that I had it not in my
power to collect the fleet together to renew the fight at that time,
and that, from their not being able to follow me, I conſequently
could not advance with them; that I did not haul down the ſignal for battle till it ceaſed to be capable of producing any good
effect; that, during the whole time I ſtood towards the enemy,
I endeavoured by the moſt forcible of all ſignals, the ſignal for
the line of battle, to call the ſhips together in order to renew the
attack; that I did avail myſelf of the ſhips that were with the
vice-admiral of the Red as far as circumſtances admitted; and
that

that I therefore did do the utmoſt in my power to take, ſink,
burn, and deſtroy the French fleet, which had attacked the Britiſh fleet.

*Anſwer to the Fourth Article.*

The French fleet having wore and begun to form their line,
on the ſtarboard-tack, by the wind, which, if they had kept,
would have brought them cloſe up with the centre diviſion, ſoon
afterwards edged away, pointing towards four or five of the diſabled ſhips, which were at a diſtance to leeward, and with evident intention to have ſeparated them from the reſt of the fleet;
to prevent which, I made the ſignal to wear, and ſtood athwart
their van, in a diagonal courſe, to give protection to thoſe crippled ſhips, keeping the ſignal for the line flying to form and collect the fleet on the ſtarboard tack. As I had thus been obliged
to alter my diſpoſition, before Captain Sutton left the Victory
with my former meſſage, I deſpatched him with orders to the
vice-admiral of the Red to form with his diviſion at a diſtance
a-ſtern of the Victory, to cover the rear, and keep the enemy
in check, till the vice-admiral of the Blue ſhould come into his
ſtation with his diviſion, in obedience to the ſignal. Theſe orders the vice-admiral of the Red inſtantly obeyed, and was
formed in my wake before four o'clock, when, finding that
while by the courſe I ſteered to protect the crippled ſhips, I was
nearer the enemy, the vice-admiral of the Blue ſtill continued
to ly to windward, and by ſo doing kept his diviſion from joining me, I made the ſignal for ſhips to bear down into my wake,
and that it might be the better diſtinguiſhed, (both being ſignals
at the mizen-peak,) I hauled down the ſignal for the line for
about ten minutes, and then hoiſted it again. This ſignal he
repeated, though he had not repeated that for the line of battle; but by not bearing down himſelf, he led the ſhips of his
diviſion to interpret his repeating it as requiring them to come
into his wake inſtead of mine.

Having now accompliſhed the protection of the diſabled ſhips,
and the French fleet continuing to form their line, ranging up
to leeward, parallel to the centre diviſion, my only object was
to form mine, in order to bear down upon them to renew the

battle;

battle; and therefore, at a quarter before five o'clock, after having repeated the fignal for fhips to windward to bear down into
my wake with no better effect than before, I fent the Milford
with orders to the vice-admiral of the Red to ftretch a-head,
and take his ftation in the line, which he inftantly obeyed; and
the vice-admiral of the Blue being ftill to windward, with his
fore-to-fail unbent, and making no vifible effort to obey the fignal, which had been flying the whole afternoon, I fent out the
Fox, at five o'clock, with orders to him to bear down into my
wake, and to tell him, that I only waited for him, and his divifion, to renew the battle. While I was difpatching thefe frigates,
having before hauled down the fignal to come into my wake, I
put aboard the fignal for all fhips to come into their ftations,
always keeping the fignal for the line flying. All this producing
no effect on the vice-admiral of the Blue, and wearied out with
fruitlefs expectation, at feven o'clock I made the fignal for each
particular fhip of the vice-admiral of the Blue's divifion to come
into her ftation; but, before they had accomplifhed it, night
put an end to all farther operations.

It may be obferved, that, amongft thefe fignals, I did not
make the Formidable's. If the vice-admiral chufes to confider
this as a culpable neglect, I can only fay, that it occurred to
me to treat him with a delicacy due to his rank, which had
fome time before induced me to fend him the meffage by Captain Windfor, the particulars of which he has already faithfully
related to the court.

I truft I have little reafon to apprehend that the court will be
inclined to confider my conduct as I have ftated it, in anfwer
to this fourth article of the charge, as difgraceful to the Britifh
flag? After I had put upon the fame tack with the enemy, to
protect the difabled part of my fleet, and to collect the reft together, there would have been little to do to renew the battle,
but bearing right down upon the enemy, if my accufer had led
his divifion in obedience to the repeated fignals and orders which
I have ftated. The Victory never went more than two knots,
was under her double-reefed top-fail, and fore-fail much fhattered, which kept the fhips that were near her under their top-
fail, and fuffered the French fleet, which might always have
**brought**

brought me to action, if they had inclined to do it, to range up parallel with the centre, under very little fail. It was to protect the five difabled fhips above-mentioned, and to give the reft time to form into fome order, that I judged it might be expedient to ftand as I did under that eafy fail, than to bring to with my head to the fouthward. The court will judge whether it was poffible for any officer in the fervice really to believe that thefe operations could give the appearance of a flight, or furnifh a rational pretence to the French admiral to claim the victory, or publifh to the world that the Britifh fleet had run away.

### Anfwer to the Fifth Article.

On the morning of the 28th of July, the French fleet, (except three fail which were feen upon the lee quarter) was only vifible from the maft-heads of fome of the fhips of the Britifh fleet, and at a diftance from me, which afforded not the fmalleft profpect of coming up with them, more efpecially as their fhips, though certainly much damaged in their hulls, had not apparently fuffered much in their mafts and fails. Whereas the fleet under my command was generally and greatly fhattered in their mafts, yards and rigging, and many of them unable to carry fail. As to the three French fhips, I made the fignal at five o'clock in the morning for the Duke, Bienfaifant, Prince George, and Elifabeth, to give them chace, judging them to be the propereft fhips for that purpofe, but the two laft were not able to carry fufficient fail to give even countenance to the purfuit ; and looking round to the general condition of my fleet, I faw it was in vain to attempt either a general or a partial chace. Indeed my accufer does not venture to alledge that there was any probability, or even poffibility, of doing it with effect, which deftroys the whole imputation of his charge.

Under thefe circumftances I could not miftake my duty, and I was refolved not to facrifice it to an empty fhew and appearance, which is beneath the dignity of an officer, unconfcious of any failure or neglect. To have urged a fruitlefs purfuit, with a fleet fo greatly crippled in its mafts and fails, after a diftant and flying enemy, within reach of their own ports, and with a

frefh

fresh wind blowing fair for their port, with a large swell, would have been not only wantonly expofing the Britifh fleet under my command without end or object, but misleading and defeating its operations, by delaying the refitment neceffary for carrying on the future fervice with vigour and effect.

My accufer afferts, by a general conclufion to the five articles exhibited againft me, that, from what he ftates as inftances of mifconduct and neglect in me, " a glorious opportunity was loft " of doing a moft effential fervice to the ftate," and that the honour of the Britifh navy was tarnifhed.

The truth of the affertion, That an opportunity was loft, I am not called upon either to combat or deny. It is fufficient for me, if I fhall be fuccefsful in proving, that that opportunity was feized by me, and followed up to the full extent of my power; if the court fhall be of that opinion, I am fatisfied; and it will then reft with the vice-admiral of the Blue, to explain to what caufe it is to be referred, that the glorious opportunity he fpeaks of was loft, and to whom it is to be imputed, (if the fact be true), that the honour of the Britifh navy has been tarnifhed.

Having now, Sir, finifhed my replies, I fhall call witneffes to prove my innocence. I have heard it afferted as matter of right to alter a log-book. I will only fay, that there is a wide difference between correcting inaccuracies, and malicious alterations, for the purpofe of aiding malicious profecutions.

As to my profecutor, I have even his own letters, of as late date as the 5th of October, wherein he thus writes to me, " I " know that you would rather meet the French fleet." Yes, Sir, that very French fleet which he afterwards accufed me of running away from! I cannot produce thefe letters in evidence, but I will fhow them to any gentleman out of court who defires to fee them. I will alfo fhow to any gentleman a paper which my profecutor requefted me to fign but a very fhort time ago, and I refufed to fign it. In the news-papers my profecutor denied receiving any meffage by the Fox frigate. Captain Windfor fwore to the delivery of fuch a meffage. He proved in evidence that he received the meffage from me at five o'clock, and
delivered

delivered it to the vice-admiral himself at half past five o'clock. Captain Bazely endeavoured to refute this evidence: but I shall call witnesses to prove the delivery of the message. My conscience is perfectly clear. I have no secret machinations, no dark contrivances to answer for. My heart does not reproach me. As to my enemies, I would not wish the greatest enemy I have in the world to be afflicted with so heavy a punishment as——my accuser's conscience.

No. XX.

## No. XX.   (P. 445.)

### Admiral KEPPEL's Letter to the Admiralty.

*Victory, at fea, July* 30, 1778.

SIR,

MY letters of the 23d and 24th inftant, by the Peggy and Union cutters, acquainted you, for their lordfhips information, that I was in purfuit, with the king's fleet under my command, of a numerous fleet of French fhips of war.

From that time till the 27th, the winds conftantly in the S. W. and N. W. quarters, fometimes blowing ftrong, and the French fleet always to windward going off, I made ufe of every method to clofe in with them that was poffible, keeping the king's fhips at the fame time collected, as much as the nature of a purfuit would admit of, and which became neceffary from the cautious manner the French proceeded in, and the difinclination that appeared in them to allow of my bringing the king's fhips clofe up to a regular engagement : this left but little other chance of getting in with them, than by feizing the opportunity that offered, the morning of the 27th, by the wind's admitting of the van of the king's fleet under my command leading up with, and clofing with, their centre and rear.

The French began firing upon the headmoft of Vice-admiral Sir Robert Harland's divifion, and the fhips with him, as they led up ; which cannonade the leading fhips and the vice-admiral foon returned, as did every fhip as they could clofe up : the chace had occafioned their being extended ; neverthelefs they were all foon in battle.

The fleets, being upon different tacks, paffed each other very clofe ; the object of the French feemed to be the difabling of the king's fhips in their mafts and fails, in which they fo far fucceeded as to prevent many of the fhips of my fleet being able to follow me when I wore to ftand after the French fleet ; this obliged me to wear again to join thofe fhips, and thereby allowed of the French forming their fleet again, and ranging it in a

I      line

line to leeward of the king's fleet towards the clofe of the day; which I did not difcourage, but allowed of their doing it without firing-upon them, thinking they meant handfomely to try their force with us the next morning; but they had been fo beaten in the day, that they took the advantage of the night to go off.

The wind and weather being fuch that they could reach their own fhores before there was any chance of the king's fleet getting up with them, in the ftate the fhips were in, in their mafts, yards, and fails, left me no choice of what was proper and advifable to do.

The fpirited conduct of Vice-admiral Sir Robert Harland, Vice-admiral Sir Hugh Pallifer, and the captains of the fleet, fupported by their officers and men, deferves much commendation.

A lift of the killed and wounded is herewith inclofed.

I fend Captain Faulkener, captain of the Victory, with this account to their lordfhips, and am, Sir,

Your moft obedient,

And very humble fervant,

A. KEPPEL.

Philip Stephens, *Efq; fecretary to the Admiralty.*

*Lift of men killed and wounded, in the action with the French fleet, the 27th of July, 1778.*

| Ships names. | Killed. | Wounded. | Ships names. | Killed. | Wounded. |
|---|---|---|---|---|---|
| Monarch | 2 | 9 | Prince George | 5 | 15 |
| Exeter | 4 | 6 | Vengeance | 4 | 18 |
| Queen | 1 | 2 | Worcefter | 3 | 5 |
| Shrewfbury | 3 | 6 | Elifabeth | — | 7 |
| Berwick | 10 | 11 | Defiance | 8 | 17 |
| Stirling Caftle | 2 | 11 | Robufte | 5 | 17 |
| Courageux | 6 | 13 | Formidable | 16 | 49 |
| Thunderer | 2 | 5 | Ocean | 2 | 18 |
| Vigilant | 2 | 3 | America | 1 | 17 |
| Sandwich | 2 | 20 | Terrible | 9 | 21 |
| Valiant | 6 | 26 | Egmont | 12 | 19 |
| Victory | 11 | 24 | Ramillies | 12 | 16 |
| Foudroyant | 5 | 18 | | | |
| | | | Total | 133 | 373 |

## No. XXI. (P. 425.)

### LIST of the BRITISH FLEET at failing.

#### LINE OF BATTLE.

Monarch to lead on the ftarboard tack—Ramillies on the larboard tack.

| Ships. | Guns | Men. | Commanders. | Frigates. | Guns | |
|---|---|---|---|---|---|---|
| Monarch | 74 | 600 | Capt. Rowley | | | |
| Shrewfbury | 74 | 600 | Sir John Lockhart Rofs | | | |
| Hector | 74 | 600 | Sir John Hamilton | | | |
| Exeter | 64 | 500 | Capt. Nott | | | |
| Courage | 74 | 600 | Cofby | | | |
| Duke | 90 | 750 | Brereton | | | |
| Queen | 90 | 772 | Sir Robert Harland, Bart. Vice-admiral of the Red, Commander in 2d poft. Capt. Prefcot | Fox | 29 | Hon — Windfor |
| Cumberland | 74 | 600 | Peyton | | | |
| Berwick | 74 | 600 | Hon. Keith Stewart | | | |
| Stirling Caftle | 64 | 500 | Sir Charles Douglas, Bart. | | | |
| Thunderer | 74 | 600 | Hon. Boyle Walfingham | | | |
| Courageux | 74 | 600 | Right Hon. Lord Mulgrave | | | |
| Sandwich | 90 | 750 | Capt. Edwards | | | |
| Valiant | 74 | 600 | Hon. Levifon Gower | Proferpine | 28 | —Sutton |
| Victory | 100 | 894 | Hon. Auguftus Keppel, Admiral of the Blue, Commander in chief. Rear-admiral Campbell Capt. Faulkener | Andromeda Pluto Arethufa Vulcan Medea Rattle-fnake | 32 32 32 | a firefhip — Marfhal a firefhip — Montagu a cutter |
| Foudroyant | 80 | 650 | Jarvis | | | |
| Prince George | 90 | 750 | Sir John Lindfay, K. B. | | | |
| Bienfaifant | 64 | 500 | Capt. M'Bride | | | |
| Vengeance | 74 | 600 | Clements | | | |
| Vigilant | 64 | 500 | Kingfmill | | | |
| Worcefter | 64 | 500 | Capt. Robinfon | | | |
| Elifabeth | 74 | 600 | Hon. F. Maitland | | | |
| Defiance | 64 | 500 | Capt. Goodal | | | |
| Robufte | 74 | 600 | Hood | | | |
| Formidable | 90 | 772 | Sir Hugh Pallifer, Bart. Vice-admiral of the Blue, Commander in 3d poft. Capt. Bazely | Milford | 32 | Sir W. Burnaby |
| Ocean | 90 | 750 | Laforey | | | |
| America | 64 | 500 | Right Hon. Lord Longford | | | |
| Egmont | 74 | 600 | Capt. Allen | | | |
| Terrible | 74 | 600 | Sir Richard Bickerton, Bt. | | | |
| Ramillies | 74 | 600 | Hon. Robert Digby | | | |

The Refolution and Defence, of 74 guns each, failed afterwards, and joined the fleet.
ſhips of the line, mounting 2418 guns, and carrying 19788 men.—6 frigates, and
2 firefhips.

*A com-*

*A complete List of the French fleet under the command of M. d'Orvilliers, admiral, Compte du Chaffault, vice-admiral, and the Duc de Chartres, rear-admiral.*

| Ships. | Guns. | Men. | Ships. | Guns. | Men. |
|---|---|---|---|---|---|
| La Bretagne, | 110 | 1200 | La Dauph. Royale, | 74 | 800 |
| Ville de Paris, | 90 | 950 | Reflechi, | 64 | 650 |
| St. Efprit, | 80 | 920 | Vengeur, | 64 | 650 |
| Couronne, | 80 | 920 | Triton, | 64 | 650 |
| D. de Bourgogne, | 80 | 920 | Alexandre, | 64 | 650 |
| Diademe, | 74 | 800 | Sphinx, | 64 | 650 |
| Glorieux, | 74 | 800 | Solitaire, | 64 | 650 |
| Conquerant, | 74 | 800 | St. Michel, | 64 | 650 |
| Zodiac, | 74 | 800 | Artifien, | 64 | 650 |
| Intrepide, | 74 | 800 | Eveillé, | 64 | 650 |
| Palmier, | 74 | 800 | Actionnaire, | 64 | 650 |
| L'Actif, | 74 | 800 | Rolande, | 64 | 650 |
| Fendent, | 74 | 800 | Indien, | 64 | 650 |
| Orient, | 74 | 800 | Amphion, | 50 | 500 |
| Magnifique, | 74 | 800 | Fier, | 50 | 500 |
| Robufte, | 74 | 800 | 13 frigates, and | 4 | ftore- |
| Bien Aimé, | 74 | 800 | fhips. | | |

32 fhips of the line mounting 2270 guns, carrying 24,110 men.

*N. B.* The above fhips were all in the action of the 27th of July, except the Duc de Bourgogne and the Alexandre, who were feparated from the fleet in a gale of wind on the 25th.

## No. XXII.　(P. 446.)

*Admiralty-Office, March* 24, 1779.

*Copy of a Letter from the Honourable Rear-admiral Barrington to Mr. Stephens.*

*Prince of Wales, in the Grand Cul de Sac, in the Island of St Lucia, December* 23, 1778.

SIR,

IN my letter of the 24th of last month, from Barbadoes, (No. 21.) I informed you of the Venus's arrival there with an account of Commodore Hotham's being on his way to join me: and you will now be pleased to acquaint my Lords Commissioners of the Admiralty, that the commodore arrived there the 10th instant, with his Majesty's ships the Nonsuch, St. Alban's, Preston, Centurion, Isis, and Carcass, and fifty-nine transports, having on board 5000 troops, under the command of Major-general Grant.

To save time, and prevent the confusion naturally arising from a change of signals among the transports, I adopted those of the commodore; and, directing him to lead with the landing division, put to sea the 12th in the morning, in order to carry into execution their Lordships secret instructions; and, about three o'clock on the day following, anchored here with the whole squadron, except the Ariadne, Ceres, Snake, Barbadoes, and Pelican, which I had stationed along the coast, to intercept any vessels attempting to escape.

More than half the troops were landed the same evening, under the direction of the commodore, assisted by the captains Griffith, Braithwaite, and Onslow, and the remainder the next morning, (the 14th), when they immediately got possession of the Carenage; and it was my intention to have removed the transports thither as soon as possible, had not that measure been prevented by the appearance of the French fleet under the command

mand of Count d'Eftaing, of which I received notice in the evening by fignal from the Ariadne.

It therefore became neceffary to fecure the tranfports as well as we could in the bay; and the whole night was accordingly employed in warping them within the fhips of war, and difpofing of the latter in a line acrofs the entrance, in the order they ftand in the margin *; the Ifis to windward, rather inclining into the bay, and the Prince of Wales, being the moft powerful fhip, the outermoft, and to leeward, and the Venus, Aurora, and Ariadne, flanking the fpace between the Ifis and the fhore, to prevent the enemy forcing a paffage that way.

Almoft all the tranfports had fortunately got within the line before half paft eleven in the morning of the 15th, when the Count thought proper to bear down and attack us with ten fail of the line, happily without doing us any material injury; and at four in the afternoon he made a fecond attack upon us with twelve fail of the line, with no other fuccefs, however, than killing two men, and wounding feven, on board the Prince of Wales, and wounding one alfo on board the Ariadne, who is fince dead.   But I have reafon to believe the enemy received confiderable damage, as their manœuvres betrayed great confufion; and one of their fhips in particular, which fell to leeward, feemed difabled from carrying the neceffary fail to get to windward again.

The next day (the 16th) the Count fhewed a difpofition to attack us a third time; but on the appearance of a frigate ftanding for his fleet, with feveral fignals flying, he plied to windward, and in the evening anchored off Gros-Iflet, about two leagues from us, where he ftill continues with ten frigates, befides his twelve fail of the line; and, notwithftanding this fuperiority of force, he has been accompanied from his firft appearance by feveral American privateers, one of them commanded by the outlaw Cunningham, who laft winter infefted the coaft of Portugal.

| * Ifis, | 50 | Centurion, | 50 |
| St. Alban's | 64 | Prefton, | 50 |
| Boyne, | 68 | Prince of Wales, | 74 |
| Nonfuch, | 64 | | |

That

That night and the next day the enemy landed a large body of troops from a number of floops and fchooners which had anchored in Du Choc bay, and the 18th made a fpirited attack, both by land and fea, on our poft at the Carenage, but met with a very fevere check, having been repulfed, with great carnage, by a fmall detachment of our troops under Brigadier-general Meadows.

They have attempted nothing of confequence fince, and what may be their future plan of operations I cannot conjecture : but their continuance at anchor has afforded us an opportunity not only of getting in all the cruifers except the Ceres, and all the tranfports except one (with only the baggage of the officers of three companies on board), which has fallen into the enemy's hands, but alfo of ftrengthening ourfelves by warping the fhips of war farther into the bay, and making the line more compact, removing the Venus aftern of the Prince of Wales to flank that paffage, and erecting batteries at each point of the bay ; That to the northward under the direction of the Captains Cumming and Robertfon, and That to the fouthward under Captain Fergufon.

This being the fituation of the fquadron, and the army being in poffeffion of all the ftrong holds in the neighbourhood of the bay, fuch a fpirit of cheerfulnefs, unanimity, and refolution, actuates the whole of our little force both by land and fea, (notwithftanding the amazing fatigue they have undergone), that we are under no apprehenfions for any attempts the enemy may meditate: and from the accounts which have been tranfmitted to me from Captain Linzee of the Pearl, who arrived at Barbadoes the 13th inftant, that Vice-admiral Byron was to fail from Rhode Ifland for Barbadoes the 19th of laft month, with fixteen fail of the line, and feveral frigates, there is every reafon to hope he will foon be here ; in which cafe affairs in this country muft take a very decifive turn in favour of his majefty's arms.

Should any unforefeen accident, however, prevent the Vice-admiral's arrival, their Lordfhips will neverthelefs be pleafed to affure his Majefty, that every thing which can poffibly be

done

done by fo fmall a body of troops, and fo few fhips, againft a force fo very fuperior, will be effected.

I cannot conclude my letter without acquainting you, that, in all probability, our operations here have hitherto faved the iflands of St. Vincent and Grenada, which, we underftand from fome officers who are prifoners, were the object of Count D'Eftaing's expedition, when a floop that had efcaped from this ifland falling in with him, and giving him notice of our being here, directed his attention towards us.    I am, &c.

SAM. BARRINGTON.

P. S. I have the fatisfaction to add, that this morning the fquadron got poffeffion of an American privateer of eighteen guns, called the Bunker-Hill, which at day-break was difcovered within reach of our guns; and having ftruck, upon finding fhe could not efcape, the boats towed her within the line before any of the French fleet could get to her affiftance. She failed from Salem the 2d inftant, and was intended to cruife fifteen leagues to windward of Barbadoes, but had miffed that ifland and fallen to leeward.

24th Dec. 1778.      SAM. BARRINGTON.

*Extract of a letter from the Honourable Rear Admiral Barrington to Mr. Stephens.*

Prince of Wales, in the Grand Cul de Sac, in the Ifland of St. Lucia, Jan. 6, 1779.

SIR,

You will herewith receive the duplicate of a letter I wrote to you the 23d and 24th of laft month (No. 23), and difpatched to Governor Hay of Barbadoes, to be forwarded from thence to England by fome faft-failing veffel, that my Lords Commiffioners of the Admiralty might have it in their power to refute any mifreprefentation, which Count d'Eftaing may have tranfmitted to his court, of the fituation of his Majefty's forces in thefe feas.

From the ftate of inactivity in which the Count continued for feveral days after, I began to conceive it was his intention to form a blockade with a view of ftarving us into a furrender; but,

but, to my utter aſtoniſhment, on the morning of the 29th (having re-embarked his troops during the preceding night) he retired with his whole force towards Martinique, and left us in quiet poſſeſſion of the iſland, which capitulated, whilſt his fleet was ſtill in ſight, upon the terms I have the honour to in-cloſe *.

I ſhould be very much wanting, were I on the preſent occa-caſion to omit acknowledging the aſſiſtance I received from Major General Grant and the forces under his command, as well as expreſſing my entire ſatisfaction with the conduct, not only of Commodore Hotham, the ſeveral commanders, and the reſt of the officers of the ſquadron, but alſo of the people in general, who never in the leaſt repined at their precarious ſitua-tion and the difficulties they hourly encountered, but ſtill per-formed their duty with alacrity and ſpirit, and, ſenſible of the additional fatigue the troops underwent in occupying more ex-tenſive poſts for the ſecurity of the ſquadron, than there would otherwiſe have been occaſion for, laboured with the utmoſt chearfulneſs in conveying proviſions, &c. for them, through roads that were almoſt impaſſable, and moſt of them without ſhoes to their feet.

I likewiſe beg leave to mention to their Lordſhips the very great aſſiſtance I received from Captain Barker, the agent of tranſports, and the ſervices of Lieutenant Governor Stuart, of the iſland of Dominica, who has done me the favour of offi-ciating as an honorary aid-de-camp between the General and myſelf, having accompanied me upon this expedition, in hopes that his Majeſty's arms might afterwards be employed in reco-vering that iſland; where, from his perfect knowledge of it, he muſt be particularly uſeful, and therefore offered himſelf as a volunteer. -

What has become of the enemy's fleet ſince its departure from hence I have not had it in my power to learn; but I hope Vice-admiral Byron, who, I have the pleaſure to acquaint you

---

* The articles of capitulation for St. Lucia were merely an exchange of ſove-reigns. The peaceable inhabitants were ſecured in all their poſſeſſions, and nothing was made capture of but forts, magazines, and military ſtores.

arrived here this morning, with nine fail of the line, will very foon be able to give their lordfhips that information ; and, that Rear-admiral Sir Peter Parker and the Governor of Jamaica may be upon their guard, in cafe of its appearance in thofe feas, I have fent the Ariadne to Antigua, with letters to be forwarded to them from thence by fome faft-failing veffel, which I have requefted Governor Burt to difpatch for that purpofe.

I have great fatisfaction in hearing, fince the capitulation, that, when Count D'Eftaing was directed hither by the floop I mentioned in my letter (No 23), he was bound firft of all to Barbadoes, in expectation of finding there only the Prince of Wales, the Boyne, and fome frigates ; of which he had received intelligence from a French flag of truce I had ordered away immediately on the arrival of the Venus.

I am forry to add, that the Ceres, which was miffing when I fent away that letter, appears, by the Martinique Gazette, to have been taken, after a chafe of forty-eight hours, by the Iphigenie, a French frigate of 36 guns ; but I have no account of it from Capt. Dacres, or any of her officers.

I cannot help regretting the lofs of this floop, not only as fhe failed remarkably well, but as Captain Dacres is an officer of infinite merit. I have, however, in order to replace the Ceres, as the Bunker-Hill privateer has the reputation of being a very faft failer, (which her log-book confirms), commiffioned her as a floop in his Majefty's fervice, by the name of the Surprize, (being expreffive of the manner in which fhe came into our poffeffion), and appointed Lieutenant James Brine, firft lieutenant of the Prince of Wales, to be mafter and commander of her, with a complement of one hundred and twenty-five men. She mounts 18 carriage and 8 fwivel guns.

For further particulars, I beg leave to refer their Lordfhips to Captain Robertfon of the Weazle, who will have the honour of delivering thefe difpatches, and whofe conduct as an officer merits their Lordfhips protection, and every favour they can poffibly fhew him. I am, &c.

SAM. BARRINGTON,


F I N I S.

AUG 14 1928

AUG 14 1928

Check Out More Titles From HardPress Classics Series In this collection we are offering thousands of classic and hard to find books. This series spans a vast array of subjects — so you are bound to find something of interest to enjoy reading and learning about.

Subjects:
Architecture
Art
Biography & Autobiography
Body, Mind &Spirit
Children & Young Adult
Dramas
Education
Fiction
History
Language Arts & Disciplines
Law
Literary Collections
Music
Poetry
Psychology
Science
…and many more.

Visit us at www.hardpress.net

## Im The Story
*personalised classic books*

JANE
IN
WONDERLAND

LEWIS
CARROLL

"Beautiful gift... lovely finish.
My Niece loves it, so precious!"

Helen R Brumfieldon

⭐⭐⭐⭐⭐

UNIQUE
GIFT

FOR KIDS, PARTNERS
AND FRIENDS

*Timeless books such as:*

*Kids*

Alice in Wonderland  ·  The Jungle Book  ·  The Wonderful Wizard of Oz
Peter and Wendy  ·  Robin Hood  ·  The Prince and The Pauper
The Railway Children  ·  Treasure Island  ·  A Christmas Carol

*Adults*

Romeo and Juliet  ·  Dracula

**Highly**
Customizable

**Change**
Books Title

**Replace**
Character's Name
with yours

**Upload**
Photo for
inside page

**Add**
Inscriptions

*Visit*
## Im The Story .com
*and order yours today!*

CPSIA information can be obtained
at www.ICGtesting.com
Printed in the USA
BVHW080316270819
556819BV00007B/1191/P